China Macro Finance: A US Perspective

China Macro Finance: A US Perspective

Ronald M. Schramm

ISBN 13: 979-8-56710-659-4

China My Muse, America My Home

Table of Contents: Chapters and Subjects

Table of Contents: Case Studies and Macro Finance Insights

PREFACE

In this new edition of *China Macro Finance: A US Perspective*, we fully explore the progress made and challenges ahead for the world's second-largest economy. Beyond a mere updating, we expand our macro finance approach to understand the mechanics of how the Chinese economy works. Whether considering the cost of capital, Solow growth theory, corporate governance, asset management or real options theory, this textbook leaves no stone unturned in utilizing tools from finance and economics to elucidate China's economic performance. The United States economy is compared and contrasted with China to provide context and serve as a type of benchmark. All the while, the book shows a tender respect for the great Chinese people and their striving for a better life.

Much has changed since the first edition of this text. The Trump trade war has made China's cooperative/competitive relationship with the United States acutely apparent. Meanwhile, the COVID-19 epidemic is likely to reshape global production, finance, and trade. China's key drivers (discussed in Chapter 1) have now become a drag rather than a catalyst for economic growth. We discuss the critical role of technological progress in China and the need for rebalancing in order to create sustainable growth and returns. The e-commerce/internet revolution has resulted in a transformation of consumer finance. And all of this has happened as monetary policies have become both more sophisticated and heavily relied upon. In Chapter 10 we present the challenges in China's fiscal situation and new measures of China's efforts at expanding the social safety net. A new chapter (Chapter 11) has been added on China's financial system—an area where dramatic changes have occurred since the first edition.

I began to write the first edition of this textbook on China in 2003, but after writing one chapter I gave up on the project. At that time, it seemed there was neither enough good research being done to synthesize nor enough good data to say something meaningful. What is more, China was transforming and mutating in incomprehensible ways. *What a difference two decades make.* There has been an explosion of economic and financial research by both Western and Chinese scholars and the data are now abundant. Most impressive since the first edition has been a second wave of young Chinese scholars producing an impressive body of research with insights only possible from an insider's perspective. The country continues to change and grow at a dizzying pace.

Necessity truly is the mother of invention—the absence of a textbook with a modern approach to China's macro economy was one compelling motivation for writing this book. Another was the question that so many MBA and master's students have asked me over the years after completing the intermediate macroeconomics course I taught: "Is there an advanced macro course that follows this one that I can take?" My answer was: "No—the PhD macro course is quite technical with limited practical application and that is the only next course—someday, I will write a good advanced textbook to fill the gap." A final interest in writing this book was that I wanted to bring macroeconomics a bit back to its finance, accounting, and microeconomic roots—there are so many worthwhile frameworks in those fields that I had already incorporated into my teaching. I wanted an opportunity to explore where those roots would take me (and the student) in the China context.

This book is intended for anyone interested in understanding the Chinese macro economy and financial structure. It should be of good use to faculty teaching a general course on the Chinese economy from a macroeconomics perspective. This textbook is self-contained in that it provides the theory, data, and institutional detail needed to understand China's economic performance. It would be appropriate for students in economics departments, business schools, international studies programs, and master's programs in public policy. In the same context, students who are seeking an advanced course in applied macroeconomics where they learn the practical skills needed to work as an economist would find this book extremely useful. Given China's success as a large emerging market, this textbook could also be used in a course on emerging markets. Certainly business practitioners who seek a deep understanding of China and its institutions would find many parts of this book to contain necessary knowledge.

That the United States and China are now the world's two largest economies makes a textbook like this both inevitable and necessary. To write about China or the United States in isolation would be to write without context. I believe that this truly is a case where the whole is greater than the sum of its parts—the reader gains a deeper understanding of each economy by way of comparison.

Organization of the Text

Every chapter contains a number of Case Studies and Macro Finance Insights. Case Studies provide an in depth look at what makes China's economy unique: everything from China's Five-Year Plans to the One Child Policy to the use of the Weixin Zhifu app. Macro Finance Insights borrow and explain critical concepts from finance, microeconomics, and management in order to elucidate financial and economic phenomena in China: for example, how can we assess the financial situation of China as we would a company? What is the role of the International Monetary Fund? Why Chinese companies would prefer one capital structure over another? Included in these Case Studies and Macro Finance Insights are the many topics we read about daily with regard to China, e.g., the environment, urbanization, the depletion of the labor force in the agricultural sector and, of course, bubbles in real estate. Wherever useful, we provide the US experience as a counterpoint.

Chapter 1 presents the four key drivers for the Chinese economy, what makes China different, and why those drivers matter. Furthermore, we review some basic ideas from macroeconomics that we will need to know as we read the rest of the book. In Chapter 2 we discuss the different ways that China measures gross domestic product (GDP) compared to the United States, the quality of Chinese economic data, and how alternate measures of GDP are relevant when discussing China. This chapter also gives us the opportunity to discuss China's environment in a Case Study. Chapter 3 presents the very important topic of the balance of payments—how it is defined, measured, and determined. Here, we examine how China accumulated over USD 3 trillion in foreign exchange reserves and how that accumulation relates to its trading and financing relationship with the United States. In Chapter 4 we examine the critical question of economic growth: are growth rates of 6 percent sustainable in China, and what are the fundamental factors that cause United States growth to be so much lower?

While the earlier chapters give us a broad perspective in terms of measurement and long-run growth in China and the United States alike, the remaining chapters provide great detail regarding institutions and policies in China that are fundamentally different from those in the US. Chapter 5 examines China's famously high savings rate (or alternatively, low levels of consumption). Here we have an opportunity to provide historical context, examine myths surrounding the data, and discuss where savings and consumption are likely to trend in the coming years. We also look in detail at corporate profits, a key element in China savings. Chapter 6 discusses the counterpart to China's high savings: its high rate of investment. In a Macro Finance Insight, we look at a key player in China's investment activity—the China Development Bank—by applying some simple concepts from finance.

Chapter 7, on monetary institutions and policy, allows us to look deeply at the complex set of tools used by the People's Bank of China and why such complexity exists. Both Chapters 7 and 8 discuss how China holds its wealth and how that profile will almost certainly change in the coming years. We compare Chinese monetary policy to the United States' in recent years, especially during times of financial crisis. Chapter 9 presents the basic Keynesian framework plus more sophisticated extensions to that model that will matter to China in the future. The basic model gives us a chance to understand the significance of some unique features of the Chinese economy, such as the *hukou* system and the high degree of adaptability of the labor force. Chapter 10 shows how recent policies in times of crisis have been decidedly Keynesian and we examine China's evolving social safety net. Furthermore, we make a detailed comparison of the differing profiles of public finance, from taxation to expenditures and fiscal transfers, between China and the United States. Finally, in Chapter 11 we present China's financial system in the context of its laws and institutions. In doing so, we conjecture what the shape of China's financial system will be in the future. This chapter allows us to explore e-money, shadow banking, and the unique ways that Chinese citizens can now hold wealth (asset management).

The Case Studies should be required reading for all purchasers of the textbook. Those readers with a deep interest in understanding Chinese data would benefit from Chapters 1–4. Those with a deep interest in government institutions and policy will benefit most from Chapters 1 and 7–10. Those with a keen interest in China's key drivers would most benefit from Chapters 1 and 4–11. Chapter 9 presents theory that challenges the reader to imagine China as a fully developed economy, including actual *renminbi* internationalization. Reading all of Chapters 1–11 will move the student to the "China Scholar" level!

The reader needs only a good macroeconomic principles course that covers demand side economics and long-run growth to comprehend the content in this textbook. For the Macro Finance Insights, some familiarity with finance would be helpful, but in most cases the explanations of concepts are self-contained. Part II of Chapter 4 and the last half of Chapter 5 on corporate savings have a heavy dose of financial analysis. I intentionally did not relegate these chapters to appendices because one of my goals in writing this book was to incorporate finance into our macroeconomic understanding of China and the United States to the fullest extent possible. Students without any background in finance may find these sections challenging but mind-expanding.

ACKNOWLEDGEMENTS

There are so many people to thank. Of course, the thousands of master's students I have taught over the years at Columbia University in New York, the University of International Business and Economics (UIBE) in Beijing, Shanghai Jiao Tong University, Chinese European International Business School in Shanghai (CEIBS), Hong Kong University of Science and Technology (HKUST), IESE, and Xian Jiao Tong Liverpool University's International Business School of Suzhou (IBSS). At the other end are the 老百姓 (*lao bai xing*, or the common man in China) who have taught me so much about their daily lives, full of aspirations and challenges.

Abby Schroering, a PhD candidate at Columbia University, provided amazing editorial assistance for this 2nd edition. She carefully edited and improved my writing and found errors and contradictions using "super-power" observational skills. Then there is the excellent detailed-oriented production work of Kimberley Hutchins (Hitch) and her very patient team at BooknookBiz, part of the Amazon publishing ecosystem. The beautiful cover design was created by the extremely talented, Shelley Savoy. George Lobell, my editor at ME Sharpe (my original publisher), would certainly come out at the top of any academic's list of acknowledgements. When I explained this project to him, he immediately "got it" and has been an unflinching supporter ever since—a real intellect. Irene Bunnell, Laurie Underwood and Eva Schramm (my daughter) line edited the first edition of this text. I give particular praise to the very excellent research assistance of Jiale "Javelin" Dong, a master's student at IBSS. Able assistance has also been provided by Pan Wang, Pinpin Jiang and Tom Wang (王云飞).

And then there are the scholars and professionals who provided their gentle advice and encouragement. Dean Sarah Dixon has created a wonderful and supportive atmosphere for research at IBSS, making this task all the more satisfying. Professors Lin Guijun, Lydia Price, KC Chan, and Sun Liu have all helped in their own way. Professor Ying Wu (Salisbury University) provided extremely detailed and useful comments and corrections to the first edition of the text. A lifetime of thanks to Professors Guillermo Calvo, John Donaldson, Xiaobo Lu, Maurice Obstfeld, Paulo Regis and Nachum Sicherman for their scholarship and humanity. Tom Easton, former China editor at *The Economist* and my former student at Columbia, has taught me much regarding China. Jeremy Stevens of Standard Bank and Phillippe Wingender in the fiscal department of the International Monetary Fund shared very useful insights on the chapters related to monetary and fiscal policy in China. Thanks to David Adams of the Fulbright Scholars Program who pushed for my great year in Beijing as a Fulbrighter at UIBE. Many parts of this book were presented to the China Group (which I founded) at the Harvard Club of New York. Participants' comments have been incorporated. Insights were also gained through participation in the China Investment Group, the China Forum, the China Institute of New York, and the Hong Kong Economic and Trade Organization in New York.

Finally, I truly thank my loving family—Connie Chung-Schramm, Mark, Eva, and David—who put up with my long absences while in China (and my absent-mindedness while at home). I would be lost (literally) without my dear wife—her support has helped me see this through. I dedicate this book to Connie and all of my 12 brothers and sisters who have the misconception that I am smart.

Ron Schramm
2020

1
INTRODUCTION

书山有路勤为径

Diligence is the Royal Path to Learning

China and the United States, the world's two largest economies, operate in a complex and ever-evolving relationship. In the first edition of this book we referred to the relationship as a marriage; recent years show severe strains between the partners. In the chapters that follow, we explore their economic relationship—an important factor in all marriages.[1] It is remarkable that along almost any economic dimension, we find China and the United States as complementary partners who often operate in starkly different ways. This makes for a truly fascinating study. In most of this text, the primary focus is on China. Comparisons are made with the United States as a counterpoint; a way to highlight similarities and differences. With the ascendancy of the Trump administration in 2016 came some dramatic shifts in the United States-China relationship, making a textbook such as this all the more important.

China's economic reforms toward a market-based economy began in 1978 (two years after the death of Chairman Mao Zedong) and have continued since then without halt. Throughout the following chapters, we must keep that date in mind since most of the discussion, data, and analysis we use really applies to the modern Chinese economy—and the process of moving to a market-based economy, which started in earnest in 1978. Although China is one of the oldest civilizations on Earth (dating back to at least 221 BCE), it is, in another sense, one of the world's youngest large modern economies. We could say that China is historically and culturally older but economically younger than the United States. Many scholars have written about the significant steps in China's development process since 1978. Wu Jinglian (2005) and Barry Naughton (2018), for example, provide excellent step-by-step descriptions of China's remarkable path of economic progress from both before and after that critical year. Naughton describes how the post-1978 period represents both an abrupt departure from and a continuation of historical economic patterns. We will not attempt to cover the same ground in this book.

Instead, this textbook combines macroeconomic analysis (now and into the future) and data for China and the United States and incorporates a novel approach to macroeconomics using tools and frameworks from finance, microeconomics, and management. This approach is particularly useful when thinking about China, a country that is often managed like a company. China is an incredibly dynamic economy, and its significance in the world arena is ever increasing. In tandem with China's development into an economic powerhouse, there has been an explosion of academic research and news coverage related to the Chinese economy. In writing this textbook, we owe much to other academic scholars in China and around the world, as well as the excellent China research being done by the International Monetary Fund, the World Bank, the Organization for Economic Co-operation and Development (OECD), the Bank for International Settlements, the Chinese Academy for Social Sciences, China's National Bureau of Statistics (NBS), the Federal Reserve and its Database System (FRED), CEIC, a number of other international organizations, and of course, *The Economist* magazine. This second edition taps into much of that new knowledge, synthesizes it, and presents it in a modern macroeconomic framework.

Four Key Drivers for the Chinese Economy

At least four key drivers of the Chinese economy today distinguish it from the United States and other large countries around the world. These key drivers help to explain many of the aspects an outsider would find puzzling about China—both in terms of economics and in daily life.

1: A Large Population

China has the world's largest population; at 1.4 billion people, it remains larger than its nearest competitor (India) by roughly 88 million citizens.[2] This large population resides on a substantially smaller plot of arable land than is found in the United States, and it must be usefully employed, fed, clothed, housed, and kept healthy. Accomplishing these basics is still a daily struggle for a good portion of China's population. This vast labor pool, which is available to a cohesive political system, deeply influences which industries thrive in China and which products are traded with the rest of the world. Furthermore, economic growth relies heavily on labor growth, a key factor of production. Chapters 1, 4, 5 and 9 discuss China's economic growth, savings and consumption, demographic shifts, and employment—all of which deal with this key factor from different angles. Figure 1.1 shows the progression of China's population and employment with the gap between the two starting to widen—an issue we will turn to in Chapter 4.

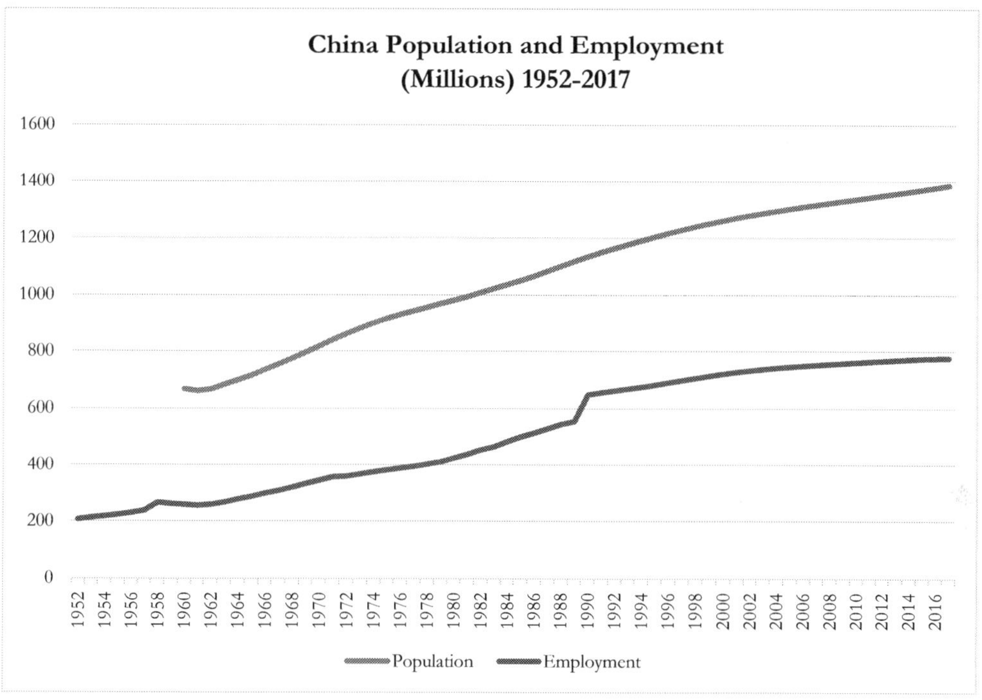

Figure 1.1 Growth in China's huge population and employment began to slow in the 1980s after the introduction of the "one-child policy."
Source: Author created based on Federal Reserve Economic Database.

2: A Very High Savings Rate

Among the world's large economies, China has the highest savings rate in the world—over 47 percent of gross domestic product (GDP) in 2017, according to World Bank data. To put this in perspective, the highest national savings rate achieved in the United States since World War II was 25 percent (in the mid-1960s). That rate has steadily declined to today's rate of around 18 percent. This large savings pool has important implications for investment, future growth, and China's current account imbalance with (and capital account lending to) the United States. In Chapter 5, we examine why China's savings rate is so high (or why its consumption is so low) and try to gauge what future Chinese savings will look like. Chapters 3, 4, and 6 look deeply into the implications of China's high savings rate both domestically and globally. Figure 1.2 shows China's savings rate over time, which peaked in 2008 at 52 percent.

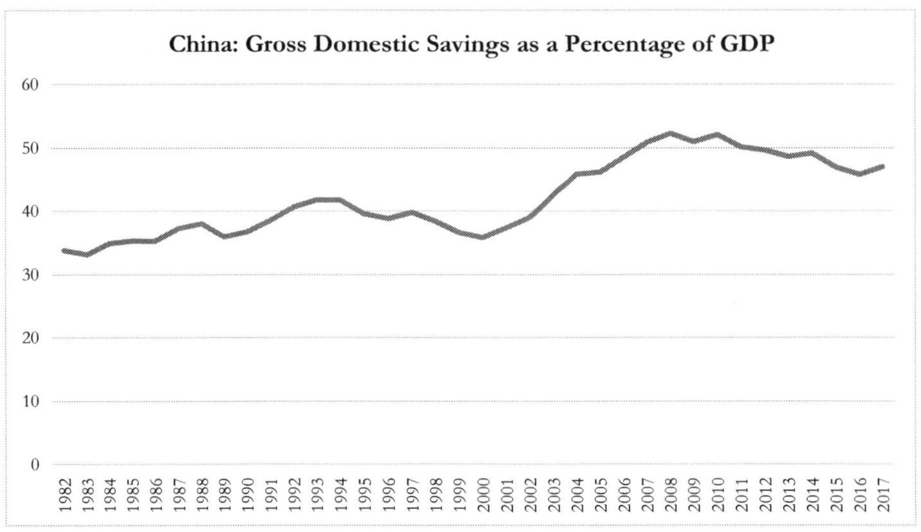

Figure 1.2 Among large economies, China, far and away, has the world's highest savings rate as a share of GDP.
Source: Author created based on World Bank World Development Indicators.

3: The Government's Role

The role of government in economic management is significantly greater in China than in the United States. The Chinese authorities establish and implement Five-Year Plans, which provide direction from the top down for China's key economic institutions—from China's central bank to provinces, townships, many companies, and even academia. The first Plan was issued in 1953. China's Central Committee and National Congress formulate these plans in conjunction with the Communist Party. While, at a microeconomic level, Chinese individuals and companies can be ferociously competitive and independent, they operate in an arena managed from the top. Paradoxically, the fierce competition at the microeconomic level is partially a result of the absence of a government role. Rule of (commercial) law and regulatory enforcement are still at an inchoate stage in much of China—particularly at the local level.

The directives in China's Five-Year Plans are not mere blandishments; rather, they are targets that anyone operating in China must understand and respond to. In many of the coming chapters, we ask how a Chief Financial Officer or Chief Executive Officer might look at a particular macroeconomic problem. This approach is intended to help us understand how top-down management works in an economy such as China's. Chapters 7–10 discuss the institutional arrangements and structures for making macroeconomic policy in China, as well as the actual policies undertaken in recent years. In Figure 1.3 we see that authorities in China have had ambitious targets for economic growth over the years and have almost always surpassed or met those targets. China's next (14th) Five-Year Plan, covering 2021–25, will no doubt continue many of the themes of the 13th, including a greater focus on the environment. Given the Trump trade war and COVID-19 pandemic, it will be interesting to find hints of China's vision of its place in the world economy in the years to come.

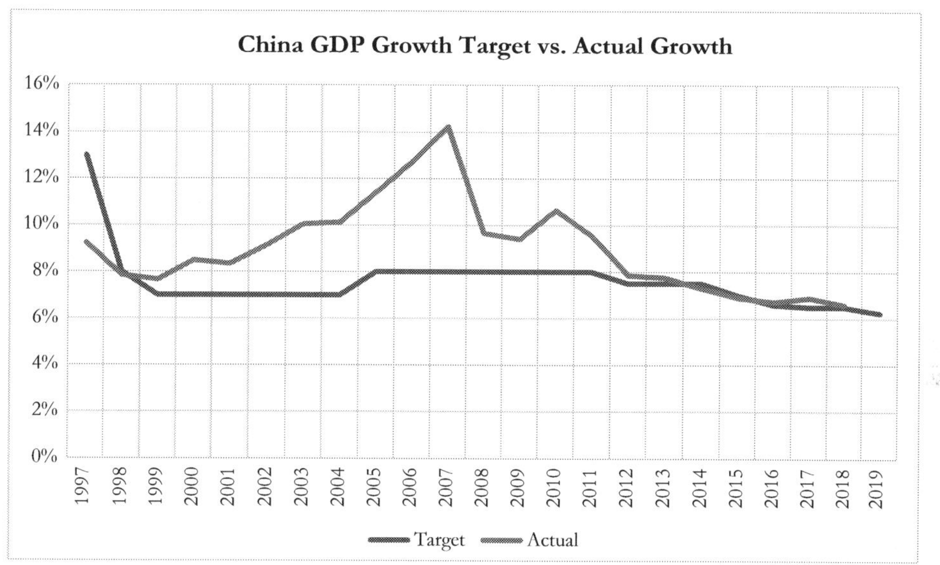

Figure 1.3 Chinese authorities set targets for GDP growth via Five-Year Plans and their updates. Actual growth generally exceeds target growth.
Source: Author created based on National Bureau of Statistics, China.

Brandt, Ma, and Rawski (2014) suggest, in their excellent survey of institutional developments over China's long history, that since 1978 enhanced state capacity has "endowed the state with unprecedented leverage over resources. Vast foreign exchange reserves, official control over the financial system, sweeping privatization of urban housing and of state-owned and town-and-village enterprise assets, and widespread confiscation and reassignment of farmland all illustrate newfound state power, often exercised through local government agencies, to accumulate and allocate assets on an immense scale…" (107).

But Coase and Wang (2012) attribute much of China's economic success not so much to the government's intervention, but rather to prudent governmental decisions to step back from involvement in the economy. Specifically, in the 1980s, allowing agricultural markets, town and village enterprises, urban businesses, and special economic zones (SEZs) to develop and operate was critical to economic development.[3]

The authors argue that, in later decades, the government's role in allowing for the integration of regional markets into a cohesive national economy permitted greater competition, economies of scope and scale, and in turn economic growth. This is a "Coasian" reminder that while some government activities, such as promotion of rule of law and political stability and infrastructure development, are critical, allowing for private markets to flourish is of equal if not greater importance. In Chapter 11, dealing with China's financial sector, we examine the nexus between government involvement, the private market, and savings.

4: Labor, The Great Economic Shock Absorber

China's workforce is extraordinarily flexible and adaptable. The willingness of the 老百姓 (pronounced *lao bai xing,* "the common man") to relocate and be relocated, work assiduously for low wages under difficult circumstances, and hold savings with negative real returns for prolonged periods (all in the hope of a better future) is arguably unmatched anywhere else in the world. At the core of China's great economic development is this great economic shock absorber. No other economy in the world boasts this extra degree of freedom. This unique characteristic allows Chinese policy-makers greater freedom as they experiment with new reforms and major shifts in economic policies. The jarring back and forth from a several-children to a one-child to a two-child policy over the past 40 years further underscores how policy-makers in China can and have exploited this flexibility. Labor force malleability is, in part, a necessary response in an economy with a large population, scarce resources, and a Confucian tradition of obedience to authority (see Case Study 1.1 below).

Description/Position (Year)	Monthly Wage Income (RMB)	Monthly Wage Income (USD)
Urban Worker (2016, National)	5,631	823
White Collar Worker (2018)	7,629	1,115
Master's Level Finance (2018)	11,810	1,727
Software Developer (2018)	11,300	1,652
Manufacturing Worker (2017)	5,000–7,000	731–1,035
Construction Worker (2017)	5,000–7,000	731–1,035
Restaurant Waiter (2018)	3,400–5,400	497–789

Table 1.1 Wages in China remain low, but since 2005 they have risen substantially.
Source: Author estimates based on various sources including city averages from www.zhaopin.com.

Table 1.1 presents recent (https://www.zhaopin.com/) monthly wages for workers in China with differing skill sets. Government officials in China are constantly trying to strike the right balance between economic progress and the pressures placed on the average Chinese citizen.[4] In Chapter 5, 7, and 9 we gain greater insight into how this flexibility plays out in China. Figures 1.4a and 1.4b show recent "help wanted" posters in China including wage offers. The government's massive and rapid response to the 2020 outbreak of the COVID-19 virus in Wuhan provides a good example of both the population's adaptability and flexibility and the powerful role of government in China. Once the threat of the virus was finally recognized, China's government engaged in a massive program of control. Wuhan, the most populous city in central China (a city of 11 million people), was completely quarantined—transportation and individuals' movements were tightly controlled. In many apartment complexes around the country (typically gated communities), exit and entry was fully restricted. Over half of China's population (https://nyti.ms/2zt53EK) experienced severe restrictions in movement. It would be difficult in any other part of the world to have such control over vast swathes of the population without public cooperation.

Figure 1.4a Unskilled workers usually have little trouble finding work but at very low wages. Looking for service workers in Hefei, capital of Anhui province in 2018.
Source: Author.

Figure 1.4b Looking for restaurant staff in Shanghai, 2019.
Source: Author.

Case Study 1.1: Confucius, Adam Smith, and Family Values

"What is prudence in the conduct of every private family can scarce be folly in that of a great kingdom."

—Adam Smith. *The Wealth of Nations* (1776)

"It is not possible for one to teach others while he cannot teach his own family. Therefore, the ruler, without going beyond his family, completes the lessons for the state."

—Confucius. *The Great Learning* (500 BCE)

Both the great economist Adam Smith (of the early Industrial Revolution) and the great Chinese philosopher Confucius, (from the 5th century BCE) tell us that the activities of individual units—such as the family—provide the basis for a strong nation (or a nation's economy). Smith argues that the state can learn how to manage its finances from the family unit, especially in terms of frugality or savings. Confucius states that a well-run family is the starting point and training ground for running the state. Family is at the base of the pyramid that has national governance at its pinnacle.

But, in *The Theory of Moral Sentiments* (1759), Smith also emphasizes the role of the individual tempered by his/her innate virtues (such as empathy) as the *primum mobile* of a fair and just society. Under such an assumption, he suggests that the behavior of individuals and individual units acting in their own self-interest leads to a greater good for society; the "invisible hand" operating via private markets would lead to good outcomes. For Confucius, virtue needs to be inculcated in both citizens and leaders because it does not come naturally. The ultimate goal for Confucius is improved state-craft in the hands of a strong, fair, and just leader.

Without doubt, the family unit continues to serve as a critical component woven into the fabric of society. Given the modern industrialized and industrializing economies of the United States and China, we ask in this textbook if national macroeconomic management can also be enhanced with lessons from a more recent basic unit in society—the corporation.

Key Drivers are Moving in the Wrong Direction

A major challenge for China presented throughout this book is that, while in the past these key drivers have worked to promote economic growth, they are now moving in the wrong direction. Specifically, the labor force is shrinking both absolutely and as a share of the population. Gross savings as a share of GDP peaked in 2008 and is gradually trending downward. The ability to move laborers from farms to urban areas has reached a limit. This specific constraint on labor flexibility is referred to as the "Lewis Turning Point," and it is discussed in Case Study 1.2. The one key driver that remains both fully active in China and even reinvigorated is the role of government. In part, this may reflect the directional drag of the other key drivers just discussed. In Case Study 1.3 and the coming chapters, we will highlight the need for and emergence of technological progress as a new key driving force in the Chinese economy to supplement the other key drivers.

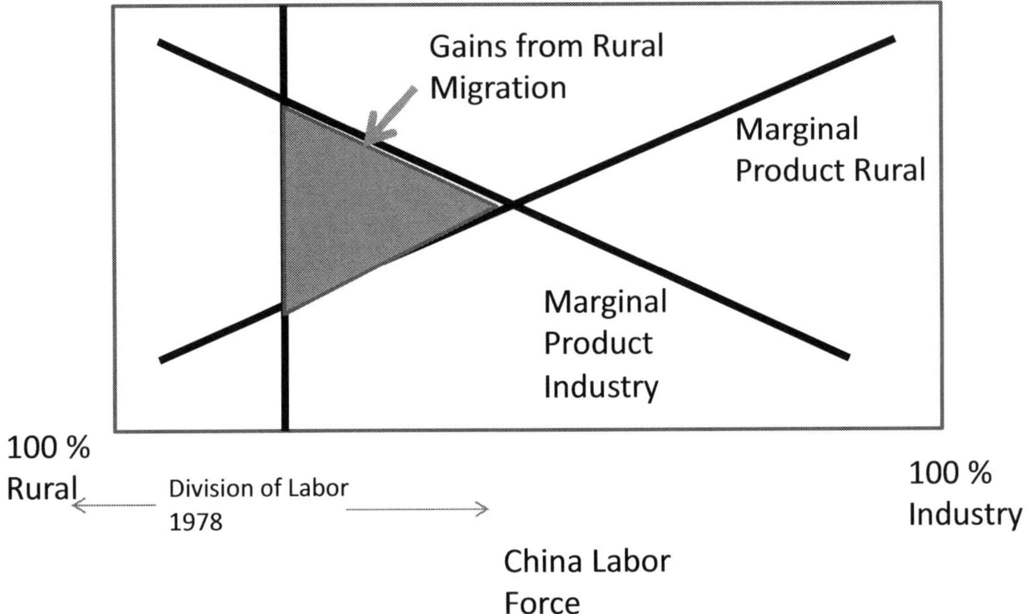

Figure 1.5 The Lewis Turning Point contends that countries eventually exhaust the total benefits of worker migration from rural employment (farms) to industry (cities and towns).
Source: Author created.

Case Study 1.2: Lewis Turning Point

As workers move from farms (rural areas) to manufacturing industries (urban areas), the marginal value of worker output rises on farms and falls in manufacturing (the law of diminishing returns). At a certain point, it is no longer efficient to continue to have workers relocate since the lost output value on the farm exceeds that which is gained in the factory. This critical point is referred to as the "Lewis Turning Point." In the past China's growth has been boosted by the movement of workers from farms to factories, but the marginal benefit no longer exists. Figure 1.5 shows the division of China's labor force on the horizontal axis between rural and urban. As the labor force migrates rightward along the horizontal axis marginal productivity rises in rural and falls in urban.

In 1980, about 19 percent of the population lived in urban areas; today, close to 60 percent live in towns and cities. This ratio is approaching that of the United States, where about 80 percent of the population lives in urban areas. Meanwhile, those remaining available for agricultural work in rural areas, tend to be either too young or too old to work. According to the World Bank (Cai Fang et al.

2012) the proportion of working-age people in rural areas is significantly smaller than that found in urban areas and will continue to shrink. It has been suggested (https://econ.st/2YWcnDp) that China is approaching its turning point in the next few years. In 2015 there were about 40 million "leftover" children in rural areas constituting about 29 percent of all rural children. These "leftover" children are individuals under the age of 18 who have been left behind to live with grandparents (or ideally other caregivers) by parents who have moved to urban areas seeking work (NBS, UNICEF). Both the shrinking population and changing demographics in rural areas make the need for introducing new technologies in agriculture urgent. In fact, the challenges created by this transformation are often depicted in Chinese television series that show rural villages bereft of working-age males and populated by small children, the aged, and females.

Macroeconomics Review and Overview

Macroeconomics is the study of a nation's economy in the aggregate. Analyzing how the national economy performs, how to enhance its performance, and how its performance impacts global linkages are all key macroeconomic concerns. As such, macroeconomics deals with questions of recession and recovery, unemployment, inflation, interest rates, savings, current accounts, investment, and long-run economic growth. Meanwhile, microeconomics deals with individual and firm (company) behavior and how distinct markets operate. In theory, we should be able to aggregate individual agent behavior in the microeconomy up to the macroeconomy and achieve meaningful results—after all, the macroeconomy should equal the sum of its parts. But this has, so far, proven difficult, especially since the individual agents are not identical (they are heterogeneous) and can interact in ways that seem irrational. An alternative approach would be to take frameworks from microeconomics, management, and finance, and assume that the macroeconomy behaves like one large firm. We often use that approach in this textbook (see the "Macro Finance Insights") and find that this does indeed provide useful insights into both the Chinese and United States economies.

The models and approaches described in the Appendix rely heavily on the experience of Western industrializing or industrialized economies. Are these experiences relevant for emerging economies such as China? Consider the question of aggregation. Do economists need to invest as much intellectual capital in this question in the presence of a Five-Year Plan, a tool China has put forth 14 times over the past 70 years? Is aggregation already accomplished via the plan, and can we more usefully adjust our macroeconomic questions to assess the rationale for aggregation rather than concern ourselves with technical questions on how to aggregate economic activity? In this text, we look to the theory of the corporation for guidance. Rarely are questions asked about aggregation when it comes to the theory of the firm or in corporate finance. Rather, it is assumed that workers work toward a goal (a strategy, a plan) and that management devises and implements that strategy.

Rather than struggling with questions of equilibrium or disequilibrium, perhaps better concerns for emerging economies are management decisions and incentives that yield the desired results of the plan or strategic mission. Instead of price flexibility or fixity, we suggest developing a pricing strategy and analyzing where the firm has market power. In this context, we assess the competitive advantages of a nation and how to exploit them. If governments have some degree of monopsony power in labor or credit markets, how will this impact the operation of markets?

Instead of making assumptions about how expectations are exogenously formed, it may be more relevant for us to think of how management can shape expectations in order to achieve desired outcomes. Specifically, can expectations be shaped by management or the government so as to build confidence? Furthermore, just as with a firm, some information is privy only to insiders, while other information is publicly known. Can expectations be controlled through the flow of information? In emerging markets, perhaps it is more fruitful to examine the asymmetry of information between insiders and outsiders than to attempt to model the expectations of individuals and firms.

Back to Supply and Demand

"All of economics is just supply and demand," or so said a sage MBA student after listening to a lecture chock full of technical detail. Figure 1.6 illustrates how simple macroeconomics is at this basic level. The level of output, employment, and price will be determined by the intersection of supply and demand. As discussed above, Western macroeconomics has wavered back and forth between emphasizing the role of demand (the basis for Keynesian economics) and the role of supply (real business cycle theory and growth theory). This difference can also be found in the Chinese and Western approach to macroeconomic policy, and—as we shall see—it is of great importance. The important role of supply shocks reared its ugly head with the arrival of the COVID-19 pandemic in 2020.

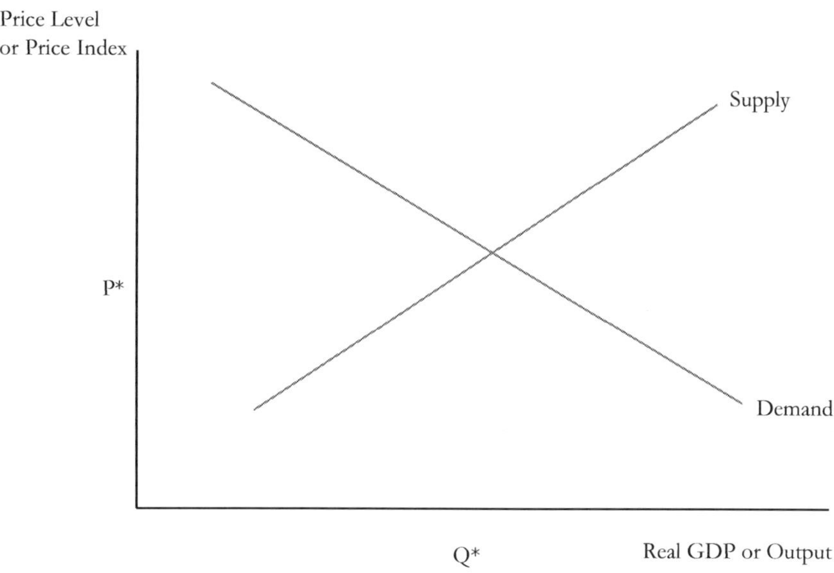

Figure 1.6 We can summarize an entire economy with an aggregate supply and demand curve. Where they intersect will determine equilibrium (average) prices and real GDP or output.
Source: Author created.

In China, the traditional macroeconomic focus has been on what to supply, where to supply output, and how it should be supplied. In Western macroeconomics, the traditional focus has been on the question of demand—is it adequate to absorb all of what is produced? Even when Western economists analyze supply, it is an abstraction rather than a careful sectoral look at who needs to produce what in order to satisfy the demands of society. Western economists are mostly concerned with how to manipulate aggregate demand so as to ensure full employment of resources. The Chinese emphasis has traditionally focused on promoting output industry by industry—demand is more or less assumed to be sufficient.

These differences are seen clearly in the way economic activity is described in national statistics. Western economists begin the measure of GDP with retail sales, corporate investment, government spending, and exports—all of which are components of demand. In fact, as we discuss later, these components are part of consumption (*C*), investment (*I*), government spending (*G*), and net exports (*XGS-MGS*)—the traditional demand-side decomposition of GDP used in Western economies. In China, GDP has traditionally been presented in terms of Primary Sector Output (agriculture, mining, and forestry), Secondary Sector Output (manufacturing and construction), and Tertiary Sector Output (services including the government's contribution to output). Further statistical breakdowns of output cover sectors within manufacturing, construction, or services. All the while, the statistical breakdown focuses on supply and output—including which provinces and important cities are producing which output.[5] In an GDP accounting sense (discussed in Chapter 2), supply necessarily equals demand; thus, the Western and Chinese approaches should be equivalent. But, as we shall see, the two have very different policy implications.

For example, we could compare the emphasis in China's 12th Five-Year Plan with a recent US Economic Report of the President. In the latest Five-Year Plan, we see the following targets:

- GDP to grow by 7 percent annually on average
- More than 45 million jobs to be created in urban areas
- Rise in domestic consumption
- Service sector value-added output to account for 47 percent of GDP, up 4 percentage points
- Annual grain production capacity to be no less than 540 million tons
- Construction and renovation of 36 million apartments for low-income families
- Expenditure on research and development to account for 2.2 percent of GDP

In contrast, in the 2011 Economic Report of the President, we see the following sections:

- Consumption and Saving
- Developments in Housing Markets
- Business Fixed Investment
- Business Inventories
- Government Outlays, Consumption, and Investment
- State and Local Government
- Real Exports and Imports

Comparing the contents of each document against the ability of the respective governments to actually implement these goals shows very different outcomes. In China, as we shall see, the tools for controlling the supply side of output are generally more sophisticated than are those of the United States; however, the United States' tools for managing demand are relatively more refined than China's.

The existence of these differences clearly reflects the differing economic histories of the two nations. In China, we see a tradition inherited from the Soviet planning model, including Five-Year Plans. We could trace events back through 20 centuries of Chinese history to consider great public works projects including the Great Wall and China's canals and water management efforts. Clearly, China has a very long history of viewing demand—particularly consumer demand—as an afterthought. Since the Chinese government was fully communist before 1978, it could and did control the means of production.[6] While government ownership of the means of production in China is shrinking, the notion that output can and should be controlled is not.

In the United States, the laissez-faire tradition combined with perhaps the world's most vibrant marketing, advertising, and branding infrastructure has established demand as a pillar of the US economy—particularly consumer demand, in which 70 percent of national output is used. The US production mix (supply) is primarily affected by how much the government demands, as well as tax policy (to some extent). The latter can also impact consumption. In the United States, production at the industrial level is determined by individual firms; in China, production at the industrial level often is still influenced by the government taking the lead, and firms from within the industry follow. In the United States, tax policy and government spending can impact consumption, investment, and (of course) government demand. In China, the tools available for influencing demand are directed at investment, exports, and the government.

An Inflection in Plan Strategies for Both Countries

Despite the obvious differences in emphasis between supply and demand, we also see some convergence in the two countries' approaches. China's twelfth Five-Year Plan discusses the need for greater consumption in China at length, while the Economic Report of the President examines issues related to innovation, infrastructure, education, healthcare, and clean energy. By 2018, both the Five-Year Plan and the Economic Report of the President had moved very far from their traditional emphases and converged somewhat in content. The 13th Five-Year Plan (2016–2020) represents a substantial shift from earlier plans in China. Here, we see less of the urgency to meet specific production targets found in the traditional plans and a greater emphasis on the broader qualitative aspirations of social welfare. Goals include:

- Inclusive Growth, allowing for those in the lower rungs of income to capture some of the gains from economic growth

- Coordinated Development, or allowing for more income equality across regions and industries
- Green Growth, or environmentally friendly growth
- Openness, or a continuation of China's long efforts at opening up trade in goods and services and financial flows across borders
- Rebalancing, or continued movement from an investment and export driven economy to an economy with consumption as the key element of demand

Even more significantly, Chinese authorities have begun to emphasize "quality of growth" over "quantity of growth"—concepts we discuss in great detail in Chapters 4 and 6. In 2015, China introduced a new kind of plan with an even longer horizon and a specific agenda emphasizing technology and innovation—see Case Study 1.3: Made in China 2025. This longer-term plan had more of the traditional flavor of aggressive targets within a central planning framework. As of the writing of this text, the Chinese authorities have decided to "play down" the significance of the Made in China agenda.

Case Study 1.3: Made in China: 2025

In the earlier sections of this chapter, we have argued that the forces (key drivers) that have propelled China's spectacular growth in the past are now acting as a drag on future economic growth. One critical solution to this problem is for the economy to rely more heavily on technological progress as a source of economic growth. Later chapters will give a more concrete definition of what that is; meanwhile, we can look at Chinese policy-makers' Made in China: 2025 policy proposals as both a response to the problem and an insight into how the government defines what is required.

Proposed by Premier Li Keqiang in 2015, Made in China: 2025 is a strategic agenda for upgrading China's manufacturing base from low-end to high-end manufacturing. The proposal was fashioned after considering the experiences of other countries with a sophisticated technological base, particularly Germany. Specific industries include advanced electric vehicles, information and communication technologies, robotics and artificial intelligence, agriculture, aerospace, materials science, power equipment, biotechnology, rail infrastructure, and maritime engineering. Of course, a key driver—the government—is to play a critical role utilizing the traditional tools of binding targets, subsidies, directed finance, state-owned enterprise investment, and the active acquisition of foreign technology.

China's proposals are a form of "strategic trade policy" (Krugman 1986)—an effort to shape (comparative) international trade advantages, rather than simply rely on inherited factor advantages (such as a large pool of labor). The goal here is to specialize (and lead the world) in industries that have a high value-added based on higher productivities or greater market power. Conversely, the goal is an attempt to move away from low-end manufacturing, low-end exports, and high-tech imports to a situation where China manufactures and exports high-tech products. Higher value-added exports implies Chinese citizens would reap a higher level of per capita income.

While the opportunities created by Made in China: 2025 are potentially great, a number of challenges lurk. A common critique is whether top-down decision making (from government down to individual firms) can best pick and nurture "winning" or successful industries of the future. As we move up the technology ladder, do we also risk falling off the ladder, relying less and less on economic considerations and more and more on the needs of special interests and political goals? Another consideration is the response of other global technology leaders in the United States, Europe and Asia. Already the United States, under the Trump administration, has launched a trade war against China with a key rallying cry related to China's acquisition of foreign technology as part of its 2025 agenda.

Finally, 2025 presents some fundamental internal challenges to the Chinese economy. Only about 10 percent of Chinese citizens between the age of 25 and 64 have a tertiary education, a third of the ratio found in richer economies (https://bit.ly/2Lp1MZQ)—though that figure is rapidly growing. Most of China's natural advantage is still in low to medium-end manufacturing. As China transitions to high-end sectors, moving more and more financial and skill-intensive resources into these industries, it is possible that a large swath of the workforce will be left behind. That result would be fully in conflict with the aspirational social goals stated in China's 13th Five-Year Plan. China, of course, is not alone in facing this dilemma. In the West, technological advances have already created great strains on the lower rungs of the labor force.

In the Economic Reports of the President (Presidents Obama and Trump) we see an evolving emphasis on supply-side issues such as infrastructure, technology and innovation, labor markets, deregulation, tax policies to promote growth. Similar to the more recent Five-Year Plan, social issues such as income distribution, inclusive growth and health care are all highlighted. Demand-side management in the Economic Report of the President, while still presented and discussed, has taken a back seat and become incidental to these broader themes.

Key Analytic Distinctions in Macroeconomics

In this book, we will introduce a great deal of economic data. It is important to keep in mind a few basic distinctions when we are looking at macroeconomic data.

Business Cycles vs. Growth Cycles

Business cycles, in Western economies, correspond to absolute declines in economic activity broadly defined to include specific indicators such as GDP, industrial production, retail sales, personal income less transfer payments, and the number of employees on non-agricultural payrolls.[5] Rapidly growing economies such as China's rarely experience absolute declines in economic output, but rather a slowing of growth. In the business cycle case, a recession would be represented by a prolonged period of negative growth in key indicators, while in the growth cycle case, growth could still be positive—just not as positive as trend growth.[7]

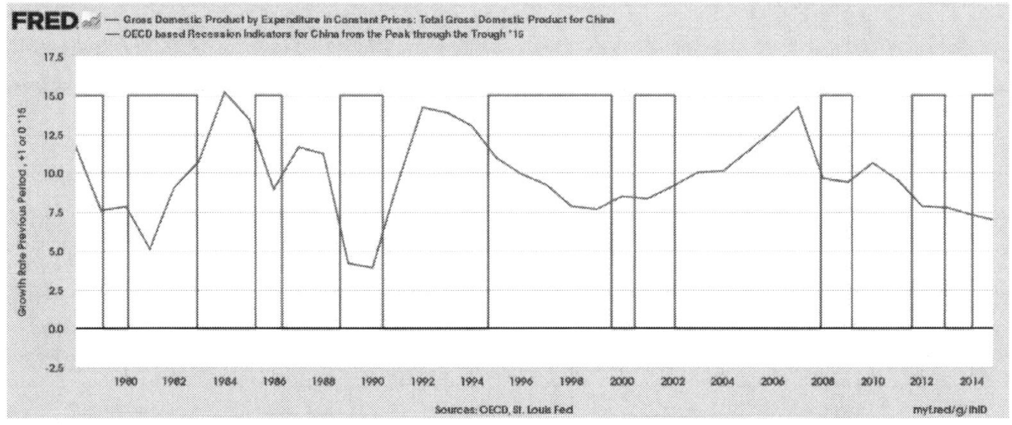

Figure 1.7 Rectangular boxes indicate growth cycle recessions set against actual real GDP growth in China.
Source: Author created based on Federal Reserve Economic Database.

Figure 1.7 shows China's real GDP growth rate from 1978–2016 along with growth cycle indicators for growth recessions (represented as rectangles) based on OECD estimates. We see continuous positive growth typical of a rapidly emerging economy such as China. In fact, China in its post-reform period has had only one outright business cycle recession according to the Conference Board (https://bit.ly/2YWkDTL) from July, 1988 to October, 1989, a time of political turmoil.[8, 9]

Figure 1.8 below shows that the United States has experienced five business cycle recessions for the comparable period (1978–present). The shaded columns indicate business cycle recessions for the entire post WWII era, periods in which there was an absolute decline in economic activity. For every shaded area, we see an outright decline in GDP levels.

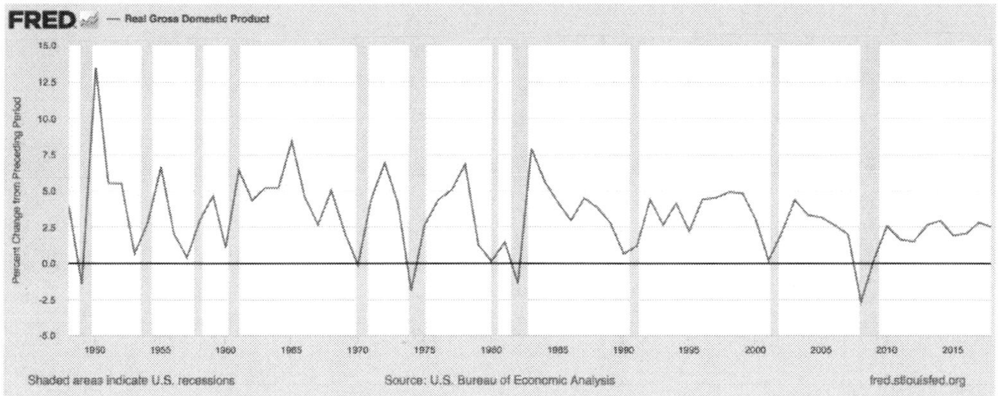

Figure 1.8 In contrast to China, the United States has experienced many outright business cycle recessions over the past 70 years.
Source: Author created based on Federal Reserve Economic Database.

Nominal Variables vs. Real Variables

Another distinction is the difference between nominal variables and real variables. Nominal variables and numbers are variables and numbers that we can actually observe in our day-to-day lives. For example, the price we actually pay for an apple or a bowl of rice at a store or restaurant is a nominal price.

In contrast, real variables are an attempt to measure physical volumes—or at least a measure that removes the effects of price changes over time. The goal here is to examine fundamental activity rather than allowing price changes to confound what is happening in a real sense. For example, between one year and the next, the nominal price of a bowl of rice may increase by 50 percent. It would be wrong, in a real sense, to say that our consumption of rice went up year over year by 50 percent if in fact we are just consuming the same single bowl each year. We might describe our real consumption as one bowl of rice each year, or *renminbi* (RMB) 1 "in constant RMBs" each year (assuming that was the initial price).

We can remove the price effect from nominal variables, converting them to real variables, through price indexes. Price indexes are numerical measures of average prices for goods and services. They are used to compare average price changes over time. If we know how prices change, we can then subtract that effect to derive the real value of an item and measure real growth.

Year	2012	2013	2014	2015	2016
Apple Price (USD)	1	1	1.05	1.08	1.15
Quantity of Apples Purchased	100	100	98	97	95
Pear Price (USD)	1	1	1.03	1.06	1.09
Quantity of Pears Purchased	100	100	102	103	107
Fixed Market Basket Indexes					
Laspeyres Index (USD)		200	208	214	224
Laspeyres Inflation			4.000%	2.928%	4.756%
Paasche Index (USD)		202	210	216	226
Paasche Inflation			3.941%	2.932%	4.653%
Fisher Ideal Inflation			**3.970%**	**2.930%**	**4.705%**

Table 1.2 Price indexes are used to both measure inflation but also to gauge the "real" changes in variables, as opposed to their nominal changes.
Source: Author created.

We must ask two central questions regarding indexes: "Which is the typical market basket that should be used to estimate inflation?" and "Should that basket be allowed to vary over time?" Table 1.2 presents differing measures of inflation depending on how we answer those questions. In the table we are considering a basket containing only two goods that are relevant—apples and pears—and that are assumed substitutes for one another. We assume the prices of apples rise faster than pears, and we note that consumption of apples drops accordingly while pears rise in some reasonable way. The fixed basket Laspeyres Index assumes that consumers keep consuming the same basket of apples and pears found in 2012 and measures how much that same basket would cost year after year. This tends to overestimate inflation since it ignores the fact that apple consumption actually drops—a phenomenon that is ignored if the same old market basket is used.

The fixed basket Paasche Index, in contrast, assumes that the 2016 market basket is consumed throughout the entire period. But this turns out to be unreasonable since it assumes that consumers have always consumed more of the less expensive pears. This index underestimates inflation. The Fisher (Ideal) Index is the simple square root (geometric mean) of the Laspeyres and Paasche Indexes, and theory suggests that this is a good compromise in correcting the flaws of these two indexes used in isolation. Finally, the Chained Laspeyres Index uses last year's basket to weight the index. It asks how much more expensive last year's basket is, if we labeled it using today's price tags. It updates the basket each year. It is a "chained index" in the sense that, in order to calculate price changes over a span of years, we must multiply the three corresponding years of inflation by each other. Constant updating of the basket keeps the index up to date at the cost of greater confusion with respect to exactly which base-year market basket is in use.

There are many price indexes employed in the United States. The Consumer Price Index (CPI) measures how much a typical market basket of goods and services consumed by an urban consumer changes over time.[10] Another index—the Personal Consumption Index (PCE)—is very similar in that it measures the cost of consumption items. Some key differences relate to coverage: the CPI measures out-of-pocket expenses for urban consumers, while the PCE measures the total cost of a good or service if the consumer had to pay the entire cost of that item. For example, consumers pay only a fraction of healthcare costs due to private insurance or government programs such as Medicare. Thus, healthcare would have a low weight in the CPI but a relatively high weight in the PCE (US Bureau of Labor Statistics). Another major difference is of a technical nature. The CPI uses a representative market basket of goods from an earlier year—a convenient solution to the inability of statisticians to know what is being consumed in real time (today). The PCE is a chained Fisher Index, using current and last year's consumption baskets as a base. This provides more reality by allowing for consumers substituting one good or service for another as prices fall or rise, and it represents an updated consumption pattern.

Another important US price index is the GDP Deflator, which is a broad measure of prices for all goods and services produced. Another is the Producer Price Index (PPI), a measure of prices at the wholesale or industrial level for goods and services absent taxes and distribution costs. The PPI measures prices from the perspective of the seller; the CPI from the perspective of the urban consumer. The GDP Deflator uses the chained approach mentioned above, while the PPI uses a market basket from a prior period.

China produces a similar set of indexes, including fixed and chained CPIs, but they are specific to China's own economic structure. For example, not only is a CPI produced for urban consumers, but a separate CPI is calculated for rural residents—about 40 percent of China's population still lives in the countryside. A producer price index with a focus on manufactured goods highlights China's role as the "factory to the world." Another index, the purchasing price index for raw materials, fuel, and power highlights China's heavy reliance on imports for these key inputs. Finally, a price index for investment in fixed assets highlights the critical role in GDP (over 50 percent in recent years) that residential construction, infrastructure, and property and equipment play. More recently, in response to concerns about housing prices, China's NBS now publishes a variety of city-specific indexes (https://bit.ly/2YXciPZ) related to residential prices. Both the United States and China provide some of these indexes on a national and a regional basis.

Flow Variables vs. Stock Variables

In macroeconomics, we see a number of economic variables being presented. Some variables are flow variables and some variables are stock variables. Flow variables represent economic phenomena that appear during a period of time. For example, a person's gain or loss of weight would be a flow variable. Stock variables are levels of economic phenomena that represent the accumulation of flows (e.g., one's total weight—the sum of the flows of weight gains and losses per year that occurred over a lifetime). At the company level, the income statement and cash flow statement contain many of the company's key flow variables; the balance sheet accumulates many of those flows into stocks. Table 1.3 provides a sampling of flow and stock variables that we will see in some of the following chapters.

Types of Economic Variables	
Flow	**Stock**
Inflation	Price Level
Savings	Wealth
Balance of Payments	Foreign Exchange Reserves
Birth Rate	Population and Labor Force
Open market Operations	Money Supply
Investment	Capital Stock
Budget Deficit	Public Debt
Current Account Deficit	External Debt

Table 1.3 Understanding the distinction between stock and flow variables is key to understanding economic models.
Source: Author created.

Exogenous Variables vs. Endogenous Variables

In economics, we explain how the economy works—specifically, what causes certain key economic variables such as unemployment or economic growth or inflation to occur.

We use economic models in our attempt to explain the behavior of these key variables. We call these types of variables endogenous, because they are the output of our economic models. Other variables are inputs into our economic models; they have a critical role (typically as a driver toward an outcome), but we accept them as a given and do not attempt to explain them. We call these kinds of input variables exogenous. For example, the weather in most economic models would be exogenous; economists are not meteorologists, they have neither the ability nor an interest in explaining the weather. But clearly weather is an important factor. For example, bad weather may cause a crop failure and inflation (an endogenous variable). Economists accept the weather as an input and a driver but do not attempt to explain or predict it. We say it is exogenous to the model.

Ten Basic Macro Facts Most Economists Could Agree Upon: A Chance to Review

We have reviewed some of the main ideas and challenges in the study of macroeconomics and highlighted how China fits into that analysis. Below are some central ideas in macroeconomics that the reader should review before progressing to the chapters that follow.

1. Demand is important. A large drop in aggregate demand can cause a recession.
2. Supply is important. A large drop in aggregate supply can cause a recession.
3. The money supply is important. High persistent inflation is caused by an overly rapid increase in the money supply relative to output over a long period of time.
4. Increased government spending when the economy is at full employment can crowd out other economic sectors: private investment, exports, and consumption.
5. Monetary policy works through several channels. A key one is known as the "transmission mechanism," in which (1) the central bank open market operations impact short-term interest rates; (2) short-term interest rates impact longer term interest rates; (3) both short- and long-term rates impact investment demand and consumer demand; (4) the change in investment and consumer demand impacts economic output and employment.
6. Lack of flexibility in wages and prices opens up the possibility of prolonged periods in which the economy is either in recession or operating above full employment.
7. There is no long-run tradeoff between inflation and the unemployment rate.

8. Fiscal policy is relatively more effective under fixed exchange rate regimes; monetary policy is relatively more effective under floating exchange rate regimes.
9. The presence of rational expectations (in which economic agents form expectations accurately and consistent with a true economic model) tends to reduce the effectiveness of activist fiscal and monetary policies.
10. Recessions triggered by financial crises have greater depth and length than recessions triggered by conventional demand and supply shocks.

Appendix

The Macroeconomic Tradition

Here, we briefly review some important paradigms for macroeconomic analysis that have proved useful. Before the expression "recessions and recoveries" came into use in the 20th century, Europe and America experienced "panics." For example, the Panic of 1819 was America's first true economic crisis involving high unemployment, bankruptcy, and declines in agriculture and manufacturing production fueled by unchecked bank expansion, credit, and a building boom, all following on the heels of the war of 1812 (this has a certain modern familiarity) (Rothbard 1962). The fact that economies could fluctuate from boom to bust formed the basis for business cycle analysis, an early attempt at classifying these crises. Early business cycle theorists tried to find regular patterns to economic declines and recoveries (e.g., Kuznet Waves, Juglar Cycles, Schumpeterian Waves), but statistical work has failed to find a regular predictable pattern for GDP growth. Later business cycle scholars made significant contributions in dating historical peaks and troughs in economic activity (Wesley Mitchell and Geoffrey Moore) and in specifying leading, lagging, and coinciding economic series (e.g., stock prices, unemployment, or retail sales). This work still finds great use today, continuing, for example, with the dating committee of the National Bureau of Economic Research (NBER).

While business cycle theory had an empirical bent, useful theoretical frameworks developed simultaneously during the latter half of the 19th and early 20th century. Say's Law posited that all goods produced and supplied would be demanded one way or another (i.e., that markets would clear based on prices that would always serve to equilibrate demand and supply). Incomes generated in the production process would always be sufficient to demand the goods and services that had been produced. Monetary theory centered around the work of political economists such as David Hume, David Ricardo, John Stuart Mill, and later, Irving Fisher.

The quantity theory of money linked the amount of money in the economy, M, the average circulation of money or velocity, V, with the price level, P, and real output or real GDP, Q. In this framework, velocity and quantity were determined by institutional or fundamental factors such that the only real role for money was to determine either the level of prices or inflation. A simple equation provides a snapshot of that relationship:

$$\text{Money} \times \text{Velocity} = \text{Prices} \times \text{Real GDP}$$

Both business cycle theory and the quantity theory of money held, as a matter of faith, the inevitability of economic outcomes. In other words, economies will settle at an equilibrium level of output and prices, and little can or need be done about it. A panic or crisis is a temporary aberration, and an economy would (on its own) gravitate to where it "ought" to be. In the wake of the Great Depression in 1929, John Maynard Keynes in the *General Theory of Employment, Interest and Money* (1936) emphatically demurred. Prolonged deviations from an economy's true potential could occur, and these deviations, in fact, stabilize at a sub-optimum equilibrium. Keynes demonstrated the significant role of money and tight credit as a potential drag on economic performance while emphasizing that the decision not to demand goods and services by consumers, investors, the government, or foreign importers could push an economy into a recession. Rather than serving as an equilibrating flexible force, prices were sticky or fixed and their inability to adjust to declines in demand was a sufficient condition for a recession or depression.

The activist approach of Keynesianism—which argues that there could be a role for the government to increase demand and output in times of economic crisis—was rejected by traditional monetarists. Keynes had concluded that, to restore the economy to full employment, using expansionary fiscal policy in conjunction with monetary policy was necessary. Monetarists such as Milton Friedman and Anna Schwarz, in *A Monetary History of the United States* (1963), argued that monetary policy intended to stabilize the economy was actually counterproductive because such efforts only lead to greater economic fluctuations. Rather, monetarists saw a need for stable and predictable monetary growth that does not react to economic fluctuations. In this way, economic fluctuations can largely be avoided.

While monetarists posited a stable and predictable demand for money, empirical evidence showing a good deal of volatility in the velocity of money suggested otherwise. New classical macroeconomics was (and is) an attempt to provide an internally consistent, more scientific approach to macroeconomics. Research in this area has contributed enormously, both technically and conceptually, to the analytical rigor of macroeconomics (e.g., Robert Lucas and Thomas Sargent). Micro-foundations using the behavior of firms and individuals are first modeled, then explicit or implicit aggregations of these individual units are built up to the macroeconomy. In this way, the role of expectations is more consistently modeled, because the expectations of firms and individuals must be consistent with the economic model in use.[11] A real contribution from this line of research is the explicit formulation of budget constraints for various sectors in an economy: government, business, consumers, and external (foreign). Any realistic economic model must acknowledge the fundamental fact that an economy has scarce resources across time and that tradeoffs exist in the use of those resources as determined by hard budget constraints.

Lucas (1976) argued that the current class of Keynesian models was unstable in the sense that too much of the structure was static and did not incorporate the response of individual agents to government policies. Once these responses were endogenized into new classical equilibrium frameworks, the effectiveness of stabilization policies was questioned. Lucas's further work (1981) emphasized the role of supply shocks (for example, technology shocks) in real business cycle theory. Economic fluctuations caused by supply shocks such as a crop failure or oil embargo had taken a back seat to the demand-side economics found in the Keynesian framework. Real business cycle models of macroeconomies allowed for simulation and parameterization of economies and, in turn, a more scientific approach in model validation.

The rapid ascendancy of Asian economies inspired other economists to develop new theories of economic growth (Romer 2011). Neoclassical models of the 1970s (Solow and Swan—henceforth, the "Solow Model") provided an accounting framework for decomposing growth and identifying exogenous drivers for growth (such as population growth and technological progress). New growth theory was an attempt to endogenize factors, which could help explain the extraordinary growth in Asia. Factors including increasing returns to scale, spillover effects, innovation, and human capital were now identified as internal and explained by these models (rather than assumed to be external factors).

Implicit in the variety of approaches to macroeconomics described above are a set of challenges that each paradigm either chooses to confront, for the sake of rigor, or ignore, for the sake of simplicity and tractability:

- Aggregation: How important is it to model and then aggregate individual economic units (firms and consumers) in order to usefully describe macroeconomic performance? A tradeoff exists between a scientific approach to modeling and aggregate models, which are closer to reality. Greater refinement of micro-foundations can diminish tractability and validity in the aggregation. Karl Popper's critical rationalism (1963) provides a basis for testing aggregation in economics; a simple counter-example to an aggregate theory allows for falsification.
- Disequilibrium vs. Equilibrium: Are well-defined markets found in the macroeconomy generally in equilibrium or are there imbalances? Do equilibrium

models provide a better notion of macroeconomic performance as opposed to models that allow for disequilibrium? In practical terms, is unemployment better thought of as a rational and optimal choice by all involved, or is it a form of market failure?

- Fixed or Floating Prices: Directly related to the notion of equilibrium versus disequilibrium models is the question of whether certain institutional factors prevent prices (for goods, labor, or assets) from moving the economy toward equilibrium. Will there be shortages or surpluses if prices cannot adjust to shifts in supply and demand in individual or aggregated markets?
- Expectations: Can economic agents reliably predict outcomes based on expectations that are internally consistent with the economic model at hand? If not, then on what basis do economic agents form their expectations? Individuals may look at past performance, or they may form no expectations at all. If expectations are often wrong or ill-formed, then what arbitrage opportunities might this present—and do such opportunities actually exist?

Different approaches to the above challenges present a unique set of valuable insights into the macroeconomy. Importantly, some are more useful for the long run and others more useful for the short run.

Challenging Questions for China (and the Student): Chapter 1

1. Go to the FRED, OECD Based Recession Indicators (http://research.stlouisfed.org/fred2/series/CHNRECM) and compare these data to Gross Domestic Product by Expenditure in Constant Prices: Total Gross Domestic Product for China: (http://research.stlouisfed.org/fred2/series/NAEXKP01CNA652S).
   a. Are the OECD recession indicators for growth cycles or business cycles?
   b. Identify the years of any outright business cycle recessions for China since 1980.
2. Schramm identifies the adaptability and flexibility of the labor force as one of the key drivers for the Chinese economy. Pick one of the "Ten Basic Macro Facts" at the end of the chapter that plays a similar role (as a shock absorber) in a traditional Keynesian framework. Explain.
3. Identify some key economic drivers (important economic/institutional/demographic factors that are fundamental and fundamentally unique) that make the United States exceptional. Contrast with China.
4. Decompose the three constituent components of investment flows into the types of stocks that they accumulate into.
5. If certain institutional structures in society, such as the family or the company, are important, compare and contrast their broader role in the Chinese and American economies.
6. During the COVID-19 outbreak of 2020, explain what key drivers were at play in the Chinese and American responses to the outbreak and how.

References

Brandt, L., D. Ma, and T. G. Rawski. 2014. "From Divergence to Convergence: Reevaluating the History Behind China's Economic Boom." *Journal of Economic Literature,* 52(1), pp. 45–123.

Chair of the Council of Economic Advisers. 2011. "Economic Report of the President." Transmitted to the Congress, February 2011. Washington, DC: U.S. Government Printing Office.

Coase, Ronald, and Ning Wang. 2012. *How China Became Capitalist.* New York: Palgrave MacMillan.

Confucius. (circa) 500 BCE. *The Great Learning.* The Internet Classic Archive. http://classics.mit.edu/Confucius/learning.html.

Fang, Cai, John Giles, Philip O'Keefe, and Dewen Wang. 2012. "The Elderly and Old Age Support in Rural China." Washington, DC: The World Bank.

Friedman, Milton, and Anna Schwarz. 1963. A Monetary History of the United States, 1867–1960. Princeton: Princeton University Press.

Krugman, Paul R., ed. 1986. Strategic Trade Policy and the New International Economics. Cambridge: MIT Press.

Leontief, Wassily W. 1986. *Input-Output Economics,* 2nd ed., New York: Oxford University Press.

Lewis, W. Arthur. 1954. "Economic Development with Unlimited Supplies of Labour." *The Manchester School,* 22(2), pp. 139–191.

Lucas, Robert. 1976. "Econometric Policy Evaluation: A Critique." In *The Phillips Curve and Labor Markets,* edited by K. Brunner and A. Meltzer, New York: American Elsevier, pp. 19–46.

Lucas, R. E., and T. J. Sargent, eds. 1981. Rational Expectations and Econometric Practice: Vol. 2. Minneapolis: University of Minnesota Press.

National Bureau of Statistics of China, UNICEF China, and UNFPA China. 2017. "Population Status of Children in China in 2015: Facts and Figures." https://www.unicef.cn/en/reports/population-status-children-china-2015

Naughton, Barry. 2018. *The Chinese Economy: Adaptations and Growth.* Cambridge: MIT Press.

Popper, K. R. 1963. "Science as Falsification." *Conjectures and Refutations,* 1, pp. 33–39.

Romer, David. 2011. "Endogenous Growth." In *Advanced Macroeconomics,* 4th ed., New York: McGraw-Hill.

Rothbard, Murray. 1962. *The Panic of 1819.* New York: Columbia University Press.

Sargent, Thomas. 1996. "Expectations and the Nonneutrality of Lucas." *Journal of Monetary Economics*, 37(3), pp. 535–548.

Smith, Adam. 1759, 2000. *The Theory of Moral Sentiments*. Indianapolis: Liberty Fund., Inc.

Smith, Adam. 1776, 1981. An Inquiry into the Nature and Causes of the Wealth of Nations: Volume One. Indianapolis: Liberty Fund, Inc.

U.S. Bureau of Labor Statistics. 2011. "Current Price Topics: Differences between the Consumer Price Index and the Personal Consumption Expenditures Price Index." *Focus on Prices and Spending—Consumer Price Index, First Quarter*, 2(3).

Wu, Jinglian. 2005. Understanding and Interpreting Chinese Economic Reform. Mason, OH: Thomson/South-Western.

Endnotes

1. As an old Egyptian saying goes "When poverty comes in the door, love goes out the window!" But one wonders what happens when riches comes in the door.
2. India's population is forecast to surpass China's around 2026.
3. SEZs are locations in China where both foreign and domestic firms are allowed to operate free of most of the restrictions typically imposed by the government on international transactions. For example, zero or lower tariffs or removal of special requirements on foreign currency earnings would provide a more favorable environment for foreign and domestic businesses to operate. The earliest SEZs were established in major coastal cities in Guangdong and Fujian provinces in the early 1980s.
4. Some websites, such as Zhaopin.com, are only presented in Chinese. The reader may use the "Help" tab in the Google browser and select "'Translate" for an English version of the site.
5. In recent years, China has begun to present GDP using the Western, demand-side approach of *C*, *I*, *G*, and *NX*, but the supply-side approach is still very much paramount in China's statistical reporting (see Chapter 2).
6. The method employed was one of input-output tables, and the primary methodology was linear programming (Leontief 1986).
7. In mathematical terms, we state that business cycles have a negative first derivative in the level of GDP while growth cycles have a negative second derivative.
8. GDP growth was still positive in the 1988–1990 period, according to official statistics, dipping to 4 percent by 1989–1990. But business cycle recession determinations are based on a broad set of indicators—not just GDP growth. The Conference Board includes manufacturing employment, industrial production value-added, retail sales of consumer goods, electricity production, and volume of passenger traffic in its coincident index.
9. The Conference Board and the NBER track similar, but not identical, sets of coincident indicators. In the United States, the NBER set of indicators provides the basis for determining when recessions start or recoveries end.
10. The CPI is presented both as a fixed Laspeyres Index and a chained Fisher Index, the former being more frequently referred to as the CPI.
11. The Phillips Curve, an artifact from the Keynesian world, assumes adaptive expectations in which future expectations represent a weighting of past or lagged information. The modeling of inflationary expectations highlights key differences between traditional Keynesian models and the new classical economics.

2
MEASURING AND ACCOUNTING FOR THE OUTPUT OF A NATION

人比人，气死人

Comparisons Cause Conflicts

In 2019, China's gross domestic product (GDP) was an estimated *renminbi* (RMB) 99.5 trillion. In the past decade, real GDP has grown at rates near 10 percent while more recent growth rates have dipped below 7 percent. In this chapter, we explore what exactly these numbers mean and how they are derived. GDP is the gross value of final goods and services produced within the geographic borders of a country over a period of time (normally, one calendar year). As we see in the paragraph below, each word used in defining GDP is significant—a highly efficient descriptor. We need a solid understanding of GDP and gross national product (GNP) because there are fundamental differences in the definition, measurement, composition, and (of course) size of GDP between China and the United States. Figure 2.1 shows GDP since 1960 for both countries in nominal US dollars (USD). We immediately observe China's accelerated growth after 1978 as compared to that of the United States. This is a normal profile for an emerging economy not yet experiencing diminishing returns. In the first part of this chapter, we take care in defining GDP and how it is measured because China and the United States approach GDP estimation from different angles.

"Gross" means before netting out (or subtracting) depreciation and the depletion of resources involved in the production of GDP. By "value," we mean the monetary value (a function of the price of products and services, as well as their quantity). By "final goods and services," we mean products and services which reach their end use (e.g., consumption, investment in plant and equipment, inventory accumulation, government goods and services, or exports abroad). "Within a country's geographic borders" means that this particular measure (GDP) is calculating output occurring domestically, as opposed to including the output from domestic firms or citizens operating abroad. The latter kind of production is included in an alternative measure to be discussed later, referred to as Gross National Product (GNP). GDP is a flow rather than a stock variable and is dependent upon the time period of that flow. By "time period," we mean the relevant month, quarter or year, e.g., the fiscal or calendar year or a particular quarter. For example, a used auto that was sold this year would not be included in this year's GDP since it was not produced this year. The services of the car dealership in refurbishing and marketing the car, however, are currently produced and would be included in this year's GDP.

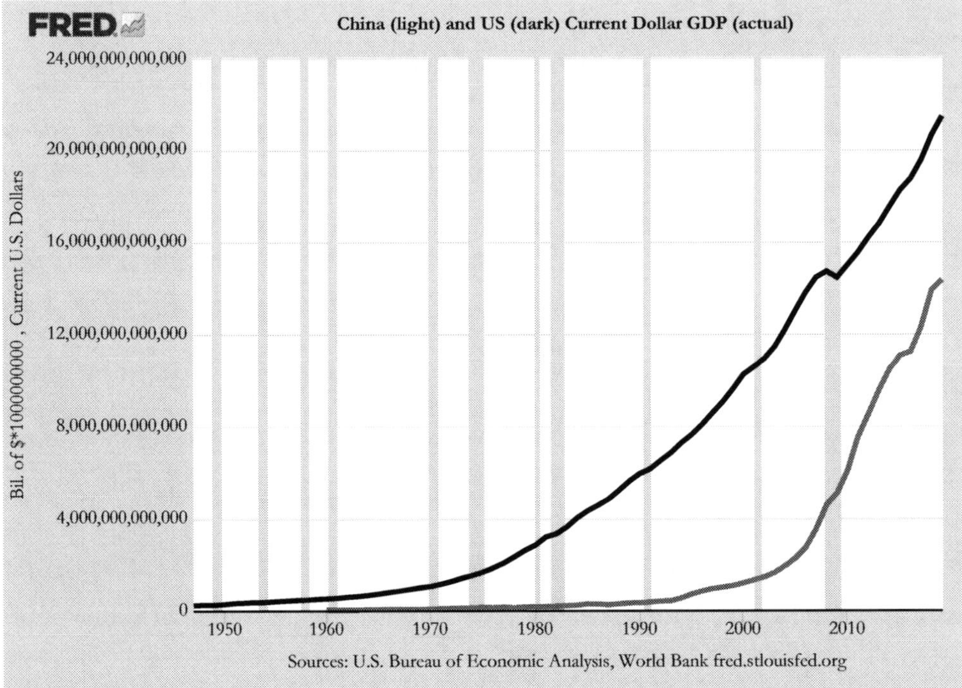

Figure 2.1 China's economic output (GDP) began its long ascent around 1978, but it is still substantially below that of the United States. (Shaded areas represent business cycle recessions in the United States).
Source: Author created based on Federal Reserve Economic Database.

Different Approaches to Measuring GDP

We will examine four basic approaches to measuring GDP: the Value of Final Goods and Sales approach, the Expenditure (Uses) approach, the Value-Added approach, and the Income approach. All four approaches are used because they enable us to (a) cross-check our measurement of GDP, and (b) allow additional insights into the basis for the creation of GDP. The Value of Final Goods and Sales approach aggregates all sales in the economy, and then makes appropriate adjustments. The Expenditure approach breaks final sales into specific final uses. The Value-Added approach breaks GDP into inter-firm stages of production. The Income approach breaks GDP into recipients of the income generated in the process of creating GDP. If (although not usually the case in such a complex statistical effort) all four measures were taken without error, they should provide an equivalent measure of GDP.

Case Study 2.1: China's Basic Numbering System

Perhaps one of the most difficult tasks for a translator from Chinese to English (or vice versa) would be a negotiation regarding buying or selling an apartment. The simplest part of the task might actually be just translating (converting) the words. But consider the following necessary conversion factors:

- The Chinese would measure the size of an apartment in terms of square meters not square feet.
  - Conversion Factor: 1 square meter = 10.763 square feet
- The quoted price would be in RMB not USD.
  - Conversion Factor: an exchange rate of USD 0.14 per RMB
- The price per square meter would be in a numbering system different from that used in the West.
  - Conversion Factor: For large numbers, Chinese use a basic unit of 10,000 [10^4] while Westerners use a basic unit of 1,000 [10^3]

Thus, a Chinese apartment quoted at RMB 五万 (5 times 10,000 or 50,000) 一米 (per meter) would come out to about USD 740 per square foot (or an overall conversion factor of about 50000/740 = 68)—a comfortable home by Chinese standards.

Because using both language skills and arithmetic skills simultaneously employs different sides of the brain, any negotiation involving numbers becomes an extremely challenging task. No wonder a wrong number is usually the outcome! The message here: Be very careful when converting Chinese numbers—it is extremely easy to make a mistake. In conversation, it is probably best to write the number down as a power, for example, "10^7." Table 2.1 shows the basic units in which Chinese (and Western) economic and financial data are typically displayed. After 1,000, the basic unit diverges—the Chinese start to use powers of 10,000 while the Western numbering system progresses through powers of 1,000. For example, in the West, the next major step after 1,000 is 1,000,000; in China, it is 10,000 (and from 10,000 to 100 million). Throughout the text in this chapter, whenever possible, we preserve each country's basic numbering system and currency—if you are working with Chinese data, you will need to get used to the differences!

Chinese Number	Spoken/Written	Western Equivalent
1	yi一	One
10	Shi 十	Ten
100	Bai 百	Hundred
1,000	Qian千	Thousand
10,000	**Wan万**	**Ten Thousand**
100,000,000	**Yi亿**	**Hundred Million**
1,000,000,000,000	Zhao兆	Trillion

Table 2.1 The Chinese numbering system starts to use powers of 10,000 for large numbers instead of 1,000 as seen in the Western numbering system. After 1,000, the bold numbers represent the different basic units that the Chinese numbering system would employ.
Source: Author created.

Value of Final Goods and Sales Approach

This is the simplest and most fundamental approach to measuring GDP, which simply measures the total quantity sold during the year—whether it be at the level of the retail consumer (i.e., to new homebuyers), other firms, the government, or exports abroad. By "final sales," we mean that the product or service has reached its final end user, rather than, say, an intermediary user such as another firm or wholesaler. We then adjust our final sales number for inventory that was added during the year but not sold to a final user (this would add to our GDP estimate) as well as inventory produced in a prior year but sold this year (this would subtract from our final estimate of GDP).

Expenditure Approach

The Expenditure (or Uses) approach identifies four major classes of users of final output or GDP. They are consumption (*C*), investment (*I*), government (*G*), and net exports (*NX*). In fact, this is the same as the Value of Final Goods and Sales approach, but with disaggregation. This approach focuses on the actual end user, rather than analyzing the intrinsic property of the good or service itself. Thus, a washing machine sold to a consumer would be classified as *C*, to the government as *G*, exported as *NX*, and—if it is added to a company's inventory or sold to a commercial launderer—as a component of *I*.[1] Consumption includes products and services that consumers buy via retail sales, as well as the flow of services provided by the housing stock (i.e., the economic benefit provided by an individual's place of dwelling during a given year, whether rented or owned).[2]

Government includes all goods and services produced during the year and used by the government. Some of these items are provided by the private sector, such as office supplies or food served within government cafeterias. Other items are produced by the government itself, such as the services of police and fire departments, the military, and government entities under income transfer programs including veterans' benefits and social security.[3] As suggested, *G* includes government purchases at the local, provincial, and national level.

CCM Data	USD (Billions)
Revenues	2.98
Domestic Sales	2.94
Export Sales	0.04
Costs of Production	2.27
Materials	1.4
Wages, Salaries	0.87
Depreciation	0.20
Operating Income	0.509
Interest to Bondholders	0.09
Taxes	0 (On "tax holiday")
After Tax Profits	0.42

Table 2.2 We can view the different ways of calculating GDP from the perspective of a single company's income statement, such as CMM.
Source: Author created.

Macro Finance Insight 2.1: One Firm's Contribution to GDP

Let's consider GDP creation from the perspective of a single firm. Our company, CMM, is a 50/50 joint venture with one partner based in the United States, the other in China, with operations in China (represented by the income statement in Table 2.2.) CMM produces computerized measuring machines that are sold to automotive and other industrial companies that require precise measurements. During the income statement period found in the table, inventories fell by USD 0.14 billion. Costs of production and interest are all paid to Chinese entities; half of the profits, however, are claimed by the US joint venture partner. Since we are measuring GDP and net product, we need to "gross up" CMM's depreciation estimate of USD 0.20 billion throughout.

Value of Output Approach

Since all output is produced in China, CMM's contribution to Chinese GDP would be (USD 2.98 - 0.14 billion), or USD 2.84 billion. We subtract the USD 0.14 billion because this inventory decumulation represents output produced in an earlier year, and it was accounted for in that year's GDP. CMM's contribution to US GDP would be 0, since no output was physically produced in the United States. When looking at GNP for China, however, we would need to subtract out half of (USD 0.42 billion + 0.20 billion = 0.62 billion), or USD 0.31 billion, since half of the pre-depreciation profits are paid in dividends to the US partner. Thus, Chinese GNP from CMM's operations would be (USD 2.84 billion - 0.31 billion) or USD 2.53 billion. US GNP from CMM's operations is USD 0.31 billion. We note that the sum of GDPs for the two countries must always equal the sum of GNPs (2.84 = 2.53 + 0.31).

Expenditure Approach

Using this approach, we assume that this product is used neither by consumers nor the government, but by firms as an addition to their plant, property, and equipment. We then base our estimate of GDP on the following uses: investment and exports. We must subtract USD 0.14 billion of inventory decumulation from domestic sales (*I*) of USD 2.94 billion or USD 2.8 billion and identify exports as USD 0.04 billion. We then have GDP for China as USD 2.84 billion, which is consistent with our Value-Added approach.

Income Approach

Income generated from CMM's sales is accrued to the following recipients: CMM's employees, CMM itself (as a corporate entity), CMM's bondholders, and to a similar (but unknown to us) set of stakeholders in the entities providing materials to CMM.

Beginning with USD 2.84 billion, we see that USD 0.87 billion goes to CMM's workers and managers. Gross income to CMM after adjusting for depreciation (+) and inventory decumulation (-) is:

USD 0.42 billion + 0.20 billion – 0.14 billion = USD 0.48 billion

USD 0.09 billion accrues to CMM's bondholders and USD 1.4 billion to CMM's material suppliers (who would distribute income to their own stakeholders). Thus, gross GDP from the Income Approach equals USD 2.84 billion for China and USD 2.53 billion in GNP.

Value-Added Approach

Value-added comprises the contribution to GDP from CMM's entire set of stakeholders—workers, investors, and lenders—plus the value added from its suppliers. Since material inputs (from outside suppliers) add up to USD 1.4 billion, the remainder of USD 2.84 billion of GDP (which equals USD 1.44 billion) must come from CMM itself. We can check this by noting that USD 1.44 adds up to USD 0.87 in wages, USD 0.09 to lenders, and USD 0.62 billion - 0.14 billion = 0.48 billion to CMM shareholders.

Investment is a very broad measure that includes new residential housing, increases in the capital stock by companies or firms, and increases in inventories resulting from current production. When inventories increase, one possibility is that the firm has chosen to use current output to build up inventory (planned inventory accumulation). Another possibility, however, is that the firm had hoped to, but was unable to, sell all of its production (unplanned inventory accumulation). Either way, the currently produced output is included in GDP as part of inventory (and more specifically, as "inventory accumulation"). Thus, inventory serves as a plug, a catchall, for goods that are currently produced but did not find their way into *C*, *G*, or *NX*.

Within the three uses covered so far—*C*, *I*, and *G*—some purchases will also include goods and services produced abroad but sold domestically, i.e., imports (*MGS*). In addition, some of the goods produced domestically will be exported. Since, in our measure of GDP, we are only interested in goods produced domestically, we somehow need to eliminate imports as a use. We also want to identify exports (*XGS*) as a use of GDP, since these goods were part of domestic output. Thus, we must subtract out imports (MSG, which are the use of another nation's GDP) and add in *XGS*. We do this by defining net exports (*NX*) as:[4]

$$NX \equiv XGS - MGS$$

where, again, *XGS* and *MGS* include both goods and services. We can summarize the relationship between GDP (using Y_{GDP} to represent GDP) and expenditure (using the Expenditure approach) as follows:

$$Y_{GDP} \equiv C + I + G + NX$$

Again, this relationship must always hold true because any good or service that is not consumed (*C*), acquired by companies for investment (*I*), bought by the government (*G*), net exported (*NX*), or otherwise "used" can always be categorized under (*I*) as inventory accumulation.

	China (2016) (RMB 100 Millions)	Percent of GDP	USA (2017) (USD Billions)	Percent of GDP
Personal Consumption	292,661	39%	13,321	68%
Investment	238,671	32%	3,342	17%
Change in Inventories	10,816	1%	26	0%
Net Exports of Goods and Services	16,412	2%	-578	-3%
Government Consumption	107,514	14%	2,731	14%
Government Investment	80,241	11%	643	3%
Gross Domestic Product	746,315	100%	19,485	100%
Net Factor Payments	-5,175	-1%	244	1%
Gross National Product	741,140	99%	19,729	101%
Minus Depreciation	98,558	13%	3,116.2	16%
Net National Product	642,582	86%	16,613	85%

Table 2.3 Gross Domestic Product, Uses or Expenditure Approach.
Source: Author created based on National Bureau of Statistics, World Bank World Development Indicators and US Bureau of Economic Analysis.

In Table 2.3, we compare uses or expenditure of GDP between China and the United States.[5] The most dramatic difference is in consumption. In the United States, most output is used by consumers (68 percent). Expressed alternatively, the product mix in the United States is geared toward consumer goods. By contrast, Chinese consumers only consume about 39 percent of the GDP pie, though this figure has been increasing in recent years. The mirror image of this difference can be found in private and government investment, in which about 43 percent of China's output (including inventories) is used for investment versus about 20 percent in the United States. We will explore the basis for these differences in later chapters; they are in part explained by savings patterns, as well as development stages for each country. One final related comparison:

China runs a relatively large positive net export surplus (around 2 percent of GDP) while the United States runs a large net export deficit (around -3 percent of GDP). In 2017, close to 60 percent of the US current account deficit can be accounted for by the US current account deficit with China. *Ceteris paribus*, in the absence of trade with the United States, China, itself, would also be running a current account deficit.[6]

Value-Added Approach

As suggested by the name, value-added recognizes that most firms in an economy utilize not only their own inputs (mainly capital and labor) to produce products and services, but also the inputs of other firms. The Value-Added approach integrates the contribution that each individual firm makes to GDP, excluding the contribution from other firms (suppliers) along the value chain. China's National Bureau of Statistics (NBS) provides exceptional detail utilizing this approach. At an abstract level, we could disaggregate any economy into primary, secondary, and tertiary activities: primary being principally agriculture, fisheries, forestry, and mining; secondary being manufacturing and construction; and tertiary being services, such as retailing or the government. We could initially think of the first stage of GDP as goods and services created by the primary sector, then passed to the secondary, then the tertiary, and finally turned over to the end user. At each stage, the receiving sector adds value and passes a further-refined part of GDP onto the next. The reality, of course, is much more complex. For example, the primary sector (agriculture), will likely purchase inputs from other sectors (e.g., accounting services from the tertiary sector). In other words, value-added is not a simple linear process running from primary to tertiary, but a much more integrated process.

In any economy, however, it is interesting to ask where value is being added. In this way, we can determine why one nation's productivity (output per worker) is higher than another's, or which sectors could achieve greater efficiencies. Formally, we can describe the Value-Added approach to GDP for an economy with (*N*) producing firms (or institutional entities) as:

$$Y_{\text{GDP}} = \sum_{i=Firm1}^{i=FirmN} (\text{Value of Output} - \text{Value of Input})_i$$

It would be a mistake to simply add each sector's output into total GDP without subtracting the value added by other sectors, as this would create a double counting of output.[7] In fact, this was a serious problem under the system of net material product (NMP) employed in China up until 1995 (see below).

Figure 2.2, Figure 2.3, and Figure 2.4 portray how value is added to create GDP in China and the United States. There has been an important shift in sector importance in recent years in China. The largest share of output in China now comes from the tertiary (services) sector, as is true for the United States. Up until 2015, the largest share of output in China was in manufacturing. The largest share of employment in China is also in the tertiary sector, a sector that has been growing rapidly in recent years. The United States sees most employment in the tertiary sector as well. Chapter 5 covers how this difference helps to explain the share of national income that workers, as distinct from companies, capture. Based on the data from Figure 2.2 and Figure 2.3, we can see in Figure 2.4 that, in China, output per worker (productivity) is highest in the secondary sector, while in the United States it is highest in the primary sector. Across all three sectors, US workers are more productive than Chinese workers; this explains the higher average standard of living found in the United States. Needless to say, these numbers reflect national differences in relative abundances of physical capital, labor, and the use of technology—issues to be explored in later chapters.[8]

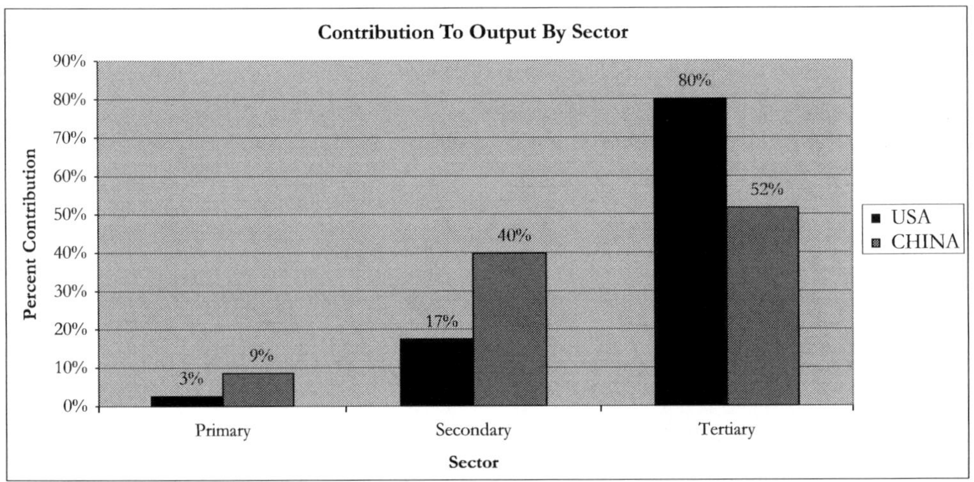

Figure 2.2 China, "the factory of the world," produces relatively (but not absolutely) more secondary (manufacturing and construction) goods than in the United States. The US services sector is still relatively large compared to China, but China's service sector is now more important than manufacturing.
Source: Author created based on National Bureau of Statistics, China and Economic Report of the President 2019.

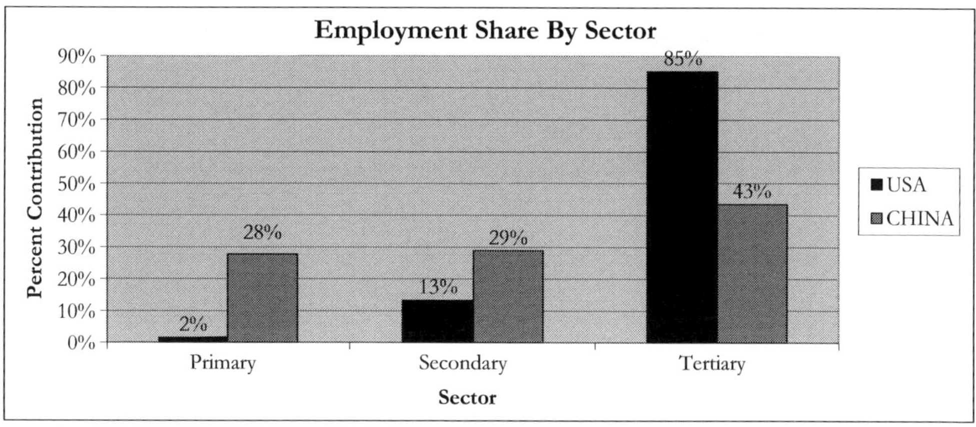

Figure 2.3 A disproportionate part of China's labor force still works in the primary sector, mainly in agriculture.
Source: Author created based on National Bureau of Statistics, China and Economic Report of the President 2019.

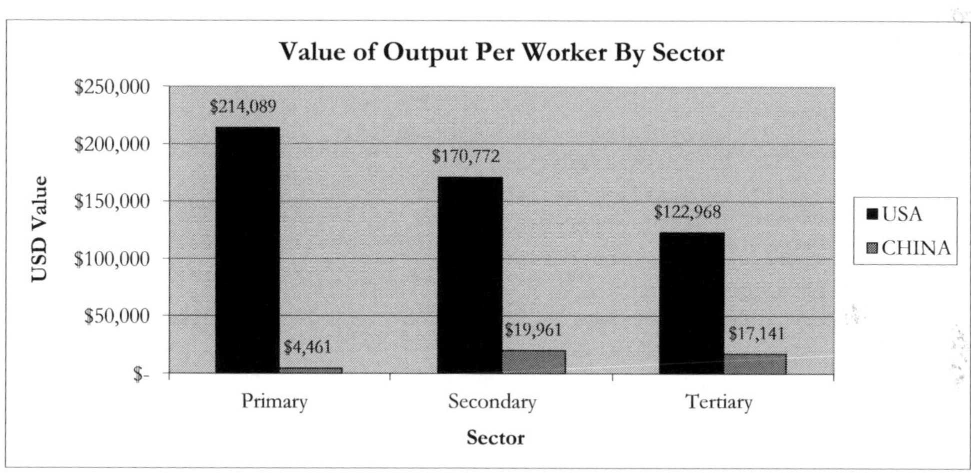

Figure 2.4 Output per worker in the United States is substantially higher across the board compared to China, giving rise to a higher standard of living in the United States. But a country's exports are determined by relative advantages, and China is relatively good at manufacturing (the secondary sector).
Source: Author created based on National Bureau of Statistics, China and Economic Report of the President 2019.

Case Study 2.2: Goldilocks Data—Who Inflated and Shrunk China's GDP?

Accuracy of Data

Given that China only began using the United Nation's System of National Accounts (SNA) for GDP measurement in 1995 (abandoning the old Soviet NMP system), the Chinese NBS has made enormous progress in measuring prices and output. If we consider the economic size of the economy (by any dimension) and the movement from a planned to a market economy that overlapped the new measurement efforts, we can appreciate the enormity and difficulty of the task at hand. Among developing economies, China fares better in terms of statistical capacity—as gauged by the World Bank (https://bit.ly/2LoySJ9)—compared to other developing economies, and its scores have gradually improved over the past 20 years. China is relatively strong in the methodology category but weak in data sources.

On virtually every economic statistic produced by China, scholars have at least two views—the number is too small, or it is too big. This uncertainty reflects both a lack of understanding of the data and systems of collection and a lack of transparency on the part of officials regarding methodology. But it also may be influenced by events such as the 2017 indictment of the director of China's NBS (https://bloom.bg/2YxuoWG) for the "illegal acceptance of huge amounts of money and property" related to the fabrication of economic data.

China has developed an accounting (https://bit.ly/3fHhJbL), regulatory, and legal framework for the collection and presentation of statistics—including serious penalties for fraudulent reporting. Furthermore, governments at all levels base their decision making (including those expressed in the Five-Year Plans and the job promotion of government officials) on the data that are published. In the past, much of the data collection effort was managed locally, which created problems of consistency across regions and, in some cases, reporting biases. In 2019 China moved to a fully centralized system of gathering and organizing data with the NBS playing a stronger role at the local collection level. This should reduce inconsistencies, particularly between provincial and national GDP data.

The United States developed its system for measuring GDP in the early 1930s, and it has made continuous improvements in its measures since then (US Bureau of Economic Analysis 2014). In 1999, the United States Commerce Department recognized its National and Product Account (NIPA) system as its greatest invention of the century. Some of the features and problems of the GDP and price statistics in China include:

Value of Output Issues

- Industrial output is likely overestimated. About 40 percent of China's GDP can be attributed to this sector. Reported growth in industrial output over time is inconsistent with the share of national output attributed to industry.
- Productivity growth in the service sector is likely overestimated (thus, the size of the service sector is also likely overstated). The tertiary sector represents about 43 percent of GDP.

- Estimates of agricultural output growth appear to be realistic but the value (level) of this sector's output may be too low. Meanwhile, the agricultural workforce is likely overestimated given the rapid and unaccounted rural to urban migration that has occurred.
- Estimates of GDP based on regional (provincial) estimates are usually larger than the what is reported in the national aggregate. This may reflect an exaggeration of output at the provincial level.[9] To correct this problem, authorities announced that data collection responsibilities of the provinces would be moved to the central government by 2019.
- Output of services is underestimated (especially government and real-estate services, including imputed rents).

Expenditure and Income Issues

- Quarterly-based measures of GDP on the expenditure and income side are still not reported (seasonal adjustment of production-based GDP began in 2011). But quarterly estimates of production-based GDP, with each quarter measured individually, was introduced in 2015; this series begins in 1992.
- In the past, GDP measurements based on the Expenditure approach exceeded those based on the Production approach, sometimes by a wide margin. But in recent years, the difference has become insignificant.
- For some years in which growth has slowed considerably, official estimates do not seem to show as large a decline—some income smoothing appears to have taken place (see Macro Finance Insight 2.2: GDP Smoothing and Earnings Management).
- Value-added measures of GDP are substantially stronger than expenditure-based measures, given that the former has deeper roots in the old Soviet methodology.
- Measures of personal income, retail sales, and consumption are underestimated. Wage data rely too heavily on public sector and state-owned entities rather than wages paid by small- and medium-sized enterprises (SMEs) and self-employed workers.
- Measures of consumption are underestimated (especially for services). The size of the consumer sector is likely underestimated due to underreporting of government consumption and imputed costs of housing. Consumption makes up about 53 percent of China's GDP on an expenditure basis (including government tconsumption).
- Measures of retail sales are underestimated (especially for services).
- Measures of Investment (gross capital formation) are not provided by industry. And they appear inconsistent with a different measure—gross fixed investment.

Index and Broader Issues in Reporting

- Scholars such as Rawski (2016) have raised a broader set of issues regarding reporting and transparency.
- Revisions to data are often made without a thorough explanation, and breaks in series due to revisions are not corrected. For example, revisions of GDP deflators have created large adjustments in how real GDP is measured.
- Statistical data used for intra-governmental purposes are not provided publicly, and they appear to differ from data published for the public.
- There is a shortage of census-based surveys in estimating national statistics (China's first economic census was undertaken in 2004).
- Political factors at times appear to infringe on an accurate and fair presentation of the data.
- There are historical discrepancies among series that should track each other reasonably closely (e.g., GDP deflator and consumer price index [CPI]; provincial GDP and national GDP; and expenditure-based GDP and production-based GDP).
- Services and imputed rents remain underrepresented in China's CPIs.

Considering the above issues, authors such as Maddison and Wu (2008) estimate that during the 1978–2003 period, for example, actual growth in real GDP was 7.9 percent compared to the official estimate of 9.6 percent. To put this in perspective, that gap suggests a real value of output of one-third lower than the official 2004 estimates. However, they also believe the level of real output was seriously underestimated before SNA was adopted, creating a difference that almost fully offsets the growth effects. In other words, on balance, current estimates of the size of China's economy are essentially correct!

Figure 2.5 depicts the official estimate of GDP (using the Value-Added approach) and compares it to an average of other estimates which use other methodologies (such as the Expenditure (Uses) approach or, in the case of Klein and Ozmucur, a broad set of other indicators.) For the period between 1978 and 2000, the official estimate is about 0.8 percent higher on average than the average estimate of outside academics. The most notable difference occurs during the 1987–1989 period, in which average estimated GDP growth was considerably lower than that of the official estimate. A similar gap occurs again in 1999. Ferson et al. (2013) make a similar comparison and come up with a similar conclusion. (See Macro Finance Insight 2.2, which highlights potential causes for biases in measuring GDP for both China and the United States.)

Outside analysts have looked at a number of other measures beyond GDP real growth to gauge the accuracy of China's official numbers; these include iron ore output, electricity use, coal output, and rail transport, to name a few. As we noted earlier, these measures do track GDP fairly well—except at the critical juncture of the 2008 financial crisis, when reported GDP growth at the trough was substantially higher than the level suggested by other indicators. China's Premier, Li Keqiang has proposed the "LI Index" which includes rail transport, bank loans, and electricity use—measures which he feels better capture economic activity. But, as we noted earlier, services have now become the largest sector in China, and these measures all fail to capture that important part of the economy. But our very broad measure of output, GDP, does include services.

The NBS has made great strides in improving the accuracy of its measurement of GDP and meeting the reporting requirements of international organizations such as the International Monetary Fund (IMF) and United Nations (UN). And, on its website, the NBS (https://bit.ly/35Ws92w) provides a good overview of its methodology with detailed definitions. For example, in 2016–2017, consistent with international standards, China began treating research and development expenditures as capital (depreciable) investments rather than as a direct expense. In 2017, more comprehensive measures for health care, new economy output, and tourism were incorporated into GDP measurements. These and other improvements led to a historical increase in the size of China's GDP by 1.3 percent without having much impact on annual growth estimates for any single year.

It appears, however, that the NBS is not the only organization that struggles to come up with reasonably good measures. The World Bank seems to face similar difficulties. Feenstra et al. (2012) estimate that a World Bank revision of GDP per capita output for 2005 was 50 percent too low! On that basis, working backward several decades from the World Bank estimate using reasonable growth rates would lead to a negative GDP for China (theoretically possible but realistically impossible). Feenstra et al. base their findings on more theoretically sound deflators of nominal consumption by including rural (not just urban) price measures and using a command GDP concept (discussed later in this chapter).

Figure 2.5 China's official GDP growth estimates of the past compared with an average of outside estimates are consistent, except at peaks and troughs.
Source: Author created based on NBS, 2012; Klein and Ozumacur, 2003 (for years 1981–2000); Keidel, 2001 (for years 1979–2000; and Wang and Meng, 2001 (for years 1979–1997).

Income Approach

The Income approach recognizes that the products and services produced and used in any given year generate income attributed to the various factors of production (e.g., labor, land, and owners of capital). This income can be earned in a variety of forms: pre-tax wages and salaries, pre-tax profits, net interest payments (to bondholders, for example), and rental payments for the use of productive capital.[10] For example, a firm's revenues (sales) will be distributed to various stakeholders in the company (employees, owners, lenders, and possibly landowners). Under this approach, China's presentation of GDP data using the income approach is incomplete; there is only a provincial presentation and quarterly data are not available.

	China (RMB 100 Millions)	Percent of GDP	USA (USD Billions)	Percent of GDP
Gross Domestic Product	746,315	100%	19,485	100%
Net Factor Payments Abroad	-5,175	-1%	244	1%
Gross National Product	741,140	99%	19,729	101%
Less Depreciation	98,558	13%	3,116	16%
Statistical Discrepancy	NA	NA	-143	-1%
National Income	642,582	86%	16,756	86%
Labor Income	395,547	53%	11,691	60%
Capital, Rental and Interest Income	186,579	25%	4,907	25%
Taxes and Transfers (Net Adjustments)	60,456	8%	158	1%

Table 2.4 China and the United States differ considerably in how GDP is used—especially with respect to consumption and investment.
Source: Author created based on Economic Report of the President 2019 and National Bureau of Statistics, China.

In Table 2.4, we see an estimated decomposition of output by GDP, GNP, and national income for China and the United States for 2016 and 2017.[11] GDP and GNP do not subtract out depreciation (capital consumption) occurring during that year for businesses, private residences, or the government. Also, remember that the difference between "domestic" measures (such as GDP) and "national" measures (such as GNP) are net factor payments (NFPs) abroad. That is:

GNP = GDP - Net Factor Payments

These factor payments represent interest payments, dividends, and employee compensation that are earned by either foreign entities or individuals located in the home country or home entities and individuals operating abroad. Since GDP represents goods and services geographically produced within the home country's borders, factor payments to foreigners must be subtracted in order to arrive at GNP.

National income is presented before corporate and personal taxes are subtracted. While national income and capital, interest and rental incomes are remarkably similar as a share of GDP for both countries, one difference is in the share of labor income. Labor income in China receives 7 percentage points less than in the United States as a share of GDP. A separate line identifies indirect taxes such as sales and value-added taxes. These are about 7 percentage points higher in China. No doubt this difference reflects the value-added (sales) tax imposed in China but not the United States—an important source of tax revenue for China, as discussed in Chapter 10. Interestingly, this measure comes close to matching the negative gap in income earned by labor in China.[12]

Macro Finance Insight 2.2: GDP Smoothing and Earnings Management

Estimates for real GDP and growth are just that, estimates. There is a fair amount of leeway in exactly determining any nation's actual output. The United States, for example, revises its quarterly GDP data twice in the quarter following the target quarter. As time passes, estimates are based less on surveys and more on realized comprehensive data. In the G7 economies, the revisions can be substantial—as much as a full percentage point. China revises its quarterly GDP data in a fashion similar to the United States. It revises annual GDP estimates in July of the year following the target year and has a comprehensive set of revisions every five years (2018 being the most recent five-year revision). Initial quarterly GDP estimates occur 15 to 20 days after the quarter. Further revisions are made two months after the quarter, and then again the following quarter. These revisions, in principle, should be largely unpredictable (unbiased).

Some scholars have suggested that China's NBS has engaged in "smoothing" (i.e., exaggerating) growth rates in times of economic slowdowns (Henderson et al. 2012). Figure 2.5 and Figure 2.6 suggest that China's estimates of growth do diverge from other estimates, notably during 1990–1991 (the United States "dot-com" recession) and 1997–1998 (the Asian financial crisis). We note, for example, that the growth rate estimate for 1998, (of 7.8 percent), while close to the planned target of 8 percent set by the government, is unrealistically low (see Rawski 2001). The GDP growth targets set in the Five-Year Plans may pressure localities within China to adjust their own production data so that targets are met. Provinces and localities compete with one another to impress the central government. Behavioral finance suggests the important role that any major benchmark plays in setting expectations and estimates; and, in this context, statisticians might rationalize a "fudging" of the data to meet a Plan target. We should remember that there are two opposing forces at play when reporting income and sales: On one hand, strong results boost the reputation of local officials; on the other hand, they invite great interest from the tax collectors at all levels of government. It is not obvious which effect is more important.

In fact, income smoothing occurs in the United States as well, but in the form of "earnings management" at the corporate level rather than the national statistical level. A large body of evidence suggests that firms try to smooth earnings using accepted accounting methods, such as accruals, rather than recognizing income or profits. For example, standard accounting principles allow leeway regarding when a non-cash sale is recognized in earnings. A variety of explanations are offered for such smoothing, including investors' preferences for a stable pattern of earnings. Thus, firms work to make their reported earnings appear smoother in order to reduce their cost of capital. In an insightful paper, Lin and Shih (2002) suggest that US firms may underestimate income in times of downturn—just the opposite of the suspected pattern in China. By underestimating income in downturns and accruing that income for a later recovery period, the authors highlight a pro-cyclical type of income smoothing. The rationale for this practice is twofold. First, since profits are down economy-wide, firms' losses in a down period are discounted by investors, but the earnings that are later booked will be rewarded. Second, bonuses in down periods are unlikely, but the corresponding earnings accrued for a later recovery period will be rewarded.

To the extent that earnings management involves accruing (deferring revenues or sales), the impact on measured GDP is direct. It is unknown to what extent pro-cyclical earnings are exaggerated by management during downturns in the United States. It is interesting, however, that China and the United States—because of the peculiarities of their respective economic systems—are probably biased in opposite directions in their GDP reporting. Particularly during downturns, China may overestimate real growth while the United States may underestimate it.

Who is Smoother: China or the US?

A study by Henderson et al. (2012) of 188 countries buttresses the notion of overly smooth GDP numbers in China. In an innovative approach, they examine nighttime luminosity growth rates of countries (use of lights) as an alternative gauge of economic activity based on observations from space by the US Air Force. For China in the 1992–2008 period, growth in luminosity was considerably slower (cumulatively, 65 percentage points lower) than the official GDP growth rates. The gap between the two was the second-largest among all countries considered.[13] What is more, reported GDP growth was substantially less volatile than luminosity growth.

By contrast, Williamson et al. (2018) compare Chinese GDP growth rates to sales growth of 150 listed Chinese companies and find that the two series moved closely together over time. Again, though, they conclude that short-term volatility is much higher for the listed companies than for reported GDP growth.

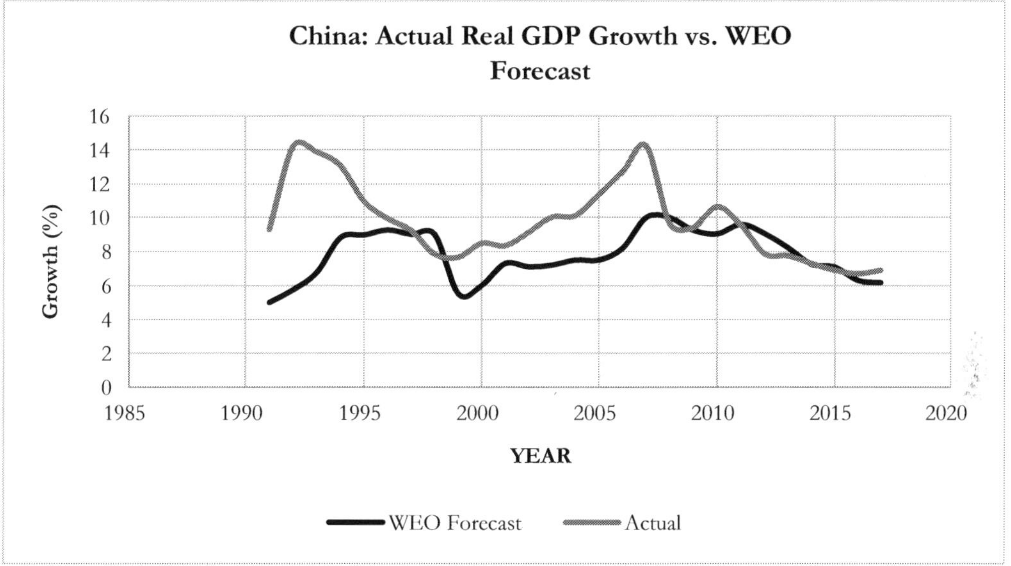

Figure 2.6 Forecasts for China's GDP by the IMF track actual growth since 2008 but had under-estimated growth in earlier years.
Source: Author created based on International Monetary Fund Database and National Bureau of Statistics, China.

In part, these differences reflect the relative abundance of labor to capital in China. From a neoclassical microeconomic perspective, the marginal product of labor is low and that of capital is high, with the marginal wage and return on capital at corresponding levels.[14] But there are other fundamental causes for this difference, relating to the use of technology and the market power of workers compared to firms' owners. China, on balance, makes net factor payments abroad, thus creating a wedge between GDP and GNP (the former being larger). The United States finds itself in the reverse position. Further examination of the underlying data shows another contrast: While China makes dividend payments on net sales to the rest of the world (representing the substantial foreign direct investment (FDI) into China), the nation also receives interest payments from the rest of the world on balance (representing its substantial holdings of foreign exchange reserves).

The United States, by contrast, finds itself in exactly the complementary position—receiving dividends but paying interest to the rest of the world.[15] As we discuss elsewhere, this difference creates an odd result, given that China is a net creditor to the United States: The high-yield investments (FDI) of the United States into China compared to the low-yielding investments of China in US assets (mainly US Treasury instruments) result in a net factor payment outflow from China to the United States. Over time, as China shifts its portfolio from US government securities to FDI in the United States, the flow will likely turn favorably toward China.[16]

Finally, we note the lower depreciation rate found in China (13 percent) compared to that of the United States (16 percent) as a share of GDP. China's ratio of capital to GDP is still lower than in the United States, meaning that the depreciation rate on capital is actually higher in China. This likely reflects several factors: (1) the newer (on average) vintage of capital stock found in China (recently installed capital depreciates at a higher rate than older vintages); and (2) the need to write off substantial investments as reflected in the substantial non-performing loan problem of the banking system (to be discussed in a later chapter).

Macro Finance Insight 2.3: GDP Smoothing and Variance Bounds Tests

"Life is full of surprises," or so they say. That aphorism holds true in finance as well. Our best guesses or forecasts about the future are often off—there is usually a surprise element. That simple concept underlies the notion of a "variance bounds test" for how well stock prices accurately represent fundamental factors such as dividends and discount rates. In his insightful research, Robert Shiller (1981) hypothesized that stock prices (what is in effect a forecast of a company's performance) should be less volatile than the actual realized fundamentals that determine stock prices (discounted dividends). To Shiller's surprise, what he found was that the opposite was true—the forecast (stock prices) were more volatile than the actual realization (the stream of dividends). In this context, he inferred that stock pricing was not fully "rational." We ask whether Chinese GDP forecasts versus realizations will surprise us in the same way.

For our purposes, we can ask whether forecasts of Chinese GDP are smoother (less volatile) than the actual realization; they should be—for the reasons described above. Figure 2.6 and Figure 2.7 show actual GDP growth and forecasted GDP growth for China and the United States. Forecasts are based on IMF World Economic Outlook (WEO) forecasts from the autumn of the prior year. If China's actual GDP is too smooth relative to its forecast, we might be suspicious that some smoothing has occurred. We find that for both China and the United States, forecasts are significantly less volatile (smoother) than the actual growth rate (as we might expect). In comparing the two countries, some other facts emerge:

- While both countries pass the variance bounds test, the United States performs better than China—actual growth is substantially more volatile than forecasts of growth in the US compared to China. Though forecasts in both countries are smoother than realizations, they are relatively smoother in the United States.
- IMF forecasters often underestimated China's growth potential in the 1990s and early 2000s.
- In absolute terms, China's GDP is more volatile than the United States'.
- Relative to its average growth rate (an inverted Sharpe ratio), GDP volatility in China is significantly less than in the United States.

The above facts suggest that either there are more surprises to economic growth in the United States compared to China, or the methodology employed in China tends to lead to smoother estimates. One possibility is that China's GDP estimates contain more forecasted components than realized data. Apparent from our discussion above, if a current measure of GDP heavily relies on a forecast rather than observed data, that measure—by definition—will behave more like a forecast (be smooth). This, in fact, would be consistent with the World Bank's assessment of weakness in data sources with regard to statistical capacity (see above). Either way, we notice that forecasts for both countries have become more accurate post-Great Financial Crisis (GFC).

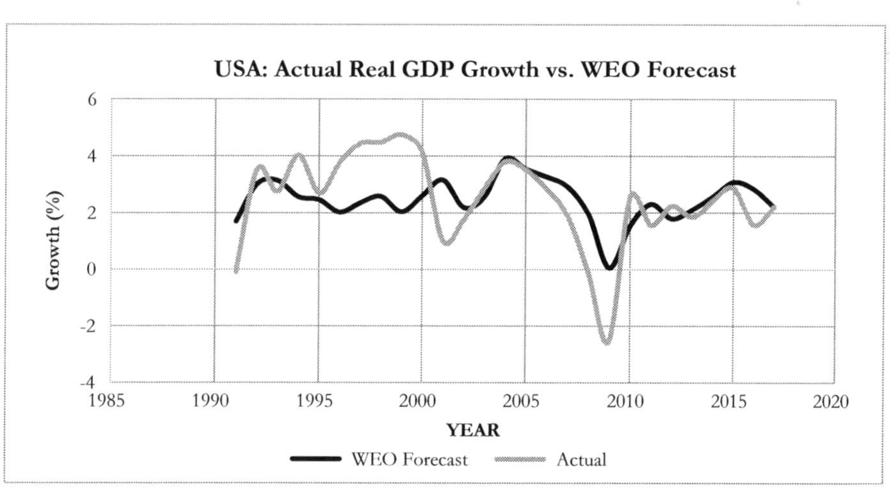

Figure 2.7 Actual GDP growth for the United States, as expected, is not as smooth as forecasted growth.
Source: Author created based on International Monetary Fund Database and IMF's World Economic Outlook.

China's Presentation of GDP Data

It is useful to understand the recent historical context of China's data collection efforts in order to gain insight into the methodological and presentational issues in China's GDP accounts. The earliest modern estimates of China's output were for the period before World War II by Pao-San Ou (1946). In the pre-reform period (1950–1978), China's GDP methodology closely mirrored that of the Soviet Union. This approach had two major underpinnings: (1) an emphasis on the production of physical volumes (as opposed to intangible production such as services), and (2) a reliance on the input-output approach consistent with that of a planned economy.[17] The latter element, in effect, allowed a central planner (rather than the "invisible hand" of a capitalist economy) to ask what outputs were desired and what combination of inputs should be produced and allocated across different sectors in order to achieve the desired output targets. The metric used in the pre-reform period was NMP. This measure excluded most services (but included material) and netted out depreciation of the capital stock. Net exports (relatively small during this period) were not independently estimated but treated as a residual. China published its first GNP measure of output consistent with the SNA and discontinued reporting NMP in 1995.

A vestige of the old system remains, however, in that the emphasis has been on measuring output as all that was produced rather than all that was used. During pre-reform China, in the absence of a market-based economy, the principal users (consumers) were de-emphasized relative to the perceived more important user (the government's investment in plant, property, equipment, and infrastructure). Without a true consumer market, effectively measuring retail sales—for example—would be difficult. In other words, China's GDP measurement relied more heavily on the Value-Added and Income approaches (especially the former), as opposed to the Expenditure (Uses) approach.[18]

In fact, China's official GDP estimate continues to be presented primarily in terms of value added and secondarily in terms of uses. The two measures have moved closer to each other over the years, and by 2018 they only differed by about 1.8 percent. As of 2019, the presentation of output using an income measure was quite limited. The presentation is provided at a provincial level by the authorities but is not readily available at the national level. The aggregate of provincial GDPs based on income have been substantially larger than China's GDP based on the Value-Added approach. For example, in 2016 the aggregate GDP for China's provinces was 4 percent larger than the more commonly used total value-added number. Furthermore, while estimates for GDP on a quarterly basis (as opposed to an annual basis) have been produced using the Value-Added approach since 1992, they are still not readily available using the Expenditure (Uses) approach or Income approach.

In contrast, the official estimate for United States GDP is based on the Expenditure (Uses) approach. In 2017, for example, estimated GDP using the Expenditure (Uses) method came to USD 19.5 trillion, but rose about 0.5 percent to USD 19.6 trillion when measured under the Income approach (also defined as gross domestic income). Given each country's belief that it will achieve a more accurate measure of output using its preferred approach, the residual approaches (e.g., Expenditure (Uses) approach for the Chinese, and Income approach for the United States) tend to be adjusted in the direction of the principal measurement.

As we will see in later chapters, these differences go beyond mere statistics. Western economists emphasize the ultimate goal of an economic system as consumption—normally the only argument found in the utility function in neoclassical economics. Traditionally, Chinese economists have emphasized the role of production and growth (the size and progress of GDP). Needless to say, both are important, and both countries are converging toward similar economic goals and ways of measuring output.

Macro Finance Insight 2.4: The Purchasing Managers' Index and the Economic Pulse

China also produces a set of purchasing managers' indexes (PMIs) to provide a timelier (and possibly forward-looking) index of current economic activity compared to GDP; GDP is reported quarterly while the PMIs are reported every month. The NBS PMI is based on surveys of large, long-established enterprises' purchasing managers. The survey asks whether certain critical business activity has gone up, down, or remained the same. This dichotomous "up or down" kind of survey is referred to as a diffusion index. For example, if new orders for products or services have gone up, a score of 100 will be given; if down, a score of 0; and if unchanged, a score of 50. The NBS looks at 13 different activities for its manufacturing index including inventories, employment, production, and delivery time for suppliers. Combining these various indicators into an overall index, one interprets a score above 50 as a positive indication of economic growth and below 50 as negative. A similar index is created for the important non-manufacturing sector, which includes nine indicators.

Because the NBS PMI contains mostly large enterprises, the media and financial data providers Caixin (https://bit.ly/2zzEH3X) and Markit (https://bit.ly/2Lojz3b) have created their own PMIs that cover 500 SMEs. In addition, they also provide a PMI general services index which covers 400 companies. While there are a number of advantages to PMI type indexes—higher frequency, earlier reporting, and no revisions—certain disadvantages remain. These indexes do not tell us about the magnitude of up or down movements, nor do they take account of increases or decreases in the number of firms in an industry. The PMI is a relatively noisy (volatile) indicator (see Figure 2.8). In the case of China's PMIs, the individual indicators are a mix of leading and coincident indicators (see Chapter 1 Appendix), so it is difficult to discern what the intended purposes of the broad indexes are: whether to forecast the future, or to describe the current economic circumstance.

Figure 2.8 shows the manufacturing PMI and an index of monthly Chinese industrial production (growth from a year ago). We can see that there is some correspondence (a correlation of around 0.65) but that the PMI is a relatively noisy indicator. The PMI is typically intended to correspond to growth rates in output. Since China is an economy that principally experiences growth cycles rather than business cycles (levels), the PMI has particular applicability.

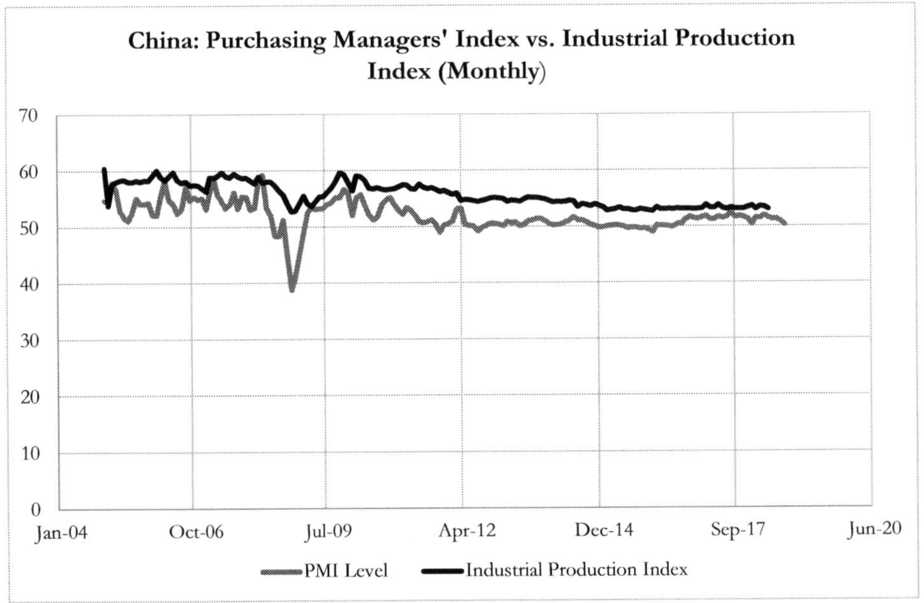

Figure 2.8 China's Purchasing Managers' Index is intended to track economic performance as measured by indicators such as industrial production.
Source: Author created based on National Bureau of Statistics, China and CEIC.

Issues in Measuring GDP

To better understand exactly what we are measuring when calculating a nation's GDP, we must look more deeply at some of the assumptions, definitions, and methodologies employed in its measurement.

Does GDP Correspond to Well-Being?

Economics is defined as the study of how best to match individuals' unlimited wants with society's scarce resources. Thus, the basic assumption of economics is that individuals seek to maximize their consumption of goods and services over some relevant timeframe. It is natural, then, to focus on the production of those goods and services (GDP) as a measure of well-being in any given economy. Economists and philosophers agree that meeting basic needs such as shelter, nutrition, and health is a desirable goal. It also seems probable that the more a country produces, the more likely it is that such a goal will be met. But at what point does the production of material goods (and services) cease to correlate with improved well-being and happiness? There is no clear answer to this question, particularly when we consider that the production of "goods" may also involve the production of certain "bads" such as pollution, congestion, resource depletion, and unhappiness (e.g., obsessive materialism). None of these latter outcomes, sometimes referred to as "negative externalities," are taken into account when measuring GDP. Similarly, GDP does not measure how much leisure time is available to individuals in an economy, nor how income is distributed among its individual members.[19]

The United Nations Development Program provides an alternative measure to GDP: the Human Development Index (HDI). This measure includes life expectancy, educational attainment, other social factors, and the more traditional measure of per capita income. China has steadily been moving up the ranking. By UN measures in 2018, China ranks 86th in the HDI (out of 187 countries), with a score of 0.752 (the range is from 0 to 1). The United States has dropped to 11th in HDI, with a score of 0.924 (Table 2.5). In terms of income distribution, estimates of Gini coefficients for the United States and China are at 0.41 and 0.47, respectively.[20] We see that China does well in comparison with its "medium human development" peers both in terms of life expectancy and education. Keeping in mind the above caveats regarding well-being and per capita GDP, but also remembering the likely high correlation between per capita GDP and economic well-being, we will focus on GDP as our main target in the body of this book.

	GDP per capita Purchasing Power Parity (USD)	Life Expectancy at Birth	Mean Years of Schooling	Expected Years of Schooling	HDI
China	15,270	76.4	7.8	13.8	0.752
USA	54,941	79.5	13.4	16.5	0.924

Table 2.5 The United Nations Human Development Index presents at a broader measure of well-being within a country than per capita GDP.
Source: Author created based on United Nations, 2018.

Case Study 2.3: The Environment and Trade with the United States

That China's economic growth is coming at a tremendous environmental cost has been well-documented. The degradation of air and water quality across the country has been enormous. It is estimated that more than half of the water sources near urban areas are unfit for drinking. About one-third of China's famous and economically significant Yellow River is too polluted even for agricultural use. And this is in a country in which water for agriculture and personal use has always been in extremely scarce supply. In many parts of China, Particulate Matter Indices (measures of the concentration of tiny but harmful particles in the air) regularly exceed 10 and sometimes 40 times the levels that the World Health Organization considers safe. In December, 2013, Shanghai had a Particulate Matter Index reading of 580, exceeding "hazardous." Air quality remains part of the daily conversation in local newscasts. It is not unusual to see citizens wearing face masks with air filters when walking outside. Some international schools in major cities have created air-filtered sanctuaries within school buildings, since students are regularly not permitted outdoors due to the poor air quality.

China now burns over half the world's coal, and evidence of that is particularly acute in major cities across the country—especially Beijing and Shanghai. China surpassed the United States in terms of carbon dioxide (CO_2) emissions several years ago. *The Economist* reports (https://econ.st/3hmRJDe) that China's cumulative emissions of CO_2 in the coming years will exceed the entire world's CO_2 output from the start of the industrial revolution to 1970. Ebenstein et al. (2015) observe that, though China's per capita GDP increased by a factor of 10 in real terms between 1991 and 2012, life expectancy underperformed by increasing by only 6.4 years in the same period. One might expect life expectancy to increase by about double that amount. Ebenstein et al.'s empirical research suggests that the shortfall may be due to increased disease rates (e.g., respiratory disease) linked to air pollution in China.

An insightful article published in the proceedings of the National Academy of Sciences (Lin et al. 2014) links China's exports (most of which are directed to the United States) to pollution not just in China but also to the US West Coast. Approximately one-third of some critical pollutant levels in China can be attributed to its manufacture (or reprocessing) and export of products to other countries. Conversely, the authors find that if these same products were produced in the target countries rather than being imported, pollution levels would be substantially higher there. Countries such as the United States are not unscathed by China's pollution. The authors find a significant impact from China's export-related air pollution on the western United States (where sulfur levels, for example, are 12 to 24 percent higher due to China's pollution spillover). In terms of improved air quality, the primary beneficiaries are those living along the US East Coast, where manufacturing that would have otherwise harmed the environment is now located in China. Another factor to consider are the massive landfills being created across the United States to ultimately dispose of these imported goods.

Since 2013, the central government has accelerated efforts to deal with air and water pollution. Specifically, a national action plan on air pollution was devised in 2013 with a number of mandates, including a reduction in coal use as large as 50 percent for Beijing and large drops for other cities between 2013 and 2018. Furthermore, output restrictions were imposed on pollution intensive industries such as steel, aluminum, and cement. The centralization of authority, such as the establishment of the Ministry of Ecological Environment (2018) under the State Council, has proven more effective in reducing pollution than the reliance on provincial enforcement. Mentioned already are Five-Year Plan targets for electric vehicles which have helped decelerate air pollution growth. As part of the 13th Five-Year Plan, China also introduced an air emissions trading system targeted to carbon emissions (Pizer and Zhang 2018). The system legally commits China by 2020 to lower carbon emission intensity of production by 18 percent from 2015 levels and to increase the share of non-fossil-fuel power sources to 15 percent by 2020. Emission ceilings will be determined as an increasing function of output, and then firms will be allowed to trade their emission "rights" with one another.

Finally, market developments, including the growth of the service sector and economically viable renewable sources of energy such as solar and wind have had an important impact. China leads the world in solar energy capacity with nearly double the amount found in the United States. Under the Paris Climate Agreement, China has agreed to rely on renewable energy sources for 20 percent of its energy needs by 2030. On some days in major cities, Particulate Matter Indices have dropped to single digits and urban skies are noticeably haze free and blue. China still relies on coal for the largest share of energy use (60 percent), but that figure is down from 80 percent in 2010. There are still concerns that actual use of coal in energy production is being underestimated.

Similar efforts are underway to meet the challenge of water pollution. For example, the "Water Pollution Prevention and Control" (https://bit.ly/2LqLsI4) law was passed and implemented in 2018. It targets water pollution from agriculture, takes measures to protect drinking waters, raises penalties for water pollution, and enhances enforcement. Based on objective measurements and policy pronouncements, it appears China is making good progress in providing a cleaner environment for its citizens, but much more work needs to be done.

Quality of Growth

Macro Finance Insight 2.5 examines the important question of quality of growth versus quantity of growth. That the above effect is important in a country such as China (in which investment use represents about 44 percent of GDP), can be shown as:

$$\text{GDP Growth} = \times \text{ Investment Growth} + (1 - \alpha) \times \text{Non-Investment Growth}$$

Here, (α) represents the share of GDP use going to investment, and (1 - α) represents the share going to non-investment uses, meaning consumption, government, and net exports. Rearranging, we have:

$$1 = \frac{\alpha \times \text{Investment Growth}}{\text{GDP Growth}} + \frac{(1-\alpha) \times \text{Non} - \text{Investment Growth}}{\text{GDP Growth}}$$

The equation above shows how much of GDP growth can be attributed to investment growth and non-investment growth. We note that China's investment is now about 44 percent of GDP, or ($\alpha = 0.44$). Historically, it had been growing at a faster rate than GDP. The first term on the right-hand side of the last equation applied to 2016 growth suggests that about 36 percent of China's growth is due to investment. Meanwhile, one-fourth of US growth can be explained by the investment component, at most. Both the share of investment in GDP and its growth combine to create this result.

In a pure accounting sense, more investment leads to higher output (by definition). Here, we are not referring to the role of investment as an input into the production function (we will discuss that later). Rather, we are making the simple accounting observation that if growth in the capital stock is large (and this is a large fraction of GDP), then GDP growth as a quantity concept will be large as well. For example, a company such as General Motors (GM) increased assets in the United States (its own capital stock) by a factor of 39 between 1965 and 2003, while increasing sales by a factor of 9. With poor financial performance, it ultimately fell into bankruptcy in the 2008 global financial crisis. Both the investment of GM and its sales were included in measured GDP over those four decades. If enough companies in any economy followed this pattern, we would see high GDP growth rates (based on asset and sales growth), but eventual value destruction and economic collapse.

The fact that so much of China's past growth is the result of measured investment (as a use of GDP) does raise certain red flags. When consumption is considered as a use, we feel more comfortable with its direct link between its pricing and economic value; after all, consumers willingly make purchases at prices determined by supply and demand (which reflects preferences). When investment goods are a primary use, the link between economic well-being and production is less clear. It may be a decade or more before we can understand whether an investment actually created value or not.

This concern becomes elevated in the presence of state-directed loans and significant distortions (such as controlled interest rates) in the financial system. We will present this distinction between quantity and quality, value creation, and value destruction in a dynamic setting in Chapter 4 within a Solow framework.

Figure 2.9 demonstrates the difference between value maximization and quantity maximization at the single-firm level. A level of investment consistent with point A, in which the return on invested capital just equals its opportunity cost, yields value maximization. Points below A (such as B) may yield higher quantities of GDP, but at the cost of value destruction. Value-destroying points below A (such as B) can occur if the cost of capital line is artificially set below its location in Figure 2.9, or if credit is directed by government fiat for excessive capital accumulation. As discussed directly below, GDP accounting implicitly pushes the return on capital line artificially high (above its location in Figure 2.9) because it neither depreciates the capital over time nor uses present value methodology.

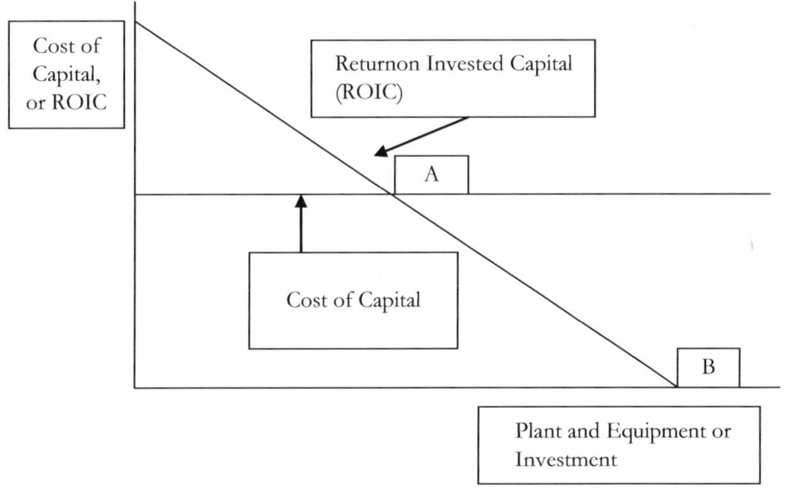

Figure 2.9 There is value creation and quality of growth as long as our capital stock is below the intersection of the two curves at A. This is where the return on investment equals its cost.
Source: Author created.

Macro Finance Insight 2.5: Quantity of GDP vs. Quality of GDP

Because GDP is measured using market prices, it is reasonably assumed that what is being measured reflects the true value of output. While for consumer goods and services this is an acceptable assumption, it is not necessarily so for investment goods. Measuring the latter is particularly problematic in economies in which investment by the private sector may be made at the behest of government policy-makers and/or with the support of a state-dominated financial sector (meaning that the cost of capital is either artificially set too low or even irrelevant to the investment decision). This situation may be an appropriate description of investments in China's past. Although we can measure the investment component of GDP by examining its selling price, this method may not truly reflect the value of that investment from a sound GDP perspective. Thus, we are now focusing on the quality of GDP rather than the raw quantity measure of GDP with respect to the investment component of GDP.

When an investment is undertaken in which its cost (the quantity measure of its GDP contribution) is greater than the present value of the profit stream it generates (its quality measure), we refer to this as value destruction rather than value creation—the latter being what GDP is intended to measure. At the GDP accounting level, we note that the investment would be measured at its purchase price (i.e., the value of its final sale in the year it was purchased). The profit stream would be measured in GDP for later years, year-by-year, as profits are generated. We immediately see two problems that create a gap between the value or quality of what is produced and the GDP measure. The first problem is that GDP is a gross measure, meaning that we never subtract out from the profit stream the depreciation of the initial investment. Thus, even if, on an undiscounted basis, the stream of profits after depreciation is less than the initial investment, we would not see it reflected in the GDP numbers themselves. The second problem is that GDP accounting, by its very nature, does not provide a present value of the stream of benefits from an investment. Thus, this is a second way in which a value-destroying project would never come to light. In summary, both an investment and its aftermath of profits will boost the raw quantity of GDP over several years without telling us directly whether that investment was in fact creating or destroying value.

These points are not intended to diminish the importance or usefulness of the GDP measure, but simply to point out that the main focus of this measure is on economic activity and employment, not necessarily value creation (or the quality) of GDP.

Prices and GDP Measurement

Several key issues must be discussed within this broad area. First, GDP is ideally measured at market prices (prices we would actually pay for the good or service in a competitive market). Second, we often are interested in real or constant dollar GDP as opposed to nominal GDP. Real GDP attempts to measure output in physical volumes rather than in current dollars (nominal GDP). The latter could create the illusion of increased output when, in fact, only nominal prices have changed (in the presence of inflation, for example). Third, we may be interested in measuring output using international prices rather than domestic prices. We would describe this as a measure of purchasing power parity (PPP) GDP. Finally, we are interested in measuring GDP through factoring in changes in the price/cost of goods and services that a country exports and imports. For example, if the cost of oil rises in world markets, and our economy is a major importer of oil, our own exports may not command as much in real purchasing power in world markets. We refer to this latter concept as "command GDP."

Price Distortions

Since GDP measures the value of final output, the extent to which prices reflect true value of output is of critical concern. If, for example, an apple is twice the price of a lemon, then the production of one apple should add twice as much to the value of GDP as would one lemon. Implicit in such a calculation is the idea that relative prices (i.e., 2:1) reflect relative values. But this will only be true in markets that operate under competitive conditions. China's entry into the World Trade Organization in 2001 accelerated the process of price liberalization that had begun in 1978. Before that, most prices had been set by the state and were thus not market determined. By 2004, Chinese officials estimated that 96 percent of all prices were market determined, but these were mainly consumer prices and did not include the many investment goods that were still subsidized. In addition, prices for certain critical products were still controlled by local price bureaus; these included electricity, transportation, fertilizer, medicine, and fuel.

Government subsidies for the production of goods and services can also distort prices, since the resulting prices that consumers or investors finally pay will generally be lower than their market value. This issue, however, has less impact if the government records the subsidy as expenditure and the value is captured under government uses.[21] Indirect taxes (such as sales taxes) are included in measures of GDP since, if consumers are willing to pay the full price for something (inclusive of taxes), we can assume that the price paid reflects the value. Sales tax, in recent years, including value-added taxes, represents about 7 percent of GDP in China.

Consider another issue in determining GDP accurately: how to factor in the wide range of products and services that are not sold in a market but are provided by the state—that is, public goods. These goods and services are normally valued at cost, since no market prices are available. In the case of China, this issue is both important and complex. Prior to 1979, all output was produced by the government (central and local) either directly or through state-owned enterprises (SOEs). After 1979, locally owned

SOEs and private enterprises tended to move into the production of private sector goods while the central government and other SOEs produced output more closely aligned with public goods (those goods traditionally provided by the public sector).

Furthermore, a significant portion of China's substantial investment occurred as a result of government directives. Accordingly, China tends to have a substantially higher proportion of output that does not result from an explicit market-based force, but rather from government decision making (especially policy-directed investments). Therefore, the value assigned to a large fraction of China's GDP may be estimated without reference to any market-determined mechanism.

It would be worthwhile to estimate the potential size of this part of GDP. As we have seen in Table 2.3, the Chinese government's explicit use of GDP for both consumption and investment purposes reached RMB 18.9 trillion, or about 25 percent of GDP—a share about 47 percent higher than that of the United States. But we can also attempt to take into account the government's indirect role in the economy. Consider that: (1) There are about 150,000 state-owned units in China (of which one third are central government units) producing at least 30 percent (https://bit.ly/2zxBVvV) of China's GDP and, (2) investment in China composed about 44 percent of GDP, and much of this investment is linked to central government directives. Even after taking account of the substantial overlap in these two figures, it remains clear that a comparatively large share (an estimated 40 percent [https://bit.ly/2zEzZBJ]) of China's GDP is due to direct or indirect government demand, with an even higher proportion related to the investment component of GDP. Compare this figure with the United States, in which about 20 percent of GDP is attributed to the government.[22,23,] In summary, a relatively large part of China's GDP may not reflect value based on conditions of supply and demand, but is instead based upon government purchasing decisions and cost.[24] Nevertheless, it is important to acknowledge the tremendous growth of the private sector, in which an estimated 25 million private firms of varying size and definition are in operation.

Converting Nominal GDP into Real GDP: The Use of Price Indexes

Nominal GDP represents the current dollar (or RMB) value of output. For example, if we only produce ten apples this year and each apple sells for USD 1, then nominal GDP for this simple economy would be USD 10. Similarly, if in Year 1 we produce ten apples and in Year 2 we produce ten apples while the price of apples rises from USD 1 to USD 1.25, our nominal GDP has risen from USD 10.00 to USD 12.50. But has there been any real change in output? No, real output has remained at ten apples. The latter real amount, of course, is of great interest since it is the amount that corresponds to our productivity, our consumption possibilities, and our economic activity. In one sense, the increase in earnings from USD 10 to USD 12.50 is not a very relevant measurement, since it simply reflects inflation. We must find a way to remove the effect of price changes from nominal GDP so as to arrive at real GDP. The tool for this adjustment is a price index. Price indexes attempt to measure price changes. As such, they help not only to measure real GDP, but also to determine intrinsic interest by allowing us to measure inflation and deflation.

Creating a price index generally involves picking a representative basket of goods and services for a particular year (the "base year"), then measuring how the price of that same basket—containing the same output in the same amounts—evolves over time. If the year 2015 is our base year, and we measure the cost of a basket at USD 100, and we find that prices are rising by 3 percent every year, we would then have the price index valued at USD 109.3 for 2019. It is as if we took a particular basket of goods for the selected base year, removed the price tags from the base year, and reattached new price tags from later years. This method clearly shows the changing cost of the same goods in different years. Typically, we assign an index value of 100 to the base year. Of course, the selection of the base year is very important in determining how the index changes. There are three main choices: (1) a market basket from a past year, (2) a market basket from the current year, or (3) a composite average basket containing a past and a current year.

Let's examine how to use price index numbers P^{2019} and P^{Base} to determine real output for 2013. If we let P^{2019} represent the price level for 2019, as measured by a price index, and P^{Base} represent the price index for the base year, then the equation below gives us a definition of nominal GDP in 2019:

$$GDP^{2019}_{\text{Nominal}} = Q^{2019}_{\text{Real}} \times P^{2019}$$

By multiplying the ratio (P^{Base}/P^{2019}) by the ratio shown below, we arrive at real GDP for 2019, but expressed in "base year dollars," as seen in the second equation (below). This is how we apply price indexes to interpret real GDP. We would refer to a price index that is used to convert nominal GDP to real GDP as a "GDP price deflator."

$$GDP^{2019}_{\text{Real}} = Q^{2019}_{\text{Real}} \times P^{2019} \times \left(\frac{P^{\text{Base}}}{P^{2019}}\right)$$

Table 2.6 provides an example of how the choice of market basket can affect the value of the price index and, in turn, our measure of inflation. To calculate how inflation would be measured using price indexes, let $Index^{2019}$ represent one of our price indexes in year 2019, then define inflation ($\prod$) between 2018 and 2019 as:

$$\prod^{2019} = [Index^{2019}/Index^{2018}] - 1$$

In Table 2.6, we assume that consumption and output are the same for two goods, candy and beer, which are the only products produced and consumed in this simple economy. Prices grow (inflation) for candy faster than for beer (3 percent per annum versus 2 percent per annum). As a result, demand and consumption grow faster for beer than for candy (5 percent compared to 4 percent). We refer to this phenomenon as a "substitution effect," which impacts how different price indexes perform over time. If we use a 2015 market basket as our base, measured inflation tends to be higher (cumulatively 11.3 percent) than if we use a 2019 market basket, for which measured inflation is cumulatively 11.2237 percent. If the 2015 basket is used, then we are implicitly assuming that consumers do not adjust their buying patterns and that output is a constant. In particular, they continue to consume candy as if relative prices had never changed. Similarly, if we use the 2019 market basket, we are implicitly assuming that consumers had anticipated the price change and, in 2015, shifted their consumption basket toward beer. Of course, neither is an accurate representation, and we infer that the use of the old basket will actually overstate inflation as experienced by the consumer, while the newer market basket will understate it.

Comparison of Different Price Indexes				
Year	**Price of Candy**	**Candy Consumed/ Output**	**Price of Beer**	**Beer Consumed/ Output**
	RMB		**RMB**	
2015	1.00	70.00	1.00	30.00
2016	1.03	72.80	1.02	31.50
2017	1.06	75.71	1.04	33.08
2018	1.09	78.74	1.06	34.73
2019	1.13	81.89	1.08	36.47

Year	Base Year: 2015	Base Year: 2019	Chained Index	Simple Square Root
2015				
2016	2.7000%	2.6919%	2.6990%	2.6960%
2017	2.7020%	2.6940%	2.6990%	2.6980%
2018	2.7041%	2.6960%	2.6991%	2.7001%
2019	2.7061%	2.6981%	2.6991%	2.7021%
Cumulative Growth Rate	11.2586%	11.2237%	11.2412%	11.2411%

Table 2.6 The table shows how we might calculate inflation for a consumer who consumes a market basket of candy and beer. Depending on whether we use an old basket, a new basket, or a mixed (chained) basket for our base year, we will come up with higher or lower estimates of inflation.
Source: Author created.

To correct for these biases inherent in using a fixed market basket, a "chain price" index can be employed. This index uses a combination of the current period's market basket and the last period's market basket. It is a geometric average of old and new baskets which, in theory, gives an accurate measure of inflation. The third column of data in the bottom half of Table 2.6 shows how a chain price index measures inflation. The cumulative estimate of 11.2 percent falls between the other two estimates. The last column shows the simple geometric average of the first and second columns. Cumulatively, it provides a good approximation for the chain index, though for any single year the differences may be larger. Meanwhile, in Table 2.6, we use quantity weights to derive a price index. Note that we could have solved a symmetric problem of determining real GDP by using price weights and allowing output to change. An overestimate of real GDP growth would have occurred if we had used an older market basket.

While the above differences in estimates may seem small, they can accumulate into large differences over time. In the United States, many programs, contracts, and benefit schemes are based on measures of inflation—including the US public pension scheme and the social security system. Thus, small differences in the measured inflation rate can make billions of dollars of difference in terms of expenditures or incomes over time. In fact, use of an outdated market-basket price index (such as is used in the US CPI) could have resulted in estimated over-payments to US social security recipients of USD 1 trillion for the period 1996–2006 (Boskin 1996). As a result, efforts to change the price index can be quite politically charged—suggesting that price indexes are not as dry a topic as one might think.

China's Price Indexes

China produces several kinds of price indexes, all of which are compiled by the NBS. Specifically, a CPI with urban and rural sub-indexes, a retail price index, industrial products price index, agricultural price index, raw materials price index, fixed asset price index, a real estate price index, and a broad-based GDP deflator price index (based on production) that began in 1985. As of yet, there is not an expenditure-based GDP deflator.

Consumer Price Index

The CPI measures how typical baskets of goods and services, purchased by average consumers, change in price over time. Since consumers are the most significant users of output, this is the most commonly used price index. China's CPI separately measures price changes for urban households and for rural households. This, of course, reflects China's substantial rural population.[25] In the United States, the CPI measures inflation for urban residents alone.[26] Monthly CPI numbers are provided about two weeks after the target month. China provides both a traditional market-basket index for the CPI (base years of 1978 and 1985) and a chain-weighted index with a most recent base year of 2015; base years are updated every five years. Updates are based on monthly survey using about 10,000 surveyors to survey 110,000 rural and urban households.

Data (https://bit.ly/35Xip8i) are collected from 88,000 prices at collection units in 500 cities and counties of the 31 provinces (including autonomous regions and municipalities), which cover shopping malls, supermarkets, open fairs, service outlets, and Internet e-commerce suppliers. Data are gathered into eight major categories, ranging from food to housing, and then 262 sub-categories. Efforts are made to survey purchases made at active marketplaces and department stores, and to conduct surveys consistently from month to month in terms of location, time of day, and market participants. Prices of domestic goods and services, as well as imported goods, are also included in the CPI. The inclusion of imports highlights that the CPI focuses on what consumers actually buy, regardless of the source. Figure 2.10 shows the CPI inflation in China from 1986 to the present, and it suggests substantial variation in the measured inflation rate with a peak inflation of over 28 percent in February, 1989.

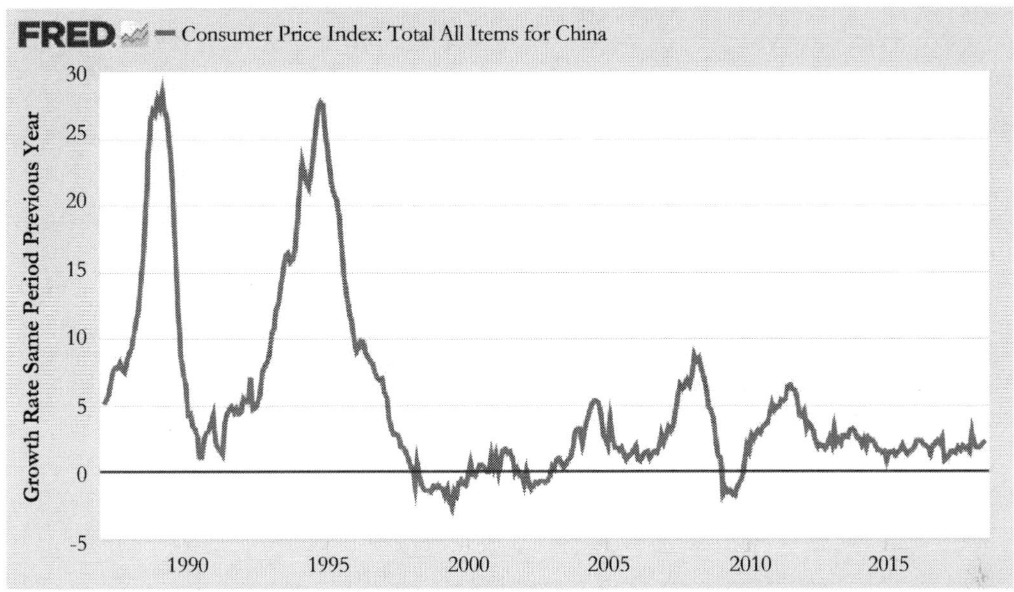

Figure 2.10 China's inflation rate has come down substantially from the double-digit growth rates of the 1980s and 1990s. Inflation since 2016 has edged upward.
Source: Author created based on Federal Reserve Economic Database.

An appropriate market basket for the CPI should include a balanced representation of how urban consumers actually spend their income. Figure 2.11 compares what Chinese consumers buy as a share of expenditure in 2016 to recent American expenditure shares. Key differences emerge; Chinese spend relatively more of their income on food and beverages compared to Americans, while Americans spend more on rent (actual or imputed) and fuel. Americans also devote a good deal of their budget to transportation (both automobiles and gasoline).

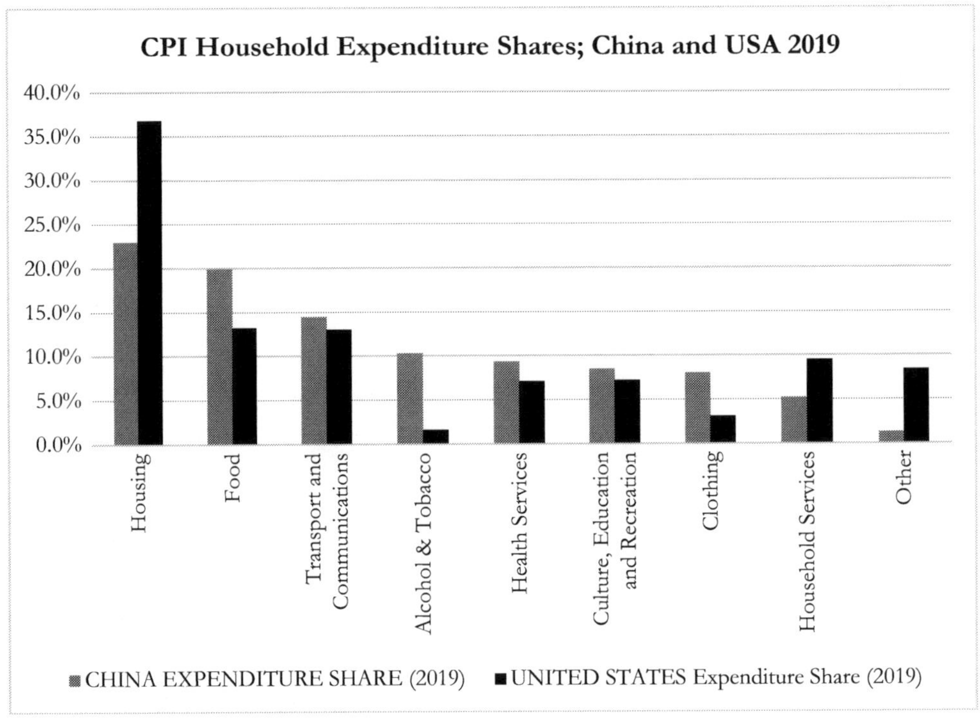

Figure 2.11 Here, we see expenditure shares for Chinese and US citizens. Some key differences emerge. Chinese spend a disproportionate amount of their income on food and beverages compared to Americans, while Americans spend relatively more on rent (actual or imputed) and utilities. Americans also devote a greater share of their budget to automobiles and transportation.
Source: Author created based on data from United States Bureau of Labor Services and David QU, Bloomberg Intelligence.
Note: Some categories such as transport and communications, culture, education and recreation and, household services did not completely align across categories. Fuel costs for vehicles was included in the transportation category for the United States.

The GDP Deflator

Unlike the CPI, the GDP deflator is a price index which measures price changes of all output produced by a country. While the CPI focuses on the consumer, the GDP deflator represents price movements for all classes of output: consumption, investment, exports, and government. It excludes imports, since these are not produced domestically. In this sense, the GDP deflator is the broadest measure of a country's inflation or deflation. China established GDP deflator base years every five years beginning in 1952, then switched to every ten years beginning in 1970, with the most recent base year being 2020. In 2005, the NBS launched its first national economic survey in order to create base year data. Determining the GDP deflator has been a complex and difficult process. It has combined outright measures of volume increases with available price deflators to apply to particular sectors (e.g., agricultural price indexes to be applied to the agricultural sector). The 2020 base year generally does not attempt to establish base year quantities, but rather uses separate price indexes (such as the CPI) to deflate nominal output for specific sectors. Though a GDP deflator is not published per se, it is implicit in official estimates of nominal GDP and real GDP, and it can be calculated quarterly. Formally we can state that:

$$\text{Index}^{\text{Real GDP}} = \text{Nominal GDP/Real GDP}$$

Figure 2.12 shows inflation as gauged by the inferred annual GDP deflator and China's actual CPI. Comparing the two, we see substantial differences in measured inflation. Both capture the dramatic slowdown in inflation in the last half of the 1990s and thereafter. But the relationship between the two varies over time; GDP deflator inflation is lower than the CPI measure through 1998 but then rises above the CPI in the 1999–2011 period. These differences are important, since the GDP deflator is used to measure real economic growth in China. The long-run consistency of the two measures suggests that, over the long run for China, average real GDP growth rates are not unduly biased by GDP deflator adjustments. The differences identified in the two sub-periods may correspond to exchange rate movements (a depreciating Chinese Yuan in the earlier sub-period and strengthening later). Recall that the CPI includes the effect of import price changes while the GDP deflator does not. For the United States, average CPI inflation tends to be larger than the GDP deflator growth over the long run and this likely corresponds to a key technical difference in the two measures: The GDP deflator allows for updating the base market basket, which in turn makes GDP deflator growth smaller in periods of rising prices.[27]

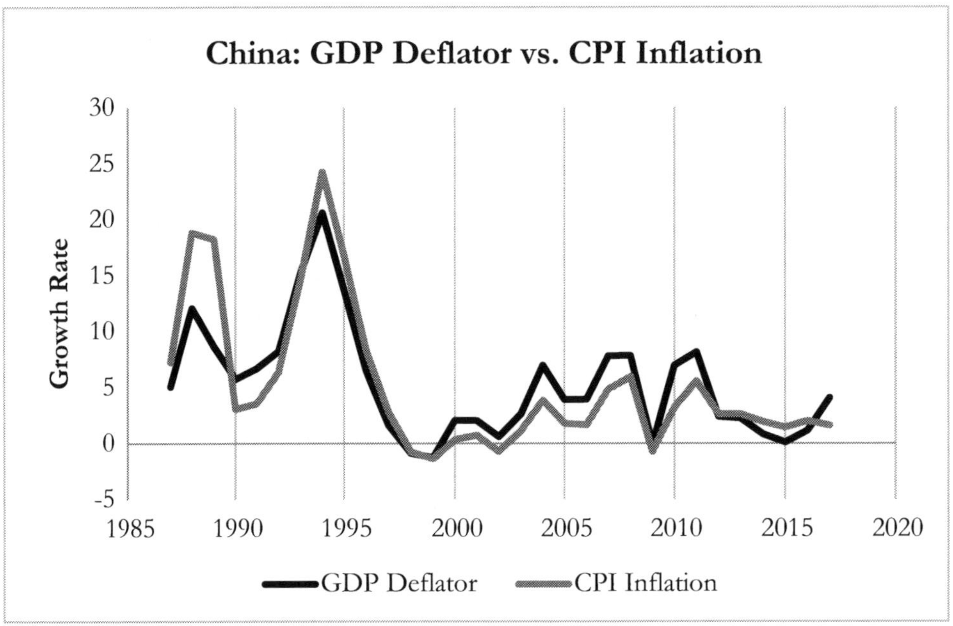

Figure 2.12 Between 1988 and 1999, the CPI measures average inflation as being larger than the GDP deflator measure, while in later years the reverse is true.
Source: Author created based on World Bank World Development Indicators.

Other Price Indexes

China's other price indexes—such as the retail price index and the industrial and raw materials price indexes—provide price information at production stages before final sale to consumers. As such, they are similar to the producer price index (PPI),[28] which provides information at crude, intermediate, and finished good production stages in the United States. These indexes differ from the CPI in that they do not cover the prices of services, distribution costs, or taxes at the point of sale to consumers.

Price Index Issues

There are several aspects in which China hopes to improve the accuracy of its indexes. One is by the greater use of chain-type indexes. This would provide more updated market baskets and take account of the substitution impact of price changes for goods and services. Another goal is to expand coverage of the services sector. Currently, both the CPI and the GDP deflator fall very short in their coverage of services—an area of rapid growth in China in recent years. Finally, coverage of export and import prices still remains weak. The trade sector continues to be treated as a residual measure rather than a sector in and of itself. Ideally, it would be independently measured for price effects.

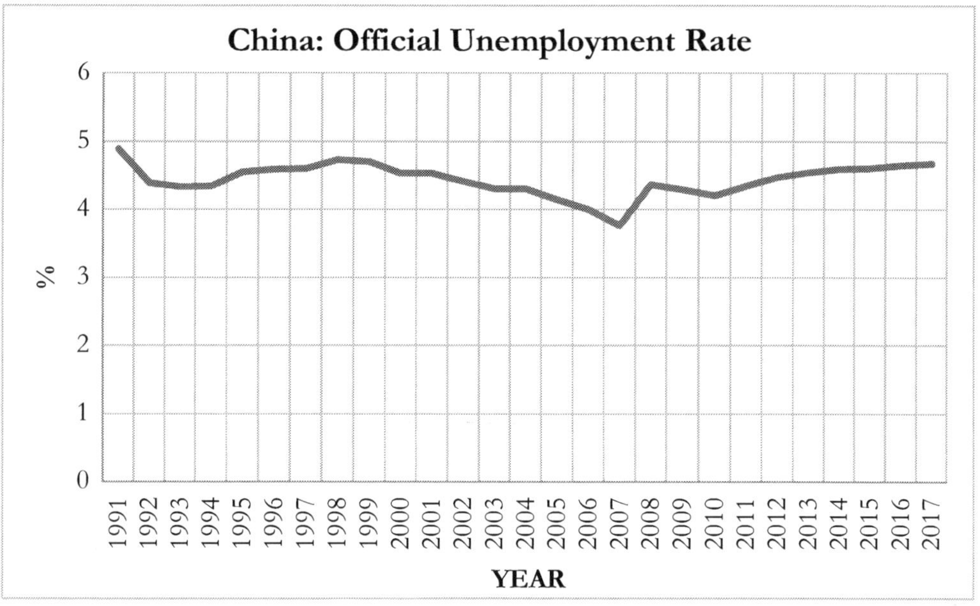

Figure 2.13 China's official unemployment rate is not a very good gauge of actual unemployment in China.
Source: Author created based on World Bank World Development Indicators.

Case Study 2.4: China's Unemployment Rate

China's official unemployment rate (registered unemployed in urban areas) was 4.7 percent in 2017. Over the past decade, it has not deviated from that number by more than a percentage point (see Figure 2.13). Most analysts believe this number seriously underestimates actual unemployment nationwide. In the past, the method of collection was based on the number of people who register themselves as unemployed at local urban employment offices. To register, one needed to be a local resident holding an official identification card (*hukou*); many unemployed do not have a local *hukou*, but a *hukou* from their home town or village. Giles et al. (2005) estimate that China's actual unemployment in 2002, for example, was closer to 14 percent (compared to the official number of 4 percent). The correlation between economic growth and the unemployment rate (referred to as Okun's Law) also seems quite low—only about 18 percent (negative)—close to half of the correlation found in the United States. Since 2002, China's economic growth has been quite strong, suggesting a decline in the unemployment rate from the Giles estimate to a number closer to 11 percent today. In February, 2018, the NBS changed its unemployment rate methodology, relying on surveys of urban workers. This will improve the accuracy of unemployment reporting in China, but more work remains (https://bit.ly/2XMP1h9), including collecting data on the close to 300 million migrant workers in China.

Collecting unemployment information through surveys, rather than self-reporting by individuals, is the preferred method. The US Bureau of Labor Statistics conducts monthly surveys to collect employment and unemployment statistics. Nevertheless, the number of unemployed in the United States is likely also underestimated due to methodological flaws. In the United States, individuals are asked if they are looking for employment. If they respond that they are not looking for work, then they are not included among the unemployed. Thus, in the United States, "discouraged" workers are undercounted in the unemployment statistics.

We can classify the unemployed into three different types: cyclical, structural, and frictional. Cyclical refers to those who have lost their jobs due to the business cycle; that is, a recession. Structural refers to those who have lost their work due to being in the wrong place or having the wrong skills while the economy is undergoing a fundamental transformation. Frictional relates to those who have left one job but have good prospects of finding another; that is, those who are between jobs. The latter kind of unemployment is actually considered a good thing, in its own way. It is one sign of a healthy labor market to see individuals matching their talents and tastes with evolving job opportunities. Cyclical and structural unemployment, on the other hand, are concerning for governments. Most governments feel pressured to respond to these types of unemployment with short-term or longer-term supply-side (structural) policies.

China's causes of unemployment are complex, and often work in complicated ways. For example, the *hukou* system adds a certain structural rigidity; but, at the same time, it allows employers in urban areas to hire workers as part of an informal economy (at lower cost). The massive movement of labor from rural to urban areas represents a frictional source of unemployment, but the movement ultimately reduces the structural unemployment rate in the long run. Investment in China remains government-mandated, which reduces the impact of the most volatile source of demand (and unemployment) in advanced economies. China's relatively low level of consumption, however, removes a stable source of demand as a basis for employment—particularly in the area of services. Table 2.7 summarizes some of these factors, which impact China's unemployment rate.

It should be no surprise that China has a relatively high unemployment rate given that it has experienced all types of unemployment, both historically and currently. The massive restructuring of SOEs in the 1980s and 1990s created a great deal of structural unemployment. The transition from agriculture to manufacturing, and now to services, is another source of structural unemployment. The global financial crisis, coupled with the ongoing slowdown in the United States and Europe, was an external shock (cyclical) that hit those employed in export-related industries particularly hard. And of course, the recent COVID-19 pandemic has both structural and cyclical impacts on the employment outlook.

Type of Unemployment	Increases Unemployment Rate	Decreases Unemployment Rate
Frictional	Dynamic Economy, "Ambitious" Labor Force, Massive Labor Migration to Urban Areas	Unemployment Benefits Do Not Exist
Cyclical	Continued Heavy Reliance on Exports, Consumption Levels Still Low	Strong Economic Growth, Government Mandated Investment
Structural	*Hukou* System, Monopsony, Power of Firms in Labor Markets, Major Shifts from Agriculture to Services and Manufacturing, Mismatch Between Skills	*Hukou* System, Absence of a Social Saftey Net, Highly Mobile Labor Force, "Flexible" Labor Force, Skill Enhancement Through Education

Table 2.7 China's unemployment rate contains elements of all three of the different types of unemployment.
Source: Author created.

Alternative Measures of GDP

Unaccounted Output

The UN's SNA stipulates that an exhaustive measure of GDP should include all transactions occurring between a willing buyer and willing seller. In addition, not only should output produced for external sale be included, but output for internal use should also be included (e.g., a farmer's consumption of some of his own crop). Nevertheless, some of the output produced in a country is simply never accounted for. This activity is referred to as "the informal economy" or, in China, *fei zhenggui jingji* (非正规经济) meaning "off the radar screen economy." In other words, these transactions are not accounted for via a nation's typical data collection infrastructure, which includes the tax collection ministry, central bank, labor ministry, central statistical bureau, and census bureau. As such, informal economy transactions are not included in GDP.[29]

Unrecorded output is economic activity that takes place but is not recorded in a nation's statistical offices because officials decide that accurate data are too difficult to estimate, or because survey methods are still too inadequate for better coverage. A good example of unrecorded output is a spouse who stays at home and does housework (a homemaker). While this activity is both valuable (e.g., caring for children) and time-consuming, it is not recorded as GDP since no explicit market transaction allows for its measurement and estimation. Another type of activity is unreported output. In this case, the official data collectors would actually like to record the economic activity, but individuals and corporations choose not to report it. This choice might be made for purposes of tax avoidance or because the activity is illegal. A repairman, for example, who works "on the side," may choose not to report this income so as to avoid paying taxes. A final category of overlooked activity is illegal activities. Although GDP attempts to measure goods and services, according to the SNA's exhaustive GDP definition, "bads" must also be included as long as the participating buyer and seller willingly undertake the transaction. Illegal gambling, drug sales, prostitution, and counterfeiting of goods are all included, even though most countries seek to eliminate these activities and replace them with legal endeavors. In most countries, illegal activities as a share of GDP would be less than 1 percent.

One strategy for estimating the size of the informal economy is to examine two separate estimates (often by different agencies or ministries) of the same economic quantity. If a large difference exists, one might infer that the gap corresponds to the informal portion of the economy. For example, we could estimate national savings from national income data but calculate changes in wealth (which amounts to the same things as national savings) from the banking and financial sector.[30] After taking into account various accounting issues, we might infer that some of the difference represents a gap between the statistical measure and the true measure—that is, the informal economy. Other approaches involve calculating alternate measures of output (such as electricity use) and inferring what actual GDP might be. Another approach examines cash transactions in an economy, since these are often undertaken to avoid taxes and regulation.

In the case of China, there is a wide range of estimates for the size of the shadow economy. Cai Fang et al. (2009) estimate the share of all workers in the informal economy in 2005 at nearly 53 percent. These are mostly migrant workers whose output may actually be recorded in GDP but who are working outside of regulated labor markets. Meanwhile, Schneider et al. (2018) estimate the informal economy as a share of GDP to be at about 13 percent, which is far below the average of 31 percent for 147 other countries but above the 8 percent figure for the United States.[31] In China, the government's direct or indirect involvement in many parts of the economy, may make hiding in the shadows more difficult.[32]

Purchasing Power Parity GDP

Naturally, a country measures its own GDP in its own currency. The United States measures the value of its output in USD and China in RMB. But the need often arises to compare or create a more standardized measure of a country's output. This process involves applying an exchange rate (e.g., RMB/USD) to China's GDP in order to calculate a dollar measure of China's output. Although this may seem straightforward, in fact, several distortions can arise. First, the exchange rate itself may be overvalued or undervalued. That is to say, its value at the point in time when the GDP conversion occurs may not be the same as its long-run, or fundamental, value. Real economic activity determines the fundamental value of a nation's currency over the long run, but short-run fluctuations (for example, shocks in financial markets) can cause the exchange rate to deviate from its long-run value. The second problem relates to relative prices in an economy. It is very unlikely that two economies have the same relative prices for all goods and services. For example, the relative price of a haircut to a steak dinner may be significantly different in China than in the United States. Yet, in applying a single exchange rate to aggregate GDP, we are implicitly assuming that relative prices are the same between two nations.

Pitfalls in Comparing GDPs in Common Currencies

	US Price	US Output	China Price	China Output
Wheat	USD 100	100 bushels	RMB 1000	75 bushels
Coal	USD 50	100 tons	RMB 250	75 tons

Table 2.8 When converting a country's GDP into a different currency, the measure will only be valid if relative prices are the same in each country.
Source: Author created.

Table 2.8 provides examples of how these two problems can create distortions. We first examine output, observing that China's output is exactly 75 percent of US output (in real terms of this hypothetical example). In USD terms, US output is USD 15,000 while Chinese output in RMB terms is RMB 93,750. There would only be one exchange rate that would give us a USD GDP for China that is 75 percent of USD 15,000: RMB 8.33 per USD 1. If the exchange rate happens to be any other rate (which it might very well be), then we would not have an accurate measure of the two nations' relative real GDP. Even if we allow relative prices to be the same in each country (e.g., allow the price of coal in China to be RMB 500), we would encounter the same problem; in that case, an RMB/USD exchange rate of 10 would be required.

Let's examine how relative prices make a difference (e.g., 2:1 in the United States and 4:1 in China for the relative price of wheat to coal). Assume that we use an exchange rate that will accurately convert the RMB price of wheat in China into the dollar price of wheat in the United States, e.g., an exchange rate of RMB 10 per USD 1. This ratio gives a USD value of wheat production of USD 7,500, or exactly 75 percent of the value of US wheat production. However, if we apply the same exchange rate to coal production, our measure of China's coal production will, in USD terms, be far too low because of differing relative prices. Ideally, we would apply USD prices to China's real output, (USD 100 × 75) + (USD 50 × 75) = USD 11,250, which would result in a measure of China's output that is 75 percent of the United States' output. But this measure can be difficult to achieve, and applying the current exchange rate is unlikely to accomplish this task. Efforts are made, however, at measuring GDP in this ideal way, and the resulting measures are referred to as "purchasing power measures of GDP."

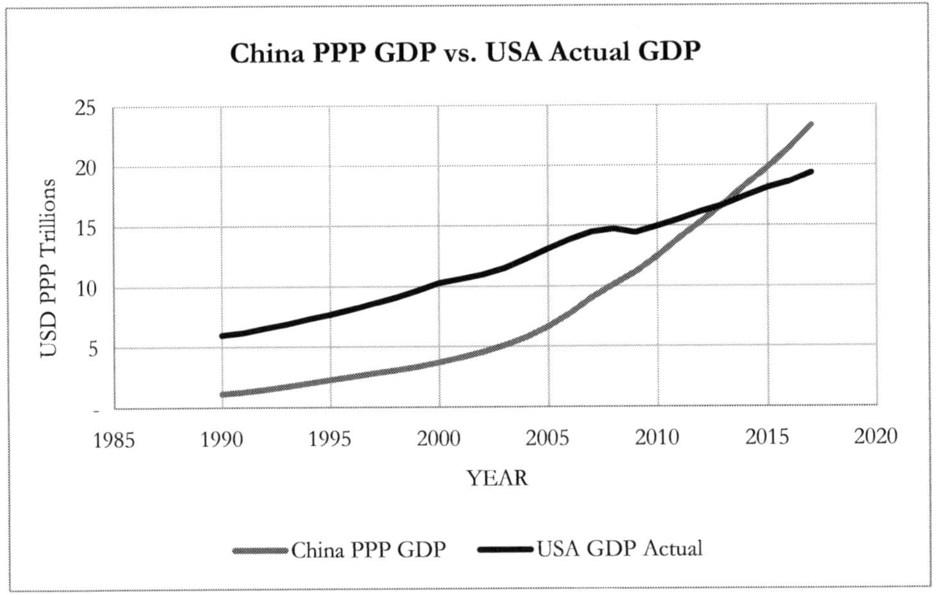

Figure 2.14 By at least one measure based on purchasing power parity, China may already have a larger GDP than the United States.
Source: Author created based on World Bank World Development Indicators.

An example based on Figure 2.14 highlights the importance of our choice of exchange rate in converting one country's GDP into another country's currency. As shown in Figure 2.14, PPP GDP for China is substantially larger than GDP measured at the actual exchange rate. This difference has become larger in both absolute as well as percentage terms, and it reflects estimates of undervaluation of the RMB relative to the USD and substantial differences in relative prices. Labor-intensive services, in particular, are substantially lower in price relative to other forms of output in China. When this type of output is assigned prices based on international markets, the USD value of Chinese GDP rises substantially. In 2014, PPP GDP in China moved higher than US GDP and continued higher throughout 2017. In 2017, estimated PPP GDP for China was about USD 23.3 trillion, while GDP based purely on a conversion using the actual exchange rate was only about USD 12.2 trillion. In the former case, China GDP would be about 21 percent higher than US GDP, while, in the latter, it would be about 37 percent lower; these are dramatic differences that highlight the pitfalls of converting one country's GDP into another country's currency using a constructed exchange rate. In late 2016, the RMB began to weaken against the USD. To the extent that market forces are at play, this would tend to weaken the estimated PPP value of the RMB.

Macro Finance Insight 2.6: Stakeholders, Their Claims, and Their Conflicts

In a modern economy with laws and institutional arrangements, different citizens and different entities have a formal claim on economic value. Who are the stakeholders in an economy? Table 2.9 details the relationship between income statement items and stakeholder claims through the lens of CMM, our typical company. As we have just described, employees in the United States lay claim to a larger share of national income than do employees in China. In the past, owners of capital received a greater share of income in China than in the United States, but now those shares are equal. Another difference is that government's share of enterprise ownership remains much higher in China than in the United States. China is also a major stakeholder in its largest banks. As such, the Chinese government is simultaneously a shareholder in the economy, a creditor to the national economy, and a collector of taxes—thus, it has a large role as a stakeholder. Unlike a single individual firm in the United States—which must compete with other firms for labor, supplies, and financing—a large comprehensive stakeholder such as the Chinese government can exert monopsony power over the acquisition of such resources. For example, Dong and Putterman (2002) suggest that, through the 1980s, the Chinese government paid a real wage less than the marginal product of labor—an observation consistent with monopsony power. The Chinese banking system has consistently paid interest rates below the market cost of funds. Also, China's SOEs have first claims to the resources of suppliers. Thus, monopsony power may lead to overuse of resources in the sectors of the economy where the state has such power, causing broader problems related to equity and fairness.

A vast literature suggests a misallocation of resources at the firm level when principals and agents have inconsistent goals, when conflicts of interest arise, or when there is asymmetric information between shareholders and other stakeholders. In China, optimal allocation of resources can break down due to monopsony power on the part of the government, and conflicts of interest can arise when the government acts as shareholder, creditor, employer, regulator, and taxing authority all at once.

		Stakeholders
Revenues	$2.98 (billions)	Customers
Domestic sales	$2.94	
Export sales	$0.04	
Costs of production	$2.27 (billions)	
Materials	$1.4	Suppliers
Wages, salaries	$0.87	Employees and managers
Depreciation	$0.20	
Operating income	$0.509	
Interest to bondholders	$0.09	Creditors
Taxes	$0 (On "tax holiday")	The government
After-tax profits	$0.42	**Shareholders**

Table 2.9 At each stage of the company's operations, stakeholders have an interest in the company's success. Only after all of those interests are satisfied are the shareholders rewarded with profits. But in China, the government serves several stakeholder roles, leading to conflicts of interest.
Source: Author created.

Command GDP

A final measure of GDP to consider is command *GDP*. The conventional measure of GDP used around the world emphasizes the production aspect of GDP rather than the consumption possibilities created by output. This focus probably relates to the tight link between production and employment; and, for most countries, employment is a central concern. Specifically, a country that produces output will see the value of that output change depending on how much output it can import (or "command") from the rest of the world. For example, a country that experiences an improvement in its terms of trade (TOT) in domestically grown coffee can now import more foreign machinery for every bag of coffee that it exports—thus enjoying an improvement in its command GDP. This improvement would not typically be measured, since traditional real GDP measures negate or offset the improvement so as not to distort the accounting measure of production. In this simple example, the number of coffee bags produced has not changed, but the price of the coffee has improved in world markets. If we wish to shift the focus from production and employment to consumption and economic well-being, then command GDP offers a preferable measure. Remember, however, that under the SNA command GDP is not given as the main GDP presentation—although some countries do present a separate measure for command GDP.

A country's TOT can change for two reasons: Either the exchange rate changes between two countries, or the relative price of imports and exports changes. The equation below shows the relationship between the TOT and the exchange rate adjusted for imports and exports. Assume that China exports machinery and imports oil. If either the RMB strengthens— that is, the ratio RMB:USD falls—or the ratio of the price of oil to the price of machinery falls, then China's TOT and command GDP will improve. In other words, China must export fewer machines to acquire each barrel of oil; or alternatively, if it exports the same quantity of machines as before, it can import and consume more barrels of oil after the improvement in the TOT.

$$\text{TOT}_{\frac{\text{MACHINERY}}{\text{OIL}}} = \frac{\text{RMB}}{\text{USD}} \times \frac{P^{\text{USD}}_{\text{OIL(IMPORTS)}}}{P^{\text{RMB}}_{\text{MACHINERY(EXPORTS)}}}$$

In fact, China's exchange rate has alternated between being fixed for prolonged periods and experiencing a controlled appreciation since 1996, but it has fluctuated against the other major currencies in tandem with the USD. In addition, relative prices between China and other countries are not static. One estimate of how the TOT has changed would be to examine a very closely related measure, the real exchange rate.[33] Figure 2.15 provides an estimate of the real exchange rate (weighted by manufactured goods data) for all of China's major trading partners. The figure suggests a substantial real appreciation of the RMB (a smaller left-hand side in the above equation) since 2005 and then a weakening since 2015. Thus, we can infer that China's command GDP has, in fact, grown faster between 2005 and 2015 than traditional GDP, but has grown slower since 2015.

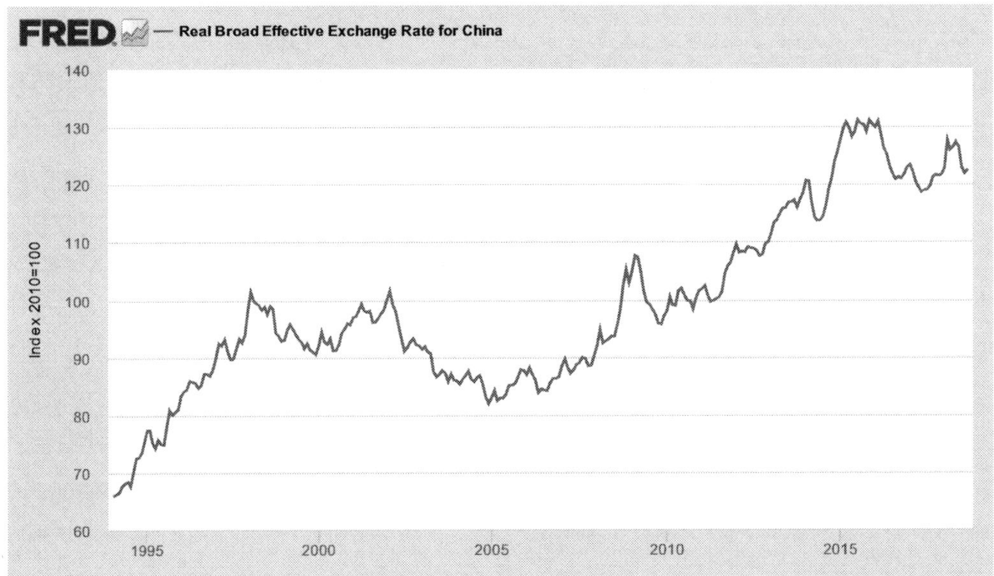

Figure 2.15 China's real exchange rate has strengthened since 2005, suggesting a more rapid rise in command GDP compared to actual GDP. But since 2015, the trend has reversed somewhat.
Source: Author created based on Federal Reserve Economic Database.

Challenging Questions for China (and the Student): Chapter 2

1. Go to FRED (the Federal Reserve Economic Database) and find three different measures of Chinese GDP. Define each measure based on its frequency (quarterly versus annual), basis for measure (e.g., Expenditure approach) and whether it is expressed in real or nominal terms.
2. Explain why, during an economic downturn, US GDP might actually be underestimated while Chinese GDP might actually be overestimated.
3. Using the table below (mind the footnote at the bottom of the table):
   a. Calculate GDP and GNP based on a method used primarily in China. Identify the method.
   b. Calculate GDP and GNP based on a method used primarily in the United States. Identify the method.
4. Assume that China's entire tertiary sector (services) is non-traded. Use the share of services in China's GDP statistics presented in this chapter to help answer some of the following questions.
   a. Is China's relative price of services to primary and secondary output prices higher or lower than in the United States (use your good judgment)?
   b. Assume that the exchange rate is at PPP for traded goods. If we use that exchange rate to convert Chinese GDP into USD, how would that distort your estimate of Chinese GDP, given your answer in (a)?
   c. Suggest a better way to approach the problem of converting Chinese GDP into USD.
   d. Observe Data Series PPPTT2CNA618NUPN (https://bit.ly/3hlPiRo) in FRED. How does this approach compare to your answer in (c)? Apply the most recent PPP exchange rate found in this series to nominal Chinese GDP. How much larger is China's USD GDP compared to when you use the actual exchange rate for the same period?
5. If a 2,000 square foot apartment in New York sells for USD 1.5 million, what is its per square meter RMB price and total RMB price? Be sure to use proper Chinese numerical units.
6. Using the table found below:
   a. Explain the classical relationship between other stakeholders and shareholders in a capitalist system.
   b. Explain the relationship among the various stakeholders in China. Compare and contrast to your answer in (a).

c. Using one of the key drivers for China presented in Chapter 1, explain the difficulties of managing a mixed-market economy such as China's.

Income Statement for a Typical Firm in an Economy*

	USD (Billions)	**Stakeholders**
Revenues	2.98	Customers
Domestic Sales	2.94	
Export Sales	.04	
Costs of Production	2.27	
Materials	1.4	Suppliers
Wages, Salaries	.87	Employees and Managers
Depreciation	0.20	
Operating Income	0.509	
Interest to Bondholders	0.09	Creditors
Taxes	0 (On "tax holiday")	The Government
After Tax Profits	0.42	Shareholders

*Assume this is a 50/50 joint venture with a foreign company and that inventories decreased during the period by 0.14.

7. Explain why investment growth leads to higher GDP growth in a short-run accounting sense but not necessarily higher growth of GDP in the long run.
8. Research Question: Using inflation, actual, and forecast data from historical IMF World Economic Outlooks (https://bit.ly/3bu6Bvo), determine whether China's inflation data passes the variance bound test discussed in this chapter.

References

Bernanke, Ben S., and Peter Olson. 2016. "China's Transparency Challenges." Brookings Institution, 8 March, https://www.brookings.edu/blog/ben-bernanke/2016/03/08/chinas-transparency-challenges/.

Boskin, Michael. 1996. "Toward a More Accurate Measure of the Cost of Living." Washington, DC: Advisory Commission to Study the Consumer Price Index.

Chow, Gregory. 2006. "Are Chinese Official Statistics Reliable?" CESifo Economic Studies, 52(2), pp. 396–414.

Dong, Lihua. 2006. "Quarterly GDP Estimation in China." Research of Methodological Issues in National Accounts—China, 9, presented at Organization for Economic Co-operation and Development on 2 December, 2009. http://www.oecd.org/std/na/44128807.ppt.

Dong, X. Y., and L. Putterman. 2002. "China's State-Owned Enterprises in the First Reform Decade: An Analysis of a Declining Monopsony." *Economics of Planning*, 35(2), pp. 109–39.

Ebenstein, A., M. Fan, M. Greenstone, G. He, P. Yin, and M. Zhou. 2015. "Growth, Pollution, and Life Expectancy: China from 1991–2012." American Economic Review, 105(5), pp. 226–31.

Eurostat, International Monetary Funds, The Organisation for Economic Co-operation and Development, United Nations, and World Bank. 1993. System of National Accounts. Brussels, New York, Paris, Washington, DC. http://unstats.un.org/unsd/nationalaccount/.

Fang, Cai, and Meiyan Wang. 2002. "How Fast and How Far Can China's GDP Grow?" China and World Economy, 5, pp. 9–15.

Fang, C., D. Yang, and W. Meiyan. 2009. "Employment and Inequality Outcomes in China." Institute of Population and Labour Economics: Chinese Academy of Social Sciences., https://www.oecd.org/employment/emp/42546043.pdf.

Feenstra, Robert C., Hong Ma, J. Peter Neary, and D.S. Prasada Rao. 2012. "Who Shrunk China? Puzzles in the Measurement of Real GDP." The Economic Journal, 123(573), pp. 1100–29.

Fernald, John, Israel Malkin, and Mark Spiegel. 2013. "On the Reliability of China's Output Figures." Federal Reserve Bank of San Francisco Pacific Basin Letter, 25 March.

Giles, John, Albert Park, and Juwei Zhang. 2005. "What Is China's True Unemployment Rate?" China Economic Review, 16(2), pp. 149–70.

He, Xinhua. 2010. "Noteworthy Discrepancies in China's GDP Accounting." China World Economy, 18(4), pp. 88–102.

Henderson, J. Vernon, Adam Storeygard, and David N. Weil. 2012. "Measuring Economic Growth from Outer Space." American Economic Review, 102(2), pp. 994–1028.

Huang, Langhui. 2005. "Compilation Method and Quality Control of CPI in China." In Statistical Commission and United Nations Economic Commission for Europe. Geneva: United Nations.

Keidel, Albert. 2001. "China's GDP Expenditure Accounts." China Economic Review, 12(4), pp. 355–67.

Klein, Lawrence R., and Sulyman Ozmucur. 2003. "The Estimation of China's Economic Growth Rate." Journal of Economic and Social Measurement, 28(4), pp. 187–202.

Koch-Weser, Iacob N. 2013. "The Reliability of Chinese Economic Data: An Analysis of National Output." Washington, DC: U.S.-China Economic and Security Review Commission.

Krugman, Paul R., and Maurice Obstfeld. 2009. International Economics: Theory and Policy, 8th ed., Boston: Pearson Addison-Wesley.

Lin, Jintai, Da Pan, Steven J. Davis, Qiang Zhang, Kebin He, Can Wang, David G. Streets, Donald J. Wuebbles, and Dabo Guan. 2014. "China's International Trade and Air Pollution in the United States." Proceedings of the National Academy of Sciences, 11(5), pp. 1736-41.

Lin, Z. X. and M. S. H. Shih. 2002. "Earnings Management in Economic Downturns and Adjacent Periods: Evidence from the 1990–1991 Recession." SSRN, 11 November. https://papers.ssrn.com/sol3/papers.cfm?abstract_id=331400.

Liu, Fujiang. 2000. "Brief Introduction on Labor Force, Retail Sales and Price Statistics of China." Presented at Workshop on Key Economic Indicators in China, Bangkok, 22 May.

Maddison, Angus, and Harry X. Wu. 2008. "Measuring China's Economic Performance." World Economics, 9, pp. 13–57.

National Bureau of Statistics of China. 2012. "Table 2.1 and Tables 2.16–2.18." In China Statistical Yearbook. Beijing: China Statistics Press.

Organization for Economic Co-operation and Development. 2009. "State-Owned Enterprises in China: Reviewing the Evidence." Presented in Working Group on Privatization and Corporate Governance of State-Owned Assets, [city], 26 January.

Orlik, Tom. 2012. Understanding China's Economic Indicators. Upper Saddle River, NJ: FT Press.

Ou, Pao-san. 1946. "A New Estimate of China's National Income." Journal of Political Economy, 54(6), pp. 547–54.

Pizer, W. A., and X. Zhang. 2018. "China's New National Carbon Market." AEA Papers and Proceedings, 108, pp. 463–67.

Prasad, Eswar, ed. 2004. Occasional Paper 232: China's Growth and Integration into the World Economy: Prospects and Challenges. Washington, DC: International Monetary Fund.

Rawski, T. 2001. "What Is Happening to China's GDP Statistics?" China Economic Review, 12(4), pp. 347–54.

Rawski, T. 2016. "Chinese Economic Statistics: A Quick and Personal Tour." Presented at "Chinese Economic Data: Users' Guide" panel, American Economic Association annual meeting, San Francisco, CA, 5 January.

Schneider, F., and A. Buehn. 2018. "Shadow Economy: Estimation Methods, Problems, Results and Open Questions." Open Economics, 1(1), pp. 1–29.

Shiller, R. J. 1981. "The Use of Volatility Measures in Assessing Market Efficiency." The Journal of Finance, 36(2), pp. 291–304.

United Nations Development Program. 2013. "Human Development Indicators and Thematic Tables." In Human Development Report, http://hdr.undp.org/en/data.

U.S. Bureau of Economic Analysis. 2009. "National Income and Product Accounts Tables." https://apps.bea.gov/iTable/index_nipa.cfm.

U.S. Bureau of Economic Analysis. 2014. "Concepts and Methods of the US National Income and Product Accounts." In NIPA Handbook, https://www.bea.gov/resources/methodologies/nipa-handbook.

Wang, Xiaolu, and Meng Lian. 2001. "A Reevaluation of China's Economic Growth." China Economic Review, 12(4), pp. 338–46.

Williamson, P. J., S. Hoenderop, and J. Hoenderop. 2018. "An Alternative Benchmark for the Validity of China's GDP Growth Statistics." Journal of Chinese Economic and Business Studies, 16(2), pp. 171–91.

Wu, Harry X. 2007. "The Chinese GDP Growth Rate Puzzle: How Fast Has the Chinese Economy Grown?" Asian Economic Papers, 6(1), pp. 1–23.

Xinhuanet (2016). "China Reveals Consumer Price Basket Changes." https://www.chinadaily.com.cn/business/2016-02/20/content_23567811.htm

Xu, Xianchun. 2009. "Zhongguo Guomin Jingji Hesuan Tixi de Jianli, Gaige he Fazhan [The Establishment, Reform and Development of China's National Economic Accounting System]." Zhongguo Shehui Kexue [China Social Science], 6, pp. 58–59.

Endnotes

1. One might ask why a government (G) would need a washing machine. For money laundering, of course!
2. We should not confuse the flow of housing services in a given year with the production of a housing (residential) unit in that year. The latter is included under I (an investment). As to whether this suggests double counting, we note that—under a net national product measure—we also depreciate the housing stock. Thus, the difference between the flow of housing services and its depreciation represents a net flow of housing services. The gross measure, however, includes the creation of the residence as a part of GDP and, in the periods that follow, as a housing service under GDP.
3. In this case, we could think of the government both producing and using the good and service.
4. We use the "≡" when presenting a definition or an identity rather than an arithmetically derived relationship.
5. China's data based on 2011; the United States', 2012.
6. This is clearly a short-run partial equilibrium result. In the absence of trade with the United States, China would surely shift exports to other parts of the world.
7. In fact, China inherited a measure, the gross value of output, from the Soviet Union, which did exactly that. This measure is no longer in use.
8. Comparisons of productivities in Figure 2.4 also reveal comparative advantages. (See, for example, Obstfeld and Krugman 2009.) Specifically, we see a comparative advantage for the United States in the primary sector and for China in the secondary sector.
9. Recently, officials in Liaoning Province were penalized for overreporting economic output for the period 2011–14.
10. Though taxes paid by both workers and corporations might be considered as "income" for the government, we are more interested in examining the link between the direct producers of output (the factors of production) and their earnings. For this reason, pre-tax wages and profits are typically used in the Income approach to measuring GDP.
11. As discussed below, input-output tables are one means by which income data for China can be obtained. These tables, however, are only published every five years.
12. Later, we will discuss the role of income taxes in both countries and whether this is an offsetting effect on the net income of labor in the United States.

13. Only Myanmar was larger; the gap for India was also large.
14. Though the product of labor and the wage rate is the total wage bill: if the supply of labor is sufficiently large, the wage will be driven down to the inelastic portion of the demand-for-labor curve, causing total employee compensation to actually decline.
15. In Chapter 5, we discuss this paradox in more detail.
16. Interest rates in the United States fell to very low levels after the GFC but have been gradually rising. The increase in yields will also cause factor payments to China to increase.
17. This approach continues even today, but in a diminished form—China's Five-Year Plans are discussed in later chapters.
18. We include the Income approach, since it is a variation on value-added measurement in which factors of production could be thought of as providing value.
19. Countries with higher per capita incomes can generally afford more leisure time than can low per capita income economies. However, among those high per capita economies, different choices are made with respect to vacation time and hours worked per week, suggesting that sacrificing GDP in favor of more leisure is perceived as welfare enhancing in some but not all economies.
20. The Gini coefficient is an index measuring the gap between a perfectly equal distribution and the actual income distribution of a country. A measurement of 0 would correspond to perfect income equality and a measurement of 1, perfect inequality. For example, in the latter case, a small percentage of the population would be receiving all of the economy's income.
21. From a purely accounting perspective, we could think of the subsidy as the government purchasing part of the good or service on behalf of the consumer or investor. From an economic perspective, however, to the extent that the subsidy distorts production and consumption decisions, our GDP measure would also be distorted.
22. The reader may use the "Help" tab in the Google browser and select "'Translate" for an English version of the site.
23. Both in China and the United States, governments not only supply but also purchase—and these purchases are included as government use.
24. Even though the government pays for something based on its cost, the price which that output would command in the market could actually be higher or lower.
25. About 40 percent of China's population is classified as rural; in the United States it is only about 2 percent.
26. In the United States, the personal consumption expenditure deflator, which is used for converting nominal GDP to real GDP, captures both rural and urban inflation.

27. Allowing the market basket to adjust allows for cheaper goods to be substituted when prices of some goods rise.
28. The PPI was formerly known in the United States as the "wholesale price index."
29. Theft, for example, would be excluded from a GDP measure, since one is not willingly robbed.
30. When calculating changes in wealth, we would also need to eliminate the effect of capital gains and losses because these would not be measured in the flow of savings.
31. The Schneider estimate tends to be smaller than other estimates because his research focuses on economic activity not included in GDP measures. Other larger estimates include unregulated activity that would still be captured in GDP by statistical surveys.
32. For both countries, the proportion identified as self-employed remains close to 10 percent. How well this sector's output is measured in each country determines the size of the shadow economy.
33. The real exchange rate considers the relative importance of different kinds of imports and exports with different countries. A variety of measures for relative prices are used, including export-import prices, unit labor costs, overall prices, etc. As a result, there are a variety of real exchange rate measures.

3

CHINA AND THE UNITED STATES AND THE BALANCE OF PAYMENTS

积少成多
Many a Little Makes a Mickle

This chapter tackles an issue that is critically important to many aspects of international finance and economics; we will discuss how a country interacts with the rest of the world, and we will assess the different tools for measuring that interaction. The balance of payments (BOP) is the main accounting tool for examining this question. The formal definition of BOP is a record of one nation's transactions with the rest of the world. In other words, it is a record of what a country imports, exports, borrows, lends, invests, pays, and receives for liabilities and investments outside of the country. For our purposes, as MBA/EMBA/Master's practitioners, we can use a much simpler and more immediately meaningful definition: The BOP answers the question, "Is a country getting or losing foreign exchange?"

Why is this question so vitally important? Many countries around the world rely on access to foreign exchange as the lifeblood of their economy. By "foreign exchange," we mean the main tradable currencies in the world that are used as a medium of exchange: the US dollar (USD), Euro, British pound, Japanese yen, and Swiss franc; the Chinese yuan (RMB) is on the way to joining this list. Most countries need to import critically important products such as oil, pharmaceuticals, and spare parts for machinery. Meanwhile, diplomatic missions abroad need to be funded. All these activities require foreign exchange, as defined above, because most countries' local currency is simply not acceptable as a means of payment.[1] The seller wants to be paid in a currency that is liquid and used widely around the world. For example, payment for oil imports for power generators are typically made in USD, and so are international debt service payments. It is therefore critical that each country has access to some of the main tradable currencies. Some countries experience chronic shortages of foreign exchange; others experience a more acute shortage in the form of a BOP crisis. Thus, the BOP lets us know whether a country is getting or losing foreign exchange and if that country might eventually run out of foreign exchange.

The Latin American debt crisis of the 1980s, the Mexican financial crisis of 1994, the Asian financial crisis of 1997, and the Venezuelan debt crisis of 2018 cover the gamut of situations in which countries can run out of foreign exchange. These foreign exchange shortages can lead to economic collapse since, for example, the nations involved may not be able to import medicines or oil, or to replace spare parts for machinery. When this happens, problems can spiral downward toward overall economic collapse. Recent red flags (https://cnb.cx/2Z4PttA) have been raised concerning the dramatic increase in loans to emerging economies under China's "one belt one road" program. Combined with growing Chinese exports to these countries, questions have been raised as to whether or not these countries will have sufficient foreign exchange to service their debts to China and other international creditors.

While the BOP for advanced economies such as the United States may not have the same level of drama as a depletion of foreign exchange reserves in developing economies, foreign exchange and BOP problems for mature countries can also be pernicious and disruptive. In the United States, for example, chronic BOP deficits in the 1960s and early 1970s ultimately led to the abandonment of the gold standard and a succession of depreciations of the USD against other currencies.

Case Study 3.1: China's Cautious (Wise) and Staged Liberalization of the Capital Account

Most economists support economic liberalization, but many academic economists and international organizations such as the International Monetary Fund (IMF) are more circumspect when it comes to a country opening up (liberalizing) its capital account to foreign financial flows.* Ill-conceived financial liberalization on the capital account has, in the past, led many countries to experience large capital inflows, an appreciating currency, current account deficits, a net loss of foreign exchange reserves, and a financial crisis. In the 20th century, Argentina, Mexico, Peru, and Egypt all allowed for financial liberalization on the capital account, then experienced a financial crisis triggered by volatile capital flows. Similarly, in Thailand, during the Asian financial crisis in 1997–1998, massive capital inflows in the context of a weak regulatory framework led to bad investments and financial collapse. Reinhart and Rogoff (2009) posit a long-term relationship between capital flows and financial crises. We need to emphasize that international capital flows in and of themselves serve a useful economic purpose. Problems can arise when these flows are allowed to occur in a system that lacks sound regulations, sound economic fundamentals, or unexploited arbitrage opportunities related to residual regulations after an incomplete financial reform. Scholars such as Guillermo Calvo (2005) have highlighted the role of policy credibility, international capital flows, and crises triggered by sudden stops of foreign capital.

Chinese policy-makers, being well aware of the problems identified above, have been both cautious and prudent in their approach to liberalizing the capital account. Specifically, the following stages have been undertaken:

1. Allowing foreign investment into China via special economic zones (1980s)
2. Liberalizing most foreign direct investment (FDI) flows into all of China (1988)
3. Initially limiting capital inflows to large foreign institutions that were permitted to invest in China's A-share market through qualified foreign institutional investor programs (2002)
4. Accepting Article VIII of the IMF Charter for full current account convertibility (1996)
5. Issuing the first RMB denominated (*dim sum*) bonds (2007)
6. Relaxing rules for foreign currency bonds issued by Chinese companies (2005)
7. Allowing RMB invoicing of exports and imports (2010)

Since 2007, capital account liberalization has picked up speed with efforts at the internationalization of the RMB. Nevertheless, as suggested above, full capital account convertibility will only be achieved when the authorities feel confident enough to take these steps:

1. Allow the RMB exchange rate to float (along with all that would entail)
2. Help develop a domestic banking system with the capacity to manage all risks associated with international capital flows
3. Declare the regulatory framework to be sufficient (after stress testing over time)

Following a large increase in capital outflows in the 2015–2016 period and the accompanying loss of foreign exchange reserves, China stepped back from its path of liberalization—particularly on capital outflows. Specifically, limits were imposed on bank card withdrawals abroad (RMB 100 thousand); restrictions were placed on outbound FDI, particularly in the hotel, real estate and entertainment industries; and, higher disclosure requirements were mandated for access to foreign exchange. But bond and equity markets in China allowed for greater foreign investor capital access in the same period. In summary, there was a crackdown on foreign currency outflows, but continued liberalization on foreign currency inflows.

*See, for example, Diaz-Alejandro (1985).

Balance of Payments

The BOP for China and the United States are presented in Table 3.1 and Table 3.2. Given that a main purpose of the BOP is to indicate whether a country is getting or losing foreign exchange, we can use a very simple rule to determine the impact of any BOP activity: Any transaction that leads to a country receiving foreign exchange can be recorded as plus (+) on the BOP; any transaction leading to a loss of foreign exchange can be recorded as a minus (-). For example, the purchase of a dress made in China by a US consumer would result in a negative contribution since it would trigger either a loss of foreign exchange on the part of America (loss of RMB), or a receipt of foreign exchange on the Chinese side (a gain in USD). Similarly, if a Chinese bank lends an American company USD or RMB, the result is either a reduction in Chinese holdings of foreign currency or an increased holding of RMB by Americans (depending on the currency of the loan). Either way, the loan would be recorded as a plus on the American BOP and a minus on the Chinese BOP.

China Balance of Payments 2017		
	Percent of GDP	**USD (in Billions)**
Current Account Balance	1.4	168
Trade Balance	4.0	481
Exports	18.4	2211
Imports	-14.5	-1742
Services Balance	-2.2	-264
Income Balance	-0.3	-36
Current Transfers	-0.1	-12
Capital and Financial Account Balance	-0.5	-57
Capital Account	0.0	0
Financial Account	-0.5	-57
Net Foreign Direct Investment	0.6	66
FDI Inbound	1.4	168
FDI Outbound	-0.8	-102
Portfolio Investment	-0.1	-7
Other Investment	-1.0	-116
Errors and Omissions	0.2	18

China Balance of Payments 2017		
Overall Balance	1.1	129
Change in Reserve Assets (-) Increase	-1.1	-129
GDP		12,015

Table 3.1 Historically, China's BOP has shown surpluses on current and financial accounts, but those surpluses have been shrinking in recent years, and the capital/financial account was negative in 2017.
Source: Author created based on data from IMF.

United States Balance of Payments 2017		
	Percent of GDP	**USD (Billions)**
Current Account Balance	-2.3	-449.1
Trade Balance	-4.1	-807.5
Exports	-8	-1,553.4
Imports	12.1	2,360.9
Services Balance	1.3	255.2
Income Balance	1.1	221.7
Current Transfers	-0.6	-118.6
Capital and Financial Account Balance	1.9	378.1
Capital Account	0.1	24.8
Financial Account	1.8	353.3
Net Foreign Direct Investment	-0.1	-24.4
FDI Inbound	1.8	354.8
FDI Outbound	-1.9	-379.2
Portfolio Investment	1.1	212.5
Other Investment	0.8	165.2
Errors and Omissions	0.4	92.4
Overall Balance	0.1	21.4
Change in Reserve Assets (-) Increase	-0.1	-21.4

Table 3.2 The United States BOP has experienced chronic current account deficits since 1992. Those deficits have been financed with borrowing from abroad (the financial account).
Source: Author created based on US Bureau of Economic Analysis U.S. International Transactions, Fourth Quarter and Year 2019 (https://bit.ly/2XZjTwv), Table 1.

Although there are many detailed items on the BOP, the simplified versions of the BOP in Table 3.1 and Table 3.2 show that there are only a few main categories. The first block of items in Table 3.1 lists current account transactions. The current account represents trade in actual goods and services, such as the shipment of steel or the consulting services of an attorney. Specifically, the trade balance represents trade in goods, while the non-factor services are those that are currently consumed or used (for example, the provision of education or a tourist visit from one country to another). Meanwhile, factor services represent income generated related to a loan or investment, or related to a foreign resident in a country who has some type of legal visa-granted status in that country and is paid for services rendered. In other words, factor services include interest on debt, dividends paid on an investment, or salaries paid to expatriate workers.

The capital and financial account represents financial flows between borders that, in turn, imply a gain or loss in foreign exchange.[2] As such, the financial account includes loans (short-term and long-term), the sale and purchase of bills and bonds, portfolio investment in equity, and FDI.[3] Errors or statistical discrepancies are a measure of the difference between the above accounts and how much the country actually gained or lost in foreign exchange.

Thus, we see that the BOP follows a very simple form, as outlined in the equation below, but with many detailed items:

Current Account + Capital Transactions + Financial Account = Balance of Payments

The overall balance in the BOP can be measured using different methods, but the international norm is to determine the total foreign exchange assets actually gained or lost by the central banking authorities. The United States uses increased holdings of foreign exchange by the Federal Reserve System and nets out official dollar reserves held by other central banks around the world. In China, the measure includes not just China's central bank—the People's Bank of China (PBC)—but the banking system as a whole. This is appropriate because, for the largest Chinese banks, the Chinese government is still the principle shareholder. In the end, it is critical to determine how much control a country's central banking authorities have over the foreign exchange accumulated in its economy. In China, that control remains substantial; in the United States, less so.

Examining the BOP for China and the United States, we see that China runs a large current account surplus and the US runs a deficit. Both countries have financial account and overall BOP surpluses. We could interpret the dual surpluses for China (current and financial accounts) as funding an increase in foreign exchange reserves. For the United States, meanwhile, the financial account surplus (borrowing from the rest of the world) funds its substantial current account deficit. For China, international trade (combined exports and imports) as a share of gross domestic product (GDP) is significantly more important, and in absolute terms is larger, than in the United States. The US is a large exporter of both factor and non-factor services, while China is an importer of such services. China remains a large recipient of FDI, while the US remains a large exporter of FDI. Finally, China's errors and omissions is about 2.3 times the size of the United States' in absolute terms, and it is of opposite sign. The large negative amount no doubt reflects capital outflows in 2017 that the national authorities have been unable to account for. All these differences reflect major underlying structural differences in the two economies, in part due to each nation being at a different stage of development. For example, the pattern of FDI no doubt reflects diminished returns to capital in the United States (a mature economy) and higher returns in China (an emerging economy).

We can learn several interesting things about China and other emerging market countries by taking a look even further below the line of the BOP. That is, we can ask—how are those balances used if they are positive, or how are they financed if they are negative?

Current Account + Capital Transactions + Financial Account = Balance of Payments = Change in Foreign Exchange Reserves of the Central Bank

If we have a BOP surplus, it becomes a part of the banking systems' holdings of foreign exchange reserves; the BOP is a flow, and foreign exchange reserves are the stock into which BOP flows accumulate. In 2017, China's overall surplus was USD 96 billion. At the end of 2016, its foreign exchange reserves were USD 3.03 trillion. We can then estimate end-2017 foreign exchange reserves as (USD 3.03 trillion + USD 0.096 trillion = USD 3.13 trillion)—the actual outcome was USD 3.16 trillion.[4] We compare this example to the situation in 2010 when China had about USD 470 billion surplus. Given end-of-2009 foreign exchange reserves of USD 2.45 trillion, we can estimate China's end-of-2010 foreign exchange reserves as (USD 2.45 trillion + USD 0.47 trillion = USD 2.92 trillion)—an even larger increase.

What happens if a country has a negative number for its BOP and is losing foreign exchange? Take the United States, for example. The United States has the luxury of simply issuing more of its currency to settle its imbalance (a solution which, we will see, cannot be used over a prolonged period of time). But what happens in a small emerging economy such as Uruguay? Uruguay in 2010 had a BOP deficit of approximately USD

400 million. In that case, its reserves served as a buffer to finance the BOP deficit. But what about a country in which reserves are insufficient to pay for a BOP deficit? The expression below suggests that "exceptional financing" may come into play:

	Current Account
+	Capital Transactions
+	Financial Account
=	Balance of Payments
=	Change in Foreign Exchange Reserves of the Central Bank
	(Exceptional Financing Items)
+	IMF Loan
+	Debt Restructuring
+	Default
=	Financing Gap

Case Study 3.2: How Did China Accumulate Over USD 3 Trillion in Foreign Exchange Reserves?

Since the BOP is just another way of measuring a country's change in foreign exchange reserves, we might ask how China came to accumulate a stock of foreign exchange reserves over USD 3 trillion. Alternatively, we could ask— how did China's foreign exchange reserves decline from their peak of USD 4 trillion in May, 2014 to just over USD 3 trillion today? Let's look at a graph of China's current account surpluses over the years (Figure 3.1). The current account has had a heavy weight in China's overall BOP in recent years because capital account mobility has been (and continues to be) highly circumscribed around FDI (see below). If we sum current account surpluses over time, as in Figure 3.2 (the integral of current account surpluses), we have a total of almost exactly USD 3.5 trillion—relatively close to China's overall reserves of 3.2 trillion. The difference between the curves in the intervening years represents financial flows, with FDI causing gross reserves to grow faster but financial outflows causing reserves to decline in recent years. Taken together, we come up with a virtually complete explanation as to how China has accumulated over USD 3 trillion in foreign exchange reserves. As suggested earlier, on a net basis, a large part of China's current account surplus is explained by the deficit that the US runs with China. The FDI surplus for China presents a more mixed picture. Scholars such as Maurice Obstfeld (2012), show that the US deficit remains a key factor when it comes to macroeconomic stability. The latter element (FDI and other gross asset positions) has added another layer of complication over the past several decades for economic policy-makers.

A country with a BOP deficit but insufficient foreign exchange reserves to support that deficit may need exceptional financing to plug the gap. (Thus, we use positive signs to indicate an addition to the available pool of resources.) We call this "exceptional financing" because it is made available not on any market-based or profit-making basis, but rather as emergency financing. In effect, it is a situation that both lenders and borrowing countries prefer to avoid. An IMF loan comes with terms of "conditionality," which imposes outside IMF policy control in order to improve the recipient country's BOP. Most countries prefer not to surrender such autonomy in terms of macroeconomic policy.[5] Debt restructuring is another possibility, but it involves rescheduling promised commitments on external debt that are located above the BOP line. Again, implicit and explicit penalties—such as loss of reputation, the collapse of short-term trade credits, higher borrowing costs, or debt/equity exchanges—may result. Default is a unilateral decision (often politically motivated) not to pay, and it may have severe short-term consequences—especially in the area of trade finance.

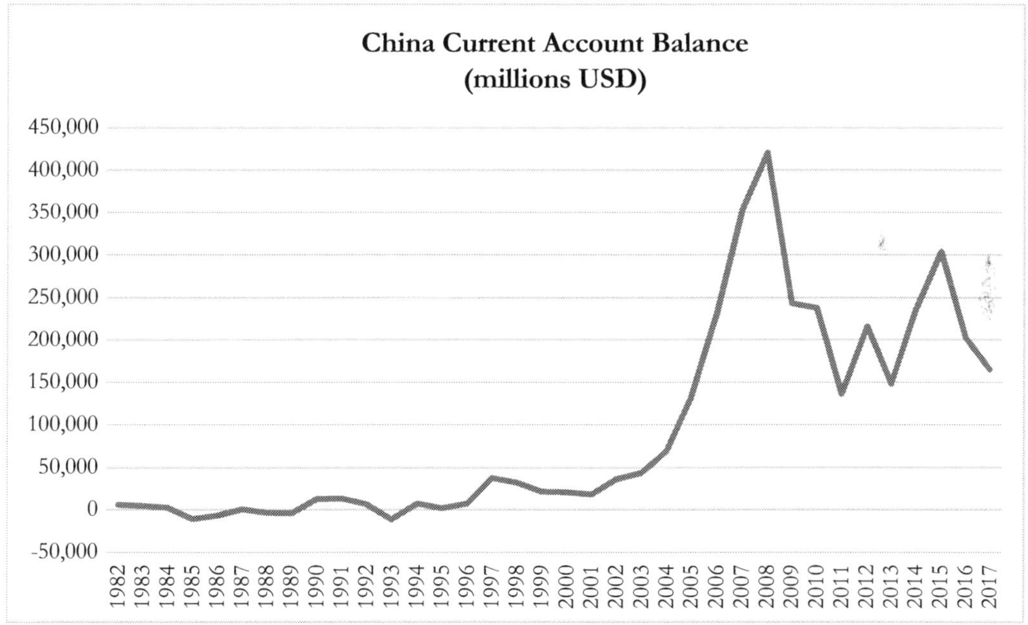

Figure 3.1 shows China's prolonged current account surpluses peaking at around USD 421 billion in 2008 but still remaining largely positive.
Source: Author created based on data from IMF.

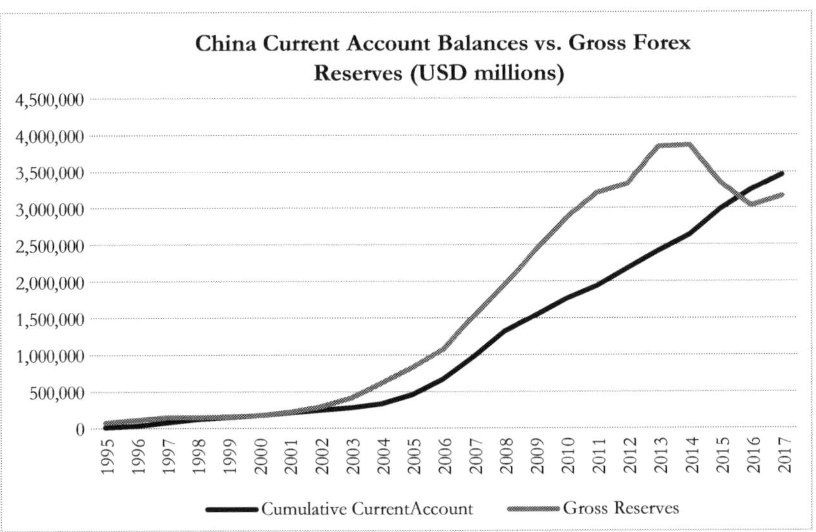

Figure 3.2 China's vast foreign exchange ("forex") reserves are the cumulative effect of continual current account surpluses.
Source: Author created based on data from IMF and FRED.3.2

If, after breaching all of these below-the-line thresholds, the country still finds itself unable to finance its BOP deficit, it is left with a hole, or "financing gap." At this point, the country is forced into "import compression"—an extremely difficult situation in which it cannot, for example, import oil, pay to keep its power plants maintained, or pay for its employees on diplomatic missions abroad. In effect, the country goes into shutdown mode from an external trade and finance perspective. By the time it reaches the default stage, the country has a "liquidity" event and is effectively bankrupt.

Macro Finance Insight 3.1: The Role of the International Monetary Fund, China, and the Paris Club

China's historically conservative approach to managing its balance sheet has enabled it to avoid externally related financial crises such as have been experienced by many other emerging economies around the world. (See Reinhart and Rogoff [2009] for an extensive catalog of crises in Latin America, Africa, Eastern Europe, and the advanced economies.) The IMF has been involved in providing exceptional finance in many of these crises. In fact, among some 188 IMF member countries, more than half have enjoyed some type of loan from the IMF, either via BOP support or structural support. Neither China nor the United States (key members of the Fund) has ever found it necessary to seek such support.

The IMF was created in 1944 along with its sister institution, the World Bank. While the latter has focused on long-term development—including everything from developing health and welfare to building roads—the IMF has a narrower mandate of macroeconomic management. Specifically, the

IMF assists countries with weak international balance sheets that are at risk of running out of foreign exchange.* In return for buttressing a country's foreign exchange holdings through its various lending programs, the IMF negotiates with the borrower to develop macroeconomic measures to avoid further international financing problems going forward. This is referred to as "conditionality," and it is often at the center of any discussion of the costs and benefits of IMF involvement with member countries.

Typically, the IMF makes a loan when commercial and government lenders are no longer willing to finance a country's BOP deficit. Needless to say, this can prevent severe harm to the borrower's economy and its citizens in the short run. But both the IMF and the World Bank (as well as other supranational lenders) take on a senior creditor status after making the loan—that is, they usually insist on being repaid first before any other lender is paid. One interesting question is whether the benefits of the Fund loan and/or macroeconomic improvements from conditionality (and the implicit seal of approval for a country undertaking a loan) outweigh the costs. Specifically, new lenders must take on a junior status to the IMF and World Bank. Will they withhold loans or charge a higher interest rate in the medium term because of their diminished rank in the payoff order?

Another interesting question concerning senior creditor status of the IMF and World Bank relates to China's surge in lending to other emerging economies. It would appear that a good deal of this lending is part of an understanding between China and the borrower that China is the de facto senior creditor (Schramm 2011). This seniority, at the time of a financial crisis, could operate through several mechanisms: directly via foreign exchange debt service to China, indirectly via first claims on the borrower's commodity exports (implicit escrow), and finally through seizure of the borrower's assets (as has recently happened when Sri Lanka [https://nyti.ms/2TlcuF9] was unable to service its Chinese debt). China took control of Sri Lanka's Port of Hambantota under a 99-year lease in partial exchange for debt payment falling due. This has led to claims that China is acting like Great Britain and other European powers when those countries enforced concessionary zones in China, including in Hong Kong and parts of Shanghai, during the 19th century.

Meanwhile, the unfolding story of Venezuela's default on its debt service highlights the problems that arise when creditors are unable to coordinate and prioritize their claims. It is estimated that, in 2019, Venezuela owed China at least USD 23 billion. Seizure of a port in that country is an unlikely solution. Between 1901 and 1903, Great Britain, Germany, and Italy became increasingly frustrated with Venezuela's non-payment of external debt related to a railroad project. They began a blockade of major ports along the coast, attempting to force payment. President Theodore Roosevelt, backed up by a recently modernized fleet of naval ships, convinced the Europeans to end the blockade as he put into practice the Monroe Doctrine of non-interference by outside nations in Western Hemisphere countries.

Should the next global financial crisis involve debt owed to China, one could envision the now-murky senior creditor question as a point of contention among China, the IMF, the World Bank, and other nation-state creditors, including the United States. China and the IMF also find areas for significant cooperation. This is particularly important because China has chosen not to participate in the Paris Club—the group of nation creditors that negotiates with borrowing countries when they fall into default. There are, however, reasons to be optimistic regarding cooperation. Recently, for example, Mongolia turned to the IMF (https://wapo.st/2y6JfhS) for exceptional financing in conjunction with receiving swap finance from China.

*In the years between 1944 and 1973, the IMF viewed its primary role as the protection of the fixed exchange rate system with the USD at the center of that system. Being a liquidity provider of foreign exchange was a key tool for the Fund in guarding the system. With the move to floating exchange rates in the early 1970s, the role of guardian of the foreign exchange system vanished. The expertise that had been developed in conditionality and international coordination, however, allowed the IMF to continue to wield the powerful tool it had used in the past—the provision of foreign exchange liquidity—to ease crises centered around countries' BOPs.

Assets			Liabilities		
End-2016 (est.)	**USD (Billions)**	**Percent**	**End-2016 (est.)**	**USD (Billions)**	**Percent**
Foreign Exchange Reserves	3,030	84	**External Debt**	1,416	34
Foreign Direct Investment 1/	727	5	**Foreign Direct Investment a/**	2,215	54
Portfolio Equity	206	6	**Portfolio Equity b/**	146	4
Portfolio Debt	154	4	**Residual c/**	340	8
Total Assets	4,116.6	100	**Total Liabilities and Equity**	4,116.6	100

Table 3.3 China's external balance sheet has become less conservative in recent years with more FDI abroad on the asset side, more external debt on the liabilities side, and more portfolio investments across the balance sheet.
Source: Author's estimates based on IMF Coordinated Direct Investment Survey (https://bit.ly/3fOyaD3); Coordinated Portfolio Investment Survey (https://bit.ly/2AlnCLg); World Bank's International Debt Statistics (https://bit.ly/3dJqUX9); and China Statistical Yearbook 2016, Tables 11-19.
Notes:

a) Assumes a 3 percent perpetual depreciation rate for capital invested. Excludes debt financing so as not to overlap with external debt figures. Data based on IMF FDI flow estimates.
b) Assumes 2 percent of China market capitalization is foreign-owned.
c) Several interpretations of this figure include statistical discrepancy, "owner's equity," or the size of China's currency exposure.

Macro Finance Insight 3.2: China's External Balance Sheet and Capital Structure

The base case assumption for a company is that capital structure does not matter. Whatever type of finance is raised—debt or equity—the weighted average cost of capital remains unchanged, and the value of the firm does not change. The fact that the assets side of a firm's balance sheet remains the same irrespective of financial structure drives this key result—commonly known as "Modigliani-Miller I" (Modigliani and Miller 1958). When taxes, bankruptcy, and agency costs come into play, capital structure can affect value. Recall, for example, that taxes on interest payments are expensed, while dividends are not, thereby creating a tax benefit to debt over equity finance.

Let's look at capital structure from the country perspective. We can examine China's capital structure vis-à-vis its relationship with external investors in Table 3.3. On the liability side, China's balance sheet resembles a typical company, with about 34 percent of liabilities due to external debt—a relatively conservative ratio by emerging market standards. In the past, FDI equity finance resulted in China relying less on external debt as a source of finance. But its external debt has increased substantially over the past decade; by 2017 external debt had surged to over USD 1.71 trillion from 1.4 trillion in 2016. FDI still represents the largest component (54 percent) of external finance liabilities. The deployment of assets remains conservative, with most assets held as liquid foreign exchange reserves.

On the assets side, we see China still holding an extremely high level of its foreign assets in a relatively liquid form—foreign exchange reserves at 84 percent, with the remaining assets held as FDI in other countries and portfolio investments. Holding such a large sum of foreign exchange reserves can be interpreted as financially conservative. Compared to past years, however, China's balance sheet has edged into riskier territory with a large increase in the share of external debt and an absolute drop of foreign exchange reserves of about USD 1 trillion. Obstfeld et al. (2010) provide a useful perspective on China's reserve holdings. They state that "a primary reason for a central bank to hold reserves is to protect the domestic banking sector and domestic credit markets more broadly, while limiting currency depreciation" (1). As such, one of the variables they focus in on in their study is a nation's money supply relative to GDP. As we discuss in Chapter 7, China is an outlier in terms of the huge amount of this ratio that citizens hold (money or M2). Money, the most liquid form of asset, can be used in an attempt to convert local wealth into foreign denominated assets (foreign exchange reserves) in times of crisis—a phenomenon well-known as a catalyst for banking and currency crises. We can infer from this research that China's historically large holdings of foreign reserves can be justified in part by the relatively large amount of money citizens hold relative to GDP.

The "residual" or owner's equity item in Table 3.3 could be interpreted as either the nation's gains from BOP activities, a statistical discrepancy, or the size of China's currency exposure to the rest of the world. Owner's equity has shrunk considerably over the past decade, reflecting the drop in foreign exchange reserves and the substantial increase in external debt. In the context of currency exposure, we note that China's currency weakened between 5 and 6 percent over 2018. No doubt, this was in response to the ongoing "trade war" with the United States (discussed in Case Study 3.3) and a weakening economy. While a weakening currency can somewhat blunt the impact of higher tariffs, one downside is that it can put strains on the ever-growing amount of Chinese external debt denominated in USD. Chinese companies and financial institutions with external debt would be most impacted by the weaker RMB.

Portfolio investment has become more significant across both sides of the balance sheet. Foreign portfolio equity holdings remain a relatively small part of the liability side of the balance sheet. Historically, China has restricted such flows into the country—something we discuss in Chapter 11. But even after China lifted some restrictions for investments in the Shenzhen stock exchange in 2014 (via Stock Connect [https://bit.ly/3cwtI9P]), and then again in December, 2016, foreign investors have been cautious about this class of investments.

In early 2018, Chinese holdings (https://bit.ly/2WvFUCl) of US financial assets amounted to USD 1.5 trillion, or about half of all Chinese foreign exchange assets. About USD 1.3 billion was in US government securities, and a relatively small amount was held in US corporate securities. About USD 194 billion was in equities. These figures, however, do not include real estate assets.[6] The obvious implication is that China still finds the United States an attractive place to invest, and the United States relies on China as a source of finance. This latter point is discussed below in the context of current account imbalances.

Being conservative has both costs and benefits. A conservative policy reduces the risk of default and financial crises. As stated in our discussion of staged capital account liberalization above, Chinese policy-makers have followed a well-thought-out strategy by encouraging FDI but heavily restricting international borrowing.[*] The cost, however, has been a lower return on the more liquid assets and the more expensive cost of equity versus debt finance. For example, between 2010 and 2020 the real return in RMB terms on US Treasury bill holdings was close to 0 percent, while the annual financing cost of raising FDI equity has been in the double digits.

Under the capital asset pricing model (CAPM), a cornerstone of modern finance, the more a company uses debt finance, the more it amplifies the non-diversifiable risk of the firm (its equity). In turn, the cost of equity finance rises with greater leverage. But, in the case of China, capital markets are not integrated, which calls into question the applicability of CAPM—at least under standard assumptions. Returns on Chinese-denominated assets are far less correlated with international markets because of capital controls. Under standard CAPM, equity returns on Chinese assets should be correspondingly lower. But, in a survey of US firms operating in China, for example, 88 percent reported profit margins that were higher in China than in the rest of the world in 2009. In summary, it would appear that China, at least until recently, has provided both less risk and higher returns to the foreign investor! Furthermore, the large short-term asset position provides a further cushion of safety. The legacy of encouraging FDI at the expense of loans appears to have had significant costs; China has moved to a more leveraged balance sheet with greater external borrowing over the past decade, decreasing the cost of capital but also increasing risk. The conservative nature of the asset side of the balance sheet should, however, be able to support the increased leverage.

[*]Technically, national statistics bureaus around the world include both debt and equity finance when measuring FDI. Even under this broader definition, China still relies mostly on the equity form of FDI.

Macro Finance Insight 3.3: The Pecking Order Theory

The pecking order theory suggests that, because of asymmetric information between firms and potential investors, firms tend to rely first on internal sources of finance (retained earnings), then debt, and finally (as a last resort) equity. The idea here is that outsiders know less than insiders and are therefore an expensive source of capital because they charge a premium in the face of greater uncertainty regarding investment. This is particularly true of an equity investment, since this requires an outright valuation of the underlying assets of the firm. In contrast, debt finance is determined more on the basis of a binomial question: Will the borrower pay the amount owed or not? Less information is required to answer this question than what is involved in equity valuation.

The above theory suggests that countries normally rely on internal savings before seeking outside finance. This conclusion is consistent with an early study done by Feldstein and Horioka (1980) which shows a high correlation between nations' levels of savings and investment; that is, a disproportionate reliance on internal versus external finance. Our conclusion is consistent with China's flow of funds, in which domestic investment is financed mostly by domestic savings. In terms of debt versus equity finance, however, China's past financial choices seem to differ from the pecking order theory. China has shown a clear preference for a particular form of equity investment, as opposed to the alternative form of external finance taken by many emerging market countries—debt finance. This interesting macro-deviation from the pecking order theory is consistent with a common concern expressed by Chinese policy-makers: FDI is a very expensive form of external financing.

Current Account Balance from Four Angles

We can look at current account balances, a critical part of the BOP, from four different perspectives. These perspectives are fully equivalent in an accounting sense, but each provides a unique insight or policy angle explaining why a country might run a current account surplus or deficit. This is particularly important in the context of China and the United States because so much emphasis has been placed on the former's surplus and the latter's deficit. We will discuss how these imbalances are really two sides of the same coin later, but for now let's focus on different ways of thinking about current account deficits.

Approach #1: Current Account Balance by Definition

The simplest approach for discussing the current account balance is to rely on its definition—the difference between the goods and services a country exports and those it imports:

$$\text{Current Account Balance} = XGS - MGS$$

In 2017, the current account balance for the United States was a deficit of about USD 449 billion, while China had a surplus of about USD 168 billion. As described above, these amounts included goods, factor services, non-factor services, and grants. In using the definitional approach to current account balance, we focus closely on trade results. Correcting a current account imbalance using this approach would rely on trade-related policies. Thus, to counteract a current account deficit, one might focus on tariffs (taxes), quotas on imports, or subsidies on exports.[7] Furthermore, countries might try to streamline relevant regulations and approvals for exporting or importing. Or, policymakers might seek to adjust exchange rates if they felt that their currency was misaligned and that that misalignment was the cause of a current account surplus or deficit.

Approach #2: Current Account Balance and Absorption

Using our second approach, we view the current account balance as the difference between a nation's supply (GDP) and demand ($C + I + G$). (Recall: C, I, and G denote consumption, investment, and government demand, respectively.) If more is being demanded than supplied, those goods and services must come from outside the country (i.e., from abroad). Conversely, if more is supplied than demanded, the excess goods must go somewhere (i.e., exported abroad).[8] We can formally state that:

Supply – Demand

or

Sources – Uses

or

GDP – $(C + I + G)$

= Balance in Goods and Non-Factor Services

Recognizing that:

$$GNP = GDP + \text{Net Factor Income}$$

We can say:

$$GNP - (C + I + G) = \text{Current Account Balance}$$

This approach emphasizes the need for demand and supply management to correct current account imbalances. For example, a country running a current account deficit may take steps to reduce demand (*C*, *I*, or *G*).[9] Alternatively, the country may need to improve productivity or its product mix to increase supply (GDP or gross national product [GNP]). For example, in the last chapter, when we discussed the Expenditure approach to GDP, we saw that US personal consumption was about 68 percent of GDP in the United States but only 39 percent of GDP in China. A shift downward in US consumption of a mere 3.2 percentage points, to about 65 percent of GDP, would yield (*ceteris paribus*) a US current account surplus equivalent to China's.

US Balance of Payments with China 2017	
	USD (in Billions)
Current Account	-338.9
Export of Goods	130.4
Import of Goods	505.6
Trade Balance	-375.2

US Balance of Payments with China 2017	
	USD (in Billions)
Export of Services (est.)	52.8
Import of Services	16.5
Services Balance	36.3

Table 3.4 The US imported close to a quarter of all Chinese exports in 2017, highlighting the fact that each country is the other's most significant trading partner.
Source: Author created based on data from National Bureau of Statistics and US Census Bureau (https://bit.ly/2WZIa3C).

Case Study 3.3: China and the United States—Fictions, Frictions, and Facts

That there is a significant financial and economic relationship between the United States and China is well known. China and the United States are now each another's largest trading partners. The BOP serves as the key nexus in which that relationship can be examined. In Table 3.1 and Table 3.2, we see that the United States has a global balance trade deficit of close to USD 807 billion, while China has a surplus of over USD 481 billion. Table 3.4 shows an estimate of the bilateral (China/US) current account relationship for 2017.

We see that the US current account deficit with China is about three-fourths of its overall (global) current account deficit, while the China/US trade deficit is between 40 and 50 percent of the overall (global) US trade deficit. And, for China, the significance of the imbalance is much larger as a share of its overall (global) surpluses. US imports from China account for about a quarter of all Chinese exports, and US exports to China account for about 7 percent of all Chinese imports. Meanwhile, China accounts for a large share of non-factor service imports from the United States and a substantial share of dividend and interest receipts to the United States (factor services).

Beginning in 2018, the United States commenced a series of escalating trade measures (principally tariffs) to restrict imports from China. In January, a tariff of 30 percent on the import of solar panels was announced, followed by a 25 percent tariff on USD 34 billion of Chinese imports in July, and then a 10 percent tariff on an additional USD 300 billion in imports in September, with a threat to increase the rate to 25 percent beginning in January, 2019.[10] Meanwhile, China responded in kind with a series of tariffs on US imports. The series of US tariffs could result in high trade barriers for close to half of China's exports to the United States and about 10 percent of China's global exports.

In January 2020 an agreement was reached between the two nations in the first phase of a trade agreement. Both countries agreed to halt tariff escalation and to reduce some of the recently elevated trade barriers. China agreed to increase by about USD 200 billion imports of manufactured and agricultural products and services in the 2020-21 period. China committed to greater protection of intellectual property rights and to reduce somewhat its efforts at technology transfer. But both countries continued to maintain recently implemented tariffs on a large swathe of products and services; in the United States tariffs covering about USD 360 billion in imports or about two thirds of imports from China were left unchanged.

The Trump administration's stated goals were to improve the US trade balance and to force China to (1) lower its own trade barriers on US exports (particularly automobiles), (2) eliminate requirements on US FDI investors in China to transfer technology, and (3) respect intellectual property rights of United States companies. Meanwhile, some Chinese viewed the increasingly hostile trade actions as an attempt to "contain" China, particularly in the context of the much touted "Made in China: 2025" strategic initiative that China announced in 2015.

Since at least the 19th century (Ricardo 1817), most economists have agreed that free trade via the mechanism of comparative advantage is welfare-enhancing for participating countries; and this, of course, is the guiding intellectual *raison d'etre* for organizations such as the World Trade Organization (WTO). There always has been, however, a counter current of strategic trade theorists who believe that free trade can be improved upon; nations can either preserve or create comparative advantage via various restrictions on free trade. No doubt, the Trump administration actions will harm certain Chinese industries, such as the electronic parts and equipment-and-machinery industries. Whether this could or would lead to a strategically beneficial ascendancy in these same industries in the United States is doubted by many economists (https://bit.ly/2AtTaif).

Based on data in Table 3.1 we can easily calculate that, as a first cut, the proposed trade barriers would impact at most about 2 percent of Chinese GDP. Furthermore, Koopman et al. (2008) estimate that at least half of the value added in Chinese exports is created by international companies ranging from South Korea to the United States. This estimation suggests that the trade barriers against China would likely impact the national income of these other countries through lower corporate profits. No doubt, these foreign companies (as well as Chinese companies) will shift production to countries other than the United States in response to the barriers targeted at China and then continue to export to the United States, if possible.

One unintended consequence of the 2018 trade barriers is a shift of China's production base (GDP) away from exports and toward greater domestic consumption. This shift has been a stated goal of the Chinese government for years now, and it is in fact a desirable goal (as we discuss in later chapters). Though tariffs may be a more abrupt force to prompt that policy shift, the events in 2018 may represent a turning point for China in this context.

Finally, regarding the issue of forced technology transfer and intellectual property protection: There is no doubt that China has been very proactive in its efforts to build up its technological base in recent years. Examples include arrangements with companies ranging from Apple to Citibank in which part of the requirement for entry into the Chinese market was the establishment of training or research facilities in China. It should be noted that there is no international mechanism or international institution that monitors and coordinates FDI between nations including technology transfer. There are, however, at least 2,600 bilateral and multilateral investment treaties between and among countries. Unfortunately, no such treaty exists between China and the United States. The Obama administration began such a negotiation, but there has been no further action since the start of the Trump administration.

Meanwhile, there is some precedent for the protection of intellectual property rights under the WTO. The 2001 Doha meetings led to a Declaration on Trade Related Intellectual Property Rights Protection—an open-ended agreement that allowed member countries to create and implement a legal framework for protecting intellectual property in the context of international trade. In summary, there are mechanisms open to nations to negotiate disputes related to technology transfer and intellectual property without resorting to a trade war. It would appear the United States, under the Trump administration, has taken the more aggressive stance.

Approach #3: Current Account Balance and the Gap Between Savings and Investment

While the Absorption approach highlights the imbalance between the supply and demand for goods and services, the Savings/Investment approach examines the imbalance between a nation's source of funds (savings) and its use of funds (investment). This is also known as a "flow of funds" approach. The gap between the savings and investment represents how a current account deficit is financed; or, in the case of a current account surplus, how much is lent abroad. The subscripts "$_P$" and "$_G$" represent the private sector and the government sector, respectively.

We recall that:

$$Y_{\text{GNP}} = C_G + C_P + I_G + I_P + \text{Current Account Balance}$$

And that:

$$S_P + C_P = Y_{\text{GNP}} - \text{Taxes} + \text{Transfers}$$

where (S_{p}) represents private savings.

Defining government saving as:[11]

$$S_G = \text{Government Savings} = \text{Taxes} - (C_G + \text{Transfers})$$

(The right side of the above expression can also be phrased as [Revenues – Current Expenses].)[12]

We have:

$$\text{Current Account Balance} = (S_G - I_G) + (S_P - I_P)$$

In other words, the current account balance is the difference between national savings and investment at both the government level and the private sector level. We could state this in an even simpler form by saying:

$$\text{Current Account Balance} = S - I$$

(Here, private sector and government sector savings and investment have been collapsed into the terms S and I.)

Although this approach toward the current account is less intuitive than the previous two, it provides highly useful insights. It makes clear that a country that saves a lot is producing while not consuming (since savings cannot exist without first producing something). Production that is not being consumed domestically must be going somewhere. Since the (I) term takes into account production being used for investment (e.g., roads or plant equipment) and inventory accumulation, the only place production must be going to (or coming from) is abroad.

The Savings/Investment approach allows us to focus on a fundamental cause of current account deficits or surpluses. If a nation saves a little and invests a lot, it will run a current account deficit. A surplus will result from high savings and low investment. This approach highlights the large difference in savings rates between China and the United States and its role in determining the different current account outcomes.

For example, if the United States wishes to reduce its current account deficit, it must either increase national savings (increase private savings or reduce dis-saving in the budget deficit) or reduce investment. Since investment in the United States is not high by international standards, the goal of improving the savings rate would appear to be a more reasonable path. Similarly, in order for China to decrease its current account surplus to more sustainable levels, it must either decrease savings (or increase consumption in the private or public sectors) or increase investment. Since China's investment is already extraordinarily high by international standards, a similar focus on less saving and more consumption (but in the opposite direction from the United States) seems reasonable.

Macro Finance Insight 3.4: Uncertainty, Real Options, and the Trade War Costs

In a thorough empirical and theoretical analysis, Handley and Limão (2017a, 2017b) examine the historical impact of uncertainty on United States imports from China and consider the implication of Trump-era trade policies. Specifically, they consider the pre-WTO accession of China (before December, 2001) and the years that followed accession. They measure the reduction of uncertainty that Chinese exporters experienced relative to the prior pre-WTO accession of China. The source of uncertainty in that period was largely due to annual US congressional reviews and a vote to determine whether China should receive "most-favored nation" status. Such status would allow China to export a broad set of goods into the United States at the most favorable tariff rates (the best rates granted to other countries who were already part of the WTO) and avoid a 30 percent "non-favored status" tariff level.

In their study, Handley and Limão take a "real options" approach to model the impact of uncertainty on Chinese exporters' decision to enter the United States market. Specifically, they establish that Chinese firms have significant sunk costs in order US markets. That is, the required investment by Chinese firms to enter US markets cannot, by and large, be recovered. What this implies is that there is an option value (also known as an "option premium") to waiting before undertaking an investment. In other words, in the presence of uncertainty, there is an additional hurdle to investing—we need to be sure that our timing of entering the US market is not premature. There are other markets or opportunities that Chinese exporters would consider while they wait for the uncertainty in the United States to get resolved. The greater the uncertainty, the greater the option value of waiting, and in turn the more likely that market entry into the United States would be delayed.

The authors show that, in the case of China's accession to the WTO in 2001, up to one-third of the succeeding growth in Chinese exports to the United States could be explained by the reduction in uncertainty due to WTO entry. They find that the impact on related prices was a decline of about 15 percent. Applying their research to the current situation, the authors estimate a 4- to 5-fold increase in trade policy uncertainty since Trump's election. Their results suggest that this uncertainty will cause a decline in Chinese exports to the United States over time, a rise in related prices, and a decline in US consumer welfare. At a minimum, the authors indicate that the increase in uncertainty could be akin to a 13 percent increase in tariff levels, and that it would cause a welfare loss of at least one-third of that caused by a complete ban on Chinese exports.

In summary, it is not just the tariff itself that impacts trade flows between the US and China, but trade policy uncertainty as a whole that can have a longer-term and perhaps even more insidious effect.

Approach #4: Current Account Balance and External Debt

If we imagine the current account as simply "trading in tangible goods," ignoring trade in services for the moment, then we can think of a current account deficit as "purchasing more tangible goods from the rest of the world than we sell to the rest of the world." What would our trading counterpart receive to settle the balance due? Clearly, the counterpart would need something, if our own goods are not settling the imbalance. Some type of financial obligation (more graphically, a piece of paper, or an "IOU") would be needed. That financial obligation might take the form of currency, a debt instrument, or an equity instrument. One way or another, we need to offer some credible financial instrument of sufficient value to offset our shortfall in exports to imports.

Thus, we can think of the current account balance as a change in our net external debt position. When we run a current account deficit, we need to finance that deficit via a financial instrument or via the counterpart's willingness to hold our own currency.[13] When we run a surplus, we increase our own holdings of foreign financial obligations, decreasing our net debt or increasing our net creditor position. Even if foreigners settle the difference using our own currency—USD—then our net external debt position falls or our net creditor position rises.

Formally:

$$\text{Current Account} = \text{Change in Net External Debt}$$

The right side of this expression is negative (-) for a current account surplus and positive (+) for a deficit.

This perspective on the current account highlights the notion that a deficit must be financed (via the financial account or reserves), and that this act of financing alters our net external debt position. From a policy perspective, it tells us that countries that cannot obtain external finance (i.e., borrow from abroad) will be constrained in running a current account deficit. Countries that experience current account surpluses, such as China, are (by definition) lending to the outside world. For other countries whose creditworthiness is in question, the inability to finance a current account deficit leads to painful import compression, as discussed at the start of this chapter.

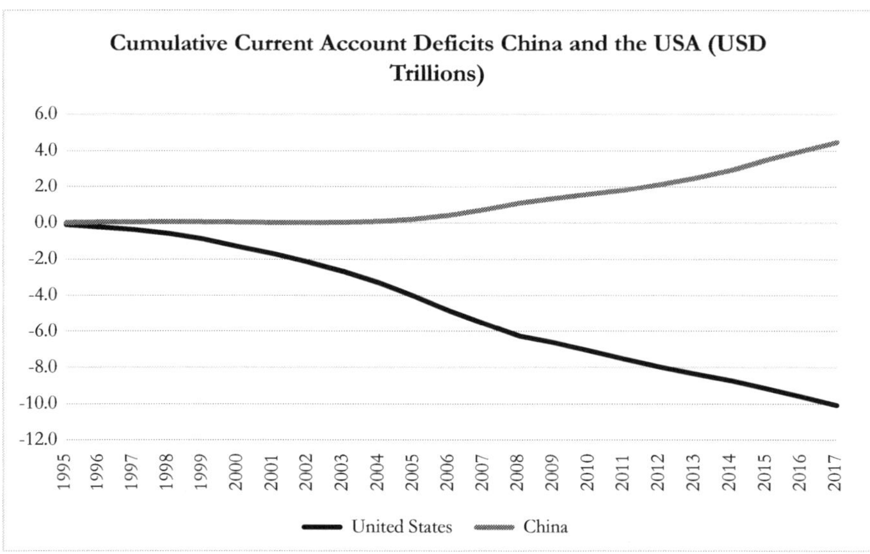

Figure 3.3 Cumulative current account balances (an estimate of external debt of assets) with the rest of the world suggests that, since 1995, China has financed about 45 percent of United States borrowing in global financial markets on a net basis.
Source: Author created based on data from IMF and FRED.

Figure 3.3 shows cumulative current account surpluses and deficits (net external debt) for China and the United States. On a net basis, between 1995 and 2017, China had lent about USD 4.5 trillion to the world (including the United States), while in the same period the United States had borrowed from the rest of the world (including China) a little over USD 10 trillion. In other words, on a net global basis, China has financed about 45 percent of US external borrowing.[14]

Financial Cash Flow	**Macroeconomic Cash Flow Assumption**	**Row**
Net Operating Profits	Domestic Savings (*S*) Corporate + Private + Government	A
Change in Net Fixed Assets	Gross Investment (*I*)	B
	Corporate + Private + Government	
Inventory Accumulation	Included in Gross Investment (above)	C
Accounts Receivables–Accounts Payable	Constant at 0	D

Financial Cash Flow	Macroeconomic Cash Flow Assumption	Row
Necessary Cash Holdings	Constant at Initial Months of Sales or Imports	E
Other Current Assets	Constant at 0	F
Other Non-interest Liabilities	Constant at 0	G

Table 3.5 shows the correspondence between corporate cash flow and national cash flow. Source: Author created.

Macro Finance Insight 3.5: What is the Cash Flow for an Entire Economy?

In corporate finance and financial accounting, a central question relates to the cash flow of a company: What is the cash flow for an entire economy? Both finance and accounting have different answers to this fundamental question. As we shall see, we can ask the same question regarding a country as a whole. The BOP and current account discussion above provides some useful tools for evaluating the cash flow for an entire country. The BOP is conceptually close to an accounting measure of cash flow, since it includes both operations (the current account) and financing items (the financial account). We now proceed to show how to measure a country's cash flow from the perspective of finance or valuation.

Measuring a Company's Cash Flow

Recall that, when measuring a company's cash flow, we are interested in identifying outflows and inflows in actual cash. Specifically, we want to look beyond the income statement and balance sheet—although these tools do help answer an investor's fundamental question, "Is this company generating or losing cash?" After all, when investors give cash to the company, their principal question is, "When and how much will I get paid back in cash?" Net income, assets, turnover ratios, etc., are all useful accounting terms, but they do not directly translate into a measure of cash generated. Reviewing the basic steps for determining free cash flow (FCF) for corporate valuation purposes, we calculate:

$$\text{NOP (Net Operating Profit)} = \text{EBIT} \times (1 - \text{Tax Rate})$$

where EBIT is earnings (net income) before interest and taxes are deducted. We can then estimate FCF for any given year using:

$$\text{FCF} = \text{NOP} - \text{Change in NFA} - \text{Change in Working Capital}$$

where NFA is the firm's net investment in plant, property, and equipment, and "working capital" is equal to (current assets – "excess cash" – non-interest current liabilities).

Moving from the Corporation to the Nation

One critical insight in accounting for a nation's cash flow is that national savings comes partly from corporate profits, while the rest comes from personal savings and government savings (surpluses or deficits in the case of dis-saving). Similarly, corporate investment is a critical part of national investment. Our approach then is to build up net income in a very natural way.

We let EBIT or NOP correspond to the (S) in the ($S - I$) macro accounting framework, and (I) (change in NFA) corresponds more broadly to corporate investment, government investment, and individual investment. In dealing with such elements as taxes and transfer payments, we recognize that national level intra-sector payments of interest and taxes are netted out and sum to 0. It is only when these payments are made abroad that they would affect national cash flow. And we note that interest payments across borders are accounted for in the current account balance. Finally, we note that the BOP "change in reserves" bottom line is equivalent to the accounting "statement of cash flows" bottom line, a different metric. The latter includes financing (the financial account) items such as loans and FDI; we are not interested here in this accounting measure of cash flows. Instead, we are measuring cash flows from the valuation perspective of corporate finance, which is akin to the operational cashflow of corporations.

Table 3.5 presents a highly simplified correspondence between measuring cash flows at the financial level and the macro (national) level. A number of basic assumptions are made, particularly with regard to the working capital component. Given the simplified correspondence between measures of financial cash flow and macroeconomic cash flow, we can say that a measure of macroeconomic cash flow consists of a refinement of ($S - I$ = current account). Instead, we use the relationship based on GDP, and not GNP, to define macro cash flow:

$$\text{Macro Cash Flow} = S - I = \text{Trade Balance} + \text{Non-Factor Services Balance}$$

As we can see in Figure 3.4, starting in the early 1990s, the United States' negative cash flow has grown increasingly large as a share of GDP, but it has improved somewhat since 2005. This negative cash flow has been financed from abroad via the financial account—broadly defined to include the holding of USD reserve assets abroad. We will discuss the sustainability of this pattern and its implications for the valuation of the United States later. But we do note that prolonged negative cashflows are unlikely to be sustainable, since they imply an ongoing need for external finance.[15] Since negative flows are unsustainable, counterparty positive flows (for China) must also be unsustainable. This fact presents one more juncture for conflict and potential crisis to add to those already highlighted in Case Study 3.3. The reverse picture holds for China, as shown in Figure 3.5. Here we see a positive cash flow in virtually all years since 1990. As the US saw negative cash flows surge in the 2000–2010 decade, positive cash flows correspondingly surged in China; but, since the peak in 2007, Chinese positive cash flows have declined steadily.

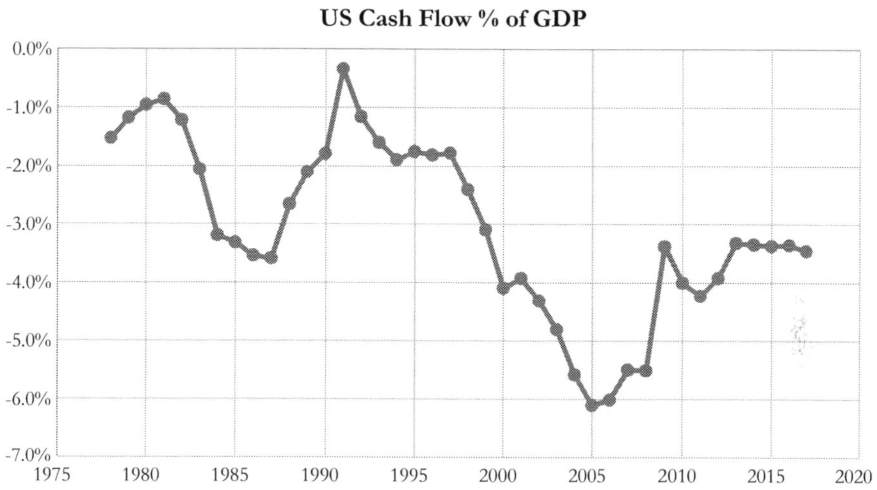

Figure 3.4 The United States has had prolonged negative cash flows as a share of GDP, but the situation has improved since 2005.
Source: Author created based on data from IMF and FRED.

China Cash Flow
% of GDP

12.0%
10.0%
8.0%
6.0%
4.0%
2.0%
0.0%
-2.0%
-4.0%
-6.0%
1980 1985 1990 1995 2000 2005 2010 2015 2020

Figure 3.5 China has had positive cash flow as a share of GDP, but it has been shrinking since 2007.
Source: Author created based on data from IMF and FRED.

Challenging Questions for China (and the Student): Chapter 3

1. Go the Federal Reserve Economic Database (FRED) and update China's current account balances and foreign exchange reserve holdings both graphically and numerically (see Table 3.1 and Figure 3.3). Determine the implied value of China's (financial account + capital account + errors) for the most recent three years.
2. Explain why the chapter argues that China's foreign exchange capital structure has been "conservative" in recent decades. Relate this to questions of capital mobility and financial crises.
3. Consider the current account balances for China and the United States:
   a. Explain the four different ways of looking at a current account deficit.
   b. Discuss: If China stopped buying US Treasury bills, the US current account deficit would shrink. Which of the four views of a current account deficit is useful in this context?
4. Choose among the four different ways of looking at a current account deficit or surplus and explain why China has historically run a large current account surplus and the United States has historically run a current account deficit.
5. Discuss the validity of the following statements:
   a. The BOP is a measure of a country's accounting cash flow, while the current account is a measure of a country's financial cash flow.
   b. In recent years, the United States has had a negative financial cash flow while China has had both a positive financial and accounting cash flow. The opposing balances are related.
   c. We should not worry about cash flows for either China or the United States since a country is not a company and having too much or too little cash flow is not important.
6. Determine the cash flow of the United States and China based on Table 3.3. Then update the data using FRED.
7. Explain why, as a conventional accounting measure, the BOP is equivalent to "the statement of cashflows," while for financial valuation purposes the current account is almost the same as "cash flow."
8. Go to the Federal Reserve Database (https://bit.ly/3d2U6Yq):
   a. Calculate the change in China's gross foreign exchange reserves between December, 2018 and December, 2019. We can call this China's overall BOP for 2019.

b. Go to the IMF (https://bit.ly/2C4pcSO) database and find China's Current Account Balance for 2019.

c. Estimate (assume Errors = 0) China's 2019 capital/financial account by using the accounting identity:

   (Current Account + Capital/Financial Account + Errors ≡ BOP ≡ Change in Reserves)

d. Compare to the most recent estimates presented in this chapter.

9. Explain the "real options" mechanism by which trade barrier uncertainty impedes exports and imports between China and the United States.

References

Calvo, Guillermo. 2005. *Emerging Capital Markets in Turmoil: Bad Luck or Bad Policy?* Cambridge, MA: MIT Press.

Diaz-Alejandro, Carlos. 1985. "Good-Bye Financial Repression, Hello Financial Crash." *Journal of Development Economics*, 19(1–2), pp. 1–24.

Eichengreen, Barry. 2011. "The Renminbi as an International Currency." *Journal of Policy Modeling*, 33(5), pp. 752–59.

Feldstein, M., and C. Horioka. 1980. "Domestic Savings and International Capital Flows." *Economic Journal*, 90, pp. 314–29.

Glick, Reuven and Michael Hutchison. 2009. "Navigating the Trilemma: Capital Flows and Monetary Policy in China." *Journal of Asian Economics*, 20(3), pp. 205–24.

Greenwood, John. 2008. "The Costs and Implications of PBC Sterilization." *Cato Journal*, 28(2), pp. 205–17.

Handley, K., and N. Limão. 2017a. "Policy Uncertainty, Trade, and Welfare: Theory and Evidence for China and the United States." *American Economic Review*, 107(9), pp. 2731–83.

Handley, K., and N. Limão. 2017b. "Trade Under TRUMP Policies." In *Economics and Policy in the Age of Trump*, edited by Chad P. Brown, London: CEPR Press, pp. 141–152.

Knight, John and Wei Wang. 2011. "China's Macroeconomic Imbalances: Causes and Consequences." *World Economy*, 34(9), pp. 1476–506.

Koopman, Robert, Zhi Wang, and Shang-Jin Wei. 2008. "How Much of Chinese Exports is Really

Made in China? Assessing Domestic Value-Added When Processing Trade is Pervasive." NBER Working Paper no. 14109.

Modigliani, Franco, and Merton H. Miller. 1958. "The Cost of Capital, Corporation Finance and the Theory of Investment." *The American Economic Review*, 48(3), pp. 261–97.

Mundell, Robert. 2012. "U.S. and China in the World Economy: The Balance of Payments and the Balance of Power." *Journal of Policy Modeling*, 34(4), pp. 525–28.

Myers, Stewart C. and Nicholas S. Majluf. 1984. "Corporate Financing and Investment Decisions: When Firms Have Information That Investors Do Not Have." *Journal of Financial Economics*, 13(2), pp. 187–221.

National Bureau of Statistics. 2012. "Table 2–32." In *China Statistical Yearbook*. Beijing: China Statistics Press.

Obstfeld, Maurice, Jay C. Shambaugh, and Alan M. Taylor. 2010. "Financial Stability, the Trilemma, and International Reserves." *American Economic Journal: Macroeconomics*, 2(2), pp. 57–94.

Obstfeld, Maurice. 2012. "Financial Flows, Financial Crises and Global Imbalances." *Journal of International Money and Finance*, 31(3), pp. 469–80.

Reinhart, Carmen and Kenneth Rogoff. 2009. *This Time is Different: Eight Centuries of Financial Folly*. Princeton: Princeton University Press.

Ricardo, David. 1817. *On the Principles of Political Economy and Taxation*. London: John Murray.

Ryan, Vincent. 2011. "China's Currency Conversion." *CFO Magazine,* 15 July.

Schramm, Ronald M. 2011. "China: Inroads to Kenya, 'It's a Long Road That Has No Turning." Chinese European International Business School: Case Centre, no. CC-111-012.

Tang, Guoxing. 2000. "A Model Study of Balance of Payments and Money Supply of China." In *Econometric Modeling of China,* edited by Lawrence R. Klein and Shinichi Ichimura, Singapore: World Scientific, pp. 9–65.

Zhang, Liqing. 2004. "Coping with China's Balance of Payments Surplus: Why and How?" *China and World Economy*, 12(4), pp. 79–87.

Zhu, Yiping. 2010. "Trade, Capital Flows and External Balance: Is China Unique in Two Hundred Years of Globalization?" *Journal of Chinese Economic and Business Studies*, 8(1), pp. 1–22.

Endnote

1. We see in Table 3.1 that China's BOP is measured in USD rather than RMB. Most countries will provide a USD presentation for their BOP. This highlights the central role that foreign exchange plays in the BOP.
2. A confusing set of definitions involves the capital account and the financial account. The latter used to be known as the former! The capital account now represents a rather insignificant item which takes account of such transactions as land sales to foreigners.
3. The distinction between what constitutes portfolio investment and FDI is definitional. FDI entails a degree of ownership and control; a rule of thumb cutoff between portfolio and FDI defines more than 20 percent of the company owned by a group of foreign investors as FDI.
4. There are also "valuation effects," that is, capital gains or losses due to currency fluctuations on non-USD reserve holdings.
5. Emergency lending could also come from another government or institution, such as the European Union. But, again, such lending would come with strings attached, or "conditionality."
6. Some of the USD 194 billion may overlap with the FDI figures found in Table 3.3.
7. Most economists, since at least the time of David Ricardo in the 19th century, would agree that such policies are more likely to cause harm than good.
8. Note that we exclude the possibility that excess goods fall into inventory accumulation since such inventory accumulation is already accounted for by the "I" term in $(C + I + G)$.
9. Keep in mind that investment includes housing—an acute source of excess demand in the United States pre-financial crisis.
10. In December, 2018 Presidents Trump and Xi Jinping agreed to defer implementation of those tariffs for 90 days pending further negotiation.
11. Government savings is the same concept as a budget deficit or surplus.
12. Note that, consistent with accepted corporate accounting practices, we do not include IG as a current expense. Fiscal accounting practices around the world do, however, include this IG in the definition of the budget deficit or surplus.
13. Holding of country A's currency by country B is a legal obligation of country A to provide something of value in the future to country B, and in this sense it constitutes a debt-like obligation.

14. Other top contributors to the global savings pool are northern European economies, developed Asian economies—including Japan and South Korea—and oil exporters in the Middle East.
15. Recall that these negative cashflows do not include interest and dividend payments or receipts. Even though these latter categories still remain positive for the United States, should they also turn negative the situation would become even less tenable.

4

LONG-RUN ECONOMIC GROWTH

冰冻三尺，非一日寒

Only a Long Winter Yields Thick Ice—Beijing Was Not Built in a Day

We now turn to one of the most important and challenging question in macroeconomics: What determines the long-run growth of an economy? "Long-run growth" refers to the secular real growth in gross domestic product (GDP) that occurs over decades after smoothing out (filtering) short-run business cycles. While macroeconomic analysis often focuses on the latter (for good reason), it is long-run growth that ultimately determines the economic well-being of a nation's citizens. More immediately, we are interested in the question: Why does China consider a growth rate below 6 percent to be disappointing, while the United States considers a growth rate of 4 percent to be extraordinarily good? How sustainable is China's growth rate, and how do we know that—over time—China's rapid growth will gravitate toward the same rates found in the United States and other advanced economies?

A careful analysis of what determines long-run growth is warranted for at least three reasons:

1. Small differences in growth rates can make huge differences in standards of living over a relatively short time. For example, a real GDP growth rate that is just 25 basis points higher (.0025 points) in Country A than in Country B will result in one's grandchildren having a standard of living approximately 20 percent higher in Country A. In 1980, China's USD GDP was only 7 percent of US GDP; by 2011, it had reached nearly 49 percent of USD GDP, and by 2018, 67 percent of US GDP. That ascent reflected GDP growth for the period (in real terms) of around 9.6 percent and 2.7 percent, respectively. In Figure 4.1, we see that China's real US dollar (USD) per capita income has moved from 5 percent of the United States ratio in 1997 to close to 18 percent today. The International Monetary Fund (IMF) estimates (https://bit.ly/363NOps) that, by 2030, China's overall GDP could surpass that of the United States.

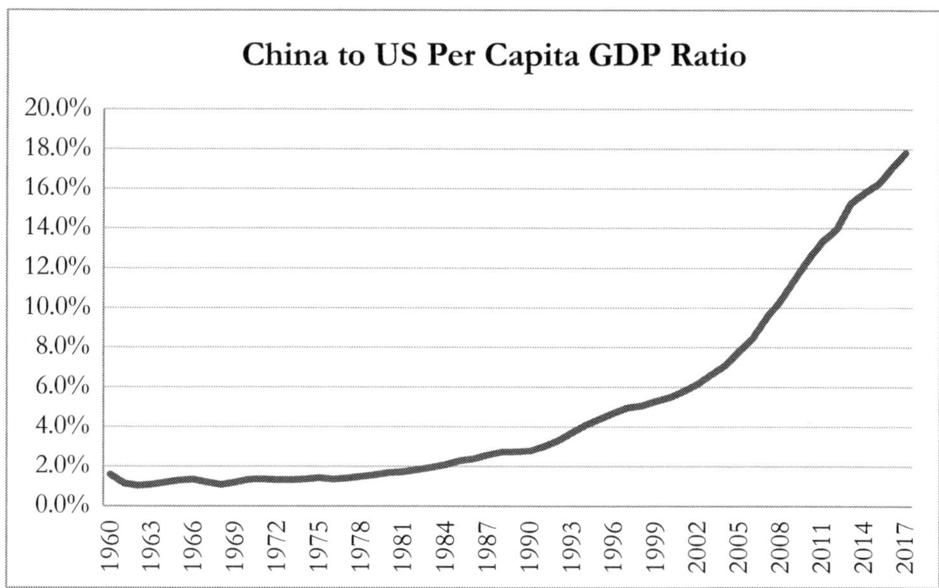

Figure 4.1 In real 2012 USD terms over the past half century, China's per capita GDP has grown from less than 2 percent of that of the United States to close to 18 percent; economic reforms beginning in 1978 accelerated the convergence. Source: Author created based on data from FRED.

2. Higher long-run growth allows for the economic pie to expand over time, which reduces potential conflict among society's various stakeholders (government, companies, investors, and citizens). In China, this has allowed a consensus to form among society's stakeholders regarding a broad range of policies in recent decades.
3. Any discussion of economic growth allows us to introduce key macroeconomic concepts and definitions, including average productivity, technical progress, and value-creating growth. Furthermore, through comparing China and the United States, we gain a deeper insight into what it means to categorize China as "labor intensive" and the United States as "capital intensive."

Figure 4.2 shows real GDP growth in the United States and China from 1978 to 2017. Despite the considerable short-run fluctuations, we can see China's long-term growth rates have been significantly above US growth rates since 1978 (beginning with the period of economic reform), with a dramatic widening from 1990 to the present (reflecting substantial rises in productivity). In this chapter, we discuss the causes and meaning of these differences. Part I presents the standard Solow accounting framework, the Solow-Swan growth theory (Solow growth theory), and then various extensions and theoretical challenges to the Solow model. Along the way, we will examine specific examples related to China's astounding GDP growth and gain insights into the future outlook. Part II examines the related and important question of quality of growth in China, borrowing concepts from corporate finance.

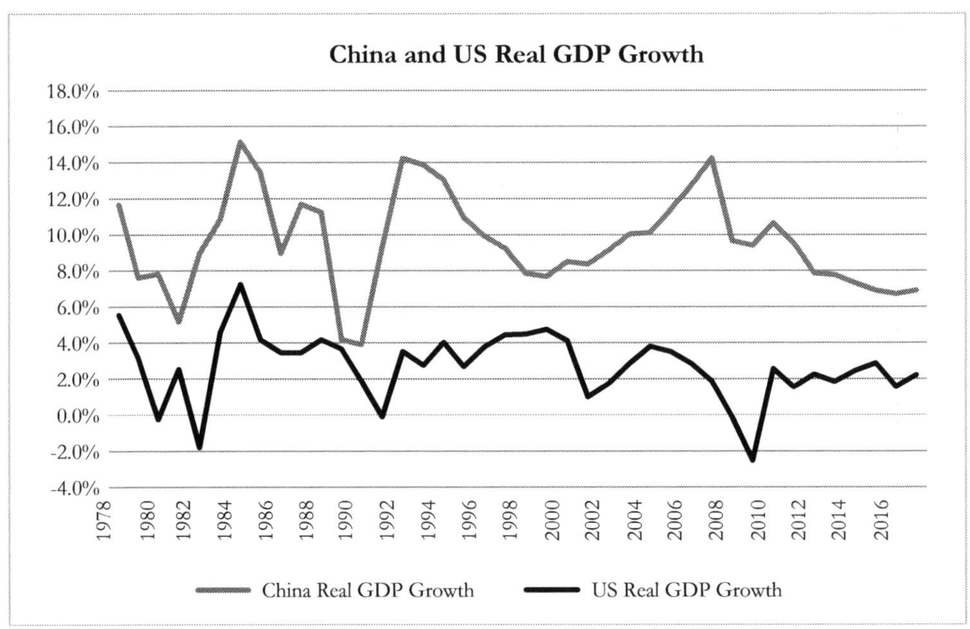

Figure 4.2 China's real GDP growth has been higher than the United States' over the past four decades with a consistently wide gap after 1990.
Source: Author created based on data from the IMF.

Part I: Economic Basis for Long-Run Growth

The Accounting Framework for Long-Run Growth

A good starting point for any discussion of economic growth is the Solow accounting framework, which decomposes growth into component factors of production including: capital (*K*), labor (*L*), and an exogenously determined factor referred to as "technological progress" (*A*). Since long-run equilibrium growth in these neoclassical models is determined by assumed outside forces (such as population growth), they are commonly referred to as "exogenous growth models."

For now, we assume (in our accounting decomposition) a closed economy, full employment of resources, and the absence of short-run business cycle fluctuations such as recessions and recoveries. (We can always relax these assumptions to add specific relevance.) Let's assume only two factors of production: capital (*K*) and labor (*L*). These factors are needed to produce goods and services in the economy, including capital itself. Thus, we can say,

Equation 1:

$$Y = A \times f(K, L)$$

in which, as always, Y represents GDP or output. Here, we somehow combine capital and labor in our economy in order to get output or GDP. This combination will be adjusted based on how much technology (A) we have at our disposal. Further, we can make each variable dependent on time (t)—where t represents one year—and give more specificity to Equation 1, as seen in

Equation 2:

$$Y(t) = A(t) \times K^{\alpha}(t) \times L^{\beta}(t)$$

Here, (α) and (β) can be interpreted in three different ways: (1) returns to scale, when we increase (K) and (L) by the same proportion; (2) elasticities of output (Y) with respect to inputs (K) or (L); or, (3) in the case of constant returns to scale (CRS), shares of national income received by the two factors, (K) and (L), as compensation for their contribution to national income. These interpretations can be seen more clearly if we take the natural logarithm of each side of Equation 2, yielding,

Equation 3:

$$\mathrm{Ln}(Y(t)) = \mathrm{Ln}(A(t)) + \alpha \mathrm{Ln}(K(t)) + \beta Ln(L(t))$$

For example, if we increase (K) and (L) by 1 percent, output increases by ($\alpha + \beta$) percent. For now, we are assuming that (A) grows exogenously over time, allowing us to focus on the path of (Y), (K), and (L). Taking the first derivative of Equation 3, with respect to time, and using Δ to indicate change, we have,

Equation 4:

$$\Delta Y(t) \,/\, Y(t) = \Delta A(t) \,/\, A(t) + \alpha \Delta K(t) \,/\, K(t) + \beta \Delta L(t) \,/\, L(t)$$

Equation 4 provides an obvious but important relationship: economic growth relies on growth in inputs and the degree to which technological progress ($\Delta A(t) / A(t)$) occurs.

Simply put, if we consistently lack sufficient growth in capital or labor, it will be difficult to increase output. This is true both when we measure growth and output over time as well as against a cross-section of countries. Small countries tend to have small GDPs, while large countries (such as the United States and China) have large GPDs; this outcome results from the pool of available inputs. However, we must always acknowledge the important role of technology (A) in qualifying these results.

The term ($\Delta A(t)$ / $A(t)$), is commonly referred to as "technological progress," "total factor productivity," or "the Solow residual." Historically, we can estimate economic growth (the left side of Equation 4) and derive estimates of how fast our factors of production, such as (K) and (L), have grown. This allows us to infer or estimate the term, ($\Delta A(t)$ / $A(t)$); it serves as a catch-all for any growth that cannot be explained by factor of production—(K) and (L)—growth. Economic growth is caused not only by the raw accumulation of inputs, but also by the other factor we call technological progress. In fact, technological progress may also be called "ignorance," since the ($\Delta A(t)/A(t)$) term reflects whatever remains unexplained by our accounting model (i.e., everything we have left out). In other words, the term really serves as an accounting plug. Since close to half of economic growth is represented by this term, optimists say that broadly defined technology is vital to economic growth, while skeptics say there is much we do not know about why economic growth occurs.

Case Study 4.1: China's Growth Since the 1978 Economic Reforms

Beginning in 1978, China embarked on a dramatic new course for economic management. Moving from the dirigiste communist-bound tradition of central planning to a market-based system of economic organization (described as either "Socialism with Chinese Characteristics," "Socialist Market Economy," or "Capitalism with State Planning and Intervention"), China's economic landscape had been transformed. Between the death of Mao Zedong (in 1976) and the return of Deng Xiaoping in 1978, initial reforms began in the agricultural sector across locations ranging from Sichuan to Guangdong provinces. Lin (1992) discusses this process, which began by reforming agricultural pricing structures and production. These reforms are referred to as 改革开放 (*gaige kaifang*), meaning "to reform and open." Reform involved allowing for market-based decision making on inputs, outputs, pricing, entry and exit of businesses, and competition. Brandt et al. (2008b), however, remind us that while China's economic structure was similar to the Soviet model in terms of its use of Five-Year Plans, one major difference was that no input-output mechanism dictated by the central government had been fully implemented by 1978.

Reform began in the agricultural sector due to its large size, importance to human survival, and likeliness to result in all-around gains with very few economic losers. Under China's new household responsibility system, beginning in the early 1980s, peasants were allowed to grow and sell their output using land leased from the local municipality rather than work on collectivized plots of land. Critically, although output quotas were still kept in place, rural production beyond the quota was allowed to be sold in quasi-private markets. Rather than central planners deciding key inputs, such as how much fertilizer to order, farmers were permitted to make these decisions on their own. In this way, individual incomes quickly became linked to the individual farmer's efficiency and efforts; the reforms reduced the role of the state and enhanced the role of markets in agricultural production. By the early 1990s, there was a virtually complete liberalization of China's agricultural economy.

With these reforms in place, a dramatic improvement occurred in agricultural output, freeing up workers to move to town and village enterprises (TVEs) where their productivity was up to 13 times greater than in the agricultural sector (Zhu 2012). Yasheng Huang (2012) points out that TVE is in fact a geographic, and not a commercial, distinction. Beneath that geographic definition were economic entities that could be classified as collectives, individual businesses, and alliances (private partnerships). Collectives continued to have local government participation. The latter two economic categories comprised the groups of businesses that demonstrated the greatest productivity gains in the early reform period. Collectives—partnerships between local governments, local managers, company founders, and local workers—served as bridges between the previous communist system and the emerging corporate structure. The dynamic private TVEs located in eastern China, in cities such as Wenzhou, became very profitable and important sources of foreign exchange earnings from exports. Huang further emphasizes financial liberalization in the rural economy, linking agriculture and TVEs to both formal (rural cooperatives) and informal sources of finance. The financial reform in these early years was later reversed in the 1990s to redirect finance to large-scale industry.

During the 1980s, privatization moved into the industrial sector (Chow 1993). Some state-owned enterprises (SOEs) were privatized, many moved from central government control to provincial/local control, and the largest in key industries—such as in mining, steel, and chemicals—remained as they were. While SOEs were also allowed to sell their above-quota output at market prices, the key development in this period was the growth in a vast periphery of private enterprises, including the above-mentioned TVEs (collectives, share-holding companies, and various types of family-owned businesses). Brandt et al. (2008a) find that the greatest impact on technological progress in the first decades of reform derived mainly from privately-owned industrial enterprises—a combination of private TVEs and large-scale enterprises.

From 1978 through the mid-1990s, the agricultural and manufacturing private sectors carried most of the burden for China's spectacular growth in productivity. Meanwhile, reform of SOEs lagged behind. Reform moved more slowly here because employees were a direct responsibility of the state and reform would inevitably lead to massive unemployment. By the mid-1990s, the financial drain involved in supporting these enterprises became unsustainable. Ever greater autonomy was given to SOEs in terms of employment, wages, investment, inputs, and the retention of profits. Special economic zones (experimental geographic areas in which government intervention in markets was vastly reduced and foreign investment was encouraged) flourished in certain provinces, including Guangdong, Jiangsu, Zhejiang, Shanghai, and other areas in eastern China.

Other reforms included increased openness to foreign direct investment (FDI) and liberalization of international trade—which culminated in China's accession to the World Trade Organization in 2001. Institutional reforms in corporate governance, regulations, and the law continued in the early part of the new millennium. Financial reform, involving the evolution of China's Big Four state-owned banks into true financial institutions, also began in the late 1990s.

What was the impact of this massive effort at economic and institutional reform in China? A number of authors including Lin (1992), Hu and Khan (1996), and Chow (1993 have employed the Solow accounting framework to address this question. Table 4.1 uses a Solow accounting perspective to present representative results of China's spectacular growth. These results show an incredible 60 percent increase in economic growth rates during the post-1978 reform period versus the prior decades of state intervention and planning. While much of pre-reform growth was due to the use of a key input—capital—in production, total factor productivity, also known as technical progress, played a significant role in the period of reform. By these estimates, close to half of the growth rates or all of the increment in growth can be attributed to this progress alone.

Other researchers provide a more nuanced explanation. Alwyn Young (2003), for example, estimates growth in total factor productivity in the industrial sector as only 1.4 percent in this period, with labor productivity rising 2.6 percent.* He suggests that these growth rates, while significant, are no different from those of other East Asian emerging economies during economic reforms. Young's careful analysis of the data suggests that increased labor participation rates, enhanced human capital, and agricultural reforms that freed up labor for industry were the key drivers for economic growth in the industrial sector (see below). Zhu estimates that, for the entire period 1978–2007, total factor productivity in China grew by 3.6 percent. He attributes about 40 percent of this growth to agricultural productivity growth and the remaining part to the non-state sector. Meanwhile, the

SOE sector balanced pre-1998 negative growth with post-1998 positive growth, netting a zero contribution to total factor productivity for the entire period.

Table 4.2 decomposes total factor productivity into key components. Here, we see that labor migration played an important role. The process of agricultural reform allowed many workers with previously low productivity to shift into the higher productivity industrial sector. Furthermore, the reorganization of work around a market-based system allowed the agricultural sector itself to grow at an unprecedented pace. Agricultural reform allowed productive workers to increase output sufficiently while releasing non-productive workers to move into high-margin activities. We can now understand the very broad impact of "technological progress" (*A*). Not only does it include education, new technology, and the results of research and development (R&D), but it also comprises how work is organized and managed.[†]

Lin (1992) estimates that nearly half of the increase in China's early reform output was triggered by the new Household Responsibility System.[1] For example, shifting into a more market-based system is a significant form of technical progress. A similar phenomenon was observed during the enclosure movement of the 17th through 19th centuries, when European agricultural land was permitted to be fenced off for private rather than communal production. The above results are also consistent with a number of academic studies on the US economy (Denison 1974). It is estimated (https://bit.ly/2yTe1ey) that, in the United States, between one-third and one-half of real GDP growth in recent decades was due to growth in total factor productivity.

Finally, Table 4.3 estimates technical progress and contribution of capital and labor to economic growth between 2011 and 2018. We see that, in this period, technological progress can explain only about 8 percent of China's real GDP growth—a substantial decline in share from the earlier post-1978 years of reform. This is surprising given some of the new technologies we have seen impressively implemented in China in recent years. In an accounting sense, it would appear that the rapid growth of the capital stock has crowded out the space for technological progress. We discuss the possibility of value destruction (negative technological progress) when capital is so rapidly deployed later. Another possible explanation is that GDP measurement simply has not kept pace with the intangible benefits of technological progress; in other words, if GDP growth is underestimated, so too will the contribution of technological progress be underestimated.

Today, China is a hybrid of fiercely competitive capitalist microeconomic markets for products and services managed from above by short- and long-term government plans at all levels. In effect, the state sets the macro rules for political and economic goals to be achieved, but within those boundaries anything is possible in terms of competition and market innovations. Under President

Xi Jinpin, however, central government SOEs have received increased support—a different direction from the broad trend described above.

*Young also estimates a lower growth in industrial output for a similar period.

†Of course, this is the very notion that professors of management teach in their courses.

Estimates of the Sources of China's Growth			
	Hu and Khan (1996)		**World Bank (1997)**
Growth Rates	1953–1978	1978–1995	1978–1995
Output (Percent Per Annum)	5.8	9.3	9.4
Contribution to Growth (Percent of Total Rate)			
Physical-Capital Input	3.8	4.2	3.5
Labor Input	1.0	1.2	0.7
Human-Capital Input	NA	NA	0.8
Total Factor Productivity	1.0	3.9	4.3

Table 4.1 China's rapid growth has been driven in equal part by capital accumulation and growth in total factor productivity.
Source: Francis, Painchaud, and Morin (2005).
Note: Percentages are rounded and therefore do not add up to 100.

Estimates of Sources of TFP Growth in China (Percent)					
	Heytens and Zebregs (2003)				
Year Range	**1971–1978**	**1979–1994**	**1985–1989**	**1990–1994**	**1995–1998**
Total Factor Productivity	-0.53	2.78	2.11	2.81	2.30
Structural Reform	0.38	0.94	0.76	0.83	0.39
Labor Migration out of the Primary Sector	2.34	2.01	1.52	2.15	2.08
Exogenous Trend	-3.25	-0.17	-0.17	-0.17	-0.17

Table 4.2 Total factor productivity growth has been a major source of China's economic growth since reforms began in 1978. A key component of this source was the movement of labor from agriculture to manufacturing and construction.
Source: Francis, Painchaud, and Morin (2005).
Note: Percentages are rounded and therefore do not add up to 100.

Variable	Real Growth	Weight	Weighted Growth
ΔY(t)/Y(t)	7.4%	1	7.4%
ΔK(t)/K(t)	12.8%	0.52	6.7%
ΔL(t)/L(t)	0.2%	0.48	0.1%
ΔA(t)/A(t)	Derived	1	0.6%

Table 4.3 In recent years, China has experienced a sharp slowdown in technological progress.
Source: Author created based on World Bank World Development Indicators.

Accounting for Growth in Labor Productivity

In competitive markets, the entire economy benefits from improvements in labor productivity, and each worker benefits from his or her enhanced productivity. With that premise in mind, we now examine the factors that determine growth in labor productivity from a growth accounting framework. We can define average labor productivity (y) as seen in

Equation 5:

$$y = Y / L$$

or total output divided by the size of the workforce. Growth in (y) is the growth in the ratio (Y / L). The growth in this ratio is approximately,

Equation 6:

$$\Delta y / y = \Delta Y / Y - \Delta L / L$$

This is growth in labor productivity, a key metric in understanding how (in a material sense) individuals in society are improving.[2] We will now assume that the economy exhibits CRS, or that ($\alpha + \beta = 1$), or that we can substitute for (β) the expression ($1 - \alpha$) in Equation 4, that is:

Equation 7:[3]

$$\beta = 1 - \alpha$$

Combining Equation 4, Equation 6, and Equation 7, we arrive at an accounting for average labor productivity growth, as seen in:

Equation 8:

$$\Delta y / y = \Delta A(t) / A(t) + \alpha[\Delta K(t) / K(t) - \Delta L(t) / L(t)]$$

Equation 8 shows that growth in labor productivity depends on two key factors: technological progress and growth in capital relative to growth in the labor force. This intuitive result implies that the more equipment and the better technology each worker has to work with, the more productive he or she will be.

From Solow Accounting to Solow Theory

Solow accounting, in and of itself, is a valuable tool for decomposing growth into its constituent components. As soon as we begin to make assumptions, we move from the realm of accounting to the realm of economic theory. We will now discuss a theoretical framework for growth (the neoclassical framework) that has a long history in economics (Domar 1946). In this basic version (Solow-Swan), we make several a ssumptions:

1. CRS or, as in above, $(\alpha + \beta = 1)$
2. An economy that is closed to international trade and capital flows (can always be relaxed)
3. Exogenous population growth, assumed to grow at a rate of $(\Delta L / L = \eta)$; this is the same growth as the labor force
4. Savings rate (as a share of income) that is exogenous at (s), and a depreciation rate for capital that is exogenous at (dep)
5. The Solow accounting framework is a valid accounting of economic growth

We will continue the convention of defining small letter variables to represent per capita versions of the corresponding capital letters. So:

$$y = Y / L$$

and,

$$k = K / L$$

and to repeat:

- (s) = the savings rate such that $(s \times Y)$ and $(s \times y)$ yields national savings (S) or per capital savings (S / L)
- (η) = rate of population and labor force growth
- (dep) = the rate of depreciation of (K) and (k)

Employing our CRS assumption and Equation 2 above, we can say:
Equation 9:

$$Y(t) = A(t) \times K^{\alpha}(t) \times L^{(1-\alpha)}(t)$$

Expressing this in per capita terms, we divide Equation 9 by labor (L) as expressed by:
Equation 10:

$$y = A \times (k)^{\alpha}$$

Diminishing Returns in Output Per Unitof Capital

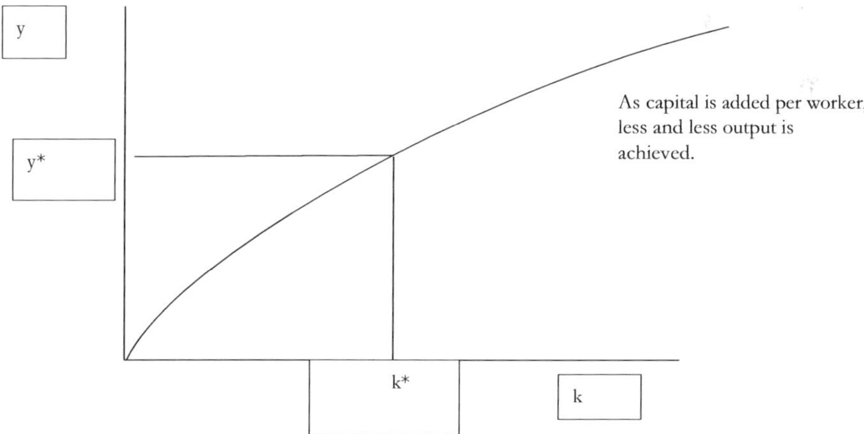

Figure 4.3 Adding more capital per worker will increase output, but with diminishing returns.
Source: Author created.

Figure 4.3 shows the relationship in Equation 10 between (y) and (k). It is concave downward because, under our assumed production function (with CRS), increasing the ratio of capital to labor (k) causes diminishing returns.[4] Once again, we can use the relationship between the growth rate of a ratio and the numerator and denominator of that ratio, analogous to Equation 6.

Equation 11:

$$\Delta k / k = \Delta K / K - \Delta L / L = \Delta K / K - \eta$$

We will refer to Equation 11 as "Step 1."

Secondly, we note that (ΔK) is the net increase in the capital stock or net investment. Net investment is the difference between gross investment and depreciation, shown in:

Equation 12:

$$\Delta K = I - dep \times K$$

where (I) is gross investment.

We note that, in a closed economy, (I) in Equation 12 equals savings, or ($S = I$). We note further that ($S = s \times Y$). Combining these definitions and Equation 12, we can say:

Equation 13:

$$\Delta K = s \times Y - dep \times K$$

We will refer to Equation 13 as "Step 2."

Substituting (ΔK) from Step 2 in Equation 13 into Step 1 in Equation 11, we have:

Equation 14:

$$\Delta k = s \times y - (\eta + dep) \times k$$

Or,

$$\Delta k = \text{Sources of Capital} - \text{Uses of Capital}$$

In other words, if we hope to increase the amount of per capita capital (how much capital each worker works with), we must ensure that per capita savings (sources) exceed the uses of capital. Savings are a source of capital because savings are the part of output not consumed (or exported) in an open economy. Thus, the remainder can be used as capital. Depreciation (*dep*) is clearly a use of capital, but what about population growth (η)? Population growth is akin to the notion of shareholder dilution in finance; the larger the workforce (or, the greater the number of shares), the less capital with which each worker can work (or, the less valuable a fixed set of assets per share). Population growth dilutes the pool of capital; thus, in this sense, population growth is a use of capital (on a per capita basis) and has the same mathematical effect as depreciation.

Case Study 4.2: China's Population Controls

Over the course of the 1970s, China began a set of policies to slow the growth of its population. These included establishing a minimum age for marriage (22 for men, 20 for women)[*] and other family planning requirements.[5] By 1978–1979, the government's family planning policy (more commonly called the "one-child policy") was formalized, and it included—as its centerpiece—the limitation of one child per urban family. The policy was a response to the strain on resources (ranging from food and water to energy) caused by China's vast population and years of economic mismanagement.[†] By 1978, China's population had reached almost 1 billion people. Despite an overall decline in birth rates between the founding of the People's Republic of China in 1949 and 1978, China's population had actually grown during this period due to greater life expectancy (which, in part, reflected lower infant mortality rates). The family planning policies of 1978 were the government's response to the overall growth. Figure 4.4 depicts an overall slower rate of population growth beginning in 1978. From 1978 to 2017, the population grew at a compounded rate of about 0.009 (0.9 percent)—virtually identical to that of the United States in the same period. While much of the US population growth has been due to immigration, (recent Trump policies could impact this key source of growth), China's population growth reflects a number of exemptions to the one-child policy.[‡] Rural families and ethnic minorities, for example, were allowed to have more than one child. In addition, greater freedom to move from one part of the country to another led to the one-child rules being flaunted due to a lack of ability to track births. Originally, the policy was intended to last only one generation.

Figure 4.5 shows the initial steady state at point A (with a relatively high rate of population growth), then point B (in which population growth has slowed). At B, we have a higher level of per capita income in the long run. However, as with all steady states in the Solow framework, growth of overall output ($\Delta Y / Y$) equals growth in population (i.e., a slower rate of output growth). This is paradoxical: higher per capita income but slower long-run growth. The key to understanding this is to realize that countries that ultimately increase the ratio of capital (or other key factors) to the labor force have a higher standard of living. But when one key input (such as labor) grows more slowly, this eventually causes a bottleneck that reduces growth in output. In other words, over time, China's family planning policy will surely make the population better off, but it will just as surely force down China's current double-digit growth rates.

As often happens with well-intentioned government plans, unintended consequences can occur. A preference for male heirs has led to an imbalance in the population toward boys (https://bit.ly/3ftm3u3). In addition, as discussed in Chapter 5, the one-child policy has led to an ever-aging population in China. These outcomes have caused the government to rethink the program and, in recent years, to grant further exemptions. In 2013, the authorities began allowing parents who were themselves both single children to have two children. In 2015, a new two-child policy was introduced (implemented on 1 January, 2016) allowing all parents to have two children. By 2019, the government was outright encouraging parents to have more than one child. The upshot of these policies, from a Solow perspective, was to increase the uses of savings slope (η + *dep*) in Figure 4.5 and move the steady state back to point A.

In the above discussion, we have focused on China's overall population growth, however some significant sub-trends in the actual labor force are or will become important. First is China's increase in labor force participation in the industrial sector, which resulted from the nation's massive agricultural reforms. Second is China's changing population demographics from working age to old age—a shift in the dependency ratio that will reduce the availability of workers. In research, Donaldson et al. (2018) show, in an intertemporal setting, that the labor shortfall arising from the one-child policy has increased the ratio of capital to labor in China. This, in turn, has reduced the need for (in effect, crowded out) FDI. In the broader context of this chapter, FDI has been an important—if not the most important—source of past technological progress in China (Liu and Wang 2003). The one-child policy, then, might even be having a harmful impact on one of China's key goals: technological progress.

*This is the highest regulated marriage age in the world.

†One measure of this demand on resources is that, in China, the ratio of people to acres of arable land is about 6.6 times higher than in the United States.

‡There were an estimated 22 different exemptions (https://nyti.ms/2AJG7cO) to China's one-child policy.

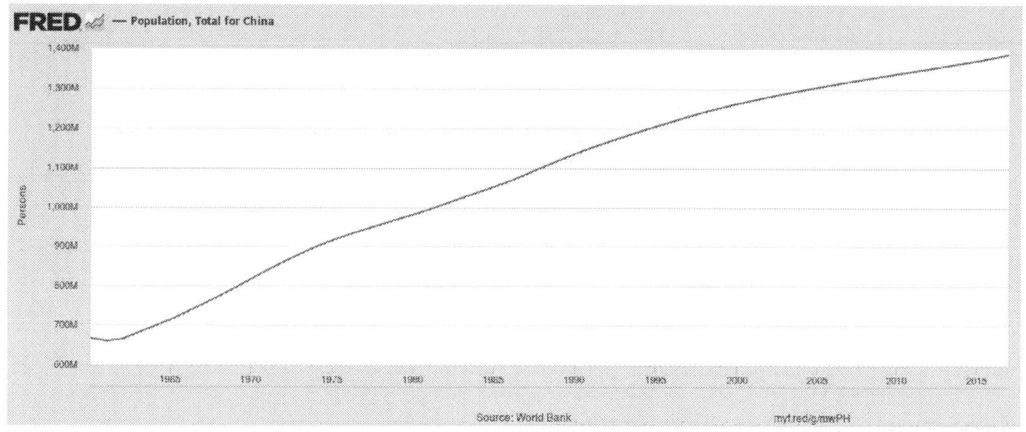

Figure 4.4 China's population started to level off at the imposition of a one-child policy beginning in 1977–1978.
Source: Author created based on FRED.

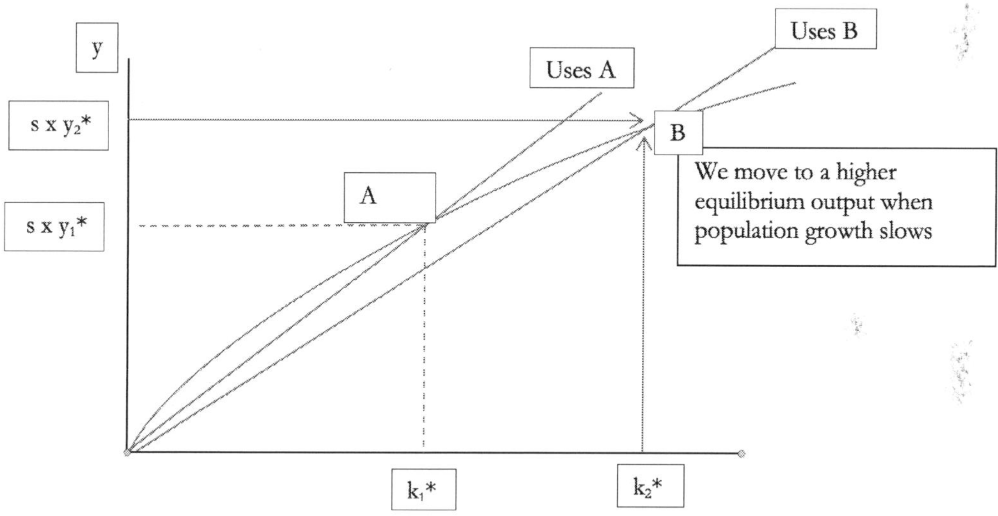

Figure 4.5 In the Solow framework, equilibrium per capita savings moves up from point A to point B when population growth slows (Uses A to Uses B); per capita income moves up in tandem with per capita savings.
Source: Author created.

With Equation 14 established, we can now find a steady state. The steady state is the point at which sources just equal uses in Equation 14 and (Δk = 0). We call this a "dynamic equilibrium" because it is a point at which the system is stable and toward which the economy gravitates. If (Δk = 0), then we can also see from Figure 4.6 that (y) will also be unchanging. The equilibrium is dynamic in the sense that, although (y) and (k) are constant, the variables that lie beneath (y) and (k) are still changing (i.e., (Y), (L), and (K)). Setting ($\Delta k = 0$) in Equation 14, we have the conditions for a steady state in our simple growth model, as seen in:

Equation 15:

$$s \times y = (\eta + dep) \times k$$

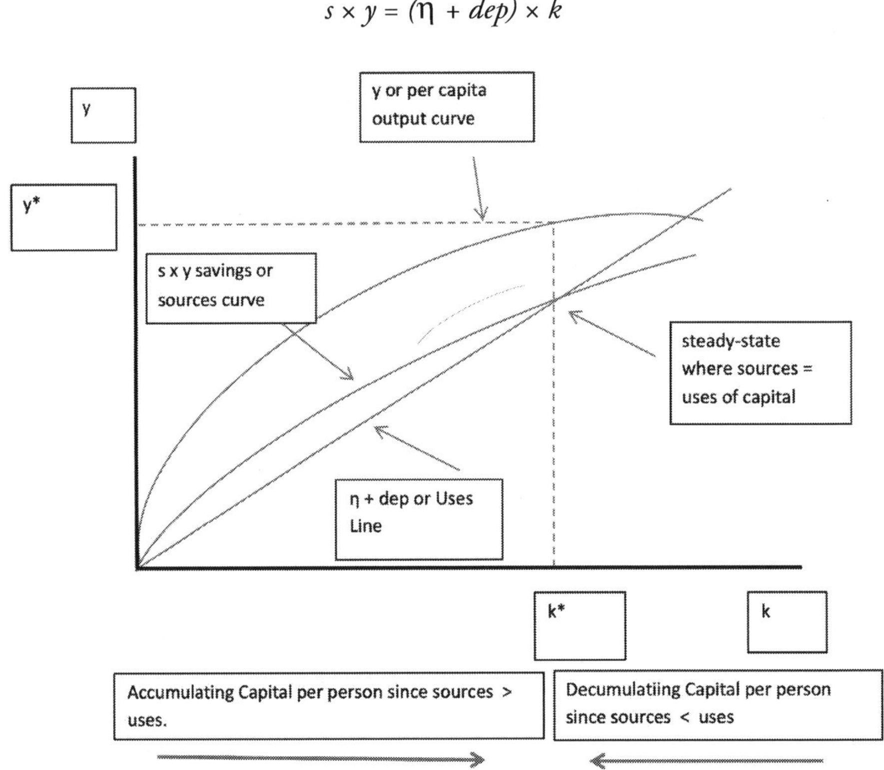

Figure 4.6 In the Solow framework, the steady state is where the sources of capital (savings) just equal their uses (population growth plus depreciation).
Source: Author created.

In Equation 15, we have a critical result, stating that the long-run destination of an economy is the point at which the sources of capital just equal its uses. Significantly, at that point, (y) and (k) will be unchanging; therefore, we have specific solutions for (y) and (k) which we can call (y^*) and (k^*). Figure 4.6 shows such a possible combination. Given that ($y = Y / L$) and ($k = K / L$), and that (y) and (k) are constant at (y^*) and (k^*), and that labor (L) is assumed to be growing at a constant rate (η), we reach another key result. At the steady-state equilibrium:

Equation 16:

$$\Delta Y / Y = \eta = \Delta K / K$$

That is, at the steady-state equilibrium (the point where we believe the economy will end up), the growth in output and capital stock will equal (or be constrained by) our assumed growth in the labor force (η). This key result is worth restating: assuming that a key input into the production process—such as labor (L)—is limited or grows within limits, then it is natural to assume that this will ultimately hinder economic growth. In other words, the economy cannot grow much faster over the long run than one of its key inputs.[6]

What drives this result in an economic sense? Three key factors drag an economy down to its steady-state equilibrium:

1. As more capital is accumulated in the face of constant growth in the labor supply, diminishing returns set in.
2. As an economy increases its capital stock, more of its sources of capital (savings) are used just to cover the depreciation of the ever-larger capital stock.
3. As an economy increases its per capita capital stock, each new entrant (labor force member) requires more capital just to maintain the same level of per capita income as the previous cohort of workers. A key use rises.

One critical assumption in this simple model of growth is the constant growth rate of the labor force. Despite the limitations of this assumption, we have some critical insights into the causes of very rapid economic growth and what, over time, constrains that growth.

Case Study 4.3: Why China Grows Faster Than the United States and Europe

We now have some basic tools for assessing why a country such as China can grow at nearly three to four times the rate of the United States for a number of years. Figure 4.6 shows the algebraic results of our analysis, depicting our sources (savings) and uses (population growth and depreciation) of capital lines. In addition, we also see our per capita income, or y-line. Recall that both the savings and income line are concave downward due to diminishing returns. The point at which the sources and uses line intersect is a key point: the steady state. Beneath this point of intersection lies Equation 16, in which growth in capital and output (total, not per capita) just equals population growth. This point represents dynamic equilibrium.

China, like all emerging economies, lacks the legacy of a large capital stock. Even though capital has steadily been added to the economy (especially infrastructure) since 1978, per capita capital still remains well below industrialized economies such as the United States. Figure 4.6 shows that China is well below its steady state (to the left of (k^*)). Since 1978, and continuing in the decades to come, China has been moving rightward in the direction of the steady-state point of ($s \times y^*$), (y^*), and (k^*). Thus, both (y) and (k) are growing.

Since (y) and (k) are (Y / L) and (K / L), respectively, and since (y) and (k) are rising, we can infer that (Y) and (K) are growing faster than the labor force (L). Thus, growth in capital, labor force participation, and technological progress will be the key drivers of growth. Meanwhile, as a mature economy, the United States is already at or near its steady state. Its growth has been dragged down by the forces of depreciation, diminishing returns, and the need to bequeath an ongoing high standard of living to each additional entrant into the population. In the United States, growth in the labor force and technological progress will be key drivers of growth.

Beyond China's greater ability to accumulate capital, other key factors come into play. Although China's savings rate is higher than that of the United States (as discussed in Chapter 5), and China has been creating, adopting, and adapting technology from all over the world (causing the y-curve and $s \times y$-curve to shift upward over time), its per capita savings is still close to one-third of the US rate. This is caused by China's larger population and the fact that it has not yet reached the steady state. In other words, although China's long-run savings curve is above that of the United States, it must move to the right along that curve for some time (likely several decades) before matching the per capita savings ratio of the United States. (See Figure 4.7) In the future, given a higher per capita savings rate and technological progress, China will accumulate capital (K) faster than the United States, and its growth rates will continue to be higher than those in the United States. It will take a long time, however, for China to be able to create as much capital per person as the US.

Table 4.4 illustrates the rapid buildup of capital in the industrial sector in China versus the United States following the 1978 reforms.* In China and the United States, growth in capital exceeded growth in output by about 1 percentage point between 1978 and 2017. As mentioned earlier, China's employment growth in the industrial sector represented a shift from agricultural to manufacturing. As a result, employment growth exceeded population growth for the same period. Another important factor was a demographic shift in China as more of the population reached working age in the 1980s and 1990s. In the United States, meanwhile, the constraints of the Solow steady state seem to be at work; both capital and labor are growing at relatively low rates.

In Table 4.4, we also examine the key ratios of capital per worker (K / L), output per capital (Y / K), and output per worker (productivity, or Y / L) in China and the United States. We note that:

$$Y / L = Y / K \times K / L$$

We see that the important measure of labor productivity (Y / L) has grown substantially (almost by a factor of 10) in China between 1978 and 2017, but productivity still remains far below that of the United States. What has spurred this growth? In China, the rapid growth of capital per worker (close to a 14-fold increase) has allowed workers to utilize more plant, property, and equipment (PP&E) and be more productive. But this has been offset by a substantial decrease in China's output per unit of capital (Y / K)—by nearly 45 percent; in other words, a sharp drop in the average return to capital. China's rapid buildup of capital has come at a steep cost—lower returns to capital and investors, or the nation's savers. We would expect the (Y / K) ratio to be consistently higher in China (or any emerging economy) than in the United States (or any developed economy) from a Solow perspective (see Figure 4.8); but, through the reform period up until 2003, and most recently in 2017, this ratio stood below that of the United States. We address this shortfall in the questions at the end of the chapter.

*The numbers differ between tables mainly because Table 4.1 shows weighted growth rates (by α and β) while growth rates in Table 4.4 are unweighted.

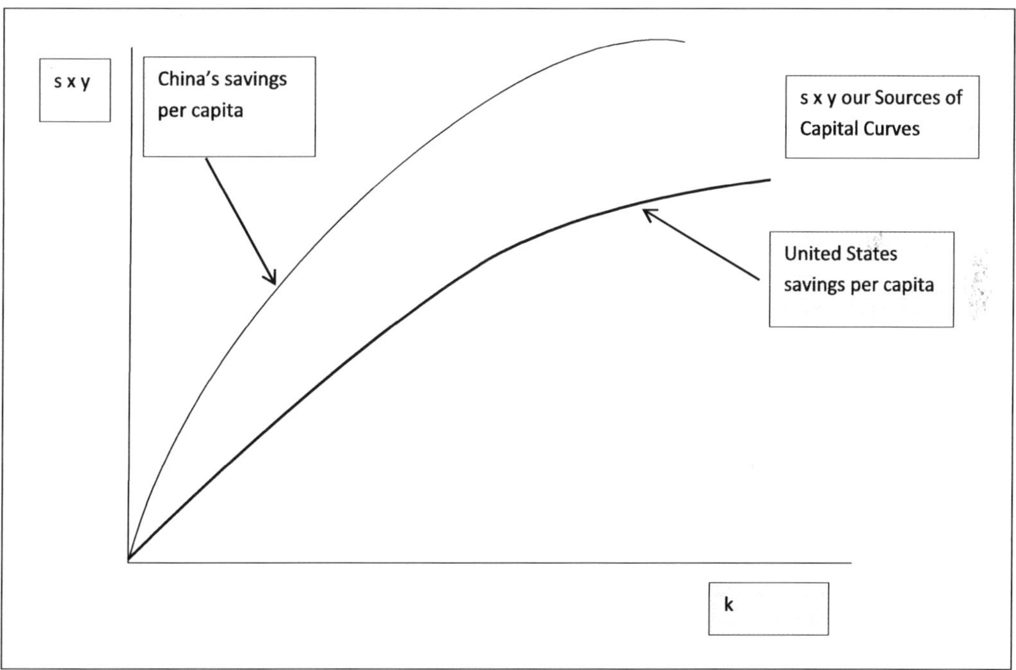

Figure 4.7 China's per capita savings is still well below the United States', even though its long-run savings curve is above that of the United States.
Source: Author created.

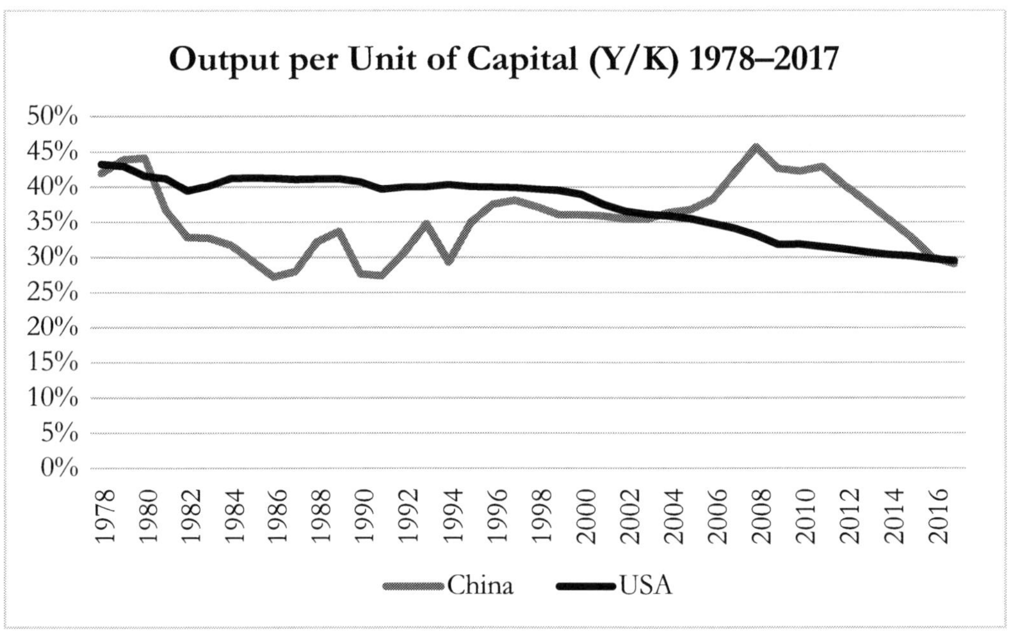

Figure 4.8 Output per unit of capital (asset efficiency) was higher in China beginning around 2005 but has since declined to US levels.
Source: Author created based on data from World Development Indicators and FRED. For capital estimates, we employ the perpetual inventory valuation method, with initial capital stocks and depreciation measured as averages, from Feenstra et al. (2015).

Real Growth Rates 1978–2017		
	China	**United States**
Output	7.8%	2.6%
Capital	8.8%	3.6%
Labor	1.8%	1.3%
Capital/Labor (K/L, Constant) (2014 USD)		
	1978	**2017**
China	3,759	52,086
United States	164,047	413,555
Output/Worker(Y/L, Constant) (2014 USD)		
	1978	**2017**
China	1,577	15,136
United States	70,904	122,045

Output/Kapital (Y/K ratio)		
	1978	2017
China	0.42	0.29
United States	0.43	0.30

Table 4.4 China has relied heavily on growth in the capital stock. Since 1978, capital stock growth has exceeded growth in real GDP. Consequently, output per worker in China has increased dramatically.
Source: Author created based on data from FRED, World Bank World Development Indicators, and author's own estimate for China's and the United States' capital stock, which assumes a 3.5 percent depreciation rate for both countries using a simple perpetual investment model.
Note: All data are measured in 2014 constant USD. Labor for the United States is defined as the civilian labor force, and for China as total employed workers.

Case Study 4.4: Are China's Provinces Converging?

One conclusion from Solow growth theory is that, if countries have access to similar technology (similar production functions), population growth rates, availability of savings, and factors of production, then they will all converge (over time) to similar levels of per capita income or development.* This conclusion is based on the notion that countries with low levels of capital grow faster than those with high levels of capital that have reached a steady state. Prima facie, this conclusion is false. The 20th century appears to show greater divergence between clusters of countries (i.e., Europe and North America versus. Southern Hemisphere economies, or Asian Tigers such as Singapore, South Korea, and China versus. Southeast Asian economies). Instead, economists speak of conditional convergence—that is, convergence that depends on factors including education levels, openness to trade, political systems, or even religious tradition such as Christianity, Hinduism, and so forth (Barro 1991; Sala-i-Martin 1997).

Regional convergence is more likely to occur at the state or provincial level because labor and capital tend to be mobile across state or provincial boundaries, and because access to technology is similar. Furthermore, many of the conditional factors—such as culture or religion—are similar within a country. Figure 4.9 shows convergence patterns based on US states since 1930 by measuring the standard deviation of per capita real income across states. As we can see, divergence by this measure has decreased from about 0.4 to 0.14. Much of this convergence is due to more rapid growth in per capita incomes in the southern United States. Other authors (DiCecio and Gascon 2008) suggest that US state convergence is far less important than the convergence of individual incomes in the country, irrespective of state boundaries. Their research points to urbanization in the United States (from rural to urban areas) as the key factor driving individual incomes to converge. Urbanization of the labor force allows for higher productivities, better paying jobs, and (in turn) individual income convergence.

By contrast, since the start of major economic reforms in 1978, China has seen increased divergence rather than convergence across provinces. This divergence has become particularly acute since 1990 as seen in Figure 4.10. There, we see two measures of per capita income dispersion across China's provinces—an inverse Sharpe ratio (the ratio of the standard deviation to the mean of provincial per capita income) from 1952–2017, and Gini coefficients over time for the set of 31 provinces.[7] Before reforms began, China's provincial income dispersion was relatively stable.

Clearly, the post-reform divergence indicates that not all provinces have benefitted equally from economic reform. Specifically, the urbanized eastern and southern seaboard benefitted from a resurgence of manufacturing, comparative advantages, and exports, while western China remained mired in outdated modes of agricultural production. For example, in Table 4.5, we compare one of China's richest provinces, Jiangsu (along the eastern seaboard) with Suzhou, a city in Jiangsu, and the rest of China and the United States. Within-province/city Gini coefficients show the greatest inequality in those locales with the highest per capita incomes. This suggests that, before any country can expect convergence, it may first see some regions (clusters) surge ahead. In other words, in order to converge, some successful pace setters must first take the lead.

While the pattern of divergence in post-reform China has been both dramatic and possibly troubling (in terms of social stability), there is good news on the horizon. The research of DiCecio and Gascon (mentioned earlier) suggests that urbanization has played a key role in creating individual economic convergence in the United States. The relaxation of China's *hukou* system (explained in other chapters), coupled with the massive urbanization now under way, suggests that China will eventually experience much greater convergence—at least at the individual level, and likely at the provincial level. Figure 4.10 does show some movement in that direction beginning around 2006.

[*]Even if savings rates differ across countries, access to international capital (global savings) allows for similar levels of per capita domestic product (though different per capita gross national incomes). An analogous concept from international trade theory states that workers in different countries with the same technology and labor force skillset will earn the same wage in a system of free trade in goods and services.

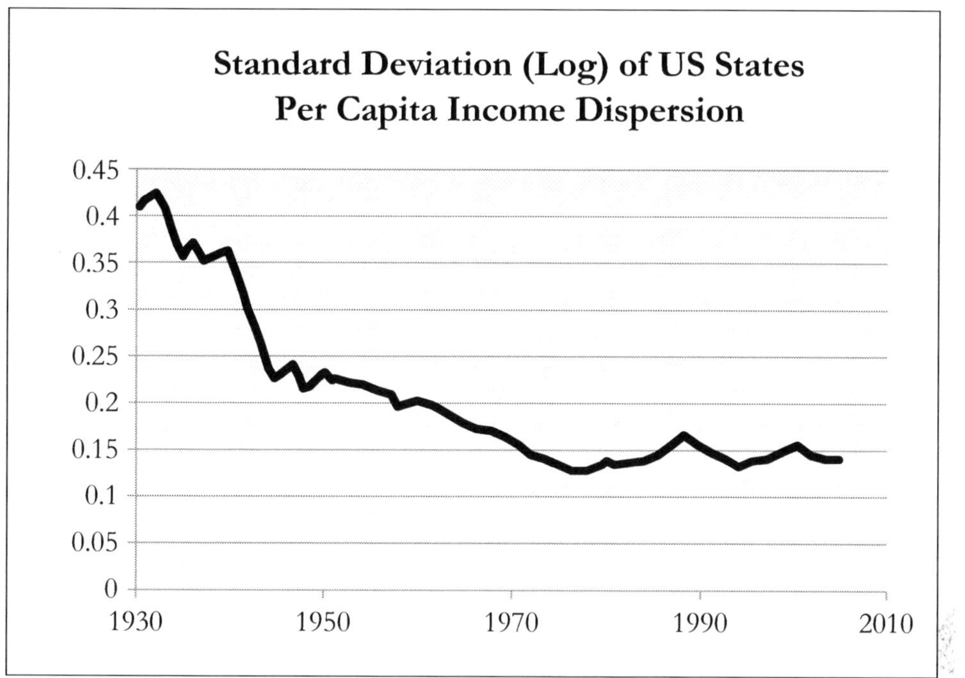

Figure 4.9 In the United States, income inequality across states has diminished tremendously in part due to the effect of urbanization.
Source: DiCecio and Gascon (2008).

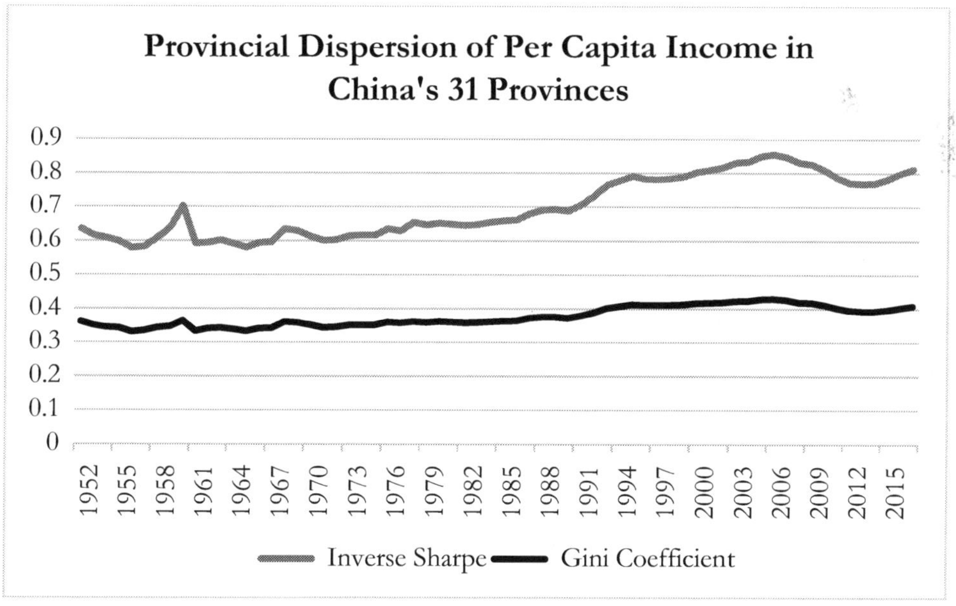

Figure 4.10 Income dispersion across provinces started to increase after the start of economic reform in China and dipped downward in 2006.
Source: Author created based on data from CEIC.
Note: Data represent the inverse Sharpe ratio by year for provinces and the Gini coefficient.

	2014 USD (Thousands)	
Location	**Per Capita GDP**	**Per Capita PPP**
Jiangsu	12.9	21.6
Suzhou	17.2	28.7
China	7.4	12.4
USA	54.4	54.4

Table 4.5 Greater income inequality across regions in China is highlighted by comparing Jiangsu with the rest of China in both current dollars and purchasing power parity PPP dollars.
Source: Author created based on data from FRED, World Bank Development Indicators and NBS.

Further Insights into Long-Run Growth

Within the Solow model described above, an economy stabilizes at a steady state (long-run equilibrium) when per capita income is constant. Given the experience of the industrialized economies, in which per capita income experiences positive growth even after these economies have matured, this result (from the base Solow framework) seems too limiting. In fact, in the Solow framework, long-run per capita income can grow if there is technological progress, that is, if ($\Delta A(t) / A(t) > 0$).

Up to now, we have assumed no technological progress, i.e., ($\Delta A(t) / A(t) = 0$). We can see this result in Equation 8, in which ($K(t) / K(t) - \Delta L(t) / L(t) = 0$) in the steady state. As long as ($\Delta A(t) / A(t) > 0$), we can still have per capita income growth in the long run (which is consistent with what actually happens in many countries). In this case, the growth rate of per capita income stabilizes (rather than the level of per capita income stabilizing) at the rate of technological progress.

Although this result gets us closer to the reality of long-run economic growth, it still does not answer the question: What determines technological progress? Some researchers (Romer 1994) have found the exogenous explanation still wanting, and they have attempted to find endogenous explanations for long-run growth in the steady state. One focus has been the possibility that the economy experiences increasing returns to scale (IRS). Figure 4.11 shows how capital is continuously accumulated during economy-wide IRS, which in turn trigger growth in per capita income. Other approaches rely on spillovers of knowledge creation. For example, as firms in a certain industry invest more in R&D, the entire industry benefits from the fruits of such research.

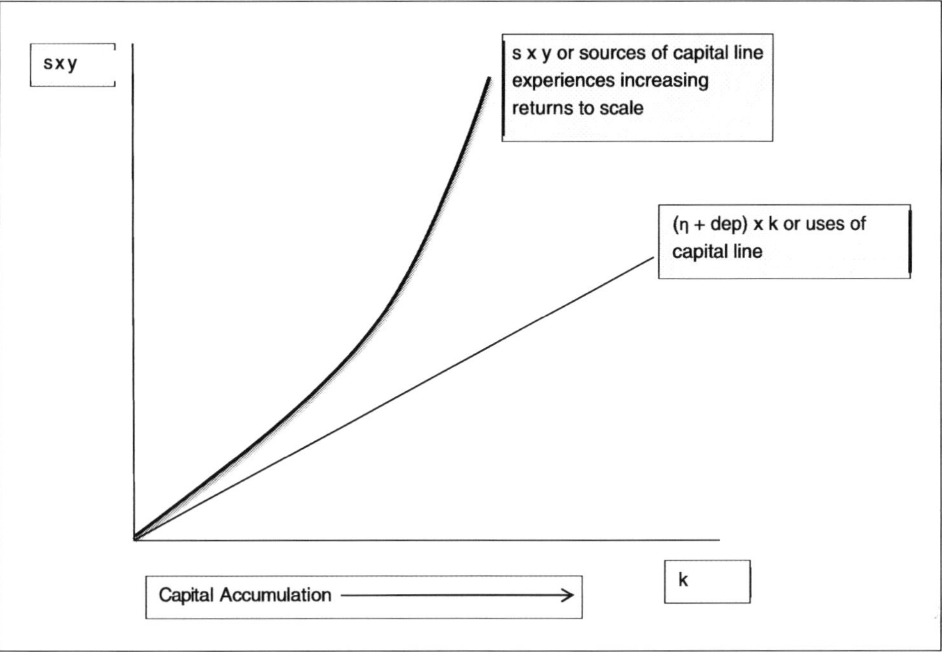

Figure 4.11 In the case of IRS, an economy can experience continuous economic growth for a prolonged period without being trapped at a steady-state level of per capita income. Source: Author created.

Case Study 4.5: Increasing and Decreasing Returns to Scale

After the death of Chairman Mao Zedong in 1976, China entered a brief period of high uncertainty regarding economic policy; should the nation continue following the same interventionist policies promoted by Mao, or should it move toward a more open economy based on market incentives? 1978 was a critical year in which economic reformers took the helm and (among other things) began opening the economy to FDI.

Under the theory of the firm, a common assumption is that firms first experience IRS, then CRS, then decreasing returns to scale (DRS). This is the basis for the U-shaped long-run average cost curve for firms in a competitive industry. What if we applied this theory to an entire economy instead of a single firm? Figure 4.12 shows a sources line, with all three returns to scale, in which the uses line intersects the sources line in the CRS region.

In this example, there are three possible steady states: point A (famine), point B (unstable/intermediate), and point C (feast). A country that initially finds itself at point B, if bumped slightly to the left (by an economic shock or by bad policy decisions), will tumble inexorably to a very bad steady state at point A. Uses will continuously exceed sources of capital, and things will only get worse. On the other hand, a country at point B that is bumped slightly to the right by a positive shock (for example, economic reforms) will move to a very good new steady state at point C. This simple example provides a basis for aggressive policy intervention in emerging markets, allowing them to achieve more feast-like steady states instead of heading into famine. Given China's unprecedented growth since 1978, Figure 4.12 suggests that good policy decisions were made at the time—and that a much worse alternative path was possible.

Other models with learning-by-doing technology (where workers learn from undertaking higher level tasks) posit that capital accumulation serves dual purposes: the traditional goal of serving as a factor of production, as well as—just as importantly—the goal of building up human capital. In other words, when new equipment is introduced into the workplace, workers are transformed through acquiring the new skills necessary to operate that equipment. Consider that a new computer is not only a new tool, but also a form of education for the user. By using this new technology, the worker is positively transformed. In the process, capital accumulation triggers an even greater impact than was envisioned in the traditional Solow framework, thus allowing positive per capita income growth in the long run.

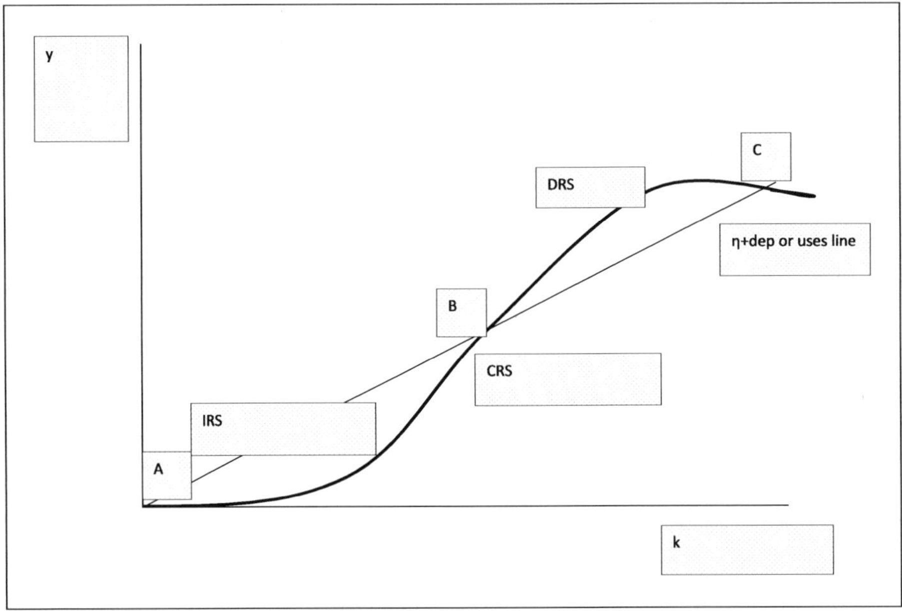

Figure 4.12 If countries were to resemble firms with IRS, CRS, and DRS, there would be two stable steady states in the economy and one unstable one. Depending on policies, a country might end up at point A, a state of famine, or point C, a state of feast.
Source: Author created.

The Organization for Economic Co-operation and Development (OECD) (https://bit.ly/361pvbM) estimates that while only 18 percent of the population of China received a tertiary education (post-high school education) in 2017, 67 percent in the cohort between 25 and 34 years of age will receive some type of tertiary training, compared to an average of 65 percent in OECD economies. Today, about 2 percent of those at the tertiary level in China study abroad, but they comprise about 23 percent of all foreign students in OECD countries. China's most recent Five-Year Plan targets a key area of tertiary education—vocational training and education. Overall, the data point to the great potential for learning-by-doing and technological progress in China.

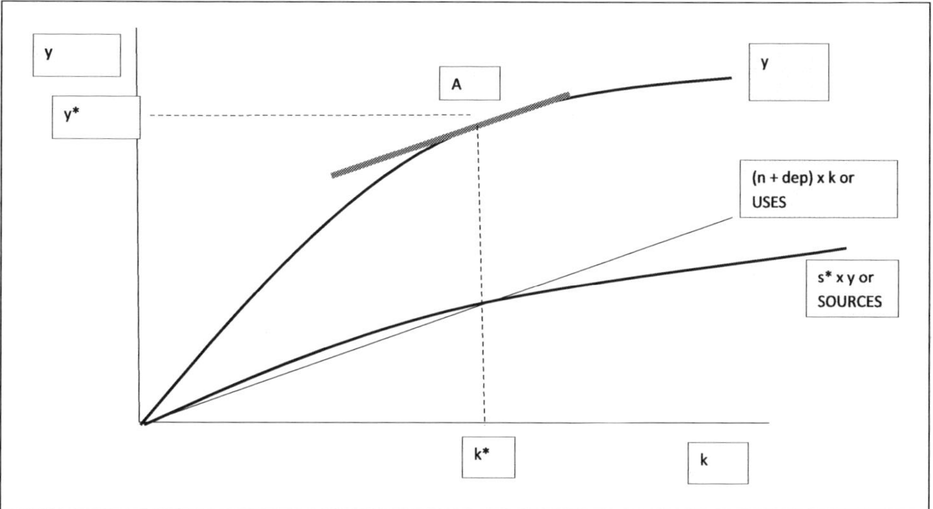

Figure 4.13 At point A the distance between per capita savings and per capita income is maximized; in other words, per capita consumption is maximized in the steady state—a desirable outcome.
Source: Author created.

Macro Finance Insight 4.1: Sustainable Growth I—National Returns on Capital

We can gain insight into which growth rates and returns on investment are sustainable over the long run by using either the Solow model or another simple model borrowed from finance: the Dupont model. Let's first examine sustainable growth and returns using the Solow model.

Figure 4.13 shows our standard framework at the optimal level of consumption. By "optimal level of consumption," we mean a particular savings rate and a corresponding steady state that maximizes steady-state consumption given all of our other parameters (e.g., technology, population growth rate, and depreciation rate). The steady state that maximizes consumption always corresponds to a point along the uses line ((η + *dep*) × *k*). Consumption will be measured as the difference between savings and income wherever our steady state ends up along the uses line. The maximum point of consumption (the largest gap between the uses line and (*y*)) will occur at the point where the slopes of the uses line (η + *dep*) and the *y*-curve (f'(*k*)) are the same. This occurs at point A in Figure

4.13. Maximum steady-state consumption ($y - c$) is measured as the vertical distance between the y-curve and the uses line.

We can now state that the optimal steady state in the Solow framework (or the point where consumption is maximized) occurs when:

Equation 17:

$$f'(k) = \eta + dep$$

or,

$$f'(k) - \text{dep} = \eta$$

However, ($f'(k) - dep$) in Equation 17 is simply the real return on capital. Thus, in the base Solow framework, the real return on capital (or assets or investments) is anchored and constrained by a country's population growth, just as GDP growth is locked in by population growth. This is an important benchmark for both China and the United States. Ultimately, the bottleneck for growth and returns is the growth of one key factor—the labor force—over the long run. The significance of this result cannot be overstated for a country such as China, in which (as discussed earlier) the labor force is shrinking. But this is a base case. Changing the analysis from the long-run overall economy to include the short-run specific industry analysis, we see other factors can come into play, specifically:

- Technological progress allows economic growth to surpass the population growth rate, breaking the bottleneck constraint both in the short and long run.
- Countries (including China), still far below the steady state, can see growth rates and returns surpass population growth for a long time period.
- Specific economic sectors (e.g., real estate or manufacturing) can reward investors with a risk premium, thus exceeding the economy's overall return on capital.
- Those parts of the economy that experience IRS need not be constrained by population growth.
- Monetary and fiscal policies can have an impact on both nominal and real returns in the short run.

Summarizing these results, we find that short-run real return on capital can be expressed as a function of,

Real Return = f'(per capita capital, population growth, distance from steady state, technological progress, economies of scale, risk, and monetary and fiscal policies)

Notwithstanding these other factors, it is important to keep in mind the benchmark case: the growth rate of an entire economy and the overall real return on capital are unlikely to stray far from each other or from the growth of a fundamental factor of production—its labor force.

Case Study 4.6: Cautionary Tale of Two Cities—Singapore vs. Hong Kong

As shown in Table 4.1, Table 4.3, and Table 4.4, a key driver for China's growth has been the accumulation of capital, which has been growing at double-digit rates in tandem with GDP. China has the world's largest share of GDP devoted to investment in PP&E and infrastructure. Is this necessarily good for China? We addressed a related issue in Chapter 2 on GDP accounting: the question of growth versus value creation. The experiences of Hong Kong and Singapore shed light on these questions. We will use our growth framework to highlight the key issues (Young 1992).

Both Hong Kong and Singapore are small island economies linked to greater Asia through China or Malaysia. Both are former British colonies with large ethnic Chinese populations. Both have a tradition of open international trade and capital mobility. Both have moved successfully from trade to manufacturing to high-end industries, including banking and finance. Finally, both economies have enjoyed extraordinary growth rates; between 1960 and 2010, Singapore's per capita real income grew at 5.5 percent, while Hong Kong's grew at 5.1 percent.

Despite these similarities, there are major differences between the two economies related to economic policy. Hong Kong has relied mainly on a laissez-faire economic policy. The city simultaneously built strong legal and regulatory frameworks and allowed industries and firms substantial leeway in terms of microeconomic choices. Singapore, meanwhile, played a more direct part in encouraging its industries—by targeting key areas for development and, at a macro level, requiring a high level of savings via a mandatory pension plan. In part, these differences reflect Singapore's later start in industrialization and its desire to catch up to Hong Kong.

These policy differences have led to dramatic differences in macroeconomic balances. For example, primarily due to its pension scheme requirements on savings, Singapore's savings rate has been at least 50 percent higher than Hong Kong's (45 percent of GDP versus 30 percent) since 1998 and up to 2010. By the late 1990s, Singapore's savings rate exceeded 50 percent of GDP—a rate that compares to recent levels in China. The flip-side of the savings coin was that Singapore's investment shares reached nearly 40 percent of GDP, compared to "only" 20 percent of GDP in Hong Kong. In the growth theory context, Hong Kong achieved similar growth to that of Singapore through technological progress, while Singapore relied heavily on the raw accumulation of capital. Meanwhile, per capita annual national income reached USD 56,000 in Singapore and USD 48,000 in Hong Kong; both countries appear to be close to the same steady state.

Figure 4.14 provides a stylized, bare bones description of these differences. To highlight the differences in savings rates and technology, we assume that both countries have similar rates of depreciation and population growth; Singapore shows higher savings, while Hong Kong shows greater total factor productivity. On balance, we assume the two effects offset one another such that they have the same sources ($s \times y$) curve but different per capital output curves, (y).

At point A, we see identical steady states in terms of capital stocks. But one key difference lies in the measured levels of per capita consumption: ($y - (s \times y)$), or output minus savings. In Hong Kong, the difference at the steady state is (point C – point A), while in Singapore, the distance is (point B – point A). Clearly, Hong Kong enjoys much greater consumption than does Singapore, despite sharing the same steady state. Why is this? Again, by relying so heavily on capital growth rather than efficiency improvements, Singapore suffers from diminishing returns, depreciation, and the need to bequeath to the next generation.

Several studies support these results. An examination of returns to capital and corresponding returns to public pensions shows Singapore as lacking when compared to other developed economies worldwide. By the 1990s, the Singaporean government had recognized the problem of overreliance on a rapid buildup of domestic capital. Singapore's Central Provident Fund (its mandated savings and pension plan) has increasingly looked beyond its borders for international investment opportunities, particularly in China. While this reduces the problem of diminishing returns, the other two problems still remain.

The lessons for China should be clear: Relying too heavily on savings and investment as vehicles for growth creates problems later, as an economy moves closer to its steady state.* In particular, if savings grow too large, consumption—a key measure of economic well-being—falls too low. In this scenario, we see a merging of two of China's Five-Year Plan goals: the need to stimulate short-run demand via consumption and the need to accomplish long-run economic well-being.

*Economies, including Hong Kong and northern European countries such as Germany, have likely found the "Goldilocks" levels of consumption and savings. Their savings rates are above the sub-optimal levels of the United States and other parts of Europe, but below those supra-optimal levels of Singapore and China.

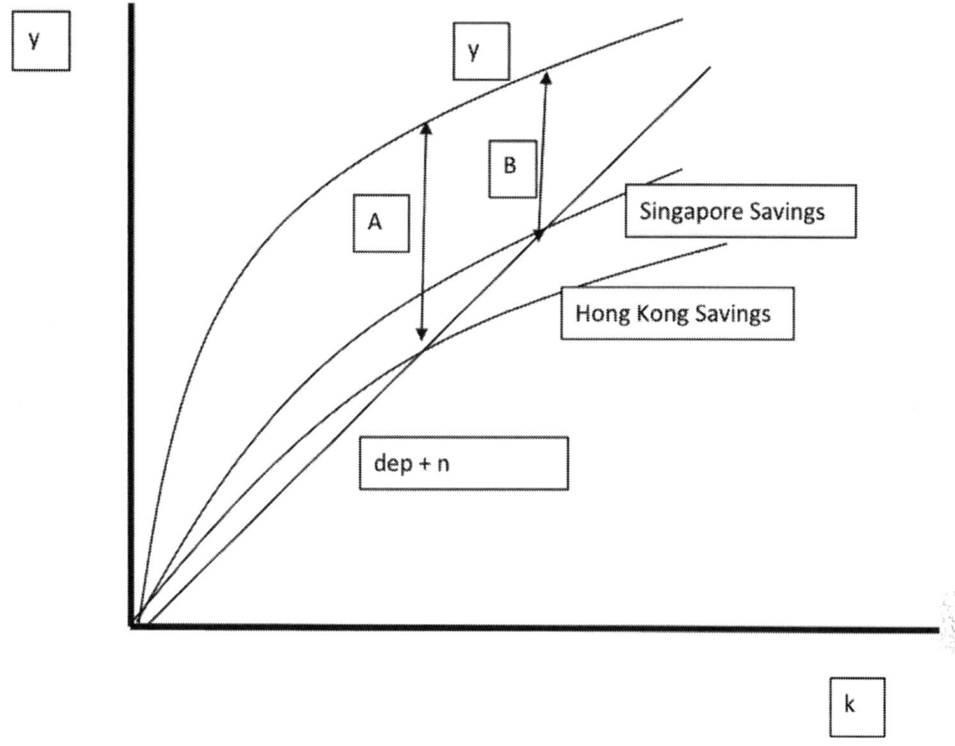

Figure 4.14 Assume Singapore and Hong Kong have the same access to technology, population growth rates, and rates of depreciation. The only difference, we assume, is that Singapore has a much higher savings curve than Hong Kong. Even though Singapore will achieve a higher steady-state (*y*) and (*k*), its steady-state consumption (gap A) will be smaller than Hong Kong's (gap B).
Source: Author created.

Part II: Financial Basis for Long-Run Quality Growth

Part I of this chapter dealt mostly with the question of raw economic growth without looking deeply into the question of the quality of growth. In Chapter 2, for example, we discussed the case of General Motors, a company whose production and investment prior to the Great Financial Crisis (GFC) contributed to growth in United States GDP but did not create quality growth or sustainable growth. Rather, General Motors destroyed value and ultimately required government support to survive. In Part II, we apply a finance-based approach to our country-growth analysis in order to analyze the quality of growth more carefully. First, we examine the equilibrium relationships between returns on capital and cost of capital. Next, we discuss measuring the return and cost of capital independently.

Using ROIC and WACC to Evaluate the Quality of Growth

Two related formulas from financial valuation link together a firm's weighted average cost of capital (WACC): the return on invested capital (ROIC) and the growth rate of operating profits (*g*). Equation 18 and Equation 19 below show that a firm only creates value (economic profits, defined as profits above and beyond the opportunity cost of capital):

Equation 18:

$$\text{Economic Profits} = (\text{ROIC} - \text{WACC}) \times \text{Invested Capital}$$

Meanwhile, Equation 19 links long-run firm value with ROIC, WACC, and firm growth, Where operating profits are equivalent to earnings before interest and taxes,

Equation 19:

$$\text{Long-Run Firm Value} = \text{Operating Profits} \times \left(1 - \frac{g}{\text{ROIC}}\right) / (\text{WACC} - g)$$

In Equation 18 and Equation 19, we see that if ROIC is high and the cost of capital (WACC) is low, then the firm's value is larger.[8] If these conditions are met, growth will cause economic profits to be positive and increase long-run firm value. Importantly, however, if the cost of capital is greater than the returns to capital, then growth actually destroys value, and the firm's long-run value is negative.[9] As we emphasize many times throughout this text, high growth rates do not imply value creation. Only when ROIC exceeds opportunity cost does growth lead to value creation. And even this assumes that the ROIC is truly measuring value—something we discuss below.

In terms of a country's economy, Equation 18 and Equation 19 show that economic growth is good if it occurs when the opportunity cost of growth (foregone consumption) is less than the returns from investments currently undertaken. Later, we will present estimates of WACC and ROIC at a national level. In this chapter we mostly discuss quality of growth as a financial measure where (ROIC > WACC). In other areas of finance and economics, the same condition is expressed in other ways:

Equations 20:

$$\text{Extra Benefit} \geq \text{Extra Cost}$$

$$\text{Marginal Revenue From Adding Capital} \geq \text{Marginal Cost of Adding Capital}$$

Or,

$$MP_K \times \text{Price of Output} \geq \text{Rental Cost of Capital}$$

Or,

$$MP_K \geq \text{Real Rental Cost of Capital}$$

Or, equivalently,

$$\text{ROIC} \geq \text{WACC (expressed in real terms)}$$

In other words, ROIC is equivalent to the marginal product of capital (MP_K).

Finally, rearranging Equation 4 from our Solow accounting framework:

Equation 21:

$$\Delta A(t) \,/\, A(t) = (\Delta Y(t) \,/\, Y(t)) - (\alpha \Delta K(t) \,/\, K(t) + \beta \Delta L(t) \,/\, L(t))$$

The right-hand side of this equation is the growth in output minus the weighted growth in inputs. If the right-hand side is positive for a prolonged period, we will have quality of growth by definition. How might we achieve this?: By having technological progress (the left-hand side of Equation 21) be positive for prolonged periods. The relationship tells us that, if we can find cost-effective ways of utilizing our inputs (technological progress), then we will have quality of growth.

Measuring ROIC and the Cost of Capital à la Wicksell

Figure 4.15 and Figure 4.16 show Swedish economist Knut Wicksell's explanation for how an economy-wide interest rate is determined through the flow of available savings and investment (the supply of loanable funds and the demand for loanable funds) in a closed economy. (The equilibrium interest rate is described as the natural or long-run interest rate.)[10] We could think of the natural rate as the base rate that determines the equilibrium cost of capital and returns on investment in each country. The equilibrium (i.e., the intersection of the savings and investment curves) shows the natural or base rate in a closed economy for each country. The solid line depicts identical equilibrium rates in economies that are fully integrated to international capital flows. In Figure

4.15 (which corresponds to the US situation), the base rate exceeds the integrated world rate (point A > point B). In Figure 4.16 (which represents China) the base rate is below the world natural interest rate, or the integrated rate (point C < point D), illustrating the hypothetical rate in an economy completely open to international capital flows. By implication, the base rate is higher in the United States than in China. How can we know if these two figures accurately reflect the relative rates between the two economies?

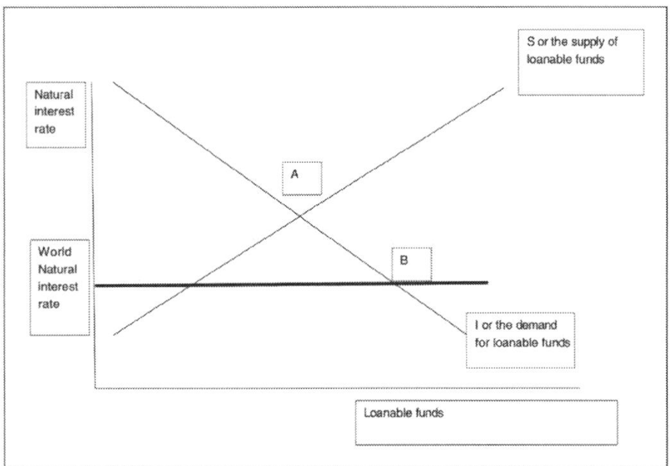

Figure 4.15 A closed economy would have an equilibrium between national savings and investment at point A. In an open economy such as the United States where there are substantial capital inflows, the world borrowing rate of point B obtains well below what the cost of capital would be if the US did not have access to foreign capital.
Source: Author created.

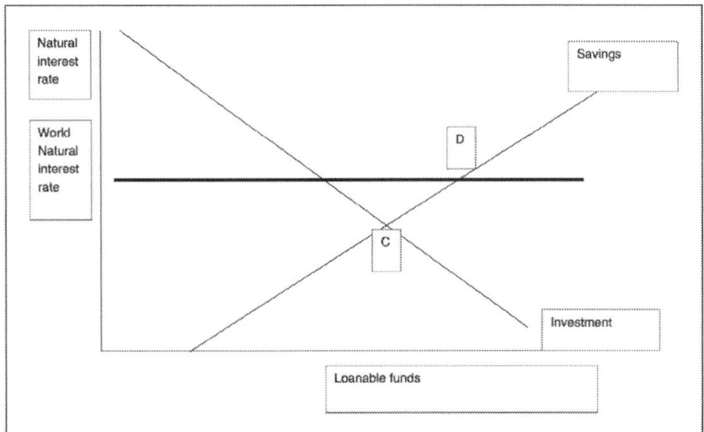

Figure 4.16 In an economy such as China (where capital controls still exist) the equilibrium is somewhere between point C and point D. China is a net lender to the rest of the world, and saving exceeds investment.
Source: Author created.

Recall that the gap between savings and investment represents how much each country is borrowing or lending to cover a current account surplus or deficit. Since the United States is running a current account deficit with China (the gap between savings and investment at some world rate) and China is running a complementary current account surplus, we can infer that the US base rate is above the world rate, while China's is below that rate.

One critical assumption in the Wicksellian approach, however, is that we have market-based decision making regarding capital flows. In fact, capital flows from China to the United States have been traditionally invested in US Treasury instruments at the behest of China's State Administration for Foreign Exchange and the People's Bank of China (PBC). The Wicksellian model is incomplete when examining China and the United States. This analysis does show, however, that current account deficits must be financed; and, when financed, they tend to push interest rates lower than they would otherwise be in the borrowing country and higher than otherwise in the lending country.

In summary, China's base rate for cost of capital and investment returns would be lower than the United States' if China were truly closed in terms of lending and borrowing internationally. The fact that China can lend abroad (specifically to the United States) acts as a relief valve, which has, in recent years, kept China's overall interest rates higher and US rates lower. Despite China's enormous demand for loanable funds (via its vast investment effort), its supply of savings is even more substantial. In fact, a large portion of those savings find their way into the US market for loanable funds—especially funds representing US government credit demands. What Wicksell tells us is that there are forces at work (international capital flows) that would cause costs of capital to move toward each other in China and the United States. This equilibrating mechanism plays out in terms of our discussion of the returns to and costs of capital below.

Measuring Returns on Capital

We now examine the ROIC, which corresponds to the demand for loanable funds or the investment curve.

The Solow Approach and ROIC

One approach to measuring the return on capital economy-wide is to use Equation 4 in the Solow accounting framework itself. We have,

Equation 22:

$$\Delta Y(t) \,/\, Y(t) = \Delta A(t) \,/\, A(t) + \alpha \Delta K(t) \,/\, K(t) + \beta \Delta L(t) \,/\, L(t)$$

Maintaining the usual assumption of CRS, we have ($\beta = (1 - \alpha)$). Recall that the coefficients α and $(1 - \alpha)$, when summed in Equation 22, represent either: (1) returns to scale (1 in this case, since the sum of α and $(1 - \alpha)$ is 1); (2) elasticities of output with respect to input; or, (3) shares of national income received by the factors of production (capital and labor). Using interpretation 2, we see in:

Equation 22a:

$$\alpha = (\Delta Y(t) / Y(t)) / \Delta K(t) / K(t)$$

which in turn can be rearranged as:

Equation 22b:

$$MP_K = \alpha \times Y(t) / K(t)$$

in which MP_K is our gross marginal product of capital—or, more importantly, our gross return on capital in a competitive market. With a little effort, we can determine the gross return to capital (since Equation 22 corresponds to gross domestic output), then subtract out depreciation to determine the real return to capital.[11] Note that we also need to know the output-to-capital ratio. We take this approach in Figure 4.17a for returns to total capital in each country (after subtracting out depreciation). United States returns have gradually declined over the years, and they have stood below China's over the past two decades. Meanwhile, China's returns surged between 2000 and 2008 (above 20 percent) but have since declined to the point they are now (around 10 percent), close to the United States. Figure 4.17b measures the ratio of net operating surplus to capital for China and the United States. This is a GDP-based measure of returns (national income approach) for businesses. Though showing consistently higher returns in China for the post-reform period, we also see a steady decline in returns post-GFC in this data. The more dramatic shifts in China's returns after the GFC reflect a combination of:

- Changing shares of labor income relative capital owners' income
- Rapid capital accumulation (which results in lower returns to capital)
- Changes in the profitability (part of national savings) of enterprises

Figure 4.17a Two effects have reduced returns in China relative to the US: Labor is capturing a larger share of national income, and there has been a surge in gross investment (and, in turn, capital) in China since the GFC.
Source: Author created based on World Bank World Development Indicators WDI, CEIC, FRED, and Chong-En Bai et al. (2006).

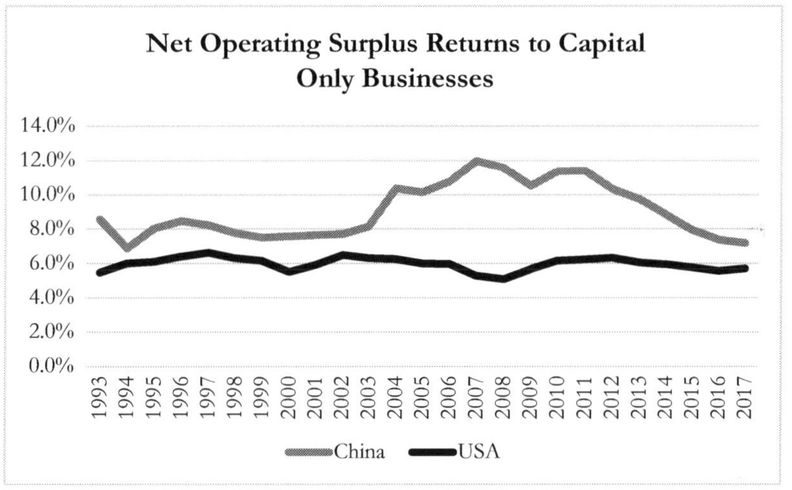

Figure 4.17b Business savings (operating surplus) for enterprises in China and the United States account for almost all of national savings. In China, this is because of the high level of corporate savings; in the United States, the low level of personal savings.
Source: Author created based on BEA (https://bit.ly/2Z8azHF) and CEIC.
Note: Net operating surplus is calculated by both China and the United States in their income presentation of their national income and product accounts. It includes corporate profits, rental income, proprietor's income, other income, and dividend payments income (excluding depreciation, government net income, and taxes, but including net interest receipts/payments of these various businesses). Because of data limitations, China's operating surplus ratio is calculated on a net operating surplus to net domestic savings basis. US figures are calculated on a gross operating surplus to gross domestic savings basis. Data for China are based on provincial aggregates, which only begins in 1993.

Bai, Hsieh, and Qian (2006) use a similar approach to estimate returns to capital in China between 1978 and 2005. For returns to all capital excluding urban residential housing, they find gross returns through the 1990s to range between 30 and 35 percent. In later years (1998–2005) those returns decline to the 20–25 percent range. When inventories are added in to the above capital stock measure and various taxes are taken into account, returns diminish to the 10–15 percent range, a range not too different from those found in Figure 4.17a. The difference in returns highlights an area in which Chinese companies could continue to make improvements: the management of working capital, especially inventories.

Actual Profits and ROIC

An economy-wide business estimate for the United States, based on actual survey data (https://bit.ly/2LvqvLM) of US non-financial corporations' profits and capital employed, shows after-tax real returns of around 8 percent in recent years, as seen in Figure 4.18—still below the estimated returns in China (Figure 4.17a and Figure 4.17b).[12] These figures exclude returns to infrastructure, residential housing, and the agricultural sector, and so they are not fully comparable to those in Figure 4.17a. In summary, regarding returns to the overall capital stock, China's returns appear to have been higher than the United States' since 1997, but they have moved closer to the United States' returns post-GFC.

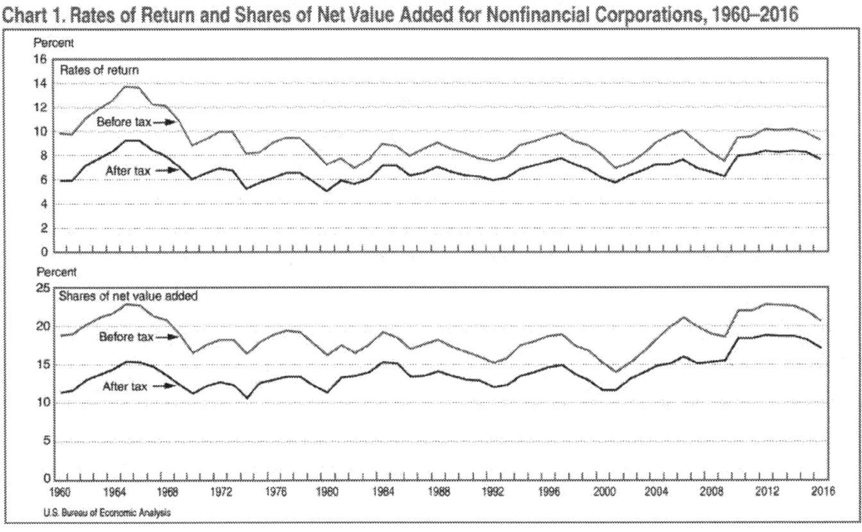

Figure 4.18 United States pre-tax returns for non-financial corporations have hovered in the 8–10 percent range in recent years. When using GDP data (an alternate approach), estimates for US returns are higher by several percentage points.
Source: US Commerce Department, Survey of Current Business (https://bit.ly/2LvqvLM).

Macro Finance Insight 4.2: Return to Capital—ROIC and ICOR

In looking at questions of the efficiency of resource utilization and diminishing returns to capital, a common ratio used in the macro-growth literature is the ICOR (the incremental capital to output ratio). More formally:

$$\text{ICOR} = (\text{Real Investment} / \text{Real GDP}) / \text{Real GDP Growth}$$

Or more intuitively:

$$\text{ICOR} = \Delta K / \Delta \text{GDP} = 1 / \text{Marginal Productivity of Capital}$$

The ICOR ratio describes how much additional capital is required in order to increase real GDP—all measured in constant dollars. The ratio is, in effect, the inverse of the marginal productivity of capital measured at a national level. The lower the ratio, the more likely that additional units of capital will be value-creating. Thus, it is simply the inverse of our formula in Equation 22b, which is charted in Figure 4.17a.

ROIC as a Measure of Returns Compared to ICOR

A technical (and literal) rearrangement of the ICOR is the ROIC, which we have already introduced as a concept borrowed from finance. We showed in Equation 20 that the ROIC is equivalent to the marginal productivity of capital (MP_K). This implies that

$$\text{ICOR} = 1 / \text{ROIC}$$

We note that neither ICOR nor ROIC, standing alone, tell us very much about value creation and quality of economic growth. In Equation 18 and Equation 19, we have already shown that we need to compare ROIC to the cost of funds within society—WACC in a corporate context, or a broad measure of WACC in society's context. ICOR, in the absence of some measure of the cost of capital (WACC) within a country (particularly countries such as China that are by and large isolated from international capital markets) gives us virtually no insight into value creation or economic returns.

Cross-Country Comparisons and ICOR

In the short run, country-to-country comparisons present challenges because an ICOR that is considered efficient for one country may not be efficient in another. In equilibrium, a country with high wage costs relative to low labor productivity will use more capital in production and, in turn, have a higher ICOR and a lower ROIC. Two countries, then, may have identical production technologies (be equally efficient) but have different returns due to differing factors of production intensities.* This would suggest that the ICOR and its inverse may be more useful in a time series than in a cross-sectional (cross-country) context. But, over the long run, with free movement of capital, ROICs and ICORs would tend to be equal across countries, which would then allow for cross-country comparisons. All of the above discussion remains with the caveat that we still need to take into account the cost of capital in each country—not just its returns—when discussing economic efficiency.

*This would be true if technologies differed between countries, and if trade in goods across borders were impeded. The Heckscher-Ohlin theorem (from international trade) implies that—in the long run—marginal productivities and returns will be equalized between trading countries due to free trade and identical technologies.

Case Study 4.7: High Speed Rail in China

Li et al. (2018) detail the impressive development of China's high-speed rail system (HSR) since 2008. China's HSR is one of the hallmarks of its remarkable economic development, and it leaves a lasting impression on those foreigners lucky enough to enjoy a journey on one of its trains. The trains travel at a maximum speed of about 155 miles per hour, compared to the conventional train ride in China of around 30 miles per hour. Virtually all cities with a population over 500,000 now have access to the HSR system. With annual growth in system miles of about 20 percent, and passenger growth double that, a natural question to ask is whether that growth has had a positive impact on HSR-connected cities' GDP. The authors, in effect utilizing an ICOR approach, find that it does.

One thing that we can learn from this type of research is just how complicated the question of value creation is. While GDP has grown in response to HSR investment, does that necessarily mean that value has been created? At one level, as discussed in the context of General Motors in Chapter 2, investment in HSR itself is measured as a part of GDP. As a result, using GDP growth itself (on a year to year basis) to measure ROIC raises logical issues. For example, a single company would not measure its capital expenditure as part of its own revenues and value-added. To do so at the national/macro level would be a mistake. Secondly, as we discussed in Macro Finance Insight 4.2, ICOR itself tells us very little. We also need to gauge the opportunity cost of capital to understand whether the extra revenues from additional HSR investments exceed their capital costs (WACC). No doubt the authors are correct in pointing out a bump in GDP due to HSR investment. And certainly, China's train system has expanded commerce and facilitated travel for both business and leisure. The question of value creation is a different one, however. At the margin, have the benefits outweighed the costs?

A Broader Measure of ROIC: The Dupont Model and Macro Aggregates

We can implement the Dupont model (expressed below in Equation 23 and discussed in Macro Finance Insight 4.3) using macroeconomic data for each country. This will help us decompose the returns for China described in Figure 4.17a and Figure 4.18. Recall that we proposed using national savings as the counterpart for company income and GDP as a measure of sales in our macro finance approach. Estimates for a nation's assets are based on annual measures of investment in each country and models of perpetual depreciation. Both the US Bureau of Economic Analysis (BEA) and China's National Bureau of Statistics (NBS) provide sufficient data to arrive at an estimate for the national capital stock, or producible assets: Equation 23 provides the firm-level relationship:

Equation 23:

$$\text{ROIC} = \text{Net Income} / \text{Assets} = \text{Sales} / \text{Assets} \times \text{Net Income} / \text{Sales}$$

Or in words,

$$\text{ROIC} = \text{Asset Efficiency} \times \text{Profit Margin}$$

In the context of macro analysis, we can tweak the corporate finance concept (Equation 23) into a more appropriate form for our purposes, as:

Equation 24:[13]

$$\text{ROIC} = (\text{GDP} / \text{Fixed Capital}) \times (\text{Net Savings} / \text{GDP})$$

Equation 24 expresses ROIC in terms of the amount of capital needed to produce output (the first term on the right-hand side in the equation) and the profit margin equivalent, where net savings is savings after depreciation.[14] The ROIC being measured is then (net savings / fixed capital). Unlike more common measures (i.e., in the Solow formula, or ICOR), the numerator contains a savings measure rather than a GDP measure. We suggest here that, when analyzing the returns to an economy, factoring in savings is more appropriate in terms of finance, accounting, or policy-making.

At a financial and accounting level, Equation 23 measures corporate profits, or net income. When shifting to a national level, that same measure is included in national savings. To be consistent, we should also include corporate savings as an appropriate measure for national returns. But this also suggests that we should include the profits of households (or what is described in national income accounts as "personal savings"). We consider that, although individuals do earn income, the portion of income used for consumption is clearly the counterpart to a firm's cost of doing business and needs to be netted out. In other words, a household's expenditures on food, shelter, and transportation are all inputs into the household production function, and that production function yields a net return—savings.[15] We thus include corporate savings, personal savings, and government savings (dis-savings), as a measure of a macro economy's returns. Using savings as a measure of return is consistent (in an accounting sense) with the accumulation of capital for the firm and, more broadly, the accumulation of wealth for the entire economy.[16]

In elaborating further on the parallels between profitability and national savings, we must recognize that corporate income already makes up more than half of the national savings in both China and the United States (as discussed in Chapter 5). Government savings (deficits or surpluses) are also already included. Including personal savings is a natural extension of the accounting concept. Some economists might argue that we should look at disposable personal income (DPI) as the appropriate counterpart to value creation or net income in addition to the corporate and government savings. Because economics is the study of how to match society's unlimited wants with its limited resources, some would argue that DPI can be considered the means to that end and therefore would be a more reasonable measure of returns.

But DPI is a different metric from savings; savings is the difference between revenues and costs, while DPI is more closely aligned with revenues (which is already included in Equation 23). One interpretation is that personal savings can be included as a measure of value creation, given the assumption that the goal of a household is to create residual value. If our goal is wealth creation (the building up of equity), then all savings in the nation—business, government, and personal—must be consistently taken into account. In Chapter 5, in particular, we highlight why this view is more consistent with Chinese rather than Western households.

Figure 4.19 and Figure 4.20 decompose Equation 23 into asset efficiency (output per unit of capital) and savings as a share of GDP (a profit margin measure). Consistent with our approach, the ratio of output to fixed capital in China gradually rose in the initial 17 years of reform, but it peaked in 2008, and since then it has declined close to the United States' level. From a Solow perspective, we would expect average output per unit of capital to be higher in China (the slope of a ray from the origin in Figure 4.3 would have a higher slope for China than the United States). For the years 2004–2016, this is true, but from1978 to 2004 it was not. Likely explanations for this difference are explored in the problems at the end of this chapter.

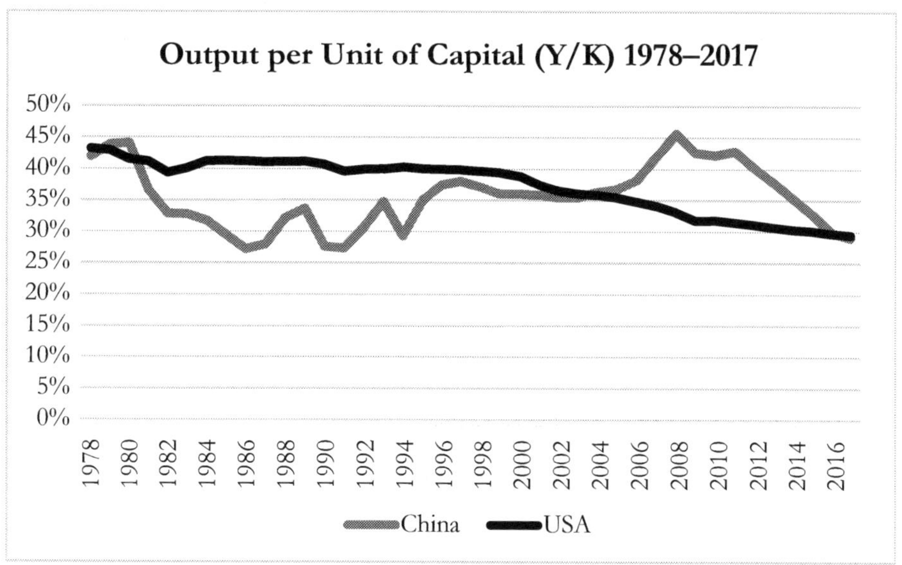

Figure 4.19 Output per unit of capital (asset efficiency) was higher in China beginning around 2005. but it has since declined to US levels.
Source: Author created based on data from World Development Indicators and FRED. For capital estimates, we employ the perpetual inventory valuation method, with initial capital stocks and depreciation measured as averages, from Feenstra et al. (2015).

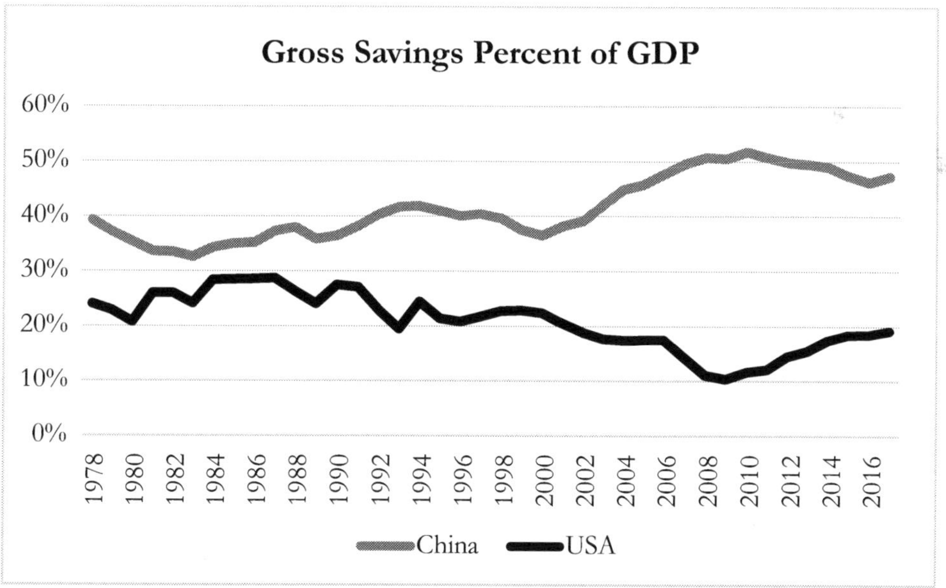

Figure 4.20 Gross savings as a share of GDP—which includes household, business, and government savings—has consistently been higher in China than in the US, and the gap widened in the late 2000s.
Source: Author created based on data from World Development Indicators and FRED.

Examining the net domestic savings to output ratio, we see that China's ratio has been substantially higher than the United States' since 1991, but it has been declining since the start of the financial crisis. Given what we see in Figure 4.19 and Figure 4.20, we can now better explain the decline in returns (the ROIC or marginal productivity of capital) that started in 2008.

- There was a surge in the capital stock beginning around 2008 that continued in the decade to follow.
- The savings rate peaked in 2008 and has steadily declined.
- Capital's share of national income began to decline in 2007–2008.

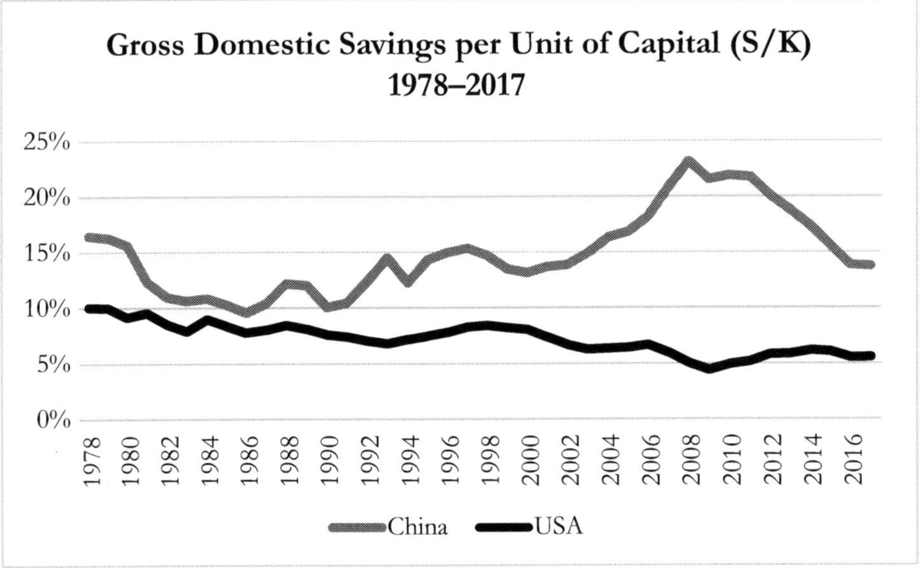

Figure 4.21 Gross savings to capital is consistently higher in China than the United States reflecting, in part, higher household savings.
Source: Author created based on data from World Development Indicators and FRED. For capital estimates, we employ the perpetual inventory valuation method, with initial capital stocks and depreciation measured as averages, from Feenstra et al. (2015).

Nevertheless, in 2017 China's savings to capital ratio remained 8 percentage points higher than in the United States in nominal terms (in 2009, the gap was even higher at around 18 percentage points), as seen in Figure 4.21. By definition, the difference in returns reflects differences in corporate savings, personal savings and government savings. After a closer consideration, several key factors stand out in explaining the overall difference between US returns and Chinese returns:

1. Each economy is located at different points along the Solow growth curve. Thus, it should be no surprise that China (an emerging economy) has both higher growth and higher returns than the United States (a more mature economy)—particularly when both economies are segmented in terms of international capital flows.
2. Since we are measuring returns according to savings (not GDP, or sales), we must also consider personal savings, not just corporate savings. Personal savings in the United States has been incredibly low, which has acted as a heavy weight dragging down the overall US rate of return as measured here.
3. The cost of labor relative to capital is lower in China than in the United States. Therefore, in the production process, more capital is substituted for labor in the United States than in China. This pushes down the returns to capital in the United States (due to diminishing returns) compared to China.

Macro Finance Insight 4.3: The Dupont Model, Manufacturing, Huawei, and CISCO

We can refine and expand our use of the Dupont model by examining the manufacturing sector for China and the United States and looking at two major companies engaged in information, communication, and technology: CISCO and Huawei.* Huawei is the world's largest telecom supplier and second-largest phone manufacturer. Huawei Technologies, founded in 1987 in Shenzhen, Guangdong, is one of the world's largest manufacturing and technology companies in the ICT industry. It provides routers, switches, and cables that are the backbone of the internet, and its equipment is used in 170 countries by most of the world's telecommunication companies. CISCO, founded in San Francisco in 1984, is a technology leader in the same industry, and it is one of the world's largest providers of internet-related equipment. In an industry with such rapid changes, it is inevitable that these two giants would clash on a variety of fronts. In the expanded Dupont model used here, we will present leverage as an additional factor in order to gain some additional insights:

Return on Equity = (Sales / Assets) × (Net Income / Sales) × (Assets / Equity)

The last term on the right-hand side measures the degree to which the company is using shareholder equity as a source of finance or, alternatively, debt. We will first compare overall manufacturing industries in both countries and then examine Huawei and CISCO specifically. Table 4.6 shows how the two countries' manufacturing industries compare based on the Dupont Model. Here, we see asset efficiency in China at double that of the United States. What is the explanation for this surprising result? China, with its abundance of labor, still heavily uses labor in the production process, while the United States employs capital-intensive techniques. Over time, we would expect this ratio in China to converge to that of the United States as newer capital-intensive technologies dominate the production process. And, similar to what happened in the United States experience, this will create low-skilled labor dislocation—a process already underway.

Meanwhile, we see the United States performs close to 50 percent better in terms of manufacturing profit margins. Once again, the explanation is interesting. Branding, profitable niche markets, and cost efficiencies can all contribute to higher profit margins; historically, the United States has had advantages in these areas. Leverage across manufacturing looks broadly similar for the two economies, with slightly higher reliance on debt for United States companies—no doubt a result of equity buybacks in the United States in recent years. The overall result is for a substantially higher return on equity (ROE) for Chinese companies—consistent with other results found in this chapter.

Examining the same ratios for CISCO and Huawei in Table 4.7, we see similar results aside from the critical difference in leverage. Huawei has more than double the leverage (reliance on debt) than does CISCO. Huawei has become one focal point in the Trump trade war. Since at least 2018, Huawei has become the target of various sanctions and sales restrictions in the United States. One area of concern for United States officials regards the easy access to state-owned bank finance that companies such as Huawei have, as seen in the difference in leverage between Huawei and CISCO. A different explanation may simply be China's very different financial structure, as discussed in Chapter 11. When strategic trade policy (discussed in Chapter 3) intersects with strategic finance, red flags arise and issues of efficiency and fairness are brought to the fore.

*Although Ericsson and Nokia are typically identified as Huawei's top competitors, CISCO is an American company competing with Huawei in the router and other networking hardware area.

Dupont Model, Manufacturing Industry		
	China	**United States**
Sales/Assets	101.0%	51.7%
Net Income/Sales	6.7%	4.0%
Assets/Equity	224.4%	242.6%
Net Income/Equity	15.0%	5.0%
Net Income/Assets	6.7%	2.1%

Table 4.6 The Dupont decomposition shows that, at least in manufacturing, China's asset efficiency is higher due to a greater use of labor as an input in the production process.
Source: Author created based on data from CEIC, NBS, Chapter 13, and Bureau of Economic Analysis BEA (https://bit.ly/37xefov) for manufacturing data.
Note: Chinese data are for all 2017 industrial enterprises with sales greater than RMB 20 million and for all US manufacturing firms.

Dupont Model Ratios (in 2017)		
	CISCO	**Huawei**
Sales/Assets	0.37	1.19
Net income/Sales	0.20	0.08
Assets/Equity	1.35	2.88
Net income/Equity (ROE)	0.10	0.27
Net income/Assets	0.07	0.09
Sales/Employee (USD Millions)	658,436	513,889

Table 4.7 CISCO and Huawei can be compared using the Dupont decomposition. Representative of fundamental differences, Huawei has higher asset efficiency but lower profit margins than CISCO. Huawei also has a capital structure that is highly leveraged. Source: Author created based on annual reports for Huawei (https://bit.ly/2zK91sp) and CISCO (https://bit.ly/2zDt1Nw).

Although we have indicated higher returns since 1997 in China, there remain some concerns. The rapid buildup of capital and the rising cost of labor (labor's share of national income) have increased in recent years. This has pushed returns downward. We must also remember that most of the nation's savings have been used domestically as investment—just as a company would use retained earnings to finance its capital expenditure. Whether these investments (a substantial share is in residential housing) have higher returns in later years remains to be seen. This point highlights another level of important inquiry in measuring the quality of growth. Not only are we asking whether (ROIC > WACC), as seen earlier in Equation 18 and Equation 19, but we are also asking a deeper question: When items produced and measured are considered as investment goods (e.g., housing in the case of the United States, and PP&E in the case of China), can we be sure that the real economic value of these goods is being measured properly? In other words, when measuring ROIC, it is far more difficult to measure the economic value of an investment good than a consumption good, which is actually purchased, used, and valued by consumers.

Macro Finance Insight 4.4: Sustainable Growth II—The Dupont Model

The sustainable growth model used in finance describes the rate at which we expect a company to grow sustainably. By "sustainable," we mean that growth in sales and assets will be consistent with a stable (unchanged) capital structure). For companies, this is an important question. Finance theory establishes an optimal capital structure that balances risks with returns such that companies do not stray too far from some ideal ratio of debt to equity.[17]

We make the following assumptions:

1. No additional equity (outside finance) is raised.
2. The capital structure remains the same (debt as a share of assets and equity as a share of assets is unchanged).
3. CRS: in order to increase output by a certain percent, we will also need to increase inputs by the same percent.
4. The payout ratio, (*R*), or dividends as a share of net income is 0. (Changing this assumption does not alter our main results.)

What is the basis for this set of assumptions in the corporate context? Raising outside finance in the form of equity can be expensive and impacts control of the company—particularly between outside and inside shareholders. Assuming the capital structure remains constant presumes an optimal capital structure; relying on too much debt as a source of finance (increased leverage altering the capital structure) can be risky (even leading to bankruptcy), and this raises overall financing costs. Too little debt can also result in a rise in overall financing costs, and it may reduce the beneficial impact that outside creditors can create. CRS is assumed (as in the Solow framework), which serves as a useful, empirically-based benchmark.[*] Given CRS, if sales grow by 10 percent (for example), then assets must also grow by 10 percent. However, since the capital structure on the firm's liability side of the balance sheet cannot change, debt and equity must also grow by 10 percent. Altering the payment of dividends or changing the retention ratio, (*R*), is bound from below by 0 and from above by 1; this serves as a constraint in helping us define what is sustainable.[†] Recall that, for a firm:

Change in Equity = Net Income + New Equity Raised

And since new equity raised, by assumption, is 0, we have:

Change in Equity = Net Income

And dividing the above by equity, we have:

Change in Equity / Equity = Net Income / Equity

Or,

Growth in Equity = ROE

Let's assume an ROE of 10 percent. Then, growth in equity will grow by 10 percent. Given our assumption of an unchanging capital structure, the debt (and in turn) all assets must grow by 10 percent. And, given our CRS assumption, sales of the company will also grow by 10 percent. If ROE is greater than sales growth, we need to either reduce the share of debt (lend, violating our assumption) or increase sales (which may not be possible). If ROE is less than sales growth, we need to either increase our share of debt (borrow even more, violating our assumption) or accept slower sales.

Translating this into a macro context, GDP growth (sales growth) will be sustainable as long as it is consistent with growth in assets (domestic savings/assets), which will be equal to the ROE (in a macro context we assume this is the ROE where we are at an optimal capital structure) and growth in debt.[18] If GDP is growing faster than the return to investors (ROA) or equity (ROE), then one of three scenarios will emerge: (1) accelerated borrowing from abroad, (2) lower dividends from firms to individuals (more retained earnings), or (3) more inbound (FDI) equity. Employed on an ongoing basis, all of these outcomes are fraught with problems, and they are thus unsustainable. For example, increased borrowing could lead to a financial crisis, and relying on ever-increasing foreign ownership (equity) of one's country is usually not politically feasible. The ability to change the payout ratio has a lower bound of 0, and investors (citizens) ultimately would like to capture the gains from the economy's capital.

At the macro finance level: If GDP growth (or the corresponding growth in assets) is greater than the ROA (10 percent in our earlier example), external finance (FDI or debt) will be required. If GDP growth is slower than the ROA, then external lending (outbound FDI or loans) will occur. The United States would be consistent with the former case and China with the latter case. We refer to Figure 4.21, which provides estimated returns in each country based on the broadest measure of returns (domestic savings) and broadly supports the above results. Finally, we remind the reader that returns on assets in the macro context represent all of the nation's saving (government, individual, and corporate) as a share of the nation's total wealth.

If ROA does not equal GDP growth, then we can turn to our Dupont model to see how an economy can be rebalanced over the long run. Recall that in the Dupont Model:

ROIC = Sales / Assets × NI / Sales = NI / Assets

And by analogy at the macro level:

$$ROA = GDP / Assets \times Savings / GDP = Savings / Assets$$

An economy must either alter the efficiency in which it uses its assets (GDP / assets) or alter its profit margins (savings / GDP) to allow ROA to again equal GDP growth. If these cannot be adjusted for some reason, then growth in GDP (sales) must be shifted either upward or downward to accommodate ROA.

It is interesting to note here that, in both the Solow and the Dupont/sustainability models, GDP growth equals the growth in capital or assets at a steady state. Solow takes us deeper in the direction of labor force growth as a key driver; the sustainability approach takes us deeper in the direction of returns on equity and assets, asset efficiency, and the savings margin as key drivers. We can think of ROE or ROA and labor force growth as competing for the position of "key bottleneck" to economic growth. We would generally think of labor force growth as the more rigid exogenous driver—but, in the case of China, with its one- and various-child policies, that variable apparently can also be endogenized.

Once again, we see China and the United States at different points along the macro finance spectrum financial when examining Figure 4.20 and Figure 4.21. The above analysis suggests China's ROA (as measured by the net savings to capital stock ratio) has been unsustainably high compared to its current rate of economic growth (6 to 6.5 percent). For China, both returns and economic growth are slowing, narrowing its margin for lending to the rest of the world. In the transition, given its vast foreign exchange reserves, it still has room to adjust its capital structure to more lending. But the forces of the Dupont model discussed above are increasingly making that path more difficult. Figure 4.22 provides net domestic savings as a share of capital (a measure of macro returns after deducting depreciation) and qualitatively tells the same story as Figure 4.21.

Meanwhile, the United States' ROA is below its long-run GDP growth rates (2.6 percent).[19] It's capital structure vis-à-vis the rest of the world is becoming increasingly precarious. It will need to either increase its savings rate or its efficiency ratio (GDP to assets). China's divergence, in part, is clearly related to the fact that the nation remains far from its steady state, which will self-correct over time. But an important example of the divergence, for both economies, is the difference in the savings to GDP rate, which is too high for China and relatively low for the United States. China must channel more of its corporate savings into the hands of citizens and, in turn, boost consumption. The United States will need to increase savings, particularly at the personal level, and boost the size of GDP to assets—which may, in part, come from a diminished role for housing as a national asset. Finally, it is important to note that, if we were to add in human capital and the need to invest in that resource (education and training), China's high rate of savings moves closer to GDP growth rates and appears more reasonable.

The above analysis in stocks or levels can also be viewed analogously from the perspective of the flow variables savings, investment, and current account balances.[20] The above discussion was framed in a national balance sheet framework. In what follows, we take a flow approach based on sources and uses of funds. Recall that:

$$\text{National Savings} - \text{Gross Investment} = \text{Current Account [Surplus (+) or Deficit (-)]}$$
$$= \text{Change in Net External Liabilities}$$

Assume as above, but at the macro level, that the net external liability to domestic equity ratio is optimally constant at:

$$\text{Domestic Equity / Domestic Assets} = \alpha$$

And,

$$\text{Net External Liabilities / Domestic Assets} = (1-\alpha)$$

And,

$$\text{Domestic Equity} = (\alpha / (1-\alpha)) \times \text{Net External Liability}$$

And so,

$$\text{Growth in Domestic Equity} = \text{Growth in Net External Liabilities} = \text{Growth in Domestic Assets}$$

And since,

$$\text{Growth in Domestic Equity} = \text{National Savings} / (\alpha \times \text{Domestic Assets}) = \text{ROE}$$

we once again see the same result as in the discussion above: a constant ROE will drive the growth in external liabilities and domestic asset growth and, in turn, GDP growth.

Finally, after a simple rearranging of the following relationships:

National Savings / (α × Domestic Assets) = Change in Net External Liabilities / ((1– α) × Domestic Assets) = Gross Investment / Domestic Assets

we can see that the growth in national savings will equal the growth in external financing (growth in net external liabilities), which will also equal the growth in gross investment. We can reasonably infer that growth rates in these flow variables would need to equal GDP growth in the steady state.

What we have shown above is that the ROA or ROE will equal GDP growth. Earlier in the chapter, we have presented a Solow framework where GDP growth equals population growth. So, once again, we have shown population growth, GDP growth, and investment returns all linked in a steady state.

*Do not confuse this assumption with the law of diminishing returns, in which only one input (capital per person) is increased and output or sales increases at a diminishing rate.

†Of course, firms do buy back shares, which, in effect, moves (*R*) to a negative number. But then we move ourselves further away from the optimal capital structure.

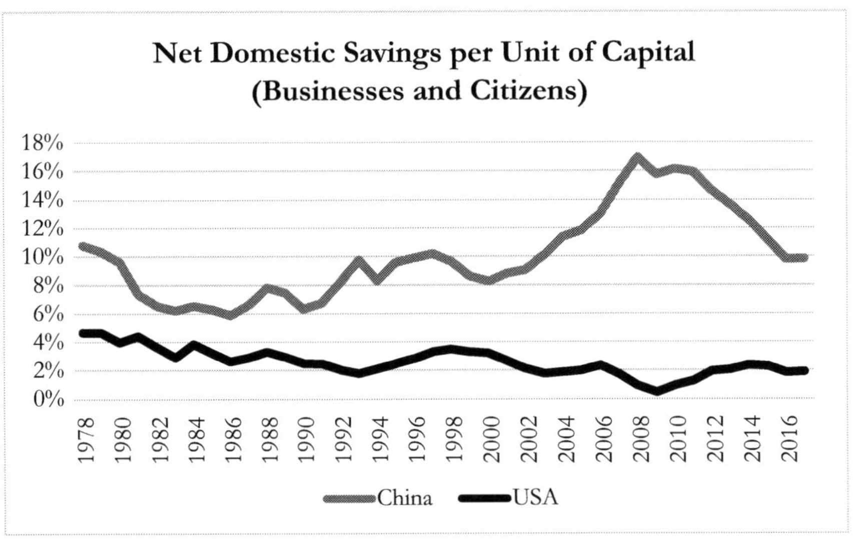

Figure 4.22 Net savings to capital shows low returns to capital in the United States relative to China—a function of the low personal savings rate in the United States.
Source: Author created based on data from World Development Indicators and FRED. For capital estimates, we employ the perpetual inventory valuation method, with initial capital stocks and depreciation measured as averages, from Feenstra et al. (2015).

Summary of the Returns to Capital in China

Figure 4.23 summarizes our varied methods of measuring returns to capital in China. A few conclusions stand out. Overall, there has been a substantial decline in the returns to capital in China since 2008. The average of the four different indicators of returns suggests a real return of about 10 percent (12 percent, nominal) by 2017–2018. And this figure is approaching some of our estimates for the United States. Several factors happening simultaneously have led to this decline.

1. Long-term factors such as convergence to the Solow steady state and slower population growth
2. An uptick in labor's share of income cutting into corporate profits
3. Short-term factors such as China's surge in investment (pushing down the marginal product of capital)
4. Short-term business cycle problems such as occasional tightening of credit (discussed later in Chapter 8), trade frictions, and (more recently) COVID-19

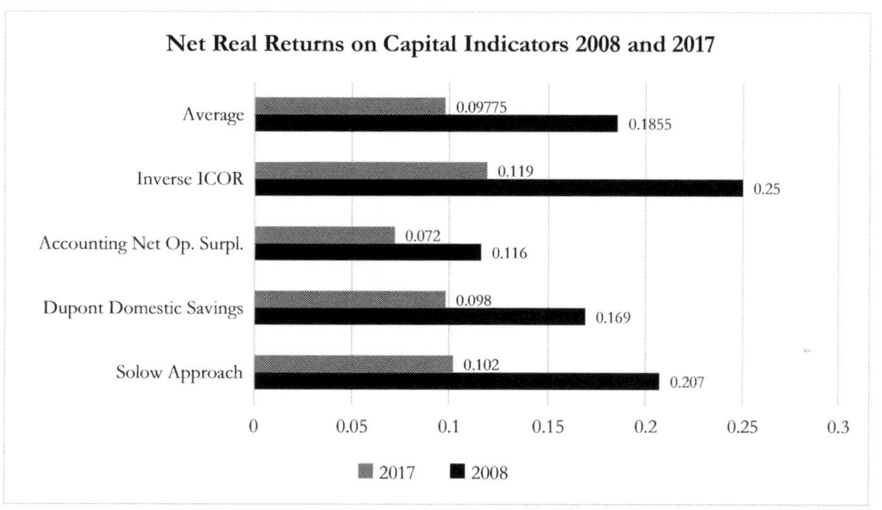

Figure 4.23 Comparing all four methodologies in terms of net (after depreciation) real returns before taxes (EBT) on capital, we see a substantial decline in returns in China post-GFC. The average of the four methods suggests that Chinese returns had declined to a little under 10 percent by 2017, not too far from that of the United States.
Source: Author created.

The latter two short-term challenges are likely easier to reverse than the longer-term first two causes. Figure 4.24 presents a diffusion index (https://bit.ly/2WZ8dbk) for enterprise profits in China. We can see some downward pressure on returns beginning around 2010, consistent with our results above. Nevertheless, the index has remained above 50. We note that diffusion indexes do not tell us how large or small returns are—only if they have risen or fallen.

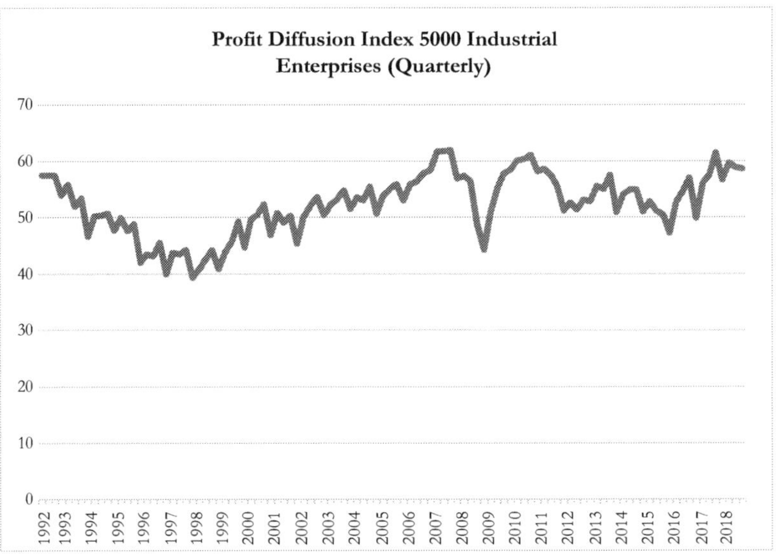

Figure 4.24 The profit diffusion index is an up-or-down measure of how many industrial companies in China report improved profits or deterioration in profits over the past quarter. This measure shows some weakness in profits from 2010 through 2016.
Source: Author created based on data from CEIC.

Measuring the Cost of Capital

Now that we have spent some time on the returns to capital in each country, we next turn to the cost of capital. Nan Geng and Papa N'Diaye (2012) provide estimates for both WACC and ROIC in each country. Based on data for Chinese listed firms (many of which have the Chinese government, directly or indirectly, as a majority shareholder), the authors find the real cost of capital to be significantly lower in China than in the United States.[21] Real WACC, by their estimates, is comprised of borrowing costs of around 3 percent (compared to nearly 4 percent in the United States) and a real cost of equity of about 5 percent (compared to about 10 percent in the United States). The authors stress that China's low payout ratio on dividends—(around 18 percent) compared to a global average of 33 percent and a US average of roughly 20 percent—is an important factor in their cost of equity calculation.

Our own calculations, taking a different approach suggests that in recent years the cost of debt in each economy is quite similar on short-term rates and longer-term rates. Table 4.8 shows real interest rates for China and the United States over the past decade on bank deposits (one year), the prime rate (United States), base lending rates for one-year loans (China), and base longer-term interest rates for 30-year high quality corporate bonds.[22]

Real Interest Rates on Deposits and Loans 2017–2018			
	Deposit Rates on One-Year Deposit	**Loan Rates on One-Year Working Capital (China) or Prime Rate (US)**	**Corporate Bond Yield on High Quality Borrowers (30 years)**
United States	-1.9%	2.5%	2.0%
China	-0.6%	2.7%	2.7%

Table 4.8 Real interest rates on deposits and loans in China and the United States have been relatively low and within the same range in recent years.
Source: Author's estimates based on FRED and China Central Depository and Clearing Co. (https://bit.ly/3byHHur).
Note: PBC still restricts rates from straying too far above the deposit rates or below the lending rates indicated.

While China's borrowing rates are not too far below the US rates, it would be wrong to conclude that the distribution of interest rates are similar. In fact, particularly for Chinese SOEs, access to credit at a below market rate is common. The difficulty in assessing credit quality for the full spectrum of China's SOEs means that many entities which would otherwise face higher borrowing costs from the banks in China (BBB-rated or even C-rated firms), receive rates close to or even below the base rates found in Figure 4.25. It is evident that these SOEs would not receive any loans if purely commercial criteria were the sole determinant of credit access. This phenomenon is accentuated by the close links between state-owned banks and borrowing SOEs (OECD 2005).

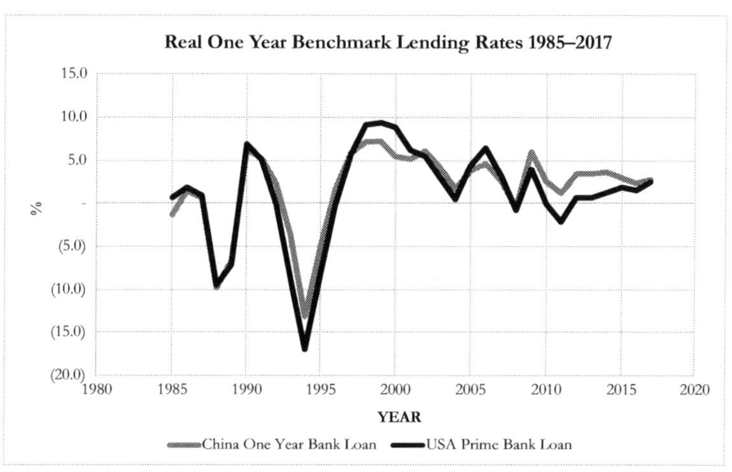

Figure 4.25 One-year real borrowing rates to the most credit-worthy customers track each other closely in China and the United States
Source: Author's estimates based on FRED and China Central Depository and Clearing Co. Ltd. (https://bit.ly/3byHHur).

If some borrowers are receiving below-market interest rates, some borrowers inevitably face above-market borrowing costs. Estimates of an underground lending market (shadow banking) are as high as RMB (*renminbi*) 70 trillion (see Chapter 11).[23] He, Chen and Schramm (2018) estimated that up to 25 percent of China's savings is channeled through an informal market. Schramm and Lin (2009) showed that, in earlier years, up to one-third of China's savings was informally channeled. Some estimates indicate borrowing costs in certain cities as high as 180 percent (Ma 2011). These numbers are in stark contrast to the base lending rates implied in Table 4.8. But the fact that depositors face very low deposit rates while SOE borrowers face low lending rates creates an arbitrage opportunity that, in turn, fosters China's underground market. If access to credit is restricted to SOE firms in the formal market, an overflow of demand for credit in the underground market will be created. Both depositors in the formal market and those with access to credit at below market rates in the formal market eventually exit this market—taking with them their demand for credit and their access to credit. They enter the informal market as a way to arbitrage between a market with price controls and one that does not contain such controls.

Outright Price Earnings Ratio 2019	
United States	19.8
China	13

Table 4.9 Price earnings ratios for Chinese and US firms in recent years suggest that the cost of equity is, in fact, relatively high in China.
Source: Author created based on CEIC PE data for China and Robert Shiller (https://bit.ly/2WxHwLQ) data for the United States.

On the cost of equity side, we can take an alternative approach to that of Gang and N'Diaye in measuring the cost of equity. Gang and N'Diaye measured cost of equity based on current earnings and dividends payout. This approach is problematic in China because growth is an essential part of the pricing equation for equities and the cost of capital. Furthermore, parsimonious dividend payments in China obfuscate other types of obligations of firms when the principal investor is a government entity.[24] We can examine price earnings (PE) ratios to infer what the cost of equity might be (see Appendix). The PE ratio is the ratio of the price of a stock to its earnings per share. Table 4.9 presents recent PE ratios for China and the United States. Inverting these indexes gives us an indication of returns expected by investors (earnings / price) as seen in Figure 4.26 and Figure 4.27. These ratios are for the broad market indexes of the Shanghai Stock Exchange (SSE) and the Standard and Poor's (S&P) 500 indexes.

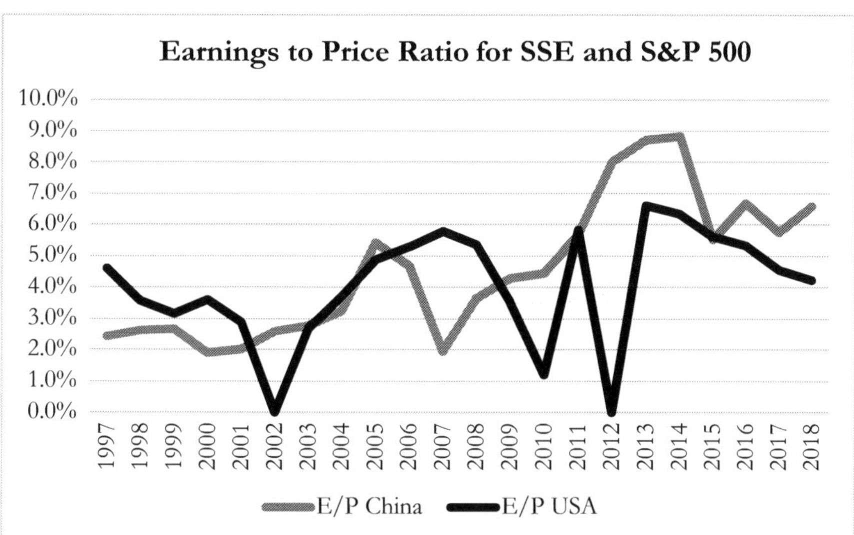

Figure 4.26 The earnings to price ratio shows how much return a company must offer in order to attract investors. In recent years, it has been higher in China.
Source: Author created based on CEIC PE data for China, and based on Robert Shiller (https://bit.ly/2WxHwLQ) data for the United States.

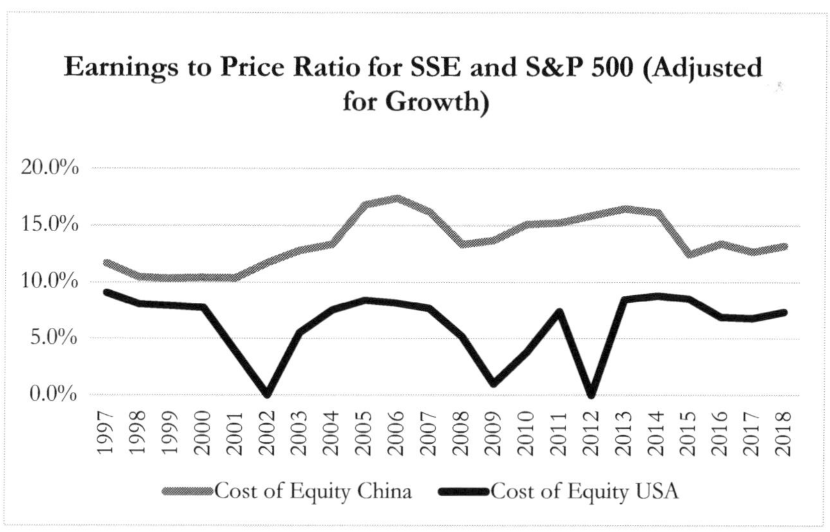

Figure 4.27 The earnings to price ratio adjusted for growth shows how much return a company must offer in order to attract investors, if we assume growth potential in earnings (using current year GDP growth). The required ROE investment by this measure has been consistently higher in China.
Source: Author created based on CEIC PE data for China and based on Robert Shiller (https://bit.ly/2WxHwLQ) data for the United States.

Here, we see that since 2009, Chinese company owners must offer shareholders a bit higher return than that found in the United States. Put simply, the cost of equity in China has been generally higher since 2009. Prior to that, the costs for each country trended together. When adjusting for the fact that companies in China are likely to have earnings that grow faster than in the United States (we assume current GDP growth rates in each country to make the adjustment), we see that the cost of equity is even higher in China going all the way back to 1997. No doubt, the higher cost of equity in China (even after adjusting for inflation) may very well explain why Chinese companies such as Alibaba have chosen to list (have initial public offerings) in the United States. An alternative way to look at this would be to say that a United States company listing in China would need to have higher growth potential in order to receive the same valuation as in the United States. In this discussion, we have not taken into account differences in risk—a key variable. But qualitatively, we can state that a Chinese firm listing in the United States, *ceteris paribus*, would likely face a lower cost of capital than at home given the lower cost of equity in the United States and the unique diversification opportunities offered to American investors.

China, the United States, and the Overall Cost of Capital

In thinking about the cost of capital, we note that Chinese firms continue to rely more heavily on debt finance than do firms in the United States, so the cost of debt (which is similar across economies) has a heavier weight in China's capital structure. Meanwhile, in the United States, less expensive equity plays a heavier role and has a heavier weight. On balance, the cost of capital is slightly lower in the United States than in China, but not dramatically so. Damodaran (https://bit.ly/2AxVpkF) estimates an average of about 7 percent for the United States, and our overall estimates for China are around 7.5 percent. This is notwithstanding the fact that Chinese firms are more highly leveraged with relatively cheap debt. We find that the cost of capital (a weighted average of debt and equity) are surprisingly similar, despite China's much larger pool of savings relative to GDP. Why is this? As with many comparisons between China and the United States, the story is complicated. Several factors seem to be at play:

1. While we may expect China's vast savings to keep the cost of capital low, we must also remember that the demand for savings in China is extraordinarily high—both savings (supply of loanable funds) and investment (demand for loanable funds) take up close to 50 percent of China's GDP. This is a simple story of supply and demand.

2. The cost of capital equals the opportunity cost of capital at the margin. We have shown that returns are higher in China (the demand for loanable funds is higher in Wicksellian Figure 4.16) and this would push up the cost of capital in China.
3. Although China's sources of funds (savings) are greater than its uses of funds (investment), the excess is shipped out (lent) to the United States. This triggers both lower US interest rates and higher Chinese rates, as shown in Figure 4.16 and Figure 4.17a .
4. We may have generalized a bit too much in our conclusions regarding the cost of debt and equity in China. The loans of the banking system in China tend to cluster around the floor rates, leading borrowers (a disproportionate number of whom are SOEs) to receive the same lower rates. Thus, for those SOEs with access to bank credit, the average borrowing cost may in fact be quite low. In other words, in China, a C-rated borrower may very well receive a rate quite close to that of a AAA-rated borrower. This is caused by the lack of a reliable rating system for China's SOEs and the continued preferences they enjoy in borrowing. In contrast, corporate borrowers receive the entire spectrum of interest rates in the United States, thus making borrowing costs higher for approximately half of the borrowers. China's risk-adjusted borrowing rates, then, may still be substantially lower than US rates: In China, interest rates tend to spike around the floor, while in the United States, the distribution is more even.[25]
5. On the equity side, we have only provided information on listed companies. Companies that are not publicly traded in China and do not have access to retail investors (but rather the wholesale intra-company investment market) are likely to experience even higher cost of equity. Credit in China is still very much a matter of segmented markets. Those with access to bank credit (especially SOEs) can tap into the vast pool of Chinese individual savings (available at a low-ceilinged interest rate). Those outside of this market (such as small- and medium-sized enterprises) face a much higher cost of funds. Another level of segmentation is between the private intra-company financing market, in which returns and the cost of funds can be extraordinarily high, and the *lao bai xing* (common man) market, in which risk-adjusted returns are relatively low (bank deposits, the stock market, and real estate). It remains difficult for the common man to tap into the higher returns offered by private companies seeking finance. But we should note that China's financial markets are becoming more integrated via the shadow banking system, as discussed later in Chapter 11.

In summary, while factors (1) and (2) above provide a compelling macro story for convergence of the cost of capital in the United States and China, examining the question at an industrial organization/micro level shows that the cost of capital may be distorted: in the dynamic private market segment in China, the cost of capital is too high; in the SOE segment, the cost is too low (both in absolute terms and relative to the United States). In other words, underperforming firms appear to have access to relatively inexpensive credit—which undermines China's more value-creating private firms.

Basic Growth	Intermediate Growth	Advanced (Sustainable) Growth
Political stability	Basic growth factors, +	Intermediate growth factors, +
Macroeconomic stability	Solid national savings rate	Sophisticated financial system
Microeconomic freedom	Solid national investment	Transparency
Rule of law	Basic education	Strong regulatory framework
	Open trading systems (international)	Strong legal system
		Strong universities with advanced degrees

Table 4.10 We can classify countries into different growth leagues and what is required for increased sustainability going from left to right.
Source: Author created.

Macro Finance Insight 4.5: Growth and Competitive Advantage

Michael Porter has suggested a framework of advanced and basic factors for the competitive advantage of nations (Porter 1990). We can think of economic growth in the same terms, building on our earlier discussion of value-creating growth compared to growth for growth's sake. Table 4.10 provides a list of factors that tend to create basic economic growth as compared to intermediate or advanced economic growth. "Basic growth" refers to raw economic growth that may or may not create value, while "advanced growth" refers to sustainable, value-creating growth. "Intermediate growth" represents economies with more sustainable growth rates than basic, but are unlikely to achieve the per capita income levels found in the industrialized economies.[*] Some countries (for example, North Korea) have not even achieved basic growth, due to enormous political and institutional constraints

As we move from basic to advanced economic growth, we shift to more sophisticated, rule-based, research-intensive economies (what Porter calls "advanced factors"). Importantly, we are moving toward societies in which institutions provide the levels of trust and security necessary to allow for ever-more-complex economic transactions and relationships. Countries that have achieved basic economic growth may encounter bottlenecks to achieving more sustainable economic growth if legal and regulatory frameworks are not present. In effect, we are moving from basic economies with the necessary "hardware" for economic growth to more advanced economies that have the necessary institutional "software." Economies, including the United States, have achieved advanced economic growth, but they are always wary of slipping back into lower stages. Meanwhile, China is arguably at an intermediate economic stage and working to develop the institutional software to move to a higher, more sustainable growth path.

*We could classify all countries at different stages of economic growth. China is at the intermediate stage, having achieved most of the benchmarks of basic growth; the United States is at the advanced and sustainable stage.

Summary of the Returns and Cost of Capital

By applying several concepts from finance at the macro level, we can qualitatively identify differences between China and the United States. China's growth in the near to medium term is likely to be larger than US growth for reasons already described. As an emerging economy, China is still likely to have an ROIC greater than its cost of capital, especially when we measure China's return on a national savings basis (à la Dupont model) and consider that China's capital structure is heavily weighted to debt rather than equity. On an ongoing basis, China remains below its steady state, and so it has greater potential for value creation than the United States. But whether China's financial system can leverage that advantage and also generate technological progress is open questions.

Given what we now know about the cost of capital from our discussion above, we see that there is still room for expansion of the capital stock and continued growth in both China and the United States (but particularly in China). And we should emphasize that a key component of capital stock growth is the potential growth in human capital. There are two main factors clearly at play in China's gap between investment opportunity and realization:

1. Adjustment costs involved in building up capital at too rapid a pace may require a slower pace of growth in the capital stock.

2. The segmented nature of China's capital markets, combined with restrictions on capital inflows and outflows, hinder development of the most productive segments of the economy—the dynamic private sector.

The positive portrayal of investment opportunities for China comes with some serious caveats, particularly related to how we measure the value of an investment. Since so much of output in China is in the form of investment, we really need to understand the quality of that investment more deeply and whether the cost of that investment is truly reflective of its economic value. We return to this question in Chapters 5 and 6.

Appendix

Linking the PE Ratio to The Standard Dividend Growth Model

Assume a country's composite stock index has total earnings, (*E*), which are assumed to grow at rate, (*g*), and are somehow consistent with cashflows to investors. Investors have an opportunity cost (the rate at which they discount earnings), (*r*). Then, using the formula for discounted earnings, we can say the value of the overall index should be (*P*), where

$$P_0 = E_0 + (1+g) \times {}^{E_1}/_{(1+r)^1} + (1+g)^2 \times {}^{E_2}/_{(1+r)^2} \cdots$$

Which sums to,

$$^{P}/_{E} = {}^{1}/_{(r-g)}$$

And, if growth is 0,

$$^{P}/_{E} = {}^{1}/_{(r)}$$

Alternatively, we can say (E / $P = r - g$) (with growth) and (E / $P = r$) (with no growth). In the section of this chapter where we work with Chinese and US (P / E) ratios, we assume the observed (E / P) ratios reflect both opportunity costs and growth rate prospects (assumed positive); that is, we assume they are represented by,

$$E / P = r - g$$

Therefore, in order to measure the true opportunity cost in each country before growth (if growth prospects were 0), we need to add (*g*) to the (E / P) ratio:

$$E / P = r - g + g = r$$

Challenging Questions for China (and the Student): Chapter 4

1. Go to the Federal Reserve Economic Database (FRED) table "Purchasing Power Parity Converted GDP Per Capita Relative to the United States, average GEKS-CPDW, at current prices for China" (http://research.stlouisfed.org/fred2/series/PGD2U2CNA621NUPN).
   a. Update and explain the graph found here and in the chapter.
2. Explain, using the Solow framework, why China's economic growth will inevitably slow in the coming years. Pay particular attention to what factors drag a country down to the slower-growth steady state.
3. Using the standard Solow framework, explain how China's past one-child policy affects per capita incomes in the short run and the long run. Explain how it will affect economic growth in the long run.
4. Urban residents from one-child families can now have two children in China. Discuss this policy and how it will affect the growth of the labor force in China in the coming years à la Solow.
5. Using the World Bank estimates in Table 4.1 and the estimates for 1978–1998 in Table 4.3, provide an estimate for the Solow alpha and beta we discuss in the growth accounting equations in the chapter
6. Linking the Solow framework with real returns on capital:
   a. Use the Solow framework to explain why faster population growth would increase the real returns to capital in the long-run steady state.
   b. At China's current stage of development, what are the factors that make its returns to capital so much higher than that of a mature economy such as the United States?
7. Utilizing the Solow growth framework:
   a. Explain the sources of economic growth for China in the past and what the sources will be in the future using the following equation:

$$\Delta Y(t) / Y(t) = \Delta A(t) / A(t) + \alpha \Delta K(t) / K(t) + \beta \Delta L(t) / L(t)$$

   b. Explain why we say that China's growth rate will surely slow in the future.
   c. Explain why China's high savings rate is an unlikely source of sustainable growth.
8. In a manner as detailed as possible, discuss the quality of China's growth compared to the quantity of China's growth. Use equations, facts, and data in your discussion.

9. We discussed different stages of growth for economies around the world—from basic growth to advanced growth. Provide different periods in China's recent economic history that might correspond to the different phases. Include what will happen in the future. Be specific about the necessary ingredients for each stage.
10. Explain the intuition behind the DuPont model of sustainable growth, which specifically links the growth in GDP (sales) to a nation's ROA. Is this consistent with what is happening in China and the United States?
11. Why is (Y / K) lower for China in the years 1978–2004? Use the standard Solow model to explain why it should be, and then explain think why it is not.
12. Strategic trade theorists have sometimes used Boeing as an example of state support of an industry for strategic trade purposes. Go to Boeing's most recent annual report (https://bit.ly/2UJLdwH) and determine Boeing's assets to equity ratio. How does it compare to American manufacturing in general, and how does it compare to Huawei?
13. Research Question: Determine whether or not China's high-speed rail system is generating quality growth.
14. In Case Study 4.3, we see that the (Y / K) ratio fell below that of the United States. Using a standard Solow (y vs. k) graph, show how this might happen, and explain in words what is going on.
15. Explain the historical role that urbanization has on income distribution. Explain fully what the implications of this are for China.

References

Bai, Chong-En, Chang-Tai Hsieh, and Yingyi Qian. 2006. "The Return to Capital in China." NBER Working Paper no. 12755.

Bai, Chong-En, and Qian Zhenjie. 2010. "The Factor Income Distribution in China: 1978–2007." *China Economic Review*, 21(4), pp. 650–70.

Barro, Robert J. 1991. "Economic Growth in a Cross Section of Countries." *Quarterly Journal of Economics*, 106(2), pp. 407–43.

Brandt, L., C. T. Hsieh, and X. Zhu. 2008a. "Growth and Structural Transformation in China." In *China's Great Economic Transformation*, edited by L. Brandt and Thomas G. Rawski, Cambridge: Cambridge University Press, pp. 683–728.

Brandt, L., T. G Rawski, and Sutton. 2008b. "China's Industrial Development." In *China's Great Economic Transformation*, edited by L. Brandt and Thomas G. Rawski, Cambridge: Cambridge University Press, pp. 569–632.

Chow, G. 1993. "Capital Formation and Economic Growth in China." *Quarterly Journal of Economics*, 108(3), pp. 809–42.

Denison, Edward F. 1974. *Accounting for United States Economic Growth*. Washington, DC: The Brookings Institution.

DiCecio, Ricardo, and Charles S. Gascon. 2008. "Income Convergence in the United States: A Tale of Migration and Urbanization." Federal Reserve Bank of St. Louis Working Paper no. 2008-002C.

Domar, Evsey. 1946. "Capital Expansion, Rate of Growth, and Employment." *Econometrica*, 14(2), pp. 137–47.

Donaldson, J. B., C. Koulovatianos, J. Li, and R. Mehra. 2018. "Demographics and FDI: Lessons from China's One-Child Policy." NBER Working Paper no. 24256.

Feenstra, Robert C., Robert Inklaar, and Marcel P. Timmer. 2015. "The Next Generation of the Penn World Table." *American Economic Review*, 105(10), pp. 3150–82.

Francis, Michael, Francois Painchaud, and Sylvie Morin. 2005. "Understanding China's Long-Run Growth Process and Its Implications for Canada." *Bank of Canada Review*, pp. 5–17.

Geng, Nan, and Papa N'Diaye. 2012. "Determinants of Corporate Investment in China: Evidence from Cross-Country Firm Level Data." IMF Working Paper no. 12/80.

He, Ming, Yang Chen, and Ronald Schramm. 2018. "The Financial System." In *The SAGE Handbook of Contemporary China*, edited by Mark Fraser and Wu Weiping, New York: SAGE Publications.

Hodge, Andrew W., Robert J. Corea, James M. Green, and Bonnie A. Retus. 2011. "Returns for Domestic Nonfinancial Business." *Survey of Current Business*, 91(6), pp. 24–28.

Hu, Z. and M. Khan. 1996. "Why Is China Growing So Fast?" IMF Working Paper no. 96/75.

Huang, Y. 2012. "How Did China Take Off?" *Journal of Economic Perspectives*, 26(4), pp. 147–70. International Human Dimensions Programme on Global Environmental Change and United Nations Environment Programme. 2012. *Measuring Progress Toward Sustainability: Inclusive Wealth Report*. Cambridge. Cambridge University Press.

Lau, Chi Keung Marco. 2010. "New Evidence About Regional Income Divergence in China." *China Economic Review*, 21(2), 293–309.

Li, H., J. Strauss, H. Shunxiang, and L. Lui. 2018. "Do High-Speed Railways Lead to Urban Economic Growth in China?: A Panel Data Study of China's Cities." *The Quarterly Review of Economics and Finance*, 69, pp. 70–89.

Lin, G., and R. Schramm. 2009. "A Decade of Flow of Funds in China: 1995–2006." In *China and Asia: Economic and Financial Interactions*, edited by Y. W. Cheung and K. Wong, London: Routledge.

Lin, Justin Yifu. 1992. "Rural Reforms and Agricultural Growth in China." *American Economic Review*, 82(1), pp. 34–51.

Liu, X., and C. Wang. 2003. "Does Foreign Direct Investment Facilitate Technological Progress?: Evidence from Chinese Industries." *Research policy*, 32(6), pp. 945–53.

Ma, Guangyuan. 2011. "What Do We Have for Wenzhou's Rescue?" *China-U.S. Focus,* 16 November.

Martin, Michael E. 2012. *China's Banking System: Issues for Congress.* CRS Report for Congress no. 7-5700, R42380. Washington, DC: Congressional Research Service.

Organisation for Economic Co-operation and Development. 2005. *Economic Survey of China*, 13, pp. 19–40.

Pedroni, P., and J. Y. Yao. 2006. "Regional Income Divergence in China." *Journal of Asian Economics*, 17, pp. 294–315.

Porter, M. E. 1998. *The Competitive Advantage of Nations*. New York: Free Press.

Romer, P. M. 1994. "The Origins of Endogenous Growth." *Journal of Economic Perspectives*, 8(1), pp. 3–22.

Sala-i-Martin, Xavier X. 1997. "I Just Ran Four Million Regressions." NBER Working Paper no. 6252.

Solow, Robert M. 1956. "A Contribution to the Theory of Economic Growth." *Quarterly Journal of Economics*, 70(1), pp. 65–94.

Swan, Trevor W. 1956. "Economic Growth and Capital Accumulation." *Economic Record*, 32(2), pp. 334–61.

Szamosszegi, Andrew, and Cole Kyle. 2011. *An Analysis of State-Owned Enterprises and State Capitalism in China.* Washington, DC: U.S.-China Economic and Security Review Commission, 26 October.

University of Groningen and University of California, Davis. "Share of Labour Compensation in GDP at Current National Prices for United States." Federal Reserve Bank of St. Louis, accessed 27 January 2019, https://fred.stlouisfed.org/series/LABSHPUSA156NRUG.

Wicksell, J. G. Knut. 1898/1936. *Interest and Prices*, translated by R. F. Kahn, London: Royal Economic Society.

Wu, Jinglian. 2005. *Understanding and Interpreting Chinese Economic Reform.* Mason, OH: Thomson/South-Western.

Young, Alwyn. 1992. "A Tale of Two Cities: Factor Accumulation and Technical Change in Hong Kong and Singapore." In *NBER Macroeconomics Annual 1992,* edited by O. J. Blanchard and S. Fischer, Cambridge: MIT Press, pp. 13–54.

Young, Alwyn. 2003. "Gold into Base Metals: Productivity Growth in the People's Republic of China During the Reform Period." *Journal of Political Economy*, 111(6), pp. 1220–61.

Zhu, Xiaodong. 2012. "Understanding China's Growth: Past, Present, and Future." *Journal of Economic Perspectives*, 26(4), pp. 103–24.

Endnotes

1. As we noted earlier, Brandt et al. (2008) and Huang (2012) assign a more significant role for TVEs and private sector industry in overall technological progress. Certainly, agricultural reform, private TVEs, and industry broadly-defined were all critical—the significance of share importance remains debated.
2. In continuous time under certainty, Equation 6 is exact; in discrete time, it is an approximation.
3. A common assumption across economics, which we discuss below.
4. Note the subtle difference between diminishing returns and decreasing returns to scale; the former holds an explicit input constant (as demonstrated above), while—in the latter case—all explicit inputs increase in proportion, but output increases by a smaller proportion (due to some implicit background constraint).
5. This restriction was codified in a 1980 law in which forced arranged marriages were also banned.
6. In chemistry, the same idea applies to chemical reactions. Le Chatelier's Principle states that the speed of a chemical reaction is constrained by the slowest link in the chain of the necessary sub-reactions.
7. A Gini coefficient ranges from 0 to 1 with 0 representing perfect equality of per capita incomes by province and 1 representing extreme inequality (one province having all income and the remaining 30 having no income). The inverse Sharpe ratio represents how disperse incomes are across provinces after normalizing for average per capita incomes.
8. Operating profits are also described as EBIT, or earnings before subtracting out interest and taxes.
9. Throughout we assume that (WACC and ROIC > g). This prevents our valuations from exploding to infinity—something we assume is economically not possible. If (ROIC > WACC > g), then growth will create value. If (WACC > ROIC > g), then growth will destroy value.
10. As opposed to the short-run rate, which is determined by the demand and supply of money, where the supply of money is determined by monetary policy.
11. We assume that (K / Y) is a ratio of two real numbers measured using the appropriate deflators for each, thus obviating the need to convert our gross return from a nominal to a real number.
12. The BEA also produces a different estimate for US non-financial corporate returns, which is higher based on the national income and product accounts. Our estimates

in Figure 4.17a and Figure 4.17b falls between the two estimates found in the *Survey of Current Business.*

13. In place of GDP, we could use retail sales, which does not include inventory accumulation as in GDP, but unfortunately excludes most investment, government spending, and net exports. In place of gross savings, we could also use net savings, which is net of depreciation. In place of fixed assets (which includes inventories), we could use all assets of the economy. Choices among all of these variables depend mainly on what national data are actually available for each country and which definition is most useful for a specific interpretation.
14. Consistent with historical averages since 1978, we assume that United States depreciation is 12.5 percent of GDP, while in China it is 13.6 percent.
15. One might exclude expenditure on recreation and leisure and include these with savings.
16. We will show a much broader measure of a nation's wealth or assets later.
17. We note that every company (country) is different, having differing volatilities and correlations in sales, costs, and cashflows. Similarly, tax consequences of new debt may vary by company—something not relevant to countries.
18. Alternatively, we could make the assumption of an all equity financed country—which, up until recently, could describe China, a country that relied heavily on FDI as a source of external finance).
19. Our net domestic savings measure is expressed in nominal terms, but even after adjusting for inflation, the rates presented are still unsustainable.
20. A review of these relationships in Chapter 3 would be useful.
21. The authors typically compare China to the "developed Americas," which includes the United States and Canada.
22. Over the years, China has had both ceilings and floors on interest rates for bank deposits and loans: what economists call "financial repression." As one tool in its efforts to enhance bank profitability and bank capital, it has removed the ceiling on interest rate loans, installed a floor on those rates, and put a ceiling on what could be paid on deposits. This, in turn, has created a sizeable profit margin for Chinese banks. Note: China's largest banks still have, as their principal shareholder, the Chinese government.
23. In the 2011 lending crisis in Wenzhou, a dynamic center for economic growth and exports in Zhejiang Province, borrowers defaulted on loans with interest rates

estimated to range from 14 percent to 70 percent (Martin 2012). See "China to Control Shadow Banking and Private Lending," (https://bbc.in/3fsT9Kt).

24. In the past, SOEs were required to provide some of the traditional services that governments typically provide, such as health, education, and other community services. Although these obligations have largely vanished, the majority shareholder (usually the government) may demand other forms of compensation. When a majority shareholder transfers assets of the firm to itself at the expense of minority shareholders, we refer to this as "tunneling."
25. Net interest paid to the large banks, e.g., Industrial and Commercial Bank of China (ICBC), Bank of China (BOC), Agricultural Bank of China (ABC), and China Construction Bank (CCB) are relatively close to the base lending rates suggested in Table 4.8, suggesting such clustering.

5
CONSUMPTION AND SAVINGS

大富由天小富由俭

Great Wealth Comes from Plain Luck, Plain Wealth from Great Thrift

Among large economies, China has the highest savings rate in the world—currently estimated at over 47 percent of gross domestic product (GDP), having peaked in 2008 at around 52 percent.[1] China's share of GDP saved exceeds even that of some of its high-saving neighbors, such as South Korea (32 percent) and Japan (22 percent); and it vastly surpasses the United States (18 percent). Figure 5.1 shows China's consistently-high domestic savings rate over the past four decades and how it has increased to even higher levels over the last decade. Since savings is the absence of consumption, we will take dual perspectives on China's high savings rate/low rate of consumption. The first sentence of this chapter could just as correctly have been written to say, "China has the lowest rate of consumption among the world's major economies." As a share of GDP, Chinese consumption has been only around 38 percent over the past decade—a rate far below the global average of 61 percent and the US average of over 68 percent. (See Figure 5.2 for Chinese household consumption share of GDP compared to the United States.) Household consumption rates in the United States and China were approximately equal in the early 1970s, then they diverged in the years to follow. Note that those earlier years of high consumption rates for China are typical for most early-stage emerging economies in which incomes are low and just sufficient to support subsistence consumption. Very few countries (https://bit.ly/3g8wjJz) today have a lower rate of consumption than does China.

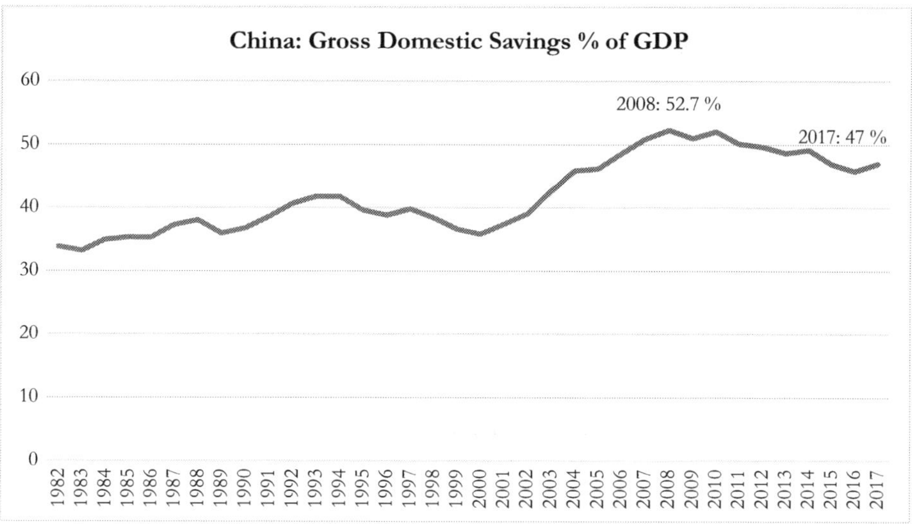

Figure 5.1 Remarkably, China's already-high savings rate continued to increase through the decades. It remains high even after declining a bit since the financial crisis.
Source: Author created based on World Development Indicators.

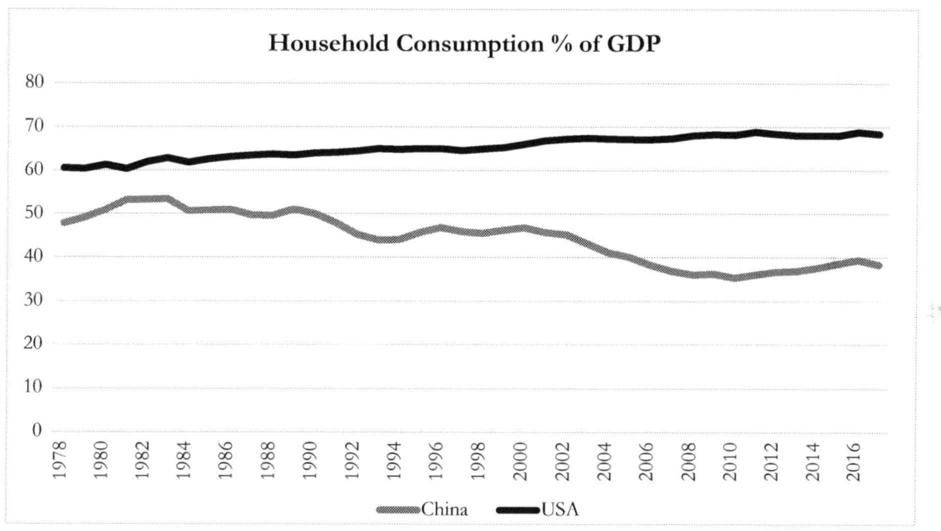

Figure 5.2 Notwithstanding spectacular growth in GDP, China's rate of consumption declined over the 2000s, rising a bit since the GFC.
Source: Author created based on World Bank Development Indicators.

Today, China's high level of savings is a key driver for other salient features of its economy, such as its current account balance, high level of investment, and rapid economic growth. Beyond China's borders, its high savings rate has implications for global imbalances on current and capital accounts in the balance of payments, world interest rates, and inflation and commodity prices. It is therefore very important to understand the factors behind China's high savings rate and how those factors are likely to evolve in the coming years. Examining China's savings rate will also allow us to look at the role that credit markets, corporate governance, and demographic factors (just to name a few factors) come into play.

China's Current Savings Rate

China's 2017 savings rate of around 47 percent of GDP is equivalent in US dollar (USD) terms to approximately USD 5.7 trillion.[2] China's savings rate has been high for decades; but, beginning in 2003, it surged even higher and continued to increase until the Great Financial Crisis (GFC). Meanwhile, in the United States, gross national savings has declined as a share of national income from about 25 percent in 1965 to an estimated 19 percent in 2018. Figure 5.2 shows the corresponding trends in consumption for each country over the past half century. While the data discussed here generally refer to national savings, we will focus our discussion on the savings of the private sector, broadly defined to include savings of individuals (households), non-government organizations, and businesses (enterprises). Specifically, we will not attempt to explain government savings or dis-savings in this chapter—this topic is covered in Chapters 9 and 10 on fiscal institutions and fiscal policy. We focus mainly on households and enterprises because they make up the lion's share of savings in China, and because these sectors' savings patterns can be explained more easily by economic and financial fundamentals: Government budget surpluses and deficits often result from policy-based decision making—an area of expertise for political scientists. It is important to note that, for the United States, government budget deficits (dis-savings) have been larger than private households' savings in recent years.

We recall that Gross Domestic Savings can be decomposed into household savings (S^H), corporate savings (S^C) and government savings (S^G). We have in:

Equation 1:

$$\text{Gross Domestic Savings} = S^H + S^C + S^G$$

And, since (Gross Domestic Savings – Investment = Current Account Balance). or external lending/borrowing ($-S^{CA}$) we also have in:

Equation 2:

$$\text{Investment} = S^H + S^C + S^G + S^{CA}$$

which shows that domestic investment can be financed via four different channels of savings: households, companies, the government or external sources. Table 5.1 provides a breakdown of the sources of domestically sourced savings in both countries by employment (labor), businesses (profits, rents, and interest income), and general government (budget deficits and surpluses). Recall that in Chapter 3 we discussed external savings, (S^{CA}). Business savings, here, is the broadest possible measure in each country's national income and product accounts—the operating surplus coming from corporate profits, rental income, proprietor income, and interest income of financial institutions. In effect, it measures returns to capital, whether owned by companies or individuals.

Sources of Gross Savings	China	United States
Broad Business Income	73%	95%
Government	-4 %	-4%
Individual Savings	31%	9%
Total	100%	100%

Table 5.1 Surprisingly, most of China's savings comes from business, not individuals, just as in the United States. Nevertheless, most theories attempting to explain China's high savings rate relate to individuals' behavior.
Source: Author created based on, CEIC, National Bureau of Statistics, Flow of Funds, Table 2–30 for China and US Bureau of Economic Analysis.
Note: Broad business income includes corporate, rental, proprietor, and interest income, including interest income to financial institutions.

Some interesting results and comparisons emerge. In both countries, most savings come from the business sector (possibly as high as 73 percent of all savings for China and 95 percent for the United States). For the United States, business income has increased in importance as a share of national savings in recent years. Notwithstanding high household savings rates in China (28–30 percent of disposable personal income [DPI]), DPI still remains a relatively low share of national income in China—thus limiting the possible contribution of savings generated by employment. We return to this point later in the chapter.

Meanwhile, in the United States, household savings as a share of personal income has been in the single digits for most of the post-WWII era, and it actually turned negative in 2009-2010 during the GFC. Though income from employment has a heavier weight in national income in the United States, the lower savings rate of individuals mitigates this effect. On balance, business income—not employee wages—are the main source of savings in China and in the United States. In both countries, governments reduce the national savings pool as measured by their net borrowing from the private sector. Part of operating surplus of businesses, as presented in Table 5.1, is corporate profits. Profits of large Chinese industrial enterprises (revenues over *renminbi* [RMB] 20 million) alone contribute about 21 percent of all of China's national savings, while in the United States (https://bit.ly/3cOKEZo) all corporations' gross after-tax profits contribute about 47 percent of all national savings.[3]

While the above discussion has focused on savings as a share of GDP, we can get a broader perspective by looking at per capita savings. Consider the following identity and corresponding ratios for each country in:

Equation 3:

$$\text{Per Capita Savings} \equiv (\text{Savings / GDP}) \times (\text{GDP / Population})$$

Table 5.2 compares the two countries using this savings relationship. Even though the United States saves much less as a share of GDP, on a per capita basis it saves three times as much as China. Clearly, the difference is in the much larger US GDP and the much larger Chinese population.[4] In terms of creating individual wealth and individual investment, the Chinese may view their savings rate as too low! As we discussed in Chapter 4, this paradox can be partially explained once we consider that each country is at a different point along the path of long-run economic growth.

Savings/GDP (×)	**GDP/Population**	**(=) Savings/Population**
	(2017 Current USD)	(2017 Current USD)
0.47	$8,827	$ 4,149
0.19	$59,532	$ 11,311

Table 5.2 Even though China saves much more than the United States does as a share of GDP, its large population dilutes national savings, thus resulting in a per capita level of savings that is actually smaller than in the United States.
Source: Author created based on World Bank World Development Indicators.

In both countries, investment including new homes, plant, property, and equipment, and infrastructure is the primary use of savings. Some of China's savings are lent to the world ($-S^{CA}$); the United States has had to borrow other countries' savings ($+S^{CA}$) in order to cover its own investment and consumption needs.

Theories of Savings

The theories below apply mainly to households. But for China and the United States, as we have just seen, the largest contributor to national savings is the business sector. (To the extent that the corporate sector is profitable, national savings will, of course, be higher.) We discuss corporate savings in the second half of this chapter. The government component of national savings (budget deficits and surpluses) are analyzed in the chapters on fiscal policy and institutions.

Disposable Income, Consumption, and the Interest Rate

In discussing different theories of household or personal savings, we begin with the accounting identity for the household in:

Equation 4:

$$\text{Personal Savings} \equiv \text{DPI} - \text{Personal Consumption}$$

Given the accounting identity above, a change in DPI would be exactly matched by a change in savings for a given level of consumption. Moving from accounting to theory, the Keynesian approach posits consumption as positively related to DPI, as is savings. As we shall discuss later, from a theoretical perspective, savings and consumption are more likely to be directly related to DPI when constraints exist on spending current wealth or borrowing against current wealth or future income. Classical economists have emphasized the role of interest rates in determining savings, since income is generally taken as a given at full employment. DPI, interest rates, and consumption are three key variables that both theoretically and empirically help to determine the level of savings.

Life-Cycle, Permanent Income, and Wealth Effects

Modern theories of savings and consumption emphasize the role of savings as a means to an end—where the ultimate goal is a smooth pattern of consumption over either a finite horizon (typically an assumed lifetime) or an infinite horizon for overlapping generations.[5] These theories of savings emphasize savings in its role as smoothing consumption, either in the short term or the longer term. In other words, savings act as a buffer to either unanticipated shocks to income or anticipated long-run changes in income, such as retirement. Most important to consider are the types of income (temporary or permanent) and the actual or projected income earned by different demographic groups for a given economy. This approach allows for more comprehensive theories of savings. Temporary changes in income have a smaller impact on consumption than do permanent changes (Friedman's [1957] permanent income hypothesis [PIH]). For example, a temporary increase in income will tend to be saved—so as to maintain a smooth (balanced) consumption pattern over time. This approach helps explain the smoothing of consumption over the short run when income experiences random shocks.

In the Ando-Modigliani life-cycle hypothesis (LCH) (Ando and Modigliani 1963), an individual recognizes three ages of man—youth, working-age, and retirement[6] Before retirement, he/she saves money; during retirement, he/she dis-saves. Roughly speaking, the saving that is undertaken during our employment years matches the consumption undertaken during years of retirement. Youth (for example, a student reading this text), neither earn nor save—only consume and dis-save. Clearly, LCH suggests a strong role for age distribution and the dependency ratio (defined below) within a society in determining the savings rate.

Figure 5.3 illustrates a typical consumption/savings pattern for an adult whose life-cycle is (*L*) years. For simplicity, we assume that the interest rate is 0, but income grows at a constant rate for (*L* – *N*) working years until retirement date (*N*). Savings during the working years must sum to the (*L* – *N*) years of consumption during retirement. This simple model explains the smoothing of consumption across the long run where income fluctuates predictably.

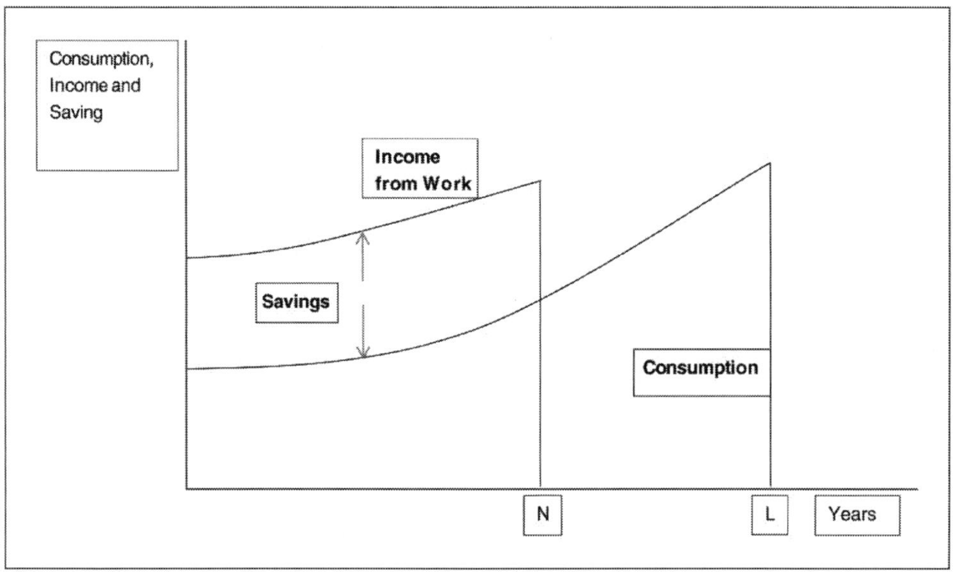

Figure 5.3 In the life-cycle approach, individuals save and accumulate wealth for retirement (at point N), thus smoothing consumption over their lifetime (at point L).
Source: Author created.

Both the PIH and the LCH, in emphasizing some type of planning horizon, suggest an important role for wealth in determining consumption. Here, "wealth" is broadly defined to include both accumulated wealth-to-date for an individual and the present value of future income; that is, the lifetime budget constraint. The LCH is really a special case of intertemporal income smoothing found in modern finance. Much of modern finance focuses on the role of identifying assets that can help smooth consumption across time or states of nature. Using wealth (or dis-saving) is an important way in which individuals can smooth lifetime consumption against both the long-run fluctuations in Figure 5.3 and shorter run fluctuations that might occur over the business cycle.

Figure 5.4 shows two extremes (points A and C); at point A, consumption in the earlier employment years is very low but high in retirement, while at point C the reverse is true. Clearly such consumption patterns would be unusual and undesirable. Point B represents a better point, where some income in the employment years is saved for consumption in retirement—a smoother pattern of consumption. Common sense and empirical evidence tell us that most people prefer points such as B.[7] Savings during employment allows individuals to obtain this smoother pattern. The higher the return on savings, the greater the consumption possibilities across both periods (a steeper slope for the line in Figure 5.4). Savings is the key element in allowing income to be smoother and utility to be higher across both long-term income imbalances and short-term income fluctuations. While governments may not explicitly impose restrictions on savings, policies which discourage savings or which make savings risky (for example, an unstable banking system) may have a disincentivizing effect, and this would push individuals toward points such as A.

From the LCH, we can also infer an increase in the savings rate in periods where economic growth accelerates from the norm. Here, the desire to smooth consumption (either absolutely or relative to an anticipated growth in income) causes one to save a disproportionate share of income earned from growth surges in order to maintain higher levels of consumption in retirement.[8] Conversely, if growth is anticipated to surge in the future, then current consumption will rise in anticipation of the future higher income. In this way, research attempts to show that the rapid growth in East Asia, and in China specifically (Modigliani and Cao 2004), is central in explaining the high savings rates found there. Modigliani and Cao incorporate the unique aspect of the one-child policy, begun in the late 1970s in China, which reinforced the need for savings by the working generation.

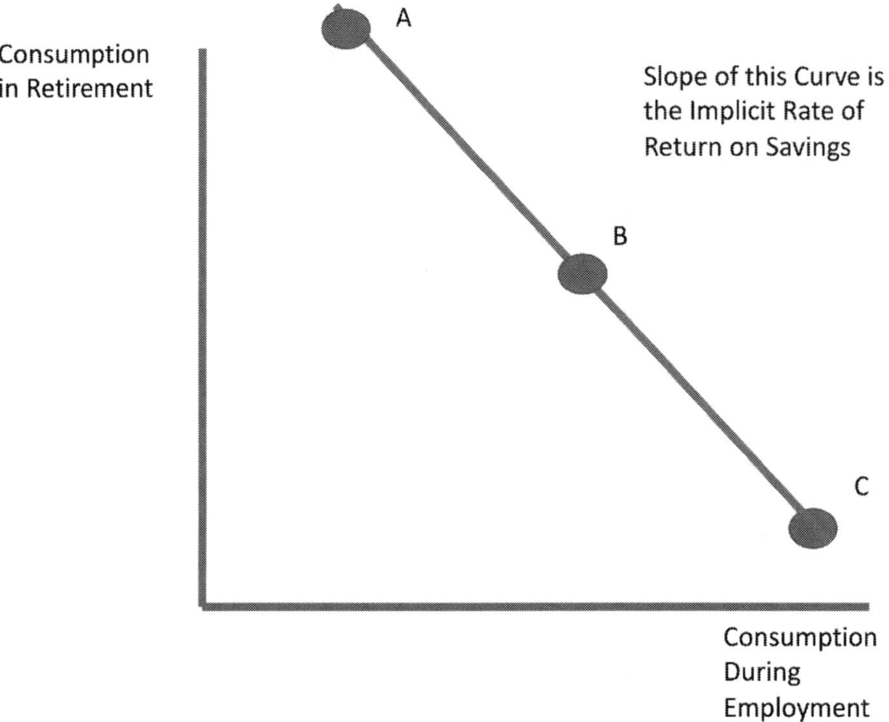

Figure 5.4 Smoothing consumption over their lifetime (at point B), individuals achieve an overall higher level of happiness than at the extremes (at points A and C).
Source: Author created.

As we noted above, another implication of the life-cycle approach is that higher growth rates today relative to the future will result in higher average savings rates today. China's simple average growth rate in real GDP from 1978 through 2017 has been above 9.6 percent. Figure 5.5 shows that, while China's growth rates surged up until the GFC, the following years have seen slower growth. The LCH suggests higher savings in those earlier years than in the years to follow. Our Solow model discussion in Chapter 4 tells us that these spectacular historical rates of growth cannot be sustained. As discussed, when the ratio of increments to income are so large, a larger portion is saved so as to smooth out consumption over the retirement period (Modigliani and Cao 2004).

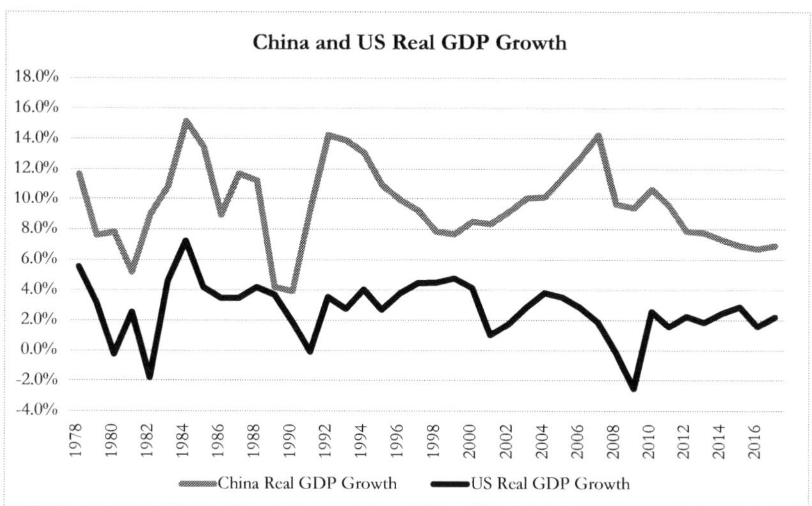

Figure 5.5 China's real GDP growth began to slow after the GFC after the spectacular growth rates of earlier years. As such, an optimal savings pattern consistent with income smoothing would be to save relatively more in periods of high growth and less post-GFC. Source: Author created based on Federal Reserve Economic Database.

Case Study 5.1: Symbiotic Savings, and Is Consumption (消费) Just a Waste?

Cultural differences are often cited as a reason for generally higher rates of savings in China compared to those in the United States. China's one-child policy, which began in the late 1970s, tends to force the current generation of workers to save rather than rely on the earnings of several offspring. Even in the absence of this policy, there is still a cultural bias toward saving (even the Chinese characters for consumption, 消费 [*xiao fei*], suggest waste and loss). Furthermore, an intergenerational simultaneity form of savings exists in China that no longer exists in the West. Consider that a typical urban worker in China has recently migrated from the countryside. He/she tends to be a low-skilled worker. Housing and food consumption are often part of the wage package and are covered by the employer. These workers save and remit a large share of their income (even though it is low) to their parents in the countryside. Meanwhile, the parents—whether working or retired—save their income as a bequest to the very same children who are saving for them! Such symbiotic saving helps keep China's savings rates high. An open question is whether future generations of young Chinese will maintain the same ethos of providing private support for the older generation, rather than coming to rely on a publicly funded social security system (as discussed in Chapter 10).

Liquidity/Borrowing Constraints

Liquidity and/or borrowing constraints represent another major determinant with respect to savings. This is similar to the situation we just examined in which savings or wealth accumulation is not permitted. In the presence of a binding liquidity or borrowing constraint, consumption cannot exceed the flow of income. In other words, savings cannot be negative. "Liquidity constraints" and "borrowing or capital market constraints" are terms often used interchangeably but, in fact, are different. Liquidity constraints represent the inability to convert accumulated wealth (financial or produced wealth) into purchasing power with ease. For example, penalties for early withdrawal from a retirement account or a certificate of deposit are forms of liquidity constraints.

Borrowing or capital market constraints represent the inability to easily borrow against accumulated wealth (e.g., use financial wealth as collateral for a loan) or future income (returns to human capital wealth). The impact of either liquidity or borrowing constraints, when they are binding, is that individuals consume up to their income (in contrast to consuming potentially up to their wealth—human and financial capital). Savings and consumption become a function of income; in other words, consumption and savings will only exceed income when the borrowing/liquidity constraints are relaxed. It has been suggested that these types of constraints are more likely to occur in developing economies where wealth is low and capital markets are undeveloped. Therefore, consumption and savings as a function of disposable income (as opposed to wealth) may be an appropriate description of savings and consumption for these emerging economies.

Liquidity or borrowing constraints allow saving but prevent dis-saving, and they have a particularly important impact in home, automobile, or other high-cost durable goods purchases.[9] Individuals typically must save for the down payment or purchase price of these items in the absence of a financing option. In the case of autos or other durables, purchases may simply not occur, which by definition reduces consumption and increases the savings rate.

We note that liquidity constraints, in the absence of borrowing constraints, would still allow for dis-saving or consumption above income. Borrowing constraints, in the absence of liquidity constraints, on the other hand, tend to encourage savings (while permitting dis-savings at a later date) because individuals understand that wealth accumulation is the only means for making large purchases. Furthermore, shocks to income that cannot be financed externally must be financed from savings. This suggests a higher savings rate. In a symmetrical fashion, shocks to consumption—a health care emergency causing health care consumption to rise, for example—will also need to be paid for out of savings when financing against future income is not available.

To the extent that constraints on lending by financial intermediaries (for example, usury laws) reduce returns to depositors, savings could be negatively impacted. Those with savings may choose to increase their own purchases of automobiles or other durables, since their savings cannot be profitably intermediated to an outside borrower.[10] Furthermore, in the presence of both liquidity and borrowing constraints (such as the situation in some developing economies) combined with negative real interest rates, one may choose to consume and not save at all—since the benefits of saving are small, if not negative.

Figure 5.6 shows the supply and demand for savings in the presence of constraints on either interest rates (a lending rate ceiling) or financial intermediation between household and corporate savers and household borrowers. Instead of lending supply occurring at the equilibrium level (*S*) where supply equals demand, it takes place at the level of (*S'*), because of either the interest or the financing constraint. Credit rationing is more likely as the demand for loans increases.[11] Empirical work suggests that the presence of lending or borrowing constraints increases the national savings rate. Specifically, if an increase in current income highly correlates with an increase in consumption, the presence of liquidity/borrowing constraints is likely (Hall 1978; LeBaron 2006).

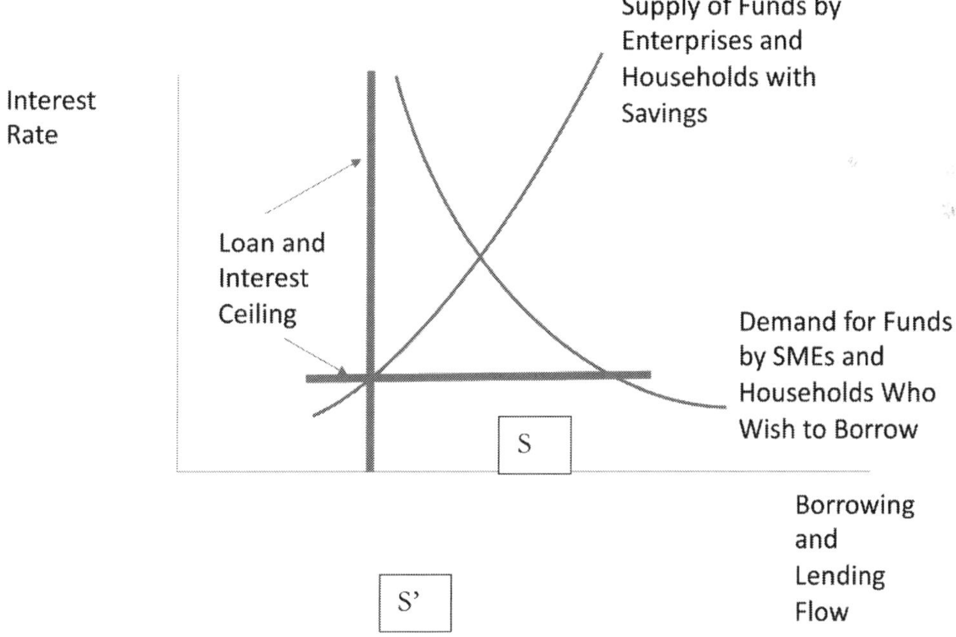

Figure 5.6 When there are constraints on lending such as at point S', borrowers face either credit rationing or "black market" interest rates, compared to the free market lending and rates at point S.
Source: Author created.

Precautionary Motive for Savings

Similar to the Friedman argument, uncertainty in income is an additional factor impacting savings—the so-called "precautionary motive." Here, the financial notion of income smoothing appears again, but at a point in time (rather than over time) across different states of nature—for example, a recession or an economic recovery. Figure 5.7 shows what consumption would be in two states (points A and B) where there is no savings by the individual to buffer the changes in income. The solid line shows the level of consumption when there is savings. Most individuals would prefer the stable consumption represented by the solid line rather than the volatility seen at points A and B. Case Study 5.2 provides the historical context for China's high savings rate and the precautionary motive for savings.

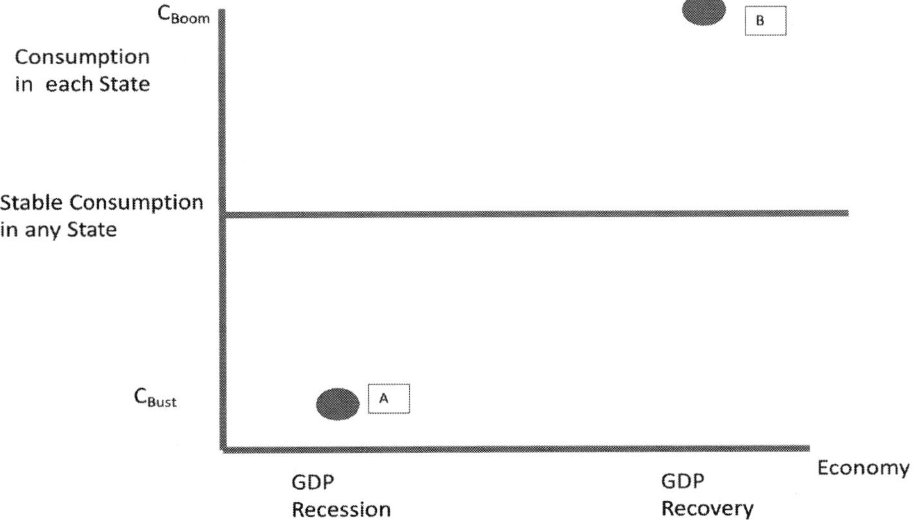

Figure 5.7 Rather than the volatile outcomes in consumption represented by points A and B, individuals smooth their income through use of savings and can achieve a more stable level of consumption.
Source: Author created.

Aggregating to the national savings rate, a key question is how open the economy is to financial and trade flows. A national income that is highly variable—due to exchange rate (terms of trade) shocks in which international trade is important, for example—may or may not be able to buffer those shocks through international borrowing and diversification. Such shocks that cannot be buffered due to either liquidity or capital market constraints (including the inability to diversify) at both the domestic and international level will result in countries choosing to save more as an alternative. Feldstein and Horioka

(1980) concluded that, in fact, markets still remain largely segmented from international borrowing and diversification. This finding implies that countries must, in effect, self-insure against shocks to real income via higher savings rates. Feldstein and Horioka's conclusion is not at all surprising to those steeped in the world of finance—companies also turn to internal funds before they turn to external sources of finance. This practice is referred to as the "pecking order" in financial theory, and it is discussed below.

At the macroeconomic level, the presumption is that increased uncertainty increases savings; however, the microeconomic foundation for this conclusion is less clear. Uncertainty has a dual effect—an income effect and a substitution effect. The income effect is the same as the precautionary motive discussed above; the certainty equivalent of our income is lower in future periods when there is greater uncertainty, so we need to save more. The substitution effect states that, since future consumption (and happiness or welfare) is less certain, we should "live for today," substituting current consumption for future consumption. That is, consume now and save less for the uncertain future. Which one of these effects dominates will determine savings in a microeconomic framework.[12]

Specific Savings Motives

In an interesting empirical work based on survey data, Horioka and Watanabe (1997) examine the motivation for savings by Japanese households. They find that the motivations for gross savings, in order of importance, are: retirement, housing, peace of mind, illness, education, marriage, consumer durables, leisure, bequest, business, and tax purposes. Most of these motivations can be subsumed under the broader theories discussed above.

Why Has China's Savings Rate Been So High?

China's Precautionary Motive

In the case of China, perhaps the most commonly cited explanation for the high savings rate is the precautionary motive—the desire to save as a precaution against uncertain fluctuations in income. Beyond the normal uncertainties of an agrarian society confronted with a rapidly rising population, blight, and drought, we see a rather amazing series of political events in China over the past 200 years, which clearly impacted its ability to produce income.[13] (See Case Study 5.2.) These events have combined with a still-weak social safety net (health insurance, unemployment insurance, and retirement benefits, as discussed in Chapter 9) to generate a clear need for significant personal savings.

Case Study 5.2: Recent Chinese History and the Precautionary Motive for Savings

Over 200 years of turmoil in China has undoubtedly formed a solid basis for precautionary savings. The intensifying encroachment of foreign powers into China in the 19th century reached a climax when Japan seized large parts of the country. The clash between Chinese imperial society, Western powers, and Japan served as a backdrop (and then set the stage) for a number of specific catastrophic events and movements. To name just a few, the Opium Wars (1839–1860), the Taiping Rebellion (1850–1864), the Boxer Rebellion (1899–1901), the collapse of a two millennia-old system of dynastic rule in the fall of the Qing (1911–1912), a period of warlordism and civil war between the Communists and the *Guomindong* (1911–1949), the Japanese progressive seizure of most of modern China (1915–1945), the massacre of Nanjing (1937–1938), establishment of a communist government (1949), the Great Leap Forward (1958–1962), the Cultural Revolution (1966–1976), and finally the movement toward a market economy beginning in 1978. Most of these events have become more or less a part of the vocabulary of anyone familiar with China. But the enormity of their impact on individuals living through these periods is difficult to fathom.

Never in the history of humanity have so many citizens of one country suffered such a series of disruptive events over such a prolonged period. Needless to say, the sum of the loss of life across this stretch of misery would total in the millions. Similarly, the loss of income for those who managed to survive the famines and other conflict-related hardships was enormous. Given the relatively recent movement toward a system in which individuals in China can actually save on their own, it is no surprise that those savings would be huge and would reflect the need to buffer against potential fluctuations in income, which in the past had led to outright starvation.* By way of comparison, volatility of real GDP in China from 1952 to 1977 (pre-Deng Xiaoping reform) was 10.5 percent per year; volatility in the industrialized economies over an overlapping period was about 2.5 percent.

But the events described above are of diminished significance to China's younger generation—especially those born after 1978. Table 5.3 gives the projected percentage of the population expected to be born post-1978 by year in China. In Figure 5.8 we see that, by 2020, a majority of China's population will have been born after 1978, and presumably the events pre-1978 will become a matter of increasingly historical—rather than personally—meaning. In turn, one would expect that the precautionary motive for savings will dampen.

*Prior to 1978, any savings or surplus was extracted from individuals as part of the central plan.

Year	Chinese Population Born after 1978
2020	56%
2025	61%
2050	83%

Table 5.3 The share of Chinese population born after the turbulent pre-1978 era suggests that the precautionary motive for savings is becoming less important to the younger generation.
Source: Author created based on United States Census Bureau International Database: IDB Database (https://bit.ly/3dedq51).

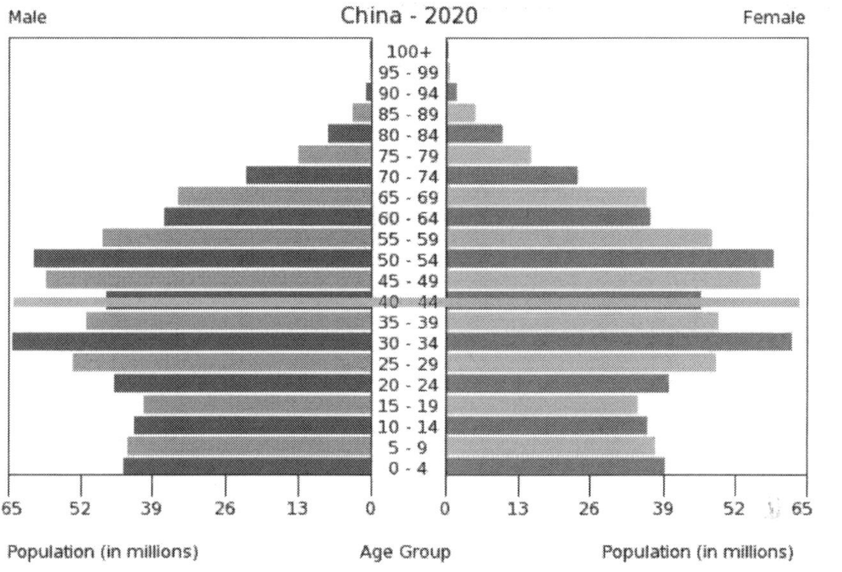

Figure 5.8 By 2020, all those in the age cohort below the thin (40-44 age cohort) line will have been born after 1978, a relatively stable social and economic period.
Source: Author created based on United States Census Bureau International Database: IDB Database (https://bit.ly/3dedq51).

Examining China's official GDP growth estimates during 1952–1978 against the post-1978 (reform) period, we see a large drop in GDP variance: from 10.5 percent to about 3 percent per annum. The latter number is not far above the output variability of the Organization for Economic Co-operation and Development (OECD) economies. If the set of impressive reforms that began in 1978 continues, the variability of output is likely to remain low, and this would tend to reduce the level of precautionary savings. But the kinds of uncertainty that existed in the past were essentially caused by political upheaval—as opposed to economic fundamentals. How well the economy is managed in the future will determine whether (economic) stability continues.

An alternate view is that post-1978 growth has created a different kind of uncertainty. According to Chamon, Liu, and Prasad (2010), high growth rates are accompanied by greater fluctuations and uncertainty regarding the future sustainability of growth.[14] They find that the greater uncertainty accompanying growth and structural shifts in the economy explains roughly 4 points of the 20–25 percent savings rates for 20- to 30-somethings. Taking a life-cycle approach, they also find that pension reform implemented in 1997 effectively reduced retirement income (after the age of 60) by about one-third. This has resulted in a higher savings rate among older Chinese workers on the verge of retirement. As growth rates move to more sustainable levels, if the social safety net is both widened and deepened, savings rates are expected to diminish with higher rates of consumption.

The Life-Cycle Hypothesis and the Dependency Ratio

Since the LCH posits that individuals save based on their age, it is important to examine the current demographic structure of China. A particularly useful metric is the dependency ratio—the ratio of those considered either too old or too young to work (over 64 and under 15 years of age) to those of working age (15 to 64). The higher the ratio, the lower the expected savings rate. Those between the ages of 15 and 64 have both DPI and consumption in the formula presented earlier in Equation 4. Those outside this range have mostly consumption and very little income from current employment, and this pushes savings and savings rates down. China's dependency ratio in 2017 was 42 percent, which is substantially lower than that of the United States (52 percent). But China's ratio has been on the rise in recent years. China and the United States' ratios compare favorably with the dependency ratio found in the Euro Area (55 percent) or Japan (66.5). No doubt this bulge in the working-age population in China plays a significant role in the high national savings rate

China's retirement age ranges from 55 (for females at enterprises) to 60 (male government workers) years of age, which is significantly lower than that of the United States (between 62 and 67).[15] China established (https://bit.ly/3cTpSrF) mandatory retirement ages in 1978. This has two offsetting effects. First, it forces China's dependency ratio to be higher. Second, given China's average life expectancy of about 74 years, the shorter working period necessitates greater savings to cover the longer retirement.[16] Since, at present, the demographic balance is still weighted more heavily toward those under 50, we have the second positive effect outweighing the first negative effect.[17] Overall, the life-cycle approach suggests China's lower dependency ratio has a positive impact on the savings rate of China.

Curtis et al. (2015) examine, in an overlapping generation model, the impact of China's changing demographic structure resulting from China's one-child policy. Specifically, they consider three effects, all of which would tend to increase household savings: (1) Fewer children per household lowering household consumption relative to income, (2) The increase in the share of the working-age population, and (3) Longer life spans of retirees combined with fewer children, which would require a greater reliance on savings rather than intergenerational transfers in retirement. Overall, though all three effects appear to have a positive impact on China's household savings rate, they find that the first effect of fewer children per household has the greatest effect.

Demographic Factors in the Coming Years

Figure 5.9a indicates that China's population in the coming decades will become, on average, older. By 2030, both China and the United States will have a higher share of older people (65 years and over) in the population than young people (15 years and below). China's dependency ratio at that point will be about 49 percent and the United States' about 64 percent. By 2050, the United Nations (https://bit.ly/2LNnWF0) estimates that both the United States and China will have similarly high dependency ratios, in the neighborhood of 60 to 66 percent. Figure 5.9b, for the United States demographic pattern, shows a more even transition to an aging population.

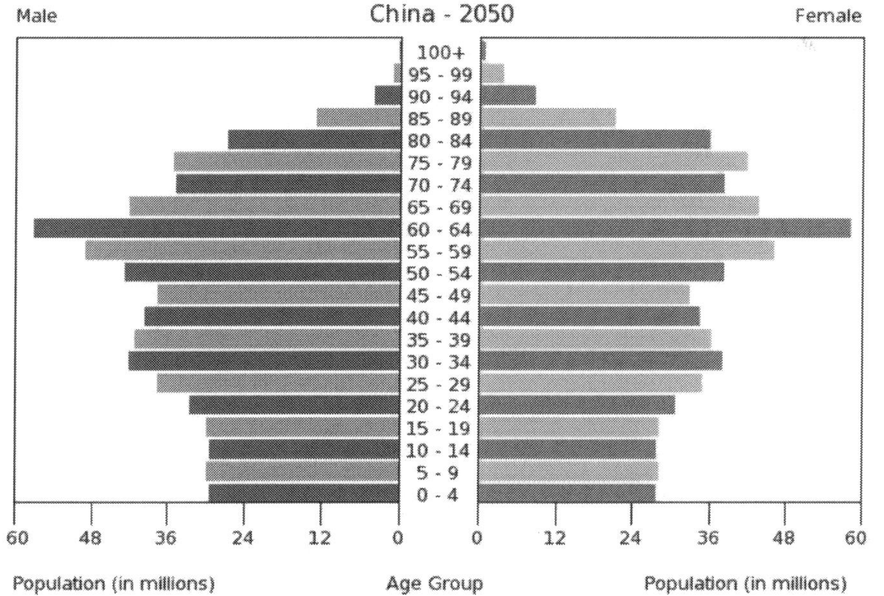

Figure 5.9a China's population will be challenged with a higher dependency ratio in 2050. Source: United States Census Bureau International Database IDB Database (https://bit.ly/3dedq51).

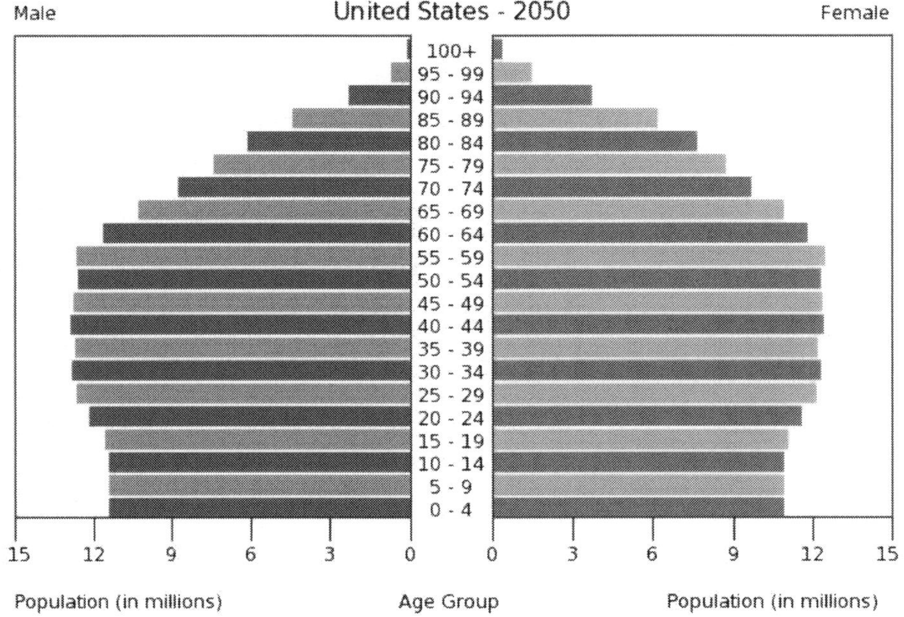

Figure 5.9b: In 2050, the United States will still have a relatively large cohort of the population of working age.
Source: United States Census Bureau International Database IDB Database (https://bit.ly/3dedq51).

A quick snapshot can be taken by observing that the largest cohort in 2020 was the 30- to 34-year-old group, which implies that, in 2050, the largest cohort will be the 60- to 64-year-old group. The implication for national savings is downward—but by how much? McMorrow and Roeger (1999) estimate that for every single percentage point increase in the dependency ratio, the average propensity to consume (1 minus the average savings rate) increases by about a quarter of a percentage point. Using the traditional definition of the dependency ratio and United Nations data, we see that, between 2015 and 2050, China's dependency ratio is expected to rise from about 38 percent to about 66 percent. This rise suggests a decrease in the savings rate of about 7 percentage points. If we examine the increase in the traditional dependency ratio out to the nearer horizon of 2025, we see a much smaller drop in the savings rate, of about 3 percentage points, from a 2015 base (for a retirement age of 65). Clearly, China's policy regarding retirement will be a critical factor in determining savings. The longer the typical retirement age of 55 to 60 years remains in place, the more dramatic the drop in the savings rate will be, due to demographic factors. Another factor in the coming years will be the impact of China's relaxing rules related to family size in 2016 (see Case Study 5.6). In all scenarios, however, the direction of average savings (from a demographic perspective) is downward.

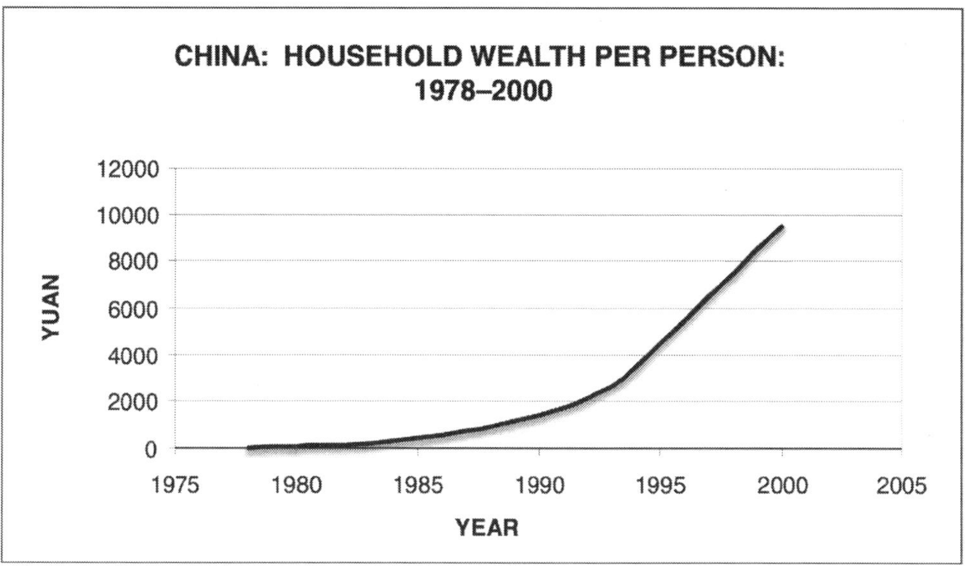

Figure 5.10a: With its high savings rate, China's average household wealth took off in the 1980s, and it has continued to grow.
Source: Author created based on National Bureau of Statistics.

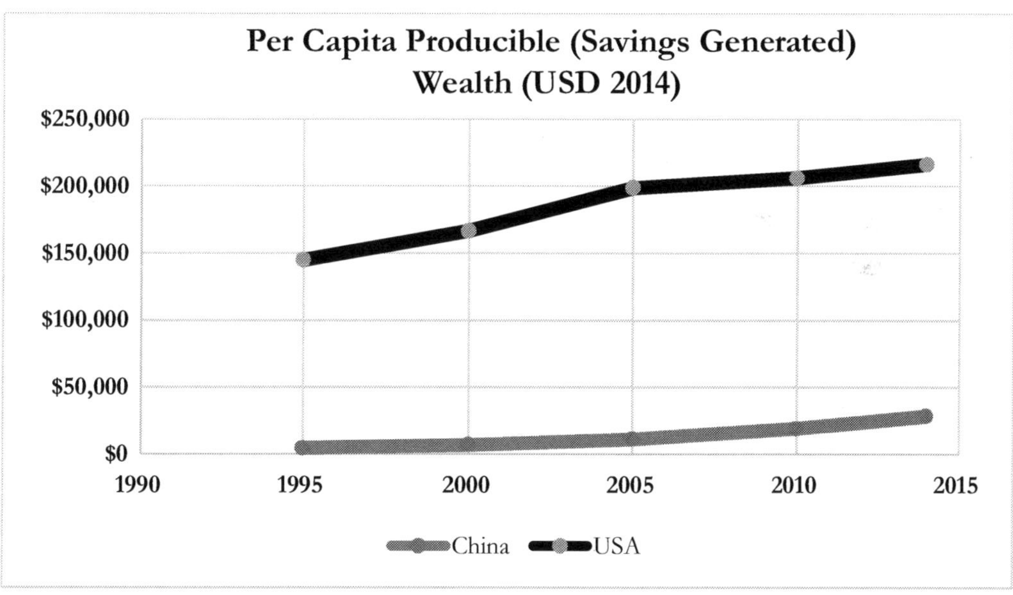

Figure 5.10b Though per capita wealth in China had grown to over USD 28,000 by 2014 (current exchange rates), it still remains far below that of the United States.
Source: Author created based on United Nations estimates.
Note: Figures are for producible wealth, which can be defined as wealth that is depreciable in the national accounts. It thus excludes human capital and national natural resources such as land, forests, and mines.

Finally, the LCH implies that consumption will be determined by the level of wealth. We approximate that private wealth in China was at USD 0 in 1978, then it rapidly increased thereafter (Figure 5.10a). Figure 5.10b and the United Nations (https://bit.ly/2XpSQJk) provide an updated estimate of per capita produced wealth in China at USD 28,600 and in the United States at USD 216,200 in 2014 (Lange et al. 2018).[18] Notwithstanding China's rapid accumulation of wealth, the country remains far from a steady-state level of wealth accumulation. Wealth accumulation is based on savings, and if China's citizens hope to become as wealthy as Americans, a continued pattern of high savings will be needed. But, as we discussed in Chapter 4, there is a difference between high and optimal savings.

Case Study 5.3: Keeping Up with the Wangs (Joneses)—Unbalanced Income Distribution

It has been argued that one of the reasons for high consumption rates in the United States has been the "keeping up with the Joneses" phenomenon, a colloquial formulation of the relative income hypothesis of the Harvard economist, James Duesenberry (1949). Specifically, individuals try to maintain consumption levels consistent with their neighbors and their own past peak levels of consumption. Besides having a remarkably prescient relationship to modern behavioral finance notions of anchoring and benchmarks, the theory also provides a unique twist on Chinese citizens' behavior. What if Chinese citizens, rather than trying to match their neighbor's consumption, try to match their neighbor's (higher) wealth? When income distribution becomes unequal, such a desire necessitates significantly higher savings on the part of those (large numbers of people, in the case of China) at the lower rungs of the income distribution.

Figure 5.11 shows an increasingly unequal income distribution in China across provinces. China's Gini coefficient between 2014–2016 has averaged around 0.47 (https://bit.ly/2AUjsKV), based on Chinese estimates (the United States' is estimated at 0.42 in 2016). This puts China in league with Latin American economies, who are known for their unequal income distribution. Since 1978, China's income distribution (virtually equal in 1978) has been growing evermore unequal alongside economic growth. In the United States, conspicuous consumption is the counterpart to China's conspicuous wealth—lavish homes and a foreign education for one's children are all ways of attaining status and "having face." These symbols of wealth do not go unnoticed by those in the bottom half or so of the income distribution; advertising and the media provide ready access to the rich and famous.

In an insightful paper by Jin, Li, and Wu (2011), the authors find that the widening gap in income has, in fact, led to increased savings by those at the lower end, particularly by those furthest down the income scale and by younger households. The one exception (remarkably consistent with what we know about China) is with respect to education. Those at the low end of the scale tend to increase spending on education—defined by GDP accountants as consumption, but in reality, a form of savings and investment in human capital.

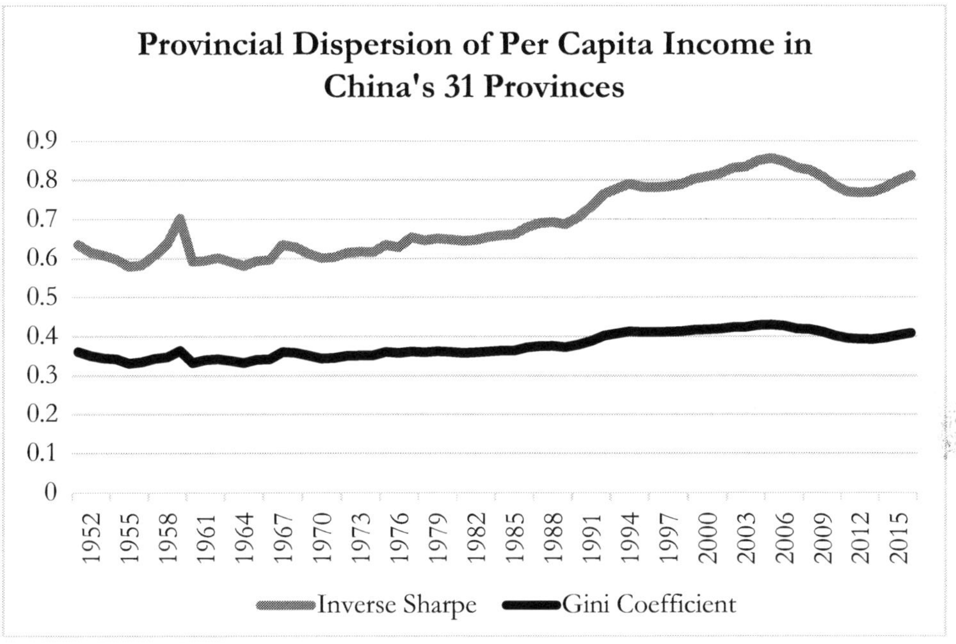

Figure 5.11 Income dispersion across provinces started to increase after the start of economic reform in China, and it slightly improved starting in 2006.
Source: Author created based on data from CEIC.
Note: Data represent the inverse Sharpe ratio by year for provinces and the Gini coefficient.

Borrowing/Lending Constraints and Consumer Credit in China

In the past, consumer credit has been an important bottleneck in China's efforts to spur consumption demand as an alternative to exports and investment as the primary drivers of short-term economic growth (see Case Study 5.4). Consistent with low levels of consumption, consumer debt (defined here to include everything from home mortgages to loans for a vacation or a credit card purchase for consumption) has historically been below that found elsewhere around the world. In Figure 5.12, we see that while overall credit to the private sector in China has historically been substantially below that of the United States, it is now approaching United States levels. Table 5.4 shows that the lion's share of loans still goes to businesses; but, as we discuss below, the growth in lending that started with the GFC has seen a relative shift to households and local governments.

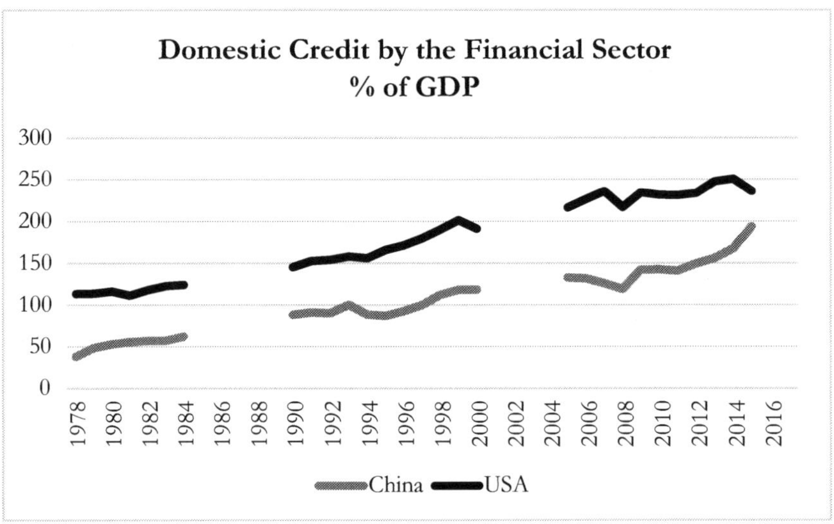

Figure 5.12 Domestic credit expansion as a share of GDP began a steep rise in 2011, and the ratio itself is now approaching that of the United States.
Source: Author created based on World Bank World Development Indicators.
Note: Breaks indicate missing data.

Borrowing Entity	2014	2017
Households	17%	19%
Corporates	56%	53%
Local Governments	18%	19%
Central Government	9%	9 %

Table 5.4 Household and local government shares of total non-financial institution debt have risen in China.
Source: Author created based on data from the 2018 IMF Article IV (https://bit.ly/3fCnBlu) Report, Table 6.

We note that, in China, over half of credit represents bank credit, and most of this is directed to large companies—the large banks still have the Chinese government as their principal shareholder (we discuss this further in Chapter 7, which describes China's monetary institutions). Figure 5.13 and Figure 5.14 show the dramatic increase in aggregate finance (also known as "total social financing," https://bit.ly/2Tv7tcX), which measures the full gamut of finance to private and state-owned enterprise (SOE) sectors. This includes equity and bond obligations, bank loans, and a variety of other financial instruments. In the United States, credit is provided by private lenders to private borrowers. Relatedly, Table 5.4 shows that only about 19 percent of total credit in China goes to the household sector—the lion's share of credit (about 54 percent) goes to the corporate sector. Finally, the private sector as defined in China includes many enterprises that still have the government as a major shareholder.

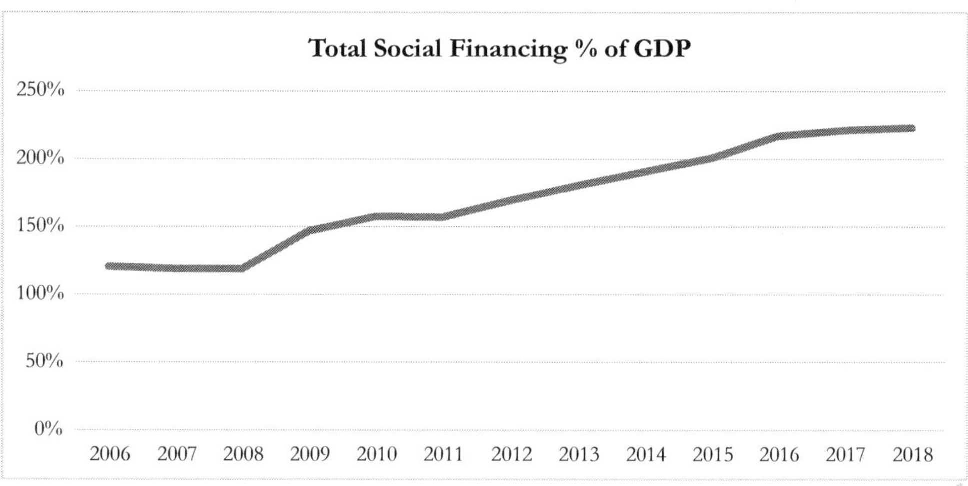

Figure 5.13 "Total Social Financing" represents finance to the private sector via banks, other institutions, securities, and instruments including RMB loans, foreign currency loans, entrusted loans, trust loans, undiscounted bank bills of acceptance, corporate bonds, non-financial corporate domestic equity financing, insurance company repayments, finance for investment property, and financing via other financial instruments. Source: Author created based on CEIC.

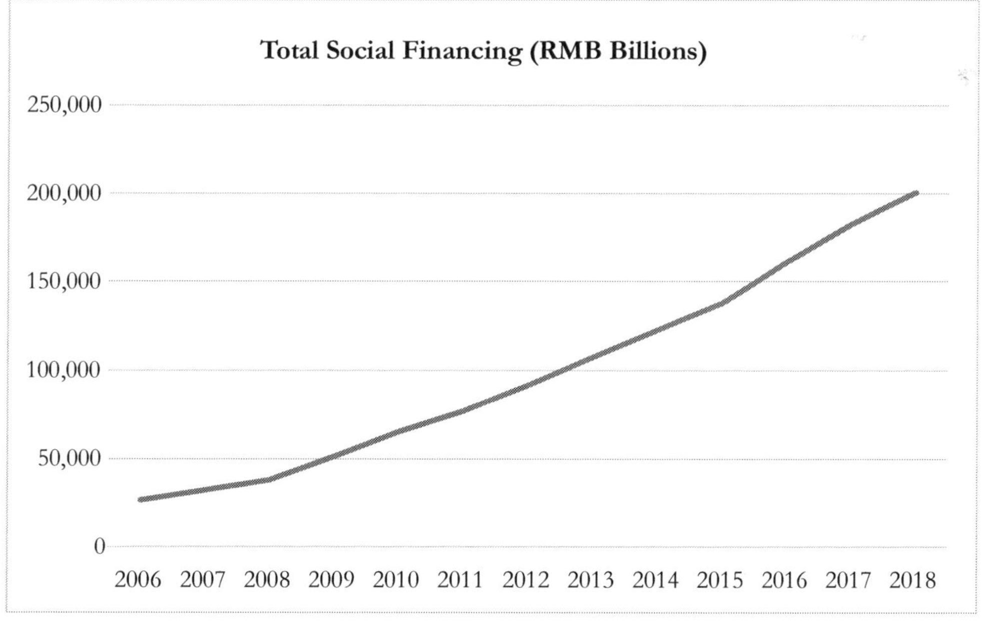

Figure 5.14 Total social financing has surged in China, particularly since the GFC. Source: Author created based on data from CEIC.

Notwithstanding the above qualifications, credit to consumers in China has surged in recent years from 12 percent of GDP in 2007 to close to 42 percent in 2018 (Figure 5.15). This figure is still well below the US rate (100 percent) or even that of China's Asian neighbors.[19] Following the GFC, this ratio has been growing in China and shrinking in the United States. An estimated RMB 40 trillion in household debt now exists in China, an increase from RMB 23 trillion in 2014. Most of this debt represents residential mortgages. In part, this reflects liberalization in the credit markets, as we discuss below. We discuss some specific areas where credit market activity is particularly important. Table 5.5 provides typical terms on major classes of consumer loans (including mortgages) in China.

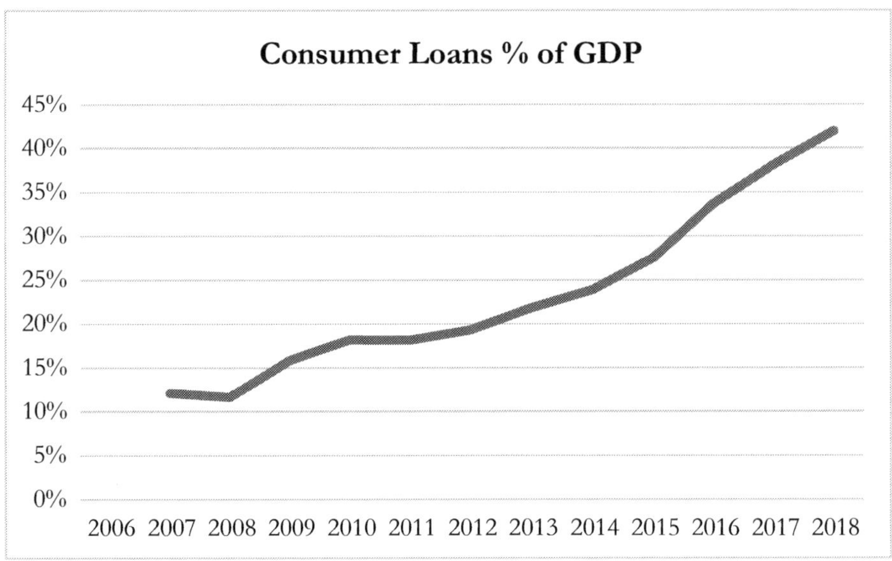

Figure 5.15 Consumer lending in China has grown rapidly since 2013, with the largest part being for residential mortgages.
Source: Author created based on data from CEIC.

Type of Loan/Term of Loan	Interest Rate	Maturity	Limit
New Housing Purchase	PBOC Guideline can Float	30 Year Maximum	**80% Value of underlying**
Automobile	PBOC Guideline can Float	3–5 Year Maximum	**60% Value of underlying**
Study Abroad USD Loan	PBOC Guideline	1–6 Year Maturity	**90% of Tuition and Living Expenses**

Type of Loan/Term of Loan	Interest Rate	Maturity	Limit
Personal Investment and Business	PBOC Guideline	5 Year Maximum	**RMB 30 thousand to RMB 3 million**
Revolving Credit	**PBOC Guideline can Float**	**1 Year Maximum**	**Maximum of RMB 500 thousand**

Table 5.5 Typical terms for consumer loans in China.
Source: Author created based on data from Bank of China.

Progress in Consumer Credit Markets

In recent years, perhaps one of the most dramatic changes in China has been in the greater availability of consumer finance. Clearly, a major relaxation of borrowing and liquidity constraints is under way in China. Inevitably, this change will have the impact of greater consumption and its mirror image of lesser savings. Whether or not China will evolve into a consumer society with a borrowing culture similar to that of the United States is unclear. Recent liberalization in credit markets suggests that Chinese consumers will indeed increase borrowing and spending. But China will still need some institutional developments in order to foster credit market growth while minimizing the risks of a consumer-led credit crisis. We discuss the great progress that has been made, and what areas still need improvement, below:

Yan et al. (2018) discuss the main set of players in the now dynamic consumer finance industry:

- Banks
- Licensed Consumer Finance Companies
- Large Internet Companies
- Peer-to-Peer (P2P)
- E-Commerce Companies

Banks and Consumer Finance Companies

The late 1980s saw the start of formal consumer sector loans with banks making loans for the relatively durable goods. Over the years, banks gradually expanded their consumer loan portfolio to include the areas listed in Table 5.5, as well as travel, home improvement, and, for some banks, health care (https://reut.rs/3bSrel2). Licensed consumer finance companies such as Home Credit Group (https://bit.ly/3e7lRzZ) began to operate and compete with banks for specific market niches as early as 2007. In the past decade there were a number of new entrants to the industry, with a total of 28 consumer finance companies in China by 2019.

Internet Companies

The three giants in China's internet industry—Baidu, Alibaba, and Tencent (BAT)—began to enter consumer finance markets around 2004. Tencent's popular Weixin payment mechanism commenced in 2013. With the introduction of e-wallet (phone-based electronic payment mechanisms) such as Alipay and WeChat (https://bit.ly/3e9G7Be), an estimated 62 percent of transactions in China are now undertaken with these new innovative modes; use of debit and credit cards and cash, meanwhile, has fallen behind. Remarkably, in China, it is common for many young people to only carry their cell phone embedded with a payment application and QR code (https://bit.ly/2ZD5IhZ) as they go out to make a purchase or buy a meal from a street vendor. An estimated 700 million users use Alipay. It should be kept in mind though, that these payment mechanisms generally do not provide credit from a financial institution—rather they provide a mechanism to debit (withdraw and transfer) cash out of one's bank account.

This "fintech revolution" has and continues to transform consumer finance in China, presenting both great opportunities and risks. Of 27 global fintech startups (https://bit.ly/3bQyxJV) to reach a value of USD 1 billion in 2018, eight were Chinese, and of these, two were related to consumer finance.

P2P

There are around a dozen large peer-to-peer lenders in China. P2P refers to the use of financial technology to link individual borrowers directly to individual creditors, bypassing the traditional banking system. PTP lending, often Internet-based, is part of the broader world of microfinance lending. Entrepreneurs directly link those who wish to lend with those who wish to borrow. This is a different model from the traditional financial institution model of pooling deposits into a fungible source of funds for making loans. The critical risk management question related to PTP lending is, how much of their own capital do PTP shareholders (owners) actually have at risk? In the past, very little information was available about the financial situation of these entities.

Firms such as Credit-Ease (https://bit.ly/2WRz5eh) were established in tandem with the growth in internet usage. P2P lending targeted small individual borrowers, such as farmers and students. Several thousand P2P lenders entered the market in China—a market that had threadbare regulation. In fact, PTP is part of a new and rapidly growing shadow banking system (see Chapter 11) creating yet-undetermined risks. As problems developed in the industry, including the spectacular collapses of several firms such as Ezubao (https://reut.rs/3bV1ILW), regulators closed several thousand P2P lenders—a process that continues to the present. In turn, the remaining more well-established firms have shifted their focus from individual consumer loans to lending to small- and medium-sized enterprises and to the more sophisticated asset management business (e.g., the sale of wealth management products). Alipay and WeChat Pay, however, do provide small loans to individuals via their own platforms.

E-Commerce Companies

Companies from automobile manufacturers such as Geely (https://bit.ly/3cUtppE) and Mercedes, to home electronic product companies such as Suning (https://bit.ly/3ebVzNg), to China's largest online retailer JD.com (https://bit.ly/2M1GCBn), have all set up consumer finance companies to support the purchase of their products. An estimated 30 percent (https://reut.rs/2AUkZ3D) of all automobile purchases were financed with a loan in recent years.

Case Study 5.4: Credit History, Data Analytics, and Social Scores

The transformation taking place in China in evaluating creditworthiness has been both dramatic and extremely innovative. In the past China lacked credit history data and the information necessary to provide individuals with a credit rating. Information is the coin of the realm in finance. Anathema to the proper functioning of financial markets is asymmetric information. Lack of information leads to the "lemons problem," in which credit is restricted due to the absence of good information on borrowers (who have perfect information on their own creditworthiness); the end result is that the markets collapse and credit availability dries up.

With the advent of large BAT internet companies entering the consumer credit market, vast amounts of transaction data have been collected and used to assess creditworthiness. Both Ant Financial's Sesame (Zhima) Credit (introduced in 2015) and Tencents' China Rapid Finance have employed such techniques. Participation is voluntary; but, in order to borrow or lend on these social platforms, participants must grant approval to be scored. Sesame Credit gives participants credit scores ranging from 350 (worst) to 950 (best) with a score of 600 or above permitting users to enjoy some specific rewards (e.g., special sales promotions) and the right to borrow money from lenders on the online platform. For example, a score over 666 allows a short-term loan up to RMB

50,000. By 2017, China Rapid Finance (Tencent) had granted over 20 million loans employing its own credit scoring system using similar big data methodologies. Sesame Credit has teamed up with Baihe (https://bit.ly/2ALLCaB), an online dating service, to use the scoring system for better matchmaking.

Metrics of non-payment, delayed payment, frequency of credit use, assets shopping, and other transaction profiles (such as travel) and creditworthiness of social media friends are incorporated into algorithms used to come up with a score. Given that most Chinese are using these large social media platforms, it is reasonable to assume that the majority of Chinese citizens have some sort of credit score—whether they know it or not.

The potential for understanding consumer credit quality has gone from very opaque to fully permeable, and it has in turn raised issues of privacy. Meanwhile, both the central and local governments in China have been building up their own credit scoring systems. In some cases, the authorities have chosen to make public those with unfavorable scores. An estimated 9 million citizens with poor scores have received penalties, such as travel bans on the nation's high-speed train, prohibitions on purchasing property, or cancellation of mobile phone services. Given the growth in scoring by a motley group of private companies and public entities (ranging from internet companies, financial institutions, telecom companies, and local governments), the central government has decided to combine the various efforts into one national social credit score (SCS). The authorities announced their plans for the SCS in 2014, saying that it would "Forge a public opinion environment where keeping trust is glorious. It will strengthen sincerity in government affairs, commercial sincerity, social sincerity and construction of judicial credibility" (Botsman 2017).

The authorities believe that SCS will build trust among individuals and companies in China and thereby promote economic efficiency. A universal and comprehensive system is to be introduced in 2020, combining the efforts of eight major firms, including the BATs, as well as other entities engaged in gathering data and scoring of individuals and companies.[20] Participation will be mandatory; that is, data collection and scoring will be without individual or company consent.

As the word "social" implies, the SCS goes well beyond a financial credit score. It will include both online and offline data ranging from individual purchases, borrowing and lending performance, online chat and post content, tax payments, friends' scores, criminal activities, and disorderly conduct. Smoking in non-smoking areas, bad driving, and too much time playing video games have been included in some of the test pilot scoring programs in China. The score will be affected not only by negative activity, but also by what are deemed positive activities, such as the donation of blood.

Needless, to say, such a program raises a host of concerns. Who will have final control over the score determination? Who will have access to the scores? Can disagreements regarding an individual's score be resolved fairly? Some scholars (Posner 1981) suggest that privacy issues are often overstated. Posner makes an analogy between the fraudulent sale of a defective product (clearly illegal) and an application for employment by a job seeker who hides his/her own faults and failings. He suggests that greater disclosure promotes economic efficiency and a better matching of individuals in a variety of economic transactions. Markets, however, are often not rational. For example, discrimination based on religion, ethnicity, or preferences can lead to sub-par outcomes. Furthermore, when scoring has non-economic motives related to political power and control, problems will arise (Yongxi and Cheung 2017). And this is likely when the legal and judicial frameworks are weak.

In China, one could view the SCS as a response to the historical difficulty of enforcing contracts and other private agreements. In effect, its economic goal is to prevent agreements that fall apart with no legal recourse. Meanwhile, states and localities in the United States seem to be moving in the opposite direction: In an effort at giving low-level convicted criminals a second chance, California (https://nyti.ms/3cULYKr) and some localities have prevented or are considering preventing the release of conviction records and banning questions related to prior arrest and conviction records during job interviews. Only time will tell whether the efficiency gains in China outweigh the host of other potential social and political costs; and if the desire to achieve the perfect score becomes too burdensome (压力很大 [*ya li tai da*] or "the pressure is too high") for individuals in society.

Some Specific Markets

Home Mortgages

An important area of credit to individuals, in both the United States and China, is the home mortgage market. Home ownership in China (mentioned earlier) is among the highest in the world, with possibly over 90 percent of households (https://bit.ly/2A14QJ1) owning a home. US home ownership peaked at 70 percent pre-GFC, and it is now down to around 64 percent (https://bit.ly/2ylsv6q). Owning more than one home is not uncommon among China's middle class—a key investment in an economy with limited investment choices. In Case Study 5.6, we can see that home ownership brings both status and possibly a spouse. Thus, the importance of owning a home should not be underestimated.

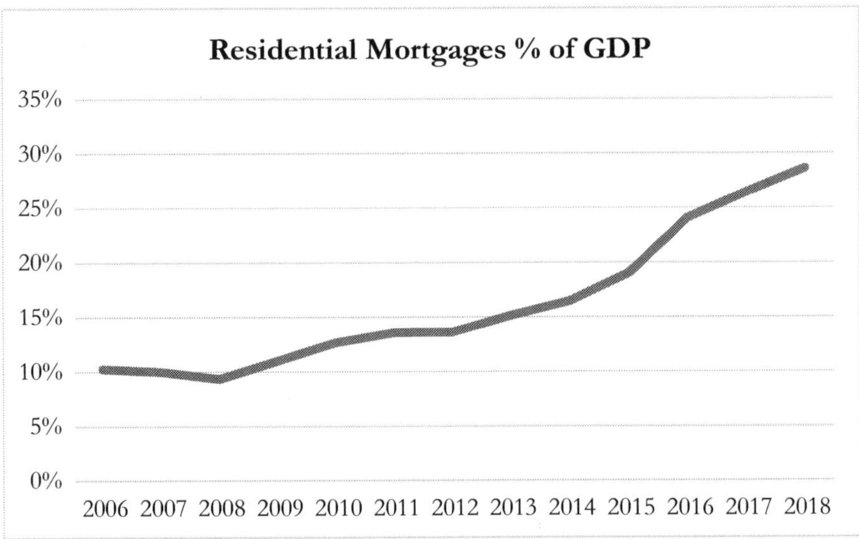

Figure 5.16 Residential mortgage growth has helped fuel the large increase in real estate prices discussed in Chapter 6.
Source: Author created based on data from CEIC.

We observe in Figure 5.16 that residential mortgage lending began to take off around 2012, and by 2018 it was valued at 29 percent of GDP in China (over 50 percent of GDP in the United States). Comparing Figure 5.14 to Figure 5.16, we see that home mortgages represent the largest component of consumer/household lending. In 2008, the value of mortgages outstanding was only RMB 3 trillion—by 2018, that figure had surged to RMB 25 trillion. In the past, only the upper echelons of the income distribution could tap into the formal credit market. But in recent years, the required down payment has been lowered and now stands at only 20 percent of the purchase price, just about the same as in the United States.[21] Most individuals still need substantial savings to acquire a home. As a proportion of all consumer loans, mortgages make up about 53 percent in China, versus around 73 percent in the United States. In part, this difference reflects the relatively expensive cost of a home in the United States and banks' greater willingness to finance debt with tangible collateral in both countries.

Student Loans

The student loan market is also still relatively small in China. Although higher education is an important symbol of status and a stepping stone to marriage, most students do not obtain loans in formal financial markets. With some effort, middle class family savings are usually sufficient to cover the costs of school, and in some cases local governments provide tuition support.

Chinese banks do offer student loans; but, for most families in China, tapping into this source of funding remains difficult (see the section on borrowing constraints). Only an estimated 10 percent of students participate in the two available government-sponsored loan programs. As one measure of the difference, average student debt (https://bit.ly/3bTCAp0) of graduating students in the United States is around USD 37,000. There are about 44 million borrowers in the United States with a combined debt of over USD 1.5 trillion. In contrast, the China Development Bank, a major student loan provider (https://bit.ly/2WRg3Vv), reported that it anticipates lending to 12 million students an average of about USD 2,000 in 2018. Of course, student lending has grown substantially in recent years. Between 2000–2004, only 830,000 students received loans in China.

Internet giant Baidu has now entered the student loan market, potentially disrupting the market. With an initial focus on lending for vocational and training programs for adults, Baidu now controls at least 75 percent (https://bit.ly/3cXTFPO) of the private market for student loans. With outstanding education-related loans of RMB 210 billion per year, covering 30 million borrowers, Baidu U anticipates making 3,000 new loans per day for education. Loans are typically less than RMB 30,000, and they target the 25- to 30-year-old market. The program is intended for those who have not had the opportunity to attend a traditional college but would like to attend one of China's many training or vocational institutions. Officially, there were only about 1,400 higher education vocational schools and 11,000 devoted to secondary-level vocational education in China, but the number of private training institutes offering some type of certificate is much larger.

A number of factors combine to limit the size of the market for student loans in the traditional college/university market. Most students are still assigned to state-run universities based on a national test (the much-feared 高考 [*gaokao*]), where the tuition is quite low (around USD 2,500 per year—a quarter of the cost of a public university in the United States, and less than one-tenth of the cost of a private university). In China, student loan programs, such as those provided by China's Development Bank, are targeted mostly to very low-income families. Once again, the contrast with the United States, where most students borrow through publicly or privately financed loan programs in pursuit of a higher education, is remarkable.

Enforcement

When borrowers default, lenders need an orderly and legal mechanism for compensating themselves and penalizing borrowers. Perhaps collateral is seized by the creditor or a new payment schedule is established. Perhaps borrowers are excluded from the credit market in the future or, as in some countries, even imprisoned. China has yet to develop an orderly process. Even when courts do make a determination regarding a default, enforcement of the ruling (collection) remains problematic. This lack of regular enforcement opens up the real possibility of non-legal, arbitrary, and sometimes criminal methods for collecting bad debts.

Case Study 5.5: Credit Reforms as an Example of a Program Rollout

In late 2013, China's Banking Regulatory Commission (CBRC) announced that its Consumer Finance Company pilot program would be expanded to cities including Chongqing, Guangzhou, and Qingdao. The program had already been introduced in Beijing, Shanghai, Tianjin, and Chengdu. The new policy allows for non-bank financial institutions with assets over RMB 80 billion to make consumer loans locally. This excludes loans for automobiles and home mortgages (unlike in the US, where mortgage loans are still the purview of regulated banks).

Consumer finance has been a relative latecomer in China's post-1978 reforms. In May 1998, the People's Bank of China (PBC) issued "Methods of Management of Personal Housing Loans," which detailed regulations related to interest rates, maturity, and eligibility in the home mortgage business. In 1999, the PBC issued "Guidelines for Conducting Personal Consumer Credit," opening the way for commercial banks to provide consumer credit across the board.

In 2003, the CBRC allowed companies with total assets of RMB 4 billion and registered capital over RMB 500 million to set up auto financing businesses. This allows the auto financing market to move outside the banking system, particularly to the major auto manufacturers themselves. Earlier reforms included allowing banks to make consumer loans and issue debit and credit cards. Today, Chinese financial institutions have issued an estimated 3 billion debit cards and 300 million credit cards, the latter seeing rapid growth in recent years. These various steps are all part of an ongoing process for freeing up and transforming China's vast savings into consumption demand.

That the recent reforms were first introduced in a few cities, then rolled out to an even broader number of Chinese cities, is unique to China and virtually identical to what a company would do with a new product being tested in the market. This method provides an opportunity to experiment, learn what bugs exist in the program, then recalibrate and improve for the final broad-market introduction. This approach has worked remarkably well for China in a number of areas, including allowing farmers to sell their produce at market prices in the late 1970s; the creation of special economic zones in the 1980s as a stepping stone to opening up all of China to foreign direct investment; the development of an interbank market in foreign exchange; the development of a corporate bond market; and plans to introduce special economic zones for allowing full convertibility of the RMB against other currencies. This methodical approach has served China well, and it has contributed to its spectacular economic performance in recent decades.

Other Factors Impacting China's Savings Rate

Policies Promoting Investment and Exports

If we consider the fundamental accounting identity in an open economy, we have in: Equation 5:

$$\text{National Savings} = \text{National Investment} + \text{Current Account Balance}$$

In an accounting sense, this identity suggests that the higher the level of the current account surplus or level of investment, the higher the level of savings.[22] Alternatively, and more intuitively, the higher the level of exports and production of investment goods as a share of some total fixed output, the less available for consumption. Thus, as a result, savings must be higher. Chairman Mao's policies in the 1950s, which followed the Soviet model of massive investment in infrastructure and heavy industry while at the same time isolating the economy internationally, effectively put China on a path of high national savings. In terms of the landscape of production, this was similar to the United States' New Deal—a period of massive public works projects. But a key difference was the role of labor working under a pervasive system of communes directed toward the goals of a planned economy. An economy directed from above (the central government) to produce investment goods will be constrained in its production of consumer goods. After 1978, China's policy-makers shifted to opening up the external sector, but with an emphasis on the export of goods. Again, in an accounting sense, the production of consumer goods would be squeezed.

Implicit Insurance of Savings Deposits

The real return on savings will impact a nation's propensity to save over the long run. These deposits become, in effect, risk-free if the government implicitly guarantees the principal on savings deposits within the state-owned banks. Confidence in China's government-backed guarantee has played a key role in its continued savings, even in the face of China's silent banking crisis (1998–2003) (see Schramm et al. 2018). One could imagine other outcomes, including a financial panic or a surge in the purchase of consumer durables. The history of financial crises worldwide is filled with such situations, but China has managed to avoid this problem due, in large part, to its ever-growing national wealth and to an implicit government guarantee.

Case Study 5.6: Love and Marriage—Unbalanced Sex Ratios

In an interesting piece of research, Wei and Zhang (2009) cite the current imbalance in the ratio of males to females in China as an explanation for half of the increase in China's savings rate since 1995. They argue that, in order for sons to find a marriage partner, parents need to save more for what is, in effect, a reverse dowry—to make their son an attractive candidate. Potential bridegrooms similarly save more in order to purchase a home.

China's one-child policy, which commenced in the late 1970s, combined with a strong traditional preference for sons, has led to the current unbalanced sex ratio. One would normally expect about 106 boys for every 100 girls in any given population—in China that ratio likely now exceeds 124 to 100. For those of age 25 in 2005, there was an estimated excess number of males relative to females amounting to 30 million—the population of Canada! Examining data from 122 rural counties and 70 cities, the authors find a strong link between sex ratios and savings rates. An interesting question not fully answered is why families with just one daughter do not save less.

In the meeting of the Third Annual Plenum of China's top leadership (2013), it was announced that the one-child policy would be relaxed. If at least one parent came from a one-child family, then those parents would be allowed to have two children. By 2016, in an implicit acknowledgement of the unintended harmful consequences of China's one-child policies, the plan was fully scrapped, and parents were encouraged to have two children. Needless to say, this has led to much soul-searching and economic calculations regarding the value of a second child; a second child brings both joys and significant additional costs.

Summary of China's Personal Consumption and Savings

As we survey the above sections, we get the sense that almost any theory of consumption can lay claim to explaining China's large savings rate on the part of individuals or households—and there are many theories of consumption.[23] But this focus on consumption in explaining savings is, to some extent, misguided, since the larger part of China's savings comes from institutions rather than private individuals. That is to say, the sum of profits of SOEs and private companies are larger than individual savings.

What is remarkable is the amount of academic research that attempts to explain China's high savings rate via the lens of the household. Unfortunately, as we demonstrate below, most of this research ignores the largest component of China's savings—corporate savings (also known as corporate income, enterprise profits, or net income).

The crux of the matter is that if Chinese enterprises take up a disproportionate share of Chinese national income, it can only mean that household income is that much lower. In turn, household consumption will be low. Meanwhile, enterprises do not consume but engage in one main activity—investment. In other words, only consumers (and the government) can consume—companies primarily save and invest. The academic research sheds a great deal of light on individual savings motivations from an economic, cultural, and historical perspective. While we do learn some important concepts from the above sections related to China's high household savings, we must now take up the issue of corporate savings.

Guo and N'Diaye (2010) suggest that, notwithstanding all of the above household consumption theories, there is in fact nothing special about China's pattern of consumption and savings when compared to a cross-section of 39 countries. In effect, these authors find that DPI in China is substantially lower as a share of national income—a fundamental difference that explains at least one-third of the difference in consumption and savings. For example, China's DPI as a share of GDP has averaged about 43 percent of GDP over the 2013–2017 period; in the United States that figure remains around 76 percent. Rather than asking, "Why is consumption so low in China?" the authors suggest that a better question would be, "Why is DPI so low in China?"

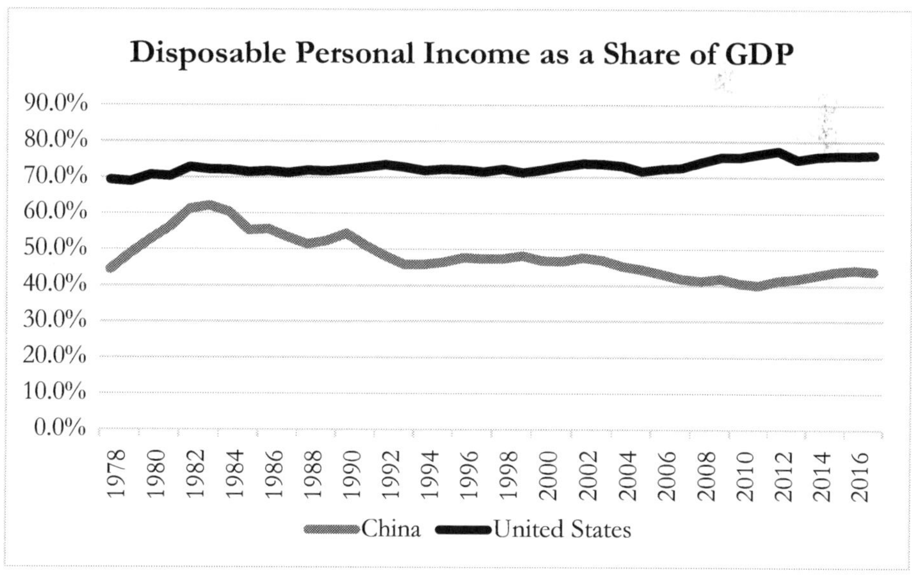

Figure 5.17a DPI as a share of GDP in China has been on the decline since 1983, with a slight uptick post-2011. Meanwhile, the comparable figure for the United States has been on a gradual ascent since 1978.
Source: Author created based on CEIC, Federal Reserve Economic Database, and National Bureau of Statistics.

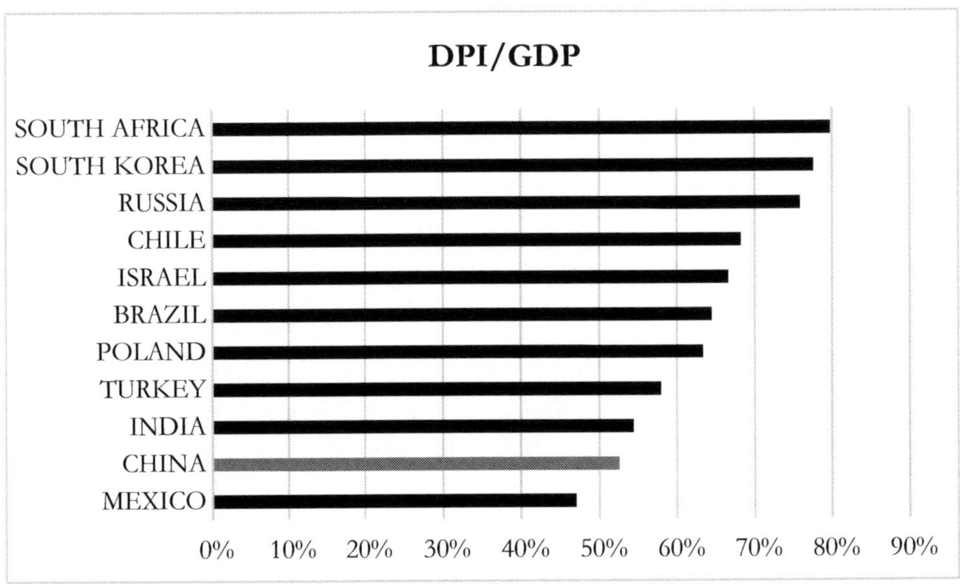

Figure 5.17b Among emerging economies China has one of the lowest shares of DPI out of GDP—explaining, in part, the low rate of personal consumption.
Source: Author created based on OECD.

Figure 5.17a shows the historical path of DPI for China and the United States. We see that, by 2017, DPI for China had been only 44 percent of GDP compared to 76 percent for the United States—and that gap has been widening since the early 1980s. DPI has not kept up with GDP growth over the past several decades. Figure 5.17b from the OECD shows China ranking relatively low among emerging economies in terms of how much of GDP goes toward DPI. Figure 5.18 shows salary and wage levels as a share of GDP for China and the United States. For both economies, wage compensation as a share of GDP has drifted downward—or at best remained stagnant—over the past several decades. Consider the relationship:

Equation 6:

$$S^H / DPI \times DPI / GDP = S^H / GDP$$

We have already seen that (S^H / DPI) is estimated at around 30 percent (https://bit.ly/3bU5zZR), and (DPI / GDP) at about 43 percent in recent years, suggesting that household savings' contribution to GDP is only around 13 percent of GDP—approximately a mere one-third of national savings.

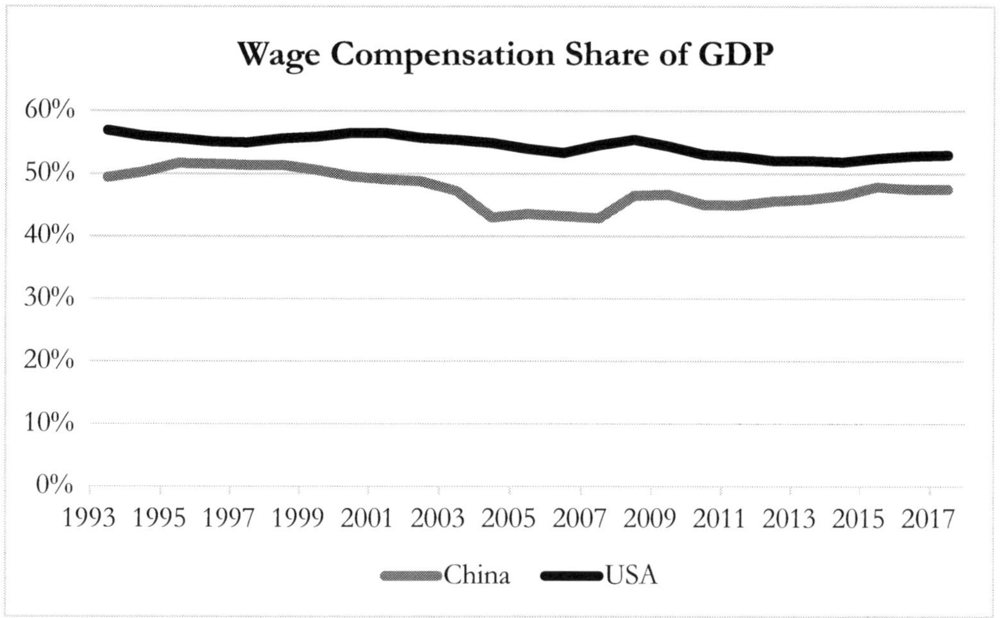

Figure 5.18 In both China and the United States, wages and salaries as share of GDP have drifted downward since the mid-1990s, highlighting the issue of income distribution between owners of capital and labor.
Source: Author created based on data from CEIC, China's MOF, and US Commerce Department's Bureau of Economic Analysis.
Note: The data here are provincial estimates.

In Figure 5.19, we gain some insight into the composition of DPI and why it is relatively low as a share of GDP difference in China.[24] There are some caveats regarding the data and comparisons of categories between China and the United States, but there are some wide enough differences to allow for useful insights. The bottom bar shows the large difference in DPI as a share of GDP already mentioned. China's household survey data (published from 2013) show a significant component of this difference is in wages and salaries—at about 24 percent of GDP in China—less than half the ratio found in the United States.[25] Meanwhile, the International Labor Organization points to a near doubling of real wages between 2008 and 2017, compared to an 80 percent increase in real GDP over the same period. In summary, real wages as a share of GDP in China remain relatively low compared to the United States, but over the past decade the gap has been narrowing (Figure 5.18).

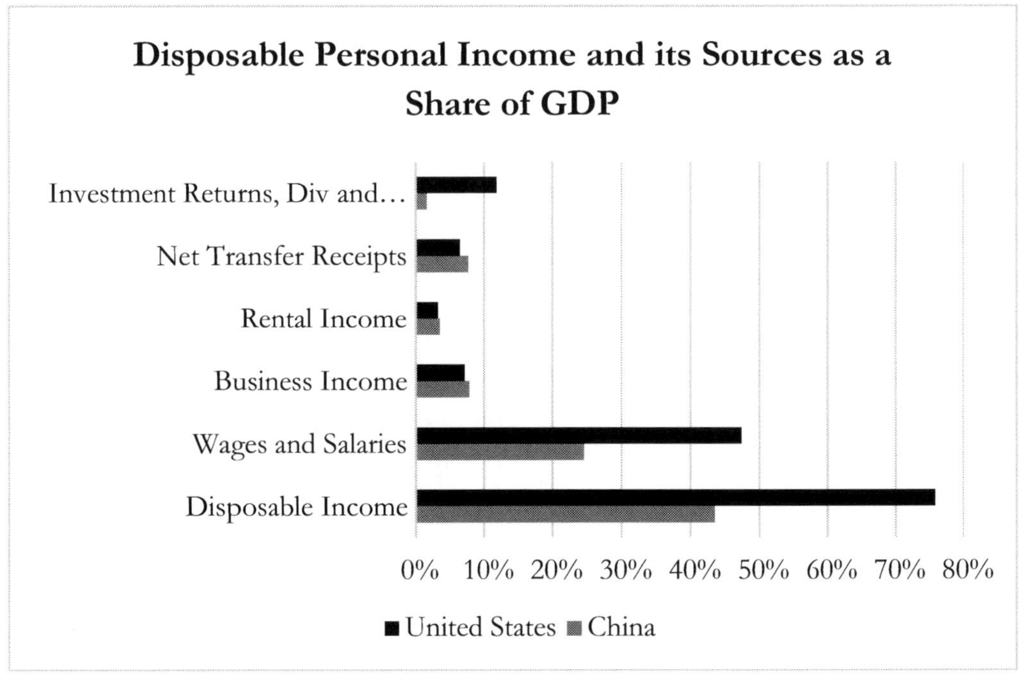

Figure 5.19 For the United States, wages, salaries, and investment returns boost DPI and contribute to the overall gap in DPI as a share of GDP between China and the United States.
Source: Author created from CEIC and the US Commerce Department's Bureau of Economic Analysis.

The top bar in Figure 5.19 shows a category not categorized in the Chinese survey data—investment returns—but for the United States represents a substantial contribution to DPI at about 12 percent of GDP, or about 16 percent of US DPI. We provide our own estimate of interest earned by the household sector in China based on deposit data and an assumed average interest rate of 1.5 percent (https://bit.ly/2TumGv4) per year. The other categories of rental income, business income, and transfer payments show similar shares of GDP for the two countries. But a word of caution related to net transfers is appropriate here; China's Ministry of Finance (MOF) shows that net transfer payments—which include social security, unemployment insurance payments, health benefits, maternity payments, and workers injury compensation—amount to only 0.5 percent of GDP, much smaller than the household survey share reported at around 8 percent. This difference likely represents government and military retiree benefits included in the household survey data but excluded from the MOF data. Social welfare coverage is discussed in detail in Case Study 10.4.

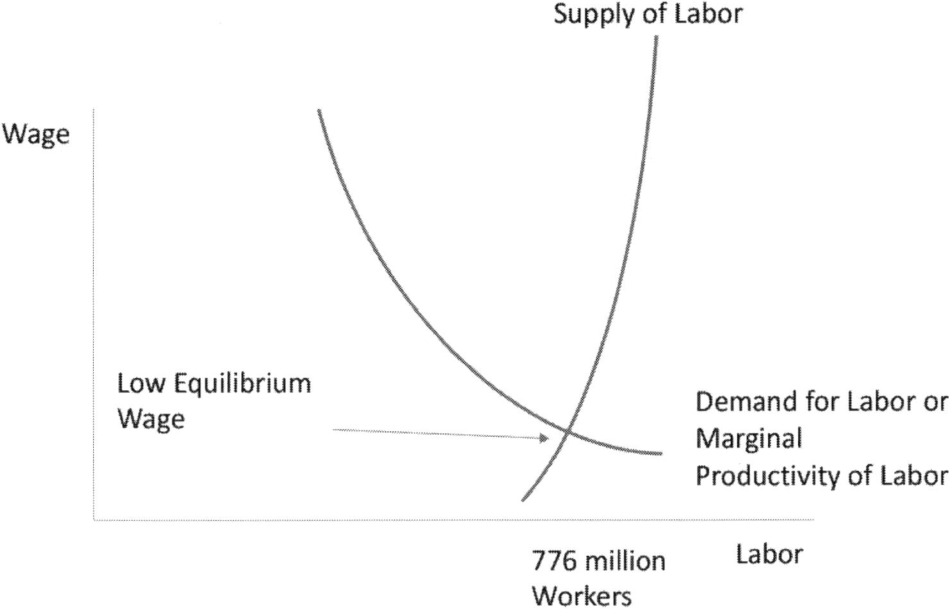

Figure 5.20 A standard explanation for China's low wage and low DPI is that one key driver, the population, is large, and it pushes down the marginal productivity of labor in a neoclassical setting.
Source: Author created.

Figure 5.20 shows the traditional or neoclassical approach for China's low wage rate—it has too much labor relative to demand, driving down the marginal product of labor and the average wage. After all, China's vast population and labor force has already been identified as a key driver in this textbook. While this explanation could be given a heavy weight in the past, its relevance has diminished over the years. As discussed in earlier chapters, China's labor force is now shrinking. Furthermore, the surge in capital accumulation over the years combined with some technological progress should boost wages. What we present below are more structural and institutional explanations for China's low wage rate—mostly related to why corporations capture such a large share of national income in China.

Case Study 5.7: The Minimum Wage in China

Both China and the United States have established minimum wage rates for labor as a way to increase equality of incomes and improve the lives of workers at the lowest rungs of society. The United States has both local and federally mandated minimum wages (currently USD 7.25 per hour at the national level and USD 15 per hour, for example, in New York City) while China's minimum wages are established at the provincial and municipal levels under the guidance of central government regulations. A 1994 law established that all provinces, autonomous regions, and municipalities were to establish minimum wages and all employers were required to adhere to the minimum wages that were set locally. Local governments were to take into account a number of factors in determining a minimum wage including the local cost of living, productivity, current market wages, the level of unemployment, and the level of development of the local economy. A new law in 2004 broadened the coverage of minimum wages to include SOEs and small businesses, and it recommended minimum wages be set at somewhere between 40 and 60 percent of the local market wage (China Labour Bulletin, https://bit.ly/2Tp1Mxh).

Minimums are set on both a monthly basis and an hourly basis. For example, at the high end, in Shanghai, the recent monthly minimum wage was RMB 2480, but in the less-developed province of Shaanxi the rate was set in the range of RMB 1600 to 1800. The gap with Shanghai is even larger for smaller cities outside of the eastern provinces. Hourly minimums stand at around RMB 20 per hour in the wealthier Eastern provinces. Provinces also establish different levels of monthly minimums that apply to specific intra-province environments.

In fact, the imposition of both a monthly and hourly minimum wage adds a layer of complexity in enforcing the regulations. Most job offers in China are based on a monthly salary (not on an hourly wage), making it difficult to accurately monitor hours per month worked. This allows employers to meet the monthly minimum wage while packing a very large number of hours into the monthly employment of the worker; in effect, diluting the hourly wage below the hourly minimum.

Meanwhile, Ashenfelter et al. (2010) show that in the case of monopsony—where firms have market power in labor markets—the effect of a minimum wage may be to actually increase employment. This is because adding a marginal worker at the new minimum wage does not require raising wages for current employees (as it would have *ex-ante* minimum wage legislation)—their wage has already increased due to the new minimum wage. As a result, the constraint on hiring an additional worker is loosened. They find significant monopsony power in United States labor markets—it would be reasonable to assume that power is even greater in Chinese labor markets.

Corporate Savings and Investment

Figure 5.21 and Figure 5.22 show business savings as a share of GDP for China and the United States and as business savings as a share of total savings. At 38 percent of GDP in China, business savings is twice the share found in the United States. Figure 5.22 shows that, by 2017, business savings made up 73 percent of all of China's savings and about 95 percent of all savings in the United States. It is interesting to note that business savings in the United States make up a relatively large share of total savings because American households save so little! Meanwhile, though China's business savings are vast, individual households in China also have a high savings rate, which moves the business share down a bit. Table 5.1 provides the most recent estimate for the breakdown for national savings for China and the United States by businesses, government, and households. We see the importance of business savings for both China and the United States. Meanwhile, households in China contribute under one-third of national savings via employment compensation. For both economies, governments dip into the savings pool due to fiscal deficits—particularly at the local government level in China.

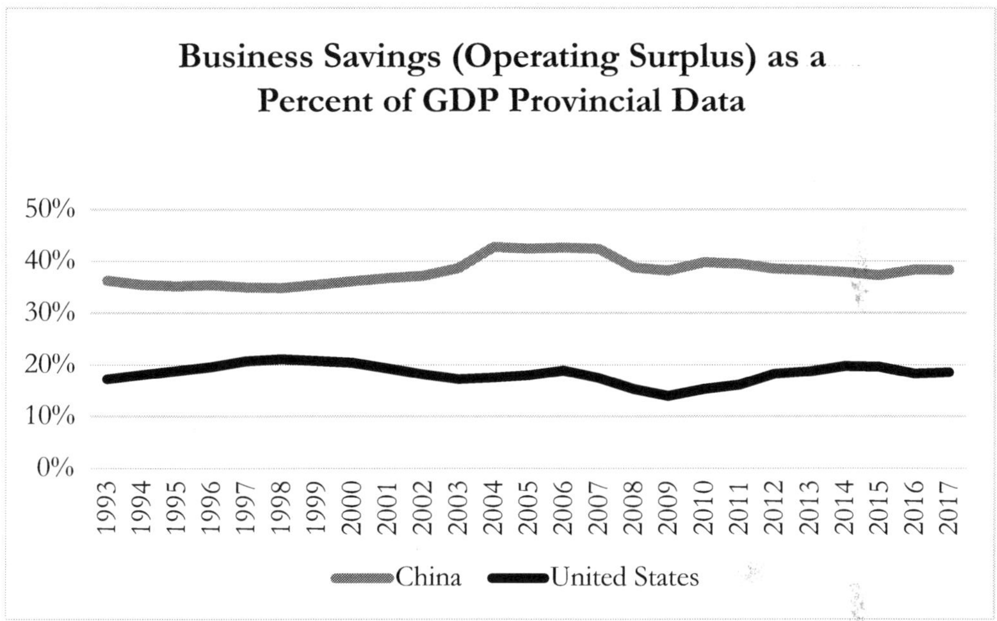

Figure 5.21 Business savings (operating surplus) for enterprises in China make up almost twice the share of GDP than in the United States, and they account for the high national savings rate of China.

Source: Author created based on data from the US Bureau of Economic Analysis and CEIC.

Note: Net operating surplus is calculated, by both China and the United States, in their income presentations of their national incomes and product accounts. The measure includes corporate profits, rental income, proprietor's income, other income, and dividend payments income—excluding depreciation, government net income, and taxes, but including net interest receipts/payments of these various businesses. Because of data limitations, China's operating surplus ratio is calculated on a net operating surplus to net domestic GDP basis. US figures are calculated on a gross operating surplus to gross domestic output basis. Total savings in these charts represent total savings of all sectors (households and businesses) and include government surpluses or deficits. Data for China are based on provincial aggregates, which only begin in 1993.

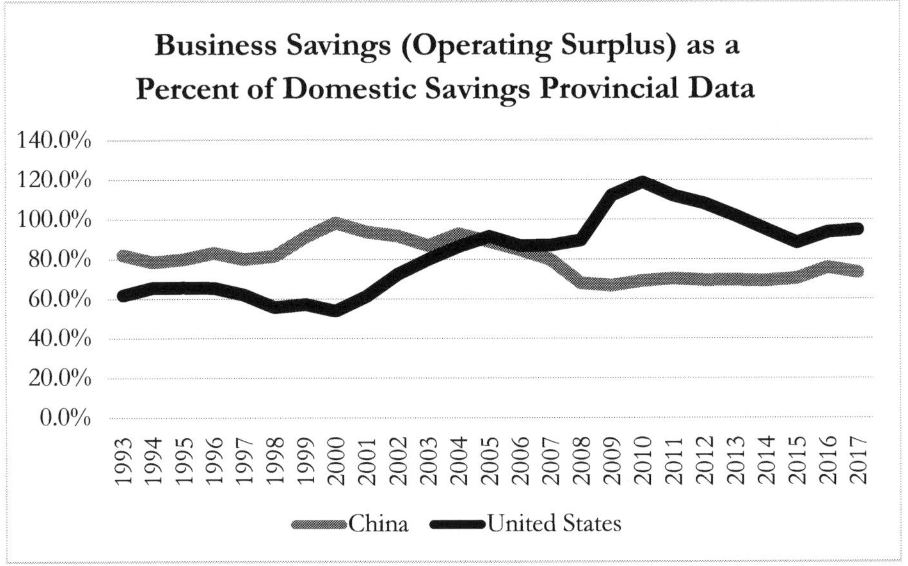

Figure 5.22 Business savings (operating surplus) for enterprises in China and the United States account for almost all of national savings. In China, this is because of the high level of corporate savings; in the United States, because of the low level of personal savings. Source: Author created based on data from the US Bureau of Economic Analysis and CEIC. Note: Net operating surplus is calculated, by both China and the United States, in their income presentations of their national incomes and product accounts. The measure includes corporate profits, rental income, proprietor's income, other income, and dividend payments income—excluding depreciation, government net income, and taxes, but including net interest receipts/payments of these various businesses. Because of data limitations, China's operating surplus ratio is calculated on a net operating surplus to net domestic GDP basis. US figures are calculated on a gross operating surplus to gross domestic output basis. Total savings in these charts represent total savings of all sectors (households and businesses) and include government surpluses or deficits. Data for China are based on provincial aggregates, which only begin in 1993.

Fortunately, there are some established relationships and frameworks that permit us to look at corporate savings (earnings) in depth. We will examine corporate net income and retained earnings from two different angles to compare the two economies. First, we will examine the determinants of net income based on the Dupont model to see why the source of corporate savings or net income may differ. Second, we will examine dividend policy to examine the wedge between net income and retained earnings (i.e., the measure included in corporate savings).

Sources of Profitability

To gain insight into differences between profitability and returns in China and the United States, we review our shorthand accounting of profits, the Dupont model, discussed in Chapter 4. As an identity, the Dupont model decomposes return on equity (ROE) into three components: productivity of all assets (sales/assets), profit margin (net income/sales) and financial leverage (assets/equity). Recall from Chapter 4:

Return on Equity ≡ (Sales / Assets) × (Net Income / Sales) × (Assets / Equity)

Table 5.6 provides an estimate of these ratios for the manufacturing sectors in China and the United States for 2017, and it highlights some likely differences in profitability between the two countries. Overall, Chinese manufacturing firms have higher ROE. This difference is consistent with China's faster growth as an emerging economy, and it helps to explain China's higher rate of overall savings. Behind this difference, the Dupont model suggests that China produces a greater amount of output per asset than does the United States. This disparity can be explained by China's enormous substitution of labor for capital. In other words, labor plays a much larger role as an input in China than do fixed assets. As a result, the ratio of output to fixed assets employed is higher.

Dupont Model, Manufacturing Industry	China	USA
Sales/Assets	101.0%	51.7%
Net Income/Sales	6.7%	4.0%
Assets/Equity	224.4%	242.6%
Net Income/Equity (ROE)	15.0%	5.0%
Net Income/Assets	6.7%	2.1%

Table 5.6 The Dupont decomposition shows that, at least in manufacturing, China's asset efficiency is higher due to a greater use of labor as an input in the production process.
Source: Author created with data from CEIC, National Bureau of Statistics, Chapter 13, and FRED's presentation of Bureau of Economic Analysis manufacturing data.
Note: Chinese data are for 2017, all industrial enterprises with sales greater than RMB 20 million and all US manufacturing firms.

Meanwhile, in manufacturing profit, margins in the United States dipped below China in 2015—a larger share of sales now goes to corporate profits in manufacturing in China. In the case of manufacturing, this reflects lower costs rather than the market power of manufacturing firms—the manufacturing environment in China remains very competitive. This competition no doubt explains the desire of manufacturing firms in the United States to move offshore to China and other relatively low-wage economies where productivity levels have become more competitive.

Manufacturing appears to be an exception to most industries in the United States, where profit margins are generally in the 10 to 12 percent range (Damodaran, 2016 and 2020) (https://bit.ly/3dftOCv). The higher non-manufacturing profit margin in the United States reflects the pricing power that US firms have, especially in the context of branding and a strong market share. Financial leverage, overall, seems quite similar.[26] Again, manufacturing appears to be an outlier—the ratio of assets to equity for all non-financial businesses in the United States was 158 percent in 2017. Macro Finance Insight 4.3 provided a more "apples-to-apples" comparison of China and the United States than does the manufacturing sector.

We turn next to the question of the share of profits returned to shareholders (dividends) and those not saved (retained) by companies in each country.

Dividend Policy

In any discussion of corporate and domestic savings, we must examine dividend policy. Dividends paid out to shareholders are the wedge (the difference) between net income and retained earnings. A business entity with a high payout ratio (PR) (dividends to net income per period) no longer has access to that share of net income paid out to shareholders. In turn, the marginal propensity to consume or save on the part of shareholders will then determine how much of what they receive in dividends goes out to domestic consumption or savings. Baker et al. (2006) examine the relationship between dividend payments, capital gains, and consumption in the United States. They find that the impact of dividend payments on consumption is "large, positive and significant" (233). As opposed to dividend payments, capital gains have a relatively small impact on consumption. They attribute this phenomenon, in part, to mental accounting, in which investors perceive dividend payments as part of current income whereas capital gains are perceived as an increment to savings. We formally summarize our discussion of dividends, PRs, and consumption as:

Equation 8a:

$$\text{PR} = \text{Dividends} / \text{NI}$$

where NI is net income,

Equation 8b:

$$\text{Retained Earnings} = \text{NI} - \text{Dividends} = (1 - \text{PR}) \times \text{NI}$$

Equation 8c:

$$MPC = MC / Dividends$$

Where MPC is the marginal propensity to consume and MC is marginal consumption from a dividend payment. And so,

Equation 8d:[27]

$$PR \times MPC \times NI = MC$$

The PR, the MPC, and corporate income will all determine consumption. Damodaron (https://bit.ly/3hE8Al9) estimates that, in 2020, the average dividend PR in the United States was 46 percent, with some industries (Food Processing) paying over 300 percent, and some paying virtually nothing (Publishing).[28] If we include stock buybacks (an alternate way to give cash back to shareholders), the average PR in the United States rises to 57 percent. In the earlier addition of this text, the average PR in China was 18 percent, with more than half of listed firms paying no dividends at all. Since then, securities regulators have encouraged companies to pay higher dividends to help boost slumping stock prices in China and allow for China's large capitalization companies (of which there are over 200) in its China Securities Index (https://bit.ly/2zobLfj) to be included (https://bit.ly/2ZEvPFh) in the MSCI set of global market indexes.[29] By 2020, regulators will require SOEs to pay 30 percent of net income to shareholders (typically state-controlled financial institutions).

It is estimated (https://bit.ly/2WRhhQB) that for Chinese publicly listed companies today, the PR has moved up to around 30 percent, with 80 percent of China's listed companies now paying dividends. As we discuss in the next paragraph, a side effect of these efforts to promote Chinese share prices and liquidity should be to positively impact Chinese consumption. In addition to a more generous dividend policy, China's National People's Congress passed a law (https://bloom.bg/3gcYzdL) allowing companies to buy back shares with two-thirds board approval. The move was intended to give companies more flexibility in supporting the price of their shares, but—again—a side effect will be to put more income in the hands of consumers.

Assuming a consumption rate (MPC) of 72 percent for China out of DPI, and a 30 percent PR, we have, from Equation 8d, the product ($0.30 \times 0.72 = 0.22$). In other words, for every RMB 1 of net income generated, consumption conceivably could be boosted by RMB 0.22: an improvement from an estimated 0.13 in 2015.[30] But it is still below the comparable figure for the United States of 0.47 (where the MPC in the United States is a key factor and we assume an average PR, averaging in buybacks, of 0.5). Examining how changes in the PR would impact consumption and savings, we have:

Equation 9a:

$$PR \times MPC \times NI = MC$$

And,

Equation 9b:

$$MC / GDP = PR \times MPC \times NI / GDP$$

Or,

Equation 9c:

$$\frac{\Delta(MC/_{GDP})}{\Delta PR} = (NI / GDP) \times MPC = 0.27$$

Since in China we estimate (NI / GDP) at 0.38 and MPC at 0.72.

In other words, for every 1-point increase in the PR, consumption in China would rise (or savings would fall) by 0.27 percent (27 basis points). If China raised its PR by 20 percentage points (close to the US PR), its domestic savings rate could decline by (0.27 × 20 = 5.4) percentage points, a significant change.

Dividend Policy Caveat: The Issue of State Ownership

All of this assumes that dividends actually end up in the hands of households. In China, we cannot be sure of this assumption because, in many large SOEs and private corporations, the key shareholders are another set of SOEs (e.g., an insurance company, holding company, or financial institution). In this case, dividends would have to go through several layers of institutions and may just end up recycled into retained earnings along the chain of entities. Or, as Milhaupt and Zheng (2016) point out, if the government is ultimately the shareholder, the dividends may simply be reinvested. Figure 5.23 shows the significant share of investment that has been undertaken by SOEs over the past decades averaging about 42 percent of all investment. If we add in government investment to this share, we see that easily over half of the capital created in China over the past several decades has been created by a government owned entity or the government itself. In this case, dividend payments (no matter how large) simply get recycled into China's vast investment pool—never entering into the household consumption stream.

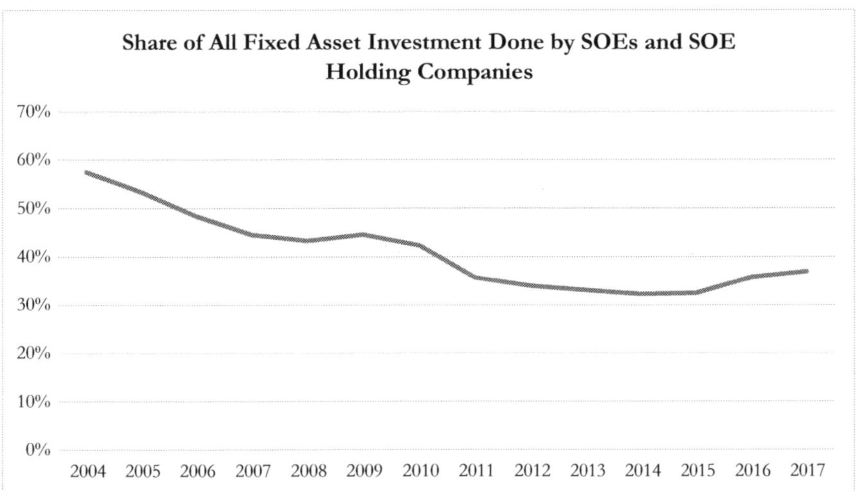

Figure 5.23 Chinese SOEs, though few in number, have an outsize importance in terms of how much investment is undertaken in China overall.
Source: Author created based on data from the Bureau of Economic Analysis and CEIC.

Finally, it should be noted that an unknown amount of corporate savings may be channeled into China's now vast shadow banking sector. Lin and Schramm (2006) estimated that about one-third of China's savings was unaccounted for by the mid-2000s. Much of that missing savings, the authors speculated, was from intra-company loans (corporate sector savings), and nowadays it has likely become part of shadow banking.[31] The question at hand, and an area for future research, is—how much of shadow banking assets ends up as consumer finance, and how much as investment?

In the section below, we discuss some theories as to what might determine a company's (or government policy) decision on the dividend PR.

Macro Finance Insight 5.1: When Dividends Are a Problem

Most of China's listed companies still continue to have the state as a major shareholder. One example highlights the difference this type of structure makes in terms of dividend policy. Shares were issued to various SOEs at only a fraction of their true value. However, a number of restrictions have been placed on the shares in terms of resale (when they can be resold, at what price, and to whom, i.e., another SOE). In response, shareowners have sought ways to somehow cash out of the shares at something closer to market (higher) valuations. In the past, establishing a generous dividend policy or high PR has proven to be a creative solution. Sometimes the payout would come as a distribution of new shares in the form of a bonus to inside shareholders/management, effectively diluting the value of stock. This practice has been described as a form of "tunneling"—a process whereby non-state minority shareholders see their ownership stake clandestinely and unfairly transferred.* In this and many other ways, we see traditional agency theory turned on its head in China. One normally thinks of dividends as a solution to—not a cause of—an agency problem; and, as discussed, dividends have been too low in China in the past, except for those lucky enough to be a majority shareholder!

*While this does provide the means for such a cash event transfer to occur, in fact, the legal transfer occurred long before, when the initial underpriced shares were issued.

Theories of Dividend Policy

Just as different theories exist as to why consumers choose to save, there are different theories as to why corporations choose to retain earnings (save) instead of releasing some share of net income to shareholders. Central to this discussion is the notion that businesses assess their own opportunities for reinvesting net income into their own or related businesses against returning some of the net income to shareholders (for them to consume or reinvest on their own). If a company, for example, has access to many investment opportunities with high returns and low risk that shareholders do not have access to, then profits should be reinvested by the company for the benefit of all stakeholders. But if the company only has the same opportunity set for investments that shareholders face, then the company should return a large share of net income to shareholders for their own use. Layered onto this approach is the notion that the firm may have better information regarding opportunities and is more likely to be exposed to the "real" options that are available than the shareholders would be.

The above paragraph hints at the distinction between a growth company versus a more stable, mature company. The former tends to conserve cash for investing in ever-growing opportunities. The latter, while still profitable, returns net income to its shareholders. Microsoft, in its first 18 years of operation, paid no dividends—its opportunities were too great. Only as it reached a more mature stage in its life-cycle, in 2004, did it begin to pay dividends.

If we assume that a company reinvests up to the point where its returns just equal the opportunity cost of capital from the market (shareholders), then—in the absence of tax and bankruptcy issues—the dividend policy of corporations is irrelevant. In other words, what is paid out as dividends does not impact the company's share price. This is known as the "dividend irrelevance theory" (Modigliani and Miller 1958). In perfect capital markets, any payment of dividends to current shareholders results in an exactly offsetting share dilution as the firm raises new capital through share issuance. Alternatively, original shareholders can themselves raise the same amount of cash as provided by a dividend through selling some of their shares.

Alternate Views

Though Modigliani-Miller dividend irrelevance serves as a benchmark—a null hypothesis if you will—regarding whether dividend payments matter, we will briefly highlight other theories that are particularly relevant in the China-US context:

Bird-in-Hand Theory (BIH)

Authors such as Graham and Dodd (1934) have argued that, both conceptually and empirically, it is preferable to receive a dividend now rather than letting management reinvest income. The former is risk-free while the latter is merely a promise of a higher return or capital gain resulting from reinvestment. The former is safe; the latter risky and nebulous. Conclusion: firms should have a high PR.

The Presence of Taxes

In both the United States and China, dividends are taxed more heavily than capital gains. In the United States, for example, a high-income individual could pay a tax rate as high as 37 percent on dividend income but as low as 0 percent on capital gains. In China, the highest tax rates are 45 percent for individuals and 25 percent for corporations. Meanwhile, capital gains taxes can range from 0 to 20 percent. This should create a bias toward not paying dividends. Furthermore, there is greater flexibility (discretion) for shareholders in terms of when they reap capital gains as opposed to a business-determined dividend payment. Conclusion: firms should have a low PR.

Pecking Order

This approach states that firms tend to pay fewer dividends because retained earnings are the preferred source of finance for firms that need funding. It is argued that retained earnings are a cheaper source of finance than, for example, new share issuance. The cost difference results from asymmetric information. While a firm may have inside information regarding a good investment opportunity, that may not be understood by those providing external sources of finance. Share issuance may also be interpreted by external markets as an indication that managers view the current share price as overvalued. As a result, new share issuance can be more expensive relative to the use of retained earnings. Conclusion: firms should have a low PR.

Agency and Misappropriation of Funds

This theory suggests that dividends are likely to be paid when management cannot be trusted to use retained earnings wisely. More specifically, a more rigid requirement on dividend payments will put pressure on management to ensure that the dividend target is met and not waste company resources. Conclusion: firms should have a high PR.

Dividends as a Signaling Device

Dividends also may support share prices as a way of communicating that a company believes that its cash flow going forward is sufficient to cover operations and investments. Otherwise, those dividends would be held as cash balances in anticipation of either profit losses or constraints on outside sources of finance. Companies that unexpectedly halt dividend payments often suffer a decline in share price because investors view this as a signal that the company is generating insufficient cash flow to meet capital expenditure and investor needs. Conclusion: firms should maintain a high PR, if possible.

Dividend Theory and China

Table 5.7 summarizes the relevance of each theory for China versus the United States. For example, tax differentials on income versus capital gains suggest that dividend payments are disadvantageous to shareholders. This is more important in China, where such differentials are substantial, especially taking into account taxes on short-term capital gains in the United States.

Theory	Implication for Dividend Payment	China Significance	US Significance
MM Irrelevance	Neutral	Low	Medium
Growth Opportunities	Low Payout	High	Low
Bird-in-Hand**	High Payout	Low*	Medium
Tax Differentials	Low Payout	Medium	Low
Pecking Order	Low Payout	High	Medium

Theory	Implication for Dividend Payment	China Significance	US Significance
Agency Issues**	High Payout	Low	High
Signaling**	High Payout	Medium	High

Table 5.7 Relevance of different theories of dividend payouts for China and the United States
Source: Author created.
*Depends on type of business; for SOEs, the effect is high in a perverse way.
**Less relevant for companies that are not held broadly by the public.

The dividend irrelevance theory is probably less relevant for China than the United States because the theory relies on perfect capital markets—especially the ease with which companies and shareholders can raise cash through a share sale. Transaction costs are substantially lower in the more mature US financial markets.

Relatively high-growth opportunities continue to exist in China compared to the United States. In Chapter 4, which deals with economic growth, we show that overall macroeconomic growth is closely related to business returns. Clearly, emerging economies such as China enjoy substantial growth opportunities, and companies in such economies require financing in order to take advantage of both growth and the presence of real options. As such, the PR tends to be lower for Chinese companies, which need to retain earnings to invest further. Just as significantly, the opportunity cost to shareholders of retained earnings in China is extremely low. Shareholders in China currently have very few methods for holding their wealth and earning a positive real interest rate. Regulated ceilings on the interest rate paid by banks on bank deposits make for negative real returns, while real estate valuations that are speculatively high make the retention of earnings by shareholding companies attractive.

The flip side of the argument for growth opportunities is the pecking order theory. Chinese companies that are neither large nor state-owned continue to face great difficulty borrowing from banks. Banks continue to have the state as their largest shareholder and, therefore, as a matter of both policy and convention, they find it easier to lend to SOEs. The vast majority of Chinese firms find it difficult to access bank credit—especially small- and medium-sized firms.[32] The corporate bond market also remains limited as a source of finance. The primitive information on credit histories for most companies is a significant barrier for arms-length finance—bank or bonds. Regional pools of informal finance, such as in Wenzhou, have become available (as discussed earlier), but these are neither cheap nor consistent sources of finance. The very presence of these pools is an exception that proves the point. The upshot of these limitations is that most firms understand that they will need to rely on their own retained earnings or the retained earnings of a small circle of other firms for finance. The dividend PR, as a result, tends to be low.

While the BIH, agency, and signaling explanations seem directly relevant to the circumstances in China, they are not completely relevant; this is because most Chinese companies are not listed. At present, some 3,500 companies are listed on Chinese exchanges while nearly 380,000 companies in China have revenues greater than RMB 5 million. Many of these companies are larger than those listed. For most of these companies, especially those that are private or otherwise closely held, the incentives between management and owners are closely aligned. In other cases, where non-listed companies have either minority or non-state shareholders, their stake is too small to impact dividend policy.

The tax bias toward capital gains over dividends appears to be more pronounced in China than in the United States, which also suggests a lower PR. In summary, though some theories point to a higher PR, these theories are not directly relevant in China, while those pointing to a lower PR are directly relevant. Therefore, we can conclude that there are some financial and economic fundamentals at work causing Chinese firms to disburse less of their net income to shareholders. As a result, corporate savings is higher, personal income is lower, shareholder consumption is lower, and China's domestic savings is greater.

Ultimately, a new set of theories on agency and signaling will evolve related to China's unique SOE situation. Recent policy proposals for growing consumption and reducing savings (in addition to the factors mentioned above) include:

1. Measures that would improve corporate governance, including giving shareholders a greater say in a company's dividend policy. Putting money in the hands of shareholders, as we have seen, will lead to greater consumption because companies do not consume but save and invest. Ultimately, though, questions about the PR are better asked on a company-by-company basis, rather than as a one-rule-fits-all policy. Some companies with high growth potential and inside information should retain their earnings for the sake of new investment. China's Third Plenum announced (in November, 2013) that SOEs would be required to raise their current regulated PR of 5–15 percent to 30 percent by 2020. But

mandating dividend policy from above, rather than at the shareholder/stakeholder level, is one more blow to the ultimate goal of quality of growth via a rational allocation of resources to consumption, savings, or investment.

2. A broad range of new policies, from greater empowerment of labor unions to enhanced minimum wage laws that redistribute corporation profits to workers. Currently, China has one of the highest ratios in the world of national income accruing to capital as compared to labor (see Chapter 4 on long-term growth).

A more promising path for China (one that it is slowly following) is the introduction of a wider range of assets for citizens to hold beyond the current mix of cash, bank deposits, home ownership, and stock market investment. Specifically, developing the corporate bond market, consumer credit (allowing individuals to short their wealth), and the ability to hold short positions in equity would be major steps forward. Allowing a broader range of assets, both in terms of instruments and underlying assets, would allow savers to diversify and, in turn, hedge their portfolios more efficiently (in the sense of different portfolios for different individual preferences). Because wealth would be better protected against adverse shocks in a hedged portfolio, individuals would not hold as much wealth and would not need to save as much to meet the needs of an uncertain future. Furthermore, the increased competition for funds would force companies to engage in more investor-friendly policy. In Chapter 7 (on monetary policy), we show the stark differences in the way Americans and Chinese currently hold wealth.[33] Without a doubt, the overweighting of money holdings in the typical Chinese portfolio relates to the lack of a broader range of investment opportunities. Chapter 11 discusses both the progress and setbacks that China is experiencing in offering its citizens a more complete financial system.

Summary Outlook for Savings and Consumption

What the above discussion suggests is that, for China's consumption to rise, particular components of DPI need to increase. Specifically, higher workers' wages and salaries, higher returns on financial investment, higher taxes on enterprises, a higher PR on corporate earnings, and a broader distribution of transfer payments to private citizens would all lead to a higher DPI and, no doubt, greater consumption. In later chapters, we discuss the role for banks in shifting the balance of interest charges and payments away from enterprises in favor of households. For companies that are already private, improved shareholder participation and corporate governance would allow for higher dividend payments where appropriate. For SOEs, some movement toward privatization would allow for DPI to rise via capital gains, higher dividend payments, higher wages, and possibly greater tax revenues, thereby allowing for more transfer payments to consumers. Greater skill-intensive service sector employment, organization of labor, deregulation of financial markets, and opportunities for investing in a wider range of assets would all be a means to achieving the ends discussed here.

What becomes clear in the above discussion is that almost all the factors that we have cited for China's high per capita savings rate and low rate of per capita consumption are now moving in a direction that will lead to lower savings and higher consumption. Whether we are considering demographics and dependency ratios, borrowing constraints and consumer finance, the precautionary motive for savings, declining corporate savings (profits), or higher dividend payments, each factor appears to be moving in a direction that suggests less savings and higher consumption. There are some open and important questions regarding how fast disposable income will increase as a share of GDP and how wide and deep the social safety net will be cast. Notwithstanding these considerations, we can reasonably project that China's national savings rate is set to decline in the coming years, and that it will ultimately have a similar profile to its Asian neighbors with a savings rate in the 20 to 30 percent of GDP range.

Challenging Questions for China (and the Student): Chapter 5

1. Go to the Federal Reserve Economic Database (FRED). Using the relationship (National Savings – National Investment = Current Account Balance), determine China's savings as a share of GDP over the past decades. Hint: Use the data in FRED for China's "Gross Capital Formation."
2. Explain why China's savings rate is so high and why the United States' savings rate is so low.
3. In terms of its impact on savings:
   a. Discuss which is more relevant for China: liquidity constrains or borrowing constraints.
   b. Discuss which is more relevant (liquidity or borrowing constraints) for each of these activities:
      i. Purchase of a product at Carrefour or Wal-Mart.
      ii. Use of a debit card.
      iii. Use of a credit card.
      iv. Loan (mortgage) for the purchase of a new home.
      v. Restrictions/penalties on sale of stock/equity holdings before a specified holding period has expired.
4. Select some theories that we discussed in this chapter and use them to explain what will happen to China's consumption and savings in the coming years. Be specific about which theory you are using.
5. Discuss whether decreased uncertainty about the future will cause Chinese to save more or to save less. Rely on the discussion about the precautionary motive and the substitution effect in your explanation.
6. Estimate the impact on China's overall savings rate if the dividend PR rises halfway between China's PR (30 percent) to what is found in the US (58 percent).
7. Pick one of the theories of dividend policy in Table 5.6 and discuss why you think it is more relevant to China than the textbook (Schramm) suggests.
8. A major theme in corporate finance is that, when firms have excess cash, they should pay it out to their shareholders.
   a. What are the interpretations/implications of this concept for China's dividend policy, national savings, and consumption?
   b. How might Chinese firms' excess cash holdings lead to greater consumption, even if dividends do not increase? Hint: Who is another major stakeholder in a company other than shareholders?

9. Why is savings not the likely path for China to increase its citizens' standard of living in the long run? Using a Solow approach, what then is the likely path for long-run sustainable improvements in China's standard of living?
10. Are symbiotic savings important in the United States? Explain what factors make them important in China.
11. Discuss the pros and cons of China's SCS system. What criteria would you want to include and exclude in the system? If the alternative to a SCS system in China is use of extra-legal measures for debt contract enforcement (threats of or actual physical harm to borrowers in default), how would you modify your assessment?
12. Would you maintain, abolish, or reform the minimum wage system in China? Explain.

References

Ando, A., and F. Modigliani. 1963. "The" Life Cycle" Hypothesis of Saving: Aggregate Implications and Tests." *The American Economic Review*, 53(1), pp. 55–84.

Ashenfelter, O. C., H. Farber, and M. R. Ransom. 2010. "Labor Market Monopsony." *Journal of Labor Economics*, 28(2), pp. 203–10.

Baker, M., S. Nagel, and J. Wurgler. 2006. "The Effect of Dividends on Consumption." NBER Working Paper no. w12288.

Botsman, Rachel. 2017. "Big Data Meets Big Brother as China Moves to Rate Its Citizens." *Wired UK*, 21 October, https://www.wired.co.uk/article/chinese-government-social-credit-score-privacy-invasion.

Chamon, Marcos, Kai Liu, and Eswar S. Prasad. 2010. "Income Uncertainty and Household Savings in China." NBER Working Paper no. 16565.

Chen, Yongxi, and Anne S. Y. Cheung. 2017. "The Transparent Self Under Big Data Profiling: Privacy and Chinese Legislation on The Social Credit System." *The Journal of Comparative Law*, 12(2), pp. 356–78.

Curtis, C. C., S. Lugauer, and N.C. Mark. 2015. "Demographic Patterns and Household Saving in China." *American Economic Journal: Macroeconomics*, 7(2), pp. 58–94.

Damodaran, Aswath. 2016. *Damodaran On Valuation: Security Analysis for Investment and Corporate Finance*. Hoboken: John Wiley & Sons.

Duesenberry, James Stemble. 1949. *Income, Saving, and the Theory of Consumer Behavior*. Cambridge, MA: Harvard University Press.

Fama, Eugene F., and Kenneth R. French. 2004. "The Capital Asset Pricing Model: Theory and Evidence." *Journal of Economic Perspectives*, 18(3), 25–46.

Federal Reserve Board of Governors and U.S. Commerce Department. 2014. *Federal Reserve Statistical Release*. Washington, DC: Bureau of Economic Analysis, https://www.federalreserve.gov/releases/z1/default.htm.

Feldstein, M., and C. Horioka. 1980. "Domestic Saving and International Capital Flows." *Economic Journal*, 90, pp. 314–29.

Friedman, Milton. 1957. *A Theory of the Consumption Function: A Study by the National Bureau of Economic Research*. Princeton: Princeton University Press.

Graham, Benjamin and David Dodd. 1934. *Security Analysis*. New York: McGraw-Hill.

Guijun, L. I. N., and Ronald M. Schramm. 2006. "A Decade of Flow of Funds in China (1995–2005)." In *China and Asia, Economic Interactions*, edited by Yin-Wong Cheung and Kai-Yiu Wong, New York: Routledge.

Guo, Kai and Papa N'Diaye. 2010. "Determinants of China's Private Consumption: An

International Perspective." IMF Working Paper no. 10/93.

Haldane, Andrew G. 2010. "Global Imbalances in Retrospect and Prospect." Remarks given at Global Financial Forum, Chatham House Conference on The New Global Economic Order, 3 November, London, England, http://www.bis.org/review/r101223f.pdf.

Hall, Robert. 1978. "Stochastic Implications of the Life Cycle-Permanent Income Hypothesis: Theory and Evidence." *Journal of Political Economy*, 86(6), pp. 971–87.

Horioka, Charles Yuji and Wakö Watanabe. 1997. "Why Do People Save? A Micro-Analysis of Motives for Household Saving in Japan." *The Economic Journal*, 107(442), pp. 537–52.

International Human Dimensions Programme on Global Environmental Change and United Nations Environment Programme. 2012. *Inclusive Wealth Report 2012: Measuring Progress Toward Sustainability*. Cambridge: Cambridge University Press.

Jin, Ye, Hongbin Li, and Binzhen Wu. 2011. "Income Inequality, Consumption, and Social-Status Seeking." *Journal of Comparative Economics*, 39(2), pp. 191–204.

Kimball, Miles S. 1990. "Precautionary Saving in the Small and in the Large." *Econometrica*, 58(1), 53–73.

Lange, Glenn-Marie, Quentin Wodon, and Kevin Carey, eds. 2018. *The Changing Wealth of Nations 2018: Building a Sustainable Future*. Washington, DC: The World Bank.

Lau, Chi Keung Marco. 2010. "New Evidence About Regional Income Divergence in China." *China Economic Review*, 21(2), pp. 293–309.

LeBaron, Blake. 2006. "Agent-Based Computational Finance." In *Handbook of Computational Economics,* edited by L. Tesfatsion and K. L. Judd, New York: Elsevier, pp. 1187–233.

McMorrow, K. and W. Roeger. 1999. "The Economic Consequences of Ageing Populations (a Comparison of the EU, US and Japan)." *Economic Papers*, Working Document no. 138, Brussels: EU Commission.

Milhaupt, Curtis, and Wentong Zheng. 2016. "Why Mixed-Ownership Reforms Cannot Fix China's State Sector." *Paulson Policy Memorandum*, 5(11).

Modigliani, Franco, and Merton H. Miller. 1958. "The Cost of Capital, Corporation Finance and the Theory of Investment." *American Economic Review*, 48(3), pp. 261–97.

Modigliani, Franco, and Shi Larry Cao. 2004. "The Chinese Saving Puzzle and the Life-Cycle Hypothesis." *Journal of Economic Literature,* 42(1), pp. 145–70.

Nabar, M. 2011. "Targets, Interest Rates and Household Saving in Urban China." IMF Working Paper no. 11/223.

National Bureau of Statistics. 2012. "Table 2–30." In *China Statistical Yearbook*. Beijing: China Statistics Press.

Obstfeld, Maurice. 1986. "Capital Controls, the Dual Exchange Rate, and Devaluation." *Journal of International Economics*, 20(1), pp. 1–20.

Posner, Richard A. 1981. "The Economics of Privacy." *The American Economic Review*, 71(2), pp. 405–09.

Schramm, Ronald, Ming He, and Yang Chen. 2018. "The Chinese Financial System." In *Handbook of the Chinese Economy*, edited by Mark Fraser and Weiping Wu. New York: Sage Publications.

U.S. Census Bureau. International Programs, International Database, accessed 18 June 2020, https://www.census.gov/programs-surveys/international-programs/about/idb.html.

Wei, Shang-Jin, and Xiaobo Zhang. 2009. "The Competitive Saving Motive: Evidence from Rising Sex Ratios and Savings Rates in China." NBER Working Paper no. 15093.

Yan, Chen, Yuan Gu, Li Chen, Yingren Wang, Yi Ying, Shuguang Zhang, and Yang Zhao. 2018. "China Consumer Finance Market Insights." Working Group of CFA, China Shanghai Crowd Research Project.

Endnotes

1. In 2017, China was only exceeded in its savings rate by Singapore (48 percent), Qatar (49 percent), Macau (the Special Administrative Regions of China (52 percent)), and the Kingdom of Brunei (56 percent).
2. This figure includes household, business, and government sector savings.
3. In the case of the United States and China, these measures exclude rental and proprietor's income. In the case of China alone, non-industrial enterprises are excluded, e.g., financial institutions, construction, and services.
4. The calculation was done using the average market exchange rate. But the result would qualitatively hold for any reasonable purchasing-power-parity-based exchange rate.
5. Overlapping generation models typically assume three generations (children, adult workers, and retirees) who incorporate each other's consumption, investment, and income into their own decision making.
6. For Shakespeare, there were seven ages: the whining infant, the schoolboy, the lover, the soldier, the wise and just man, the old slippered man, and the child again. This would be far too complex a life for the economist to model.
7. There is a vast finance literature that argues that assets (and the means for acquiring assets—savings) are more valuable the more they allow for the smoothing of income and consumption in the presence of uncertainty. See, for example, the "Capital Asset Model" (Fama and French 2004).
8. Recall that Solow theory tells us that countries' growth rates will initially surge and then ultimately slow, suggesting that savings rates will be higher in the earlier boom years.
9. We note that, under national income accounting, an individual's purchase of a home or business using accumulated wealth would not impact the savings rate during that period. Instead, it would represent merely a shift in assets from one type of wealth (e.g., a savings account in a bank) to another kind of investment (a home or business).
10. Note that the purchase of an automobile or other durable is treated as consumption (thus reducing savings), while a loan for the construction of a new home leads to an investment—the counterpart to that investment is a use of savings.
11. Figure 5.7 represents the market between household and corporate savers and household borrowers only. Although these savings may not flow to other households due to lending constraints, we can assume that savings can still flow to corporate borrowers, to the government, and externally. To the extent that the demand for these loans is high relative to the household market, the constraint on household lending

will not be binding. In turn, the total level of savings will not be reduced by the constraint effect described in this figure.

12. The result depends on the shape of the individual's utility function—a concept known as "prudence" (Kimball 1990).
13. Of course, China's long history affords a discussion of many periods of dramatic and devastating change, but the last 200 years seem particularly harsh.
14. The study is based on census data from the China Health and Nutritional Survey, a randomized sample from 4,400 households in nine provinces comprising 19,000 individuals. Survey years are 1989, 1991, 1993, 1997, 2000, 2004, and 2006.
15. The precise age for retirement in China depends on both gender and whether you are employed in the government or the private sector. In the United States, retirement ages are less determined by economic sector than on a particular employer's retirement policy.
16. The current life expectancy at birth in the United States is about six years longer than China's. Given a ten-year lead in retirement age, the Chinese would need to save for an additional four years of retirement compared to the Americans.
17. In the United States, those over the age of 65 spend about 15 percent more than their income (most income comes from retirement benefits); whether the thrifty Chinese retiree manages to spend less is a question for further research.
18. Produced wealth or capital includes wealth created through production or labor; it excludes human capital, health, and natural resources of wealth—a much larger figure for both countries.
19. This difference gets magnified when we consider that personal income as a share of GDP in the United States is nearly twice that of China.
20. In 2018, the central government approved Baihang Credit to be the only government-sanctioned individual credit rating agency. It is 36 percent owned by the central government, with other internet giants and institutions holding an 8 percent share each, and it will be a key part of the SCS project in 2020.
21. Given the recent history of defaults on zero-down-payment mortgages in the United States, this is probably a good thing.
22. Here, we are referring to physical investment in plant, property, equipment, housing, or inventory accumulation.
23. The multitude of theories of consumption no doubt relates to the central role of consumption in recessions and recoveries identified in the early work of Keynes and the scholars who built upon his basic framework. Furthermore, in most economies worldwide—with China as one important exception—consumption represents

the largest component of macroeconomic demand. Keynes's approach continues to spawn much interest in how consumption, a key component of economic demand, is determined.

24. In Figure 5.18 and Figure 5.19, wage data as a share of GDP is not consistent. Figure 5.18 is based on household survey data, while Figure 5.19 is based on national income account data.
25. A much higher estimate from aggregate provincial data shows that around 48 percent of GDP comes from wages and salaries in China, which would put that share on par with the United States. We might view these two percentages as boundaries to the actual figures.
26. These results are based on aggregate sales, net income, assets, and equity for each country. Results differ substantially if we look at typical (or median) firms for each country. Aggregation gives a much heavier weight to very large firms in each country.
27. We assume tax rates are 0 without loss of generality.
28. In order have a dividend PR higher than 100 percent, some companies engage in stock buybacks—borrowing and using the funds to buyback shares. This alters the capital structure, creating more risk, but presumably lowers the cost of capital. In the United States, stock buybacks amounted to somewhere between USD 700 billion and USD 800 billion in 2018.
29. Chinese companies in the past were referred to as iron roosters, 铁公鸡 (*tie gongji*, "no eggs delivered, no feathers to pluck"), because of their unwillingness to release dividends to shareholders.
30. For ease of exposition, we are assuming a 0 tax rate on dividends.
31. The entrusted loan sector of China's shadow banking system is the quasi-formal counterpart to the missing savings in Lin and Schramm (2006), and it is estimated at USD 2 trillion in 2018.
32. This is certainly true in the United States as well; the government-sponsored Small Business Administration, with its provision of small business loans, attempts to alleviate this problem.
33. The financial crisis beginning in 2008, in which the financial sector had grown to an unprecedented share of the national economy, suggests that Americans may have developed too many ways of holding their wealth. Meanwhile, the surge in stock and housing prices in China suggests that Chinese citizens may have too few. The latter effect has been further exacerbated by a rapid growth in the money supply, discussed in Chapters 7 and 8.

6
CHINA'S PATH OF INVESTMENT

欲速则不达
Haste Makes Waste

The tremendous growth in savings in China discussed in the last chapter has been matched by an equally significant increase in gross fixed investment (also called "gross capital formation," or GCF) over the past decade. When discussing investment in this chapter, we are referring to physical investment, that is, the flow of new plant, equipment, housing, and inventories that accumulate into the national capital stock, broadly defined.[1] This type of investment is in contrast to "financial investment," which is more commonly used in everyday conversation; the latter refers to the channeling of savings into different asset classes such as savings accounts, stocks, and bonds. Although the two concepts are clearly related, we must keep in mind that investment (in the context of this chapter) involves actual current production of output (investment or capital goods) that will be used to produce more output in the future. In contrast, financial investment in the context of asset management may not result in any current production of output at all, but rather may simply involve the reallocation of financial assets. We do briefly discuss, in this chapter, fixed asset investment (FAI)—a measure that does include physical and financial investment. "Gross capital formation" refers to investment in plant, equipment, and housing, but excludes inventory accumulation (also known as "stock building)"; total investment includes the latter.

Figure 6.1 shows the high rate of real investment in China during the reform period rising above 40 percent in the early 2000s and peaking in 2011 at close to 48 percent of gross domestic product (GDP). By 2018, investment as a share of GDP was about 44 percent. The figure also suggests that the increase in investment was not solely an artifact of economic growth; instead, investment took up an increasing share of economic output. Figure 6.1 also shows the much smaller share of economic output devoted to investment in the United States. China's share of GDP devoted to investment in recent years has been the highest worldwide for any large economy. China, in absolute terms since 2009, has spent more on investment than the United States and is now the world's largest investor.

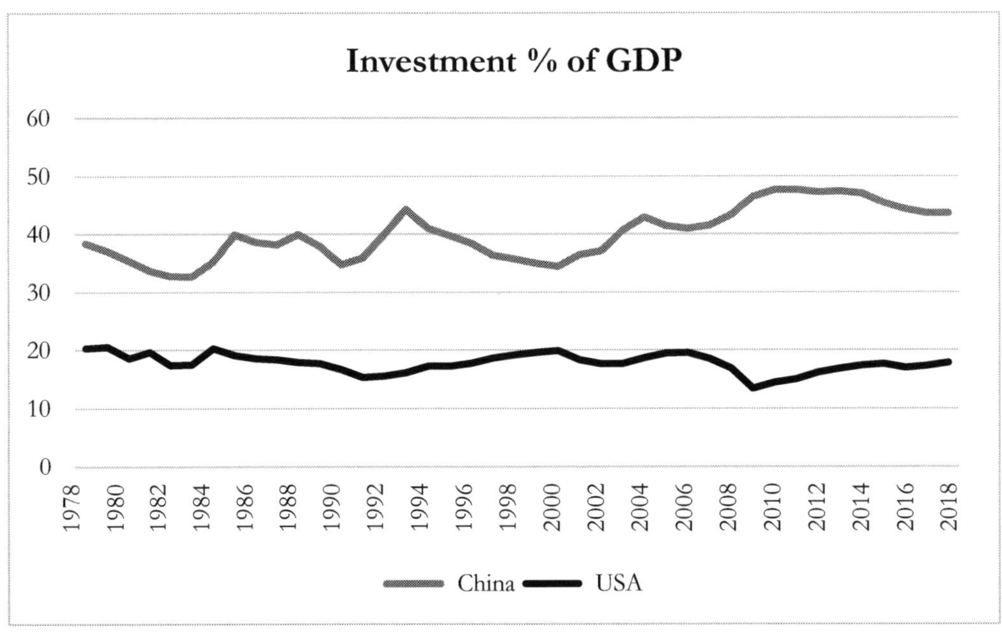

Figure 6.1 Investment as share of GDP in China has consistently been the highest among large economies of the world and over twice the share found in the United States. The share peaked in 2011 at around 48 percent.
Source: Author created based on data from the Federal Reserve Economic Database and World Bank World Development Indicators.
Note: For China, we use gross capital formation (percent of GDP); for the United States we use investment (percent of GDP).

We can compare that level to other middle-income economies—in which the share of investment reaches only around 25 percent—and to the United States, where the share is approximately 18 percent. As was discussed in Chapter 2, investment growth in China can explain, in a GDP accounting senses, about one-third of GDP growth for 2017. Figure 6.2 shows the fraction of GDP growth that can be attributed to investment growth in a GDP accounting sense (as opposed to a Solow long-run theoretical sense). We see in Figure 6.2 that, during the Great Financial Crisis (GFC) and the earlier dot-com bubble recession, China relied heavily on investment growth as a source of GDP growth.[2] In the United States, we would typically see investment fall in a recession rather than rise in importance as in China.

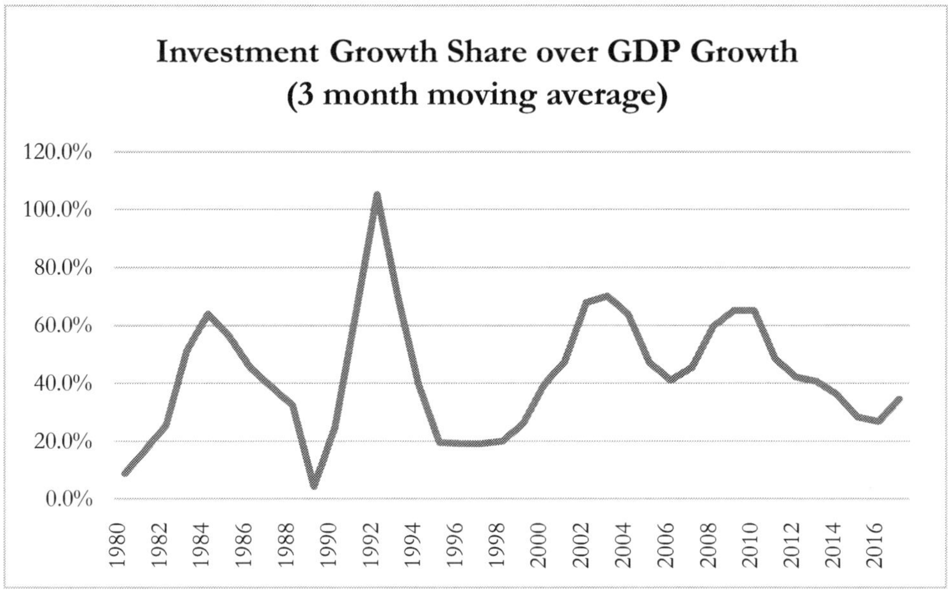

Figure 6.2 Though we must be careful when using GCF data for China, the figure suggests that, in periods of slow global growth, China surges its investment to support GDP growth. Here we see that a large share of China's GDP growth in 2009 was due, in a GDP accounting sense, to investment growth.
Source: Author created based on data from the Federal Reserve Economic Database and World Bank World Development Indicators.
Note: For China we use gross capital formation (percent of GDP), and we weight real investment growth by its share of GDP (the numerator) and divide by real GDP growth (the denominator).

That China's creation of new fixed capital on an annual basis (GCF) moved from just RMB (*renminbi*) 870 billion in 1980 to RMB 34 trillion by 2017 in real terms has implications not just for the types and level of economic activity in those intervening years, but also for economic growth in the years to follow.[3] Such a massive accumulation of capital raises questions about which economic agents were involved in the decision to invest, what their motivations were, and what can be inferred about the quality of investment taking place. In other words, will these investments yield returns sufficient to offset their initial costs, and who are the potential beneficiaries (or losers) from such investment? Finally, we note that—in developed, market-oriented economies—investment has played a critical role in short-run economic fluctuations (that is, the business cycle). Of the various components of demand for these advanced economies, investment is, by far, the most volatile.

		China	United States
a	Real GDP Growth	9.5%	2.7%
b	Volatility of GDP Growth	2.7%	1.8%
c	Coefficient of Variation (Row b / Row a)	28.3%	69.7%
d	Real Investment Growth	10.1%	3.6%
e	Volatility of Investment Growth	7.7%	8.4%
f	Coefficient of Variation (Row e / Row d)	76.5%	234.7%

Table 6.1 Growth in China's investment has been both more rapid and less volatile than in the United States since 1978.
Source: Author created based on data from the Federal Reserve Economic Database and World Bank World Development Indicators.

Table 6.1 presents the volatility of GDP and investment in both countries. Though volatility of investment in China has increased in recent years, it is still below that of the United States in absolute terms. After adjusting for the larger average growth in investment in China (the coefficient of variation), we see that investment in the United States is substantially more volatile than in China. Furthermore, compared to GDP volatility, US investment is relatively more volatile than in China. The higher relative volatility in investment in the United States overall contains both good news and bad news for China. The good news is that a key component of economic demand is stable; and, in turn, the overall economy has relatively more stable GDP growth (a macroeconomic plus). But the bad news is that stable investment growth is one symptom of an economy that still relies heavily on economic planning in which investment is not reflective of market forces, but rather of government mandate (a microeconomic/financial minus).

The latter phenomenon is suggested by David and Venkateswaran (2019). They examine the dispersion of the average productivity of capital in the United States and China and its causes. Dispersion in productivity can either be a sign of the inefficient allocation of capital or a rational response to factors such as high adjustment costs or the inability to substitute capital for other factors of production. Dispersion of returns is substantially higher in China than in the United States. The authors detect ongoing factors (such as government policies) that may be leading to the misallocation of capital in China. They also detect that firm size may influence access to capital, suggesting that smaller firms may have limited access. Overall, removing some of these inefficient factors, they estimate, could lead to improvements in total factor productivity in China by 36 to 38 percent.

Finally, we note that China's investment growth rates vary as a result of long-term trends, while in the United States growth rates can swing dramatically over the short term. This, of course, is consistent with the definition of growth cycles versus business cycles discussed in Chapter 1. Given China's movement away from a planned economy to a market-based economy, we must understand the implications for investment in both the long run and the short run.

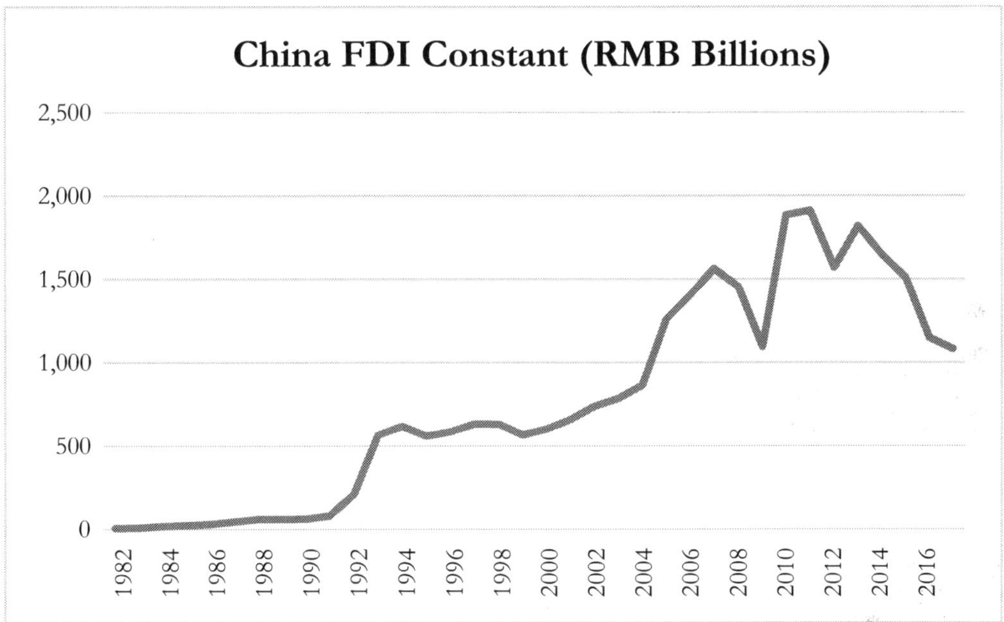

Figure 6.3 China is one of the world's largest recipients of FDI, but it has come to play a more important role in China's quest for technological progress than in its sources of physical capital.
Source: Author created based on International Monetary Fund Database.

Figure 6.3 shows a dramatic increase in foreign direct investment (FDI) into China over the past several decades in real terms. In the same period, however, overall investment increased even more—by a factor of 6—rising from 38 percent of GDP to close to 44 percent.[4] As seen in Figure 6.4, FDI contributed only about 17 percent of China's total investment at its peak in 1994; by 2017, the amount fell to only 3 percent.

Figure 6.4 FDI represents a decreasing share of GDP and total investment in China: By 2017 only 3 percent of all investment was funded from abroad.
Source: Author created based on International Monetary Fund Database.

China's Investment: Uses and Sources

Uses

It is worth repeating that, in a macroeconomics accounting context, investment, consumption, government, and export spending or demand is defined by its use, rather than its source. If something is used by the government sector and is consumed (for example, meals), we define that product's use as "government," even though the product was produced in the private sector for the purpose of consumption in a colloquial sense. Similarly, a washing machine purchased by a consumer is defined as "consumption," whereas, had it been purchased by a commercial launderer, it would be classified as an "investment" good. New residential housing construction, meanwhile, is treated as an investment good (even though a consumer is "using" the house), and the homeowner is classified as an investor. Police or fire department services provided by a municipality are included as government spending (as are military services) because they are public goods that are, in effect, demanded by the government. Public education is another interesting example. Provided by the government but used by consumers, its classification might seem ambiguous. But, to the extent that parents do not directly pay tuition for public education (tax revenues do), we would classify public education as a government service—something demanded by the government.

For developed economies, the interesting nexus of classification is between consumption and investment uses. In China, however, more interest is placed on the government and investment nexus. Investment represents a relatively large fraction of China's GDP. Historically, however, most of the decision making on investment has taken place at the behest of the government. About 38 percent of FAI in China (discussed below) is by state-owned enterprises (SOEs) or state-owned holding companies. A further complication is that many consumer goods have been produced by SOEs, which are owned by the government. In developed economies, much of that same production would be undertaken by the private sector.[5] Given these differences, our definition of investment as a use becomes an important tool to keep in mind.

Fixed investment includes both business fixed investment and residential fixed investment (housing). Business fixed investment includes new plant, property, and equipment (PP&E) (but excludes land) as well as software development. Another type of investment that is not considered "fixed" is the flow of new inventory (stock building). In summary, investment includes gross new PP&E (including residential housing, business software development, and inventory accumulation.[6]

Figure 6.5 Residential property prices have surged in China over the past two decades, increasing by a factor of 4.
Source: Author created based on data from CEIC.

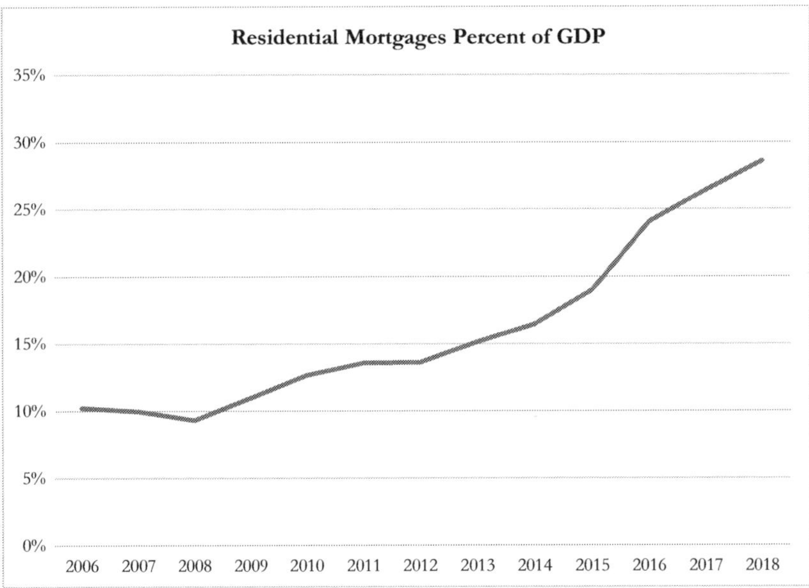

Figure 6.6 The ability to borrow from banks to purchase a home in China is a relatively recent phenomenon.
Source: Author created based on data from CEIC.

Case Study 6.1: Is There a Housing Bubble?

A "financial bubble" is an increase in an asset price unrelated to fundamental factors (such as a higher anticipated return or cash flow, or a decrease in the cost of capital). Rather, a bubble is defined as price increases based solely on the expectation of further price increases. Here, we ask one of the most popular questions in China related to finance: "Do housing prices today represent a bubble?" A classic bubble example comes from the South Sea Company (1718–1721): one of the earliest attempts to securitize debt—in this case, the national debt of the United Kingdom. Although lacking in actual income, the company was able to attract investors, so much so that the price of stock in the company rose from around 100 pounds sterling to close to 1,000. One investor, who bought the stock at around 700 pounds (hoping to follow the momentum) and sold at closer to 300 pound (missing selling at the peak of 1,000 pounds), was the great physicist Isaac Newton. He lost close to USD (US dollar) 3 million in today's dollars in the venture, leading him to famously state: "I can calculate the movement of stars but not the madness of men." There are two well-known characteristics of bubbles: (1) they are unsustainable, and (2) they are notoriously difficult to identify in terms of their existence and the timing of their collapse. Or, as attributed to the great economist (and investor) John Maynard Keynes, "Markets can remain irrational longer than investors can remain solvent."

Since 2000, housing prices in China have more than tripled; and, in some major cities such as Beijing, they have increased by a factor of 6 to 8. Beijing is now over four times more expensive than the national average on a per-square-meter basis. During the same period, land prices doubled on average for residential buildings. And again, in specific cities, land prices have risen by a multiple of that. In a single quarter of 2013 (the first quarter), land prices nearly doubled in Shanghai. Figure 6.5 shows the steep rise in residential prices per square meter—a 9-fold increase since 1995.

Glaeser et al. (2017) note that, between 2003 and 2014, 5.5 million new apartments were built in China every year, with 16 percent of urban employment in 2014 engaged in the construction industry. Meanwhile, housing vacancy rates in China's Tier 1 cities were estimated at 20 percent in 2012—in the United States, at the start of the GFC in 2008, vacancy rates were only 3 percent. Since residential housing represents about 22 percent of national investment (or about 10 percent of GDP), the impact of a bursting bubble would be significant in China—likely triggering a contagion effect on financial markets, investment, and consumer demand. The recent US financial crisis serves as a poster child for such a possibility.

From the founding of the People's Republic of China through 1978, land and property in China has been state-owned. In 1979, limited privatization of housing began, mainly in cities along the east coast. The government took another important step toward privatization by implementing a 1988 constitutional amendment allowing for 70-year leases of land for residential purposes. The government continues to own all land in China, but individuals can "lease" homes in 70-year time slots. Another critical year for housing was 1998; work units (*danwei*) were no longer responsible for the direct provision of housing. Instead, it became the responsibility of individual citizens to rent or purchase their own housing. This was the start of a truly private housing market. Banks started to grant residential mortgages around the same time. As seen in Figure 6.6, residential mortgages across China have seen a steep ascent since 2012.

On the supply side, from 1998 to 2008, China saw its available residential floor space more than triple. Between 1999 and 2018, residential construction grew at a 20 percent annual rate—twice the rate of growth of real GDP (Cook et al. 2018). In some cities, more than half of the housing construction taking place during the past decade was completed by SOEs. These enterprises, as discussed in this chapter and Chapter 7, have access to bank finance at subsidized borrowing costs. The high involvement of SOEs raises a question: "Are China's housing price increases driven by supply-and-demand fundamentals, or are they a vestige of a planned economy?"

On the demand side, we have seen massive urbanization (i.e., the movement of the population from rural to urban areas) encouraged by policy announcements and Five-Year Plan mandates. In fact, in 1978, less than 18 percent of China's population lived in urban areas; by 2017, over half of the population lived there—a change of about half a billion people. Alternatively, since 1995, about half a billion people have moved into urban areas; meanwhile, only about 100 million single-family housing units were added since then. In the same period, per capita income in USD terms increased by more than a factor of 6. Tier 1 and Tier 2 cities (cities that are the largest in terms of size and economic significance) have seen housing price rises outstrip increases in disposable income, but not so in Tier 3 cities.[7] These factors point to housing shortages conditional on location and family income. Comparing China's situation with that of the United States suggests that the problem may persist long into the future: 40 percent of Chinese citizens still live in rural areas, while only 15 percent of Americans live in rural areas, and only 2 percent of the US population works in agriculture. Thus, it is likely that China's urban migration will be a long-term phenomenon. Finally, on the demand side, there is a shortage of relatively secure assets to invest in for China's citizens with ever-growing wealth. Real estate has traditionally been viewed as a safe way to hold wealth.

Chinese authorities, meanwhile, have been concerned about rising housing prices. Beginning in 2017, a number of measures have been instituted to curb speculation in housing markets. At the time, an estimated 20 percent of homeowners owned multiple dwellings; and, in 2018, an estimated 70 percent of all new homes were purchased by those who already owned a first home. Beijing has imposed at least 30 restrictions on aspects of new home buying ranging from acquiring a mortgage, to purchasing a second home, to working around the restrictions by shell organization purchases. Shenzhen, for example, requires a 3-year holding period after a new home is purchased.

In examining house-price-to-annual-rent ratios (a form of price-earnings [PE] ratio), Wu et al. (2011) find that, in seven large Chinese cities, ratio estimates range from 25 to 45.[*] In the United States, the range would be from 16 to 20. They employ an approach suggested by Poterba (1984) to see if the ratios in China make economic sense:

$$\text{User Cost} = (1 - t)(r + p) + m + \delta + \beta - \pi^e$$

Here, we employ a specific form of the "user cost," defined as the cost of owning a home, per home price. In the equation above, (t) is the individual tax rate (a home interest deductibility benefit), (r) is the borrowing or financing cost, (p) is the property tax rate, (m) is the maintenance fee, (δ) is the depreciation rate, (β) is the risk premium on home ownership (in percent), and (π^e) is the expected appreciation rate of the property (home price increase). In theory, this cost should just equal the rental rate, or the inverse of the PE ratios mentioned above.

China's parameters for the above relationship differ fundamentally from those of the United States. It is useful to discuss these differences qualitatively. Interest on mortgages is not tax deductible in China, but it is in the United States. In 2018, mortgage rates in China were around 5.7 percent. Property taxes clearly exist in the United States, but not yet in China (though there are plans to implement them). Maintenance fees are generally quite low in China, and in turn maintenance expenditure is low. Due to lack of preventative maintenance, absentee owners, and—in some cases—hasty construction, the depreciation rate of property in China is likely higher. Home ownership is such an important asset in citizens' portfolios that it may, in and of itself, define the market beta and as such equal one. Finally, if expectations are formed adaptively (i.e., based on what has happened in the past), then China will continue to see high expectations of home price appreciation. Wu et al. (2011) find that the structure of some of these parameters render current PE ratios unsustainably high (i.e., actual home price appreciation is far from what is expected—implying a possible collapse of China's housing prices in the near future).

The authors also examine home-price-to-annual-income measures, but here (as suggested above), the picture is more mixed. Given the factors discussed above, Wu et al. (2011) and others suggest that China's housing market prices do reflect an asset pricing bubble.

Our view, however, is that current prices do not necessarily represent a bubble, but they may instead represent fundamental economic factors which have driven prices astronomically high in the short run. Specifically, much of China's rapid increase in prices no doubt reflects an inelastic supply of land in the cities where much of the population is migrating.[†] Fang et al. (2016) point out the key role that local governments have had in the monopoly sale of land. Land sales have been a way of raising revenues for cash-strapped localities. As such, the authors point out that, on the supply side, local government involvement through land sales and zoning regulations may serve to limit the supply of housing and keep prices artificially high. In effect, they are arguing that localities are acting as rational monopolists.

Basic microeconomics clearly segregates short-run from long-run prices. In the former, prices can surge, but ultimately prices will moderate in the long run with new entrants and new supplies in the market. What both "bubbleists" and fundamentalists do agree on is that, in both situations, those who invest and assume that current high prices and price increases are sustainable will lose money. The rational investor is able to observe the market fundamentals, understand that other cities may offer opportunities for quality urban living, and thereby moderate demand and price increases. In contrast, those in the bubble economy irrationally ignore fundamentals and, thus, economic outcomes tend to be worse. Figure 6.7 shows basic short- and long-run supply curves and demand in the housing market. In the long run, market entry prices fall from point A to point B.

In China, an industry's outlook is often very much contingent on government policies, and this is particularly true in real estate; the state owns and leases all land for development. If the government allows for even more construction, property prices will soften; if it restricts supply, prices will remain high (and out of reach for purchase by the average citizen). Finally, we note that China's real estate market has a different financial structure than did the United States' pre-GFC. In China, fewer mortgages are granted, and those that are granted require large (20–30 percent) cash down payments. Many Chinese buyers save and acquire a home fully with a cash payment, not relying on any mortgage at all. Employee-based savings plans have also been institutionalized by the government (housing provident plans). In summary, while China's home prices are likely far above their long-run equilibrium value, the housing market also appears to be driven by basic (short-run fixed) supply and measurable fundamental demand, rather than only by champagne fizz (a bubble).

*For an eighth city, Hangzhou, the ratio peaked at around 65.

†As we noted earlier, part of this may be artificial due to the participation of bank-financed SOEs.

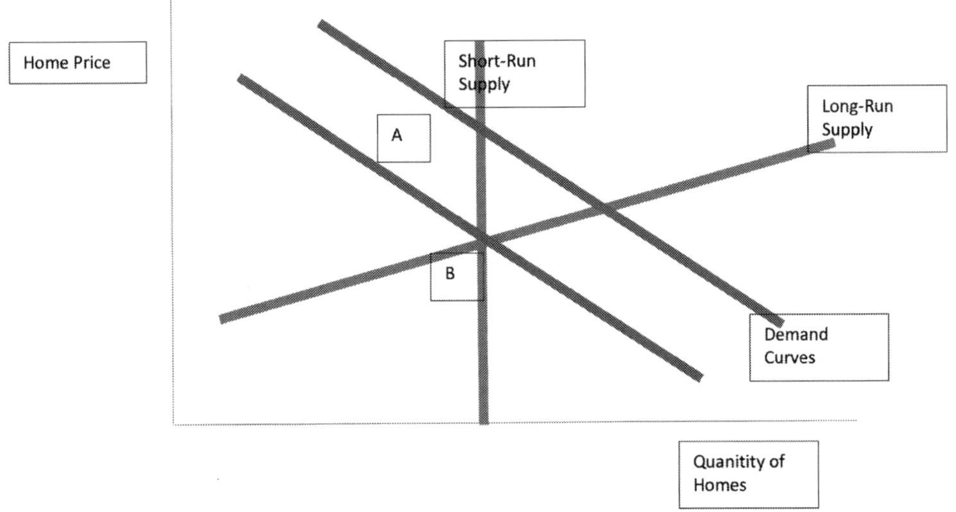

Figure 6.7 In the short run, an increase in demand for housing is met by a rise in prices; but, in the long run, the increase is met by an increase in supply of housing—possibly with very little impact on prices.
Source: Author created.

Table 6.2 provides a comparative breakdown of investment types in China and the United States. In order to make such a comparison, we must identify the share of investment undertaken by the government in demanding investment goods. In the case of China, it is difficult to separate out investment demand by the government because a substantial part of investment is undertaken by SOEs. Some of this investment will ultimately be used by the government sector, but much of it will be used by the private sector—and this is where our "uses" concept for measuring GDP comes in handy. Table 6.2 assumes that government investment demand or use is limited to those investment activities that are formally part of the central, provincial, township, and village government budgets; that is to say, they represent spending by those government entities and are financed by either taxation or public borrowing.

	US 2018 (In USD Billions)	Share of GDP	China 2017 (In RMB 100 Millions)	Share of GDP
Gross Investment Total	4,330.90	21.1%	360,625	43.6%
Non-Government and Government				
Non-Government, Fixed Gross Investment	3,595.70	17.5%	257,141	31.1%
Government Gross Investment	678.7	3.3%	88,898	10.7%
Non-Residential, Residential and Government				
Non-Residential	2,800	13.7%	176,580	21.3%
Residential	795.3	3.9%	80,561	9.7%
Government Gross Investment	678.7	3.3%	88,898	10.7%
Change in Inventories				
Change in Inventories	56.5	0.3%	14,586	1.8%
GDP	20,500.6		827,122	

Table 6.2 Residential investment and government investment are relatively more important in China than in the United States. All classes of investment in China are larger as a share of GDP.
Source: Author created based on data from CEIC and the Federal Reserve Economic Database.

As a share of GDP, China's gross investment is over twice as large as that of the United States. Across all major categories, investment is higher by similar orders of magnitude. In both countries, non-residential investment comprises the lion's share, and this was also true before the 2008 global financial crisis. Non-residential investment includes investment in PP&E—mostly on the part of companies—but also infrastructure investment. Residential, government, and inventory investment categories are all disproportionately larger in China than the United States. Even in the pre-financial crisis era, residential investment in the United States never reached the share of GDP that it currently holds in China. The large share of investment in China from residential investment (close to 10 percent of GDP) highlights the economy's sensitivity to that key component of demand; Other broader estimates (https://bit.ly/3gfjb59)(which include both real estate investment and real estate services) in China are even higher, at around 12 percent of GDP. Cook et al. (2018) estimate that a 10 percent decline in real estate construction in China would lead to a 2.2 percent decline in China's GDP—a huge impact on economic growth (see Case Study 6.1). The high level of government investment (which overlaps somewhat with SOE investment) presents a stabilizing force to overall demand, but it comes with some potentially costly tradeoffs discussed below. The relatively large share of inventory accumulation in China suggests an area where there is room for efficiency improvements.

Gross Capital Formation vs. Fixed Asset Investment

In the above paragraphs we have been using the measure GCF, which is the appropriate measure of national investment (after we add in changes in inventory) for the (I) component of GDP (recall $Y = C + I + G + [X - M]$). Investment (or GCF plus change in inventories) measures all new construction (residential and commercial), PP&E, infrastructure, and government investment. China also provides a broader measure of investment, FAI, which would not be consistent with a GDP measurement approach. It includes everything in GCF plus land purchases, acquisitions from mergers and acquisitions, and the purchase and installation of used capital equipment. Because it includes items not produced in the current year, it is not an appropriate measure for GDP expenditure/uses purposes. Nevertheless, it provides another useful angle on what individuals, companies and the government are doing in the investment space.

Figure 6.8 shows GCF, FAI, and change in inventories. It is odd that, up until 2005, FAI is less than GCF when the latter should be a subset of the former. Several explanations have emerged for this discrepancy, but the most likely explanation is a conflict between provincial/local data collection and the need to "fit" investment uses into a GDP expenditure/uses framework at the national level. (Recall our discussion of GDP measures in Chapter 2). Local governments collect FAI data and the National Bureau of Statistics (NBS) then derives an estimate for GCF for the sake of estimating GDP (production approach). What both measures do tell us, however, is that investment activity started to decline as a share of GDP around 2013.

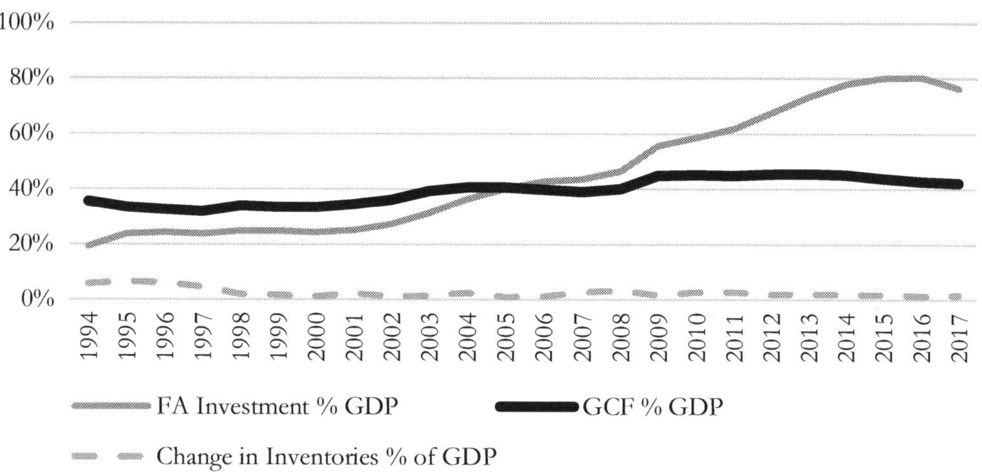

Figure 6.8 Beginning in 2005, the non-GDP metric of FAI surged past the GDP measure of GCF. FAI includes land acquisition and merger/acquisition activities whose impact positive on future economic growth is open to question.
Source: Author created based on data from CEIC and World Bank World Development Indicators.

We observe FAI sharply rising above GCF after 2005. There are at least two possible interpretations of this phenomenon. A positive interpretation would be that the Chinese economy has refocused investment away from the hard investment approach of PP&E and infrastructure to the softer side of technological progress: a reshuffling of assets, for example, via mergers and acquisitions, or land sales that improve efficiency. A negative interpretation, however, would be that the economy has moved into a speculative mode fueled by the financial sector, where "real" investments are not being made but are rather being replaced by speculative financial ones.

In 2017, infrastructure investment in China accounted for about 30 percent (https://bit.ly/2WRRdVD) of total investment, and since 2015 growth in infrastructure investment has accelerated while private investment growth has slowed. Case study 6.2 discusses one of the key funders of China's infrastructure investment: the China Development Bank (CDB). China is usually held out as a model for the efficient creation of massive infrastructure such as transportation, public housing, and industrial park projects. Furthermore, it has been argued that these types of investments have huge spillover effects, benefitting other parts of the economy. Ansar et al. (2016) have a more nuanced view. They find that, while China completes projects at a faster pace and completes projects on schedule, its performance with respect to cost overruns is no different from developed economies (actual costs about 31 percent over budget). They state that even the rapid completion has tradeoffs in terms of safety and reliability. They find that the benefit to cost ratio is remarkably low with a large number of inefficient projects—specifically, the construction of roads that are either underutilized or over-utilized. Finally, they discount the impact of positive spillovers, suggesting that negative spillovers (e.g., environmental impact) are often not taken into account. Meanwhile, He, Chen, and Schramm (2018) examine this question at the firm level in China's key electronics industry and find significant productivity gains from public investment, including infrastructure.

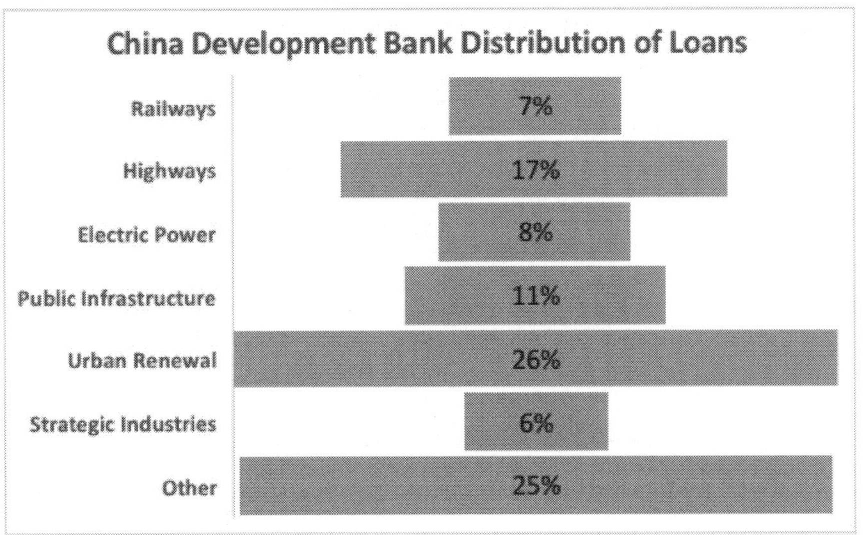

Figure 6.9 CDB, the largest lending institution in the world, invests a significant amount of funds in urban areas and highways.
Source: Author created based on data from China Development Bank (https://bit.ly/2ATnHXj), Annual Report 2018.

Total Assets	15,959.288
Liabilities	14,718.813
Equity	1,240.475
Net Income	0.114
Interest Expense	0.380

Table 6.3 CDB key financials (in RMB billions).
Source: Author created based on data from China Development Bank (https://bit.ly/2ATnHXj) Annual Report 2018.

Case Study 6.2: China Development Bank—A Fannie Mae Freddie Mac Redux?

One institution at the center of the Chinese government's investment effort is the CDB, which was founded in 1994.* Its mandate is to finance the vast collection of infrastructure projects that result from China's Five-Year Plans. Owned by the central government, half of its capital comes from the Ministry of Finance, and the other half from Central Huijin Investment Corporation and the nation's social security fund—all government-owned entities. A good fraction of the CDB's loan portfolio is for public highways, subways, airports, power, and other large infrastructure projects across China and in developing countries (Figure 6.9). The Three Gorges Dam and Shanghai's Pudong International Airport were financed primarily with funds raised by the CDB, as were deluxe sports complexes and hotel resorts both inside and outside of China. Many of its loans are to provincial and local governments (Chapter 10 provides some context for this). Its main source of funds is through the issuance of bonds with maturities ranging from short-term (under one year) to over ten years. It is the second-largest issuer of bonds in China, after the Ministry of Finance itself. Most of these bonds are held by other large state-owned financial institutions such as banks and insurance companies.

By the end of 2017, its assets (loans and other investments) had totaled almost RMB 16 trillion (over USD 2.4 trillion), an amount that was nearly double its 2012 portfolio (which was double its 2008 portfolio). Table 6.3 and Figure 6.9 highlight some key financials and a sectoral breakdown for some of CDB's loans. Meanwhile, its outstanding negotiable instrument liabilities (bonds, etc.) had increased by about 58 percent, reaching RMB 8.4 trillion. In 2017, the CDB lent around USD 103 billion. By comparison, in the same year, the entire World Bank Group had provided new financing commitments totaling USD 62 billion. Any financial institution with such a breathtaking pace of asset growth in such a short period of time warrants a careful inspection of its financial position.

CDB was responsible for funding about 2 percent of all investments undertaken in China in 2017 and about 8 percent of all Chinese government investment. About 25 percent (https://bit.ly/2zmIP7r) of its outstanding loans are foreign loans, and around half of this amount is related to China's Belt and Road Initiative. With these foreign loans, an interesting question going forward—who will take senior creditor status should borrowers encounter difficulties in repaying their debt: China, or international organizations such as the International Monetary Fund (IMF) and World Bank?†

Since the CDB issues debt with an implicit government guarantee, its debt instruments are considered risk-free—it has been able to borrow at a lower cost than would an institution without such support. One of its principle sources of finance is the large state-owned banks (the Big Four) that hold the vast savings of China's citizens. A natural question to ask when governments are so heavily involved in both borrowing and lending for projects at such a break-neck pace is whether or not a crisis is brewing. Are there echoes here of Fannie Mae and Freddie Mac and the supercharged lending for residential construction that occurred prior to the GFC in the United States (and other parts of the world)? At a macro level, government-mandated borrowing and lending has a very different set of goals (for example, employment, foreign relations) than the traditional one of explicit value maximization. These priorities can and have led many intermediating financial institutions into trouble around the world. At a micro level, access to an eager lender can lead to slack project evaluations and corruption, as seen in the 2008–2009 US financial crisis. Most CDB loans, however, are not directly related to residential construction, but rather to infrastructure.

Various key financial ratios—such as CDB's return on assets (0.75 percent), the capital adequacy ratio (close to 11.6 percent), and non-performing loan ratios (0.70 percent)—compare favorably to major private US banks today. One way of quickly assessing whether CDB is a value-creating entity is to examine how well its investors are doing. Again examining Table 6.3's snapshot of key financials, we see that equity holders (the government) provide about 8 percent of the bank's assets, and they earned a nominal return of around 9.2 percent in 2017; lenders (including the Big Four banks) provided the remaining 92 percent of its finance and earned 2.6 percent. (Depositors/citizens in banks have earned about 2 percent on their deposits in recent years, suggesting that financial institutions lending to the CDB earn a sizeable "haircut" before paying depositors.) The weighted return on invested capital (ROIC) has been around 3.1 percent. Inflation, meanwhile, has averaged around 1.8 percent in recent years, suggesting a real return for lenders of about 0.8 percent and a real ROIC of about 1.3 percent. We note that CDB returns are far below the estimated returns to capital suggested in Chapter 4, which still hovered around 10 percent. The gap between 1.3 percent and 10 percent suggests that borrowers from the CDB may be benefitting at the expense of savers/taxpayers (the ultimate stakeholders in CDB). Figure 6.10 shows that returns on equity peaked in 2014, but they have now moved down close to where they were during the GFC.

CDB's Vice President, Ding Xianqun, stated in the context of a concessionary (low interest) 40 year loan in Indonesia (https://reut.rs/2ZroQiP) (without Indonesian government guarantees) that CDB does not seek to "maximize profits." In 2013–2014, the interest rate charged to CDB by creditors had risen by almost 50 percent to close to 6 percent, suggesting some concerns about risks of lending to CDB. Since then, borrowing costs have moderated to the 2 to 3 percent range. Furthermore, CDB appears to have no trouble raising funds in international capital markets with a number of international bond issuances (https://reut.rs/2XcqRwg). Only after a better understanding of each CDB project's merit will we be able to understand the true quality of its loans. Good projects will yield social returns, which taxpayers will gladly pay for via the low returns on their savings; bad projects will weigh heavily on the real returns anticipated but never received by China's thrifty citizen-savers. In this light, a natural question would be, why does the CDB (and then another layer of financial institutions) need to act as an intermediary between these projects and the end-investor at all? Could project-specific bonds be rated and sold directly to the public? Alternatively, what is the value-added in terms of information gathering and credit-decision making of CDB and other related financial institutions? In the last chapter, we will examine developments in China's financial system to see if China's financial system is up to this task.

Finally, we might compare the financing of public projects in the United States with the role that the CDB plays in China. Taxes and bond issuance are two principal modes of finance for public finance in the United States. In contrast, China taps directly into its vast pool of individual and corporate savings via the banking system to finance public projects. Readers should consider the tradeoffs that exist under each method related to ease of access to capital for infrastructure investment versus the actual quality of the target infrastructure project.

*Other major government banks with a mandate for development include the Agricultural Development Bank of China, the China Export Import Bank (CHEXIM), and the Guangdong Development Bank (provincial level); their names suggest their role in development.

†Both the IMF and World Bank view themselves as the senior creditor to countries.

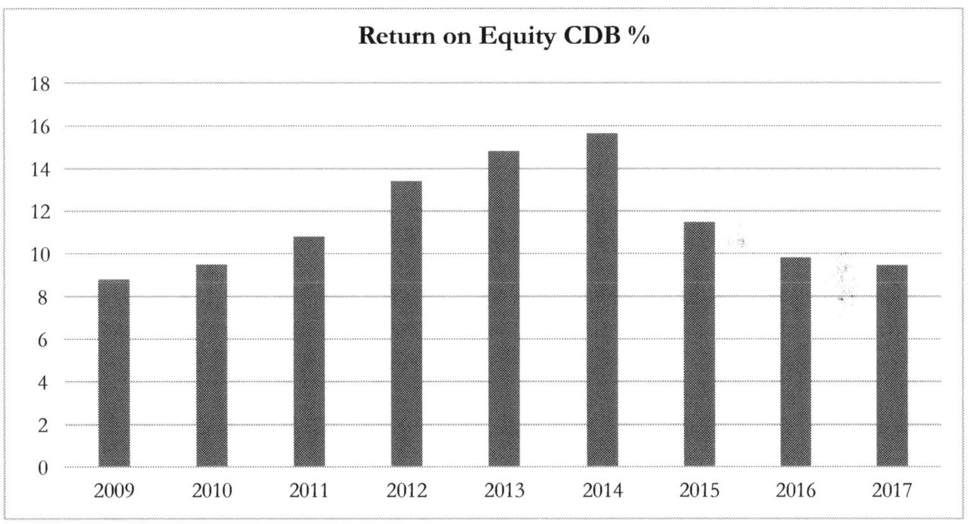

Figure 6.10 Returns to equity for the CDB have fallen since 2014, and they are now back to the rates found during the GFC.
Source: Author created based on data from CEIC.

Sources

The largest share of investment in China is now undertaken by private enterprises—about 57 percent of all investment—a ratio that has risen substantially over the past decade. SOEs, collective enterprises, and various combinations thereof make up about

39 percent of total investment, a ratio that has risen since this book was last published (but below the level in 1995, when the share of SOE investment was close to 44 percent [Lin and Schramm 2009]). Other important investment categories include the government (around 10 percent, overlapping with some SOE investment) and foreign firms (about 3 percent of total investment).

Both in China and the United States, non-financial corporations rely overwhelmingly on internal funds (retained earnings or profits) to finance investment. In China, despite its substantial investment, the very profitable production sector has been a substantial lender to other sectors—including indirectly financing the US current account deficit with China. In the United States, in recent years, the non-financial corporate sector has used its ample profits to finance its relatively low levels of domestic investment, and it has used the surplus funds to finance other economic sectors ranging from consumer borrowing to FDI into China. In the United States, companies in recent years have been buying back rather than issuing new equity.[8] In contrast, Chinese firms have been net issuers of equity, and they have been borrowing from banks despite their strong cash flow from operations. No doubt some of these funds are recycled (via China's shadow banking system, as discussed in Chapter 11) into other firms with low or negative cash flows. Some of the funds borrowed, however, may simply represent the arbitrage opportunity that SOEs enjoy through borrowing from state-owned banks at low rates, then investing in outside opportunities including foreign investments.

As Lin and Schramm (2009) point out, a key difference between the United States and China, in terms of investment and production, is the presence of SOEs in the production process. The Chinese NBS provides definitions of the broad types of production units still found in China.

Definitions of Entities Involved in Production of Output in China

State-Owned Enterprises

There are over 100,000 entities—that have not been incorporated and that are engaged in the production of goods and services both of a public and private nature—whose assets are entirely owned by the central government, provinces, or local governments. Most SOEs are owned by provinces and localities. Over 100 SOEs are owned by the central government, and these entities are both large and economically significant. Not included here are state-funded enterprises registered as limited liability companies.

Collective-Owned Enterprises

Economic units where the assets are owned and operated by members of a group are referred to as a "collective" (collective-owned enterprise, COE). Typically, the collective would represent residents of a town or village—the definition therefore comprises town and village enterprises. The collective leadership decides on how revenues of the enterprise are to be distributed among the collective members and any outside stakeholders. Management typically receives some fixed percentage of profits. One type of COE is the cooperative enterprise in which capital is contributed mainly by the workers of the entity. COEs have a great deal of independence in terms of management decisions, strategic direction of the entity, distribution of profits, and wage remuneration.

Private and Quasi-Private Enterprises

Economic entities that have assumed either a limited-liability corporate structure, share-holding corporate structure, individual proprietor structure, or some type of foreign-funded investment structure are private or quasi-private enterprises. Included in this group are share-holding companies that are listed on stock exchanges but whose principal shareholder remains the Chinese government (former SOEs that have been listed).

Because the state still has a major role in the production process, certain complications in measuring output and investment can arise. Assigning roles for GDP—for example, whether goods and services are consumer goods or government goods—is relatively easy. This classification (as discussed earlier in the chapter) is based on the user of the end product, not the producer. Thus, at least in principle, an SOE producing consumer goods would correctly have its output included in consumption under GDP measurement methodology.

Difficulties arise in deciding how to assign SOE surpluses (profits) or deficits (losses) when measuring flows of funds (the sources of funds for investment [savings] versus its uses [investment]). Are SOE gains or losses assigned to the government sector (particularly at the local level) as deficits or losses, or are they kept off of the government's balance sheet? A similar question arises when we try to assign the amount of investment undertaken by the government: should SOE investment be included or excluded? Recognizing that SOE investment is often directly linked to a Five-Year Plan adds another layer of complexity. Since the start of the reform period in 1978, the share of investment attributed to the government has risen, while long-run SOE investment has diminished in importance (Figure 6.11). It would appear that the investments previously attributed to

SOEs (such as for health, housing, and general welfare) are now being undertaken by all levels of government in China.

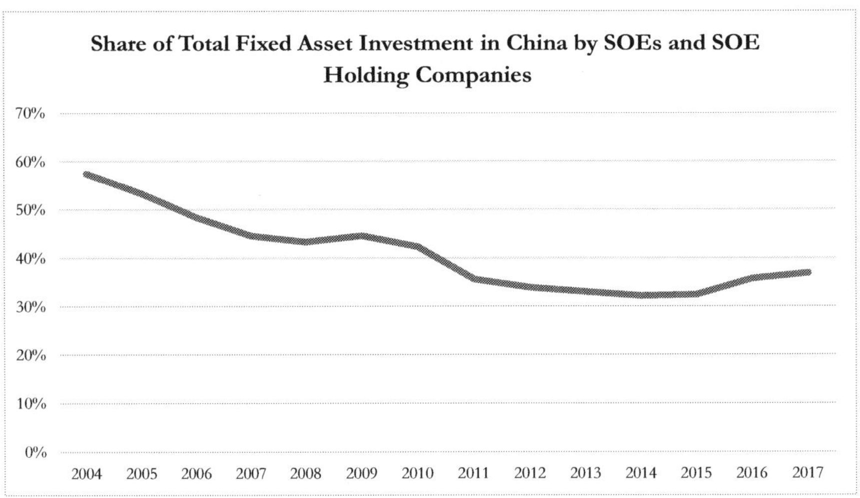

Figure 6.11 Though not as high as the early 2000s, SOEs and their holding companies remain a very important factor in overall Chinese investments.
Source: Author created based on data from CEIC.

Investment Demand Theories

How an investment decision is made is a complex issue in any nation, but especially so in China. The fields of microeconomics, macroeconomics, and finance have provided a variety of models with which to explain the investment level in an economy, both theoretically and empirically. This work has a long tradition, dating back to at least the beginning of the 20th century. The neoclassical models are truly at the center of a capitalist framework, in which owners of capital (capitalists or investors) make rational decisions on how much capital to allocate to a firm or a project being considered by the firm.

As we have seen above, however, a disproportionate share of investment in China has been undertaken by the government and by SOEs at the behest of the government. In the past, much of this investment was financed either by grants or with "soft" loans (i.e., loans whose payment terms are either more favorable than market rates or which, in effect, become grants, and are never actually required to be serviced or repaid). By definition, when the government is the principal investor or giver of grants to a company, that company is an SOE. When investment is determined by government decision makers, there may be an entirely different set of objectives from those that a private value-creating capitalist might have to consider. This section is set in this context, and it analyzes the question: "To what extent can the mainstream (traditional) models of investment behavior explain China's investment behavior?" Given that investment is highly variable in advanced economies, and given its reputation for being at the center of business cycle fluctuations in the short run and economic growth in the long run, the issues covered here are critically important.[9] In China's economy today, we see two extremes. At one end of the spectrum, we see investment undertaken by central and local governments that, although serving a public policy purpose, may have little or no relation to the mainstream model assumptions and outcomes. Meanwhile, at the other end of the spectrum, we see investment undertaken by private entrepreneurs (including foreign ones) that fits very comfortably within the confines of these very same models. Over 95 percent of Chinese enterprises are privately held; but, as we have seen, very large SOEs continue to have an outsize importance in terms of production, employment, and investment.[10]

Models of Investment Behavior

Neoclassical Model

If we begin to consider investment at the firm level, we can examine the standard model for decision making on the part of the firm. Here we imagine managers who have a range of possible projects that will yield incremental increases in profits (Π) over some future horizon.[11] The manager must weigh the anticipated benefit (more profit) against the incremental cost of achieving these profits. The incremental cost includes the ongoing cost of financing the investment needed for the project. That cost (r) includes either the opportunity cost of using the owner's own funds or someone else's funds for the project—in other words, what those funds could have earned in their best alternative risk-equivalent use during each time period. An additional cost to factor in is depreciation of the fixed investment during each time period, either as a result of wear and tear or because the investment has lost value due to obsolescence. The opportunity cost of these funds plus the depreciation must be compared with the anticipated profits in order to see if the investment should be undertaken. We refer to the sum of opportunity costs and depreciation as the "user cost of investment."

In summary, at the firm level, greater anticipated profits (Π) can be associated with increased investment, while higher opportunity costs (r) (often defined as the "cost of capital") are associated with lower levels of investment. This relationship is summarized in the following equation:

$$\text{NPV} = -I_0 + \Pi_1 / (1 + r) + \Pi_2 / (1 + r)^2 \dots$$

where I_0 represents the initial outlay for investment. The term net present value (NPV), in effect, measures the difference between the increased profits and the increased cost of undertaking the project. A positive value suggests that the investment should be undertaken. In Macro Finance Insight 6.1, we establish a link between marginal productivities of capital and cash flows.

Macro Finance Insight 6.1: Optimal Investment, Neoclassical Model, and Project Valuation

A basic microeconomics course establishes the following equilibrium condition between the cost of capital and returns to capital in a competitive economy:

$P \times$ MPK = rental cost of capital (or r)

where (P) is the price a firm receives when selling its output, MPK is the marginal product of capital (or the extra output derived by adding one unit of capital), and (r), the rental cost of capital, is an all-inclusive measure of the opportunity cost of using one more unit of capital. Sensibly, this means that a firm should add more capital up to the point at which the extra benefits just equal the extra costs. Implementing this rule in practice has many formulations. For example, we could identify the left-hand side of the above equation with the ROIC and the right-hand side with the weighted average cost of capital (WACC), restated as:

$$\text{ROIC}(K) = \text{WACC}(K)$$

If the left-hand side is greater than the right-hand side, then one should continue investing, creating more and more value, until they are equal.

Similarly, the neoclassical model discussed here can be simplified and rearranged by examining (K), our level of capital, and assuming a perpetually level cash flow that can increase as a result of new capital (K).[12] Thus, we have:

To maximize with respect to (K), we set

$$\Delta(\text{NVP}) \,/\, \Delta K = 0$$

Where,

$$\Delta K = \text{Investment}$$

which yields,

$$0 = -1 + (\Delta \text{CashFlow}(K) \,/\, \Delta(K)) \,/\, r$$

which yields,

$$P \times \text{MPK} = r$$

where, MPK can be defined as the increment to perpetual cash flow from an increase in one unit of capital.[13]

Researchers examining the efficiency of investment in China use these various measures to examine China's decisions. As discussed above, many economists find distortions related to both the right-hand side and the left-hand side of this fundamental condition for optimal investing in China.

Profits are the difference between revenues and expenditures. Anything that might increase profits will increase NPVs and result in more investment. Since firms seek to ensure that marginal revenue equals marginal cost, any factor that either increases marginal revenue or decreases marginal cost will increase profits—which, in turn, will increase output and increase investment. What we have just established is a positive link between output and investment. While it may seem obvious that more output requires more investment, the subtle point is that increased output derives from either lower anticipated costs or higher anticipated revenues; a change in anticipated costs or revenues, in turn, alters (increases) profits, the optimal level of output, and the optimal level of investment.

In summary, the equation above shows that a lower opportunity cost, a lower rate of depreciation, or an anticipated permanent increase in profit-maximizing output will lead to greater investment. We can summarize this result in a linear equation (where (*a*) is a constant term and (*B*) and (*C*) are sensitivities of investment to the opportunity cost and anticipated output:

$$\text{Investment} = a - B \times (\text{opportunity cost}) + C \times (\text{anticipated output})$$

Of course, other factors—such as exchange rates, the price of capital, and how quickly new capital can be added—must be included in such an equation when we actually attempt to estimate coefficients using econometric techniques.

Tobin's Q

An alternate but equivalent approach to the neoclassical model is to examine the relationship between how financial markets value a firm's investment prospects compared to the purchase price (also referred to as the replacement cost) of new capital. We refer to this approach as "Q theory" or "Tobin's Q." Tobin's Q is defined as the ratio of the firm's market value to the replacement cost of the firm's capital.[14] The firm's market value is the market value of the sum of debt and equity issued by the firm. The Q theory states: If the firm's market value is high relative to the replacement cost of capital, then it would be worthwhile for firms to issue new debt or equity and purchase even more capital. For every share issued with a value of one dollar, less than a dollar would be used to purchase new capital without any dilution of current shareholder value; the residual would reflect the added value that the market believes the firm can contribute when employing the new capital. Clearly, such an expansion of financing and new capital is worthwhile for current shareholders. Thus, Tobin's Q is a theory based on the ratio (*Q*). If (*Q*) is greater than 1, we expect to see an increase in fixed investment on the part of firms in the economy; if it is less than 1, the reverse happens.[15]

Referring to the equation above, we recall that profits (Π) are a function of both revenues and costs. Optimal long-run revenues, costs, and (in turn) profits will only expand if output expands. Long-run output will only expand if capacity or fixed investment expands. In summary, profits (Π) will increase as a function of investment (*I*). We can formalize the Q theory, then, by using the following equation and assuming (for the moment) that (NPV = 0) at the margin. Thus, the firm has invested up to the point of optimality. We have:

$$I_0 = \Pi_1 / (1 + r) + \Pi_2 / (1 + r)^2 \ldots$$

In the above equation, the left-hand side represents the replacement cost of capital while the right-hand side represents the market valuation (given the market's opportunity cost and profit expectations). The ratio of the right-hand side to the left-hand side is, of course, Tobin's Q, and it is equal to 1 in this special case. If the ratio is greater than 1, then the NPV of the investment would be positive, and we would expect the investment to be undertaken.[16] We see that this formulation of Tobin's Q is fully consistent with our NPV rule.

Macro Finance Insight 6.2: Has China Pulled the Trigger to Quickly?
Real Options and Optimal Timing for Investment

Consider a hiker who, walking along a path, encounters a snake to his left and sees a threatening bear in the distance to his right. He has a gun with only one bullet and his aim is poor (has a variance). If he exercises his option to shoot the bear in the distance (pulls the trigger), traditional finance says that his opportunity cost (the best option or alternative use of the bullet) would be to shoot the snake. There is, however, another opportunity cost to consider, and that is the approach used in real options theory (Dixit and Pindyck 1994). Suppose that we have the option to wait (allow a bit of time to pass) for the bear to get closer before we fire; that might be the best option—our true opportunity cost, especially since we are not a sharpshooter. Real option theory says that if we do not consider the option to delay and only consider the present option (the snake), we might be overinvesting now (using our bullet too early); our perceived opportunity cost (shooting the snake) is too low. At a more sophisticated level, there is not just a contemporaneous optimal decision (what project to select), but an optimal time for that decision (when to invest). The theory of real options helps us determine when that optimal time is.

Real options are more likely to be lurking and valuable when compared to the traditional NPV approach if we have flexibility in the timing of investment. For example, competitive pressures are not so great that we must make the decision now or lose the opportunity—there is great uncertainty about the future (our marksmanship is bad); the passage of time may allow for a more profitable decision later as uncertainty gets resolved.

China, in its rush to develop and grow, may have been blindsided by the snake, foregoing valuable new opportunities that may emerge in the future. While its vast investments in infrastructure have in many cases been very impressive, perhaps the timing has not been optimal—particularly, when we think of investments in residential buildings, bridges, roads, and power plants that are location-specific. There would appear to be enough flexibility to allow for later investments in these projects after uncertainty (related to demand for example) gets resolved. High levels of uncertainty (volatility) makes real options more valuable; and China, as we have seen, has relatively more volatility than the United States.[17] A corollary to the real options approach is that it is a good idea to lay the groundwork for investments (create options) so as to be prepared to invest if the opportunity arises. As China moves forward with China 2025, certainly the concept of real options helps us to think deeply about the costs and benefits of moving too fast in the highly uncertain but competitive arena of new technologies.

Is China's Investment Too High?

The fact that China's level of investment as a share of GDP is so high naturally raises the question of whether or not it is too high. As we saw in the chapter on economic growth, emerging economies on a sustainable path to growth will naturally have high levels of investment. That is because the marginal productivity of capital (the slope of the production function in a Solow framework) is much greater than that of advanced economies, which have moved further along the development curve. But what constitutes too high a level of investment relative to some optimum level? Economists have broken this question into different parts, logically looking at the MPK in China (its return), then comparing that to the opportunity cost of capital (its cost). Figure 6.12 shows an equilibrium in which the demand for more capital (investment) corresponds to a declining MPK. The supply of greater capital (investable funds) only willingly increases with higher returns.

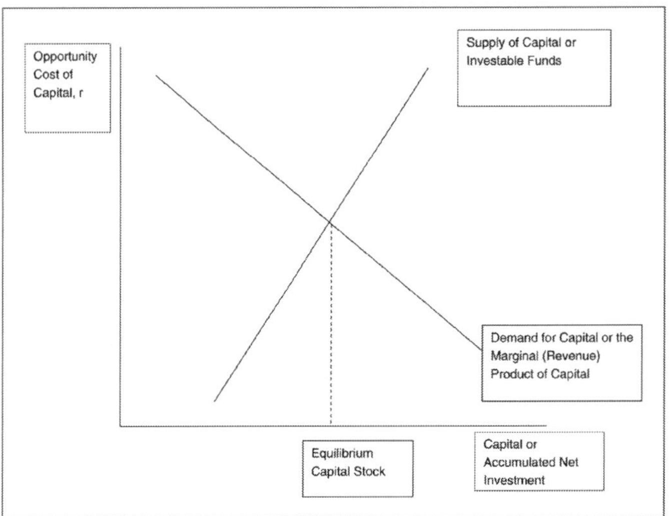

Figure 6.12 The supply of loanable funds (based on savings and financial wealth) and the demand for loanable funds (based on the MPK) will determine the equilibrium capital stock.
Source: Author created.

A related question regarding China's massive investment described above is: "To what extent has this investment been determined by market forces, and to what extent by government decision making?" In the former case, we can use a variation on the models mentioned above to explain China's investment; in the latter case, we must identify the government's possibly diverse motivations for investing. This latter set of motivations is more complex, as it ranges from the traditional public good approach to developmental approaches to purely political motivations.

As discussed in other chapters, analyzing investment in China presents additional layers of complexity beyond these questions. Specifically, when measuring the returns on investment, much of production (44 percent of GDP in 2018 and over 47 percent in 2013) is an investment good rather than a consumer good. Determining the value of an investment good requires us to assume that our estimate accurately reflects the value of goods and services that investment goods will yield in the future. In contrast, an investment good used to produce consumer goods and services can be valued based on our knowledge of what consumers willingly pay for that good or service currently—an easier task. Regarding the cost of capital (discussed in Chapters 4 and 7), China's capital markets are segmented both domestically and internationally. Identifying a cost of capital that truly reflects all risks with opportunity costs is very difficult.

Authors such as Bai et al. (2006) look at aggregate data and find that China's marginal productivity of capital is still high but declining. Consistent with that notion, Figure 6.13 shows an increasing incremental capital to output ratio (ICOR) for China. But, as indicated in Chapter 4, marginal productivities remain above those of the United States and other developed economies. Qin and Song (2009) examine investment across provinces and find evidence of both inefficient allocation of capital across sectors of the economy and inefficient use of capital once it is put in place. They find greater efficiency along the eastern and central regions of China compared to the western regions.

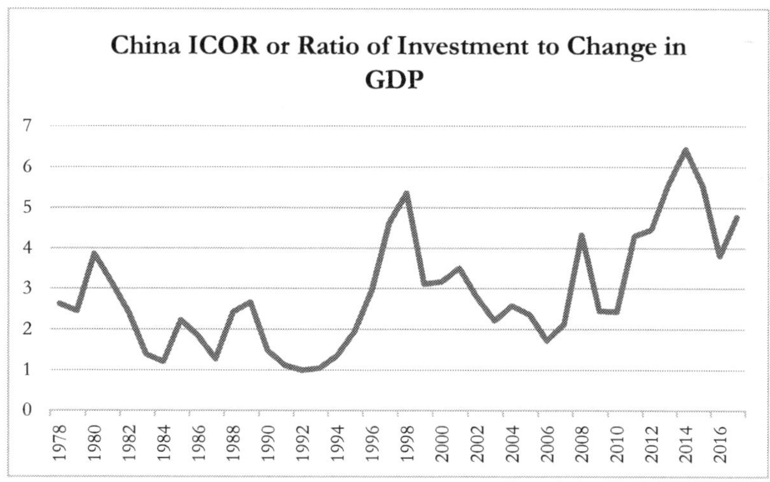

Figure 6.13 The ICOR is a traditional measure of how effective additional capital is in boosting output. The recent increase suggests diminishing returns in China (where an increase indicates more capital is required to boost output).
Source: Author created based on data from the Federal Reserve Economic Database and CEIC.

Other authors examine disaggregate data at the firm or industry level to determine cash flows and marginal productivities. Ding et al. (2010) examine more than 100,000 firms in China and find that overinvestment is pervasive across both private firms and SOEs; they find that one-third of China's firms overinvest, and those that do so have capital that is too large by about 25 percent. The authors suggest that private firms overinvest because of the presence of excessive cash flow and an absence of outside stakeholders—in particular, a lack of private bondholders. SOEs tend to overinvest because of easy access to credit from the banking system, which is lacking in screening and monitoring capabilities.

Lee et al. (2012) take a comprehensive look at investment using both a neoclassical approach and a model of dynamic optimization. They find that, in China, actual investment as compared to optimal investment has been consistently too high—and it may now be up to 10 percentage points too high (i.e., as a share of GDP investment, it should be closer to 40 percent rather than 50 percent).

A simple approach to answering the question of whether China's investment is too high is to examine what steady-state investment would be for a country such as China and then compare this figure to the actual level. Recall our simple Solow steady-state condition used in Chapter 4:

$$s \times y = (n + \text{dep}) \times k$$

In other words, sources of capital (on a per capita basis) equal uses of capital. We can transform this to a condition in terms of savings per output, and capital per output (k') (rather than per capita); if we allow for the accounting identity of (Savings $\equiv$ Investment) and assume future economic growth to equal population growth, we have:

$$i' = (g + \text{dep}) \times k'$$

where (i') and (k') are investment-to-output and capital-to-output ratios, respectively. Currently, China's capital-to-output ratio from Table 4.4 in Chapter 4 is around 3.4 which is close to the current United States ratio. Let's assume China ultimately hopes to raise its ratio at an eventual steady state to that of South Korea's current ratio of somewhere between 4 and 5. Furthermore, let's assume a steady-state growth for China of around 3 percent and a depreciation rate close to 3.5 percent. The equation above shows steady-state investment for China in the neighborhood of 26 to 32.5 percent of GDP.

Note that, in the presence of technological progress, China would need to invest (and save) even less. We note that this national investment (and savings rate) is close to the level of some of China's Asian neighbors, and it suggests that the gap between today's investment rates and steady-state levels in China is too large. It also suggests that US investment as a share of GDP is too low.

The theoretical models above are rooted in the neoclassical framework in which rational firms and investors respond to market forces when making investment decisions. A number of studies have examined this approach econometrically. Specifically, authors such as Lee at al. (2012), Geng and N'Diaye (2012), and Song et al. (2001) have attempted to estimate the responsiveness of investment in China to real interest rates (the cost of capital), real economic growth, the real exchange rate, and availability of credit—just to name a few variables. Overall, the data suggest that, in fact, investment in China does respond to market forces in a predictable way. Recent policy developments show that the role of market forces should become ever more important. Further research is needed to prove whether or not such changes are taking place in a meaningful way.

Financial Repression

While the above models are increasingly useful in showing how future investment will be determined, the reality regarding a significant share of investment determination in China (especially before 1998) is that the key determinant has been government decision making. Through its control of virtually all financial intermediation in the post-reform period—especially its control of lending decisions by the four major banks (which manage most of the nation's loanable funds)—the government has been the ultimate decision maker in the level, patterns, and types of investments made. The term "financial repression" describes a set of policies that, in effect, remove most of the market-based mechanisms we expect to operate in financial markets. Specifically, financial repression refers to an institutional arrangement in which the following conditions apply: profitability is not the main objective of financial institutions; there is an absence of competition among financial institutions; lending and borrowing rates are not determined by supply and demand conditions; and lending and borrowing decisions are not based on anticipated NPVs (as suggested in the models above), but rather by other criteria (e.g., a social or public good objective). We can still describe China's financial system as financially repressed, but it is rapidly transforming into a market-based system. In Chapter 7 and Chapter 11, we look more deeply into some of these issues. Under a financially repressed system, one does not see the usual supply curve of loanable funds.

Rather, we see, as in Figure 6.14, interest rate ceilings below the equilibrium level and rationing of credit (investable funds) to select borrowers.

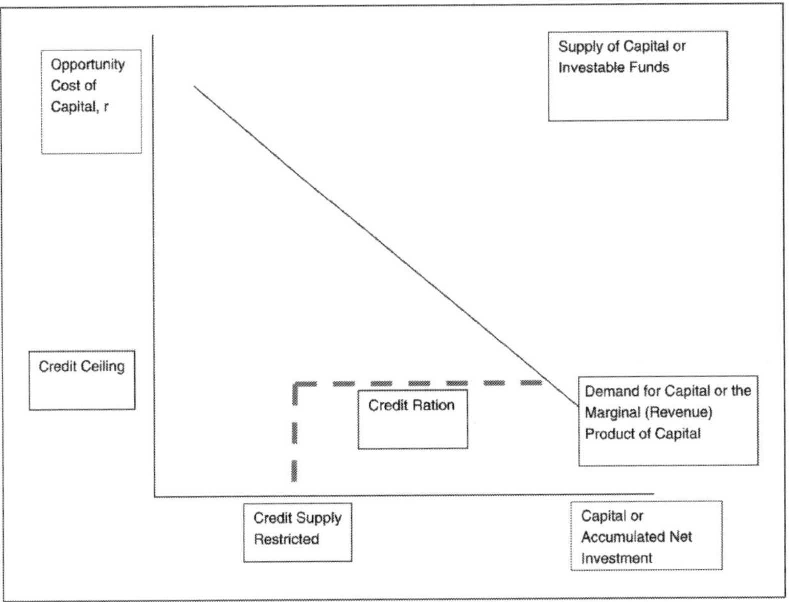

Figure 6.14 Ceilings on lending rates harm the economy by allocating capital to those entities that cannot use it most efficiently.
Source: Author created.

The fact that investment has been determined by lending policies (which in turn reflect government decision making) is only half the story. The other half is control over the real economy and investment at the firm and industry level. China's central government has, at times, felt the need to directly control investment spending in the aggregate; and, at other times, to directly control investment spending in specific industries in which either investment is perceived as part of a broader public policy or over-investment (a bubble) is occurring. The government accomplishes this control by restricting specific industries to specific levels of investment. Thus, the government can and has directly controlled investment both at the financing (lending) end and at the industry (decision-making) end.

A Growing Periphery

In contrast to the processes described above, a growing periphery of newly introduced investor classes (such as venture funds and private equity funds) and small businesses have emerged on the investment scene. These new entrants are still guided by China's Five-Year Plans in making sectoral investment decisions, but they likely base specific investment decisions on financial criteria. The new set of investors, however, represents only a sliver of China's total investment activity.

On the positive side, relatively small private firms now comprise over 95 percent of the productive units in China (but, of total FAI, SOEs and state-owned holding companies still account for close to 38 percent of all FAI). We can assume that, for this group of private enterprises, the models presented earlier in this chapter have become more relevant. As in the United States, small businesses now represent China's most dynamic sector. Since 1998, new policy loans to SOEs have been substantially cut back and, in turn, SOE goals have also changed in a way more consistent with our market-based models. Improved financial decision making by SOEs is very important if China is to have quality growth, given that the role of SOEs in China has seen somewhat of a resurgence over the past decade.

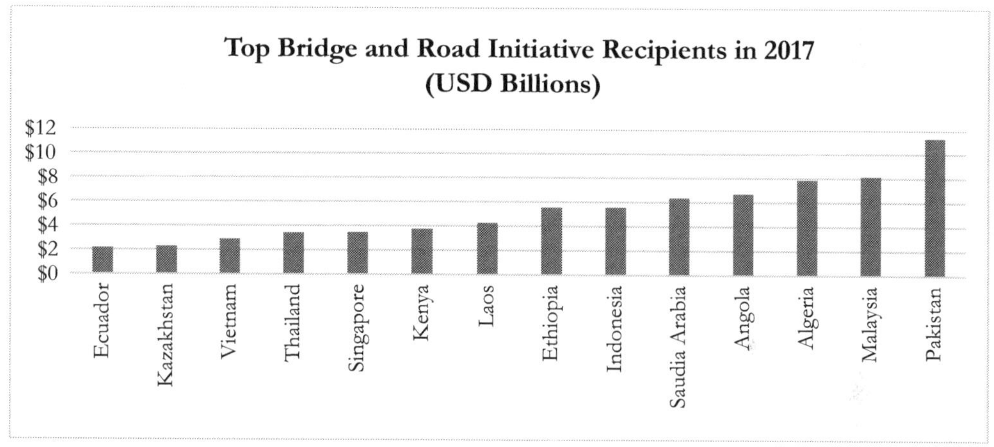

Figure 6.15 China has lent and invested heavily in a broad range of countries, many of which have poor credit ratings.
Source: Author created based on data from CEIC.

Case Study 6.3: China's One Belt One Road Program

China's One Belt One Road (OBOR) program is a visionary initiative to recreate the old trading routes that once traversed central and south/southeast Asia linking China with Europe and beyond. The critical feature of the historical Silk Road was a series of trading outposts and routes linking China with the West. "One belt" refers to overland routes through the various "stans" (e.g., Pakistan) and other countries such as, Iran, Turkey, and ultimately western Europe. "One road" refers to sea routes connecting countries such as Malaysia, Sri Lanka, and Kenya. For example, most recently, on the western front, the Chinese government signed an agreement with Italy (in March, 2019) to redevelop the port at Trieste as a forward point in its efforts to expand trade with Europe; something that harks back to the Silk Road relationship between renaissance Italy and China. In most of the agreements with target countries, China has agreed to provide loans, equipment, labor, and technology for the construction of roads and bridges (also known as the "Bridge and Road Initiative") to tie the country into the OBOR network. Figure 6.15 shows some top recipients of OBOR resources from China in 2017.

China's broad investing relationship with the rest of the world comes in two main forms. One is FDI outflows, which totaled around USD 1.4 trillion over the past decade. FDI represents ownership and control on the part of China. A second major category, in which China provides external finance to target countries, is described by Chinese authorities as "Economic Cooperation." This is where China builds, lends, and transfers (BLT) to a target country, typically infrastructure. Over the past decade China has made about USD 1.8 trillion commitments in BLTs. Actual annual disbursements have averaged around USD 150 billion. About half of these disbursements are part of the OBOR set of projects. One of the largest recipients of OBOR funding has been Pakistan. Pakistan has, for example, received about USD 19 billion in economic cooperation funding since OBOR's inception. An estimated 70 percent of FDI into Pakistan in recent years has come from China.

From a global perspective, this initiative makes a great deal of sense. Many of the target countries are emerging economies with a great need for infrastructure and the accompanying financing. China has a glut of savings in which, as we have pointed out, the rapid pace of investment has pushed returns downward. China also has an excess supply of companies engaged in construction and capital equipment manufacturing and a large number of underemployed workers. Using these otherwise idle resources abroad makes economic senses. In Chapter 2, we pointed out that China's asset side of its balance sheet has been foreign-exchange-heavy, and a rebalancing away from US Treasury instruments to other international assets is in order. China, in the coming years, will rely more heavily on internal consumption, but in order to do so it will need ever-increasing quantities of commodities. These commodities can be acquired through increased trade with the target regions—China already has substantial trading links with Africa and south and southeast Asia. Finally, establishing strong economic relationships with these regions will also establish greater goodwill and harmony—no different from one of the main goals of creating a common market in Europe. Figure 6.16 shows that China, itself, on a per capita basis still has far less capital than the United States.[18] One could argue that China, rationally, has chosen to deploy (and lay claim to) capital wherever in the world it feels returns will be highest

Some concerns about OBOR's effects have been raised. Particularly, whether the target countries will be caught in a debt trap with China. Pakistan, for example, has large current account deficits, relatively low foreign exchange reserves, and a national savings rate of only 12 percent. Will it have the domestic political will to raise taxes to service its debt to China, if needed? Will it have the foreign exchange wherewithal to repay China? At least half of the top OBOR countries have very poor credit ratings (C or below). Meanwhile, the IMF and World Bank have struggled to keep track of the murky (non-transparent) contracts between China and borrowing countries. The agreements in some cases rely on assumed barter-like repayments, or "golden share" rights by China to use the foreign infrastructure it has constructed. Furthermore, China is not a party to the Paris Club or the Arrangements on Guidelines for Officially Supported Export Credits. Should countries find themselves unable to repay China, a crisis could develop with no clear institutional framework to determine issues such as senior creditor status among multilateral institutions, China, and other country lenders.

We have already discussed, in Macro Finance Insight 3.1, Sri Lanka's need for a debt-to-land-lease swap with China after Sri Lanka was unable to service its debt. At the time of this writing, the COVID-19 pandemic has wreaked havoc on many OBOR economies; they are currently seeking debt relief from China. In the short run, one wonders whether the debt can be restructured in an orderly fashion. The ultimate question for China, still to be answered, is, are these various projects creating value? When international lending goes awry, historical precedent shows that both the lender and the debtor countries suffer. After all, it is CHEXIM, the CDB, and various state-owned banks that are involved. And of course, the sources of funds for these institutions are the Chinese taxpayer and corporate profits. Will they capture a reasonable all-in return from China's new Silk Road?

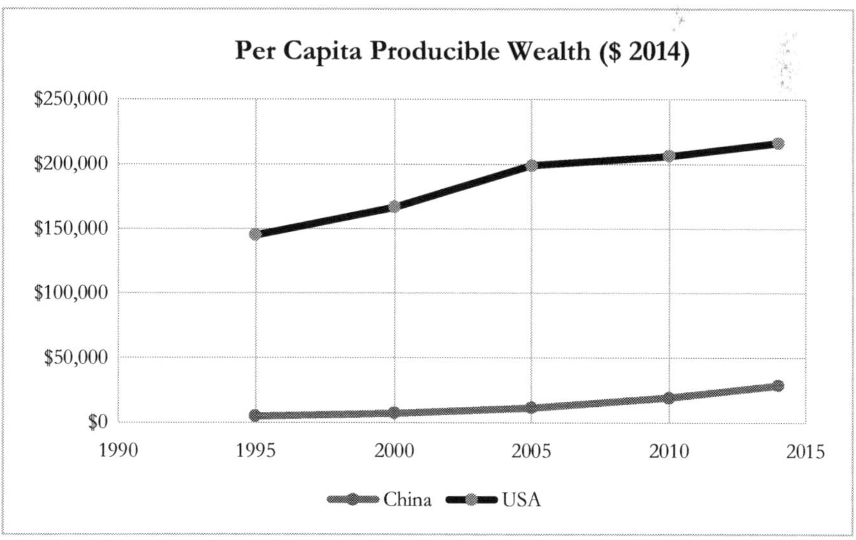

Figure 6.16 China's per capita capital stock remains far below that of the United States. Nevertheless, China has chosen to invest heavily through its OBOR initiative.
Source: Author created based on World Bank Changing Wealth of Nations 2018 (https://bit.ly/2XdXUjK).

Summary

The long-term future of China's citizens and all its stakeholders depends heavily on the investment decisions of China's production sector. The medium-term return to households on their financial and real estate investments are likewise dependent on these decisions. The huge scale of China's investment relative to other components of GDP reinforces these points. In any society, the ability to generate investment depends on a number of steps working in a synchronized fashion (Donaldson and Danthine 2014):

$$I = \text{Efficiency} \times (\text{Investing} / \text{FI}) \times (\text{FI} / S) \times (S / Y) \times Y - \text{Rate of Depreciation} \times K$$

On the left-hand side, we have actual investment (I); on the right-hand side, we have a nation's savings (S) out of GDP (Y) being channeled to financial institutions (FI), which in turn make loans and invest. How efficiently the productive entities use those funds will determine the true size and value of the investment taking place (I). In contrast to the United States, China has a vast pool of internal savings relative to GDP (S / Y). This is both a blessing and a curse. It allows for a great deal of leeway in terms of how those funds are used—in the short run, mistakes can be made without being noticed, but those mistakes can accumulate into large economic losses. Furthermore, academic research suggests that, at the corporate level, the greater the availability of funds, the more likely they are to be used inefficiently. Meanwhile, the United States has a much more sophisticated financial system ("Efficiency," in the equation above) than does China, but it has less savings to work with. The tendency toward overconsumption in the United States has led to underinvestment, particularly in infrastructure. The United States' capital stock is significantly larger than China's, which is also a blessing and a curse. While a higher standard of living results, the absolute amount of capital depreciation is that much higher, and diminishing returns act as a drag on economic growth.

Investment is not only important as a source of future output, but also as a source of demand for economic output in the short run. In recent years, over half of China's GDP growth can be attributed to investment demand growth. Fortunately for China, it is not as volatile a demand component as that found in the United States; fluctuations in investment demand are often the major contributor to business cycle fluctuations. Once again, though, the silver lining for China comes with a cloud. When investment is that stable, we can question the extent to which market forces, rather than government mandate, are driving China's investment decisions.

Challenging Questions for China (and the Student): Chapter 6

1. Go to the Federal Reserve Economic Database (FRED) and update Chinese investment as a share of GDP.
2. In terms of measuring the size of the government sector in China, explain why it is important to understand how GDP's components of C, I, G, and NX are being measured in a GDP accounting sense?
3. In this chapter we derived: $P \times \text{MPK}$ = rental cost of capital (r)
   a. From the cash-flow valuation approach, assume that cash flows are growing at a rate of (g). Derive the above equilibrium condition in this case.
   b. Based on your answer in (a), explain in a neoclassical sense why China's investment rates are so high compared to the United States'.
4. When investment is a large fraction of GDP output, as in China, why does this present a special challenge in measuring the quality of economic growth as compared to the quantity of economic growth?
5. Consider the neoclassical framework compared to Chinese investment decision making:
   a. Provide the neoclassical framework for investment and link that to the traditional cashflow NPV approach.
   b. Discuss whether the approach in (a) is applicable to China. Is it more relevant for some sectors instead of others? Which sectors of the economy?
   c. Why are the questions in (a) and (b) vitally important for China in the coming years?
6. Explain the costs and benefits of funding public works projects (infrastructure) via the financing mechanism of the CDB as opposed to a taxation mechanism (let's say a property tax or personal income tax) in China.
7. In this chapter we discussed the user cost of capital and PE ratio (the home price to annual rental ratio): where (user cost = $(1 - t)(r + p) + m + \delta + \beta - \pi^e$) where ($t$) is the personal tax rate, (r) is the borrowing cost of financing a home, (p) is the property tax rate, (m) is the cost of maintenance, (β) is the risk premium on property, (π^e) is the expected appreciation of property values, and (δ) is the depreciation rate on residential property (all expressed in nominal percent).
   a. If, in the United States, home prices are expected to increase by 3 percent, r = 4 percent, the tax rate is 25 percent, property tax is 1 percent, the maintenance fee is 0.5 percent, depreciation is 3.5 percent, and the risk premium is 2 percent, calculate the PE ratio

b. If some Chinese cities have a PE ratio of 30, calculate the implicit value of π^e. Provide justification for the other numbers that you used in the formula for the China case. Do you think π^e is based on rational or adaptive expectations?

c. In this chapter, Schramm suggests that the housing market price surge in China represents fundamental factors and not a bubble. Buyers may still end up losing money over the long term, however. Explain this argument using basic supply and demand curves. If Schramm is correct, then why haven't rental rates risen as dramatically as home prices? Is Schramm wrong? Explain.

8. Why can the stability (that it fluctuates so little year to year) of China's investment as a share of GDP be viewed as a "blessing," a "curse," and a worrisome omen?
9. Explain why measuring the cost of capital (a difficult task anywhere in the world) is particularly difficult in China.
10. As indicated in this chapter, FDI has declined as a share of overall investment in China. Discuss whether this is a positive or negative development for China's economic well-being.

References

Ansar, A., B. Flyvbjerg, A. Budzier, and D. Lunn. 2016. "Does Infrastructure Investment Lead to Economic Growth or Economic Fragility? Evidence from China." *Oxford Review of Economic Policy*, 32(3), pp. 360–90.

Axtell, R. L. 2001. "Zipf Distribution of US Firm Sizes." *Science*, 293(5536), 1818–20.

Bai, Chong-en, Chang-Tai Hsieh, and Yingyi Qian. 2006. "The Return to Capital in China." NBER Working Paper no. 12755.

China Development Bank. 2014. *Annual Report*. Accessed 20 June, 2020. http://www.cdb.com.cn/English/bgxz/ndbg/ndbg2014/.

China Development Bank. 2018. *Annual Report*. Accessed 20 June, 2020. http://www.cdb.com.cn/English/bgxz/ndbg/ndbg2018/.

Cook, Thomas, Jun Nie, and Aaron Smalter Hall. 2018. "An Inter-industry Analysis of China's Housing Market and the Macroeconomy." *The Macro Bulletin*, 12 September, https://www.kansascityfed.org/publications/research/mb/articles/2018/chinas-gdp-slowdown-housing-activity.

David, J. M., and V. Venkateswaran. 2019. "The Sources of Capital Misallocation." *American Economic Review*, 109(7), pp. 2531–67.

Ding, S., A. Guariglia, and J. Knight. 2010. "Does China Overinvest? Evidence from a Panel of Chinese Firms." Department of Economics Discussion Paper Series, no. 520. Oxford, UK: University of Oxford.

Dixit, Avinash K., and Robert S. Pindyck. 1994. *Investment Under Uncertainty*. Princeton: Princeton University Press.

Donaldson, J. B., and J. P. Danthine. 2014. *Intermediate Financial Theory*. New York: Elsevier.

Dong, H., W. Zhang, and J. Shek. 2006. "How Efficient Has Been China's Investment? Empirical Evidence from National and Provincial Data." HKMA Working Paper no. 0619, Hong Kong: Hong Kong Monetary Authority.

Fang, H., Q. Gu, W. Xiong, and L. A. Zhou. 2016. "Demystifying the Chinese Housing Boom." *NBER Macroeconomics Annual*, 30(1), pp. 105–66.

Geng, N. and P. N'Diaye. 2012. "Determinants of Corporate Investment in China: Evidence from Cross-Country Firm Level Data." IMF Working Paper no. 12/80.

Glaeser, E., W. Huang, Y. Ma, and A. Shleifer. 2017. "A Real Estate Boom with Chinese Characteristics." *Journal of Economic Perspectives*, 31(1), pp. 93–116.

He, M., Y. Chen, and R. Schramm. 2018. "Technological Spillovers in Space and Firm Productivity: Evidence from China's Electric Apparatus Industry." *Urban Studies*, 55(11), pp. 2522–41.

Lee, I. H., M. Syed, and L. Xueyan. 2012. "Is China Overinvesting and Does it Matter?" IMF Working Paper no. 12/277.

Lin, G. and R. M. Schramm. 2009. "A Decade of Flow of Funds in China (1995–2006)." In *China and Asia: Economic and Financial Interactions*, edited by Y. W. Cheung and K. Y. Wong. London: Routledge.

Poterba, James. 1984. "Tax Subsidies to Owner-Occupied Housing: An Asset Market Approach." *Quarterly Journal of Economics*, 94(4), pp. 729–52.

Qin, Duo and H. Song. 2009. "Sources of Investment Inefficiency: The Case of Fixed Asset Investment in China." *Journal of Development Economics*, 90, pp. 94–105.

Song, H. Y., Z .N. Liu, and P. Jiang. 2001. "Analysing the Determinants of China's Aggregate Investment in the Reform Period." *China Economic Review*, 12, pp. 227–42.

Wu, Jing, Joseph Gyourko, and Yongheng Deng. 2011. "Evaluating Conditions in Major Chinese Housing Markets." NBER Working Paper no. 16189.

Endnotes

1. Also included is investment in software which, in the United States, was first included in 1999.
2. Such high shares for investment correspond to negative growth in net exports and consumption during those specific growth recession periods.
3. We discuss the link between the accumulation of investment (the capital stock) and economic growth in Chapter 4. Here, it is worth noting that, in recent years, investment demand growth comprises over half of China's economic growth rate.
4. FDI is defined as a degree of both foreign ownership and foreign control of an economic entity in another country. This contrasts with portfolio investment, which represents a degree of ownership but absence of control. The IMF defines FDI as an investment with a "lasting interest" in the enterprise. Both the IMF and Organization for Economic Co-operation and Development suggest at least a 10 percent voting interest in an enterprise as a necessary and sufficient condition for having a lasting interest.
5. In 1995, the World Bank conservatively estimated that approximately 42 percent of state investment could be undertaken by the private sector. Clearly, that would be an upper bound today, given the substantial privatization in China since then. Most countries now split government spending into government investment and government consumption. Budget deficits or surpluses, however, continue to be reported after expensing government investments (unlike accounting practices for firms).
6. Generally speaking, if something is permitted to be depreciated under the tax code (as certain software development is now, for example), it can be considered an investment
7. Chinese cities are ranked by a tier system based on population and economic importance. Tier 1 includes major cities that are the most economically developed such as Beijing, Shanghai, Guangzhou, Shenzhen, and a recently added set of 15 other cities ranging from Hangzhou to Ningbo. Tier 2 cities tend to be smaller commercial centers, and Tier 3 includes many provincial capitals.
8. For example, in February, 2014, Apple Inc. repurchased USD 14 billion of its own shares.
9. In the US post-WWII period, it is estimated that business fixed investment is 3–4 times more volatile than output.
10. The relative importance of very large firms in production is a reality in most economies, including the United States. Often described as a "power law" distribution (Axtell 2001), or more colloquially the "80/20 rule," only the largest (approximately) 20 percent of the firms in an industry comprise 80 percent of production.

11. Most important in finance is not accounting profit, but cash flow. "Cash flow" is defined as profits after adding back non-cash expenses (such as depreciation) and certain cash expenses (such as interest payments) while subtracting out the tax benefits accruing from these accounting expenses. Although the accounting treatment of depreciation is not included, investment required to replace depreciated capital is a cash item and is therefore subtracted from profits. In this way, it is included in actual cash flow. In summary, the reference to profits above is actually a reference to all cash revenues and expenditures, as well as new investment.
12. What we are doing here is essentially a version of Tobin's Q. Comparing the replacement cost of capital (K) with the market value, as measured by discounted cashflows that would be generated by (K), gives us economic value. Technically, taking the derivative: (d(Economic Value) = -dK + d(CF)dK / r = -Investment + Discounted Incremental Cashflows) provides us with our traditional NPV formula.
13. If we assume depreciation (d) and a proportional reduction of cashflow ($((1-d)_n \times$ CF(K_n)), we can derive a discount factor of ((1 – d) / (r + d)); we would have an optimization result where ($0 = -1 + ((1-d) / (r+d)) \times (\Delta \text{CF}(K) / \Delta K)$), or (($P \times$ MPK) $\times (1-d) - d = r$), or the same qualitative result of equivalence with the marginal product formula in terms of net returns on capital rather than gross returns.
14. Named after the great Nobel Prize–winning economist, James Tobin.
15. When (Q < 1), the firm's current capital is worth more than its market values. It should then either sell off some of its physical capital or allow it to depreciate without replacement.
16. In fact, Tobin's Q relates to the existing capital stock and existing opportunities projected off of that capital stock within the traditional valuation approach in finance. In the analysis presented here, we assume that, if valuations exceed the replacement value of the current capital stock, then the same will hold true for the marginal investment opportunity.
17. One of my former students at Columbia, Julia Giuliani, pointed out that the Chinese government—a key driver—intervenes in the economy with such force that it can control the future and reduce uncertainty, obviating any concern about missed opportunities. In effect, the government can create opportunities and mitigate downside risks. This argument takes us outside the realm of traditional economic thinking—something that makes the study of China quite interesting.
18. Here, we measure physical capital using the World Bank's producible wealth measure. Data go through 2014.

7
MONETARY POLICY AND INSTITUTIONS IN CHINA AND THE UNITED STATES

钱能通神

Money Lets You Converse with the Gods

In this chapter, we will define what money is, discuss the supply and demand for money, and learn about Chinese monetary policy. In the process, we will understand what money is not only conceptually, but also institutionally. How money is supplied to the economy is, at its core, an institutional question based on how a country's central bank and banking system operate and are structured. The question of why individuals and institutions in an economy want to hold on to money—the demand for money—raises interesting conceptual and theoretical questions (addressed in Chapter 8). In this chapter, we focus on the institutional framework for monetary policy in both the United States and China. These two large economies make for some interesting comparisons and contrasts in terms of monetary economics both historically and contemporaneously. We care about money not only because of its relationship to institutions and its role as a key asset, but also because the amount of money in an economy has profound effects on inflation, interest rates, short-term economic growth, and employment.

Defining Money (Conceptually)

Money is anything that is generally accepted as a medium of exchange. This broad definition highlights the open-ended possibilities of what constitutes money. As long as individuals willingly accept and make payments with an instrument, that instrument constitutes money. Tea, black and white shells (wampum), printed deer skin, gold, silver, cigarettes, and pieces of paper have all served as money at one point or another.[1] Not too long ago, the French franc or the Dutch florin represented money for those countries; but, by 2001, these currencies had been fully replaced by the euro. Whether Bitcoin will ever make it to the class of world monies will ultimately depend on its general acceptability as a form of money.

Case Study 7.1: The Invention of Paper Money

China was the first country to introduce paper money ("flying money," made of mulberry bark, was used as banknotes) in the Tang Dynasty (618–907 CE). Printed money (using wood blocks) gained widespread use in the economically-sophisticated Song Dynasty (960–1279 CE). Bronze coins with a square in the middle could be looped around a string and thus easily transported. Spades and knives were also used as money in China, and currency later kept the shrunken shape of those implements. In 19th-century China, centrally issued paper money and copper coins (*wen*) circulated alongside foreign coins of silver and gold, and were all used as money. As late as 1995, a separate currency for foreigners circulated alongside the Chinese yuan (RMB). The Foreign Exchange Certificate (FEC) served to control how and where foreigners could spend money in China. Because the FEC's value in terms of actual foreign currency was different from the official RMB rate of exchange for foreign currency, a black market developed, ultimately leading to the elimination of the FEC as a separate form of money in China.

In the colonial United States, settlers used wampum to trade with Native American tribes. Gold, silver, and banknotes also served as forms of colonial monies. In the first half of the 19th century, a number of banks issued their own paper currency, and these forms of payment were not always acceptable across state lines. Eventually, hundreds of different kinds of money circulated alongside gold and silver in the United States. By mid-century, the US government refused to accept tax payments in the form of paper money (the Specie Circular [1836] specified gold and silver as the only legitimate form of tax payment), and most of these locally issued monies became worthless. In order to help finance the Civil War, the US government (the North) began issuing United States Notes (greenbacks) in 1862. This launched the creation of a truly national currency—accepted across the nation.

The terms "yuan" and "RMB" have been used interchangeably to describe the Chinese currency since the founding of the People's Republic of China (PRC) in 1949. Yuan is the basic unit in the Chinese monetary system (like the dollar) in which all other coins or denominations are expressed as a fraction thereof. The term *yuan* (元)or *kuai*

(块)is used more colloquially than RMB. In foreign currency markets, the Chinese currency is identified as the CNY, or Chinese yuan, and the US dollar is the USD. Offshore RMB is referred to as CNH in international currency markets. The RMB (人民币) stands for *renminbi*, or "People's Currency."

Defining Money (Institutionally)

The section above provides an overview of what constitutes money at a conceptual and historical level. But how do we define money at a practical level, for the sake of policy and measurement? Countries worldwide use very similar definitions of money. But, as we shall see, there are large institutional differences in the types of bank accounts and other financial institutional assets offered in different countries. Every nation attempts to use the conceptual definition above to drill down to an implementable definition of money, but—because of institutional differences—countries inevitably come up with the same name for a technically-different type of asset and classify it as money. For example, is a sight deposit (checking account) that typically backs up a mobile payment (as found in China) an identical asset as a checking account that backs up a debit card (as found in the United States)? Both will be clumped together in each country's definition of money. Or, in the United States, we find money market funds as an established component of the supply of money, while in China, money market funds are still evolving (see Case Study 7.6).

United States (2018)				China (2018)			
Components of M1	**USD Billions**	**% M1**	**% GDP**	**Components of M1**	**RMB Billions**	**% M1**	**% GDP**
Currency	1,582.6	42.9	7.7	**Currency**	7,320.8	13.30	8.1
Demand/ Checking Deposits	2,103.3	57.1	10.3	**Demand/ Checking Deposits**	47,849.2	86.70	53.1
Total M1	3685.9	100	18	**Total M1**	55,170	100	61.3
Components of M2		**% M2**	**% GDP**	**Components of M2**		**% M2**	**% GDP**
Total M1	3,685.9	26.1	18	**Total M1**	55,170	31.2	61.3
Non-M1 Components	10,419.2	73.9	50.8	**Non-M1 Components**	121,852.4	68.8	135.3
Total M2	14,105.1	100	68.8	**Total M2**	177,022.4	100	196.6
Total GDP or GNP	20,494.1		100	**Total GDP or GNP**	90,030.9		100

Table 7.1 Components of M1 and M2 for China and the United States, and the actual and percent of M1, M2, and GDP.
Source: Author created based on data from the Federal Reserve Economic Database.

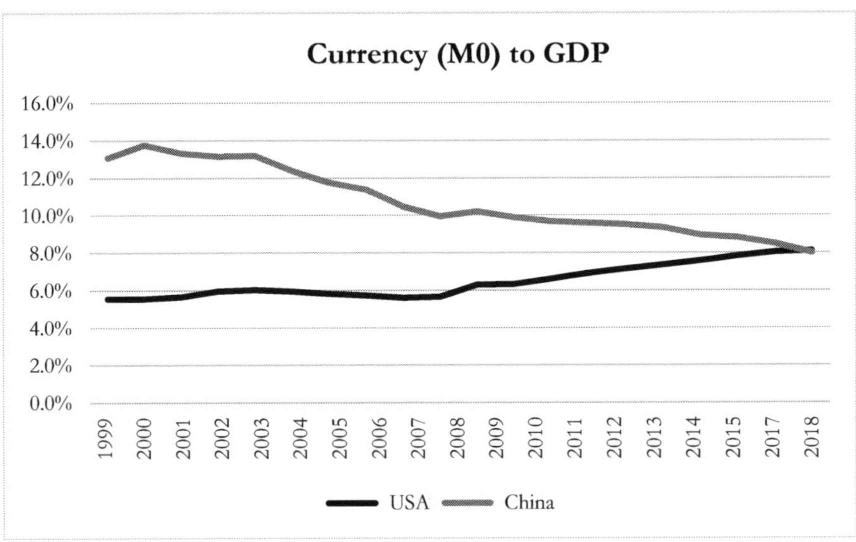

Figure 7.1 Chinese citizens' holdings of currency as a share of GDP has dropped dramatically and is now on par with the United States.
Source: Author created based on data from the International Monetary Fund Database.

Table 7.1 shows the different definitions of money used in the United States, China, and virtually the entire world. M1, or narrow money, includes currency in circulation or cash—what most people (who have not taken a macroeconomics course) assume is money. In 1999, the ratio of currency holdings to gross domestic product (GDP) was twice as high in China as in the United States. By 2018, with the greater use of mobile payments, China and the US had about the same ratio at 8 percent as seen in Figure 7.1.[2] Demand deposits make up an even larger share of what constitutes money (about 57 percent of M1 in the United States, 87 percent in China—referred to as sight deposits or checking accounts). These typically provide an instant means of payment via an ATM, debit card, mobile phone, computer, or written check. M2 includes everything in M1 plus time deposits and savings accounts; access to one's savings via these latter accounts may be restricted in terms of withdrawals or making payments for purchases of goods and services. Figure 7.2 and Figure 7.3 show a steep ascent in M1 and M2 in China since the Great Financial Crisis—something we will discuss in Chapter 8. In 2018 and 2019, this growth accelerated even further in response to slower GDP growth in China. But the growth also reflects a broadening (https://bit.ly/2Xukp4e) of the definition of M2 to include the expansion of the shadow banking sector; over the past decade, banks have offered off-balance sheet investment vehicles for depositors, which pay higher interest (money market funds and wealth management products). In 2011, deposits of non-banks at financial institutions were included in M2; and, later in 2018, money market fund deposits and some wealth management products were added in to the M2 measure. We discuss these developments in Chapter 11.

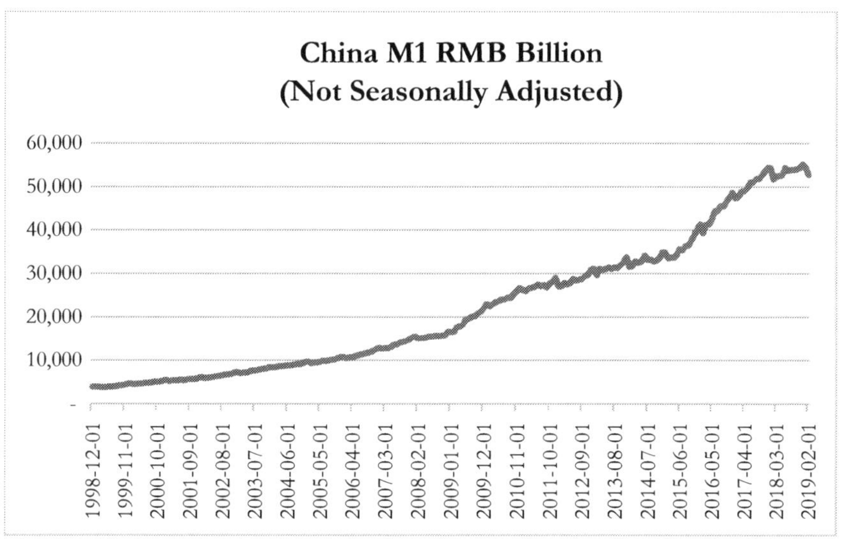

Figure 7.2 China's monthly M1 money supply has grown rapidly over the past two decades.
Source: Author created based on data from the International Monetary Fund Database and the Federal Reserve Economic Database.

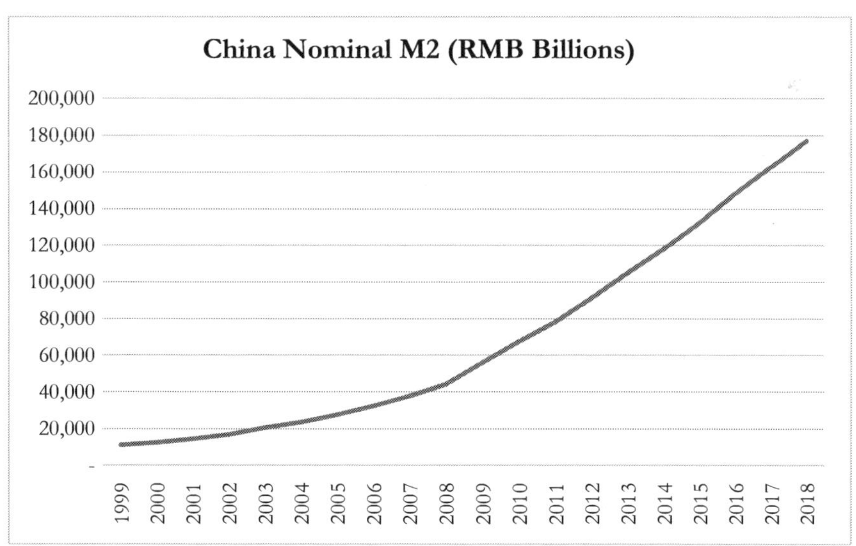

Figure 7.3 China's M2 measure of money has also grown rapidly, but its definition was broadened in 2011 and 2018 to include some of the shadow banking liabilities of the traditional banking system.
Source: Author created based on data from the International Monetary Fund Database and the Federal Reserve Economic Database.

We can see that, as we move from M1 to M2, we are shifting into forms of money that are less liquid. We define "liquidity" as the ease with which we can convert one asset into purchasing power without a loss in that asset's long-term value.[3] Clearly, cash is a very liquid asset, since we can buy goods and services without affecting the face value found on either the dollar or the yuan. Meanwhile, use of a time deposit to make a purchase may involve some explicit or implicit transactions costs. For example, we might have to pay a penalty for early withdrawal, or we may have to physically go to our bank to make a withdrawal. Assets such as time deposits, corporate bonds, equity, and jewelry are clearly less liquid than cash.

Another way of looking at the movement from M1 to M2 is that we are moving from more transaction-based motives to more investment-based motives—that is, a greater focus on return as opposed to liquidity. Most countries around the world, including China and the United States, choose M2 as their main definition of money.

M2 can be used for transactions with relative ease, and it would also be the type of money implicit in the response of a typical consumer or company to the question: "How much money do you have in the bank?"

We also need to highlight some of the institutional differences in the definition of money. Interest rate ceilings on bank deposits, used at different times in both countries, have been a key difference. China's banking institutions, which really only became true financial institutions in the early 1990s, have managed to jump past one of the most common features of banking in the United States—checking. (Checking involves writing a check, or assigning value that is held in the bank—a checking account—to another party via a signed, legally binding document, i.e., the check). Instead, customers use China's demand deposits via an ATM (which involves paper money), mobile payment, or a debit card (neither of which involve paper money). In the past, a surprising amount of business in China has been transacted in cash—not checks or debit cards. Consumer transactions, however, are increasingly conducted using mobile payments, debit cards, and credit cards (especially the former).

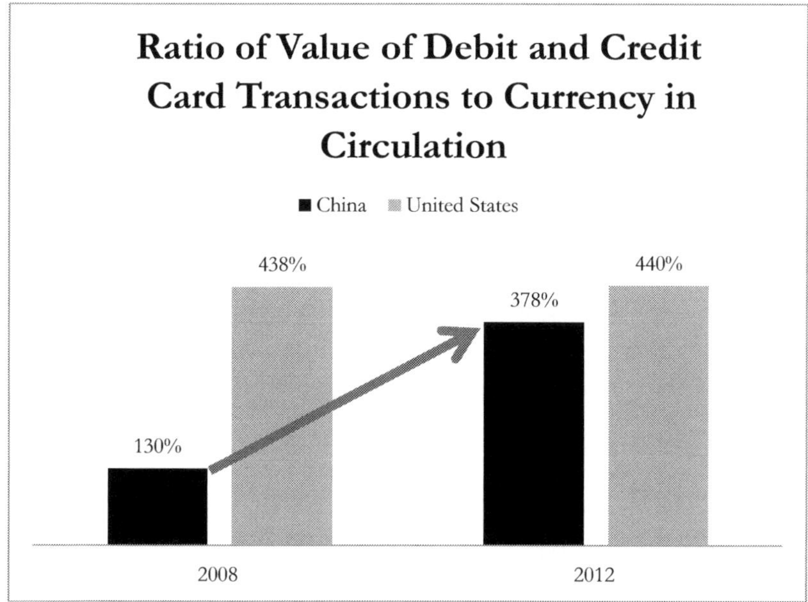

Figure 7.4 Non-cash modes of payment have been rising by 20–30 percent annually over the past decade. Relative to the level of currency in circulation, debit and credit card transaction values are now approaching the same levels in China as in the United States.
Source: Author created based on data from the Bank for International Settlements and the Federal Reserve Economic Database.

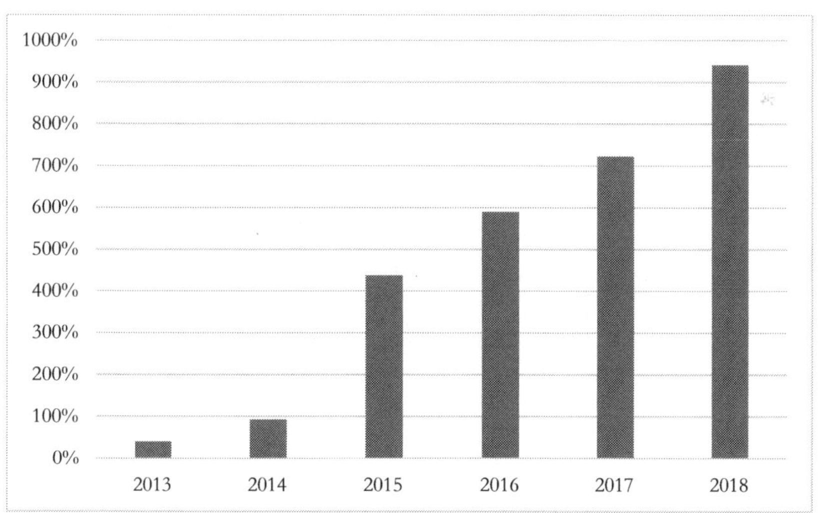

Figure 7.5 Ratio of value of electronic (mobile) bank-only transactions to currency in circulation.
Source: Author created based on data from CEIC.
Note: In fact, the ratio is about four times larger for each year. These data, remarkably, only included mobile payments via a bank app, and they do not include those channeled through non-bank mobile platforms such as Alipay and Tenpay; the latter make up about three-quarters of the mobile market.

Case Study 7.2: The Shift from Cash to Cards to Mobile Payments

The largest currency denomination in China is the RMB 100 note, introduced in 1988. At today's exchange rate, that is worth less than one USD 20 note. In the past, the small denomination combined with the continued use of cash for large transactions led to some odd situations in China. The *New York Times* reported on the purchase of a new BMW in Shanghai that involved the exchange of USD 60,000 at the auto dealership; nearly 10,000 RMB 100 notes stashed into duffel bags. The China Banknote Printing and Minting Corporation employs 30,000 people at the behest of the People's Bank of China (PBC) and prints 40 percent of the world's total currency note output.[4] But the use of cash has declined dramatically as newer technologies have emerged in China

Figure 7.4 and Figure 7.5 show the remarkable progression that Chinese individuals and companies have made from the use of cash to the use of debit and credit cards, and then—beginning around 2013—the dramatic shift to mobile payments. Total estimated 2018 transactions (https://bit.ly/2ZHrwJl) in China that are undertaken with a mobile app is estimated at an astounding USD 45 trillion when both bank and non-bank transactions are included. Approximately three-fourths of all mobile transactions are channeled through non-bank financial institutions such as Alipay and WeChat Pay. By 2019, about 78 percent of smartphone users made a mobile payment with their device. It appears that China and the United States are converging—at least in terms of non-cash consumer transactions (for the United States, credit and debit cards, and for China, mobile payments). The QR code (Figure 7.6)—for most Chinese—has become a ubiquitous identifier in both mobile transactions and social media applications. Individuals use their code for all kinds of transactions, from groceries to a quick snack at a convenience store to donating to panhandlers on the street.

Figure 7.6 The ubiquitous QR code is used for virtually all sorts of mobile payments and social platform communications in China. It is the unique application user's identification.
Source: Author created based on WeChat's communication application.

What is most striking about what we see in Table 7.1 is the significantly higher share of GDP that M1 and M2 constitute in China compared to the United States—about three times as high. One would think that, if transactions are the main motive for holding money (as we have defined it), then these ratios should not be too different; and, if anything, it should be lower in China because consumer transactions (as we have seen in Chapter 5) are substantially lower. Holding M1 and especially M2, however, is also a vehicle to save or to store our wealth—a relatively risk-free but very low-yielding method.[5] China has a relatively limited array of assets for holding wealth safely and profitably; corporate bonds remain inaccessible, the stock market contains only a fraction of existing companies, government bonds and treasuries remain limited to institutions and inaccessible to the public, and foreign-based assets are not yet legally available.[6] As a result, Chinese citizens and companies hold a greater share of their wealth (or savings) in the asset that is available via the institutions that do exist—mainly banks. The now-similar currency holdings relative to GDP in both countries (as seen in Table 7.1 and Figure 7.1) and the widely different shares of non-currency money holdings (which move us closer to the wealth motivation) suggest that Chinese citizens view money as a store of wealth. Finally, we recall the argument presented in Chapter 3 (Macro Finance Insight 3.2), initially posited by Obstfeld et al. (2012), that these very liquid money holdings could be a cause for holding excess currency reserves.

A Simple Example of Walras's Law			
	Supply	**Demand**	**Excess Demand (-) or Supply (+)**
Money	200	160	40
Stock/Equities	100	140	-40
Total Assets	300	300	0

Table 7.2 An excess demand in one financial market implies an excess supply in some other financial market.
Source: Author created.

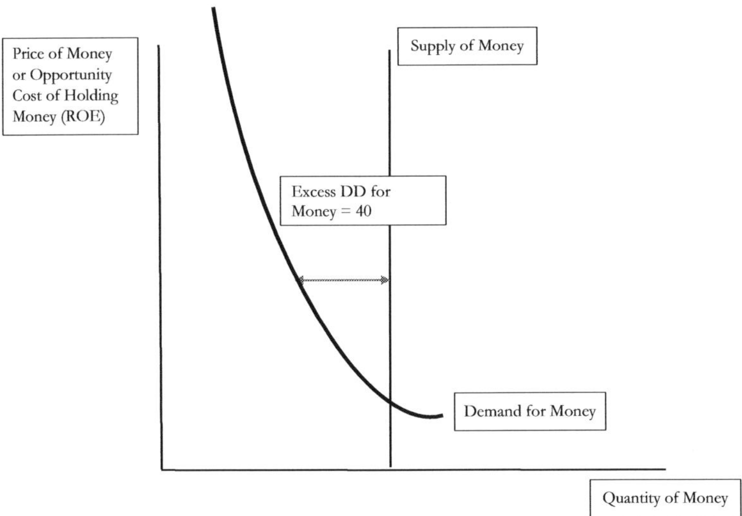

Figure 7.7 If the price of holding money (the interest rate or opportunity cost of holding money) is too high, there will be an excess supply in the market. By Walras's Law, there will be an accompanying excess of demand for other assets with an anticipated higher return.
Source: Author created.

Macro Finance Insight 7.1: Walras's Law and How China and the United States Hold Wealth

Walras's Law states that, for a complete set of related markets, the value of excess supply must equal the value of excess demand. Formally, for a set of related markets in which (P_i), (D_i) and (S_i) are the price, demand for, and supply of a particular asset, good, or service, then:

$$\sum P_i \times (S_i - D_i) = 0$$

Walras's Law is a form of budget constraint on wealth holdings stating that, in order to effectively demand something in one market, you must offer something from another market. (Note that money is a key vehicle for doing this.) The acquisition of one form of wealth (for example, a bond) requires something in exchange (such as cash). Let's assume that the goods market has, on balance, no excess demand or supply; that is, it is in equilibrium. This assumption allows us to focus on the market for financial assets including money, bonds, stocks, and non-financial assets such as real estate and direct ownership of companies. Some of these markets will have excess demand, and some will have excess supply. Walras's Law states that these excesses must balance out to 0. Consider Table 7.2 for example. Here, we only have two financial assets: money and stocks. The sum of these two assets (USD 300) represents our nominal financial wealth. In the short run, the quantity of these assets is fixed, meaning that we don't have new issuances of equity or changes in the money stock.

The prices of these assets can change, however, depending on wealth holders' perceptions of risk and return.

Table 7.2 shows an excess supply of money (more than individuals want to hold) of USD 40. Where has this excess money supply moved to? The only other available market is equities. Thus, the desire to move USD 40 out of money must also be a desire to move USD 40 into equities. In other words, the fact that the sum of 40 and -40 is 0 is not a coincidence, but a consequence of Walras's Law. Because of disequilibrium in the separate markets, either the price of money will decline or the price of equities will rise (or the return on equity [ROE], which is the implicit price of holding money, will fall). Some new nominal wealth will be established if the price of equity rises. Again, we can assume that the quantity of equities or money will not change; however, the nominal value of equity (its price) may change. Figure 7.7 shows the initial disequilibrium in the money market and where the equilibrium point (A) where the price of money (the ROE) will need to fall.

Looking at the distribution of wealth across different asset classes through the lens of Walras's Law provides some useful insights. Figure 7.8a represents a rough index of how China and the United States hold their wealth as a share of producible wealth in each nation in 2019-2020. The first key difference is the share of wealth in China held as money (M2) compared to the United States (33 percent versus 21 percent). Americans hold far greater shares of wealth in bonds and equities when compared to the Chinese.

The value of China's residential housing (https://on.wsj.com/2D2O7qD) stock is now both larger and a more significant share of producible wealth than that of the United States (https://bit.ly/39H5kBP). Home ownership in China (https://bit.ly/2A14QJ1) is even higher than in the United States (about 90 percent in China versus 64 percent (https://bit.ly/2WUqVlq) of households in the United States). In Chapter 11 we discuss emerging ways of wealth holding in China which the shadow banking sector is now providing.

Overall, the picture that emerges is that Chinese citizens hold a disproportionate amount of their wealth in money and real estate relative to the United States while falling short on financial assets, with the exception of net foreign assets.* Through the lens of Walras's Law, the suggestion is that there is an excess supply of money (more money than is actually desired or optimal) and a counterpart excess demand for other types of assets. Alternatively, the lack of publicly available bonds and equities in China, leads to excess demand and prices in the real estate market. Figure 7.9 shows how this law would work in the real estate market. There, we see the excess demand for real estate (excess supply of money) putting pressure on prices to rise toward where the real estate market is back in equilibrium. Underlying the excess demand for alternative assets is the desire to diversify portfolios and mitigate risk. Meanwhile, the shortfall in the range of asset holdings in China may reflect higher state ownership of real underlying wealth.

Finally, we take a deep dive into how China holds net foreign assets. Net holdings of foreign assets by China is a positive number (4 percent), while in the United States it is close to zero percent. Figure 7.8b shows China's investment holdings in the United States amount to about USD 1.5 trillion. This figure is behind holdings in the US by Japan (USD 2.5 trillion) and the United Kingdom (USD 2.1 trillion). What is remarkable, though is that the latter two countries have built up their ownership of US assets over many decades; China has built its portfolio in the span of 15 to 20 years.

China is second only to Japan in its holdings of US government debt instruments. Both the United Kingdom and Japan hold a much more diversified array of assets in the United States than does China. Specifically, these other countries have substantial foreign direct investment in the United States. China's large holdings of US Treasury instruments is in contrast to the substantial foreign direct investment of the United States into China. This difference, paradoxically, has led to China paying the United States a net positive amount on the bilateral services balance, notwithstanding China's net position as a creditor.

'Historically, China has had too few ways to hold wealth, while some suggest that the United States presents a confusing array of too many ways to invest in financial securities.

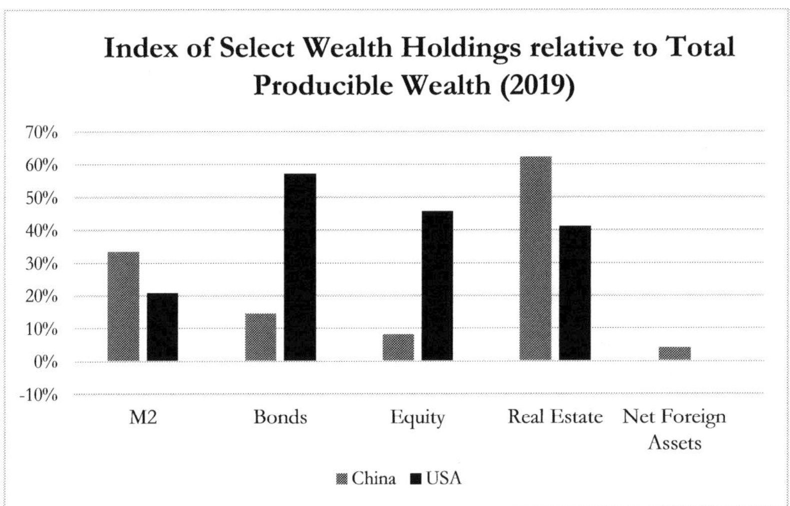

Figure 7.8a China holds more of its wealth in the form of money, real estate and net foreign assets relative to the United States. The United States holds relatively more bonds and equity and its net investment position (net foreign assets) vis a vis the rest of the world is slightly negative.

Source: Author created based on data from the World Bank, FRED and NBS.

Note: The numerator for the index is non-human capital as presented in the World Bank publication The Changing Wealth of Nations 2018 (https://bit.ly/2BcAfcy). Real estate holdings for China is estimated from residential construction as a share of total fixed investment, provided by the NBS. Net foreign assets for China is estimated from cumulative current account balances.

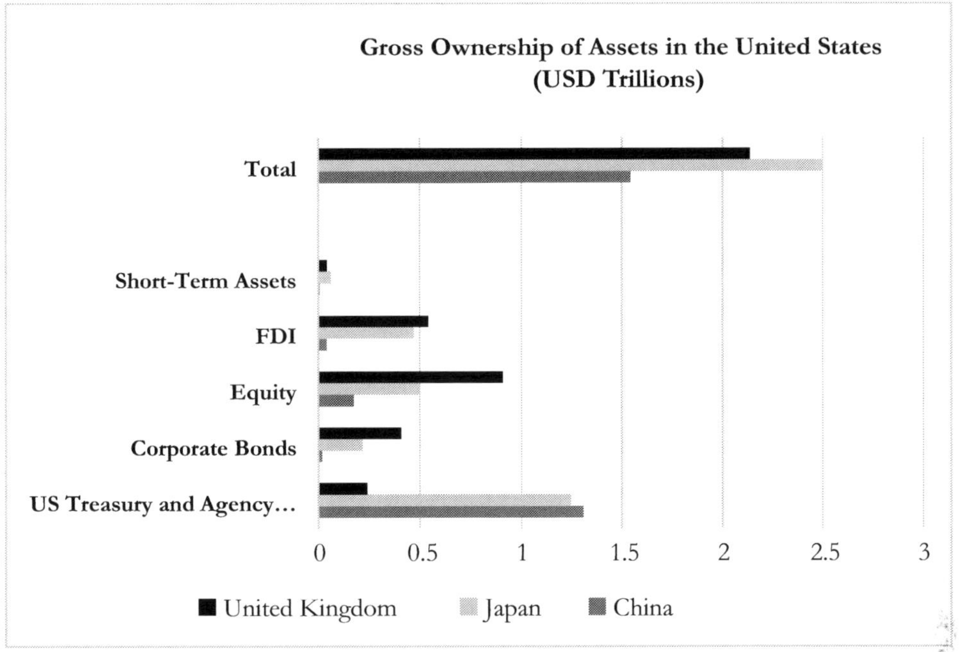

Figure 7.8b China is the third largest gross holder of United States assets, but most of those holdings are in low-yielding treasury instruments.
Source: Author created based on data from *Rest of the World: International Portfolio Investment Holdings of Long-term Securities by Country* in Tables 1 through 1e (https://bit.ly/2VaPDwz) and Bureau of Economic Analysis news release (https://bit.ly/3exLPNJ).

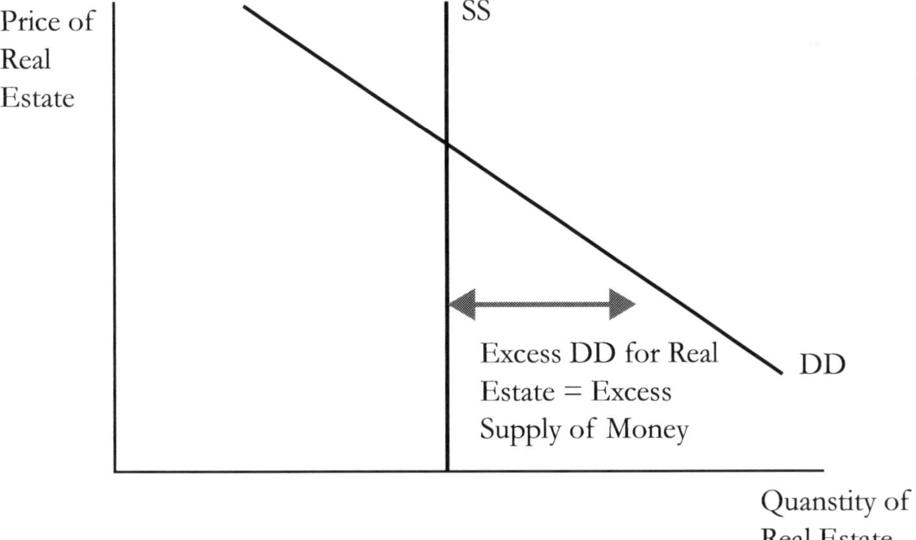

Figure 7.9 China's excess demand for real estate can be attributed in part to the corresponding excess holdings of money. This relationship is a result of Walras's Law.
Source: Author created.

Defining the Velocity of Money

Another way of comparing China's money supply to that of the United States is to look at the velocity of money. "Velocity" is defined as the average number of times the money supply needs to turn over in order to purchase one year's GDP. More formally:

Velocity = Nominal GDP / Money Supply

We can calculate M2 velocity by substituting M2 into the above formula. For 2019, China's M2 velocity was around 0.5, that is, the money supply was more than enough (by almost a factor of 2) to purchase all of China's GDP in a single year. For the same year, velocity in the United States was around 1.5—three times as fast. Do United States financial institutions and individuals really utilize money that much more efficiently than Chinese, or is there another explanation? A likely interpretation is that much of M2 is not held for GDP transactions, but rather as a way of holding savings and wealth (as discussed earlier) in China. In other words, the turnover of M2 is significantly higher in the United States because M2 is an asset used more for transactions than as a store of wealth—higher yielding outside assets serve the latter purpose.

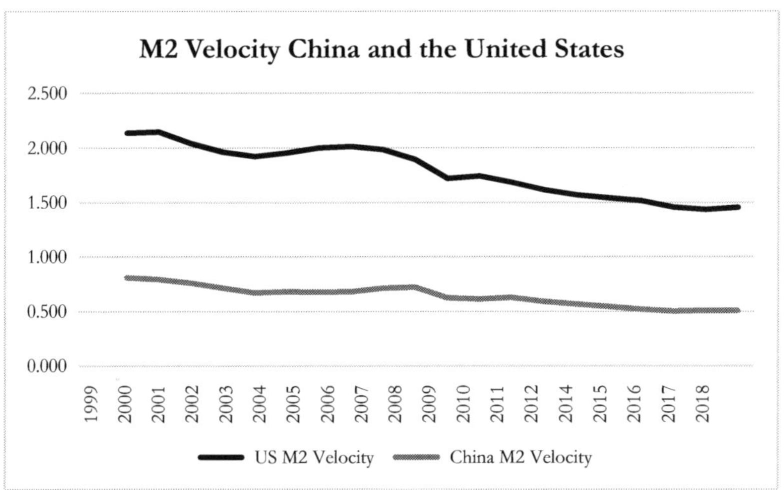

Figure 7.10 Consistent with Chinese holding an excess of cash, we find that the velocity of money is much lower (GDP/M2).
Source: Author created based on data from the International Monetary Fund Database and the Federal Reserve Economic Database.

Figure 7.10 shows M2 velocity for the United States and China in earlier years, where the difference appears even greater. One measure of the sophistication of a financial system is the speed of its velocity. China's velocity of money will trend closer to that of the United States and other financially-developed economies as its financial system continues to evolve, offering other ways beyond M2 to hold wealth.

Case Study 7.3: Did the Chinese Invent Velocity, Too?

In his epic work, *Science and Civilization in China* (1954), Cambridge University scientist and historian Joseph Needham details the many early Chinese discoveries and inventions in science and technology, from paper to agricultural water pumps. Many economic insights also have their roots in early China; for example, one of the earliest discussions of the velocity of money is by Shen Kuo, a finance minister in the Song Dynasty (Chaudhury 1990). He stated, in 1077:

> The utility of money derives from circulation and loan-making. A village of ten households may have 100,000 coins. If the cash is stored in the household of one individual, even after a century, the sum remains 100,000. If the coins are circulated through business transactions so that every individual of the ten households can enjoy the utility of the 100,000 coins, then the utility will amount to that of 1,000,000 cash. If circulation continues without stop, the utility of the cash will be beyond enumeration. (82)

Other key concepts in monetary theory were presented by Chinese scholars long before their introduction by Western scholars in the 18th century and later. Table 7.3 lists some of these concepts and the Chinese scholars who discussed them across various dynasties. No work similar to Needham's has yet detailed early Chinese contributions in finance and economics. Perhaps a student/reader of this textbook will someday make that contribution!

Theory	Scholar	Dynasty
Seignorage	Guan Zi	645BC (春秋) Spring/Autumn
Gresham's Law	Jia Yi	Han
"Money as a Veil"	Many Scholars	Han
Velocity of Money	Shen Kuo	Song
Demand for Money	Shen Kuo	Song
Fractional Reserves Against Deposits	Zhou Xing	Song
Quantity Theory of Money	Lu Zhi	Tang
The Gold Standard	Wang Maozi	Qing

Table 7.3 In the area of monetary theory, Chinese scholars over the centuries have introduced concepts later formalized by Western economists.
Source: Author created.

The Money Supply Process

How does money enter into an economy? What you may have observed in Table 7.1 is that most of money (M2) is demand deposits and other types of savings accounts. These vehicles, used for transactions and as a store of wealth, are not created by either governments or central banks. Rather, they are financial instruments created by commercial banks and other financial institutions. While currency (cash) is deposited at these financial institutions, that same currency is re-lent by banks many times over and re-deposited in an ever-growing cascade of checking accounts and other deposits. In this sense, most money is actually created by the banking system. While this may seem like an artificial form of money, if one were to ask each depositor how much money they have in the bank, their response would correspond to the value held in their checking and various savings accounts. If consumers and investors accept (believe) that something is money, and they can use it for all the purposes that money is used for, then—in fact—it is money.

The most significant way for a piece of paper to become acceptable as money is for a government to create laws making it acceptable as a means of payment. In effect, holding money becomes the same as holding a legal document, such as the title to a home or a land lease giving the bearer a variety of rights. Specifically, governments create "legal tender," which is acceptable for tax payments and legally mandated as acceptable for the settlement of debts. This governmental imprimatur effectively guarantees money's acceptability as a medium of exchange.

But what about cash itself? Who creates that? Of course, that is created by central banks with varying degrees of government involvement. Currency in circulation is called M0. The portion of the money supply that includes currency in circulation, currency held in vaults by banks, and currency on reserve by banks at the central bank is the "monetary base" or "high-powered money." It is the base from which all the other types of money-like accounts are created by the banking system; as such, it is truly high-powered. As we mentioned at the beginning of this chapter, mobile phone technology—no different from a debit card—is just a means of accessing our money (M1 or M2), which is held at a financial institution and backs up the ability to transact via mobile or card technologies.

The monetary base enters the economy through the actions of the central bank as it interacts with the government and the private economy. Central banks can and do print money or issue electronic credits for money and then trade that money for government, central bank, and sometimes even private securities.

In summary, while central banks create what is traditionally thought of as money (pieces of green or red paper printed with official portraits of current or former leaders and official language), financial institutions, including commercial banks, create most of what constitutes money. The M2 money multiplier (the ratio of M2 to the monetary base) was 3.9 for the United States and 6.1 for China in 2018.[7] In other words, the actual money supply (M2 in China) was six times larger than what was created by the central bank. China's money multiplier has increased over the past decade, reflecting lower reserve requirements and expanded lending—topics discussed later in this chapter. Notwithstanding the difference between actual currency and the money supply, the central bank still exerts almost complete control over the overall size of M2 via the various tools at its disposal.

Monetary Policy Tools

Table 7.4 provides a summary of monetary tools and their uses by the PBC and the Federal Reserve (the Fed). Specifically, we can think of these tools as instruments of monetary policy that the central banks can directly affect. Employing these tools, central banks hope to affect intermediate targets such as the money supply (usually measured by M2), the availability of loans within the financial system, interbank rates, and the exchange rate; these targets, once met, should impact longer-term interest rates such as those for mortgages and corporate loans. In turn, it is hoped that these intermediate targets affect final targets such as economic growth, employment, and inflation in a positive way. As we discuss in Chapter 8, the United States and China have monetary policy agendas that differ (at least at this point in each country's development) in terms of the tools employed (for example, the use of reserve requirements), intermediate targets (monetary growth instead of a targeted overnight interbank rate), and final targets (relative tolerances for inflation versus slower GDP growth).

Monetary Policy Tools	China	United States
Open Market Operations	Active	Active
Adjusting Reserve Requirement	Active	Rare
Discount Window Lending	Active	Occasional
Window Guidance	Active	Rare
Interest Rate Ceilings	Implicit Active	Not Used
Directed Credit	Active	Rare
Govt. Deposit Management	Active	Rare

Table 7.4 Monetary policy tools and their use by China and the United States.
Source: Author created.

Open Market Operations

Open market operations (OMOs) are the most widely used tool by central bankers worldwide. On an ongoing basis, central banks buy and sell securities of short-term maturities and undertake repurchase agreements ("repos") and reverse repos with financial institutions.[8] When a central bank buys a security, it pays the financial institution with high-powered money or reserves. This increases the money supply. When it sells a security, the money supply shrinks. Repos tend to be short-term (less than a month), allowing central banks to both add and drain liquidity from the economy as needed, at known repo prices. OMOs are intended to affect the monetary base (or, the availability of reserves in the banking system) and the interbank market interest rate. In China, the interbank market determines CHIBOR (China interbank offer rate, based on actual transactions for Chinese banks) and SHIBOR (Shanghai interbank offer rate, based on a poll of 18 banks of the estimated cost of funds on eight different maturities ranging from overnight to a year in Shanghai). Meanwhile in the United States, the interbank rate is called the "federal funds rate." When banks lack available reserves (usually due to OMOs of the central bank), they tend to cut back on lending to one another, thereby increasing their own reserves. This practice impacts interbank interest rates.

Both the Fed and the PBC buy and sell via primary dealers.[9] One difference reflecting fiscal surpluses and a limited supply of government debt is that the PBC deals mainly in government-owned institutions' debt, corporate bonds, and (in the past) its own central bank bills for OMOs, while the Fed has traditionally used government-issued securities.[10] Maturities tend to be substantially shorter (bills) for China's OMOs as compared to the United States' (bonds). In recent years, the United States' Fed has moved to even longer maturities to lower its cost of funds. A final critical difference is that the PBC at times buys and sells foreign exchange so as to maintain the exchange rate within a range of values. In the United States, there is no target exchange rate, and intervention in the foreign exchange market is rare. On those rare occasions where there is an intervention in currency markets, the Fed and the US Treasury coordinate their activities.

In summary, OMOs in China involve both the sale and purchase of its own bills, securities, and foreign exchange; while, in the United States, OMOs (under normal circumstances) are conducted using government securities alone. Since 2012, the PBC has gradually been moving toward using OMOs as its main tool for implementing monetary policy. Up to that point, the PBC had relied mostly on adjusting reserve requirements to affect the money supply. Via twice-weekly auctions of bills and bond repos, the PBC undertook approximately RMB 1 trillion in transactions from July to December of 2012—representing the estimated equivalent of a 1 percent hike in overnight interest rates. Apparently, the flexibility of open market repos compared to the more rigid reserve requirement ratios outweighed some of the cost considerations discussed below. Figure 7.11 shows the benchmark 7-day CHIBOR rate—a rate akin to the shorter-term federal funds rate in the United States: both central banks attempt to affect market-determined interbank rates via OMOs.

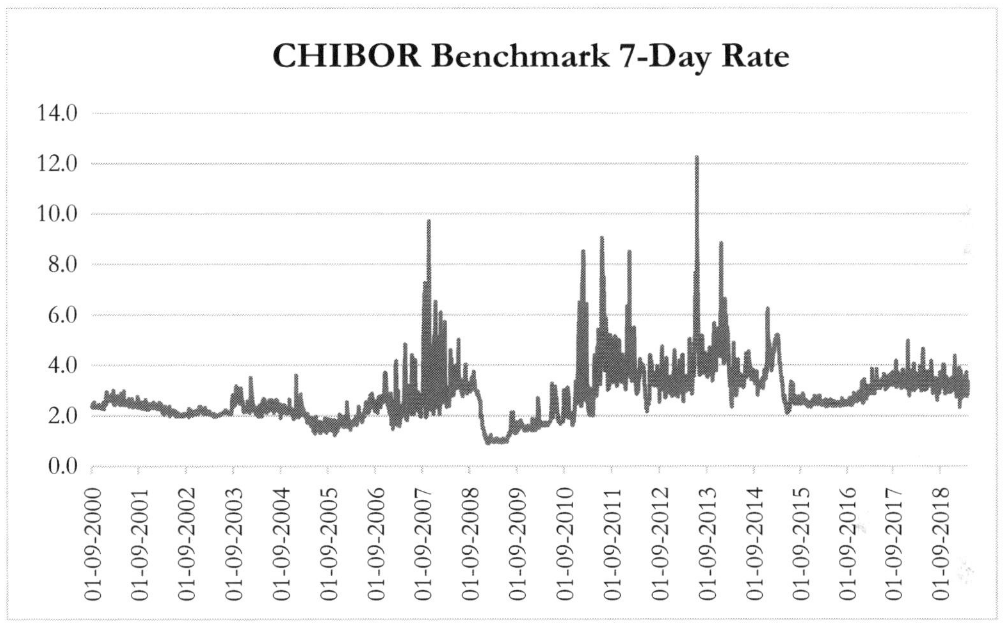

Figure 7.11 The CHIBOR provides one measure of market rates, and it is based on actual transactions between banks for funds at different maturities.
Source: Author created based on data from CEIC.

Discount Window Lending

Discount window lending is targeted to specific banks that borrow short-term on collateral in order to meet their reserve requirement. Borrowing banks are required to pay an interest rate (the discount rate or rediscount rate) that is above the interbank market rate. The discount interest rate also serves as a clear signal regarding the intent of central bank policy, since it is not subject to daily market fluctuations but rather a rate fixed by the monetary authorities. When set above the interbank rate, it serves as an indicator of the upper bound of rates acceptable to the monetary authorities.

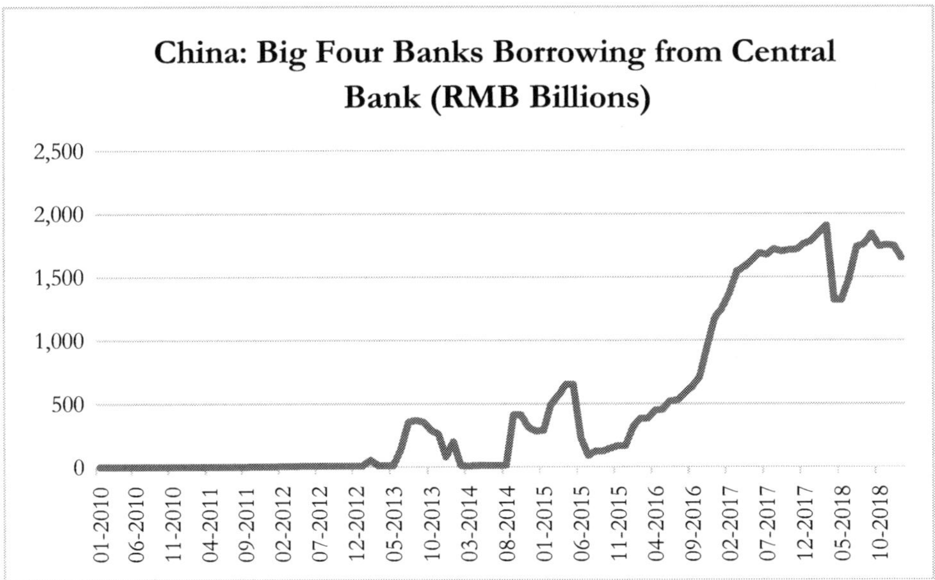

Figure 7.12 Chinese banks make far greater use of the central bank's lending facilities than do United States banks.
Source: Author created based on data from CEIC.

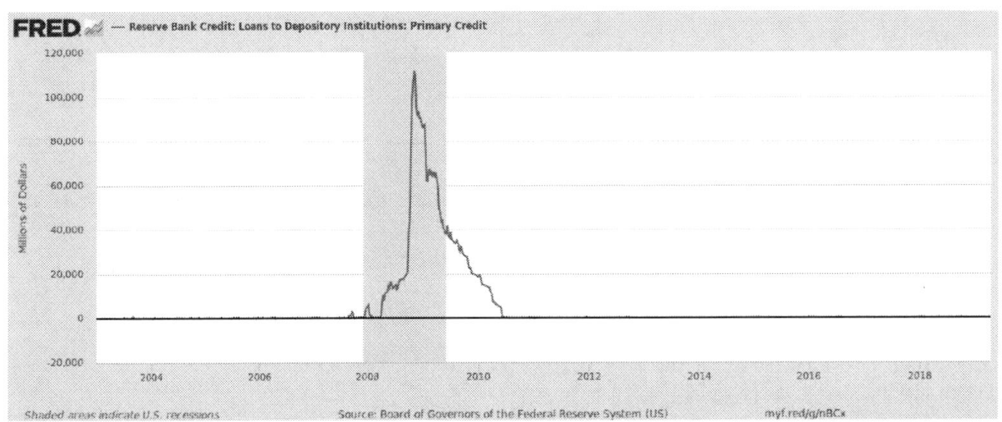

Figure 7.13 During the Great Financial Crisis, United States Banks' discount borrowing from the Federal Reserve surged.
Source: Author created based on Federal Reserve Economic Database.

China uses the discount window as a tool of monetary policy on a more regular basis than does the Fed. Discount window lending in the United States tends to be for exceptional circumstances, such as when a bank is having difficulty in meeting its reserve requirements—a serious problem suggesting that the bank is lacking adequate liquidity to cover the cash demands of its depositors.[11] Figure 7.12 and Figure 7.13 show discount window utilization by financial institutions in China and the United States and the pattern of discount rates in both countries. During the financial crisis, we see a peak in usage, but it drops to negligible amounts both before and after the 2008–2010 period in the United States. At the end of 2018, PBC credit to financial institutions via various collateralized lending arrangements—referred to as "standing lending facility" (1- to 3-month maturity), "medium-term lending facility" (3-month to 1-year maturity), and the newer "pledged supplementary lending facility" (over 3-years maturity)—made up around 25 percent of the monetary base—reflecting a significant role for discount-type window lending in China. In the United States, by 2018, the ratio had become negligible.

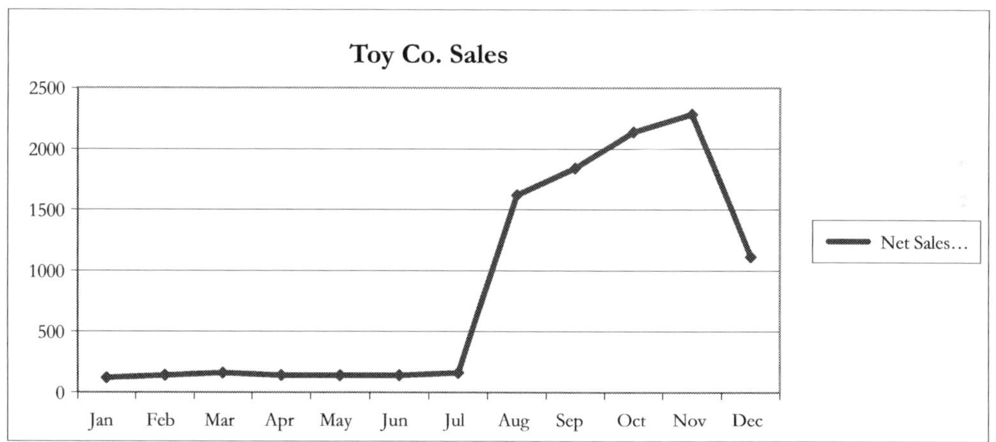

Figure 7.14a A typical company may see a seasonal increase in sales leading up to the Christmas holiday in the United States.
Source: Author created.

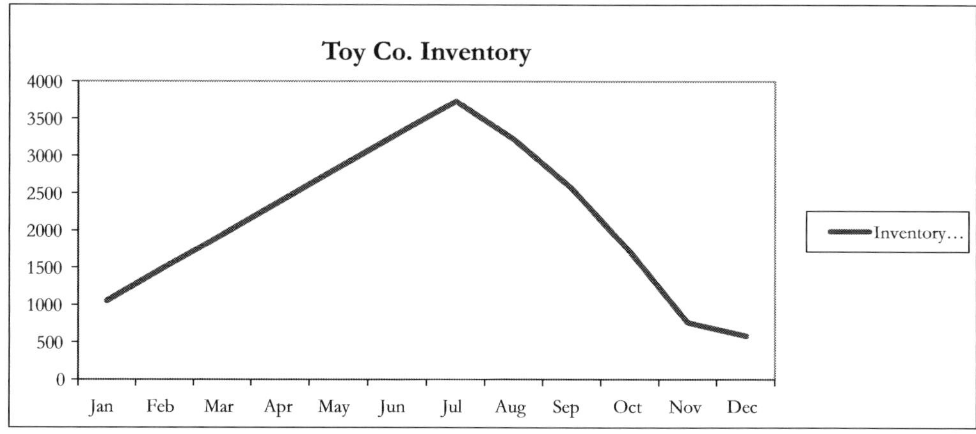

Figure 7.14b There is a seasonal decline in inventory leading up to the Christmas holiday.
Source: Author created.

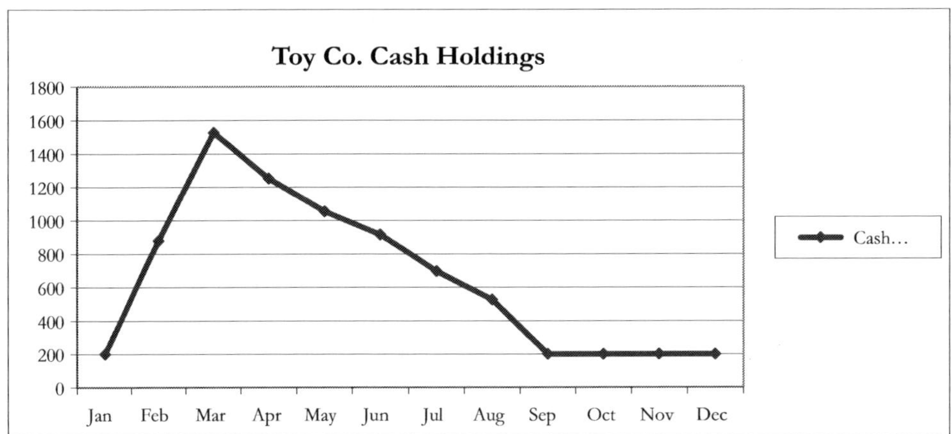

Figure 7.14c Over the year, as production ramps up for the holidays, there is a seasonal decline in cash holdings.
Source: Author created.

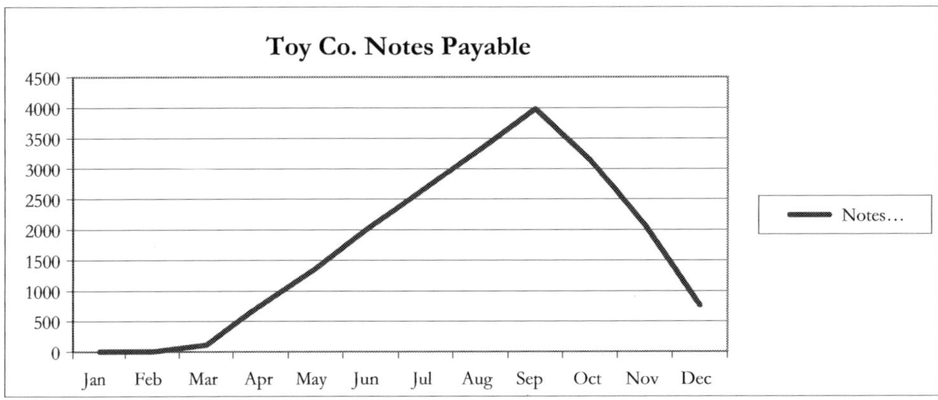

Figure 7.14d Over the year, as production ramps up for the holidays there is a seasonal increase in short-term debt.
Source: Author created.

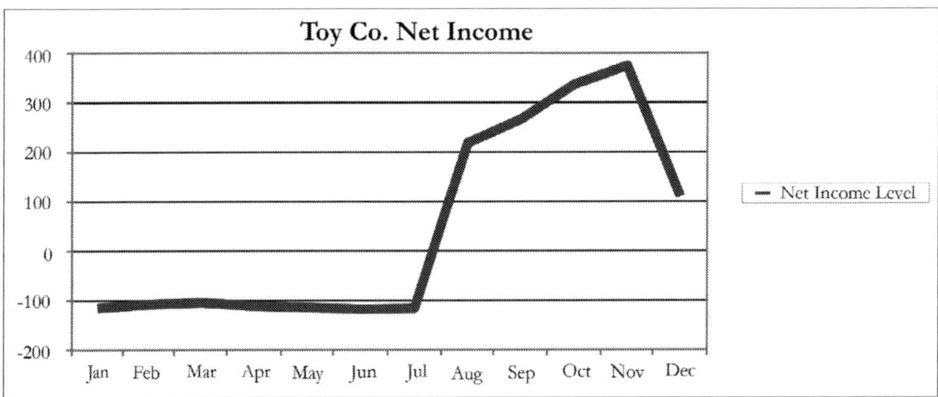

Figure 7.14e Profits experience a seasonal surge as holiday sales pick up.
Source: Author created.

Macro Finance Insight 7.2: Seasonality and an Elastic Currency

The Federal Reserve System was established in 1913 in response to a series of financial crises (known as "panics"), including the Panic of 1907. Beyond the broader goal of promoting financial stability, the Federal Reserve Act specified that the Fed should supply an "elastic" currency. What this provided, in practice, was a method for meeting the seasonally determined needs of consumers and private businesses for money and credit (loans). These needs might be large in some months of the year but smaller in others. During times of high demand for credit, the Fed expands the monetary base to allow real economic activity to proceed smoothly. In times of low demand for credit, the Fed ought to shrink the monetary base (or slow its growth) to prevent rapid credit expansion and overheating. At the turn of the century, when the Fed was created, the United States was still an agrarian economy, and seasonal patterns consistent with crop cycles were important.

Figures 7.14a–e show the pattern of a toy manufacturing firm in the United States whose production is fairly constant year-round, but whose sales rise in the last half of the year in the run-up to Christmas. The firm builds up inventory in the first half of the year, drains down cash holdings, and borrows to finance its working capital. The company must pay for production in the abeyance of sales that will occur later in the year. It is in the second and third quarters that financing is critical for this firm's survival. Even though its accrued (non-cash) net income rises, its obligations to suppliers rise, its cash holdings decline, and its short-term debts rises. The Fed plays a role here by providing an elastic currency that ensures the financial system is not constrained when supporting the seasonal needs of this firm and others like it.[*]

Figure 7.15 and Figure 7.16 show the seasonal patterns for China and the United States for retail sales beginning in 1993. Figure 7.17 shows the ratio of the seasonal patterns; if the two countries had the same seasonal pattern, the line in the last chart would be smooth rather than having a continued heartbeat like pattern. Clearly, it is not. In both countries, activity is highest in the last quarter of the year. China has relatively low activity in the second and third quarters of the year, while the United States has normal activity in those quarters. China's annual Spring Festival (Chinese New Year) boosts first quarter activity compared to the same period for the United States.[†] Table 7.5 summarizes the seasonal pattern in each economy. The increased economic activity in China in the first quarter requires an elastic currency response by the PBC. We see their response in Figure 7.18: Where China's currency spikes the first quarter of each year, we note that the PBC seems to have been more actively engaged in more recent years. On the consumption side, China experiences a burst of consumer activity in late January or February, during the run-up to Spring Festival. In fact, the British Broadcasting Corporation reported that China injected over RMB 255 billion into the financial system in January, 2014 to meet the increased liquidity needs of the vast travelling and *hongbao*-carrying Chinese population en route to their hometowns for the Chinese New

Year.[‡] Apparently successful, interbank short-term rates, which had surged to 6.5 percent, dropped abruptly to 5.25 percent (BBC 2014).

In contrast, if we look at China's seasonal GDP in Figure 7.19 (production rather than demand), we see a sharp decline in output in the first quarter. The surge in retail sales in the first quarter, matched by a drop in production, suggests declining inventories (built up in earlier quarters) and, in turn, an increase in cash flow. A Spring Festival for companies, indeed! Given that China's economy still weighs production and investment more heavily than consumption, we can guess that the production seasonality effect (rather than the consumer finance effect) is more pronounced relative to the United States.

So, why is an elastic currency needed at all? If, in China, consumer expenditures are outpacing income in the first quarter, while firm revenues are simultaneously exceeding costs, could not the latter sector lend to the former, i.e., finance their purchases? The situation would be symmetric in the United States if, when consumer sales surged in December, firms were able to finance consumers. Or, taking the question to an international level, if an entire economy has a seasonal imbalance, shouldn't it be able to borrow internationally? To some extent, this does happen, both domestically and internationally. However, the financial intermediation process can experience periods of uncertainty, lack of information, risk aversion, and irrationality (fear), and it often does not provide a smooth and predictable intermediation from quarter to quarter. This can create severe working capital shortfalls for both firms and consumers in the short run, and it can even potentially trigger an economic crisis. Thus, the role of the Fed and the PBC in providing an elastic currency remains critical. Eventually, no doubt, some clever hedge fund will find a way to lend across the seasonal cycles between these two major economies, helping residents in each country smooth economic activity (and of course, helping him/herself to newfound profits).

[*]Prior to the creation of the Fed, most financial panics of the 19th century occurred in the spring and fall seasons, when farmers needed to support planting and harvesting production but lacked adequate cash. Investment and inventory accumulation required cash (working capital), but these activities typically occurred at different time periods from peaks in consumption and cash receipts.

[†]The Chinese New Year occurs at an irregular date in the first two months of the Gregorian calendar, as the holiday is based on the Lunar calendar. Cash needs are further exacerbated by companies giving several months of salary in the form of a bonus immediately before the Chinese New Year begins.

[‡]A *hongbao* (红包)meaning, "red envelope," is an envelope containing cash that older relatives give as a gift to the younger generation on the Chinese New Year; of course, with the admonition that it should be saved.

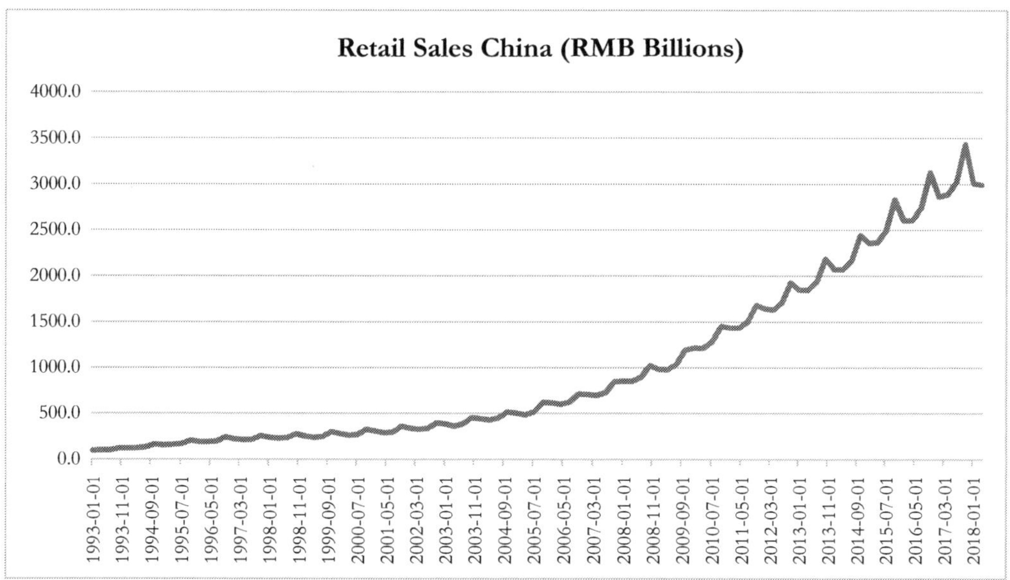

Figure 7.15 China's Spring Festival shows a distinct bump in retail sales in the first quarter of each year followed by a lull in the second quarter.
Source: Author created based on data from CEIC.

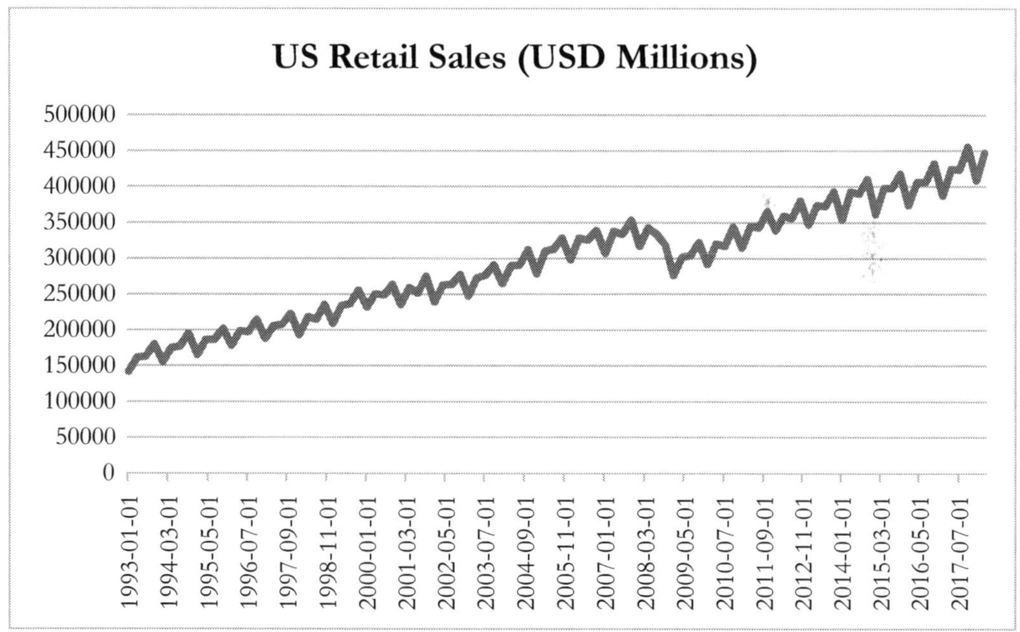

Figure 7.16 In the United States, there is a surge in retail sales during the final quarter (Christmas) followed by a lull in the first quarter.
Source: Author created based on data from the Federal Reserve Economic Database.

Figure 7.17 The ratio of the two countries seasonal patterns would be relatively flat if they were identical. We see, below, evidence that the two seasonal patterns are not the same.
Source: Author created based on data from the Federal Reserve Economic Database.

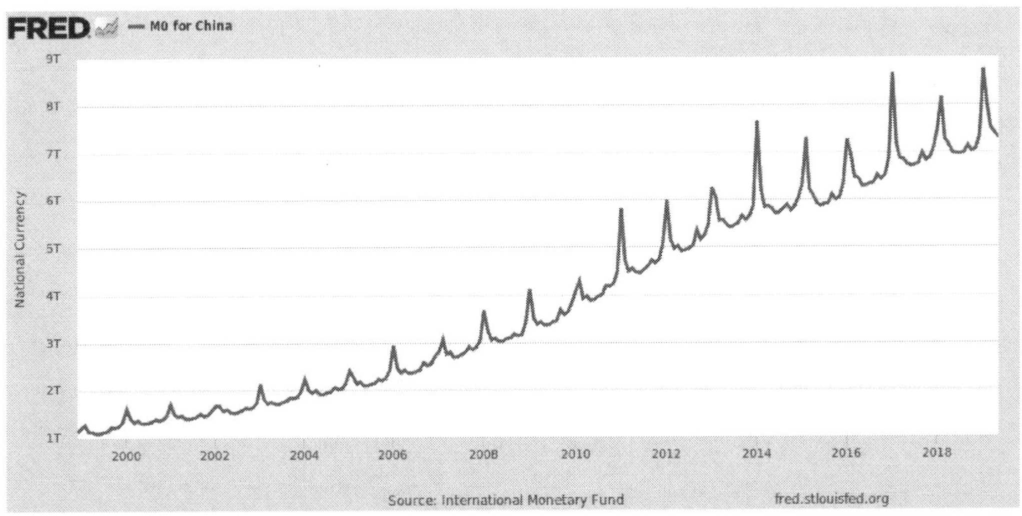

Figure 7.18 In recent years, we see China's monetary authorities increasingly responding to the seasonal pattern by providing an elastic supply of currency.
Source: Author created based on data from the Federal Reserve Economic Database.

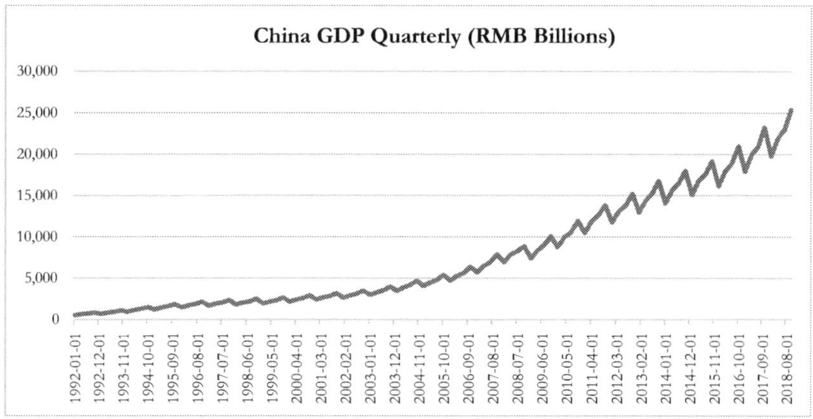

Figure 7.19 China's quarterly GDP shows the same seasonal surge in the first quarter and lull in the second quarter as do its retail sales.
Source: Author created based on data from the Federal Reserve Economic Database.

Retail Sales Seasonal Pattern		
Quarter	**China**	**United States**
I	High	Low
II	Low	Normal
III	Low	Normal
IV	High	Very high

Table 7.5 Seasonal patterns for retail sales in China and the United States are different, especially in the first quarter of the year.
Source: Author created.

Window Guidance

"Window guidance" is a broad term describing how the central bank can persuade financial institutions to follow stated monetary policies. It is an attempt to actually affect the operational aspect of financial decisions through communication, persuasion, and even regulatory threat. Specifically, a central bank would like to affect how much is lent by banks in the overall economy. The PBC, for example, stated in its Fourth Quarter Report for 2006 (https://bit.ly/2Z5xYrh):

> By communicating with the commercial banks and other financial institutions on a regular basis, the central bank is in a better position to have the market anticipate its monetary policy and thus to make its policy more effective. China's experience in recent years indicates that improving transparency through window guidance is not only conducive to

> reducing costs of monetary policy operations, but also to helping the central bank realize its policy objectives and enhance the effectiveness of monetary policy. (16)

Or, in the 2017 Annual Report (https://bit.ly/36naHoc) of the PBC:

> The PBC spearheaded efforts to issue guidance on providing financial services to build China into a manufacturing power, especially increasing financial support to "Made in China 2025" strategy. At the year-end, outstanding medium and long-term loans to the manufacturing sector posted RMB 3.1 trillion, up 3.6 percent year on year. To help reduce excess capacity, the PBC guided financial institutions to provide financial services to promote the transformation and upgrading of, and to overcome difficulties in the iron and steel and coal industries. (30)

The PBC actively engages the banking system (the principal shareholder of the largest banks remains the central government) to follow its directives. Specifically, the PBC announces regular targets for lending growth during the year, and it attempts to ensure that banks in the aggregate meet these targets. Furthermore, as we see in other PBC statements, the guidance regarding which industries need more credit and which need less goes even to the disaggregated industry level. This PBC guidance naturally flows from and is consistent with the central authorities' Five-Year Plan. The PBC's top policy-makers meet with the banks on a monthly basis and provide more formal window guidance pronouncements on a quarterly basis.[12] In the United States, the Fed has not provided anywhere near the level of window guidance found in China. On the contrary, some have argued that there has been an absence of transparency in Fed policy goals and targets over the years. Perhaps that perception comes from the Fed's careful distance from financial markets, ensuring that traders cannot unfairly take advantage of imminent market movements resulting from Fed actions. Furthermore, central banks have historically been wary of establishing specific goals and targets that might tie their hands in certain exigencies.

The chair of the Fed is, however, required to testify before Congress twice a year to set out monetary policy goals. Between 1978 and 2000, the Fed set growth targets for monetary growth as a result of congressional legislation known as the Humphrey-Hawkins Bill. Since 1990, the Fed has published a target range for the interbank (federal funds) rate. In January, 2012, the Fed announced a formal long-run inflation target of 2 percent as part of an effort at greater transparency.

In summary, the Fed provides broad, general guidance regarding future policy targets. It then relies on market forces to summon an appropriate response. China's guidance also comprises the provision of policy transparency, but it involves telling financial institutions what they must do—operationally—to help the PBC and the central government implement both broad and specific policy goals.

Reserve Requirements

Reserve requirements represent how much cash financial institutions are required to hold, either in their own vaults or on deposit (typically as a credit) at the central bank. Reserve requirements serve two main purposes:

1. As a precautionary amount, providing the bank with adequate liquidity should depositors withdraw an abnormal amount from the bank
2. Even more importantly, as a tool for controlling the amount of money (i.e., M2) in circulation

Regarding the latter role, recall that banks create money through receiving a deposit in, for example, a checking account, re-lending that amount, and then accepting further deposits from those who have borrowed from the banking system. Thus, a recycling of high-powered money sets off a chain reaction of new bank deposits. These new deposits are all captured, by definition, in M2, and they thus become bank-created money.

When financial institutions have higher reserve requirements, they can lend out less. Reserve requirements, in effect, create dead-in-the-water money. In fact, while these amounts, held as reserves, are part of the monetary base, they are not part of either M1 or M2 and—by definition—are not part of the money supply. Technically, if (r) represents the fraction of deposits that are held in reserve (the reserve ratio), and (c) represents the fraction of deposits held by citizens in actual cash (the currency to deposit ratio), we can say that the broad M2 money multiplier mentioned above (the ratio of M2 to the monetary base) is:

$$\text{M2 / Monetary Base} = \text{Money Multiplier} = (1 + c) / (r + c)$$

There is a substantial difference in the way China and the United States use this tool for controlling the money supply. From January, 2010 to June, 2019, the PBC raised the reserve requirement 27 times, and it currently has one of the highest reserve requirement ratios in the world at 11.5 percent. Both in terms of the reserve ratio and the degree to which this tool is used, China, among all large economies in recent years, relies on this tool more. Recent utilization involves lower reserve ratios and expanding the money supply in response to weakening economic growth and the Trump trade war. We estimate that a 1 percent drop in the ratio (*r*) would allow for about an RMB 800 billion increase for large banks alone, or about a 0.5 percent increase in M2. In January, 2019, the fifth cut in the span of year was announced, lowering reserve requirements for large banks to 13.5 percent and for small banks to 11.5 percent. In contrast, over the past 54 years, the Fed has rarely changed reserve requirements as a tool for monetary control. It does, however, provide frequent updates (https://bit.ly/3giErH9) on how reserves are to be managed. Most of these changes are a minor part of monetary control and are technical in nature, rather than part of a targeted monetary policy. In the United States, for example, banks must maintain a marginal reserve requirement of 10 percent on transaction-based accounts (e.g., checking accounts) with bank holdings over USD 124.2 million, 3 percent with holdings of USD 16.2 to124.2 million, and 0 percent with under USD 16.2 million—a much narrower base for reserves than China's all-deposits base.[13] Figure 7.20 shows the average reserve ratio for US commercial banks.

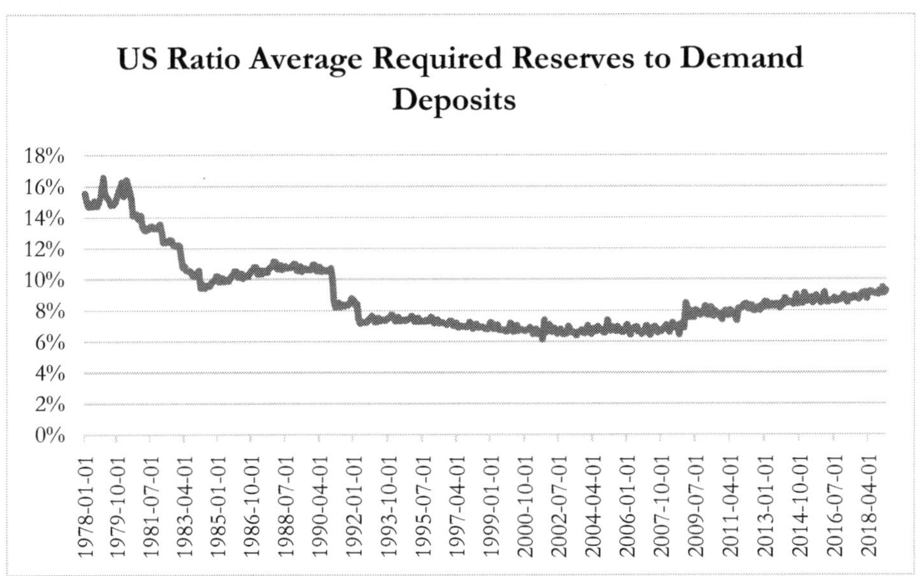

Figure 7.20 In the United States, the reserve ratio change is not used as a tool to conduct monetary policy.
Source: Author created based on data from the Federal Reserve Economic Database.

The Federal Reserve Bank of San Francisco (https://bit.ly/2A62B77) explains why the FED rarely uses reserve requirements to conduct monetary policy:

> There are several reasons why reserve requirements are not frequently changed, the most important of which is that OMOs provide a much more precise tool for implementing monetary policy. When the Fed purchases $10 billion in securities for its own portfolio, it adds $10 billion to bank reserves.
>
> The impact of changes in reserve requirements is difficult to estimate; each change has the potential to affect thousands of depository institutions in different ways, depending on each institution's deposit base. Changes in reserve requirements also typically lead to changes in pricing schedules for some bank services, because some bank fees and credits are set based on reserve requirements.

In this context, we can understand why changing the reserves ratio would be a more commonly used tool in China: greater precision can be achieved in China's banking sector since the Big Four banks have historically dominated the banking scene and, what is more, they are state-owned. However, with the growth in the number of medium-size and smaller banks both privately and publicly owned, management of the monetary conditions via reserve changes has become more complex. This helps explain China's efforts at (1) moving toward more market-based mechanisms, particularly open-market operations, and (2) applying different reserve ratios for large versus small- and medium-sized financial institutions.

Remarkably, as a share of GDP, China's required reserves for the Big Four banks alone are near 10 percent; in the United States, the share is less than 1 percent. Figure 7.21 shows a decreasing pattern of reserve requirements since 2011 as China has tried to boost economic growth rates related to both short-term factors and long-term factors already discussed in this book. It should be noted that real long-term secular declines in economic growth (Solow factors) are unlikely to be ameliorated via stimulatory short-term monetary policies.

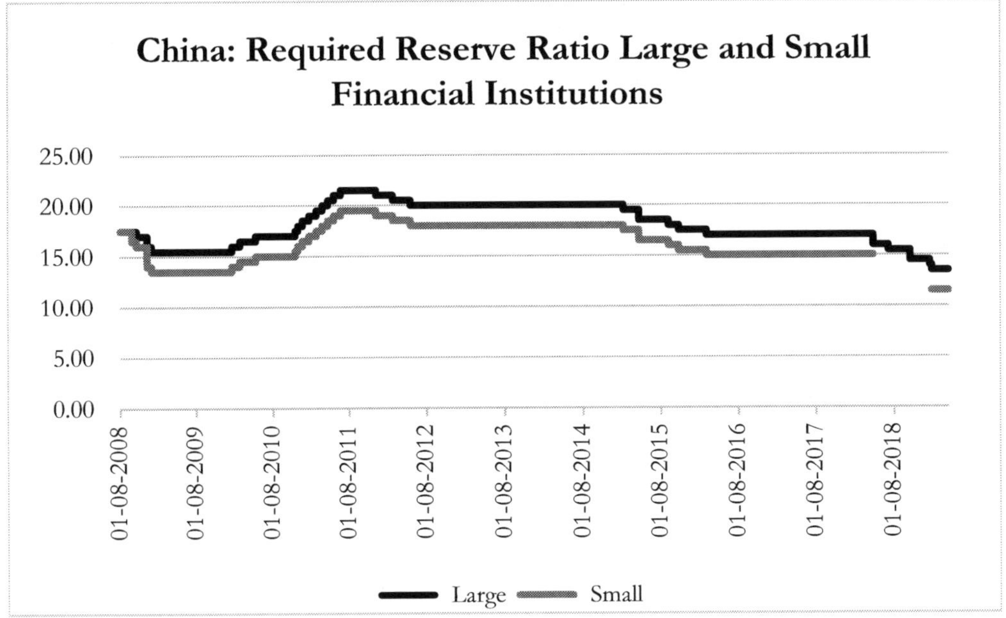

Figure 7.21 On an ongoing basis, China has adjusted the reserve ratio for banks as a tool for monetary policy.
Source: Author created based on data from CEIC.

Interest is paid on required reserves in both the United States and China.[14] In the United States, the current rate on reserves is 1.6 percent, while in China the corresponding rates are 1.62 percent on required reserves and 0.72 percent on excess reserves. In the United States, interest on reserves and on excess reserves is the same, and it is now used as a key tool of monetary policy. In China, the rates on required and excess reserves differ, and they are just one of many tools that the central bank employs.

China's extensive use of reserve requirements is consistent with its efforts at controlling monetary growth instead of overnight interest rates (i.e., controlling the quantity rather than the price of money); this practice, in turn, is related to China's massive efforts to sterilize the foreign exchange inflows since 2007 in order to halt rapid monetary growth. Furthermore, it has been a less expensive alternative form of monetary control—the interest rate paid on required reserves in China is less than the amount needed to pay banks to hold additional debt instruments through OMOs.

In both countries, the holding of excess reserves is large by international norms. In the United States, this is a recent phenomenon reflecting asset purchase programs implemented by the Fed during the financial crisis which, in turn, increased cash holdings by the banks. In China, excess reserve holdings are chronic, reflecting longer-term monetary policies to control the amount of money circulating in the Chinese economy.

Macro Finance Insight 7.3: Return on Equity and the Money Multiplier

The money multiplier links the monetary base with the actual amount of money (M1 or M2) circulating in the economy. The ratio of currency held by the public to bank deposits (*c*) and reserves held against deposits by the financial institution (*r*) will combine with the amount of high-powered money created by the central bank (*H*) to magnify out to the money supply (*M*).

$$M = H \times (1 + c) / (r + c)$$

The money multiplier ratio above also serves as a constraint in terms of how fast the money supply can grow. But another very important constraint is often overlooked in macroeconomic discussions on determining the size of the money supply: the capital adequacy ratio (CAR). CAR represents the required ratio of capital or investor funding (beyond citizen deposits) to the amount of loans granted by financial institutions. The underlying purpose is to ensure that owners of banks have an adequate amount of their own capital at risk in order to ensure that banks appropriately consider the risks of making new loans. The Bank for International Settlements, based in Switzerland, has recommended ratios and relevant metrics for CAR, referred to as BASEL I, II, or III.

Let's simplify the complex set of guidelines by saying that financial institutions in a country are required to hold a minimum ratio of capital or equity (*E*) against loans or domestic credit (LC), and the ratio of capital or equity to domestic credit we define as (*e*), that is:

$$E / \text{LC} = e \text{ or } \text{LC} = 1 / e \times \text{E}$$

Furthermore, let's summarize an entire nation's financial system with the balance sheet and accompanying panels of ratios shown in Table 7.6. There, we include all financial institutions, from the country's central bank down to the lowest-level regulated small financial institution. Equity includes everything from paid-in-capital and retained earnings to holdings of other acceptable forms of capital by the financial system. Loans or credits include both domestic and foreign loans, on a net basis. Thinking of money as "broad money," or M2, we substitute our ratios into the original balance sheet. Finally, dividing by (*E*), we have the final panel in Table 7.6.

Assuming that (*e*), (*c*), and (*r*) are constants, and that the balance sheet remains in balance, the above balance sheet says: if (*H*) grows (the monetary base grows) then (*E*) must grow at the same rate. But the growth rate of (*E*), (meaning $\Delta E / E$) is the same as the ROE for banks. If (*H*) grows faster than ROE, banks will be constrained from making loans by their capital requirements; as a result, banks will hold excess reserves. If (*H*) grows slower than ROE, banks will lack adequate liquidity to offer loans.

During an economic recession, the economy-wide ROE declines (the companies' ROEs that banks have lent to), so banks' ROEs (profitability) will also shrink, or possibly turn negative. Providing greater liquidity through (*H*) may not create greater lending in this situation because banks are constrained by their capital inadequacy. It is this situation that corresponds to shrinking collateral and credit rationing in times of financial crisis (Bernanke and Gertler 1995). In the case of China, banks (as discussed below) have had artificially high ROEs due to interest rate ceilings and other favorable treatment from their main benefactor/investor—the government. This artificial growth in ROE has, in turn, permitted more rapid loan growth—and this may very well harm the allocative efficiency of investment and the overall quality of China's growth.

Assets	Liabilities
	Money (*M*)
Loans or Credits (LC)	Equity (*E*)

Assets	Liabilities
	$H \times (1 + c)/(c + r)$
$1 / e \times E$	E

Assets	Liabilities
$1 / e$	$H / E \times (1 + c) / (c + r)$
	1

Table 7.6 Growth in the monetary base needs to be consistent with banks' (and by inference the economy's) ROE. During a recession, the ROE can slump, requiring a pro-cyclical (harmful) slowdown in lending in order to meet Basle capital adequacy requirements. Source: Author created.

Interest Rate Ceilings and Floors

Interest rate ceilings and floors are a form of financial repression; an effort at bypassing market-determined interest rates with fixed ones. Ceilings and floors can appear on both deposits and loans, and they are intended—at one level—to control interest rates in the economy. At another level, they are a means of either subsidizing banks (when deposit rates are ceilinged) or subsidizing borrowers (when lending rates are ceilinged).[15] In the case of controls, interest rate ceilings can be viewed as another tool in the monetary policy toolkit. In the case of a subsidy, the goal is usually to enhance bank profitability or encourage certain types of investments. While possibly achieving certain short-term credit market goals, ceilings and floors tend to be distortionary at a microeconomic level, and they can lead to financial disintermediation, rationing, and black markets for borrowing in the long run.

Figure 7.22 shows the supply and demand of investable funds in an economy against the interest rate (or cost of capital) charged. If a ceiling is set below the equilibrium rate (where the two curves intersect), a shortage results and the potential for credit rationing and shortages exist.

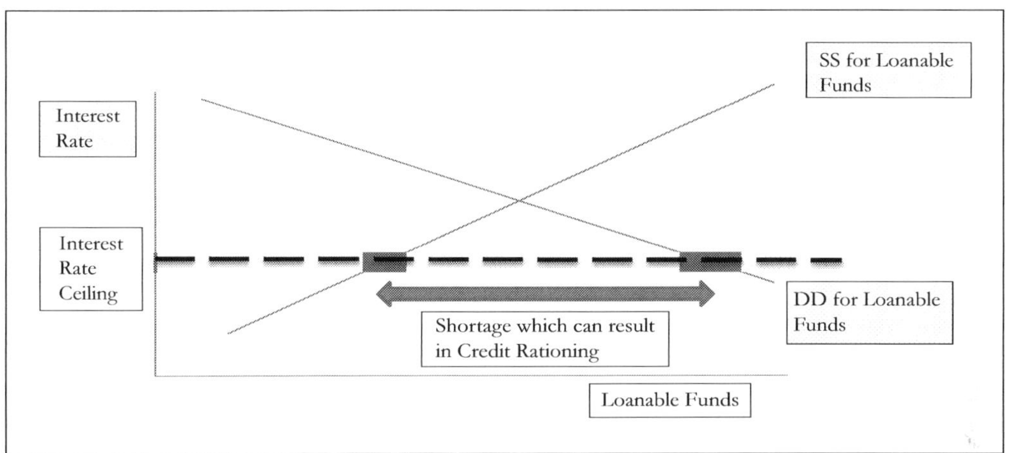

Figure 7.22 Imposing an interest ceiling on bank deposits will create an excess of demand for loanable funds.
Source: Author created.

The United States eliminated ceilings on interest rates for bank savings accounts in 1980; and, by 2010, ceilings on rates for demand deposits were also fully eliminated.[16] China had floors and ceilings on lending and deposit rates until fairly recently. An important role of these interest rate controls was to guarantee a hefty profit spread for China's banks after the national banking crisis of the early 2000s; at the time, China's major banks were technically bankrupt. The policy of interest rate ceilings and floors was a long-term solution to recapitalizing the banks—but, as always, it came with costs in terms of allocative efficiency and the quality of growth and loans. In July 2013, floors on lending rates were completely eliminated in a critical step toward liberalizing credit markets. China continued to have ceilings on deposit interest rates for bank deposits until October, 2015. Table 7.7 provides current bank deposit and lending rates and Figure 7.23 presents the historical path of these regulated rates; we note the widening spreads starting in the late 1990s, a result of policies that were intended to (and successfully did) restore profits to the troubled banking system.

	Commercial Banks (2018)	
Term (Months)	**Deposit Rates**	**Lending Rates**
0	0.3	3
3	1.35	NA
6	1.55	4.35
12	1.75	4.75
24	2.25	4.75
36	NA	4.9
60	2.75	4.9
Personal Loan	NA	6.4

Table 7.7 A sampling of interest rates offered in China's banking system, where the PBC continues to provide guidance for deposit and lending rates.
Source: Author created based on sampling of banks in Financial Advisory. com (https://bit.ly/2Czmuot).

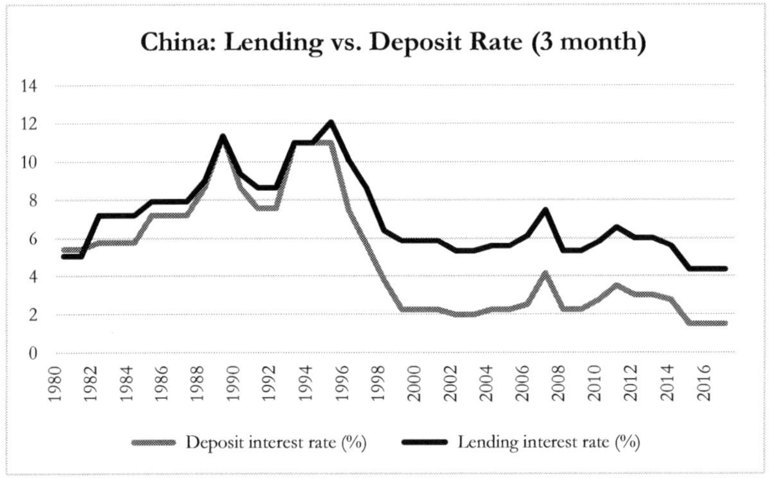

Figure 7.23 A widening mandated spread between deposit and lending rates has created large profit margins for the troubled banking system since 1998.
Source: Author created based on data from CEIC.

Directed Credit

Directed credit involves a central bank targeting specific industries or companies to receive financing. This could take two main forms:

1. A central bank could instruct financial institutions to lend to these target industries. Or,
2. The central bank could directly purchase a targeted company's financing instruments.

Figure 7.24 illustrates how a central bank interfaces with end-user firms or industries. We typically think of central banks as making credit available to financial institutions through OMOs or discount window activity. These institutions, in turn, lend to the private economy (companies and consumers) based on their own assessment of risk, return, and opportunities. This is the generally accepted practice for central banks. Most countries prefer to see private financial institutions make decisions regarding creditworthiness and borrowing or lending opportunities. Central banks are charged with the task of broad macro aggregates (not corporate creditworthiness, valuation, or industry selection), including inflation, economic growth, unemployment, and setting the overall level of nominal interest and exchange rates.

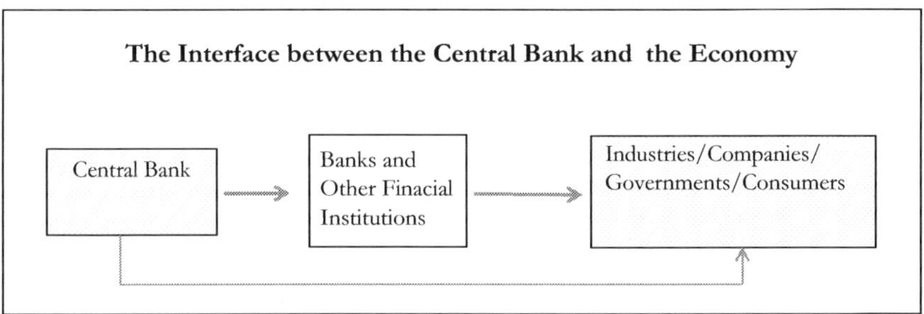

Figure 7.24 Normally we think of the central bank interfacing with the financial sector and the financial sector providing finance to the "real economy" based on profitable opportunities. Sometimes (as in the case of China, or the US during the recent financial crisis) the central bank bypasses the financial system and interfaces directly with the real economy. Source: Author created.

When central banks require or encourage financial institutions to target industries or companies for lending, we have a form of directed credit. The central bank may also interface directly with companies, target industries, governments, or even local consumers by buying their securities or making loans.[17] This practice would be a direct form of directed credit. In both instances, the central bank typically acts on behalf of the government to establish industrial policy or to meet the more short-term goal of rescuing a company from bankruptcy—or an industry from collapse.

Until the mid-1980s, the PBC was engaged in direct lending to companies and industries in China. Virtually all companies, at the time, were state-owned, and loans were considered to be part of the industrial policies set out in the government's Five-Year Plans. When China's Big Four commercial banks (see Case Study: 7.5) were eventually carved out of the PBC and allowed greater independence, they undertook more and more lending. They still, however, made most of their loans at the behest of the PBC and central government—a very clear form of direct lending. A more decisive step was taken in 1994 with the creation of a separate category of policy-lending banks (China Development Bank, Export Import Bank, Agricultural Bank of China [ABC]). However, policy-lending still continued with encouragement from local governments. After China's major banking crisis in 2000–2003 (a result of the prior policy loans turning into non-performing loans), policy lending was further curtailed, and banks were allowed to make lending decisions on more market-based criteria. As evidenced by China's Central Government 2016 State Council Directive (https://bit.ly/2A1B5Iw) for the 13th Five-Year Plan for the development of strategic emerging industries, we still see a substantial role for directed credit in China:

> Explore the establishment of an investment and financing information service platform for strategic emerging industries to connect banks to enterprises. Encourage the establishment of a system for determining, assessing, pledging, and transferring intangible assets in digital creative, software, and other areas and advance financial product innovation, such as intellectual property rights pledge financing, equity pledge financing, supply chain financing, and technology insurance. Guide policy and development financial institutions toward increasing support for strategic emerging industries. Promote the development of a number of financial leasing and lending companies that cater to such industries as the aircraft, marine engineering equipment, and robotics industries. Accelerate the establishment of a national financing guarantee fund to support the financing of strategic emerging industry projects. (47)

Directed credit in the China context can also mean targeting major markets, such as the real estate market and the stock market. The PBC formalized these efforts in April, 2014 by introducing its pledged supplemental lending facility, which channels funds to strategic industries or economic sectors (such as rural areas) that need greater support. Traditionally, in the United States, the Fed's policies have been directed at the broader notion of financial market stability and have specifically avoided policies directed at the stock market.

The Fed was structured as an independent entity; not subject to day-to-day political pressures from the United States government. As such, it has viewed its mandate as applying to the broad macro targets mentioned earlier, rather than to directed credit. That being said, the financial crisis that began in 2007 has seen a more intrusive role for the Fed in specific industries—the acquisition of AIG securities, the purchase of mortgage-backed assets, and the broader purchase of government agency debt.[18] While the Fed balance sheet expanded tremendously after 2007, it is gradually returning to its pre-2007 level. (Total Fed assets were about USD 900 billion at the end of 2006; but, by mid-2011, they reached USD 2.3 trillion.) In the Fed's view, this expansion was consistent with maintaining stability in the financial system during the financial crisis, and it did not target specific industries for economic development. Rather, it prevented the broad financial system (with a focus on real estate finance) from collapsing.

Case Study 7.4: Developments in China's Financial Markets

As mentioned above, China's financial sector and markets remain a "work in progress." The PBC served, in effect, as the financial sector up until the early 1980s, before the Big Four state-owned banks were reconstituted as deposit-taking institutions. In December, 1990, the Shanghai Stock Exchange (SSE) was reopened, as was the Shenzhen Stock Exchange. In October, 2009, a Shenzhen-affiliated NASDAQ-like exchange was established (CHINEXT). Notwithstanding this short history, China's combined equity markets had the second-highest market capitalization in the world (USD 3.6 trillion) by the end of 2012, after the United States. Virtually all of the approximately 2,000 companies traded still had the state as their majority shareholder.

If the 1980s was the decade for banking institutions, and the 1990s focused on equity institutional development, the first two decades of the new millennium were the period for bond market development. Today, China's bond market is the world's fourth-largest, valued at around USD 3.1 trillion. Most bond trading occurs in the interbank market. Central bank notes and bills are the most actively traded short-term instruments in the interbank market. In addition, government bonds for a wide range of maturities are also traded. Central bank bills and government bonds (central and local governments) are used primarily in PBC OMOs (with central bank bills used more often in recent years). The majority of transactions in the interbank market are repurchase agreements with virtually all of the instruments mentioned here or below used as collateral. Table 7.8 details some of the key institutional developments in the monetary and banking sector. From the table, we see that, in the 1979–1998 period, institutional buildup of the banking system occurred; then, in the 1998–2015 period, liberalization of interest rates and financial market developments took place; and, finally, between 2015 and the present, the tools needed for proper operation of the transmission mechanism were put into place.

Financial bonds are the most actively traded long-term instruments in China.* Other long-maturity bonds include enterprise bonds, which are issued by either state-owned enterprises or private corporations. The private issuances are still a relatively small share of the bond market, and they are traded on the Enterprise Bond Exchange rather than the interbank market. In summary, the bond market grew from insignificant levels in the 1990s to an important tool for short-term liquidity management and long-term yield by 2013. That being said, the instruments that continue to dominate the market remain government-related instruments (PBC notes and bills, government bonds, policy bonds, and a majority of enterprise bonds). In China, only about 8 percent of bonds and commercial paper instruments are issued by private companies, as compared to about 28 percent in the United States. The remainder, in both countries, is government-related.†

*Financial bonds represent loans to financial institutions, especially the policy banks: China Development Bank, Export Import Bank of China, and ABC. These loan projects, in turn, are used for large infrastructure projects. Financial bonds are also issued by commercial banks and other financial institutions, such as large insurance companies.

†Estimates from Goldman Sachs Liquidity Management. FAQ: China's Bond Market (https://bit.ly/2CAnp8i) and Federal Reserve Board of Governors. Credit Market Debt Owed by Financial Sector. Report Z.1, Table L.2 (https://bit.ly/2VcxKgY).

Institutional Development	Date
Movement from a mono-bank system (the PBC) to a group of state-owned banks with specific sectoral responsibilities Agricultural Bank of China (ABC), Bank of China (BOC), China Construction Bank (CCB) and Industrial and Commercial Bank of China (ICBC).*	1979
Conversion of local/rural cooperatives into local commercial banks	Mid-1980s
Interest paid on excess reserves of banking system	1987
Establishment of a maximum loan to deposit ratio to control credit expansion	1994
Interbank market deregulated	June, 1996
Introduction of CHIBOR: 7- to 120-day actual average lending rates on interbank funds	1996
Interbank bond market inaugurated and accompanying repurchase agreements market becomes active	June, 1997
Open market operations commence (Tuesdays and Thursdays)	October, 1998
M2 (defined 1993) identified as sole target for monetary policy	1998
China Development Bank issues market-priced bonds	1998
Central government issues market-priced bonds	1999
Big Four state-owned banks begin to act as traditional commercial banks	2002

Institutional Development	Date
First auction of central bank bills	May, 2003
Lower limit on deposit rates and upper limit on lending rates removed (upper limit on deposit and lower limit on lending still in place)	2004
Introduction of a corporate bond market	2005
Introduction of SHIBOR, an average of 18 bank quotes on lending rates used as an index for interest rate swaps—the eight tenors range from overnight to one year	January, 2007
Introduction and implementation of China Banking Regulatory Commission regulations restricting banks' lending to real estate and other risky industries (overcapacity industries)	2010–2013
Standing lending facility created to establish ceiling for interbank lending rates	January, 2013
Corridor for interbank rates established with PBC repurchase OMOs and interest on excess reserves, establishing a floor, and standing lending facilities, a ceiling	2013
Removal of base lending rate floors for commercial bank lending	July, 2013
Bank deposit insurance established, covering virtually all bank deposits	May, 2015
Removal of deposit rate ceilings for commercial bank deposits (de jure, but not de facto)	October, 2015
PBC institutes daily open-market operations via repurchase/reverse repurchase agreements (typically 7–28-day tenure)	February, 2016
Deemphasis on the quantity M2 target and heavier reliance on pricing mechanism (interest rate targets)	2016–Current
Broaden definition of M2 to include (1) deposits of non-financial institutions and (2) wealth management products of banks and money market fund deposits	(1) Fall, 2011 (2) Spring, 2018
Establishment of a new benchmark loan prime rate by the PBC to be set on the 20th of every month and used as the basis (floor) for a bank's lending to its most credit-worthy commercial customers. Loan prime rate benchmark will be based on medium-term rates generated via open-market operations	August, 2019

Table 7.8 China has steadily taken a series of significant steps in liberalizing its monetary policy since the start of major economic reforms in 1978.
Source: Author created.
*Agricultural Bank of China, Bank of China, and China Construction Bank were established in 1979. Industrial and Commercial Bank of China was separated from the PBC in 1984.

Regulatory Fiat

China's State Council, in conjunction with the PBC, has also used regulations targeted at specific markets, such as the housing market or construction industry. For example, in early 2016, the PBC lowered the required down payment on a new home purchase to 20 percent—down from 25 percent on a first home and from 30 to 40 percent on second-home purchases. This action was taken to stimulate the fragile residential housing market. In contrast, in 2011, local governments were urged to increase the supply of land available for housing to rein in rising property prices. The PBC has also intervened (https://bit.ly/3gfVoC5) in tandem with China's National Team efforts to support stock prices in China. At the time, the PBC utilized reverse repurchase agreements to lend to various state-backed financial institutions (https://cnb.cx/3cXtHft), including Central Huijin Ltd. (https://bit.ly/2yxbxSU), who then channeled that cash into equity markets. Traditionally, the Fed has not targeted specific industries or asset classes—although steep changes in equity or real estate markets are part of the Fed's broader mandate toward "maintaining financial stability." In an oft-quoted speech, Ben Bernanke, the Fed's then-chair, made his views very clear on this matter: It was beyond the Fed's mandate and ability to determine what constitutes an equity market bubble and then attempt to counter it (Bernanke 2002). China's PBC, meanwhile, includes such policies in its toolkit to complement the more traditional monetary policy tools mentioned above.

Government Deposit Management

Government deposit management involves the way in which the central authorities manage their typically large bank accounts, with respect to their impact on bank reserves. Government funds held on account with the central bank reduce (tie-up) the amount of reserves, loans, and money supply in the general economy. The reverse happens when the government writes checks (makes payments) to the private sector from its central bank account, expanding the money supply. Since central banks around the world act not only as the banker for the financial system but for the government as well, such movements from the central bank system to the private economy can have the same effect as an OMO.

The US government (the Treasury) maintains bank accounts at both the Fed and private financial institutions (Treasury tax and loan accounts). Because, in the United States, the responsibility for monetary control rests with the Fed, the Treasury is obligated not to move its funds back and forth from Fed accounts in ways that impact the money supply.[19] For this reason, the Treasury attempts to keep a fairly constant balance in its Fed account.

In China, by contrast, the PBC actually utilizes the central government's accounts as a tool for affecting the money supply in the same spirit of an OMO. For example, should the PBC wish to constrain monetary growth, it will move the Chinese government's funds from the private banking system to its own accounts.

Policy Rates and the Interbank

The difference between the two countries in terms of central bank involvement in interest rates is a matter of degree. In the United States, the central bank focuses mainly on affecting the federal funds rate (and interbank liquidity) via OMOs and interest paid on excess reserves. In China, the effort at intervention is broader: both short- and long-term benchmark rates are established, and the banking system is expected not to stray too far from these benchmarks. In effect, in China's control goes beyond mere overnight interbank rates, but extends to the whole term structure. Implicit deposit ceilings remain both an instrument for short-run monetary policy and a long-run source of profits (subsidy) to the largely state-owned banks in China.[20] In the United States, deposit and lending rates serve as an intermediate target toward the final targets of inflation, real economic growth, and employment. In recent years, deposit rates have remained exceptionally low, also serving as a source of profits for the troubled financial sector.

In China, the various facilities, including the medium-term standing lending facility, provide an upper bound (corridor ceiling) on interbank lending interest rates (CHIBOR and SHIBOR) for different maturities. These facilities now extend traditional discount window lending—another upper bound, but for shorter maturities. The discount rate also serves as a signaling device for changes in the monetary policy stance. Figure 7.25 shows China's discount window interest rate since 1990. Providing a floor for interbank lending rates are the interest rate paid on excess reserves held by banks and the rate offered for PBC-initiated repurchase agreements. Figure 7.26 provides (ceiling) 7-day reverse repurchase agreements over the past decade. The PBC offers at least five different maturities up to half a year. We note that the PBC pays a rate nearly twice as high for excess reserves as for required reserves. In recent years, it has not used the rate on excess reserves as a policy tool. Meanwhile, in the United States the rates on excess reserves and required reserves are identical; and, since 2016, the rate paid on excess reserves has become an important monetary tool for maintaining a lower bound on the federal funds rate in interbank markets.

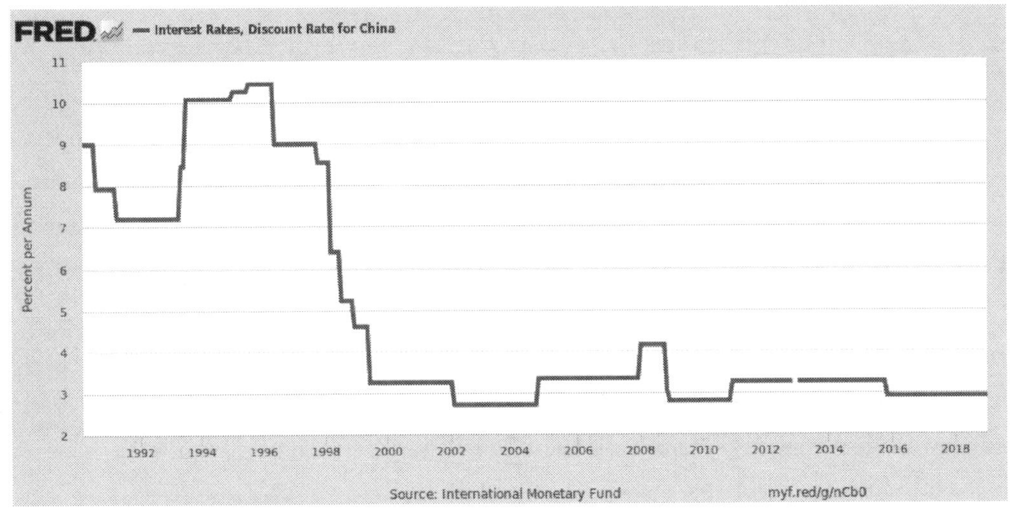

Figure 7.25 China uses the discount window as a tool for monetary policy much more than does the United States.
Source: Author created based on data from the Federal Reserve Economic Database.

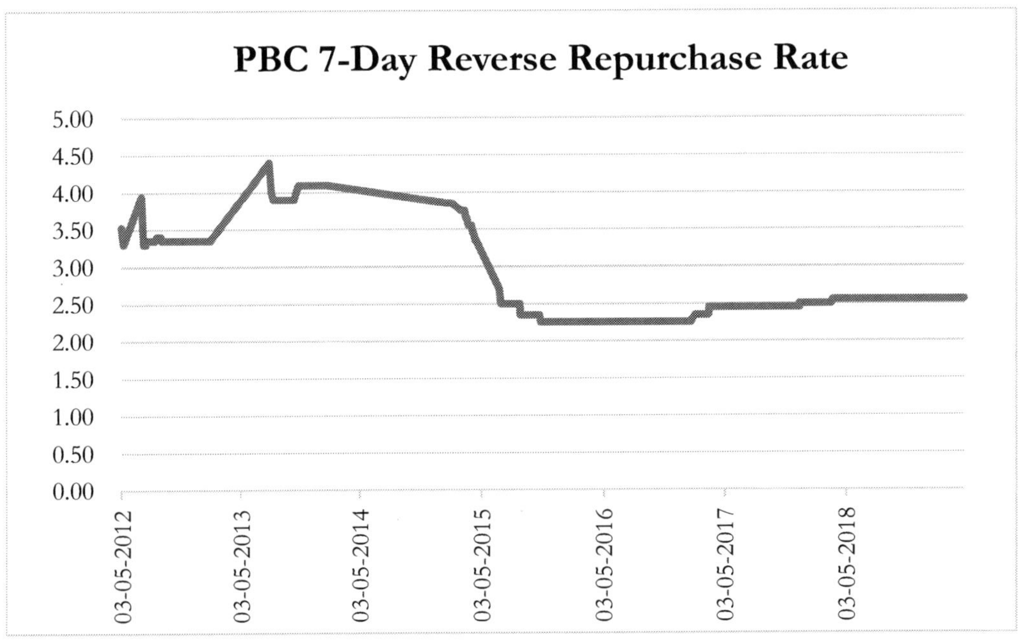

Figure 7.26 Reverse repurchase agreements are one way of lending to the banking sector via OMOs—thus establishing one type of interest rate ceiling on interbank interest rates.
Source: Author created based on data from CEIC.

Although, formally, floors and ceilings have been removed, the PBC continues to monitor and guide interest rates. The periods of flat interest rates for benchmark one-year lending rates, as seen in Figure 7.27, (rather than wiggly market-determined rates as seen, for example, in Figure 7.11) are one indication of non-market PBC control. The benchmark lending rate has served as a floor for banks' lending rate to customers. However, in August, 2020, in a further step toward liberalization, the benchmark lending rate was replaced by two market-based reference lending prime rates—one for bank loans under five years and another for longer maturities. The new rates are based on a survey of actual rates charged by 18 banks to their most creditworthy customers (SHIBOR). These rates still represent a form of interest rate guidance for loans to end-users, but this guidance is at least based upon actual market rates. The one-year benchmark deposit rate (ceiling), however, still remains in place.

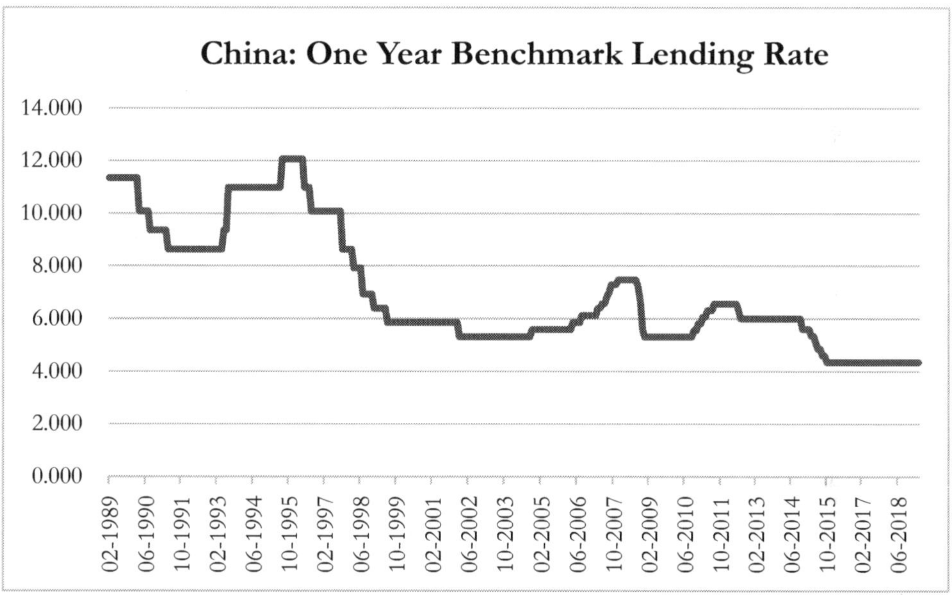

Figure 7.27 A different ceiling for one-year loans has historically been the benchmark lending rate established by the PBC. In 2019, this benchmark was replaced by a more market-based rate: the lending prime rate.
Source: Author created based on data from CEIC.

Price-Based vs. Quantity-Based; Market-Based vs. Non-Market-Based

One way to categorize the above monetary tools is to determine whether the quantity or price of an asset is being targeted, and whether the tool is market-based or non-market-based (i.e., implemented by government mandate). For example, a central bank could choose to sell a certain quantity of bills in order to affect the quantity of reserves that the banking system holds, or it could sell bills at a specific price (interest rate) in order to directly impact interbank interest rates. In a market-based system, the central bank can control either the quantity or the price, but not both. In the former case, it controls quantity by allowing the demand of banks to determine the interest rate. In the latter case, it controls the interest rate (the price) but allows banks to determine how many reserves (quantity) they wish to hold at that price.

Non-market tools (such as regulations on how much cash borrowers must provide as a share of a home mortgage) represent controls on ultimate lending by banks in ways they may not choose on their own. China has used tools in the upper-left quadrant, upper-right quadrant, and lower-right quadrant of Table 7.9. That is, in the past, China has tended to use quantity-based tools (e.g., the growth of the money supply) and non-market-based tools. It is gradually moving toward the lower left quadrant of market- and price-based tools for implementing monetary policy. In fact, since at least 2016, the authorities have deemphasized M2 as an intermediate target in favor of interbank rates now playing a more significant role. The United States has traditionally used price- and market-based tools, though—once again—the recent financial crisis and the Fed's quantitative easing have been an important exception. These differences have important implications for both the effectiveness of monetary policy and the sophistication of the downstream financial sector.

	Market-Based	**Non-Market-Based**
Quantity-Based	Short-Term Liquidity Facility	Pledged Supplementary Lending Facility
	Size of Repurchases and Reverse Repurchase Arrangements	Government Deposit Management
	Reserve Ratio Requirements	Controls on Bank Credit
		Controls on Bank Credit by Sector
		Window Guidance
Price-Based	Open Market Operations Reverse Repos and Repos	Benchmark Rates on Loans and Deposits
	Rates Paid on Excess Bank Reserves at the PBC	Regulatory Fiat (e.g., down-payment on home mortgages)
	Medium- and Long-Term Lending Facilities	Term Structure Benchmark Rates

Table 7.9 China has tended to use quantity-based and non-market-based tools in its implementation of monetary policy.
Source: Author created.

Kamber et al. (2018) find that, in recent years, China's monetary policy implementation more and more resembles what is found in the United States and other advanced economies. That is, they find that China is relying more heavily on pricing rather than quantity mechanisms in the implementation of monetary policy. They cite the interbank market interest rate corridor, in which the PBC pays interest on borrowed excess reserves and receives interest on standing lending facility loans, and the stabilizing activity of OMOs in the interbank market since 2016 as prima facie proof of policy liberalization. Going even further, they provide evidence of the interbank mechanism as having an impact on long-term bond yields, corporate spreads relative to government bond yields, and overall loan growth. They conclude that the credit channel in China is beginning to work.

Summary of Differences

Both in terms of ultimate targets (output, employment, and inflation in the United States; economic growth, the value of the exchange rate, and inflation in China) and in terms of intermediate targets (the federal funds rate in the United States; monetary growth and a kit of non-market tools in China), there is a wide range of differences in how and to what purpose monetary policy is conducted within each country.

The PBC utilizes a wider range of available tools for the conduct of monetary policy compared to the Fed. While the Fed relies primarily on OMOs to affect the federal funds rate and uses rates paid on excess reserves as a lower bound, the PBC makes substantial use of other tools that we have described above. Some of the policy rates (e.g., those used in standing, medium-term and pledged lending facilities) are tools intended to impact the term structure of rates. This is something that the FED generally does not attempt to do; rather, it relies on markets to establish a term structure based off of interbank markets and treasury instrument yields. Over the past decade, however, the PBC has moved to a heavier reliance on OMOs to impact interbank rates. From the above discussion, we can see that a jumble of policy rates remains in place in China, and—ultimately—some of the interest rate clutter will need to be cleared if monetary policy is to operate smoothly and arbitrage opportunities are to be eliminated.

One important reason that China relies on a wider arsenal of monetary policy tools is related to the complexity of tasks undertaken. Trying to control the exchange rate, interest rates, economic growth and financial stability all at once requires controlling the flow of international capital (as we discuss in Chapters 3 and 8). Juggling these many tasks requires a plethora of heterodox tools. Notwithstanding a sophisticated set of capital controls, China cannot let its interest rates stray too far from international rates lest the wall of capital controls be breached. This basic paradox creates a need for intervention in the economy at a variety of levels. How long China can maintain its balance in trying to achieve so many goals remains to be seen.

Chinese Bank	Assets (USD Billions)	Share of Total Assets*
Industrial and Commercial Bank of China	4,006.2	11%
China Construction Bank	3,397.7	9%
Agricultural Bank of China	3,233.2	9%
Bank of China	2,989.7	8%
Bank of Communications	1388.0	4%
Postal Savings Bank of China	1363.0	4%
China Merchants Bank	967.1	3%
Industrial Bank Company	985.4	3%
Shanghai Pudong Development Bank	942.5	2%
China Minsheng Bank	906.4	2%
Total Assets of Depository Institutions	38,019.9	

Table 7.10 Top ten domestic banks in China, ranked by assets as of 2018.
Source: Author created based on Global Finance Magazine (https://bit.ly/2ByObgH).
*Author estimate.

Financial Institution	Assets (in USD Billions)	Share of Total Assets
JP Morgan Chase	2218.9	13%
Bank of America	1782.6	10%
Wells Fargo	1689.4	10%
Citibank Group	1406.7	8%
US Bank NA	459.5	3%
PNC Bank	366.3	2%
Capital One NA	304.7	2%
TD Bank	360.7	2%
BNY Mellon	286.4	2%
State Street Bank	242.8	1%
Total All Commercial	17,080.2	

Table 7.11 Top ten insured US-chartered commercial banks, ranked by consolidated assets as of 2018.
Source: Author created based on Global Finance Magazine (https://bit.ly/2ByObgH) and data from the Federal Reserve Board.

Case Study 7.5: China's "Big Four" Banks

China's largest four banks now rival the largest US banks, and they are among the largest banks in the world as measured by assets (see Table 7.10 and Table 7.11). At one level, this is unremarkable given China's enormous savings rate and limited alternative asset classes. It is remarkable because these banks were, until the late 1980s, not recognizable as independent entities, but rather entities operating under the wing of either the Ministry of Finance or the PBC. All banks in China were among the first institutions to be nationalized after the founding of the PRC in 1949. Even today, the majority of shares in these institutions are owned by the government. For example, over 70 percent of Bank of China shares are state-owned. Beginning in the 1980s, however, these banks gained increasing independence from direct government control, were allowed to accept individual deposits, and—between 2000 and 2010—had each issued shares (initial public offerings) on domestic and international stock exchanges allowing for minority ownership.

Each bank's name gives a clear indication of its traditional source of deposits and loans; for example, the ABC has principally operated in rural areas, while the Bank of China has traditionally engaged in international operations, including foreign exchange activities.* These banks, however, are edging into each other's traditional lines of businesses over time. Figure 7.28 reveals two noteworthy features of China's banking system.

1. Banks in both the United States and China do not make up as large a share of GDP as do banks in many other countries.
2. If we were to draw a line from the origin through China, we would see that other countries fall below that line, indicating that the top four banks in China have a lower concentration ratio than other major economies.

*In fact, the Bank of China (not to be confused with the People's Bank of China [PBC]) has SAFE—the State Administration for Foreign Exchange—as its majority shareholder.

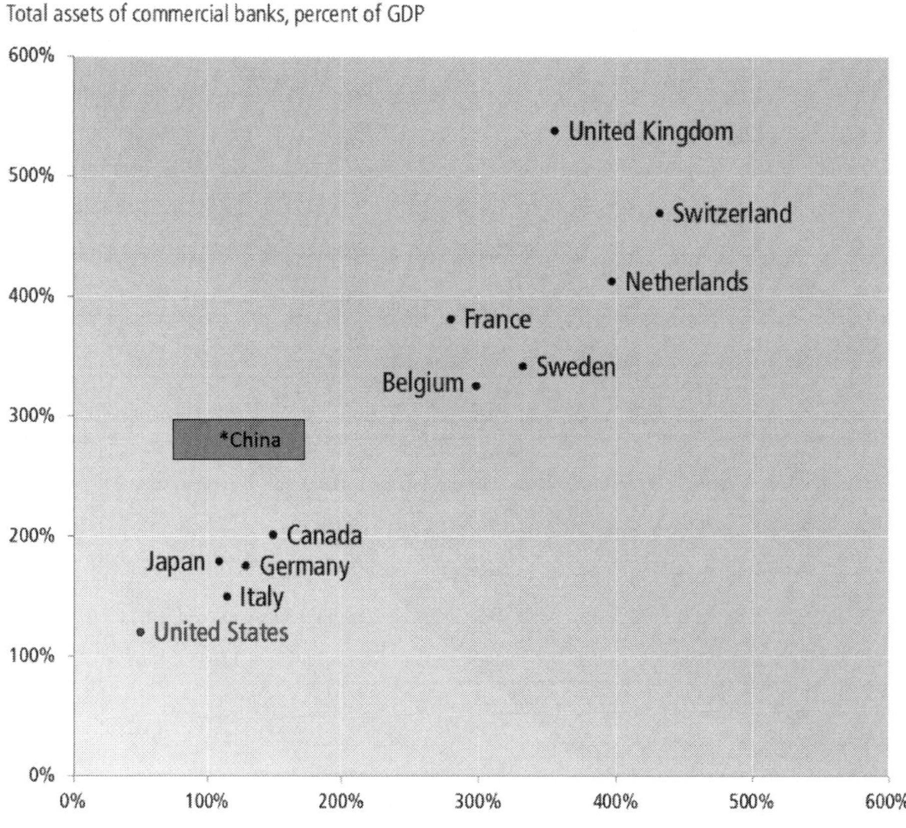

Figure 7.28 Total assets of commercial banks relative to GDP around the world. China's bank concentration is on the low side compared to other economies—particularly, those in Europe.
Source: United States Treasury and author's estimate. For a qualitatively identical update: See Bank for International Settlements, Graph 5 (https://bit.ly/2YriC1g).

State-majority ownership of the five largest banks (including the Bank of Communications) in China compared to privately owned banks in the United States is another difference that serves as a necessary condition for greater PBC intervention. China's banking system is relatively new and still evolving. Until 1979–1980, the PBC was effectively China's only bank. But, by 1994, the PBC had assigned the traditional banking role of deposit taking and lending to four major state-owned banks: Bank of China, Industrial and Commercial Bank of China, China Construction Bank, and ABC. These four major banks still dominate the banking landscape in China in terms of both deposits and loans. A plethora of financial instruments in which the private sector can invest in the United States, compared to a paucity of instruments in China, is another factor. In Chapter 8, we build on this institutional understanding to interpret actual monetary policy in recent years in each economy.

Case Study 7.6: Financial Innovation or Financial Disintermediation in China?

Taobao ("treasure chest"), the most popular online shopping site in China, has found plenty of treasure to fill its chest via its money market fund, established in 2013. Yu'e Bao ("spare cash") had, by 2018, 588 million investors with RMB 1.7 trillion under management, making it the largest money market fund in the world. By providing higher returns on money-market-like assets (now at 2–3 percent per annum, but in the past it has been as high as 6 percent), Taobao has attracted deposits from depositors at the large Big Four banks—which, as indicated in Table 7.7, now pay one percentage point less in returns. Taobao is owned by Alibaba, another Chinese online giant that provides information on suppliers of products and services around the world. The money market funds provide both a higher return and a transaction account on Taobao's site and via mobile apps. Other internet retailers, such as WeChat's Tencent, have also established money market funds (2018) that pay even higher returns. Current estimates for the size of the overall market are around USD 1.2 trillion, compared to about USD 26.4 trillion on Chinese bank deposits. Prior to 2013, a money market industry in China barely existed.

The PBC has also taken notice, and it is looking for ways to regulate but not stifle this emerging financial segment. For regulators and policy-makers, there are three key issues: First is the degree of risk to investors (depositors) and, in turn, implications for systematic risk throughout the financial system. After all, one critical juncture of the global financial crisis in the United States was when the Primary Reserve money market fund saw a decline in its net asset value from USD 1 to 0.97 in September of 2008 (it "broke the buck"); an event that had been assumed close to impossible. A second concern relates to monetary control. The PBC has relied heavily on reserve requirements and guidance to the Big Four banks as monetary policy tools. It is unclear how the same mechanisms would work for the internet-based money market funds. A final concern relates to the Big Four banks. In recent years, they have relied on a vast, reliable source of virtually free funds (in real terms), and they have become comfortable making loans under the operating assumption that this would continue. But now, the situation is changing rapidly.

Past ceilings on bank deposits had created an opportunity for Taobao and other companies like Tencent to siphon off bank deposits from the traditional banking sector. Taobao invests in both the short-term interbank money markets and some of the companies that provide products and services on the Alibaba site. It contends that it has pierced the veil of asymmetric information, since it knows the credit history of these borrowing companies. Meanwhile, China's citizens perceive this as a long-awaited opportunity for the small depositor to finally get a positive real return on their money holdings.

What no doubt worries regulators is that this phenomenon might just be the tip of the iceberg. After all, if a ` percent advantage in returns can support a shift in deposits of USD 1.2 trillion and continued double-digit growth in money market assets, regulators may be closing the barn door a bit too late—possibly, the horse has already bolted (to the shadow banking sector). Meanwhile, investors continue to pour money into funds such as Yu'e Bao in search of yield while believing that they are too big to fail.

Macro Finance Insight 7.4: Demand for Money as an Option—The Precautionary Motive

What are some of the motivations for individuals to hold money, an asset whose return or yield is either zero or very low? Economists such as John Maynard Keynes and James Tobin offer several theories: namely, the transactions-inventory motive and the speculative motive.

The transactions-inventory motive states that individuals manage money as a company would manage an inventory: based on the volume of transactions (sales), the opportunity cost of holding working capital, and the interest rate on a money market investment. Transactions occur on an ongoing basis, but income occurs at intervals. Money serves as a buffer between income and transactions, and moving wealth from less liquid assets (such as equities) into money on a continuous basis results in transaction costs.

The speculative motive states that individuals move wealth into money when bond yields are low (to avoid capital losses on bonds) and out of money into bonds when yields are high (to speculate on potential gains and avoid capital losses on bonds). The portfolio motive states that, since the return on money is constant, and capital gains and losses do not occur, money provides an anchor to one's portfolio that stabilizes its performance. While holding money has the disadvantage of a zero or low yield, that same feature yields a distinct advantage in a zero possibility for a capital loss.[*] This makes money a desirable method of holding wealth. Another motive is the precautionary motive for holding money, which states that money serves as a form of insurance against uncertain necessary transactions that might require payment with money—such as medical emergencies.[†]

Expanding on and combining the speculative motive, the portfolio motive, and the precautionary motive, we can think of holding money as having an optional value. Money gives the holder the right, but not the obligation, to acquire something without incurring the transaction cost of converting from a less liquid asset (such as an equity or real property). This transaction could occur in an unfavorable circumstance, such as during a medical emergency, or when an opportunity arises to make a purchase of something (such as a good, service, financial instrument) that randomly dips below its true (average) market value.

Consider the following variables related to this notion of money as an option, where (S_{AVG}) is the market (average) nominal price for a market basket of commodities or assets, constant over time, and

(K) is the amount of money held that gives the holder the ability (the right) to acquire (K)'s worth of a market basket of commodities or assets whose nominal value is (K). Purchase can be made up to time (T). Assume that, for the moment, (at time T_0, $K = S_{AVG}$), the nominal price level. (St) = The actual price of a market basket of goods or assets at time (t); a variable whose mean is (S_{AVG}); assumed to follow Brownian motion:‡

- σ = A measure of the volatility, or dispersion, of $(St / St - 1)$, either across time or geography
- T = The period of time for which the distribution of prices is stable with mean (S_{AVG})
- r = The excess return on the best alternative risk-free asset above the return, if any, paid on money holdings

Under the above framework, individuals receive payments in amounts of money (K), which, on average, can be used to acquire one basket of assets or commodities whose average nominal price is (S_{AVG}). At time 0, the value of receiving (K) is equivalent to receiving one market basket. These baskets, however, randomly vary in price (S_t) over time. Individuals use money to take advantage of this price variation, choosing to buy when the price is at or below the average, and not to buy when the price is above the average. Figure 7.29 shows the payoff from holding money, which is very similar to the payoff from holding a put option.**

The model above, based on option pricing theory, suggests that holding money is more valuable and therefore demanded more when:

1. (σ), the measure of volatility of price changes (inflation), or price dispersion or pricing uncertainty is higher,
2. (T) (the period in which money can be utilized in a volatile environment) or maturity is longer,
3. (K / S_{AVG}) the real purchasing power of money is higher (assumed to be 1 in the above framework),
4. The risk-free interest rate that could be earned on the best alternative asset to money is lower.

Figure 7.30 shows the demand for money with respect to the interest rate (a traditional view) and how it shifts with changes in the above parameters (non-traditional). Because money can be used to buy anything (unlike a standard financial option, which is usually tied to only one underlying asset or commodity), the multi-asset optional value of money should be higher than that of any option on a single asset. Table 7.12 compares consumer price index volatility between China and the United States and equity market volatility (SSE and New York Stock Exchange). Since 1990, both have been about five times more volatile in China than in the United States. The greater volatility suggests a greater option value to holding onto money in China (when all other aspects are equal) and this is consistent with actual money holdings. Furthermore, in this light, money is not just an anchor (as in the portfolio motive), but an actual hedge in which the return varies inversely with a basket containing many assets and commodities. While we have argued earlier in this chapter that Chinese citizens hold too much of their wealth in money, options theory points toward the opposite conclusion. Finally, we note that we are discussing the positive role that volatility of prices play in money demand—not the average negative return, also known as the inflation rate. In fact, a higher anticipated inflation rate channeled via the interest rate (item 4 above) would reduce the demand for money.

*Of course, for foreigners holding US currency, a capital gain or loss can take the form of an appreciation or depreciation. This is the exception that proves the rule—most foreign currencies do not fully meet the threshold for being "money" in another country.

†In fact, the availability of medical insurance in China is still quite limited. Most doctors, hospitals, and clinics require payment in cash prior to treatment.

‡The index (*T*) could instead be measured at a point in time but be a spatial index of geographic location where prices vary by location according to a mean, S_{AVG}. In this case, the holder of (*K*) dollars would have the option of purchasing at a particular location.

**Put options give the holder the right but not the obligation to sell something at a fixed price. As an alternative formulation, nominal prices (*K*) could be "sticky" for a time period (*T*), while the underlying equilibrium price (*St*) randomly moves above or below (*K*). In this case, the variable of interest would be (*K* / *St*). Since the purchase (sale) of money can be made at any time up to (*T*), the option would be an American rather than a European option.

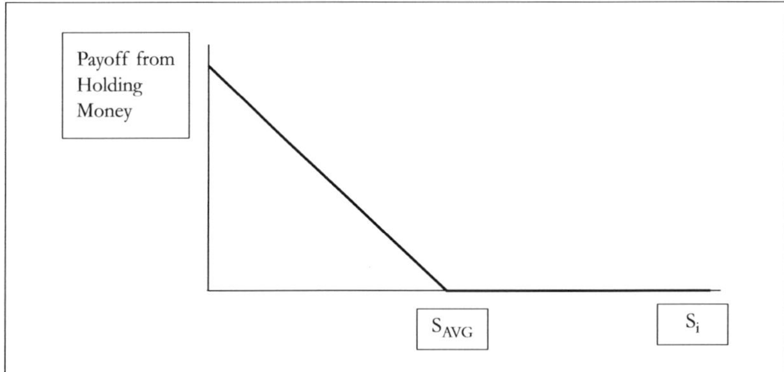

Figure 7.29 Money is a multi-asset option in which the strike price (S_{AVG}) represents some composite of either asset or goods/services prices.
Source: Author created.

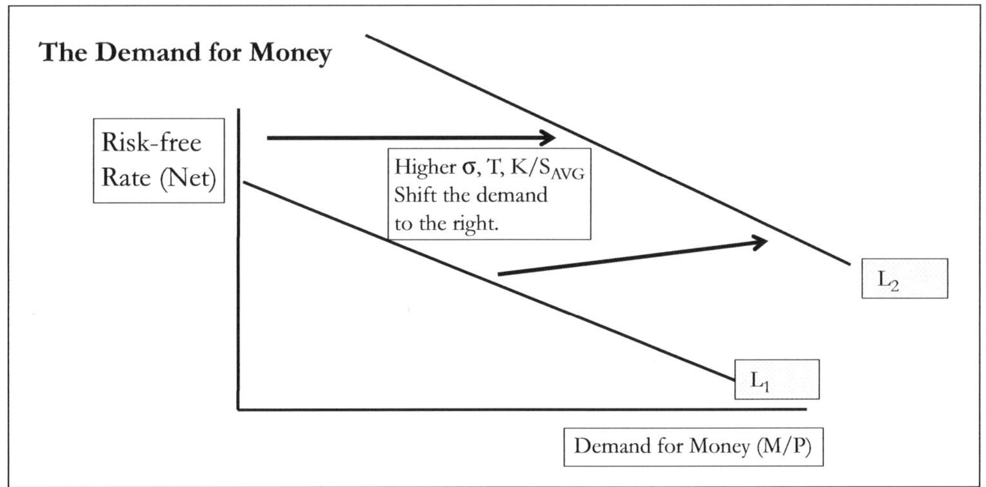

Figure 7.30 Theory predicts that the higher volatility of inflation and the higher the return on other financial assets, the greater the demand for money will be.
Source: Author created.

	Consumer Price Index Annual Inflation and Volatility 1990–2018		**Equity Market Annual Returns (Geometric) and Volatility 1990–2018 (Shanghai Stock Exchange and Broad Market Index United States)**	
	China	**United States**	**China**	**United States**
Average Percent Change	5.3%	2.6%	7.8%	6.8%
Volatility or SD	6.3%	1.2%	68.2%	12.1%

Table 7.12 Both the volatility of inflation and asset returns is higher in China than in the United States. The option value of money is one more reason to hold on to money in China.
Source: Author created based on data from the Federal Reserve Economic Database and the Shanghai Stock Exchange.

Challenging Questions for China (and the Student): Chapter 7

1. Go to the Federal Reserve Economic Database (FRED) and provide three different charts depicting China's money supply, with at least one in terms of China's real money supply.
2. Explain China's relatively large holdings of M1 in terms of the transactions motive, precautionary motive, or holding of wealth motive. In terms of excess money holdings (relative to the United States), which factor appears most important?
3. Using the Walras relationship, explain the impact of an excess supply of money on other asset prices (the prices of other ways of holding wealth) in China. Be specific about which assets you are referring to.
4. Suppose new ways of holding wealth start to appear in China (as in the case of Taobao and other internet bankers offering high-yielding money market funds).
   a. Explain the impact on bank deposits (sight deposits, for example) as Chinese citizens learn of these opportunities.
   b. Is the arrival of this alternative a good or bad thing? What might be the impact on the prices in equity or real estate markets?
   c. Why might China's Banking Regulatory Commission cast a wary (regulatory) eye toward such new asset classes?
5. Go to FRED and provide monthly seasonally-adjusted and non-seasonally-adjusted money supplies for China. Calculate (infer) the seasonal adjustment factor for China.
6. If China's capital markets were fully open (which they are not), explain how you might arbitrage the seasonal difference in credit demands between China and the United States as a hedge fund manager.
7. Explain the notion of "directed credit" and its relative importance in China compared to the United States as a tool of monetary policy.
8. Explain why, in periods of normal economic growth, capital adequacy types of rules will allow for more rapid loan growth in China than in the United States. Explain why, in times of financial turmoil when companies are losing money, such rules may slow lending growth more dramatically in China compared to the United States.
9. In the first half of September, 2014, it was estimated that China's PBC lent the five largest (including the Bank of Communications) Chinese banks around RMB 100 billion to spur slowing economic growth.
   a. Using some economic models discussed in this chapter, explain how this policy is intended to have an impact on the real economy.

   b. Because the injection of high-powered money came not through OMOs, but through some of the other monetary policy tools (such as discount window lending) discussed in this chapter, Western economists criticized the move as a step backward in terms of financial market liberalization in China. Discuss.

10. If (*r*) is 0.13, and the current money multiplier (M2 / Monetary Base) is 6.1, calculate the currency to deposit ratio (*c*).
11. Explain why China pays a lower rate on excess reserves than on required reserves, while the United States pays the same rate on both types of reserves. (Hint: The US uses the rate on reserves as a policy tool).
12. In Macro Finance Insight 7.3, we suggest that the past scheme of interest rate ceilings and floors at banks has allowed for excessive lending by banks, harming economic efficiency. Explain the mechanism under which this would occur.

References

Arora, Raksha. 2005. "Homeownership Soars in China." *Gallup*, 1 March, https://news.gallup.com/poll/15082/homeownership-soars-china.aspx.

Bernanke, Ben S. and Mark Gertler. 1995. "Inside the Black Box: The Credit Channel of Monetary Policy Transmission." *Journal of Economic Perspectives*, 9(4), pp. 27–48.

Bernanke, Ben S. 2002. Speech delivered at the National Association of Business Economists. 15 October, New York, NY.

British Broadcasting Corporation World News Service. 2014. "China Injects Fresh Cash into Banks." 21 January, https://www.bbc.com/news/business-25822544.

Central People's Government of the People's Republic of China (中华人民共和国中央人民政府). 2016. Translated into English by the Center for Strategic and Emerging Technologies at Georgetown University, https://cset.georgetown.edu/wp-content/uploads/Circular-of-the-State-Council-on-Issuing-the-National-13th-Five-Year-Plan-for-the-Development-of-Strategic-Emerging-Industries.pdf.

Chaudhury, K. N. 1990. *Asia Before Europe: Economy and Civilization of the Indian Ocean from the Rise of Islam to 1750*. Cambridge: Cambridge University Press.

Conway, Paul, Richard Herd, and Thomas Chalaux. 2010. "Reforming China's Monetary Policy Framework to Meet Domestic Objectives." OECD Economics Department Working Paper no. 822.

Federal Reserve Bank of St. Louis. 2013. "Home Ownership Rate for the United States." Accessed 9 May, 2014, http://research.stlouisfed.org/fred2/series/USHOWN.

Federal Reserve Board of Governors and U.S. Commerce Department. 2014. "Federal Reserve Statistical Release: Flow of Funds Accounts, Table Z.1." Bureau of Economic Analysis, https://www.federalreserve.gov/releases/z1/.

Franses, Philip and Heleen Mees. 2010. "Approximating the DGP of China's Quarterly GDP." Econometric Institute Research Paper no. EI-2010–04, Rotterdam: Erasmus School of Economics, Econometric Institute.

Fukumoto, Tomoyuki, Masato Yigashi, and Yasumari Inamura. 2010. "Effectiveness of Window Guidance and Financial Environment—in Light of Japan's Experience of Financial Liberalization and a Bubble Economy." *Bank of Japan Review*, 2010-E-4.

Geiger, M. 2008. "Instruments of Monetary Policy in China and Their Effectiveness: 1994–2006." United Nations Conference on Trade and Development, Discussion Paper no. 187.

Glick, Reuven and Michael Hutchison. 2009. "Navigating the Trilemma: Capital Flows and Monetary Policy in China." *Journal of Asian Economics*, 20(3), pp. 205–24.

Goodfriend, Marvin and Eswar Prasad. 2006. "A Framework for Independent Monetary Policy in China." IMF Working Paper no. 06/111.

Kamber, G., and M. S. Mohanty. 2018. "Do Interest Rates Play a Major Role in Monetary Policy Transmission in China?" BIS Working Paper no. 714.

Ma, Guonan, Yan Xiandong, and Liu Xi. 2011. "China's Evolving Reserve Requirements." BIS Working Paper no. 360.

Mehrotra, Aaron and Jose R. Sanchez-Fung. 2010. "China's Monetary Policy and the Exchange Rate." Federal Reserve Bank of San Francisco, Working Paper Series no. 2010–19.

National Bureau of Statistics. 2012. *China Statistical Yearbook*. Beijing: China Statistics Press.

Needham, J. 1954. *Science and Civilisation in China: Volume 1*. Cambridge: Cambridge University Press.

Obstfeld, Maurice, Jay C. Shambaugh, and Alan M. Taylor. 2004. "The Trilemma in History: Tradeoffs among Exchange Rates, Monetary Policies, and Capital Mobility." NBER Working Paper no. 10396.

Obstfeld, Maurice. 2012. "Financial Flows, Financial Crises and Global Imbalances." *Journal of International Money and Finance*, 31(3), pp. 469–80.

Porter, Nathan and TengTeng Xu. 2009. *What Drives China's Interbank Market?* Washington, DC: International Monetary Fund.

Porter, Ruth D. and Judith A. Judson. 1996. "The Location of U.S. Currency: How Much Is Abroad?" *Federal Reserve Bulletin*, pp. 883–903.

Shu, Chang and Brian Ng. 2010. "Monetary Stance and Policy Objectives in China: A Narrative Approach." *China Economic Issues*, 1(10), pp. 1–40.

Tor, Maria and Saad Sarfraz. 2014. "Largest 100 Banks in the World." *SNL Financial*, 9 July, https://seekingalpha.com/instablog/388783-christopher-menkin/3052135-largest-100-banks-in-the-world-snl-financial-exclusive.

Yang, Lien-Sheng. 1957. "Economic Justification for Spending—An Uncommon Idea in Traditional China." *Harvard Journal of Asiatic Studies*, 20(1/2), pp. 36–52.

Endnotes

1. Gold has often served as money because it is difficult to counterfeit, does not corrode, is easily divisible, has a limited short-run supply, and has the added advantage of easy conversion to uses in the real economy—such as for specialized electronics (its malleability and conductivity are unique) and jewelry.
2. But historical estimates (https://bit.ly/3eB588z) suggest that between 50 and 60 percent of US currency is held outside of the United States (mostly in 100 dollar bills). This suggests that Chinese still hold about twice as much currency as do US citizens as a share of GDP.
3. The flip-side of the liquidity definition is the impact on the price of what is being acquired. If purchases can be made of a good, service, or asset with virtually no impact on its price, we describe the associated market as being "liquid."
4. Some have suggested that the small denomination is one way that the government discourages corrupt practices, such as paying off government officials for special favors. One could say it promotes transparency in financial transactions. The Law of Unintended Consequences does come into play here—gifts of expensive watches or jewelry come to fill the same purpose. Citizens, meanwhile, have limited ways to hold their wealth beyond cash (see the discussion on Walras's Law). Thus, they place greater trust in cash holdings, as opposed to other ways of holding wealth. In Chapter 5, we discussed how a limited range of available assets limits diversification possibilities. This limitation, in turn, creates a need for even greater precautionary savings. The same argument would apply to holding wealth in one of its least risky forms—cash.
5. Money is generally considered risk-free because it does not suffer from capital gains or losses like stocks and bonds. It can, however, experience a gradual loss of purchasing power through inflation. Furthermore, in an international context, whenever the exchange rate moves up or down, money experiences a capital gain or loss in global currency markets.
6. China is currently in the process of allowing for greater holdings of foreign assets by individuals.
7. It is important to remember that an estimated 60 percent of the US monetary base is held outside of the United States, suggesting a larger actual multiplier in the United States than in China. Furthermore, post-financial crisis there was a surge in reserves (currency) by the Fed. In the absence of these factors, the US money multiplier would be higher and closer to that of China.

8. A repurchase agreement is an agreement to sell a security now and buy it back at a fixed date at (typically) a higher price. When a central bank sells a security, it is in effect borrowing money (draining liquidity) at an implicit interest rate. By analogy, reverse repos involve the central bank buying a security now (lending money) and returning it later at a higher price. These types of transactions have the benefits of both collateralization and hedging, since the holder of the security lends with the security as collateral but capital gains or losses on the security accrue to the borrower.
9. In May, 2012, China became the first foreign government allowed to acquire US Treasury instruments directly from the US government rather than going through one of the US-based primary dealers. Given China's vast holdings of US treasuries (at least USD 1 trillion), the United States agreed to allow purchases at a wholesale price. China's PBC interfaces with about 20 different primary dealers.
10. Since the 2008 financial crisis, the Fed has transacted in a wide range of non-public financial assets of longer maturities in order to flatten the yield curve and to increase the quantity of money. This policy is known as quantitative easing.
11. In the United States, there are three types of discount window lending rates: primary credit, secondary credit, and seasonal. The primary credit rate applies to sound financial institutions temporarily in need of funds to meet their reserve requirement. The secondary rate applies to banks that are encountering more serious liquidity needs. Seasonal borrowing applies to reserve imbalances that result from normal seasonal fluctuations, such as holiday demands. In early 2003, the Fed discontinued the use of the term "discount rate" in favor of these definitions.
12. Geiger (2008) notes that the governor of the PBC has a higher political ranking within the Communist Party than bank presidents in China; therefore, such guidance is fully effective.
13. In the United States, reserve requirements only apply to net transaction accounts—liquid demand deposits. In China, reserve requirements apply to bank deposit accounts of all maturities.
14. The United States began paying interest on reserves in October, 2008.
15. High reserve requirements are also a form of financial repression because reserves typically pay low interest rates. The government collects an implicit tax on these reserves, resulting from its ability to create and use money now while paying very little interest on it—a phenomenon known as "seignorage" or "the king's right to create money." Given China's high reserve requirements and relatively low interest

paid on those reserves, it is likely to be a significant source of revenue to the central government.

16. The Depository Institution Deregulation and Monetary Control Act of 1980 disabled these features of Regulation Q; the Dodd-Frank Wall Street Reform Act of 2010 did the same for demand deposits.
17. As part of normal OMOs, central banks buy government securities. But when the central bank is independent from the central government, these purchases typically come from the general public, not directly from the government. When central banks do buy directly from the government and fully fund the central government's financing needs, we have an accommodative monetary policy. As we shall see, this can be inflationary and/or crowd out the private sector.
18. AIG, which went bankrupt in 2009, was a global insurance company based in the United States. AIG was founded on 19 December, 1919 by Cornelius Vander Starr in Shanghai.
19. Such impacts have, on occasion, occurred, suggesting that controlling inflows and outflows is not easy.
20. China's four large state-owned banks were technically bankrupt by 2003 as a result of decades of bad policy-mandated loans. The ceilings and floors were a critical element in their return to profitability and recapitalization. Furthermore, asset management companies were created to take many of the bad loans off the books of these banks, and government assets were—in effect—substituted for the removed bad loans.

8

MONETARY POLICY IN ACTION

慈不掌兵，义不掌财

Neither Controlling an Army nor Controlling Finances is for the Timid

The tools mentioned in the last chapter are used to improve economic performance. Figure 8.1 provides the traditional mechanism by which monetary policy works—what is known as the "transmission mechanism." It also depicts the enhanced set of tools and goals included in China's monetary policy (note that enhancements are shaded). Clearly, the transmission mechanism in China is even more complex than the traditional one, since it includes multiple tools and goals. In this chapter, we will explain why. The transmission mechanism represents a chain of actions and outcomes, starting with the central bank trying to either stimulate or slow the economy using the tools identified in Figure 8.1.

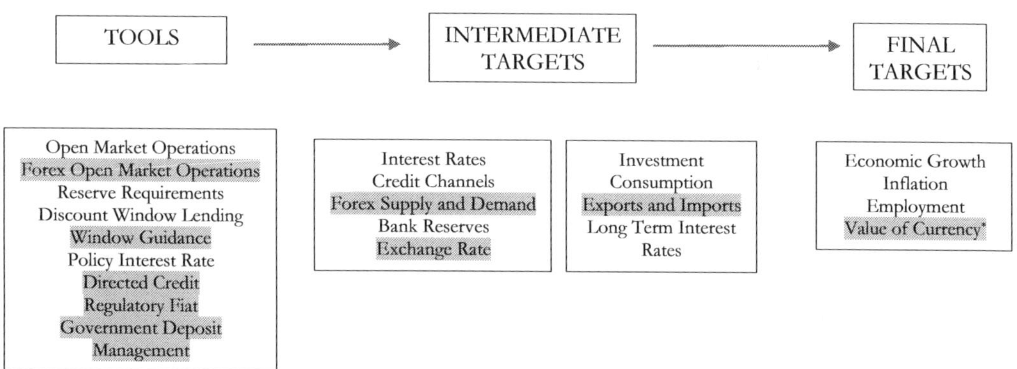

Figure 8.1 The traditional transmission mechanism in the United States and the more complex mechanism in China (shaded text indicates additional tools/targets in China).
Source: Author created.
*Value of currency is included in final target for China, since that is included in PBC main policy mandate.

The initial policy action typically impacts bank excess reserves, which in turn impact the short-term interest rates that banks charge each other (the interbank market rate), then longer-term interest rates, and finally end-users. China, historically, has implemented changes in the required reserve ratio rather than targeting excess reserves and interbank interest rates, but in recent years it has started to rely more on the latter as a policy tool. China's transmission system also affects the availability of credit—influencing the size of the loan or even the possibility that a loan application is turned down. As these types of lending constraints are passed on to companies and consumers within the economy, their decisions to purchase investment goods or consumer goods are affected. These decisions, in turn, impact overall economic activity.

The transmission mechanism can be shown graphically by using the investment-savings/liquidity-money demand (IS/LM) framework found in Chapter 9 and described in Figure 8.2. The LM curve shifts to the right due to the increase in the monetary base, which creates an excess supply of money in the interbank market. Interbank rates fall as a result of the excess money supply. Investment and other interest-sensitive components of demand rise as economy-wide, long-term interest rates fall. The increased demand triggers rising output and employment on the part of firms.

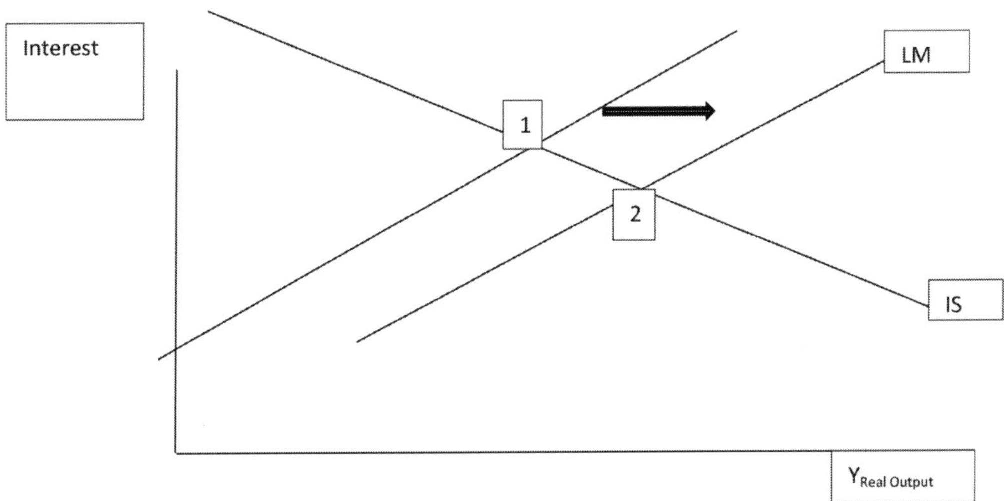

Figure 8.2 When the money supply increases, the LM curve shifts rightward, causing interest rates to fall and real output to rise from point 1 to point 2. This is the standard transmission mechanism.
Source: Author created.

Clearly, the domino-like chain reaction triggered by monetary policy is long and complex, which explains why the great economist John Maynard Keynes doubted the effectiveness of expansionary monetary policy when used alone, especially during an economic downturn. As we discussed in Chapter 7, Chinese monetary authorities have added even more tools to their toolkit for conducting monetary policy. So why are these additional tools and interventions needed in China?

Broad Goals of Monetary Policy

In a speech before the Bank for International Settlement (https://bit.ly/36qmfXQ) in 2018, Li Gang, Governor of The People's Bank of China (PBC), described the PBC's mandate by saying:

> *The Law of the People's Bank of China explicitly stipulates that the ultimate goal of China's monetary policy is to maintain currency stability and thereby facilitate economic growth. To maintain currency stability has two tiers of meanings: internally it means to maintain prices stable and externally it means to keep RMB [renminbi] exchange rate basically stable at an adaptive and equilibrium level. (1)*

In recent years, we have seen evidence of China's added goal of exchange rate management. Between 2014 and 2017, China depleted its foreign exchange reserves by close to USD (US dollars) 1 trillion. A good chunk of this amount was related to efforts to support the RMB in international currency markets by way of the PBC purchasing offshore RMB with USD. This move was precipitated by earlier efforts toward RMB internationalization (capital mobility) that came up against the policy trilemma (discussed below). As markets turned against the RMB, the PBC responded with massive purchases of its own currency. The impact was a reduction in RMB offshore liquidity at the cost of reduced foreign reserves.

Meanwhile, the Federal Reserve System has the following broad goals, as set out in a 1977 amendment to the Federal Reserve Act: "Maintain maximum sustainable output and employment and stable prices" (FRB of San Francisco 2004).

As we will discuss, this difference in goals helps to explain some of China's variations in operating policy. For example, one difference in operating policy relates to key intermediate targets. In the United States, the emphasis on the interbank market interest rate has been much greater than in China. Or, for example, a US long-run target of 2 percent inflation is a stated goal; but, in China, maintaining exchange rate stability has been a key policy target. In the next section, we present a simple theory explaining how different end-policy goals lead to divergent policy paths. In summary, both countries, like virtually all countries around the world, view monetary policy as a tool to achieve price stability and economic growth. China and the United States, however, have very different means to achieve those ends.

The Chinese Dilemma and the Policy Trilemma

The Basic Conflict

One simple way to think of China's reliance on a multiplicity of tools for managing monetary policy is in terms of the simple curves for the demand and supply of money. Figure 8.3 depicts a standard demand curve found in any introductory economics course with price on one axis and demand on the other. For any given price (P_1), there is a corresponding quantity (Q_1) determined by the shape of the demand curve (preferences). A combination of (P_1) and (Q_2) will simply not work unless we intervene in the market in some regulatory fashion. Even then, determining (P_1) and (Q_2) independently is usually only temporarily possible (in the short run). In Figure 8.4, the y-axis shows the opportunity cost of holding money—the interest rate on an asset that is less liquid than M2 (for example, a government or corporate bond). The x-axis shows the amount of real money, defined as (M2 / *P*), where (*P*) is a measure of the price level—for example, the consumer price index or a gross domestic product (GDP) deflator. This is a simple demand-and-supply figure in which quantity (M2 / *P*) represents the amount of real balances supplied and demanded, while the price of money is the interest rate (*r*) or opportunity cost of holding our wealth in a particular asset—namely, money. The higher the interest rates on alternative assets (such as treasury or corporate bonds) the lower the demand for money.

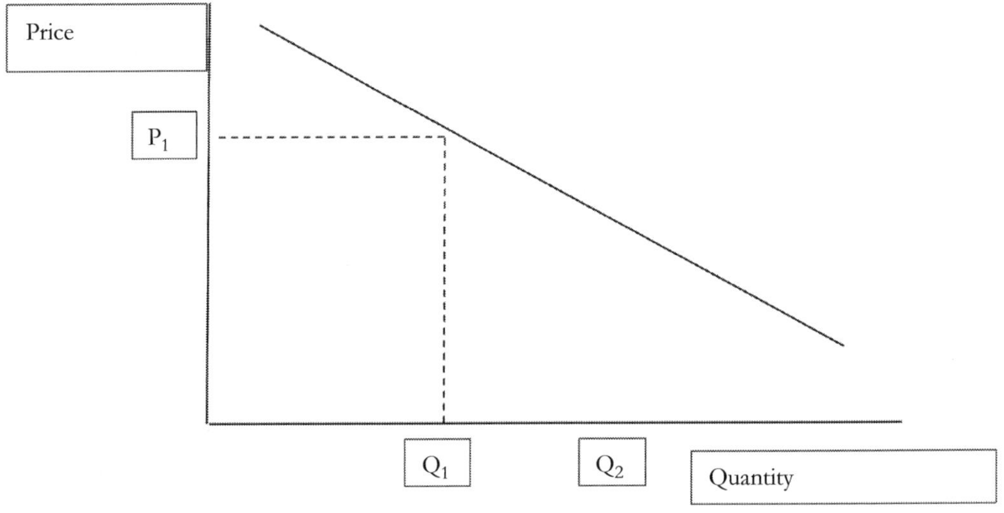

Figure 8.3 In a well-functioning market, the demand curve will determine the price if a quantity is supplied, and demand will determine quantity if a price is offered. A point at (Q2, P1) would not be consistent.
Source: Author created.

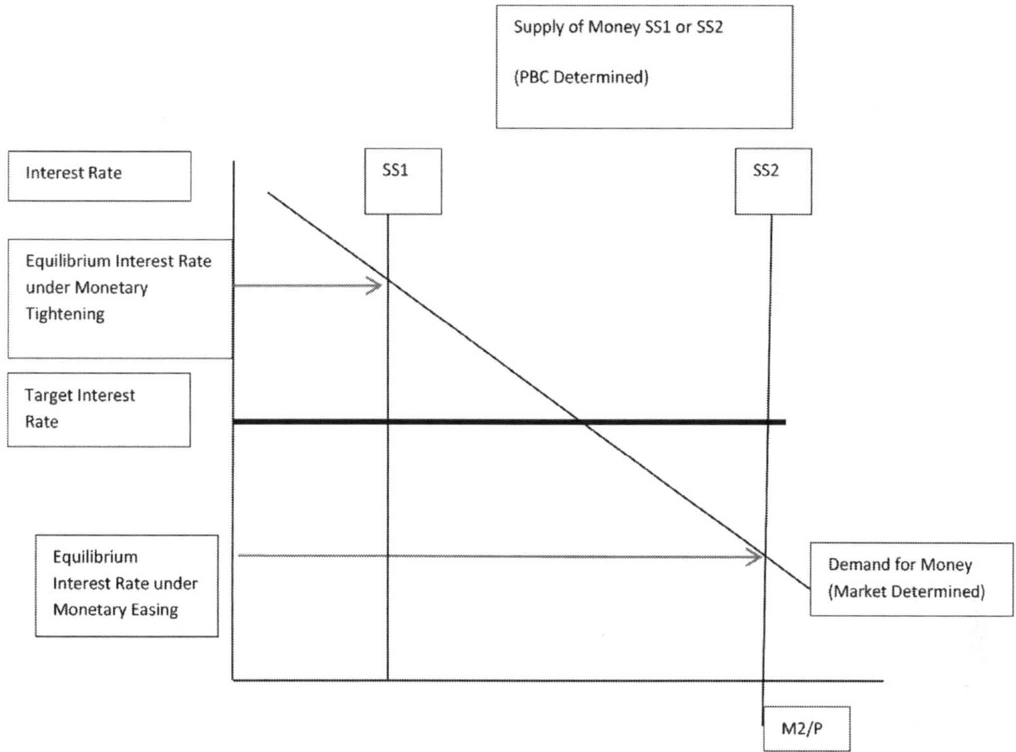

Figure 8.4 Once an amount of money is supplied to the market, the equilibrium interest rate will be determined such that SS2 and the demand for money intersect. To achieve a different target interest rate would require non-market intervention.
Source: Author created.

The vertical lines in the figure show the supply of money as determined by the PBC (central bank). Since money supply is controlled by the central bank, we assume it is vertical—the supply is constant for any interest rate. If the PBC reduces the supply of money (using the tools mentioned above), the supply curve will shift to the left (as in SS_1). On the other hand, if the PBC wishes to ease the money supply, it will shift the supply curve to the right (as in SS_2). Each shift implies a higher or lower equilibrium interest rate, in which the demand for money equals the supply of money. The dilemma for the PBC, however, is that while it may want to move the supply of money to impact either output, exchange rates, or inflation, it may prefer a different interest rate than the implied equilibrium rate. The control of interest rates might be triggered by China's desire, in recent decades, to control the exchange rate. The desire to control the amount of money and the interest rate (or, alternatively, both the quantity and the price) at non-equilibrium levels, has led to the use of multiple monetary policy tools.

Supplementary tools—such as interest rate ceilings, directed lending, or window guidance—are part of a package of efforts to control the two variables of money and interest rates. Attempting to control both can mean shortages and surpluses of money and credit—a situation in which more direct or dirigiste methods need to be employed. Most central banks only target the interbank interest rate; China targets both M2 and the interest rate (the latter in order to control exchange rates) and, as we discussed in Chapter 7, it also targets the term structure of interest rates and even interest rates in specific markets, e.g., the real estate mortgage market. After the Great Financial Crisis (GFC), even the Federal Reserve ("the Fed") found itself in the awkward position of trying to control both rates and quantities. The policy of quantitative easing, discussed below, resulted in equilibrium interbank rates below what the Fed considered desirable. As an antidote to this problem (https://bit.ly/3geXqmd), it began paying a higher rate on excess reserves held by banks—thus, establishing a floor for interbank interest rates.

The PBC's efforts at controlling both the price and the quantity of money, for the sake of controlling the exchange rate, are part of broader phenomenon seen across many countries and over many centuries (Obstfeld, Shambaugh, and Taylor 2004). It is known in the field of international finance as the "policy trilemma." The policy trilemma states that, while the following policy intermediate targets:

1. Having a fixed exchange rate;
2. Controlling monetary policy (controlling domestic interest rates);
3. Allowing capital to flow in and out of the economy (capital mobility);

are often viewed as useful and desirable by policy-makers, they are also in conflict with each other and are therefore inconsistent.

A fixed exchange rate means that a country's central bank can, in a sustainable way, act as a market maker in its own currency—buying and selling at a fixed rate. The opposite of a fixed exchange rate is a floating exchange rate that is determined by market forces and fluctuates continuously based on supply and demand. In normal circumstances, a floating exchange rate would not have a central bank intervening to achieve a particular exchange rate. Figure 8.5 shows that China's exchange rate roughly follows a step pattern, an indication that the RMB has been tied to the USD for prolonged periods of time. Contrast this with Figure 8.6, showing the USD against the Swiss franc. Here, we see the erratic movements of that exchange rate—a clear indication of a floating or flexible rate moved by market forces.

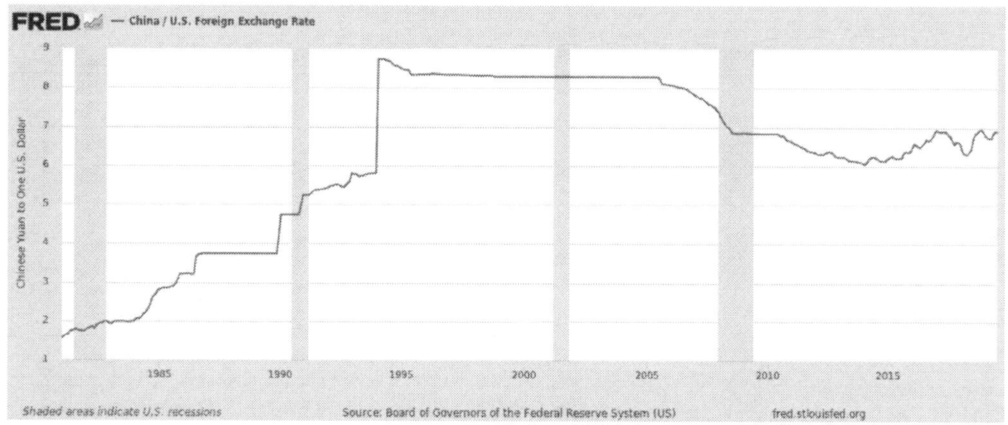

Figure 8.5 The low short-run volatility of the USD-RMB exchange rate suggests that the PBC intervenes to maintain a desired non-market-determined rate.
Source: Author created based on data from the Federal Reserve Economic Database.

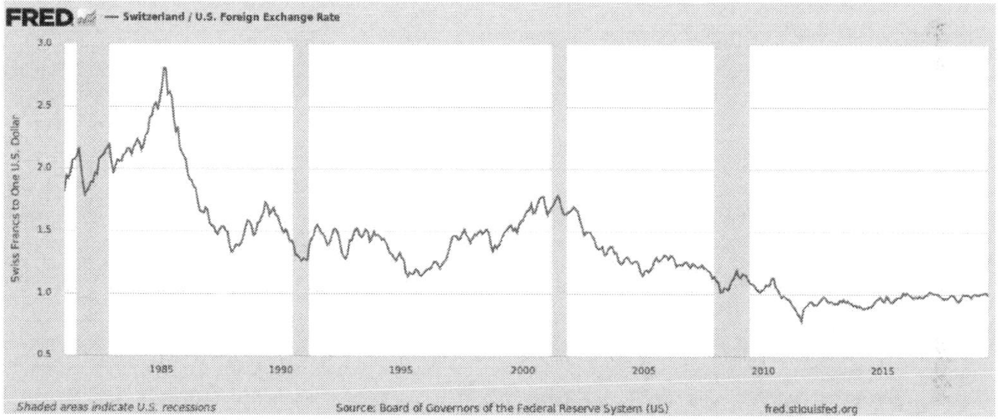

Figure 8.6 The USD-Swiss Franc exchange rate's wiggly pattern tells us that this is exchange rate is responsive to market forces.
Source: Author created based on data from the Federal Reserve Economic Database.

Controlling monetary policy means achieving a target interest rate (such as the interbank rate) via the monetary policy tools discussed earlier. Allowing capital mobility means the regulatory permission of unfettered movement of funds into and out of the country for purposes of financial investment—also known as "convertibility on the capital account." A related but different concept is "current account convertibility," or allowing unfettered access to foreign exchange for international trade in goods and services. While virtually all economists, especially those at international organizations such as the International Monetary Fund (IMF), have encouraged countries to adopt current account convertibility, they have been more cautious regarding capital account mobility.[1]

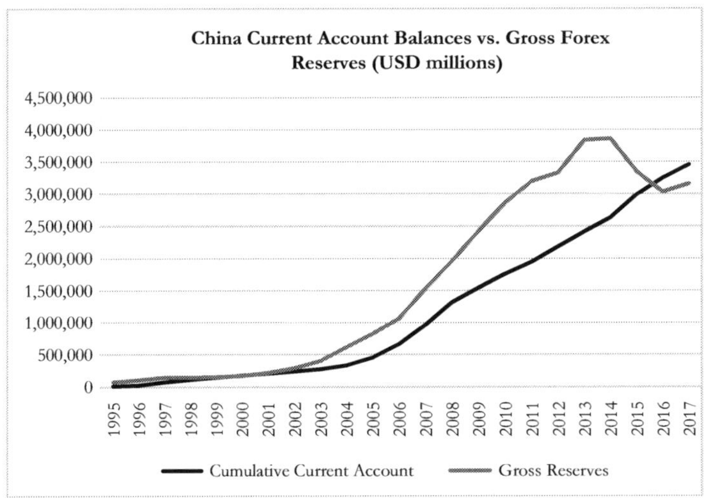

Figure 8.7 China's cumulative current account and foreign exchange reserves.
Source: Author created based on data from the International Monetary Fund Database.

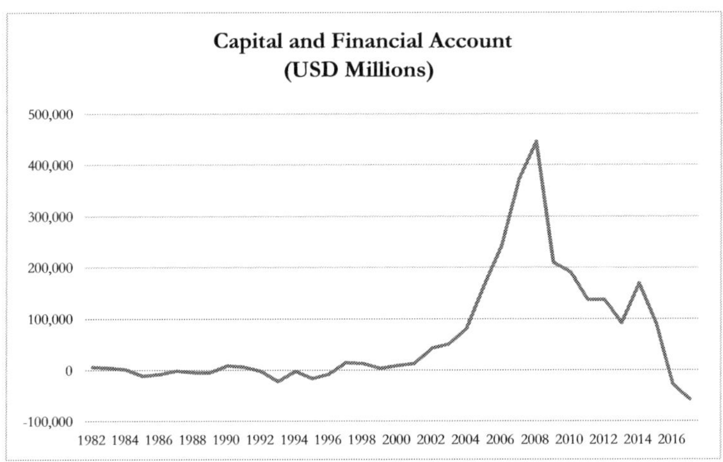

Figure 8.8 China's capital/financial account was a relatively insignificant part of the overall balance of payments picture until the 2000s.
Source: Author created based on data from the International Monetary Fund Database.

Macro Finance Insight 8.1: Current Account Surpluses and the Policy Trilemma

Figure 8.7 and Figure 8.8 show which factors have contributed to China's reserve accumulation. What is obvious in Figure 8.7 is the significance of current account items (rather than capital account items) in explaining China's foreign exchange reserve growth and, in turn, monetary growth. Capital account items (foreign direct investment [FDI] and financing flows) came to play an increasingly important role (Figure 8.8) after 2001. Figure 8.9 details the role of FDI in those capital account surpluses. After the GFC, increased borrowing on the capital account led to a large increase in external debt, as seen in Figure 8.10.

While the policy trilemma is expressed in the context of arbitrage opportunities and capital mobility, the reality for China is that, since 2004, a fixed exchange rate has presented a much simpler arbitrage opportunity: cheaper tradable goods for the rest of the world, particularly the United States. While China has largely controlled capital flows, the trade flow since 2001 (when China became a member of the World Trade Organization) has greatly impacted its money supply. In effect, China's example since 2004 is closer to the gold-specie mechanism.* This was arguably a self-correcting mechanism under the 19th-century gold standard, in which countries with trade imbalances could lose or gain gold, thereby shrinking or expanding domestic demand. This chain reaction would, either directly or via inflation, cause the country to restore balance on the current account. The gold-specie mechanism is essentially an earlier version of the policy trilemma, stating:

A country can only do two out of the following three:

1. Have a disequilibrium fixed exchange rate
2. Control monetary policy (controlling the domestic level of interest rates)
3. Have control over the trade balance

It is the second item above, in particular, with which China's monetary authorities have increasingly struggled.

*For further reading on this, see Chapters 19–20 in Krugman, Paul R., Maurice Obstfeld, and Marc Melitz. 2011. *International Economics (9th Edition)*. London: Pearson Addison-Wesley.

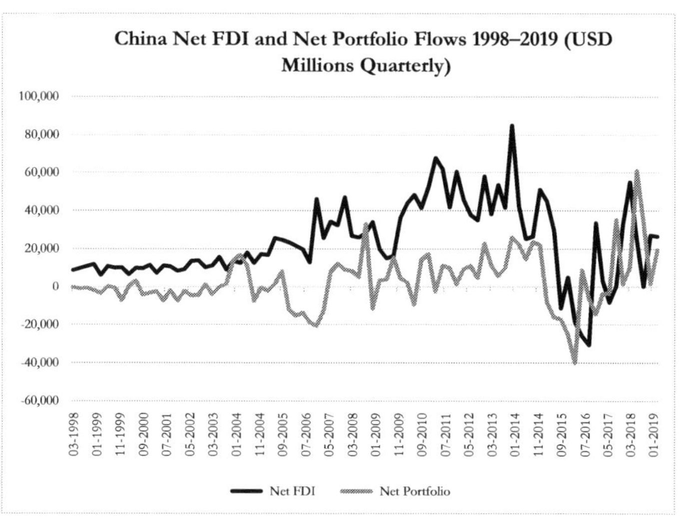

Figure 8.9 FDI and portfolio flows to China.
Source: Author created based on International Monetary Fund Database.

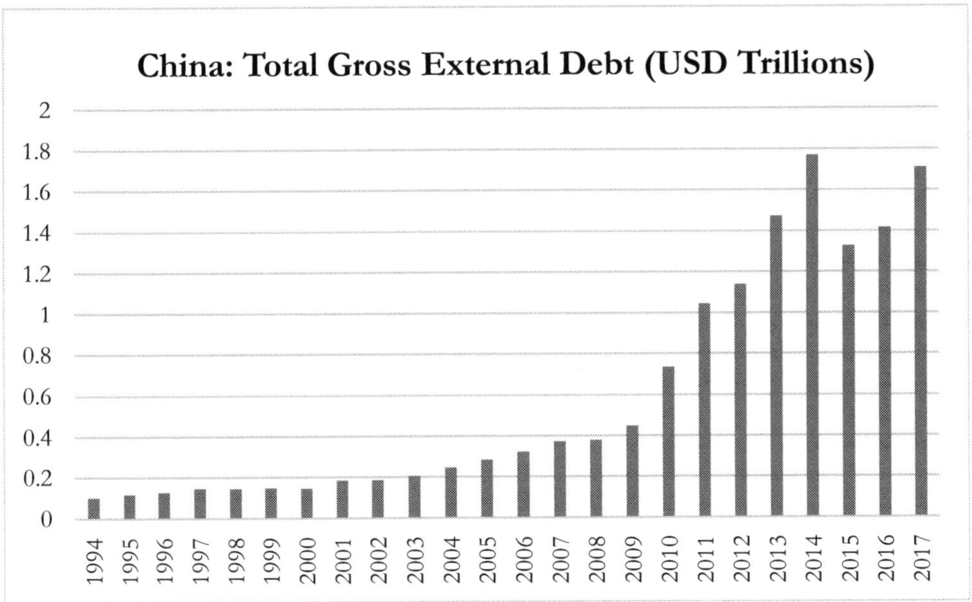

Figure 8.10 External debt in China has grown to a sufficiently large level to make currency exposure one more issue for policy-makers to consider when the RMB depreciates. Source: Author created based on World Bank World Development Indicators.

Capital Mobility and the Policy Trilemma

One benefit of greater capital mobility is either a lower cost of capital (for borrowing countries) or higher returns (for lending countries). Another benefit is global portfolio diversification. However, capital account mobility may result in destabilizing the real economy via disruptive capital inflows and outflows (hot money); thus, countries have been encouraged to ensure that their institutions and regulatory frameworks adequately support capital account convertibility. Obstfeld (1986) provides some excellent insights into the relaxation of capital controls in the post-World War II era worldwide—a practice that has gained momentum in emerging economies over the past 25 years.

To understand why a country can only achieve two out of the three policy targets mentioned above, examine Figure 8.11. The y-axis measures real returns in China versus the United States, taking into account both risk-adjusted interest rates and expected appreciation or depreciation of the exchange rate. The x-axis measures the net financial capital (money) leaving or entering China. If real returns are the same, then there will be no net movement (i.e., at the intersection of the x-axis and y-axis).

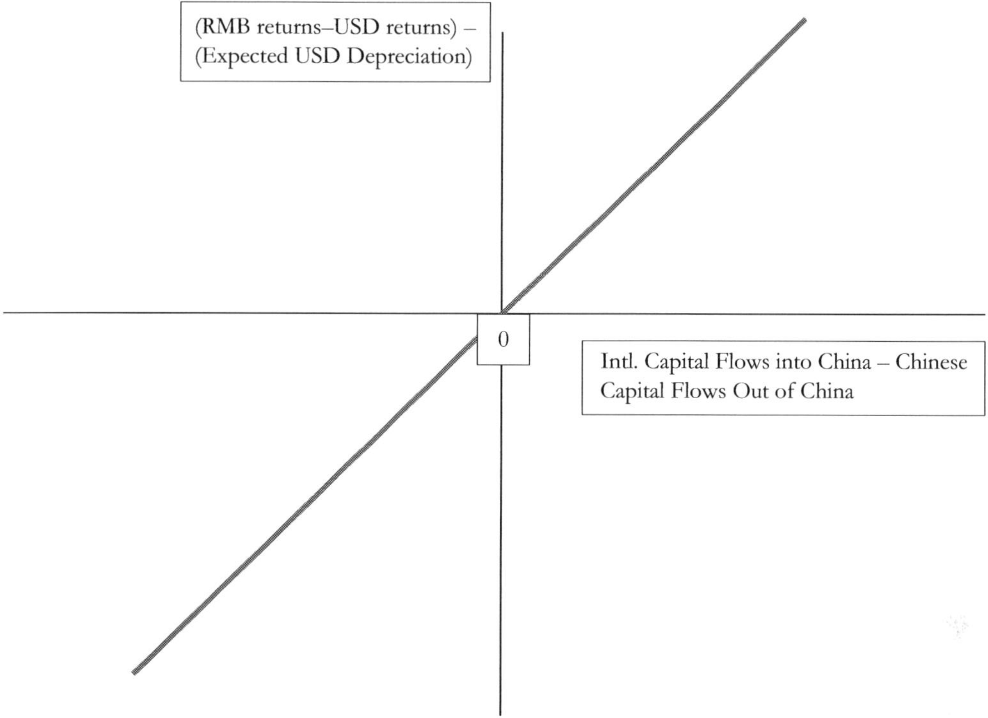

Figure 8.11 Capital will flow into and out of a country based on return differentials, including the anticipated effect of exchange rate changes.
Source: Author created.

If, however, real returns are higher in China (after taking into account anticipated changes in the exchange rate), then international capital would tend to flow into China. Consider the following expression, which represents the excess (+) or shortfall (-) of RMB versus USD returns on comparably risky assets:

Equation 1:

(RMB returns – USD returns) - (Expected USD Depreciation)

This expression is found on the y-axis of Figure 8.11—specifically, the last part of this expression "expected USD depreciation." While any positive or negative number could be used, depending on a variety of factors, let's consider two benchmark critical values. Under a stable fixed exchange rate regime, the value of this term would be 0 because the USD / RMB exchange rate would not be expected to change.

Under a floating exchange rate regime in which there is no arbitrage possibility, we would have:

Equation 2:

(RMB returns – USD returns) = (Expected USD Depreciation)

resulting in another benchmark value for the "expected USD depreciation" term above.[2]

When the interest differential equals the expected exchange rate depreciation or appreciation, we would expect that—after taking the exchange rate into account—capital movements into or out of China could not yield a return exceeding the amount earned at home. Now that we understand the framework, let's consider the first benchmark case—in which the exchange rate is fixed and the overall expression (Equation 1) equals 0. In this case, if the PBC raises interest rates (RMB returns) relative to USD returns, there will be a capital inflow into China from abroad. This capital inflow will lead, in the short run, to more money circulating in China's economy (a phenomenon we will explain shortly). This inflow, in turn, will place downward pressure on interest rates, reversing the initial efforts at raising them. Such pressure would persist until interest rates or returns in China were restored to their initial level. It is in this way that China could maintain a fixed exchange rate and international capital mobility but not maintain control over its interest rates. Other scenarios are possible, but they inevitably lead to the same conclusion. For example, a hike in interest rates that leads to a capital inflow could also be inflationary, making it difficult for China to remain competitive using a fixed exchange rate. In this scenario, China would have to stop fixing the exchange rate, and allow a weaker, more competitive RMB.

Now, let's consider the second benchmark value, (Equation 2), in which expected USD depreciation equals the return differential between China- and US-based assets. This condition would occur if the exchange rate were floating (not fixed), therefore allowing (under the trilemma) the two goals of capital mobility and control of the money supply (interest rates). In this case, if the PBC raises interest rates, any incipient capital inflow will cause the RMB to appreciate far above its fundamental long-run value such that its eventual expected depreciation just matches the return differential initially established by the PBC. In this way, we will never stray too far (and, in fact, we will return very quickly) to our 0 point on the graph. Since any return difference is exactly offset by an anticipated depreciation of the RMB, the PBC can maintain that return difference (unlike in the case of fixed exchange rates) and will have benefitted from both capital mobility and ultimate control over its own interest rates.

In the absence of capital mobility, a country's monetary policy can march to the beat of its own drum. That is to say, in the absence of the threat of capital flowing in or out of the country and subverting the goals of the central bank, a country can have a fixed exchange rate and also independently determine whether it wants a tight or expansionary (high interest rate or low interest rate) monetary policy. There are economies (such as those of Hong Kong and French-speaking West African countries) that choose not to have an independent monetary policy. Instead, they fix their exchange rate, remaining open to capital flows but surrendering their monetary policy to the partner country or region to which their currency is fixed (the United States in the case of Hong Kong; the eurozone in the case of French-speaking West Africa).

China and the United States have adopted different policy goals based on the trilemma perspective. Clearly, as with all large and important economies, both countries want to maintain control over their monetary policies (independent interest rates). Over the years, however, China has maintained a fixed and then a pegged exchange rate, while the US currency has floated freely since 1974. The third leg of the trilemma must also be different in both countries. The United States remains one of the most open economies with respect to capital flows, while China has attempted to maintain strict control over capital flows. It is clear that, as China's government moves toward greater capital account liberalization (more capital mobility), it must simultaneously allow greater flexibility in its exchange rate.

Obstfeld (2012) points out that the policy trilemma is not as stark a choice as it is usually presented to be. Rather, countries—including many in Asia—tend to adhere to more heterodox variations on the trilemma. That is to say, exchange rate policies may not be totally fixed or floating, capital mobility may not be completely open or closed, nor may monetary policy be fully surrendered or fully controlled. China would appear to be a prime example of these types of heterodox policies. For example, the IMF, in its 2018 publication of Annual Report on Exchange Arrangements and Restrictions (https://bit.ly/2Xvr4en), describes China's exchange rate as "crawl-like," something between floating and fixed. Efforts at RMB internationalization, already discussed, or the Stock Connect (https://bit.ly/3cwtI9P) program—linking Shanghai, Shenzhen, and Hong Kong stock markets for inbound equity investments—is an intermediate form of international capital mobility. Meanwhile, Ito and Kawai (2014) suggest that China's monetary policy is somewhat interdependent with United States monetary policy. Why is this? Obstfeld (2004) argues that, in fact, countries have important concerns beyond just monetary control—financial stability being a key one. In other words, Chinese authorities care not just about inflation and interest rates, but also about the stability of the banking system and the avoidance of financial crises. As such, they need to strike a balance that falls somewhere in the center, rather than at a particular corner, of the trilemma.

How does the above discussion pertain to China's need to use a much wider range of monetary policy tools? Trying to achieve all elements of the trilemma, albeit in a partial way, requires more policy intervention. Inflation, economic growth, the exchange rate, financial stability, and interest rates are just some of the many management targets that Chinese policy-makers have. More targets require more tools. Furthermore, China's comparative advantage in the production of labor-intensive goods and the broader range of assets presented by domestic financial market liberalization make outside investors increasingly eager to enter China's financial markets. The progressive integration of Hong Kong into China since 1997 has opened additional avenues for funds to flow in and out of China. (Note that Hong Kong's capital markets are ranked among the most open in the world.) China faces increasing challenges in its efforts to work its way around the policy trilemma. In short, fixing interest rates and the exchange rate when capital mobility is growing continuously is becoming more and more difficult. Chinese authorities have, as a result, evolved a broader array of monetary policy tools to temporarily offset the gravity-like force of the policy trilemma.

Sterilization and the Monetary Authority's Balance Sheet

Sterilization refers to the efforts of central banks to offset the impact of foreign exchange flows on the domestic money supply by using monetary tools such as open market operations. For example, if China receives substantial inflows of foreign exchange via exports, the financial system will exchange domestic currency for the foreign exchange receipts deposited by exporters.[3] That exchange, in turn, will increase the supply of money. To offset that increase, the PBC could either sell central bank bills or raise the reserve requirement of banks, thus offsetting the initial increase. To better understand this process, let's examine basic balance sheets of the PBC and the Fed in recent years. Macro Finance Insight 8.1 shows the important link between trade and capital flows on foreign currency holdings.

People's Bank of China	2007	2017	2019	2007–2019	2007–2019
	RMB Billions			Annual Percent Increase	Total Percent Increase
Total Assets	16,914.00	36,293.20	34,855.00	6.2%	106.07%
Foreign Assets	12,482.50	22,116.40	21,810.00	4.8%	74.72%
Loans to Government and Financial System	4,431.50	14,176.80	13,045.00	9.4%	194.37%
Total Liabilities and Owner's Equity	16,914.00	36,293.20	34,855.00	6.2%	106.07%
Currency	10,154.50	32,187.10	30,371.00	9.6%	199.09%
Liabilities to Government and Financial System	6,759.10	4,106.60	4,484.00	-3.4%	-33.66%

PBC Balance Sheet

Table 8.1 Unlike the Fed, the PBC holds substantial foreign exchange reserve assets as the basis for its money supply.
Source: Author created based on data from the International Monetary Fund Database.

Federal Reserve System	2007 (USD Billions)	2017 (USD Billions)	Percent Increase	Actual Increase (USD Billions)
Total Assets	894.3	4,448.7	17.4	3,554
Foreign Assets	16.2	(336.6)	-36.1%	-353
Loans to Government	752.3	2,271.8	11.7	1,520
Other Assets	125.8	2,513.5	34.9	2,388
Total Liabilities and Owner's Equity	894.3	4,448.7	17.4	3,554
Currency	791.8	1,569.7	7.1	778
Deposits of Financial Institutions	11.4	2,176.5	69.1	2,165
Other Liabilities and Owner's Equity	91.1	702.5	22.7	611

Table 8.2 The Fed's balance sheet ballooned with other assets, and their counterpart bank deposits, as a result of their aggressive response to the GFC.
Source: Author created based on data from the International Monetary Fund Database.

Table 8.1 and Table 8.2 present simplified recent balance sheets for each institution compared to those from just before the GFC. Central bank assets typically comprise the government obligations held by the bank and the foreign exchange cash or securities held by the bank. The central bank's liabilities are domestic currency, which it issues, and the deposits of financial institutions held at the central bank as either required or excess reserves. The Fed's balance sheet ballooned in this period due to the rapid expansion of credit facilities and credit following the GFC.

The PBC's balance sheet also grew rapidly during this period, primarily due to lending to financial institutions in response to the GFC and the secular decline in economic growth discussed in earlier chapters. Growth in foreign assets also led to a growing PBC balance sheet. Most of this growth on the asset side had, as a counterpart, the growth in currency holdings by companies and individuals. That the balance sheet in China grew more slowly than the Fed's highlights one key difference in monetary policy tools: China's PBC has relied heavily on changing reserve requirements rather than open market operations as a monetary policy tool. Reduction of reserves as a tool of monetary policy would actually shrink the size of the central bank's balance sheet. (Note the PBC's negative growth rate in the last line of Table 8.1.) Meanwhile, expansionary open market operations actually enlarge the balance sheet of the central bank. (Note the Fed's large increase in "other assets" found in Table 8.2.)

Case Study 8.1: Walras's Law, the Flow of Funds, and Missing Assets and Wealth

As we saw in the last chapter, Walras's Law establishes a correspondence (identity) between total wealth and the financial instruments that lay claim to that wealth. The relationship can be described as:

$$\text{Wealth} \equiv \text{Cash} + \text{Bank Deposits} + \text{Bonds} + \text{Equity} + \text{Real Estate} + \text{Other Assets}$$

The right-hand side of the equation above includes a much more extensive list of financial instruments in the United States than in China, encompassing everything from mortgage-backed securities to shares in a hedge fund. The quantities of the assets supplied often depend not only on real underlying wealth creation (such as via a new medicine or a new physical asset) and the need to hedge against risk, but also on the legal and regulatory structures that promote their development. After all, it is quite easy to create a piece of paper and define it as a claim on wealth. The critical question usually relates to the demand for these assets—whether other investors are willing to trade a valuable financial asset (such as money or a Treasury bill) for that financial asset. The presence (or absence) of demand has a direct impact on whether the other asset actually has value.

Walras's Law also holds in terms of first differences:

$$\Delta\text{Wealth} = \Delta\text{Cash} + \Delta\text{Bank Deposits} + \Delta\text{Equity} + \Delta\text{RealEstate} + \Delta\text{Other Assets}$$

Where the left-hand side of the equation, ΔWealth, corresponds to savings (broadly defined to include the private and public sectors). We then recall from Chapter 2:

$$\text{Savings} = \text{Current Account Balance} + \text{Investment}$$

Combining the two above, we can say:

$$\text{Savings} = \text{Current Account Balance} + \text{Investment} \equiv \Delta\text{Cash} + \Delta\text{Bank Deposits} + \Delta\text{Equity} + \Delta\text{Real Estate} + \Delta\text{Other Assets}$$

The above expression is known as the "flow of funds," and it is actually calculated by China and the United States as part of their measurements of output and financial sector activity.

Lin and Schramm (2009) examine China's flow of funds in the fashion described above and find that, in the past, up to one-third of China's vast national savings was unaccounted for by any financial instrument. That is, a large portion of China's savings was used to finance investments with no paper trail. This provides just one measure of the informal banking sector, which has become even more significant since the publication of their research. No doubt, much of this informal lending reflects investment by small- and medium-sized enterprises, as well as relationship (*guanxi*) lending at the local level. More recently, much of this informal lending has morphed into shadow banking, which is discussed in the final chapter of this text. This transition has allowed for greater asset transparency, but has also increased risks for investors due to lack of regulation. What is clear is that transparency and information are the coin of the realm in finance. The more Chinese authorities can work toward achieving financial transparency in a market-based and well-regulated framework, the better.

Once again, the United States comes out at the other end of the spectrum when compared to China. If the Chinese financial system seems under-identified with financial assets, the US financial system seems over-identified. Figure 8.12 shows the ratio of non-bank financial assets in the United States, which rose from around 10 percent of overall wealth in 1978 to 40 percent by the start of the GFC. Many of these non-bank financial assets were likely redundant in terms of hedging benefits; but, what is worse, they were excessively valued in terms of the underlying real asset or income stream supporting their existence. Furthermore, the crisis revealed that the underlying asset itself (especially in real estate and individual income streams) was often overvalued, creating a false portrayal of total wealth.

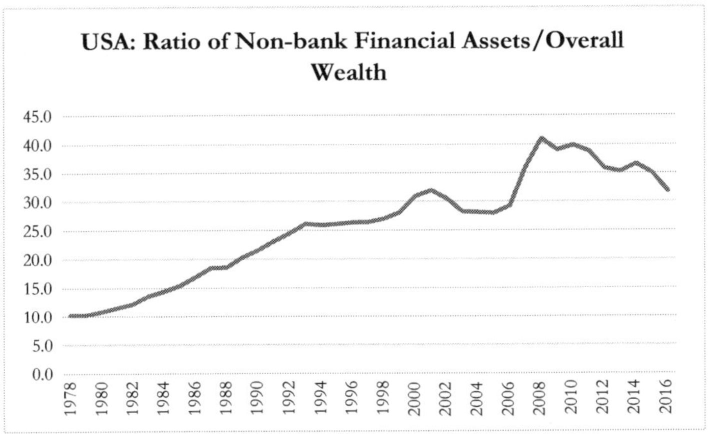

Figure 8.12 By the time of the GFC, non-bank financial assets as a share of total wealth had increased by a factor of four in the United States.
Source: Author created based on data from the Federal Reserve Economic Database.

We now examine foreign currency aspects of the two countries' balance sheets. The most dramatic difference is in the composition of assets: For China, over 60 percent of PBC assets represent foreign assets (reserves), while for the United States, the corresponding figure is close to -8 percent. Of course, these figures also reflect the PBC's past policy (created under a surrender requirement regime) of accumulating foreign exchange. In the United States, financial institutions, corporations, and individuals are allowed to hold onto foreign exchange—it becomes part of the private sector's assets. Because foreign exchange holdings are such a vital component of the PBC balance sheet, large increases in foreign exchange (prior to 2014) and then huge decreases (after 2014) have necessitated offsetting movements in lending/borrowing to the financial sector in order to maintain some measure of stability on the liability side of the balance sheet (particularly currency holdings).

In the United States, close to 51 percent of the Fed's assets are derived from its holdings of government obligations, including Treasury securities—a low figure by historical US standards, due to the Fed's emergency increase in financial institution (and other private sector) assets following the financial crisis. Rather surprisingly, most of China's monetary base (the liabilities side) entered the economy via the acquisition of foreign currency holdings—much of which is still held in US Treasury securities. In the United States, most currency has entered the economy via the Fed acquiring Treasury securities as well. In this peculiar way, the PBC and the Fed share something in common—a preference for holding US Treasury securities as a way of injecting currency into their economies. By 2019, about 20 percent of total PBC assets were in US debt obligations.

But both countries have recently reduced their holdings of these securities on a relative basis—in China, as a portfolio preference; in the United States, in response to the improving economy.

Case Study 8.2: Are PBC Holdings of US Dollars Profitable?

By end-2019, China held about USD 3.1 trillion in foreign exchange reserves of which a little over USD 1.1 trillion was in United States debt. China's rapid buildup of foreign exchange reserves began around 2000. Between 2000 and 2019, average returns (interest and capital gains) on US Treasury Bills was around 1.6 percent and on US Treasury Bonds around 5.2 percent. Meanwhile the USD weakened during the same period by about 1 percent against the RMB, and inflation in China was about 2.2 percent. Overall, real RMB returns were then -1.5 percent on Treasuries and 2 percent on Bonds. Assuming an equal mix of Treasuries and Bonds held, returns for the period under consideration were barely positive. The picture is slightly better when measured in US dollar terms; real Treasury returns were -0.6 percent and 2.9 percent for Bonds. On balance, it appears that China's earnings on its vast US dollar holdings have been disappointing. In terms of the PBC's standalone income statement (in which interest must be paid on bank reserves and discounted bills) the picture is even bleaker.

Monetary Policy Effectiveness

In Chapter 7 and this chapter, we have tried to highlight some of the important steps the monetary authorities have taken to liberalize and enhance monetary policy in China. Table 7.8 in Chapter 7 details some of the major steps undertaken. The main focus of these efforts has been to create a transmission mechanism that operates via market-determined interest rates. The PBC is moving to a system based on open market operations and a smaller set of policy rates that establish an interest rate corridor for short-term interbank rates. Kamber and Mohanty (2018) provide evidence, based on movements in the 7-day repurchase agreement interest rate, that the transmission effect appears to work in China; longer-term rates, inflation, and economic activity all seem to be impacted by standard monetary policy tools.

In an insightful article, Chen et al. (2019) find that the easy access to finance that state-owned enterprises (SOEs) have distorts monetary policy in China. In developed economies, monetary policy is often likened to "pushing on a string." That is, it is very difficult to stimulate an economy (cause a recovery) via expansionary monetary policy, but it is relatively easy to contract an economy (cause a recession) via tight monetary policy. Demand for investment is inelastic with respect to interest rates when the economy is in a slowdown (one of the many hoops that monetary policy must jump through to be effective; something we discussed earlier in this chapter). In China, however, the opposite asymmetry exists due to the importance of SOEs in the banking/monetary system. SOEs' direct links to banks combined with policy mandates can make stimulatory monetary policy very effective. Meanwhile, when the PBC contracts monetary policy, SOEs—unlike private enterprises—maintain their access to credit. Ideally, this type of asymmetry would not exist—neither in China nor in developed economies. In terms of long-term quality of growth, we can conjecture, however, that China's type of asymmetry is more harmful.

Chen et al. (2018) provide research that lends support to the monetary anomaly results in China just discussed, but from a different angle. They find that contractionary policy actually leads to an expansion of credit via local (non-state) banks and the shadow banking sector. Since banks need to meet a PBC ceiling on the loan to deposit ratio and meet a Banking Regulatory Commission restriction on lending to certain sectors (such as real estate), a monetary contraction by the PBC makes these constraints more difficult to meet. Banks can get around this regulatory straitjacket by creating special "account receivable investment" accounts, which are in fact loans to the shadow banking sector. These loans tend to be riskier than what is found on their normal asset side of the balance sheet. Consistent with Chen et al. (2019), contractionary policy is not only ineffective at contracting lending, it can actually be expansionary via loans to the shadow banking sector. Non-state banks are much more likely to confront this tradeoff between meeting the regulations with safer loans on the one hand and bypassing the regulations with shadow banking loans on the other. The largest state-owned banks are monitored too closely, and they are thus prevented from bypassing the regulatory framework. In Macro Finance Case Study 8.2, we provide an even more general formulation for policy asymmetry and the growth in shadow banking.

Macro Finance Insight 8.2: An Entanglement of Regulations for Chinese Banks

China's PBC and Banking Regulatory Commission (https://bit.ly/3ew0Q2t) impose a number of significant constraints on banks' lending activities. Combined with reserve requirements and capital adequacy standards under the Bank for International Settlements Basle Accords (https://bit.ly/3bZOGNr), these constraints make it very difficult for banks to meet the regulatory requirements and simultaneously maintain lending and depositing operations that are profitable to banks and create quality growth. We also see implications for the growth of shadow banking in China. Let's consider a simplified bank balance sheet with Deposits (D), Loans (L), Reserves (R) and Equity (E):

Typical Bank Balance Sheet:

$$D + E = L + R$$

Or, equivalently,

$$E / L = 1 + R / L - D / L$$

Let's also consider some stylized constraints on that balance sheet imposed by the various regulators:

PBC Reserve Requirement, where (*r*) is the reserve requirement:

$$R / D \geq r$$

PBC loan to deposit ratio ceiling (λ):

$$L / D \leq \lambda$$

And finally, a Basle-like requirement on capital adequacy, where (*e*) is the floor on capital relative to risky assets:

$$E / L \geq e$$

Combing our balance sheet equality with the three constraints on the balance sheet, we can derive:

$$D / R - 1 \leq \lambda (1 - e) / r$$

This is a necessary condition for all three constraints to hold. It states that the actual ratio of deposits to reserves (minus 1) must be less than the ratio of the various regulatory constraints imposed by the PBC and Basle. If, for example, the reserve requirement (*r*) were raised by the authorities (in an effort at monetary tightening), and (D) and (R) are sticky, banks would not only find it challenging to meet the reserve requirement, but there would also be implications for meeting the other two constraints represented by (λ) and (*e*). If we assume current values for ($\lambda = 0.75$), ($e = 0.105$), and ($r = 0.115$), and that (D / R) is at its regulatory boundary of (1 / 0.115 = 8.7); then we see that the necessary condition to meet all constraints cannot be met—they are internally inconsistent! An alternative solution that Chinese banks have used in the past is to hold a high level of excess reserves—a smaller (D / R): an approach with high opportunity costs relative to returns found in the shadow banking sector.

It is well known in economics and finance that over-regulation and financial repression (e.g., price controls) can lead to informal markets. No doubt, as banks struggle to meet the various regulatory constraints, they have sought and found solutions in the shadow banking sector. For example, if a bank is having trouble meeting its reserve to deposit ratio floor and loan to deposit ceiling, it might classify certain deposits as a wealth management product (off-balance sheet liability)—lowering the actual (*r*) ratio—and then, later, at another regulatory checkpoint for the (L / D) ratio, shift that accounting liability back to the deposit category to lower that actual ratio.

In the above discussion, we have not even included other constraints on banks such as requirements to lend to the real sector and not financial institutions, or to lend to small- and medium-size enterprises, or Banking Regulatory Commission restrictions on lending to sectors viewed as too risky (such as real estate). Indeed, the more entangled the banking sector is in regulations, the more regulatory arbitrage opportunities arise that a very creative set of shadow bankers can take advantage of.

Recent Monetary Policy Developments in China

For both countries, the first decade of the millennium presented a number of unprecedented challenges regarding monetary policy. In China, the goal of maintaining a stable currency in the face of ever-growing capital mobility and large current account surpluses created trade-offs for inflation and employment. In the United States, the 2008 financial crisis resulted in an epic expansion of the Fed's balance sheet in an effort to avert another Great Depression. Frequent changes in reserve requirements in China and quantitative easing in the United States became the "new normal" in any discussion of monetary policy.

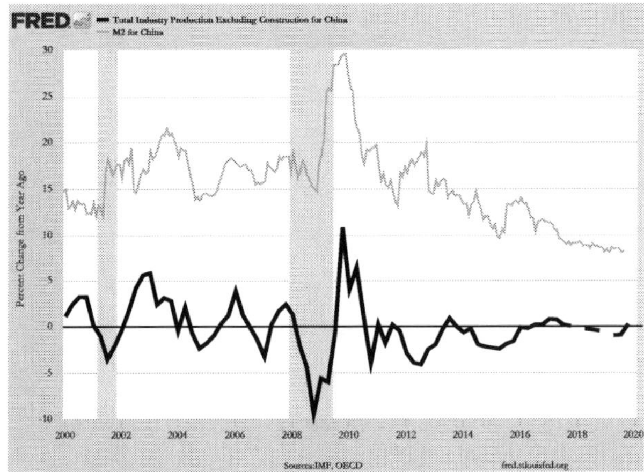

Figure 8.13 Over the past two decades, Chinese monetary policy has responded to externally generated (global) shocks.
Source: Author created based on data from the Federal Reserve Economic Database.

Figure 8.14 China's PBC makes frequent use of banks' reserve requirements as a tool of monetary policy.
Source: Author created based on data from CEIC.

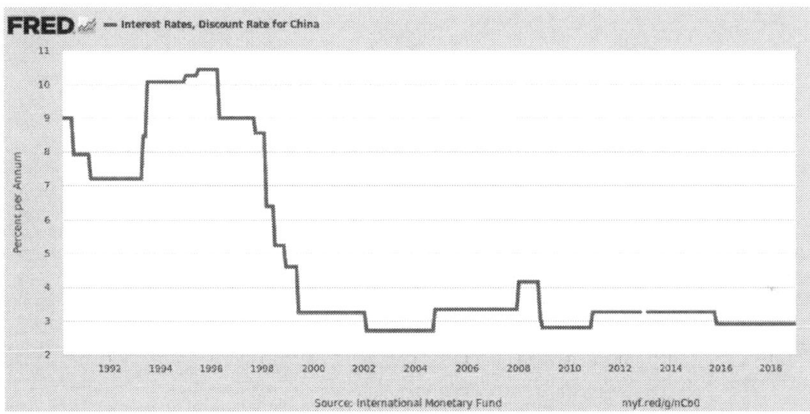

Figure 8.15 The discount rate has not been an important tool in China's overall monetary policy toolkit in recent years.
Source: Author created based on data from the Federal Reserve Economic Database.

Figure 8.13, Figure 8.14, and Figure 8.15 provide a quick snapshot of China's monetary policy, beginning with the GFC. Specifically, we see substantial loosening of monetary policy—either lower rates (market-based or regulatory), increases in the money supply, or (as discussed above) changes in reserve requirements in response to exogenous economic events. After the Asian financial crisis of 1997–1998, we saw a loosening of monetary policy. In the period building up to the 2008 financial crisis, in which China experienced a surge in prices and economic growth, we saw substantial increases in reserve requirements. During and after that crisis, we see a surge in the money supply as the PBC moved to stimulate the economy.

During the 2008–2009 GFC, China announced an RMB 4 trillion stimulus policy. In fact, according to Chen (2016), the actual monetary stimulus was much greater, at RMB 11.5 trillion. The package resulted in a remarkable 25 percent increase in M2 and a 30 percent increase in bank loans. At this point in China's monetary framework, the authorities were still relying heavily on quantity (M2) effects rather than pricing (interbank interest rate) effects. Chen et al. (2016) argue that most of this expansion of credit went to heavy industries—which includes real estate, infrastructure, and manufacturing—rather than to other areas such as health, education, or other service industries. In tandem with this approach, most of the lending resulted in more investment in China, no doubt exacerbating the quality of growth and debt problems that already existed. More controversially, Chen et al. go on to suggest that heavy industries, not SOEs, were the main beneficiaries of increased lending in this period; it would be no easy task to distinguish the class of firms identified as heavy industry from those under state ownership. In any event, the impact on real GDP growth was large, but the impact on longer-run quality of growth remains in question.

Figure 8.13 gives a measure of the dramatic increase in the growth of M2 during periods of slower industrial growth in China. The figure shows (in the shaded areas) both the 2001 US recession and the 2008 financial crisis.[4] With high average growth rates, the figure suggests that, in the last decade, monetary policy in China was used more as a response to external shocks than internal ones. In the coming decades, as long-term growth slows and domestic consumption demand becomes a significant factor, we will no doubt see the internal business cycle influencing monetary policy more heavily. To combat rising concerns over inflation, in the second half of 2010, the PBC slowed monetary growth. The central bank then reversed its monetary policy in the second half of 2011 in response to concerns over the impact of an economic slowdown in Europe, especially in Italy, Greece, Spain, and Portugal. We gain an even clearer picture of China's monetary policy by examining the movements in reserve requirements in Figure 8.14.

The Great Financial Crisis and Quantitative Easing

During the GFC, the Fed took extraordinary efforts to expand money and credit by launching at least nine different programs (https://bit.ly/3d2X3sH) beyond the standard methods of open market operations and discount window lending. Figure 8.16 shows the unprecedented nearly five-fold increase of the monetary base as the financial crisis unfolded in 2008–2009. What the Fed and other central banks engaged in during this period was called "quantitative easing" (https://bbc.in/2X2UqSp). Unlike traditional monetary easing in normal times, in which the Fed attempts to simply lower the federal funds rate through open market operations, quantitative easing attempts to create a continuous excess supply of money in financial markets and a reduction in some financial assets (including troubled assets such as mortgage-backed securities). The Fed accomplishes this by creating large amounts of money in the form of the monetary base, then it uses these funds to purchase excess financial assets. The hope is that the new money will be lent, boosting investment in property, plant, equipment, housing, and consumption.[5]

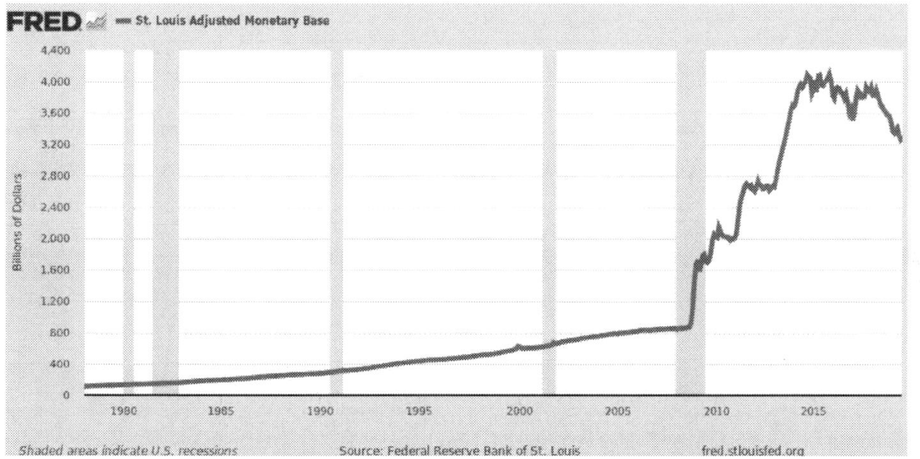

Figure 8.16 In the United States, the GFC caused the Fed to increase the monetary base (currency and bank reserves) dramatically.
Source: Author created based on data from the Federal Reserve Economic Database.

As we saw in Figure 8.1, the traditional transmission mechanism relies on a complex chain reaction of events to ultimately impact output and employment. If any link in the chain is broken, the transmission of monetary policy will be weakened. The 2008–2009 financial crisis verified the existence of what Keynes called a "liquidity trap," or an important break in the link. In that situation, interest rates cannot be pushed any lower because either the demand for money is infinitely elastic or nominal rates are at zero (the "zero lower bound"). During the GFC, individuals and corporations— out of fear caused by the risky environment—were more than eager to hold their wealth in money or Treasury bills at interest rates as low as zero, or even negative real rates. Since increasing the money supply was met by the eager demand for money, its price (the interest rate) could not fall, and the transmission mechanism would be off to a bad start.

One simple way to represent the quantitative easing response to the failure of the transmission mechanism is via the quantity theory of money. Recall that velocity is the average number of times the money supply (M) circulates in the economy in a certain year. (*P*) and (*Q*) represent the price level and real output, respectively. If velocity (V) is assumed to be constant, we have:

$$M \times V = P \times Q$$

($P \times Q$) represents nominal GDP. To the extent that monetary policy affects the availability of credit, (*M*) shifts up or down, impacting either prices or real output. The goal of quantitative easing is to bypass a faulty transmission mechanism by increasing the monetary base. This practice results in an increase in the overall money supply, which spills over directly into demand in the economy. In terms of the IS/LM framework, the role of money is no longer limited to the LM curve. Rather, in the quantitative easing variation of the IS/LM framework, consumption becomes a direct function of money, as does investment. Formally:

$$C = f(M / P)$$
$$I = f(M / P)$$

An increase in the money supply not only shifts the LM curve to the right, but it also influences the IS curve itself. Figure 8.17 illustrates a liquidity trap, in which the IS shifts to the right due to an increase in the money supply and the LM shifts into itself due to an infinitely elastic demand for money (liquidity trap).

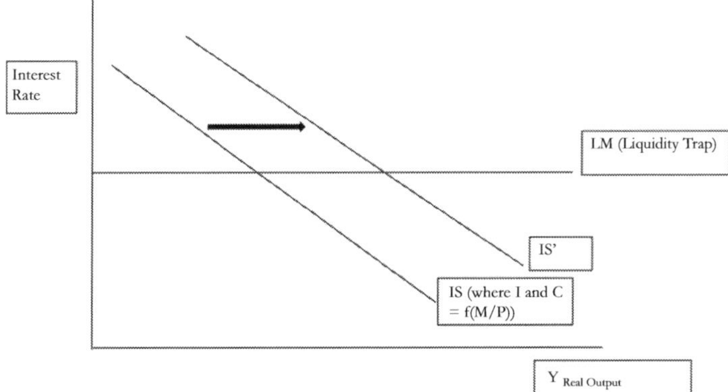

Figure 8.17 When the demand for liquidity (money) is infinitely elastic, expanding the money supply is ineffective—money holdings simply increase (in a money-under-the-mattress kind of story). This rule is also known as the "zero lower bound" because the nominal interest rate cannot fall below zero and monetary stimulus therefore bumps up against a constraint. In such situations, shifting the IS curve to the right is the best hope—and the availability of additional liquidity and credit may help in this process. Source: Author created.

In fact, the above IS/LM framework not only provides a more suitable description of the Fed's activities during a financial crisis, it may also be a way of viewing how monetary policy works in China. Since interest rates in China still represent a mix of government intervention and market determination, the direct impact of the availability of money and credit plays a more important role in China in terms of monetary policy. In this sense, monetary policy as undertaken in China—via window guidance, credit directives, and interest ceilings and floors—functions through direct shifts in the IS curve. In China, the complicated path of the LM curve shifting via the transmission mechanism is still a work in progress. Meanwhile, in the United States by 2011, credit markets were returning to the normal, traditional IS/LM mode in which the transmission mechanism could actually work.

Policy Trade-offs and Evolving Policy Responses

As we argued in the policy trilemma discussion, the effort to maintain the exchange rate, economic growth, and inflation presents some serious policy trade-offs. During the last decade, the order of importance of the goals has matched their order in the previous sentence, in which control of inflation is decidedly the lowest priority—at least for now. Early estimates of a "Taylor rule" (Taylor 1993) confirm these priorities. The Taylor rule specifies how central banks respond to deviations from full employment and inflation targets via changes in interbank interest rates. Most scholars find that monetary policy in China responds more, and more in the expected direction, to economic growth targets than to inflation targets. In other words, monetary policy is tightened when growth rises above long-term averages, and it is loosened when growth falls below the trend. The response to inflation is generally weaker; in fact, Mehrotra and Sánchez-Fung (2010) find that it may even be pro-cyclical, that is, expansionary in periods of high inflation, or vice-versa.[6] Notwithstanding spikes in the inflation rate toward the end of 2019, the authorities' concerns remain muted, which is consistent with China's emphasis on economic growth over inflation. Chen et al. (2018), in a modified Taylor rule, empirically demonstrate that the M2 response is at least three times greater to declines in economic growth as compared to upticks in inflation. Other authors (Wang 2015) come up with similar results for earlier periods.

Given the myriad of tools that the PBC uses to implement policy, it is often difficult to focus on one metric as a good measure of China's policy stance. Instead, Shu and Ng (2010) take a narrative approach by examining quarterly reports and press announcements from the PBC. They come up with a broad spectrum of measures ranging from "strong tightening" to "strong loosening." What is clear, from this and other studies, is that Chinese authorities do indeed respond (i.e., have a monetary reaction) to innovations in real economic growth and prices.

Since the start of the Trump administration's adversarial trade policy beginning in 2016, China has encountered further strong economic headwinds. Interest rates in the United States also began to rise in 2016, complicating China's efforts to expand monetary policy, control capital mobility, and maintain a stable exchange rate. As this chapter is being written, the COVID-19 virus supply shock represents the other bookend of economic woes.

Consistent with the policy implementation section above, Chinese monetary policy has continued to place a heavier weight on quantity methods or quantitative easing. Most recently (January, 2020), China injected RMB 1.2 trillion into the financial system and-at the same time—pushed these funds onto the banking systems at repurchase repo rates of 2.44 and 2.55 percent (on 7- and 14-day maturities). When China announced it was cutting its reserve requirement for banks to 12.5 percent in early January, 2020, it was the eighth time the ratio had been lowered since 2018. The series of cuts had the potential to release about USD 1 trillion into the Chinese financial system. In summary, similar to the United States' response to the GFC, Chinese monetary authorities chose to throw money at the problem (quantitative easing).

But China's monetary efforts in the 2016–2020 period present even more difficult challenges than those found during the GFC, a period in which China's economy remained relatively unscathed. The current context for the vast credit expansion is that China is already heavily burdened by debt—both domestic and external. On the domestic front, total social financing (or aggregate financing)—the authorities preferred measure of internal debt—is already around 270 percent. Adding more layers of debt to that heavy burden raises questions of sustainability. One sign of this concern is that, even as China vastly expanded credit, the authorities raised base lending rates on mortgages to 4.85 percent and 5.45 percent on first and second home mortgages. Another sign was the smaller policy response to the COVID-19 pandemic (the proposed stimulatory package, announced in May, 2020, was only about 2 percent of China's GDP).

Continuing efforts at ameliorating the domestic credit situations also involve targeting loans to the real economy and small- and medium-sized businesses. Meanwhile, as suggested above, the shadow economy will continue to hinder monetary policy implementation while presenting new surprises in the spirit of the law of unintended consequences. On the external debt side, at least USD 1.7 trillion is owed to foreigners on a gross basis, as seen in Figure 8.10. Depreciation of the RMB as a policy tool is circumscribed by this exposure. What is clear from all of this is that it is highly unlikely that China will abandon using its non-market interventionist toolkit any time soon.

Case Study 8.3: China's Capital Structure

Capital structure relates to how a company chooses to finance itself—particularly the choice between debt and equity as sources of funds. Two competing theories on capital structure in corporate finance are (1) the pecking order theory (Myers and Majluf 1984) and (2) the trade-off theory (Kraus and Litzenberger 1973). Pecking order posits that, in the presence of asymmetric information, firms rely on internal funds before external funds and debt before equity. This order will be the least expensive, since outside investors will charge a premium for funds when they have less information than inside shareholders. Furthermore, debt holders need less information about the binomial possibility of payment or default compared to equity investors' valuation concerns across an infinite spectrum of values. The trade-off theory weighs the tax benefits of more debt versus the incremental cost of risking bankruptcy when more debt is incurred.

For traditional corporate finance, then, the issues facing an individual company and its investors (in terms of capital structure) are information availability, costs of different types of capital, tax rates, and likelihood of bankruptcy. From a country's perspective, we need to qualify or modify the significance of some of these factors. In China's case, while increased debt and bankruptcy are certainly of concern, the effect may be reduced in the presence of SOEs where the government may readily step in to rescue the firm—a problem of moral hazard.* Conversely, while a company may prefer the deductibility of interest expenses on debt, countries tend to prefer more tax revenues (and, in turn, less debt). If the state can receive corporate net income via interest paid to state-owned banks, that effect is neutralized.

China's production sector has lagged, and continues to lag, behind the developed world in terms of transparency—that is, the availability of symmetric information shared between the enterprise and investors. At both the national and corporate-level, the goal is an efficient and low cost of capital. In the face of asymmetric information, achieving a low cost of capital can be difficult. China (along with many emerging markets around the world) has found that internal finance combined with bank finance is the most efficient ways of keeping capital costs low (and investment high). Sources of finance that better pierce the veil of asymmetric information include "arms around finance (such as that found in family-owned businesses), wholly foreign-owned enterprises with retained earnings, and internal pension funds or banks. "Arm's length" investors (such as outside equity investors or bond holders in public markets) remain cautious about providing finance when they do not have as much information as company insiders do.

But beyond the variables for the corporation mentioned above, in China, there are other significant factors of concern at the national/government level. (1) Control of the enterprise, for example, tends to be easier to achieve via arms around financial structures. This control becomes even more significant when the investors are local rather than foreign; that is, a domestic state-owned bank as compared to a wholly foreign-owned enterprise. (2) Privatization (or outside equity participation) of enterprises is a relaxation of control and, ideally, a move to greater efficiency. And, (3) technology transfer becomes much more important when considering capital structure. For example, a foreign joint venture with equity participation is much more likely to inbound transfer new foreign technologies than is, say, a firm whose only source of finance is a state-owned bank.

China has moved in stages, from state investment (thus the notion of an SOE) in the 1950–1980s, to state-owned bank finance in the 1980s, to stock market finance in the 1990s, to bond finance after 2000. Clearly, these stages represent China's efforts to triangulate optimally across the traditional corporate finance capital structure factors and the other macro-based factors such as control, privatization, and technology transfer.

*This occurred frequently in China, particularly in the 1990s.

Summary

China's monetary policy remains complex, but it is slowly evolving toward simpler, market-based mechanisms. Given China's size and its key trading and international financial relationships with the rest of the world, the path China takes in this regard is of global importance. China has, in recent decades, employed tools—such as changes in the reserve requirement—that focus on controlling (targeting) the money supply, a quantity approach. Changing M2 is intended to impact the ultimate policy goals of output, prices, and the exchange rate. China's recent historical focus on trade and the exchange rate and its ongoing focus on economic growth have made the nation reliant on a wider range of other tools and controls (both market- and non-market-based).

In recent years, however, open-market operations involving the outright sale of central bank bills and government debt instruments (so as to impact overnight rates) have begun playing a more important role. In turn, China is relying more on the transmission mechanism (as employed in advanced economies) for impacting final economic targets. Empirical evidence suggests that this more recent effort is impacting intermediate and long-term interest rates (Conway et al. 2010 or Kamber and Mohanty 2018). Table 7.8 in the Chapter 7 shows many of the institutional reforms that have taken place in China's banking and financial system since 1979. We note that those reforms paused in the years of and immediately following the GFC. The crisis was harmful not only in terms of the massive amount of credit released in response, as discussed in this chapter, but also in terms of its interruption of China's steady pace of financial reforms.

Both the structure of the real economy and the still under-developed financial system, however, remain a hindrance to the new approach significantly impacting the real economy. The Trump trade war and the COVID-19 pandemic have resulted in another round of stimulatory monetary policies in China (and the United States). The space for monetary maneuver now, however, is even more limited given already-high levels of domestic and external debt and long-run structural declines in growth potential.

In terms of policy response, the PBC tends to react more to output gaps than to contemporaneous inflation. It also appears that monetary policy responds more to shocks from outside of China (the United States in particular) than from inside of China. The recent COVID-19 crisis was one of the few shocks to China generated internally—followed by related external aftershocks. This situation is likely to change as investment becomes more susceptible to market forces within China. There is no evidence that monetary policy responds to changes in the exchange rate, which is consistent with a fixed exchange rate system combined with—at least until recently—the ability of the Chinese authorities to control international capital flows.

Challenging Questions for China (and the Student): Chapter 8

1. Go to the Federal Reserve Economic Database (FRED) and compare the lending-deposit spread with the 90-day interbank interest rate (graphically). Explain why one is highly volatile and the other is relatively stable (period to period).
2. What is the main difference between the stated goals of the People's Bank of China (PBC) and the Federal Reserve Bank of the United States (the Fed)?
3. Why does the PBC use so many tools to control the financial system compared to the Fed?
4. Eventually, if China is to have a high degree of international capital mobility, explain what it will have to give up in terms of a key policy variable. Explain why.
5. Go to the IMF's Annual Report on Exchange Arrangements and Exchange Restrictions (2013) (www.imf.org/external/pubs/nft/2013/areaers/ar2013.pdf) and identify how China's exchange rate regime is classified. Explain its regime classification with its monetary policy classification.
6. In terms of the traditional capital structure theories for companies, explain how China's government policies and special economic circumstances may modify the conventional approaches to capital structure.
7. Even though China does control international capital mobility, it still needs to undertake the increasingly difficult task of sterilization. Explain why China, in its efforts to control its exchange rate, has in effect lost a degree of control over its monetary policy. Discuss both the magnitude and volatility of exports as factors.
8. Explain the traditional transmission mechanism and why it is still a work-in-progress description of how monetary policy works in China.
9. Explain the difference between the capital adequacy ratio and the reserve requirement ratio. Use a typical financial institution's balance sheet to explain the difference.

References

Chen, H., R. Li, and P. Tillmann. 2019. "Pushing on a String: State-Owned Enterprises and Monetary Policy Transmission in China." *China Economic Review*, 54, pp. 26–40.

Chen, K., H. Gao, P. Higgins, D. F. Waggoner, and T. Zha. 2016. "Impacts of Monetary Stimulus on Credit Allocation and the Macroeconomy: Evidence from China." NBER Working Paper no. w22650.

Chen, K., J. Ren, and T. Zha. 2018. "The Nexus of Monetary Policy and Shadow Banking in China." *American Economic Review*, 108(12), pp. 3891–936.

Conway, Paul, Richard Herd, and Thomas Chalaux. 2010. "Reforming China's Monetary Policy Framework to Meet Domestic Objectives." OECD Economics Department Working Paper no. 822.

Federal Reserve Bank (FRB) of San Francisco. 2004. "What are the Goals of U.S. Monetary Policy?" Accessed 9 May, 2014, www.frbsf.org/us-monetary-policy-introduction/goals/.

Ito, H., and Masahiro Kawai. 2014. "New Measures of the Trilemma Hypothesis: Implications for Asia." In *Reform of the International Monetary System: An Asian Perspective*, edited by Masahiro Kawai, Mario B. Lamberte, and Peter J. Morgan, Tokyo: Springer, pp. 73–104.

Kamber, G., and M. S. Mohanty. 2018. "Do Interest Rates Play a Major Role in Monetary Policy Transmission in China?" BIS Working Paper no. 714.

Kraus, A. and R.H. Litzenberger. 1973. "A State-Preference Model of Optimal Financial Leverage." *Journal of Finance*, 28(4), pp. 911–22.

Lin, G. and R. M. Schramm. 2009. "A Decade of Flow of Funds in China (1995–2006)." In *China and Asia: Economic and Financial Interactions*, edited by Y. W. Cheung and K. Y. Wong, London: Routledge, pp. 26–44.

Mehrotra, Aaron and José R. Sánchez-Fung. 2010. "China's Monetary Policy and the Exchange Rate." BOFIT Discussion Papers no. 10/2010, Bank of Finland, Institute for Economies in Transition.

Myers, Stewart C. and Nicholas Majluf. 1984. "Corporate Financing and Investment Decisions When Firms Have Information That Investors Do Not Have." *Journal of Financial Economics*, 13(2), pp. 187–221.

Obstfeld, Maurice. 1986. "Capital Controls, the Dual Exchange Rate, and Devaluation." *Journal of International Economics*, 20(1), pp. 1–20.

Obstfeld, Maurice, Jay C. Shambaugh, and Alan M. Taylor. 2004. "The Trilemma in History: Tradeoffs among Exchange Rates, Monetary Policies, and Capital Mobility." DNB Staff Report (discontinued) no. 94, Netherlands Central Bank.

Obstfeld, Maurice. 2012. "Financial Flows, Financial Crises and Global Imbalances." *Journal of International Money and Finance*, 31(3), pp. 469–80.

People's Bank of China. "Monetary Report." Accessed 24 June, 2020, http://www.pbc.gov.cn/en/3688229/3688353/3688356/index.html.

People's Bank of China. "Objective of Monetary Policy." Accessed 24 August, 2020, http://www.pbc.gov.cn/en/3688229/3688299/3688302/index.html.

Shu, Chang and Brian Ng. 2010. "Monetary Stance and Policy Objectives in China: A Narrative Approach." *China Economic Issues*, 1(10), pp. 1–40.

Taylor, John B. 1993. "Discretion Versus Policy Rules in Practice." *Carnegie-Rochester Conference Series on Public Policy*, 39, pp. 195–214.

Wang, Tian. 2015. "Taylor Rules for China: Theory and Estimation." Unpublished Thesis. Xian Jiao Tong University, Department of Mathematical Finance.

Endnotes

1. Current account mobility allows citizens to acquire foreign exchange for current account activities such as importing, exporting, and the payment of interest and dividends on international obligations. Specifically, it excludes the use of foreign exchange for the acquisition or sale of real and financial assets. Most countries around the world, including China, allow for current account convertibility under the IMF charter (referred to as "Article VIII convertibility").
2. In international finance, this is called "uncovered interest rate parity." It occurs when the expected exchange rate movement exactly offsets interest rate differential between countries on a risk-adjusted basis. "Covered interest rate parity" is a close companion, no-arbitrage condition in which—instead of the expected exchange rate—we use the forward (contractual obligation) exchange rate.
3. China has historically had very large foreign exchange surrender requirements. These require recipients of foreign exchange, such as exporters, to turn these receipts over to the banking system in exchange for local currency. For countries around the world with such requirements, an important question is whether the conversion rate (the exchange rate used) is too favorable to the central authorities and too unfavorable to the exporter.
4. In step with the monetary stimulus, the State Council announced a series of measures that ultimately led to an additional fiscal stimulus of RMB 4 trillion in November, 2008.
5. Quantitative easing is a demonstration of Walras's Law. Creating excess demand in one financial market (the demand for bonds) is identical to increasing an excess supply in another financial market (the supply of money). The goal is that the excess money supply will spill directly into creating an actual demand for goods and services.
6. This, however, could be a spurious correlation related to the clear monetary response to economic growth.

9
THE KEYNESIAN MODEL: EXTENSIONS TO CHINA AND BEYOND

能者多劳

The Capable are Fully Employed

There is a limited body of research attempting to apply the Keynesian framework (new or old Keynesian models) to China's economic policies. Chapter 10, however, will show that in times of economic downturn, China has decisively turned to Keynesian solutions (as has the United States). But we also suggest that, during periods of greater stability, China has viewed fiscal policy as mainly investment policy and a tool for economic growth (i.e., supply-side management). Although published in 1936, Keynes's *General Theory of Employment, Interest, and Money* was not translated into Chinese until 1957; it was initially banned in China for being too pro-capitalist (Cox 2011). In this chapter, we will examine the special case of China using the investment-savings/liquidity-money demand (IS/LM) framework and aggregate demand and supply framework. This is a very useful heuristic device for understanding the constraints and opportunities of an emerging economy (such as China's). Later examples—more complex versions of the IS/LM framework—are more appropriate for advanced economies (such the United States') and the China of the future.

Traditional Keynesian Framework: Investment, Savings, and Liquidity Preference

IS/LM: A Review[1]

It is said that all of economics is about supply and demand and whether or not markets are in or out of equilibrium. This certainly holds true in macroeconomics. While a variety of macro models are now part of the economist's toolkit for analysis, the

Keynesian model remains both a benchmark and a workhorse for analyzing short-term economic fluctuations in output and employment. As we will see in the section below, in China, fiscal and monetary policy responses to the Great Financial Crisis (GFC) and earlier shocks closely followed Keynesian policy prescriptions, but with unique characteristics. In the Keynesian IS/LM framework, we examine supply and demand in two separate markets: (1) supply and demand for gross domestic product (GDP), and (2) supply and demand for money. The first describes an equilibrium in flows, the second describes an equilibrium in stocks—just as an income statement describes a flow during an accounting period and a balance sheet equates stocks of assets with outstanding equity and liabilities.

Equilibrium in the Market for Goods and Services (the Market for GDP, or the IS Curve)

Reviewing the IS/LM model, we recall that, to achieve equilibrium in the market for goods and services (the IS relationship):

$$Y = \text{GDP} = \text{Income} = \text{Supply of Output}$$

Recall the components of demand:

- C = Consumer demand for goods and services
- I = Investor demand for plant, property, and equipment; other interest-sensitive forms of demand such as auto and home purchases; and inventory (stock building) accumulation
- G = Government demand for goods and services
- NX = (Exports – imports), or net exports of goods and services
- t = (Tax rate – transfer rate on all of income)[2]
- i = The interest rate or rate of return on the best alternative to holding money—this is assumed to be equal to cost of borrowing funds for the sake of investment (I)

Setting (Supply = Demand), we have:

$$Y = C((1 - t) \times Y) + I(i) + G + NX(Y)$$

in which the expressions in parentheses represent independent variables that influence (+/–) the components of demand or dependent variables. Assuming linear relationships throughout, we have:

$$Y = C + I + [\, c \times (1 - t) \times Y] - [d \times I] + G + X - [m \times Y]$$

in which (*c*), (*d*), and (*m*) are sensitivities (model parameters) of consumption, investment, imports to net income, the interest rate, and income. Autonomous changes in consumption, investment, government spending, or exports would change the (capitalized) constants, (*C*), (*I*), (*G*), and (*X*), respectively. In Figure 9.1, we show a standard IS curve, which would shift to the right if any of the constants just described changed for some exogenous reason (such as a shift in consumer or investor behavior). The IS curve represents various combinations of (*Y*) and (*i*), in which the supply of the economy's goods and services just equals the demand for those goods and services. Above the curve, for any given (*Y*), there is too little demand (implying inventory accumulation); below the curve, there is excess demand (implying inventory reduction). In the former case, companies would cut back on production and decrease output (*Y*) over time; in the latter case, companies would increase production. Either way, output would gravitate toward the IS curve. This is another way of looking at that curve as a set of equilibrium levels of output and interest rates.

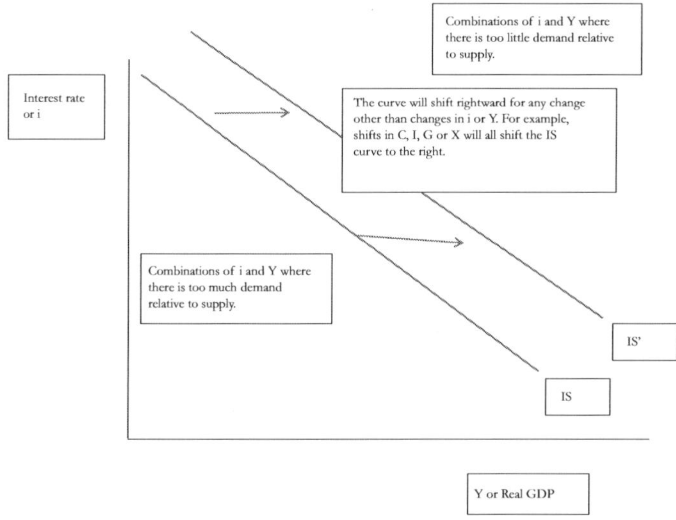

Figure 9.1 The IS curve represents the combination of output and interest rates where the goods market is in equilibrium. If we are off the IS curve, then there is an excess supply or demand for goods. Any exogenous increase in (*C*), (*I*), (*G*) or (*NX*) would cause a shift in the curve rightward.
Source: Author created.

In this framework, there are two key variables at work and one not at work: At work are investment and inventory accumulation, not at work is the overall level of prices. Let's discuss prices first. Prices are assumed to be sticky (fixed) and, for purposes of simplification, constant. As such, we don't see prices at all in our demand framework. This may seem strange—how can we discuss supply and demand without including prices?—but Keynes argued that prices at the aggregate level tend to be fixed or sticky, and this is a critical assumption in the Keynesian framework. Economists have suggested menu costs, meaning that it takes time for any firm to change its menu of prices in response to short-run fluctuations in demand. Eventually, firms do change their prices (in the long run); but, in the Keynesian world (the short run), prices are not flexible. Other economists have also suggested that changing prices (particularly reducing them) changes revenues, and that this may, in turn, trigger cost-cutting or wage reductions to maintain business profitability. Employees will resist real wage reductions despite the possibility of losing their jobs. While economists have long debated downward wage rigidity, research utilizing a behavioral economics approach—in which workers have a wage benchmark or anchor—is useful in explaining the phenomenon (Bewley 1999).

Since prices cannot (under the model's assumption) relieve much of the pressure typically resulting from demand or supply shocks, another variable must relieve the pressure in the system. This is where inventory accumulation or reduction comes into play. When demand drops, for example, instead of prices changing, inventory accumulates. In response to unwanted inventory, firms cut output. Inventory represents both planned and unplanned (unintended, unwanted) inventory accumulation. In the latter case, firms alter production in response to the unwanted and unanticipated changes in inventory.[3] Figure 9.2 shows these two critical aspects of the Keynesian system in a simple demand and supply framework.

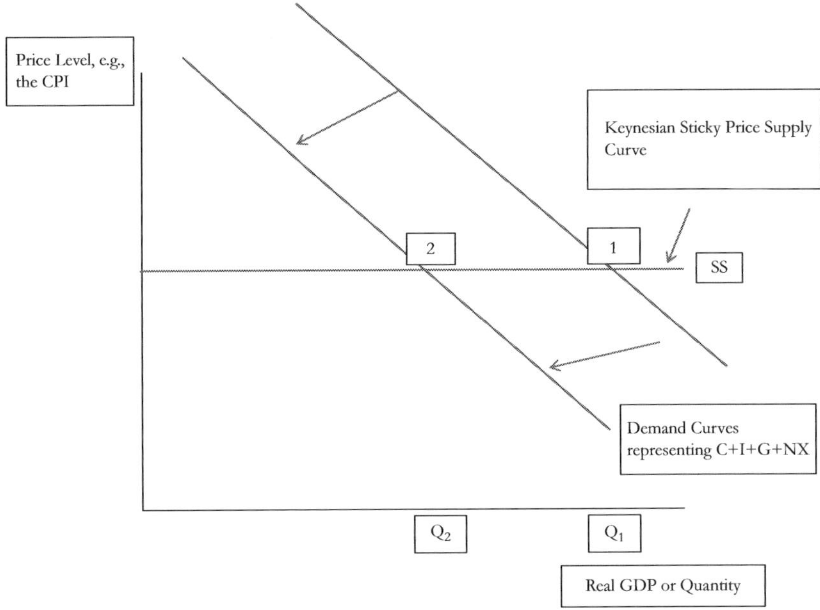

Figure 9.2 In a Keynesian framework, we represent sticky prices by a perfectly elastic supply curve—any shift in demand (either an increase or a decrease) results in GDP fluctuating rather than prices.
Source: Author created.

Equilibrium in the Money Market (the LM Curve)

As we discussed in Chapter 7, the LM curve describes equilibrium in the money market, but it just as easily (via Walras's Law) extends to equilibrium in all financial markets—whether they be equities, bonds, or currencies.[4] If the money market is not in equilibrium, then—by the requirements of Walras's consistency—at least one other market is not in equilibrium. We start with the supply of money (M), assumed to be exogenously determined by the monetary authorities and the banking system. The overall price level is represented by (P), and (i) represents the interest rate on the opportunity cost of money. The expression ($L(Y, i)$) represents the demand for the real stock of outstanding money, in which demand is positively related to real income and negatively related to the nominal interest rate. We then have:

Supply or stock of real money:

$$M / P$$

Demand for real money:

$$L(Y, i)$$

Setting (Supply of Money = Demand for Money), we have:

$$M / P = L\,(Y, i)$$

Assuming linear relationships throughout, we have:

$$M / P = e \times Y - f \times i$$

in which (*e*) and (*f*) are the sensitivities of money demand to the level of real income and the nominal interest rate.[5] For now, we assume (*M / P*) is constant. In Figure 9.3, we see the LM curve, which shows all combinations of (*Y*) and (*i*) in which the money market is in equilibrium. An increase in the money supply will shift the LM to the right. Any point above the LM curve corresponds to an excess supply of real balances relative to demand; any point below, an excess demand relative to supply.

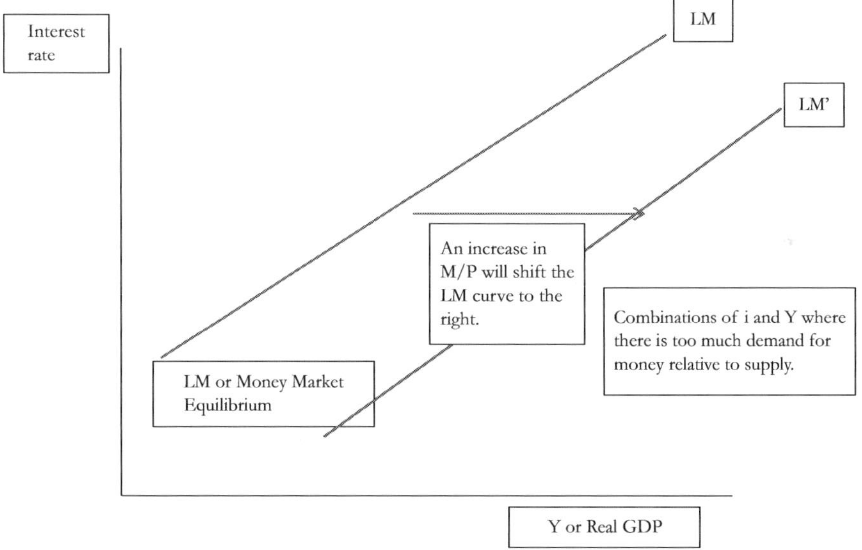

Figure 9.3 The LM curve represents the combination of interest rates and output where the money market is in equilibrium. An increase in the real money supply (from either nominal money increasing or the price level dropping) will shift the LM curve to the right.
Source: Author created.

Equilibrium in Both Markets

In the IS/LM framework, there is only one combination of levels of real income (*Y*) and interest rates (*i*) in which both the market for goods and services and the market for financial assets are in equilibrium. That is point A, as indicated in Figure 9.4. If the economy enters quadrants 1, 2, 3, or 4, we have excess supply or demands for goods and services and money. Imbalances in inventories, output, and interest rates will force a move to the equilibrium level of output and interest rates. In the China context, being off these curves is an important and relevant concept. We suggest below (Chapter 8) that because of a multiplicity of policy goals, China employs a multiplicity of tools, which allows the economy to linger off of both the IS and LM curves for prolonged periods—that is, a sustainably long period out of equilibrium.

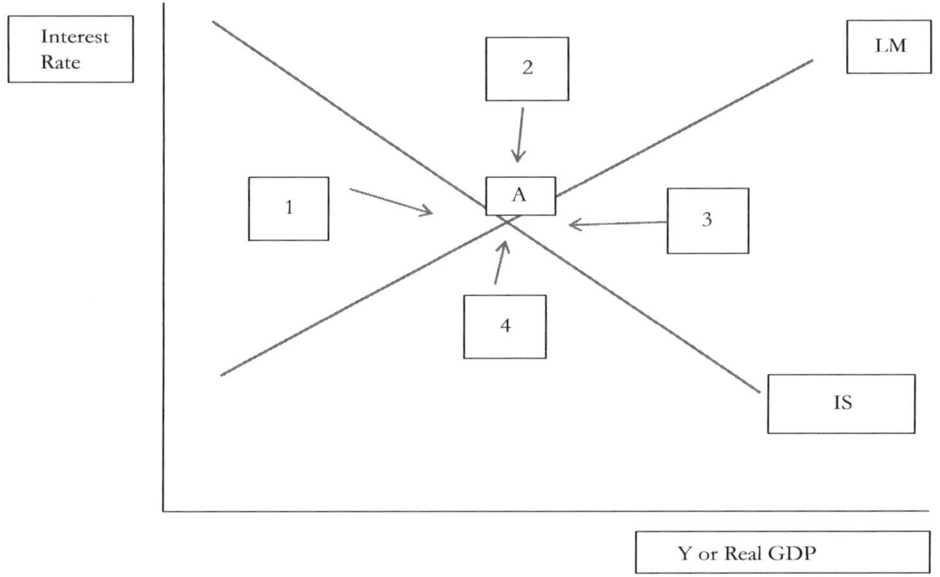

Figure 9.4 At point A, both the goods market and financial markets are in equilibrium. In quadrants 1, 2, 3, and 4 we have either inventory accumulation/decumulation, excess supply of money, or excess demand for other financial assets.
Source: Author created.

Any autonomous increase in the demand for goods—such as an increase in government spending (*G*) or an increase in consumption (*C*)—will shift the IS curve to the right. This move will cause (*Y*) and (*i*) to increase.[6] An increase in the real money supply (*M* / *P*) shifts the LM curve to the right and downward. This move also causes output to rise; but, in this case, it triggers interest rates to fall. As shown in Figure 9.5 and Figure 9.6, both expansionary monetary policy and expansionary fiscal policy result in output increasing in the standard Keynesian framework, but they will impact interest rates in opposite directions. Case Study 9.1 elaborates on the LM curve shift and what it means for China in terms of the transmission mechanism.

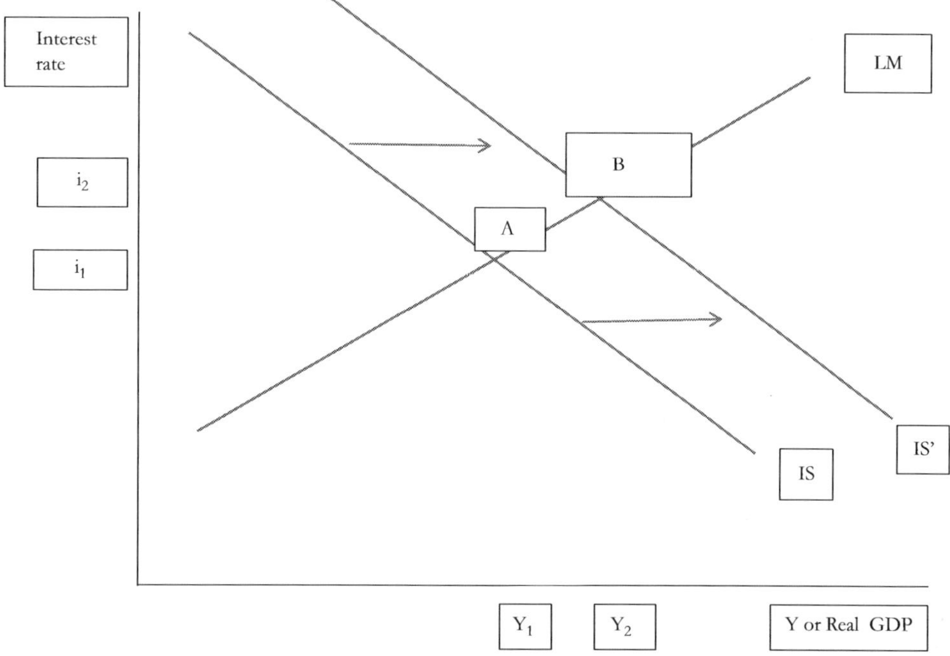

Figure 9.5 An increase in (*C*), (*I*), (*G*), or (*NX*) will shift the IS curve to the right and cause output to rise, along with interest rates.
Source: Author created.

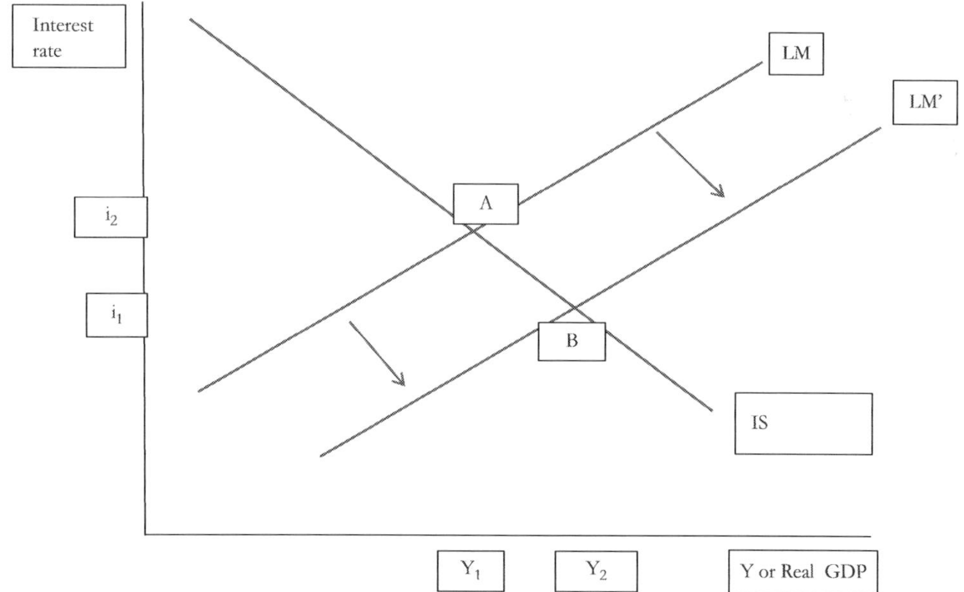

Figure 9.6 An increase in the real money supply shifts the LM curve downward, increasing output and decreasing interest rates.
Source: Author created.

There is a natural (psychological) tendency to think of equilibrium as a good situation.[7] However, that presumption is definitely false in the Keynesian framework. In that framework, equilibrium simply means the situation in which the economy stabilizes—a situation that might be good, but could also be very bad if, for example, equilibrium corresponds to high rates of unemployment and low levels of output. This is Keynes's main point: the economy could stabilize (reach equilibrium) in a situation that is very undesirable. It would then be up to policy-makers to move the economy to a better equilibrium.

Case Study 9.1: The Chopstick Economy

We have suggested, in Chapters 7 and 8, that the transmission mechanism for monetary policy is not yet fully operational in China. The transmission mechanism is the mechanism found in advanced economies whereby central banks intervene (use open market operations involving repurchase agreements) in overnight interbank lending markets (i.e., the US federal funds market). This intervention, in turn, impacts overnight interbank interest rates. Overnight rates then spill over into longer-term borrowing or lending rates, which impact interest-sensitive components of demand (such as housing or new company investments). Next, these changes in demand impact output and employment—possibly with a multiplier effect. In other words, in order for monetary policy to be effective, it must pass through a number of institutional gateways—any of which might not be open. China still faces some institutional impediments to a fully functioning transmission mechanism. The bottom line is that the pricing-of-money mechanism (the interest rate) is still under construction. As a result, China relies heavily on quantity-of-money effects, in which the availability of money operating through the lending channels of the financial system is quite important. Interestingly, this is very similar to the US Fed's quantitative easing (QE) response to the breakdown of the transmission mechanism during the Great Financial Crisis. Macro Finance Insight 7.3 sheds some light on this important issue.

In terms of deriving an LM relationship, the lack of interest sensitivity implies a steep demand-for-money curve (as seen in Figure 9.7). This curve suggests a money market that is in equilibrium over a range of interest rates, as long as the amount of money supplied is consistent with the level of economic output. The shaded box represents a range of possible interest rates and money supplies in which market disequilibrium is possible given imperfect capital markets in China. The People's Bank of China (PBC) can pick and choose interest rates and the money supply independently (both a price and a quantity) because the demand for money is inelastic and financial markets are still imperfect. (We alluded to this in our discussion of disequilibrium scenarios in Figure 9.4.)

We suggest a monetary policy closer in spirit to the quantity theory of money (QTOM) presented earlier—along with the notion of "channels of credit," or credit rationing, suggested by Laurens and Maino (2007). Rather than a neat LM line showing equilibrium points for money demand and supply, we have a box showing a range of combinations of output (*Y*) and interest rates (*i*) from which the PBC chooses (a toolkit, as shown in Figure 9.7). The upper and lower boundaries of the shaded box represent constraints—interest rates above or below the box would not be consistent with a sticky exchange rate regime; setting interest rates outside the box would create too tempting an arbitrage opportunity, inviting capital inflows or flight. However, if we move beyond the borders of the box to the right or left, we risk creating shortages or surpluses in financial markets.

China's IS curve, meanwhile, is also somewhat steep. Its slope is determined by the sensitivity of investment demand to interest rates. We can infer that investment in China remains relatively insensitive to interest rate changes and is mainly a function of access (quantity) of credit rather than to its price (e.g., Geng and N'Diaye 2012, Wen and Wu, 2019). This can be represented as a steep IS curve. Figure 9.8 suggests that China has a range of interest rates—not just a single one—that are all stable in the short run. A steep IS curve allows for many possible interest rates, as does a steep LM curve. In turn, there is a range of interest rates that the PBC can pursue without either impacting demand for goods or the demand for money very much. Furthermore, it is possible to be off our equilibrium IS and LM curves for prolonged periods in China. (For a related concept, see the discussion below on interest rate overshooting.)

The discussion above suggests that the PBC has great flexibility in terms of fiscal and monetary policy. In fact, the boxes we have drawn represent policy boundaries. The upper and lower sides of the rectangle represent the constraints on how high or low interest rates can go given China's regime of capital controls and a sticky exchange rate. The right and left borders represent constraints on China (and all economies): economic output (to the right) cannot exceed a nation's limited resources (supply). On the left, economic output is politically constrained to avoid falling too far given the high costs of unemployment and expectations about improved prosperity. China's constraint to the right is relatively soft compared to that of the United States given China's still-vast growth potential. Its constraint to the left is relatively hard given the lack of a social safety net and high expectations for economic growth.

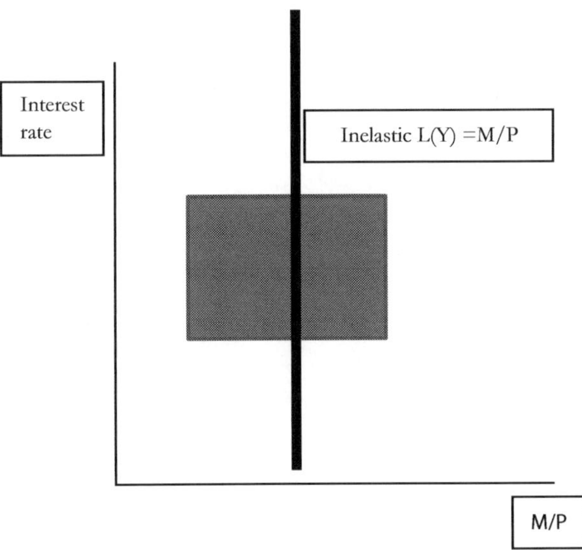

Figure 9.7 With inelastic money demand in China and imperfect capital markets, there are many possible interest rates consistent with a level of output. The shaded box shows a range of combinations of interest rates and money supplies that the PBC can attempt to manage before severe imbalances in money markets occur.
Source: Author created.

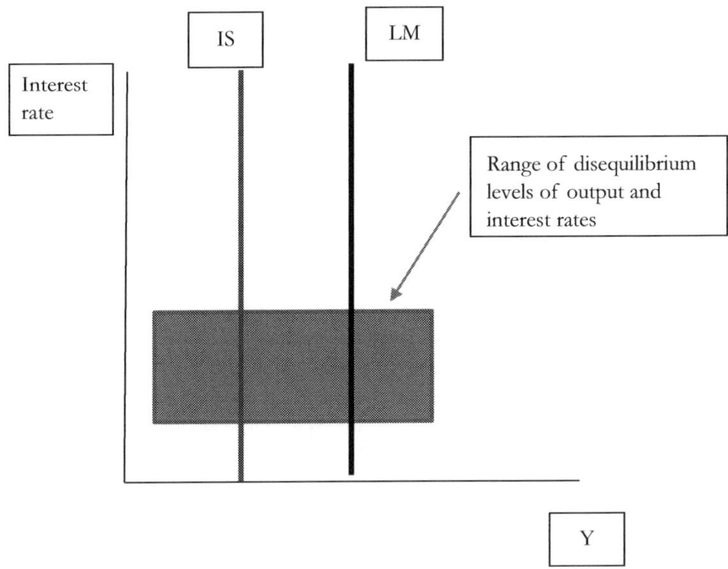

Figure 9.8 The Chopstick Economy: Rather than a single equilibrium point, China has a range of possible combinations of interest rates and levels of output. Authorities can choose to be on or off and IS or LM curve for prolonged periods as long as they operate within a range permitted by capital mobility and employment constraints (the shaded box).
Source: Author created.

Aggregate Demand and Supply

The absence of explicit roles for prices (since they are sticky) and the supply of goods are clear shortcomings of the traditional IS/LM framework. A broader framework of aggregate supply and demand (AS and AD) has proven a useful step forward (in reality, a step back to earlier macroeconomic roots). We first introduce the new element, aggregate supply. Both a short-run supply curve and long-run, full-employment supply curve are presented. Figure 9.9 shows both curves in which (as always) (*P*) represents an index of average prices, and (*Y*) represents real GDP. On the long run (Y_{Full}) curve, we have a classical supply curve—a constraint or boundary representing full employment of the economy's labor force and other key factors of production. This curve is shaped by long-run fundamental factors (described in Chapter 4). Factors of production—such as capital stock, labor force, and technology—all determine this boundary. While these can change over time, in the short run, they act as constraints. Obviously, it is difficult to quickly change the labor force or capital stock at full employment. As both increase over time (as we saw in Chapter 4 with the Solow framework), the long-run supply curve moves to the right.

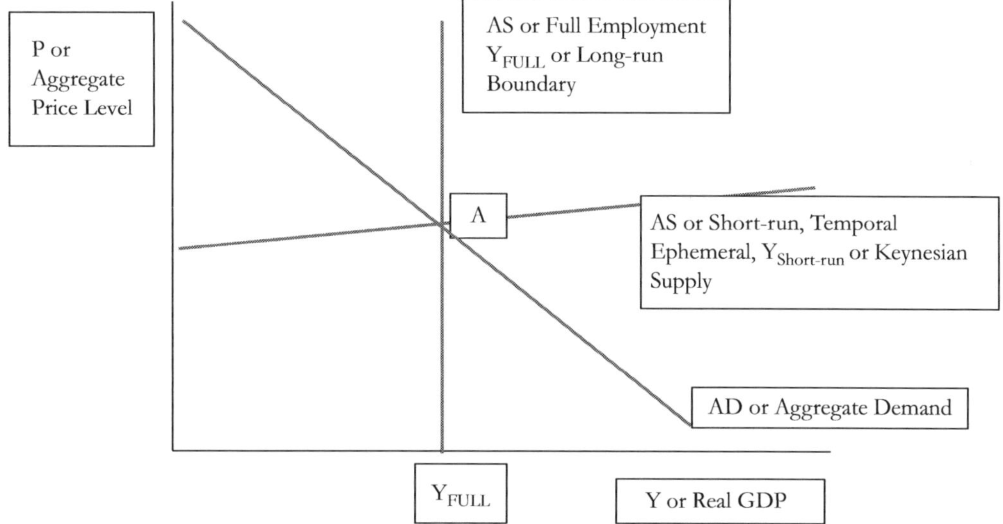

Figure 9.9 The aggregate demand and supply framework (AD and AS) is more comprehensive in that it allows for prices to play a role in the long run while allowing for sticky prices in the short run.
Source: Author created.

The short-run supply curve represents temporary possibilities to be either below full employment (to be on the short-run curve to the left of the vertical long-run supply curve) or above full employment (to the right of full employment on the short-run supply). If we are above full employment, the short-run curve gradually drifts upward, representing economy-wide price increases. If we are below full employment, the short-run curve gradually shifts downward, representing price declines caused by falling demand.[8]

The aggregate demand curve comprises all of the demand-creating components of the IS/LM framework: (*C*), (*I*), (*G*), (*t*), (*NX*), and (*M*). We can consider it as a reduced form (or summary) of the IS/LM framework. Anything that increases any of these components of demand will shift the AD curve to the right and move us along a short-run supply curve initially, then eventually to a new position on the long-run supply curve (AS).

A second, simpler, and more intuitive way to derive the AD curve is to view it from the perspective of the QTOM (discussed in Chapters 7 and 8):

$$M \times V = P \times Y_{\text{Real}}$$

Recall that (*M*) is the nominal money supply. Velocity (*V*) is the average number of times the money supply circulates to acquire GDP, and (*P*) and (*Y*) are as defined earlier. Rearranging, we have:

$$Y_{\text{Real}} = (M \times V) / P$$

Assuming that ($M \times V$) is constant, the above represents a rectangular hyperbola (or, graphically, a demand curve relating the price level with demand for real GDP). If either (*M*) or (*V*) increases, the demand curve shifts to the right. In the IS/LM framework, (*V*) will increase if (*C*), (*I*), or (*G*) increase, or if (*t*) decreases. An expansionary monetary policy, for example, would increases (*M*) and shift the curve to the right; expansionary fiscal policy increases (*V*) if we are below full employment. Therefore, this approach is fully consistent with the IS/LM approach in terms of explaining how the AD curve shifts to the right.

Figure 9.10 shows the effect of a policy causing the AD curve to shift to the right due to changes in (*C*), (*I*), (*G*), (*t*), or (*M*). If we begin at point A (full employment) and try to move the economy above full employment, we first succeed in moving to point B. However, eventually, the ephemeral (temporary, unstable) AS short-run curve floats upward until it intersects with the AS long-run curve at point C. Our expansionary policy would have only accomplished either increasing prices or crowding out some other component of demand, and we would be right back at full employment. In other words, our expansionary policy would have been completely ineffective. If, on the other hand, we had initially started at point Z, our expansionary policy might have prevented economic stagnation below full employment.[9]

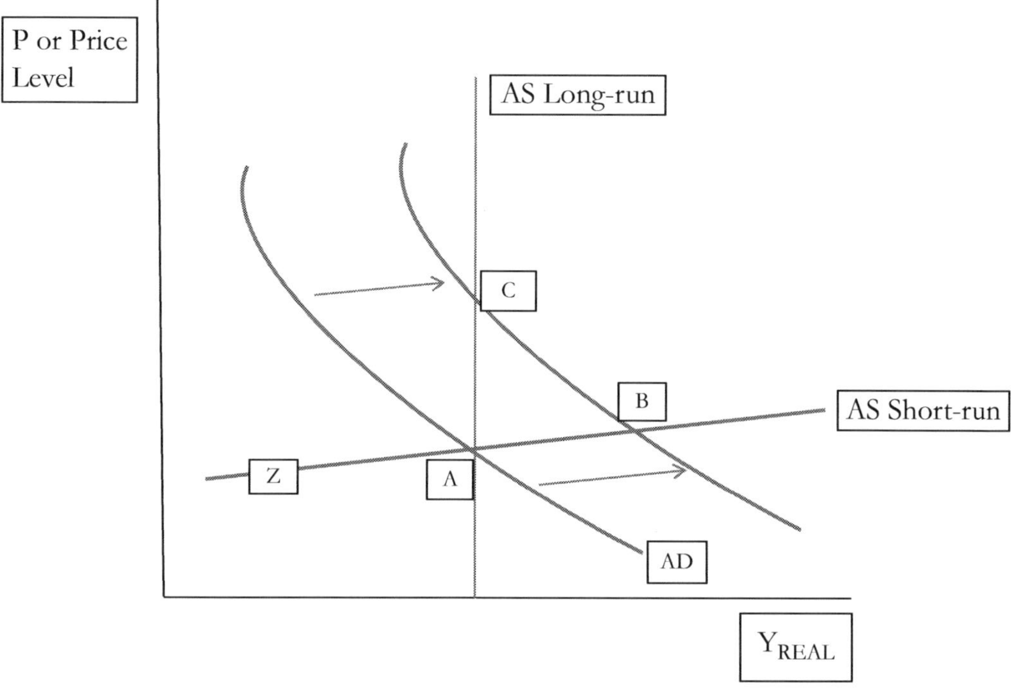

Figure 9.10 If we assume we start at full employment (point A), an increase in the money supply would cause the aggregate demand curve (AD) to shift rightward, increasing output in the short run to point B, but only causing higher prices in the long run (point C). If our initial state is one of unemployment or insufficient demand (point Z), then an increase in demand could move us to full employment (point A).
Source: Author created.

Case Study 9.2: COVID-19 and Supply Shocks

Most economists believe that economic recessions occur as a result of the cumulative effect of a series of "shocks," that is, random but economically significant disturbances—for example, a bad harvest or a change in tax policies. We can classify these shocks as supply shocks or demand shocks. For example in Figure 9.9, a shift to the left of either the short-run or long-run supply curve would result in slower growth and higher inflation, while a shift to the left of the demand curve would result in slower growth and lower inflation.[10] In fact, the impact on inflation would be one way to distinguish between a supply shock and a demand shock. Drautzburg (2019), for example (based on a model of Smets and Wouters [2007]) estimates that about half of the variation in GDP growth in the United States between 1965 and 2004 was due to demand shocks and the other half was due to supply shocks. In most cases, a combination of these two shocks played a role in output variation.

In the first quarter of 2020, COVID-19, which first struck China and then spread to the United States and the rest of the world, was clearly an economic shock relevant to economic growth and inflation. What type of shock was it? Since it resulted in restrictions on workers' supply of labor, the closure of production facilities, and a severe cutback in transportation, we can conclude that it was principally a supply shock. To the extent that consumption demand and exports fell, we could also argue that there is a demand component to the shock. In other words, our supply curves in Figure 9.9 shifted to the left, and the demand curve for China likely did as well. We could contrast this shock with the impact of the 2008 GFC on China, in which the main impact was a large decline in demand—principally a decline in export demand by 47 percent in 2008–2009.

Economists, relying on Keynesian insights, have a good set of policy tools and recommendations for demand type shocks: reboot demand via expansionary fiscal and monetary policies—shift the demand curve back to the right. Supply shocks such as COVID-19 present a much greater challenge. How does one reboot supply when workers are constrained to their homes and transportation is shut down? Similar questions played out in the United States during the oil shock of 1973–1974. Boosting demand in response to a supply shock carries the risk of accelerating inflation even further and making the situation worse. Perhaps the best strategy for a short-run supply shock is to wait it out until the source of the shock vanishes, or work to mitigate the shock itself (in this case, the virus). For longer-term supply shocks, such as a demographic shrinking of the labor force, longer-term solutions are needed. In earlier chapters, we have emphasized the role of technological progress as a key response when long-run supply encounters constraining shocks.

Keynesian Model Extensions

Goods Market Equilibrium and Interest Rate Overshooting

One extension of the standard Keynesian model presented above is to assume that the market for financial assets is always in equilibrium, while the goods market could be out of equilibrium for a period of time. Money markets, equity markets, and other financial markets usually have extremely flexible prices, responding instantaneously to news (the efficient markets assumption from finance). Because prices respond instantaneously to equilibrate demand and supply for financial assets, those markets are always in equilibrium. In contrast, prices in the goods and services markets adjust slowly (if at all), causing excess demand or supply, inventory decumulation or accumulation, and markets to be temporarily out of equilibrium. In our IS/LM framework, the implication of these assumptions about the speed of price adjustment in each market suggests that we are always on an LM curve (the original LM or a new LM, after a change in the money supply), but we can fall off of an IS curve (above or below it). In other words, unplanned inventories might be accumulating or decumulating.

Figure 9.11 shows an example of a contractionary monetary policy (i.e., a policy in which the money supply is decreased). In this case, the LM curve shifts upward, as does the interest rate—a vertical jump from (i_1) to ($i_{1.5}$) in which interest rates hop to the new LM curve. We are temporarily stuck at (Y_1), but we gradually move along this LM curve to a new, lower economic equilibrium—(Y_2) and (i_2). Note that, during the transition from (Y_1) to (Y_2), we are in goods market disequilibrium (off and above the IS curve); that curve is the equilibrium locale. While off the IS curve, we have an excess supply of goods and inventory accumulation. In response, companies will cut back production, causing output (Y) to decrease over time. In summary, interest rates adjust instantaneously, and we overshoot the long-run equilibrium interest rate (i_2), causing output to decline in a prolonged transition of disequilibrium in which the supply of goods and services exceeds their demand.

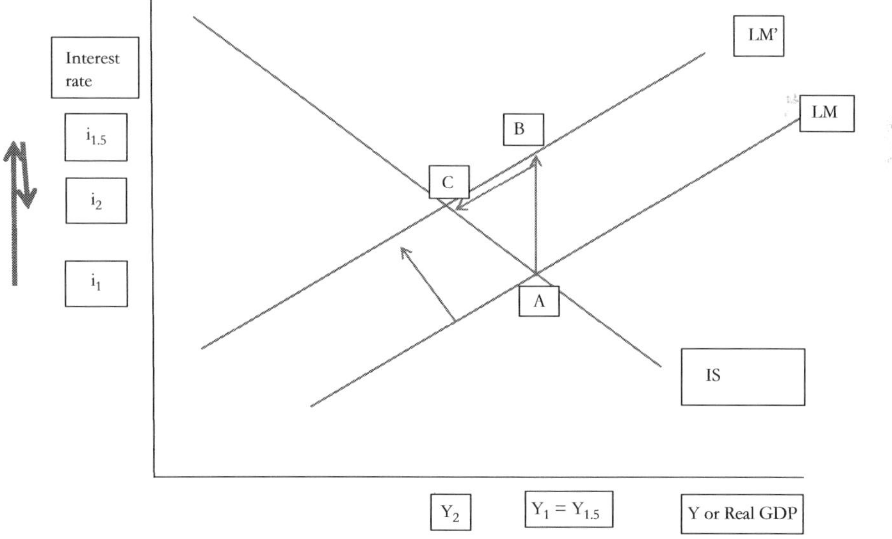

Figure 9.11 In the case of efficient financial markets that clear immediately but a goods market that does not clear in the short run, there can be overshooting. Here, a decrease in the money supply causes interest rates to first jump from point A to point B, but then output eventually falls consistent with the decrease in the money supply and we end up at point C. The vertical gap between point B and point C is referred to as overshooting. Source: Author created.

The disequilibrium situation of being off the IS curve is fully caused by the sticky price assumption. In a more classical model, only one interest rate equates savings with investment—and the IS curve would be flat at that interest rate. If the IS curve is flat at an interest rate consistent with savings equaling investment, then monetary policy (shifts in the LM) would have no impact on the equilibrium interest rate. If prices adjust in tandem with the money supply, such that (M / P) is constant, then changes in nominal money would not matter (i.e., would not shift the LM curve). With such assumptions, the economy would always operate at long-run equilibrium, and there would not be much room for policy action. However, we must question how reasonable it is to assume market clearing prices in goods markets when, even in financial markets (contrary to our assumption above), prices of financial assets do not always clear markets. The existence of circuit breakers in equity markets and the collapse of auction rate securities markets in February of 2008 are examples of financial markets not operating with complete smoothness—and these are markets with sophisticated participants in a normally-liquid environment. If even these markets sometimes fail to clear and encounter frictions, it is reasonable that the market for goods, services, and labor (which are much less transparent and less liquid) could regularly fail to clear.

Overshooting in Currency Markets

In the scenario above, we saw that the overshooting of interest rates occurs when prices are sticky (do not move in response to economic shocks) and the goods market does not immediately equilibrate. In this section, we examine a situation in which exchange rates can overshoot, prices are sticky, and the exchange rate is in disequilibrium for the short run. Disequilibrium occurs when the exchange rate does not immediately adjust to its purchasing power parity (PPP) or long-run value. Recall that PPP states that the price of a homogeneous product expressed in the same currency should have the same price—otherwise, an arbitrage opportunity exists. Both domestic prices and the exchange rate should adjust to prevent arbitrage opportunities. For example, the price of an apple in Detroit, Michigan, expressed in US dollars (USD), should be the same as the price of an apple in Windsor, Ontario, also expressed in USD. Otherwise, consumers and wholesalers would buy all their apples from the cheaper location.[11]

In the overshooting model for exchange rates, as developed by Dornbusch (1976), we utilize the following relationships:

Purchasing Power Parity

$$P^{Z}_{\text{USD}} = \text{USD / RMB} \times P^{Z}_{\text{RMB}}$$

That is, the price of product (Z) expressed in USD will be the same in the United States and China after factoring in the exchange rate. We assume this holds true in the long run but not the short run.

Uncovered Interest Rate Parity and Capital Mobility

$$r^{US} - r^{China} = \text{USD Depreciation or Appreciation (+/-) against the RMB}$$

This relationship assumes that capital flows freely across borders between two countries to seek the highest return. As such, it is an arbitrage condition for financial assets. If the risk-free return on US assets (r^{US})is higher than the risk-free return on Chinese assets (r^{China}), then the dollar must be expected to depreciate over time in order to make the returns expressed in USD the same. This is another arbitrage condition (assuming no risk premium) on asset returns. We assume that this relationship always holds true except during the initial period after an unexpected policy change.

Quantity Theory of Money

As described above, here we assume the following relationship, where (V) is the assumed constant velocity of money, (P) is the price level, (M) is the nominal money supply, and (Y_{Real}) is real GDP:

$$(M \times V) / Y_{\text{Real}} = P$$

In other words, large increases in (M) relative to (Y_{Real}) will yield increases in prices or inflation.

Short-Run Keynesian Economics with Capital Mobility

We use the same standard Keynesian model assumptions discussed in the Chapter 8, but with the additional assumption that capital can flow into or out of an economy when domestic interest rates go above or below world interest rates (Mundell 1963; Fleming 1962). With these assumptions and conditions, we can examine the impact on the exchange rate of an increase in the money supply in one country. Since capital is still not freely mobile into and out of China, we will use an example for the United States and Europe instead. Suppose our initial exchange rate in Figure 9.12 at time 0 is 1, and that interest rates in each country are initially equal. For expansionary policy purposes, the United States decides to increase monetary growth above trend. This is our initial assumed shock to the system.

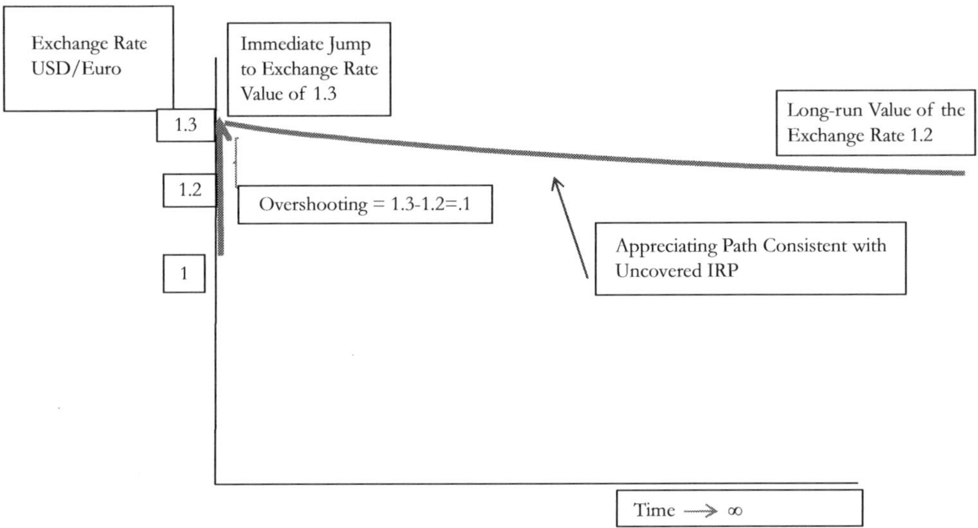

Figure 9.12 In the case of exchange rate overshooting, an increase in the money supply in the United States leads to an overshooting of the exchange rate. In this case, the dollar first weakens by a substantial amount, but then strengthens over time. It never fully recovers, however.
Source: Author created.

We solve this problem by starting at the end of time, or out toward the infinity benchmark in Figure 9.12. Following PPP and the QTOM, the long-run impact of more money in the US economy would be greater inflation and a weaker USD (at point 1.2).

Moving now to the first instant after the monetary expansion is known (the very short run), we turn to the expanded IS/LM model. In this model of capital mobility (Mundell 1963; Fleming 1962), capital flows out of the United States and into Europe due to the initial drop in US interest rates—a shift that would weaken the value of the USD. How far would it weaken the dollar? Far enough from its fundamental PPP long-run value that it would be expected, over time, to actually appreciate. That appreciation would be just sufficient (à la uncovered interest rate parity) to offset the initial lower interest rate differential caused by US monetary expansion. That path of appreciation is represented by the curved line in the center of Figure 9.12. In summary, we start off with an exchange rate of 1, immediately jump to 1.3 (after the announcement), then gradually appreciate to 1.2 over time.

The notion of overshooting assumes that we depreciate beyond what is necessary in a PPP sense by the difference, (1.3 – 1.2), or 0.1. But then the exchange rate gradually works its way back from 1.3 to 1.2. Once again, overshooting occurs when a key variable (such as price) is sticky, causing other variables to adjust more than they otherwise would in order to absorb the monetary shock.

Macro Finance Insight 9.1: Is a Nation's Exchange Rate Its "Stock Price?"

The notion of efficient markets in finance states that stock prices reflect all publicly-available information on the value of a company to shareholders, and that non-random movements in the share price reflect new fundamental information.[*] Does the value of a country's currency (the exchange rate) similarly capture fundamental information regarding the strength or weakness of an economy? In some ways, the exchange rate provides a clearer signal because it represents relative prices (against another country's currency), while the movement of a stock price must always be gauged against the overall market, a comparable industry, or another asset class.

For the special case surrounding financial crises in countries (corresponding to situations of corporate financial distress), the exchange rate plays the same role as stock prices—showing a sharp depreciation. Based on a survey of more than 80 academic studies on financial crises, Frankel and Saravelos (2012) state that the "vast majority of studies include some measure of changes in the exchange rate" (page 4)—specifically, a depreciation of 25 percent or more. In fact, financial crises are often defined in terms of sharp depreciations (relative to trend) in the exchange rate. But the story does not end here. The authors also find that the real exchange rate (the exchange rate adjusted for inflation in each country) tends to appreciate in the months before a financial crisis. That appreciation corresponds, in some cases, to a speculative bubble found in overvalued stocks. As in the case of equities, a surge in capital inflows (or investor interest) pushes up either the exchange rate or the stock price. The surge in inflows corresponds either to irrational exuberance or, in some cases, the counterpart to current account deficits. We see an overshooting of the exchange rate, devastation on the trade balance, and ultimately, a violation of the intertemporal budget constraint presented in this chapter's Appendix. Unsustainable, the path of the economy leads to a crisis.[†]

A more normal, secular, and non-crisis relationship between exchange rates was explained in Chapter 3. There, we identified ($S - I$), the adjusted current account balance, as a measure of a nation's cash flow. The larger the cash flow (corresponding to net external indebtedness), the higher the valuation; or, in our case, the stronger the exchange rate.[‡] Broadly speaking, current account deficits (negative cash flows) imply a currency depreciation (see Obstfeld 2012 or earlier arguments dating back to the gold standard to find the basis for this conclusion). In effect, depreciation of the currency rebalances current account imbalances. In the context of stock prices, bad news must result in a stock price low enough to ultimately yield a competitive return. The latter effect is, in fact, identical to the exchange rate overshooting model (see our earlier discussion) in which the exchange rate must adjust sufficiently far from its long-run equilibrium to attract foreign investors to continue holding assets denominated in that currency.

The above discussion expands on the valuable work of Calvo and Mishkin (2003) and others who examine the costs and benefits of different exchange rate regimes. They conclude that what really matters is the institutional framework, including independence of the monetary authorities and the soundness of the financial system underlying the exchange rate system. We add to that work by suggesting here that a critical benefit of a floating exchange rate regime is that it provides a clear signal regarding government policies and economic performance by providing greater transparency than fixed exchange rates. We could argue that the fixed exchange rate regime found under the euro system since 1999 hid many fundamental problems that would have been seen earlier and more clearly under a floating exchange rate regime for countries such as Greece and Spain. This is one critical advantage of a floating exchange rate over a fixed exchange rate regime.

Figure 9.13a and Figure 9.13b show China's nominal and real exchange rate. The nominal exchange rate begins appreciating substantially in 2005, while a secular and significant real appreciation of the *renminbi* (RMB) began in 1994 (rising by nearly 40 percent in that period).[12] How should we interpret this? We could interpret the pressure on the RMB to appreciate either as: (1) a reflection of its artificial undervaluation compared to very upbeat valuations of the Chinese economy by the international community; or, (2) a leading indicator of an imminent financial crisis, as discussed above.

In the first case, the causes stem from international investors' appetite to hold RMB as an investment. In the second case, the causes stem from an overvalued RMB leading to current account deficits and a precipitous depletion of foreign exchange. Frankel and Saravelos (2012) shed light on this question by pointing out that another significant leading indicator for financial collapse, in conjunction with an appreciating real exchange rate, is a secular loss of foreign exchange reserves. Figure 9.13c show that this is clearly not the story in China; rather, China has seen an enormous gain in foreign exchange reserves (i.e., its cash flow has been positive and very large) in recent years. Together, this information suggests that the strengthening of the RMB reflects the international community's fundamental assessment of the Chinese economy as growing in value. (We also observe, in Figure 9.13b, on average, a flat real exchange rate over most of the period for the United States, but overall strengthening post-GFC.) Nevertheless, the longer China maintains a quasi-fixed exchange rate with its concomitant lack of transparency, the greater the opportunity for fundamental problems to accumulate. The current arrangement also confounds efforts at financial liberalization. Finally, we note that, since the GFC, the RMB has tended to depreciate. One interpretation for this phenomenon is that global investors have become less optimistic regarding the Chinese economy; more controversially, another interpretation is that policy-makers in China are using the exchange rate as a tool to counter Trump trade-war tariffs.

*This is the semi-strong form of the efficient markets hypothesis. The strong form asserts that even non-public "insider" information is reflected in the stock price.

†Sometimes, over-valuation results from a fixed exchange rate regime combined with rapidly rising domestic prices (inflation). The outcome remains the same as described above.

‡Recall that, for valuation purposes, we exclude cash flows related to financing activities—specifically, borrowing and investing activities. From a pure accounting perspective, the cash-flow statement does include financing flows.

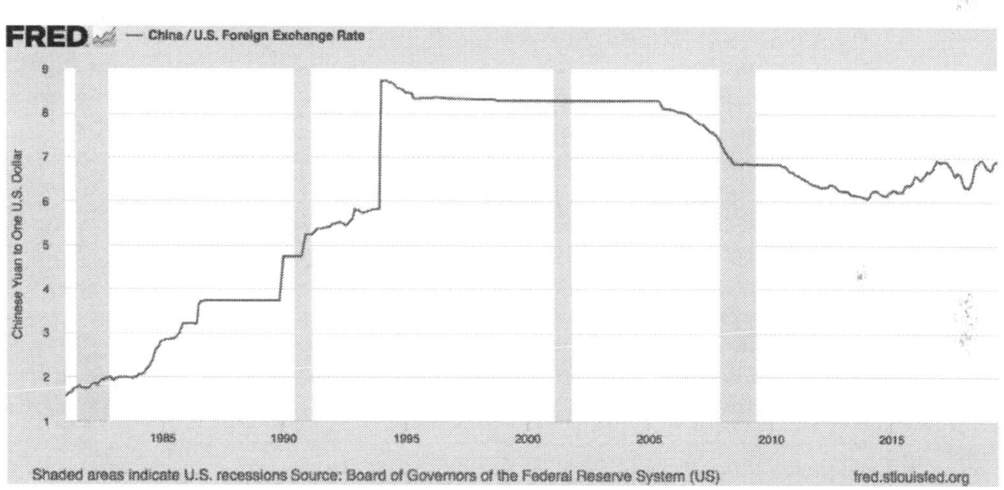

Figure 9.13a China's nominal exchange rate has depreciated by about 12.7 percent since April, 2018 (through August, 2019), and it does not fully float in response to market forces (the International Monetary Fund classifies it as a "crawl-like" currency arrangement). Source: Author created based on data from the Federal Reserve Economic Database.

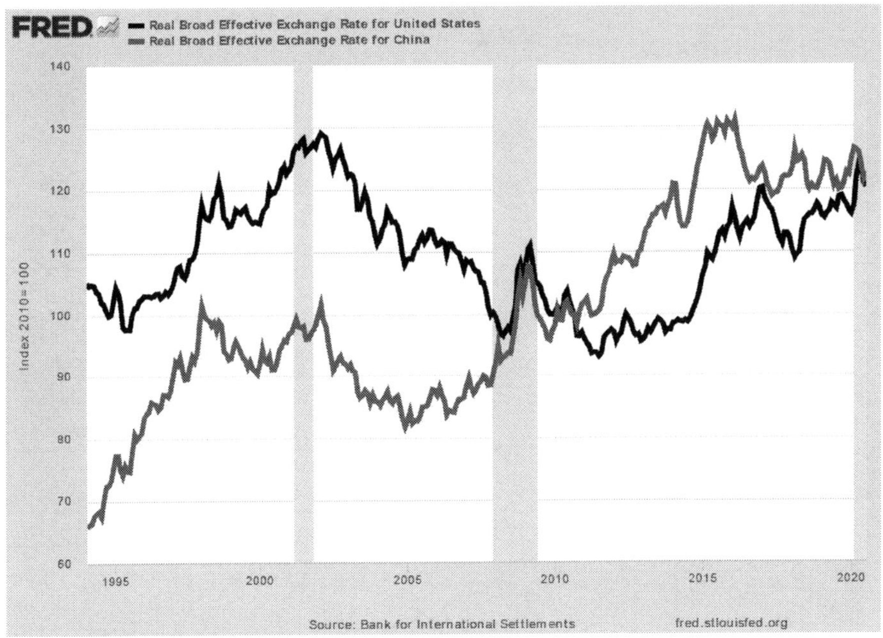

Figure 9.13b Real effective exchange rates are weighted exchange rates adjusted for inflation in the partner countries. The US and China's real exchange rates appear to move together over the long term (since the nominal exchange rate between the two countries is fairly stable), but differences in inflation do matter. Beginning in 2010, China's real effective exchange rate had appreciated more than the United States' rate, but since 2018 the difference has narrowed.
Source: Author created based on data from the Federal Reserve Economic Database.

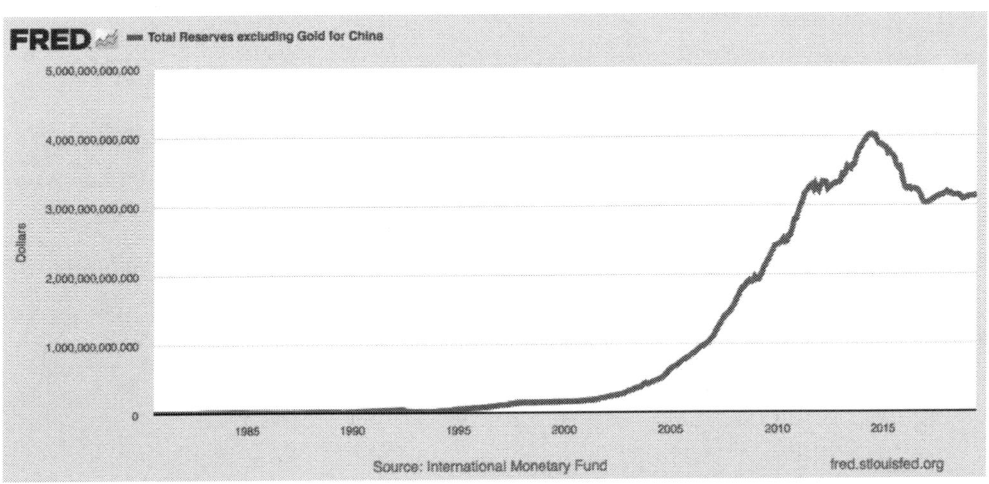

Figure 9.13c China's foreign exchange reserves peaked at around USD 4 trillion in June, 2014, but they have since declined as a result of capital outflows and shrinking current account surpluses.
Source: Author created based on data from the Federal Reserve Economic Database.

Macro Finance Insight 9.2: Sticky Capital Stock—Overshooting in Equity Markets

By now, we should be fairly familiar with the notion of overshooting and how it can occur. In this third case, we consider the role of equity markets regarding international capital mobility. Consider a country such as China that has restricted international capital flows for many years. By this, we mean that the financial flows in and out of the country have been strictly controlled.* Furthermore, we reasonably assume that the capital stock (plant, property, equipment, infrastructure, and human capital) is a very sticky variable. In other words, we cannot increase the capital stock overnight; in most countries, it takes decades to make substantial capital stock enhancements.

Finally, we introduce Tobin's Q, as defined previously:

Q = Market Capitalization of the Capital Stock / Replacement Cost of the Capital Stock†

In a normal equilibrium state, we would expect Q to be close to 1. If it is greater than 1, there would be an incentive to raise funds in capital markets and acquire additional units of the cheaper capital. If Q is less than 1, firms would sell off some of their capital and use the cash proceeds to enhance value. In fact, Q can deviate from 1. In periods of optimism regarding growth prospects and options for the firm, investors may place a premium in equity markets over the underlying cost of capital assets. Figure 9.14 shows one measure of Tobin's Q for the United States based on Federal Reserve and United States Commerce Department data.

Figure 9.15 shows the effects of a country such as China opening its capital markets fully to foreign capital. Initially, we start with a closed economy at point A, where Q equals 1 and is at equilibrium. The demand for equity (or an even broader range of local assets) is purely local, and the supply of equity in the short run is relatively inelastic (vertical). Once we open capital markets to foreign investors, the demand for equity shifts to the right.‡ Since the physical supply of capital cannot shift instantaneously (i.e., it is sticky, but it does increase over a much longer time frame), we adjust to point B in the short run. That is, the price of equity adjusts instantaneously (overshoots). The price will move sufficiently high to restore equilibrium in the equity market from the combined domestic and international investor base. The high Q will result in a compelling incentive for firms to add new capital until long-run equilibrium is restored at point C. Thus, in this case, the amount of overshooting is the gap between point B and point C.

This model demonstrates why countries must be very careful in their efforts to open capital markets. The movement from point A to point B creates an enormous capital gain for the pre-existing in-country owners of capital. In fact, they capture all future excess returns instantaneously.

This gain raises serious questions of wealth distribution and fairness. How were those initial shares acquired and then sold? If the initial wealth holders acquired their wealth in an unsavory fashion, the enormous returns generated from the opening of capital markets may very well lead to social, political, and economic problems. The cases of privatization of capital markets, foreign involvement, and transfer of state assets in Eastern Europe and Russia in the 1990s are instructive in this context. And, as China moves toward greater capital account liberalization, lessons learned there are of great use.

*If it were possible to increase the capital stock quickly, emerging economies could arrive at the same level of development as the developed economies more easily.

†Sometimes, the book value of capital is used as a surrogate for replacement cost.

‡In finance, this may sound odd. The value of companies is simply the net present value of their cash flows—so how can changes in the investor base affect that value? A change in the investor base can change value because foreigners will have different costs of capital based on different macro policies (interest rates) and different needs for diversification.

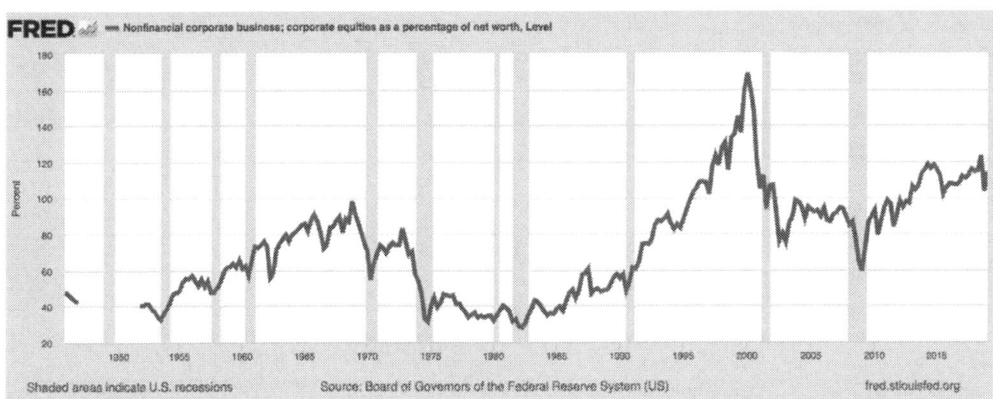

Figure 9.14 A measure of Tobin's Q shows market valuations substantially higher than book values in the United States.
Source: Federal Reserve Economic Database.

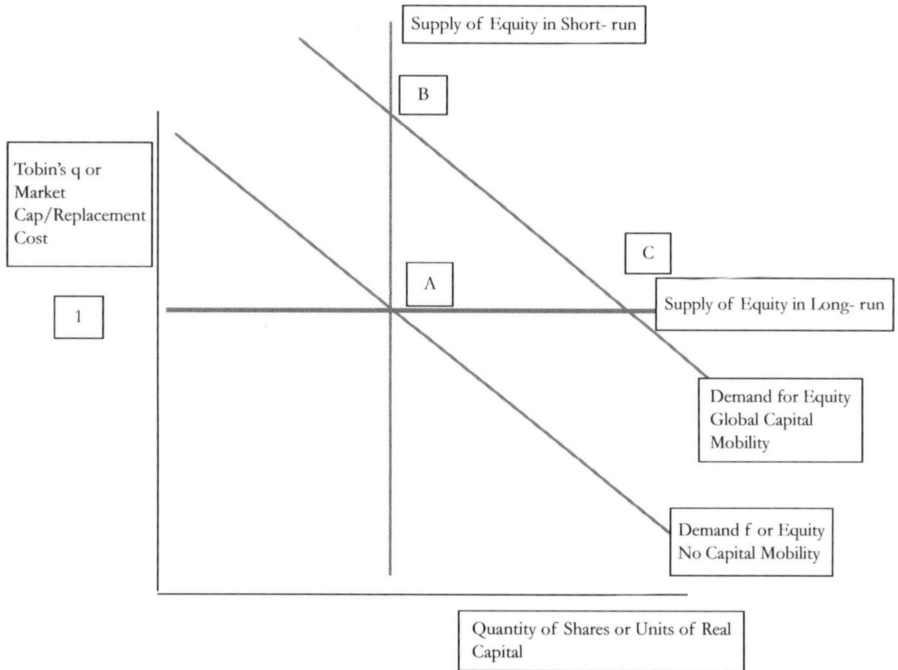

Figure 9.15 For a country that opens up its markets to foreign financial capital inflows, demand for assets could surge, causing the price to jump from point A to point B. In that initial overshooting, the stream of excess future returns (capital gains) are captured by the initial owners of the assets (local owners). It is therefore critical that the process of capital account liberalization and sale of assets be fair to all citizens, particularly to those locals who are not owners of the sold assets.
Source: Author created.

Challenges to Fiscal Policy for Economic Management

The effectiveness of fiscal policy, as we have described it above, has been questioned on a number of fronts—both economic and political. This criticism represents a generally conservative "free-market" approach regarding the role and size of government in an economy. This critique views fiscal policy as a zero-sum game in which the private sector gets the short end of the stick (loses) when the government intervenes. We now discuss economic arguments against using fiscal policies to manage an economy.

Crowding Out: The Case Against More Government Spending

The crowding out argument states that fiscal policy, particularly increased government spending, only serves to squeeze out private-sector spending. In other words, while government spending may move the economy one step forward, reduced private spending moves the economy one step back. How does this work? In the basic IS/LM framework (as we saw in Figure 9.5), an increase in government spending shifts the IS curve to the right. That shift causes interest rates to rise (assuming that the demand for money is not completely sensitive to changes in interest rates—as in all cases except for a flat LM curve). The resulting increase in interest rates leads to reduced investment and other interest-sensitive sources of demand (such as auto purchases). The more sensitive investment demand is to interest rates, the flatter the IS curve, and the greater the investment reduction. This process is known as "crowding out," since private-sector spending and the private sector's share of the economy shrinks as a result of increased government spending or fiscal policy. The financial market counterpart to this phenomenon is increased government spending that is financed with debt. This increase, in turn, collides with private-sector financing needs, driving up borrowing costs and crowding out the private sector's investment plans.

Alternatively, we could see crowding out in the AS/AD framework (see Figure 9.10), in which the AD curve shifts to the right due to increased government spending and the AS curve is vertical. The vertical AS curve corresponds to an economy operating at full employment. Thus, any rightward shift of AD leads to higher prices (from point A to point C, or P_1 to P_2)—and these higher prices correspond to either a reduction in the real money supply and higher interest rates or the same chain of events described in the earlier paragraph: a rise in interest rates, a drop in investment and a decline in overall demand. If government spending is paid for with increases in the money supply, we simply get inflation, and private consumption is crowded out due to the higher prices—with no corresponding increase in overall output.

The Keynesian response to the above critique is "of course, this is obvious." Attempting to increase output beyond full employment is indeed pointless. Rather, the Keynesian world corresponds to a special case of Figure 9.9 or Figure 9.10—where the aggregate supply curve is perfectly elastic (flat) because workers and suppliers of goods and services have such a high rate of unemployment that they are willing to supply output without constraint and without a tendency toward price increases. Instead of prices rising, real output rises from Y_1 to Y_2. Fiscal policy is fully effective in this case, with no crowding out.

An alternative way to view crowding out is shown in Figure 9.16a and Figure 9.16b. Here, the expansion of the government sector squeezes into the investment and consumer shares of GDP; meanwhile, overall GDP (the whole size of the pie) does not change at all. Figure 9.16c corresponds to the Keynesian view of the effectiveness of fiscal policy. Here, increased government spending expands the pie so that all the sectors expand—from recession to recovery mode.

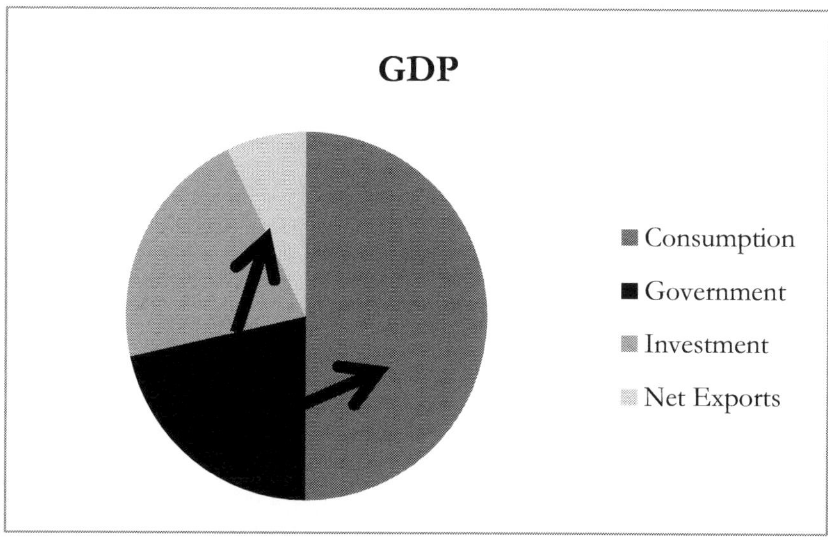

Figure 9.16a Crowding out occurs when the Government sector expands but the GDP pie remains the same size. The implication is that other sectors' share of the pie must be reduced.
Source: Author created.

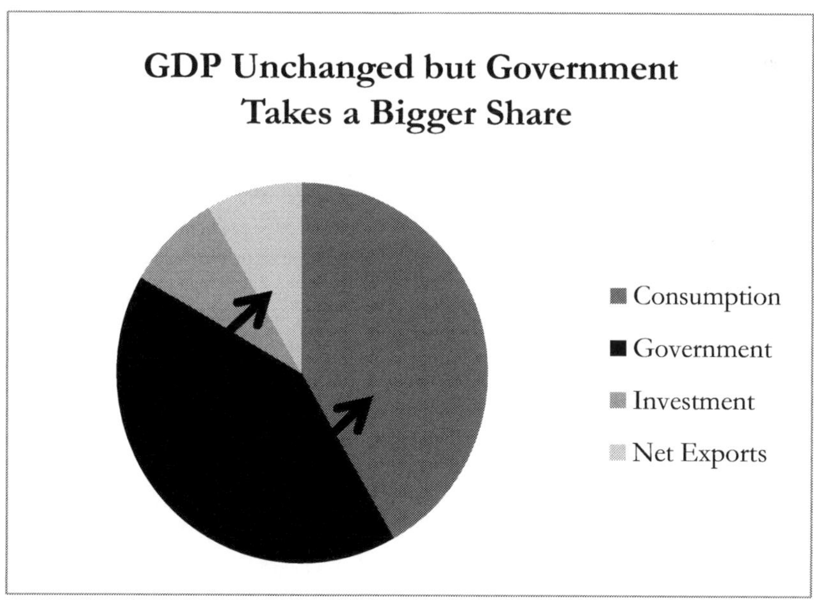

Figure 9.16b The government sector is larger but investment, consumption, and exports are all smaller.
Source: Author created.

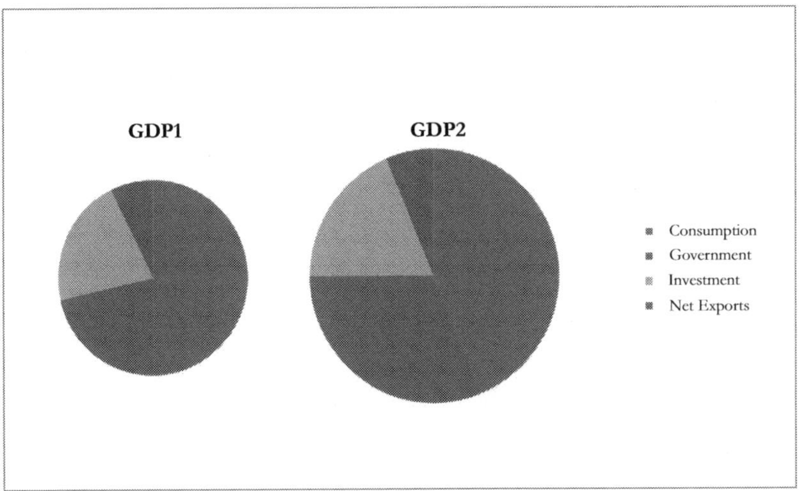

Figure 9.16c In the Keynesian case of unemployment and recession, an increase in government demand increases the size of the pie and everyone benefits from a bigger share. Source: Author created.

Case Study 9.3: Crowding Out in China

The notion of crowding out takes on a very different meaning in the Chinese context for four separate reasons: First, China is in a stage of continued rapid growth (as we have discussed) in which the risk is a growth recession rather than a traditional business cycle recession. In China, crowding out depends on whether the government is capturing a larger share of fresh economic growth, rather than a larger share of an economy that is fixed in size. Second, the role of China's state-owned enterprises (SOEs) in producing private sector goods remains significant, albeit diminishing.* For China, the question of crowding out relates more to SOEs producing private goods rather than private firms producing them. In contrast, traditional crowding out relates to the production of public goods and services at the expense of private goods and services.† Third, China's Big Four (the four largest banks) still have the government as their principal shareholder, and these banks (on a secular basis) continue to channel a disproportionate amount of funds to the state-owned sector as opposed to the private sector. Fourth, government policies related to crowding out fall just as heavily on the production side as the expenditure side. In the past, government policies biased the economy toward the production of investment goods over consumption goods, and exchange rate policies pushed the economy to export production over consumption production. These outcomes turn the Western notion of crowding out upside down; in the West, crowding out is often viewed as government expenditures squeezing out investment.

*As an indication of that: by 2010, about half of China's workforce was still employed in state-owned units; in 2001, approximately three-fourths worked in the state sector.

[†]Public goods are often defined by the characteristics of non-excludability and non-rival; the former represents goods or services which, once provided, are inevitably open-access (such as national defense). The latter represents goods in which one person's use does not preclude another person's use (such as the benefit of a lighthouse in a harbor).

Ricardian Equivalence: Linking Government Spending to Future Taxation

Ricardian equivalence is a budget constraint applied to a government's ability to borrow, spend, and tax over time. It states that governments cannot persistently borrow to finance current budget deficits if they cannot afford to service the resulting obligations through tax collections and/or reduced expenditures in the future. Alternatively, budget deficits must ultimately stabilize as a share of GDP. In this chapter's Appendix, we present a form of this type of argument adjusted for an entire country and its financial relationship with the rest of the world. There, we show that countries would be constrained by international capital markets from borrowing more internationally than they could afford to pay back via trade and non-factor service balance surpluses in the future. Recall that:

$$S - I = (G + \mathit{Transfers} - \text{Taxes}) + (X - M + NFP)$$

In other words, the intertemporal budget constraint in the international sphere corresponds to the $(X - M + NFP)$ term, while $(G + \mathit{Transfers} - \text{Taxes})$ corresponds to the budget deficit (+) and Ricardian equivalence. [13] The two constraints are linked and coexist; the domestic private sector $(S - I)$ and foreign lenders $(X - M + NFP)$ will not finance an unsustainable budget deficit (Ricardian equivalence), while international lenders will not finance an unsustainable current account deficit.

As the key corollary to Ricardian equivalence, any expansion of government spending or reduction of taxes today will require raising taxes or reducing government spending in the future in order to be sustainable. Ricardian equivalence therefore implies that fiscal policy is neutralized once taxpayers/citizens realize that today's expansion only implies a future reduction in government benefits and services or increased taxes. Today's government spending increases (fiscal policy) are offset by concurrent reductions in private-sector consumption or investment in a rational anticipation of either reduced benefits to consumers or a heavier tax burden.

These conclusions, although algebraically correct (if we assume a full employment economy), may not be valid in practice. Whether such rational calculations can be assumed to take place in an economy such as China's is an open question. In recent years, both the senior leadership and the common man (the *lao bai xing*) in China have questioned the sustainability of current policies described throughout this text. The question of sustainability has led the Chinese to seek ways to either build wealth or diversify their wealth internationally, and to increase consumption. While in some ways this shift is following the spirit of Ricardian equivalence, it is unlikely to hold much weight in discounting the effectiveness of short-run fiscal policy in China.

Macro Finance Insight 9.3: Adjusted Tobin's Q as a Measure of Economic Performance

We suggest, in Macro Finance Insight 9.1, that one gauge of economic performance is exchange rate performance. But the absence of a freely floating exchange rate in China warrants a different approach. Another method is to examine a variation of Tobin's Q. Recall that, in 1969, the great economist and Nobel Laureate James Tobin suggested that a good way to gauge stock valuations is to compare the ratio of the market price of the stock to the replacement cost of its capital net of liabilities.[*] This approach closely aligns with the thinking of value investors such as Warren Buffet.

Using macro data, Tobin's approach can be generalized to entire stock market valuations in the United States and other industrialized economies.[†] For our purposes, it is also consistent with a well-known relationship between stock market performance and economic activity; stock prices lead economic activity by a half a year or more at recessions, and they are one of the United States' leading indicators.

Although stock market capitalization data are readily available in China, replacement cost data are not.[‡] A good variation, however, which appears to track Tobin's Q very well, is the "equitization ratio"—the ratio of overall stock market capitalization to nominal GDP. This ratio has been used by a number of economists. Figure 9.17 shows the equitization ratio for both the United States and China. We see both countries experiencing substantial overvaluations at the pre-GFC peak, then a sharp drop, followed by a recovery in the United States but a leveling off in China. Thus, the equitization ratio serves as another useful indicator of economic performance. Whether the ratio itself leads or coincides with economic activity is an area for further research.

*The former is readily available from stock market data published in each country and the latter from the company's balance sheet.

†In the United States, replacement cost data are available both from the Federal Reserve Flow of Funds Z.1 report and the US Commerce Department.

‡See, for example, the Hong Kong Stock Exchange website (https://bit.ly/2B6CWMQ):

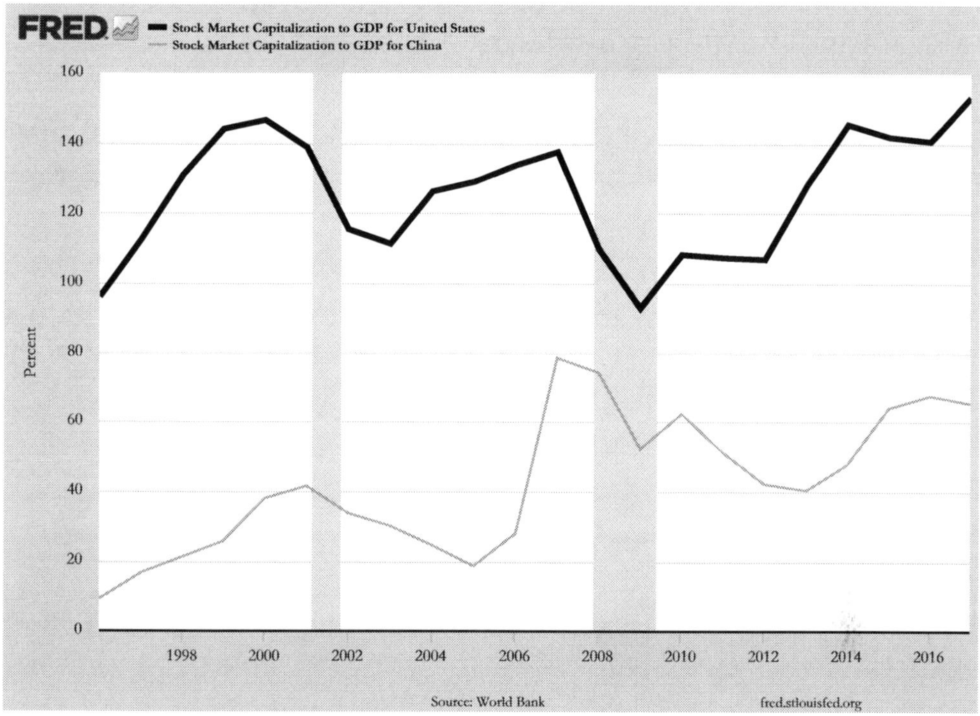

Figure 9.17 The equitization is a variation of Tobin's Q—it uses GDP in the denominator rather than replacement value, but it keeps market valuation in the numerator. US stock market value is large relative to GDP compared to China. Markets stabilized in China after the GFC, but they have surged in the United States.
Source: Author created based on data from the Federal Reserve Economic Database.

Flexible Wages, Prices, and Efficient Labor Markets

Another argument casting doubt on the stabilizing effects of fiscal policy is that, in the long run, it is unnecessary because the markets for labor and other factors of production and goods and services will move toward equilibrium through price adjustment. If there is unemployment, real wages will fall in the long run. To this argument, Keynes is said to have responded: "In the long run, we are all dead." As we have shown above, the economy normally operates on a short-run supply curve, which corresponds to either underemployment or overemployment. Clearly, the greater the flexibility of wages and prices, and the less rigid the labor markets (e.g., rules restricting hiring, firing, wages, and benefits), the more likely the economy will be to operate at full employment. That is, the less time the economy will spend on a disequilibrium short-run curve and the more time it will spend on the long-run full employment curve.

In this context, as has been posited in Case Study 9.2, approximately half of all US recessions have been caused by supply shocks rather than demand shocks (i.e., the long-run supply curve shifting to the left due to adverse events such as oil price increases, natural disasters, or technological shifts resulting in parts of the labor force becoming obsolete). If this is true, demand-shifting policies such as increases in government spending can only generate price increases without improving the long-run equilibrium level of output. Whether the source of the business cycle is a demand or supply shock, the return to full employment will be hastened when the economy is more flexible (has fewer structural rigidities). In Case Study 9.4, we examine one of the great sources of strength for the Chinese economy—the flexibility of its labor force and the adaptability of its citizens.

Case Study 9.4: The Chinese Citizen as a Great Economic Shock Absorber

Flexibility and adaptability are two key assets of the Chinese citizen as a worker, saver, and consumer—these assets are key economic drivers. These two qualities allow the citizenry to act as a "shock absorber" for economic changes occurring to the supply or demand curve. The United States' automatic stabilizers consist mainly of unemployment benefits and automatic tax receipt declines. But China is unique in that its key resource—its labor force—is critical in absorbing a wide array of economic shocks. A good example of this flexibility is the willingness of many citizens to relocate rapidly and at long distances in order to seek employment. The migration of rural workers to urban areas in China is now at a historical magnitude. One indicator is that an estimated 46 percent of China's urban laborers in 2007 were migrant workers (Cai et al. 2005). In 1978, about 76 percent of the workforce was located in rural areas; by 2010 that number had declined to 54 percent. Today, an estimated 200 million Chinese workers are floating within China seeking employment opportunities (though the number has shrunk in recent years due to a declining birth rate and greater opportunities in rural areas). The coming years should see an acceleration of this trend given that an expected 15 million rural residents will be moving to urban areas every year! This willingness to relocate in search of employment is a sign of a very dynamic and flexible workforce—and it will likely lead to better matching of positions with job applicants, resulting in a more efficient use of the labor force.

One feature peculiar to the Chinese economy, which at first seems to add rigidity to the labor market—the *hukou* system—may paradoxically make the market more flexible and competitive. The *hukou* is a system of national identification in which residents are given an ID card based on their official legal residence. Established in the 1950s, the system restricts local government benefits (such as health care, employment protection, minimum wage laws, and education) to local residents.* In the past, the *hukou* system restricted the movement of labor around the country. Today, it no longer serves that purpose; instead, its main impact relates to the non-provision of local government benefits and protections for those living in an area (typically a large city) with no *hukou* status. As such, various laws—including local minimum wage laws that might create a wedge between workers' offer price and the bid price of employers—are absent. It is estimated that migrant workers in the informal sector in urban areas earn about 70 percent less than local residents, and most of this difference cannot be attributed to skill differences. Employers, for better or worse, can hire non-*hukou* (migrant) workers at a lower overall cost (including non-payment of social welfare benefits) than is stipulated by local laws. We have already discussed the role of government monopsony power in hiring. Recent government efforts geared toward increased urbanization have opened up limited channels for changing one's *hukou* to become official urban residents (such as through the purchase of a residence).[†]

Another way in which Chinese citizens act as shock absorbers is in their role as savers. Chinese families have continued to deposit savings within the state-owned banking system, despite the negative real return earned on typical deposits. This has helped the banks remain quite profitable as they lend to both the government and the private sector. The same phenomenon occurred in the 2000–2003 period, when the large state-owned banks had a sufficiently large number of bad assets (loans) on their books to make them effectively bankrupt. In such situations elsewhere in the world, a distinctly negative outcome usually occurs; typically, when depositors lose confidence in banks' ability to protect depositor savings, a bank run occurs. Given China's lack of explicit bank insurance at the time, the willingness of citizens to continue depositing may illustrate their faith in the government's obligation to protect citizens' assets.[‡]

A central tenet of the Keynesian framework is that sticky prices serve as a form of economic sclerosis. In China, labor force flexibility acts as a shock absorber and an antidote, allowing economic growth even in times of harmful exogenous shocks. Even shock absorbers, however, wear out over time, and the most recent Five-Year Plans emphasize improving income distribution and expanding the social safety net (see the next chapter). In the coming years, China must find alternate means of managing its vast and valuable human resource and, simultaneously, maintain flexibility.

[*]Minimum wage limits do exist in China, but they differ by province and are generally in the range of RMB 1500 to 2500 per month.

[†]For the very largest cities—Shanghai, Beijing, and Chongqing—acquiring a *hukou* is still very difficult.

[‡]An alternative interpretation might be that the absence of financial transparency at the time prevented most depositors from truly understanding the dire situation of their banks.

Appendix

National Budget Constraint in International Financial Markets

In this section, we cover two key concepts: Ricardian equivalence (discussed in this chapter) and the measurement of a country's cash flows (covered in Chapter 3). Ricardian equivalence argues that current government consumption and deficits are constrained, over time, by available resources. Here, we suggest that a country's international deficits and its access to external finance are constrained by its ability to produce and service its debt. Meanwhile, in Chapter 3, we presented a definition of a country's cash flow (an important metric for providers of external finance to a country) which was equivalent to its current account balance. Any outside investor (whether issuing equity or debt) will ask a very basic set of questions: when and how much will I get paid back? An investor provides money to a company and wants to be assured of the timing and amount of payment. Of course, the more risky or uncertain the cash flows, the higher the required return. This approach can be readily applied to a country seeking finance from world financial markets. The critical question is the feasibility of repayment—and this is directly related to the country's cash flows and valuation.

Intertemporal Budget Constraint (ITBC)[14]

A country that seeks resources (finance) from the rest of the world must be able to provide resources (cash flow) over time to pay back its loans. What resources will a country have over time? Its GDP. Specifically, its sources of payment will be:

$$Y_0 + \frac{Y_1}{(1+r)} + \frac{Y_2}{(1+r)^2} + \frac{Y_3}{(1+r)^3} \cdots$$

In which (Y) represents real GDP and (r) represents the country's discount factor or weighted cost of capital. We look at the country's potential for output over an infinite horizon and discount it to its present value.

We can consider the uses of GDP as either consumption, investment, or service over time of debt to foreign creditors (foreign debt service is $r \times D_0$). We assume that (for both the private and public sectors) all uses can be collapsed into two categories, (C) and (I):

$$(C+I)_0 + \frac{(C+I)_1}{(1+r)} + \frac{(C+I)_2}{(1+r)^2} + \frac{(C+I)_3}{(1+r)^3} \cdots + (r\ x\ D_0)_0 + \frac{(r\ x\ D_0)_1}{(1+r)} + \frac{(r\ x\ D_0)_2}{(1+r)^2} + \frac{(r\ x\ D_0)_3}{(1+r)^3} \cdots$$

We can first subtract uses of GDP from sources (*Y* – *C* – *I*), then use the fact that (*Y* – *C* – *I*) is the same as the trade balance (TB). For the second term involving external debt, we can sum the infinite series to yield ((1+ *r*) × D_0). This yields:

$$TB_0 + \frac{TB_1}{(1+r)} + \frac{TB_2}{(1+r)^2} + \frac{TB_3}{(1+r)^3} \ldots - (1+r)\, x\, D_0 \geq 0$$

The above inequality states that, in order for a country to offer value to external investors, its trade balances (in present value terms) must be greater than its external debt (D_0). Alternatively, if a country has no foreign equity holders, its present value of trade balances must be at least as great as its external debt—otherwise its creditors will consider the country insolvent. Once again (as noted earlier), the role of trade balances is similar to the role of cash flow at the macroeconomic level—an exact analogy to the corporate context. While our earlier discussion covered the gap (*S* – *I*), here, we derive the resulting comparison of sources and uses of output—but the results are the same. Each provides a unique insight into policy prescriptions—similar to the discussion of current account balance perspectives.

An interesting scenario is when trade balances average zero over the infinite horizon. Even if the country has no external debt, its value to internal investors and external shareholders is zero at a macroeconomic aggregate level. If it has external debt, its value is less than zero. Does this seem reasonable? In the corporate context, such a situation is equivalent to a company having zero projected cash flows over the future horizon. While the company is able to pay its employees, suppliers, and taxes, it is unable to service its investors; thus, the situation is not sustainable. Ultimately, investors will withdraw their capital by refusing to reinvest and the company will go out of business.

We note that, when a country has a stock of either foreign debt or equity obligations, a perennial trade balance of zero is still inadequate to satisfy foreign investors. It would still need to service its obligations, implying a negative current account balance and further accumulation of external debt. Assuming that the cost of external finance (the cost of capital) is greater than the country's long-term growth rate, a perennial current account deficit and concomitant rise in external debt would lead to an ever-rising ratio of external obligations to GDP. In this scenario, 100 percent of GDP would be needed to service external obligations (interest and dividends). Once a hint of such a scenario appears, international financiers will step back, halt any further finance, and even attempt to withdraw their existing investments.

In the country context, when $(S - I)$ is perennially zero or negative, or when the equation above shows trade balances less than or equal to zero, we see international investors halting their investing (lending or equity investment) in the country for lack of returns. If the economy is in fact closed to external finance and the cash flow remains zero, we see self-financing of investment at the domestic level. Formally, we can decompose domestic savings, $(S_D - I_D)$, as follows:

$$(S_D - I_D) \equiv (S_P - I_P)\ (S_C - I_C)\ (S_G - I_G)$$

In which subs (P), (C), and (G) represent the private savings investment gap by individuals (P), corporations (C) (net income), and the government (G) (the budget surplus or deficit). In the special case in which $(S_D - I_D = 0)$, (given no international financing), a surplus in one of the sectors implies at least one deficit in the other sectors. Typically, the corporate sector would have a negative $(S_C - I_C)$ balance, which must be financed by the excess savings of either private individuals or the government. Similar reasoning applies in the international case. If private individuals do not ultimately see a surplus of cash in the corporate sector in coming years, they will stop providing their excess savings. This would cause a financing shortfall for the corporate sector. If policy-makers view this situation as untenable (since employment may be impacted, for example), the government may choose to channel funds to the corporate sector. In the past, this has been China's response to funding shortfalls in the production sector. Of course, this is much easier for the government to do if it has a surplus of savings. The real question, though, relates to whether corporations should be supported by the government if their long-run viability is in doubt.

Challenging Questions for China (and the Student): Chapter 9

1. Go to the Federal Reserve Economic Database (FRED) and graph government consumption as a share of GDP in China.
2. Suppose that China's economy in Figure 9.8 is located right between the two chopsticks in the shaded area. Using Figure 9.4, show what natural economic forces will tend to build up and move the economy in one direction or the other.
3. Explain why "crowding out" has a very different meaning in China versus the United States. Be specific about where crowding out is occurring—on the production side or the uses side—and which sectors (*C, I, G* or *NX)* are crowding out which other sectors.
4. Explain why price flexibility (or its absence) is a linchpin (a critical assumption) in the Keynesian framework. Now explain the analogous role that China's "great economic shock absorber" plays.
5. Explain why it would be important for any emerging economy (including China) to clarify, in a legal sense, the ownership of domestically-owned assets before opening its assets markets to international capital mobility. In this context, explain the advantages and disadvantages of an emerging economy delaying the opening up of its financial markets to international investment.
6. Explain what warning signs are and are not contained within China's appreciating exchange rate in recent years.
7. If China comes to rely less on exports and less on investment as a source of demand in the coming years, how will fiscal policy need to be different from its current situation?
8. Discuss: In the coming years, China's labor force will come to show increasing inflexibility, and this will present new challenges for fiscal policy.
9. In Macro Finance Insight 9.2, what assumption must we be making in the background regarding the fixity or flexibility of the exchange rate? How would Macro Finance Insight 9.2 be altered if we changed that assumption?

References

Bernanke, Ben and Mark Gertler. 1995. "Inside the Black Box: The Credit Channel of Monetary Policy Transmission." NBER Working Paper no. 5146.

Bewley, Truman F. 1999. *Why Wages Don't Fall During Recession*. Cambridge and London: Harvard University Press.

Cai, Fang, Meiyan Wang, and Yang Du. 2005. "China's Labor Market on Crossroad." *China and World Economy*, 13(1), pp. 32–46.

Calvo, Guillermo and Frederic S. Mishkin, 2003. "The Mirage of Exchange Rate Regimes for Emerging Market Countries." NBER Working Papers no. 9808.

Cox, Simon. 2011. "Keynes v. Hayek in China." *The Economist*, 17 November. https://www.economist.com/news/2011/11/17/keynes-v-hayek-in-china.

Dornbusch, Rudiger. 1976. "Expectations and Exchange Rate Dynamics." *Journal of Political Economy*, 84(6), pp. 1161–76.

Drautzburg, T. 2019. "A Narrative Approach to a Fiscal DSGE Model." Federal Reserve Bank of Philadelphia. https://www.philadelphiafed.org/-/media/research-and-data/publications/economic-insights/2019/q1/eiq119-predicting-recessions.pdf?la=en.

Fleming, J. Marcus. 1962. "Domestic Financial Policies Under Fixed and Floating Exchange Rates." *International Monetary Fund Staff Papers*, 9, pp. 369–79.

Frankel, Jeffrey and George Saravelos. 2012. "Can Leading Indicators Assess Country Vulnerability? Evidence from the 2008–09 Global Financial Crisis." *Journal of International Economics*, 87(2), 216–31.

Geng, N. and P. N'Diaye. 2012. "Determinants of Corporate Investment in China: Evidence from Cross-Country Firm Level Data." IMF Working Paper no. 12/80.

Keynes, John Maynard. 1936. *The General Theory of Employment, Interest and Money*. London: Macmillan.

Laurens, Bernard J. and Rodolfo Maino. 2007. "China: Strengthening Monetary Policy Implementation." IMF Working Paper no. 07/14.

Mundell, Robert A. 1963. "Capital Mobility and Stabilization Policy Under Fixed and Flexible Exchange Rates." *Canadian Journal of Economic and Political Science*, 29(4), pp. 475–85.

Obstfeld, Maurice. 2012. "Financial Flows, Financial Crises and Global Imbalances." *Journal of International Money and Finance*, 31(3), pp. 469–80.

Smets, Frank and Rafael Wouters. 2007. "Shocks and Frictions in US Business Cycles: A Bayesian DSGE Approach." *American Economic Review*, 97(3), pp. 586–606.

Wen, Y., and J. Wu. 2019. "Withstanding the Great Recession Like China." *The Manchester School*, 87(2), pp. 138–82.

Endnotes

1. The convention of labeling IS as the point at which supply = demand for goods and services relates to the fact that when supply = demand, savings will also equal investment in a closed economy. Savings is the absence of consumer and government demand; investment is the activity whose presence fills in the needed demand to rebalance supply and demand. We will discuss this point more fully in introducing the role of inventories as a part of investment demand. The LM label represents the demand for money or a liquid asset (L) and the supply of money (M).
2. The tax rate is an index of corporate, personal, and all other tax rates. The transfer rate represents the share of income derived from transfer payments that include social security, unemployment, welfare, and veterans' benefits.
3. Investment is clearly a critical component of demand that can trigger short-run fluctuations in output (recessions and recoveries). Plant, property, equipment, and residential investment are interest-sensitive components of demand. Unplanned inventory accumulation or decumulation are also part of investment (by definition), and they have an important impact on the output decisions of firms.
4. Recall that Walras's Law states that demand for assets cannot exceed the underlying basis for demand—the supply of wealth. In turn, excess demand for any asset must be offset by an excess supply of some other asset or set of assets.
5. In alternative financial markets, such as the bond market, there would be an excess demand for bonds (consistent with Walras's Law).
6. Recall that the rise in interest rates results from an unchanged money supply meeting an increased demand for money, which is caused by the rise in economic activity (output) and results in greater demand for money.
7. Being dead, for example, is a bad kind of equilibrium.
8. In reality, we rarely see outright deflation or declines in prices. Rather, we see a deceleration of the inflation rate.
9. One would reasonably ask why we would try to stimulate the economy if we are already at full employment (point A). One explanation might be that policy-makers are not sure exactly what the full employment level of output is in the economy.
10. In Figure 9.9 and Figure 9.10, we could just as easily have placed real GDP growth and inflation on the x and y axes instead of output and price levels.
11. There are many caveats to PPP (the law of one price). It is assumed that trade barriers and transportation costs are insignificant and that information about price differences is widely available. Empirically, relative PPP seems to hold much better than

absolute PPP. Relative PPP states that percent price changes and percent exchange rate changes tend to move in a way that prevents large price discrepancies from appearing.

12. In Figure 9.13a, a rise in the nominal exchange rate indicates a depreciation of the RMB; in Figure 9.13b, a rise indicates a real appreciation of the RMB.
13. Transfers are payments by the government to individuals or entities for non-current production. For example, veterans' benefits, social security, and unemployment compensation are all forms of transfer payments.
14. Also known as the "transversality condition" in dynamic programming, or optimal control.

10
PUBLIC FINANCE AND FISCAL POLICY IN ACTION

天不生无用之人，地不长无名之草

Heaven Does Not Create Useless People—Earth Does Not Grow Nameless Plants

Fiscal policy relates to the government's taxing, spending, investing, lending/borrowing, social welfare, and redistribution activities, and how these activities affect a country's economic performance. In China, the Ministry of Finance (MOF), the National Development and Reform Commission (NDRC), the State Administration for Taxes (SAT) and, of course, the State Council, all play important but different roles in managing fiscal policy. The MOF, in cooperation with the State Council, is responsible for establishing the national budget every year, including target budget deficits/surpluses and financing needs. The NDRC (formerly the State Planning Commission), in conjunction with the State Council, is responsible for establishing long-term priorities and policies, including economic reform via Five-Year Plans and their annual revisions. The SAT administers China's vast tax system of over 750,000 employees and 30,000 branches. As of 1994, separate administrative systems operate for collecting national level taxes (and sharing revenues with localities) and local taxes. Local tax offices are administered jointly by the local and central government.

In the United States, the US Treasury is primarily responsible for implementing fiscal policy at the national level, while Congress has sole constitutional authority over raising revenues and spending.[1] In both economies (especially China), local governments have a significant role in how fiscal policy is implemented. In any economy, investors (capitalists), suppliers of labor, and the institution that we know as "the government" are the three critical stakeholders in the production process. There are substantial differences between China and the United States in terms of the government stakeholder's role in production, investment, and claims on income (taxation)—as we shall see.

In the United States, the president submits an annual national budget to Congress each February, and Congress makes its own changes to the proposed budget in the following months. Congress sets limits on tax revenues, spending through various appropriation bills, and the national debt. After extensive negotiations over priorities, spending, tax levels, and the ultimate deficit, the budget is presented in its final form for the president's approval and signature. The US fiscal year runs from October 1st through September 30th. China's fiscal year corresponds to the January/December calendar year. In the United States, the President's Council of Economic Advisors submits its Annual Report—also known as the Economic Report of the President, (https://bit.ly/2LACWWX)—in early March of each year. This extensive document surveys the US economy and international linkages and sets out policy priorities for the coming years. Table 10.1 summarizes key differences in the policy-making framework.

	China	**United States**
Budget Period	Calendar Year	Oct. 1–Sept. 30
Key Players	MOF, NDRC, SAT, State Council (35 Members), Formal Approval by National People's Congress	President/US Treasury and Congress (Taxation and Expenditure Limits)
Key Documents	Five-Year Plan with Annual Updates	Economic Report of the President (Annual)
Relative Timeframe	Five Years	One Year
Relative Focus	Production and Macro-Management	Macro-Management over Production
Implementation	MOF, SAT, NDRC, Provincial and Local Governments, SAFE, State-Owned Banks, SOES, Society in General	Federal Government with Cooperation of Localities

Table 10.1 Comparing China and the United States' central budget processes.
Source: Author created.

Case Study 10.1: Administrative Levels in China

Similar to the governmental divisions of nation, state, county, township, and city found in the United States, China's different levels of government can be seen in Table 10.2. Below the Chinese central government, there are 31 provinces (*sheng*省), which include 26 on the geographic scale of a state (Guangdong, for example), 5 autonomous regions (Tibet, Inner Mongolia, Guanxi, Ningxia, Xinjiang), and 4 mega-cities (Beijing, Tianjin, Shanghai, and Chongqing). Within these provinces, there are prefectures (*diqu*地区—large cities or powerful clusters of smaller cities). Counties (*xian*县)

are either the urban part of a prefectural city or a rural area with no large city. Townships (*zhengqu* 镇区) are rural areas in a county and villages, and *cun* (村) are small communities with only an indirect administrative role. With respect to expenditures in China, counties play an outsize role.

Furthermore, Chinese cities are ranked by a tier system based on population and economic importance. Tier 1 cities include major cities that are most economically developed, such as Beijing, Shanghai, Guangzhou, Shenzhen, and a recently added set of 15 other cities ranging from Hangzhou to Ningbo. Tier 2 cities tend to be smaller commercial centers, and Tier 3 includes many provincial capitals.

If the mix of administrative levels described above seems complex and overlapping, that's because it is. China's long history and large population centers make it difficult to divide administrative regions in a tidy way. The current structure of provinces was formed over the last three dynasties—the Yuan, Ming, and Qing. In part, the many governmental divisions reflect a "divide and rule" policy by various emperors. By splitting powerful groups into separate entities within China's longstanding borders, emperors could prevent cohesive challenges to their power. In fact, large multinational companies do very similar things. For example, companies organized around geographic lines find that foreign subsidiary managers see only their own local interests at the expense of the goals of the entire company. The chief executive officer of a multinational company may then choose to split the company up along functional lines (e.g., finance, operations, marketing) to have managers think more broadly about corporate goals, rather than their own geographical turf. We discuss this later in Macro Finance Insight 10.3.

These same issues arise in the United States with large towns located in otherwise rural counties or suburban communities located in townships. Large population centers feel that they deserve a closer link from the central government, even though the actual geographic area that they cover may be small. Over time, these efforts at greater representation get reconciled at the cost of greater complexity.

Administrative Unit	Number
Provinces	31
of which are Municipalities	4
Prefectures	333
of which are cities including provincial capitals	293
Counties	2,851
Townships	39,945
of which are towns	21,297

Table 10.2 China's different administrative levels.
Source: Author created based on data from China Statistical Yearbook 2019.

China's budget policy is rooted in its Five-Year Plans. The 35-member State Council and NDRC in Beijing, representing the major departments of the Chinese government, establish long-term policy goals via Five-Year Plans and their annual updates. China's 13th 2016–2020 Plan, for example, establishes targets in areas including the state of the environment, size of the service sector, income distribution and growth, and enhancements to the health-care system. Every October, the People's Congress and top leadership meet to establish short-run macroeconomic goals. At this time the budget is also presented to establish priorities for the coming year, and the general stance of monetary policy is set. For example, in the 2019 budget approved by the National People's Congress in March (https://bit.ly/3fYA04h), goals were established for economic growth of 6 to 6.5 percent and an inflation rate of 3 percent. Given the uncertainties found in any economy, the targets set in the annual budget are often missed. Lam et al. (2017), in a comprehensive survey of fiscal policy in China, highlight the vacuum between Five-Year Plan policy goals and annual national budgets. Five-Year Plans contain ambitious targets, as we have seen, without providing a budget ("the devil is in the details"). Meanwhile, annual national budgets must both implement Five-Year Plan mandates, fund recurring expenditures, and meet hard budget constraints, while simultaneously fine-tuning the budget to the current economic circumstance. Caught in this vacuum, as we shall see, are local governments. Chinese authorities are currently trying to implement medium-term revenue and expenditure frameworks that would bridge the gap between long-term policies and short-term budgets. Already, 60 countries around the world (but not the United States) employ a medium-term framework for financial/budgetary planning.

Case Study 10.2: China's Five-Year Plans

The strategic planning function is an important activity for most large companies around the world. Among governments, arguably no country in the world has achieved the same level of sophistication as China in terms of planning via its Five-Year Plans. China is now following its 13th Five-Year Plan for National Economic and Social Development. The first plan was issued in 1953, with new major plans issued every five years after that—the most recent one was deliberated and approved in 2015.[2] These plans establish priorities for the Chinese government starting at the macro level and moving downward to impact all economic sectors—from industries, to companies, and even to individual townships and villages. Based on the national Five-Year Plan, sublevels of government establish their own strategies that, in turn, are used by local non-government institutions (such as banks and universities) establishing their own Five-Year Plans.

China's budget policy is rooted in its Five-Year Plans. The 35-member State Council, representing the major components of the Chinese government, establishes policy goals for the long, medium, and short term. The current Five-Year Plan is updated annually in response to the economic environment, and it provides the framework for short-term fiscal and monetary policy in its traditional role. Every October, the People's Congress and top leadership meet to establish short-run macroeconomic goals. At that time, the budget is also presented, establishing priorities for the coming year and setting the general stance of monetary policy.

More broadly, the goals of the most recent Five-Year Plan include protecting the environment, tax reform, financial system reform, agricultural modernization, new manufacturing technologies, reducing social inequality, enhancing the urbanization process, reducing poverty, improving the social safety net, expanding health care, shifting the economy from being investment and export driven to greater domestic consumption, and—finally—developing spiritual culture in the context of socialism. In the context of earlier Five-Year Plans, we see that the 2016–2020 Plan has relatively more aspirational/social goals compared to the numerical production goals of earlier plans. We should not dismiss these targets as mere blandishments; the Chinese government uses its powerful fiscal and financial (lending) tools to achieve them.

Furthermore, the Five-Year Plans can be quite specific, and they include precise targets to be met. For example, the current plan had originally set an explicit target of 6 to 6.5 percent real gross domestic product (GDP) growth for 2020, but that explicit target was scrapped for 2020 in the face of the COVID-19 pandemic. It also proposes a doubling of per capita income between 2010 and 2020, seeks a 3000 kilometer increase in urban rail lines, mandates good air quality on 80 percent of days in large cities; seeks an increase of 100 million more people with urban registration (*hukous*), sets specific fuel efficiency targets, and establishes a goal of increasing the average lifespan of citizens by one year.[3] Furthermore, it names specific industries/sectors to be supported, including health care, education, technology, and energy. Promotions of local officials are based in part on how well they meet Five-Year Plan targets. Given the uncertainties found in any economy, these targets are sometimes missed. And some targets are not mandatory but serve as recommended guidelines. However, the Chinese government's impressive track record in achieving its goals makes it essential for investors and businesses to carefully assess the Five-Year Plan when setting their own strategy for operating in China.

China's short-term fiscal and monetary policies are more formally linked to a longer-term strategy—the Five-Year Plan—than what we find in the United States (see Case Study 10.2).[4] As we shall see, fiscal policy in China has historically focused on long-term investment strategies. In contrast, US fiscal policy places a heavier weight on short-term macroeconomic issues, especially demand management related to unemployment and inflation. Recent uncertainty regarding economic growth, however, has shifted China's focus toward short-term goals as well. Since China's central bank is not independent of the central government (as in the United States), fiscal and monetary policy are highly coordinated. The People's Bank of China (PBC)'s role in allocating credit to specific sectors and industries is critically different from that of the US Federal Reserve, as discussed in Chapter 8. China's annual meetings in October also differ in that a key policy variable (the exchange rate) is an important discussion point. Also different is the focus on key sectors and industries in the economy; in recent years, China's property market has been an important part of the policy discussion, while in earlier years, cement production (for example) was considered an important topic.

Although China's State Council establishes long- to short-term policies, implementation is accomplished by various institutions and government agencies. The PBC (monetary policy), State Administration for Foreign Exchange (SAFE) (exchange rate policy), the National Development Resource Commission (NDRC—responsible for investment in infrastructure), and the SAT all play a role in implementation. But local government spending (that of province-states, prefectures, counties, towns, and villages) is perhaps the key element in implementing fiscal policy—particularly when tied to national priorities (discussed below). The International Monetary Fund (IMF) estimates that 70 percent of central government expenditures is for intergovernmental transfers (to local governments), and 93 percent of public investment is undertaken by localities. Finally, state-owned enterprises (SOEs) play a significant role in implementing policy, particularly as it pertains to investment.

Key Goals of Fiscal Policy

At one level, fiscal policy is similar to the activities of a company in that it involves the provision of goods and services, the collection of revenue, investment in plant and equipment, the raising of capital, and maintaining the quality of its balance sheet. At another level, the corporate goal of value creation becomes more complex and ambiguous in the case of governments, where maximizing social welfare or operating at full employment are important objectives. Perhaps the European corporate model, which considers all stakeholders (not just shareholders), is relevant in this context. Fiscal policy activities include:

- Providing needed goods and services that the private economy does not provide as efficiently, or at all (the provision of public goods)
- Maintaining economic output at levels consistent with full employment (counter-cyclical policy)

- Creating incentives for the private sector to engage in value-creating activities (taxes, spending policies, and subsidies)
- Investing in physical capital, infrastructure, and human capital to sustain value-creating economic growth over the long term (economic development)
- Promoting a fair distribution of income, resources, and opportunities across different regions and citizens (income distribution)

Table 10.3 provides the counterparts to the above-mentioned government activities in corporate activities. Many of the corporate sector's activities are consistent with government activities. For example, both seek full and efficient employment of their labor force.

Government Activities	Corporate Activities
Public Goods, Including Defense and Education	Private Goods and Services
Short-Term Counter-Cyclical Policy (Fiscal and Monetary)	Full Use of Resources, Including Labor, Capital and, Inventories
Long-Term Economic Development	Research and Development and Investment in Capital Stock
Income Redistribution	Corporate Governance; Allocation of Value-Added to Stakeholders
Taxes, Subsidies, and Economic Incentives	Human Resource Management and Compensation Policy

Table 10.3 Government goals and corporate goals can align at times, but governments still need to fill in the gaps when private sector activities are inadequate in meeting broad social needs.
Source: Author created.

We could think of the role of government as filling in the gaps caused by targets that are unmet or out-of-synch with the corporate sector. For example, corporate governance tries to strike a workable balance between various stakeholders—workers, management, investors, and the government. For a variety of reasons, including principle-agent problems, corporate governance may fail to provide a fair or efficient distribution of the value-added to each stakeholder. The government may want to step in and smooth out the distribution of income. We note that China's system of taxes and transfers is unique among economies around the world in that its impact on income distribution (https://bit.ly/2N2sOqt) is virtually nil.[5] Governments use their tax and spending power to encourage or discourage certain activities. For example, the US government encourages home ownership by allowing the deductibility of interest payments on first- and second-home mortgages (a tax incentive). It is generally agreed, however, that US tax rules have become too complex. As a result, the rules and regulations related to federal taxes are contained in 20 volumes, or about 17,000 pages. China's tax laws are considerably shorter, but with the tradeoff of having less transparency.

Some policy goals are long-term and, some are short-term. In this chapter, we will examine the role of policy in both time frames. First, we assess the broad outlines of taxing and spending in both countries. We will then employ the Keynesian model, the workhorse for understanding fiscal (and monetary) policy, in the context of the COVID-19 pandemic, the Trump trade war and the Great Financial Crisis (GFC). Next, we will examine fiscal policy in the long run as an engine for economic growth—something relatively important in China. Finally, in the context of decentralization and federalism, we discuss the links between central government fiscal activities and local government activities. This latter discussion allows for some interesting comparisons between China and the United States.

Overall Budgets

Fiscal budgets are significant at both the central and local level in terms of their real economic impact. In the short run, they can add or subtract from overall economic demand. In the long run, they will need to be sustainable. Defaults at the central government level (in Europe) and at the local level (in Detroit, Michigan) are cases in point.[6] Furthermore, central government revenues are often shared with local governments through grants and loans. We will first compare and contrast revenues and expenditures in China in detail at the central and local levels, then we will see how this breakdown corresponds to patterns found in the United States. Table 10.4 and Table 10.5 provide an overview of each country's overall revenues, expenditures, deficits, and surpluses at the national and local level (province, state, and local).

	Central Government	Share of GDP	Local Government	Share of GDP	General Government	Share of GDP
Revenues	8,565	10%	9,790.45	11%	18,355.2	20%
Expenses	3,271	4%	18,819.8	21%	22,090.6	25%
Surplus or Deficit (-)	5,293.95	5.9%	-9,029.35	-10%	-3,735.4	-4.1%

Table 10.4 China 2018 distribution of revenues and expenses (in RMB billions).
Source: Author estimates based on data from CEIC and IMF Article IV Consultation (https://bit.ly/3fCnBlu).
Note: IMF estimates of general expenditures and revenues are larger than official estimates. "General government" refers to the total (overall) or combined financials for both central and local governments. Central government expenditure and revenue estimate is the implied residual of the general government estimate minus the local government estimate. Expenditures do not include central government transfers to local government.

	Federal Government	Share of GDP	State/Local Government	Share of GDP	Total Government	Share of GDP
Revenues	3,559	18%	2,484	13%	5,484	28%
Expenses	4,254	22%	2,743	14%	6,438	33%
Surplus or Deficit (-)	-695	-4%	-259	-1%	-955	-5%

Table 10.5 In the United States, revenues and expenses are closely aligned. Figures given in USD billions.
Source: Economic Report of the President 2019, Table B-49.
Note: Local government revenues include transfers; federal government expenditures include transfers to localities. Transfers are netted out of each line item for the total government estimates.

China runs a surplus at the central level and a large deficit locally; the United States runs a deficit at all levels. As a share of GDP, China's overall official deficit is around 4 percent, while the deficit in the United States is close to 5 percent (after the 2008 financial crisis, it was as large as 9 percent, and it will likely mushroom during the COVID-19 pandemic). In China, the large positive savings balance found in the private sector can easily fund the relatively small budget deficit. In the United States, savings deficits occur across both the government and private sectors, and therefore they have been funded by foreign savings (international borrowing).[7] In both countries, there are constraints on local governments running deficits or using debt to finance them. As we will see, this implies substantial grants (revenue sharing) from the national to local levels in both countries.

Figure 10.1 shows IMF estimates of China's overall general government budget deficit in 2020 to be at 6 percent of GDP—larger than the official estimate of 4 percent of GDP. IMF deficit estimates are consistently larger than official deficit estimates, and the gap grew even larger during the GFC and the Trump trade war. In 2008, the IMF began to regularly report a separate estimate for general government deficits. Those estimates are based on general government net borrowing and lending. The figures include expenditures financed by the sale of land, revenues and expenditures for social security, and SOE deficits. The IMF also provides a more comprehensive deficit estimate that includes net borrowing, primarily by local governments, via special purpose vehicles (SPVs) and bond issuance.

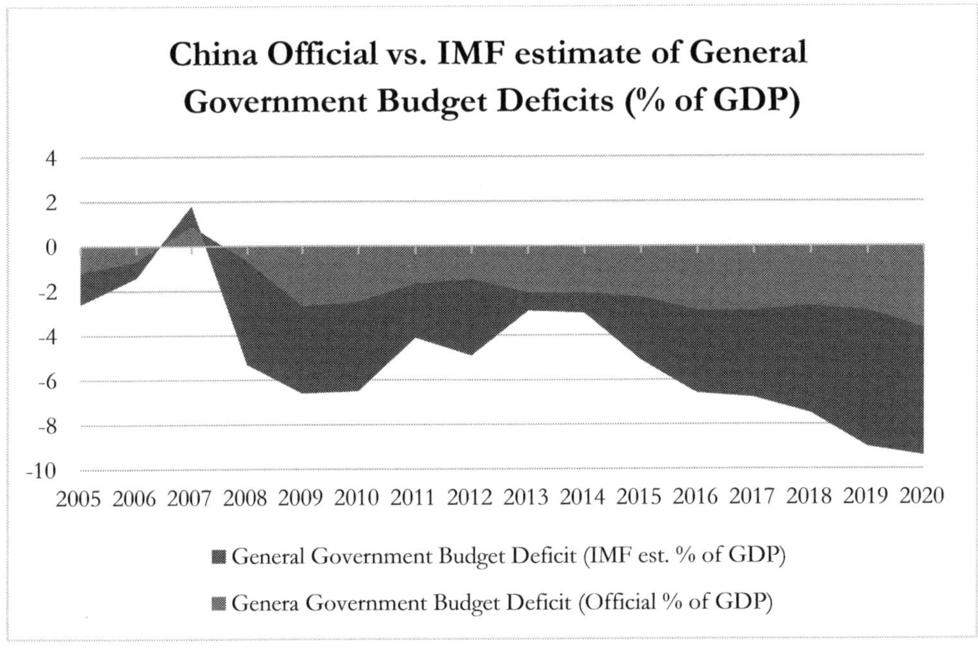

Figure 10.1 The IMF generally reports larger general government budget deficits for China than the official estimate. Various social security expenditures, SOE deficits, and infrastructure expenditures add to the required amount of financing that is required.
Source: Author created based on data from IMF Article IV Reports (https://bit.ly/3drsTzT).
Note: Deficits for 2020 are IMF projections. "General government budget deficit" consolidates central and local government spending and revenues. Since 2008, the IMF has been consistently reporting a separate estimate for general government deficits. Those estimates are based on general net borrowing and lending. It includes expenditures financed by the sale of land, revenues, and expenditures for social security and SOE deficits; the IMF also provides a more comprehensive (larger) deficit estimate that includes net borrowing by local governments via SPVs and bond issuance.

Macro Finance Insight 10.1: The Odd Accounting for Budget Deficits

In corporate financial accounting, we learn to exclude certain expenditures from the income statement. Specifically, capital expenditures are excluded because they do not reflect a cost of production but rather an increase in a firm's assets. The corresponding cost included in later-year income statements is depreciation. In contrast, GDP accounting often includes capital expenditures as an expense in the headline calculation of budget deficits. This practice undoubtedly reflects the desire to reveal the critical borrowing that governments must undertake to finance both current and capital expenditures. Meanwhile, given that the "G" in GDP stands for "gross," depreciation is usually not included in budget deficit numbers.

Governments usually do provide a breakdown, however, between activities related to government consumption and those related to government investment. Government consumption represents expenditures for providing current services, including the acquisition of goods and services from the private sector and employment of the civil service. Table 10.6 provides a comparison of the Chinese and United States governments in terms of consumption and investment. We can see once again the heavy bias toward investment, even at the government level, in China compared to the United States.* In China, about 43 percent of government expenditures represent investment, while in the United States, this figure is only 19 percent. In the United States, most government spending is consumption-related—mainly transfer payments and defense spending. This breakdown very much mirrors the balance between investment and consumption in the broader macroeconomy. A corollary is that much of the government investment in China appears to be financed through borrowing—specifically bank borrowing, since state funding appears to cover only about one-third of government investment spending.

To our main accounting point: Even if we exclude investment spending from the US fiscal accounts, there would still be a budget deficit; however, excluding investment in the case of China would turn its deficit into a surplus. Viewed from a cash flow (rather than income statement) perspective, both governments need to borrow.

*In fact, these figures probably understate true Chinese government investment, since they do not include "off balance sheet" investment or SOE investment at the behest of central and local governments. These investments, while often not funded directly by the government, are funded by the state-owned banks.

	China			United States		
	(RMB 100 Millions)	Percent of GDP	Total Percent Invested	(USD Billions)	Percent of GDP	Total Percent Invested
Government Consumption	107,514	14	57	2,845	14	81
Government Investment	80,241	11	43	678	3	19
Total	187,755	25	100	3,523	17	100

Table 10.6 Government consumption and investment spending 2017–2018.
Source: Author estimate based on data from the Economic Report of the President 2019 and National Bureau of Statistics, China.
Note: Transfer payments are not included in these figures for the United States, thus the totals differ slightly from Table 2.3 in Chapter 2 of this textbook.

Tax Revenues

China's current tax system is rooted in the tax reform laws of 1994 in which a major goal was to recentralize tax collection away from indirect taxes levied locally (e.g., sales- or transactions-based taxes) to national taxes based on both income and value-added. The end result is that provinces and localities have extremely limited taxing power in China today, either in terms of how much they receive in taxes or in terms of their control over tax structure. This practice contrasts sharply with most advanced countries worldwide. In the United States, state and local governments are free to establish sales taxes, taxes on individuals and corporations (income taxes), and property taxes.[8] In the United States, taxes that are autonomously set locally amount to about 8 percent of GDP, whereas in China the central government has virtually full control over tax powers.

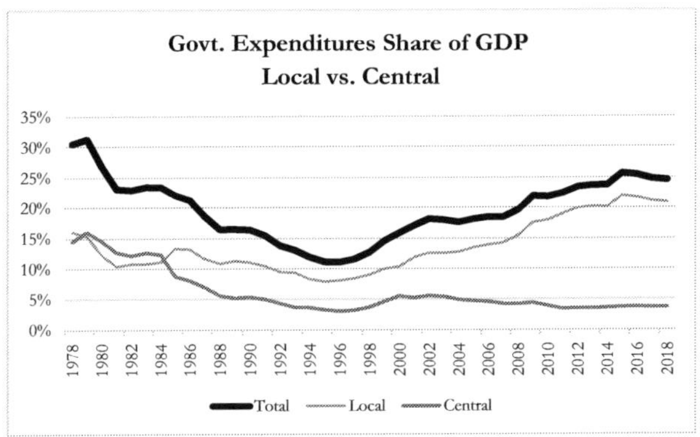

Figure 10.2 Local government expenditure burden has risen since the 1994 fiscal reform in China.
Source: Author created based on data from CEIC.

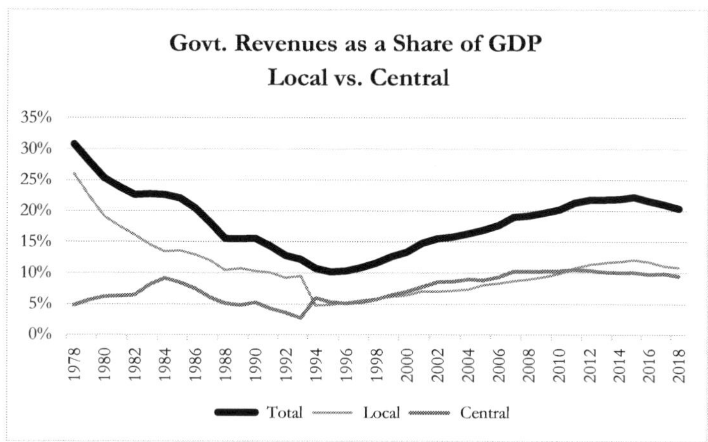

Figure 10.3 Local government revenues have not risen as rapidly as expenditures (see Table 10.2).
Source: Author created based on data from CEIC.

Meanwhile, in China, as Figure 10.2 shows, expenditures (the provision of services) have increasingly become the mandate of local governments. In fact, China—more than any other economy in the world—relies on local government spending (Wingender 2018). Revenues for localities have risen too, but not as fast as expenditures (Figure 10.3). Particularly acute is the shortfall of revenues compared to required expenditures at the rural and urban district levels. If provincial and local governments have no taxation ability, what are their sources of revenue? Case Study 10.3 delves into this question.

	Central	**Provincial**
	Legal Sharing Rate	
Central Taxes		
Consumption	100	0
Tariffs	100	0
VAT and International Trade-Realted Consumption	100	0
Refunds of VAT and Consumption	100	0
Vehicle Purchase	100	0
Cargo	100	0
Shared Taxes		
VAT	50	60
Corporate Income	60	40
Personal Income	60	40
Stamp Tax on Securities	97	3

	Central	Provincial
	Legal Sharing Rate	
Subnational Taxes		
Social Secutiry	0	100
Resource	0	100
Urban Maintenance and Development	0	100
House Property	0	100
Real Estate	0	100
Urban Land Use	0	100
Land Appreciation	0	100
Vehicle and Boal Operation	0	100
Arable Land Use	0	100
Tobacca	0	100
Deeds	0	100
Effective Average Tax Rate	47	53

Table 10.7 Legal revenue sharing rate of 1994 Budget Reform Law.
Source: Author created based on IMF Working Paper no. 18/88, 2018.

Case Study 10.3: Revenue Sharing

China's 1994 Budget Law provides a specific formula illustrating how central government tax revenues are to be shared with localities. Table 10.7 provides a breakdown based on the most recent revision of the formula (2015). On average, the central government retains around 54 percent of collected taxes and transfers the remaining 46 percent to provincial and local governments. The three main types of taxes shared in this way are the VAT, corporate income tax, and personal income tax. But this shared tax revenue represented only about 40 percent of provincial and local expenditures in 2017. As we will see, over time these regions have come to rely on even less stable and less transparent sources of revenue.

The bottom line, for purpose of comparison, is that—in the United States—localities collect a little over 40 percent of government revenues and comprise about 40 percent of government spending.[*] In China, while localities collect a little over half of all revenues, they are responsible for around 78 percent of expenditures. Both in China and in the United States, substantial revenue sharing is required. Insufficient revenue sharing in China causes substantial budgetary pressure at the local level, particularly when it comes to local government investment expenditures. Shortfalls are particularly felt in Chinese villages, which come at the bottom of the governmental "food chain"—a system in which bilateral transfers start with the central government and then move down to the provinces, prefectures, and other localities.[†]

*Since overall expenditures are greater than revenues, localities still have a shortfall in revenues that must come from the federal government.

†In China, approximately 41 percent of expenditures from provinces and localities are funded by tax transfers and direct transfers from the central government. In the United States, an estimated 23 percent of state and local expenditures require federal funding.

As a share of GDP, China general (central plus local governments) tax revenues make up around 20 percent—close to the average share collected in the United States, but far below what is collected in the (Organization for Economic Co-operation and Development) OECD economies (34 percent). China also differs from the OECD economies (including the United States) in its heavy reliance on various sales taxes (indirect taxes) on goods and services (including the value-added tax (VAT) and a variety of user fees and land usage fees). China's VAT, enhanced and broadened extensively in 2016, is 17 percent for goods and 6–11 percent for select services. For most OECD economies, personal income taxes and corporate taxes (direct taxes) are major sources of revenue, but in China personal income taxes represent only a small slice of total revenues (about 6 percent of GDP compared to an average of 25 percent for OECD economies); the rate is also low in the United States at around 10 percent of GDP. Corporate income taxes in China are slightly higher as a share of GDP than what is found in other OECD economies.

China has eleven different types of taxes on income (direct taxes) ranging from taxes on personal income and rental income to corporate income.[9] Personal income taxes follow a progressive schedule ranging from 3 to 45 percent, while corporations pay 20–25 percent on profits. Over 80 percent of households in China pay no wage/salary tax at all (Lam et al. 2017). This is because a generous taxable income threshold of *renminbi* (RMB) 42,000 is not met by most Chinese individuals. High-income individuals benefit from this allowance as well, which adds an element of regressivity (in that it benefits high-income, high-tax-rate earners more than low-income earners) to the personal income tax system. We discuss a similar regressive impact with regard to social pension contribution in a later section of this chapter on the social safety net. Virtually everyone working in China's formal economy contributes to its various social welfare programs.

China's tax system, while complex, comes nowhere close to matching the United States tax system's complexity. A long history of tax legislation in the United States has layered on ever more complex sets of rules, particularly related to exemptions and incentives. Deductions and allowances related to education, child-care, pension contributions, corporate investment incentives, and hedge fund income—just to name a few—have made the United States system unwieldy. The United States provides income deductions for size of household, while China does not.[10] But while tax preparation is the most obvious cost of such a complex system, there is likely a far greater cost in terms of economic efficiency. Creating very different effective tax rates for different economic activities can result in perverse economic outcomes, such as overinvestment or underinvestment in certain industries. Economists generally recommend simpler taxing systems in which all income is categorized as arising from labor or capital (investments). Both China and the United States could benefit from such a system in their efforts at rebalancing. Specifically, China's overinvestment in physical capital and lack of consumption and human capital investment could benefit from higher marginal rates on returns to capital and greater progressivity toward personal income. Meanwhile, the United States could benefit from taxes that reduce consumption and enhance human and physical capital.

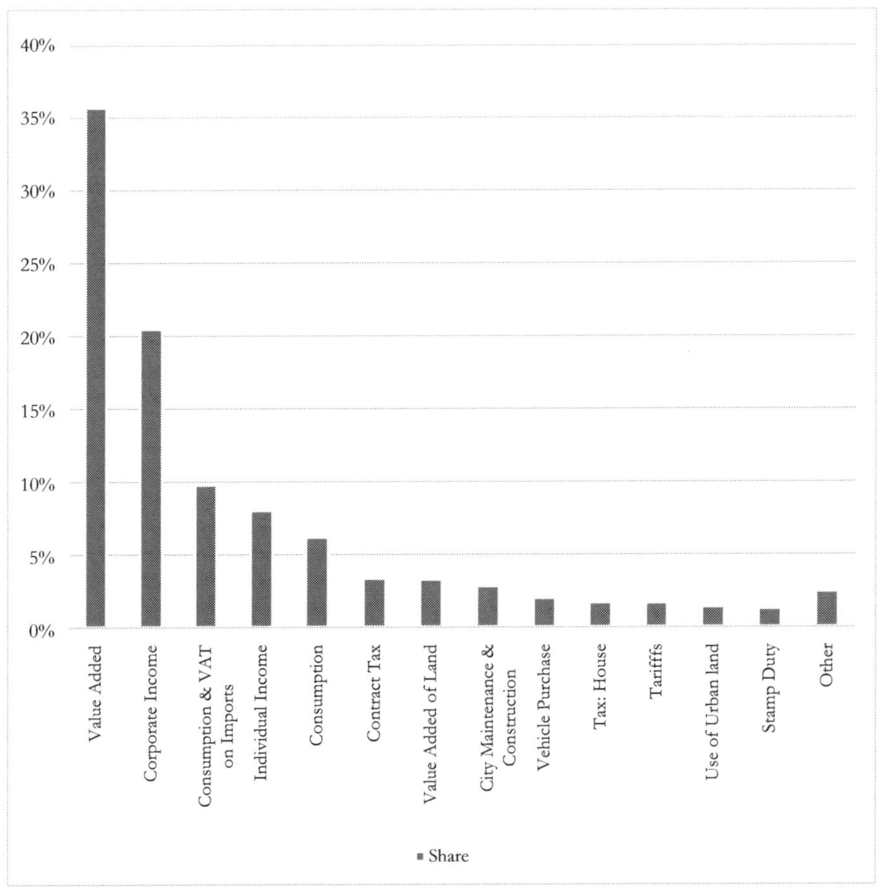

Figure 10.4 China general government main sources of tax revenue, 2018.
Source: Author created based on data from CEIC.

Figure 10.4 shows the main sources of tax revenues for general (central plus local) government in China, and Table 10.8 breaks down tax revenues for local governments. Overall, about 36 percent of tax revenue funding for general government comes from the VAT (a tax on how much value above input costs each firm generates). The corporate income tax follows in importance at about 20 percent of overall government tax revenues. For localities, the VAT is also the main source of shared tax revenue at about 31 percent, followed by the shared corporate income tax at 13 percent. The next most important tax is the tax on land improvements, which provides 5 percent of local tax revenue.

REVENUE SOURCES LOCAL	RMB Millions	Share
Local Government All Revenues	9,146,941	100
of which Non-Tax Revenues	2,279,669	25%
of which Tax Revenues	6,867,272	75%
TAX REVENUES		
Value Added	2,821,216	31%
Corporate Tax	1,169,450	13%
Value Added Land	491,128	5%
Contracts	491,042	5%
Personal Income	478,564	5%
City Maintenance and Construction	420,412	5%
Property Tax	260,433	3%
Urban Land Use	236,055	3%
Cultivated Land Use	165,189	2%
Other	333,783	4%

Table 10.8 China's main sources of local revenue. 2017.
Source: Author created based on data from CEIC.

Shared tax revenues cover about 40 percent of local expenditures, as seen in Table 10.9, while transfers from the central government cover another 41 percent of expenditures, leaving a remaining 19 percent to be funded by limited local tax and non-tax revenues—including various user fees and penalties. Table 10.10 presents the overall financing picture for expenditures broken down by tax and non-tax revenues, grants, land sales, and borrowing. Localities have large off-budget expenditures related to infrastructure and other Five-Year Plan mandates. The two largest sources of finance for these off-budget items are land leasing and—until recently—borrowing using SPVs beyond what is shown in Table 10.10. Both of these latter items have presented challenges in terms of long-term sustainable sources of funds for local governments. In fact, since 2014, the central government has pushed localities to raise funds via bond issuance as an alternative to the various off-budget mechanisms.

China Overall Revenues and Expenditures Summary 2017		
	RMB Millions	**Expenditures**
Total Expenditures	17,322,834	100%
Total Revenues	16,216,240	94%
Tax Revenues	6,867,272	40%
Non-Tax Revenues	2,279,669	13%
Transfers from Central	7,069,300	41%
Basic Deficit	1,106,594	6%
Financing from Borrowing or Land Sales	(1,106,594)	-6%

Table 10.9 Local comprehensive revenues, expenditures, and financing.
Source: Author created based on data from CEIC and IMF estimates.
Note: Revenue and expenditure data differ slightly from Table 10.4 above due to differences between aggregated and disaggregated presentations in data.

Financing China's Borrowing	RMB Trillions 2018	Percent of GDP
Local Government Financing Vehicles	4	4.4
Land Sales	2	2.2
Government Directed Loans	1.8	2.0
Bond Sales	1.4	1.6
Other	1.3	1.4
Total	10.5	11.7

Table 10.10 Local government revenue and deficit financing, 2017.
Source: Author estimates based on IMF Article IV Consultation.

Beyond tax sharing, as we see in Table 10.11, the central government provides a large amount of grants and transfers to localities. Of these transfers, at least 60 percent are for general use, mainly toward equalizing incomes across provinces and individuals. About 40 percent of grants are earmarked for specific sectors such as agriculture or health care. Liu et al. (2014) detail how transfers are determined in China. The reforms of 1994 created winners and losers across provinces, so a transfer mechanism was implemented to correct some of these imbalances. Over time, other transfer mechanisms were created for greater horizontal equity (provinces with similar incomes and wealth should have equal taxes and benefits) across provinces. Provinces with greater natural resource contributions or more minorities also received transfers. Overall, a complex mix of factors come to play in China's transfer system. In the United States, transfers are largely based on the population of local congressional districts as determined by the decennial census. Given that transfers in the United States are targeted directly to individuals and program beneficiaries (such as Medicaid recipients) rather than government jurisdictions, transfers in the United States tend to correct more for individual income disparities than in China. We repeat, for emphasis, that China's system of transfers and taxes ranks lowest among economies surveyed by the OECD (https://bit.ly/2N2sOqt) in terms of creating a more even income distribution.

	Total Revenue (Including Tax Sharing, Transfers, and Non-Tax Revenues)	Transfers	Tax Sharing	Central Government Support (Percent of All Revenues)
China (RMB Millions)	16,216,241	7,069,300	4,960,358	74.2%
United States (USD Millions)	2,920,125	657,677	NA	22.5%

Table 10.11 China and United States local revenue sources, including tax sharing and transfers.
Source: Author created based on data from CEIC and Tax Policy Center, Brookings Institute (https://tpc.io/2X6kmLI).
Note: Data for China are from 2018; for the United States from 2015. Dataset excludes funding from land sales and borrowing.

In the United States, about 32 percent of local and state revenues (excluding non-tax revenues) comes from federal transfers. About one-third of those funds are earmarked, and much of this is for Medicaid—a health care program for those who have low incomes. Table 10.11 provides an overall picture of local revenues from all sources—taxes, non-tax revenues, and central/federal government transfers to localities. We see that, as a share of all revenues, China's central government transfers more three times as much to provincial/state and local governments than does the United States. If we include tax sharing, about 74 percent of provincial/local revenue (including non-tax revenue) comes from the central government in China, while in the United States the comparable figure is only about 23 percent. Of course, this larger transfer is due to the high level of decentralization of expenditure responsibility in China. As we discuss later, a large share of US federal transfers relate to human services—such as Medicare for low-income earners—and these transfers merely pass-through localities to individuals. Figure 10.5 provides a breakdown of uses of revenue sharing in the United States. In China, transfers fund a broader range of province/state and locality activities such as education, social security, and unemployment benefits; but, in contrast to the United States, transfers are targeted not to individuals but to local government jurisdictions.

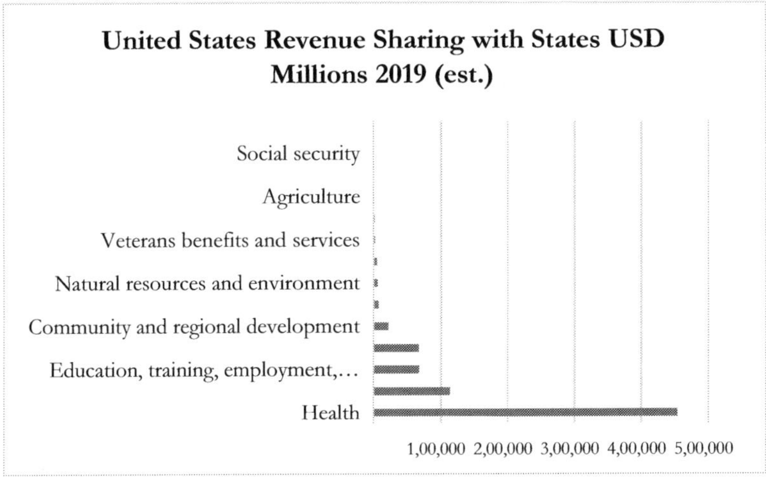

Figure 10.5 United States distribution of total revenue shared with states and localities.
Source: Author created based on Table 12.1, White House US Historical Records (https://bit.ly/2TeovMb).
Note: Total revenue sharing is an estimated 750 billion in 2019.

Macro Finance Insight 10.2: Risk Pooling, Tax Sharing, and Conglomerates

China's central government shares its tax revenues with the provinces based on a strict formula. This limits the amount of risk sharing that is possible across provinces. The financial notion of risk pooling states that individual provinces can benefit by sharing in a national pool of collected taxes rather than relying (as under the current system) solely on a share of what is collected in their own province. To see how this works, suppose that each province (i) receives a random tax rebate (TR_i) from the central government. (Note that the rebate is random because income (or output) in that province is random. Also, tax rebates to the province are proportional to provincial income. For the sake of simplicity, we assume that all provinces are alike.

Under the current system, each province will receive, in any given year, an expected rebate in an amount with variance:

$$\text{Expected Value} = E(TR_i) = \mu$$

And,

$$\text{Variance}\ (TR_i) = \sigma^2$$

Suppose now that, instead, each province receives an equal share of the entire pool, or, where (N) represents the number of provinces,

$$1\ /\ N \times \sum_1^N (TR_i)$$

In the case of China, $N = 31$. Thus, when pooling for each province, we have:

$$E(TR_i) = \mu$$

where (E) is the expected value operator, and,

$$\text{Variance} = 1\ /\ N \times \sigma^2$$

In the latter pooling case, there is no reduction in average tax rebates (μ), and the variance of the rebate has been reduced by a factor of (N). Or, in the case of China, the variance is close to 3 percent of what it would be without risk sharing.*

Because we have simplified, some caveats are needed. First, income is assumed to be independent across provinces; for example, income can be impacted locally by an area flood or crop failure. If this is not the case and incomes are highly correlated (e.g., if PBC monetary policies cause trans-province economic losses) then the reduction in risk through pooling is diminished. Second, provinces differ in size and volatility of income. Large provinces or those with higher incomes receive less benefit from pooling.† Third, if residents of one province already have the opportunity to invest and earn across all provinces, then pooling tax rebates will be less beneficial.

The above discussion parallels another topic in management and finance: Are conglomerates (for example, *chaebol* in South Korea or *keiretsu* in Japan) good corporate structures? Because, by definition, they may contain many different kinds of businesses, they may offer significant risk-sharing benefits as a form of self-insurance. When one subsidiary encounters trouble, it can be cross-subsidized by another subsidiary experiencing better times. The counter-arguments include those made in the paragraph above. But even more germane to our discussion is the question of moral hazard. Insurance comes at a price—subsidiaries, states and provinces can become too comfortable with the notion that a rescue plan is always available, losing valuable incentives for efficiency. Furthermore, they may take undue risks. It appears that China has taken a path of letting provinces bear individual risk as a way of promoting greater provincial efficiency—we could say that provinces eat what they catch. In the United States, a variety of automatic stabilizers—such as unemployment, welfare, and tax code benefits—suggest a more nuanced approach to risk pooling.

*We normally measure variability by the standard deviation, not the variance, which would yield standard deviation volatility that is less than 20 percent of the current system.

†Such provinces, in fact, may feel that risk pooling is harmful. Central government involvement then becomes necessary to force participation in a risk-pooling scheme.

Revenues in the United States

As indicated in Figure 10.6, in the United States, personal income tax makes up about 50 percent of all federal tax revenue, followed by the social insurance tax (Social Security, Medicare and Unemployment Insurance) at 32 percent. A much smaller share comes from corporate taxes (7 percent in 2017).[11] At the state level, states rely on intergovernmental transfers (https://tpc.io/2LQJlxr) from the federal government (33 percent of total revenues in 2016) and sales taxes (23 percent of total revenues) with individual and corporate taxes providing a smaller share (20 percent in total). Meanwhile, local governments rely heavily on intergovernmental transfers from the state level (about 36 percent of their total revenues), and 4 percent comes directly from the federal government. Property taxes (about 30 percent of their total revenues) are the most significant own-source revenues. Expenditures typically outstrip own-source revenues across states and localities, necessitating grants from the federal government. The amount is comparable to the amount raised locally via property taxes.

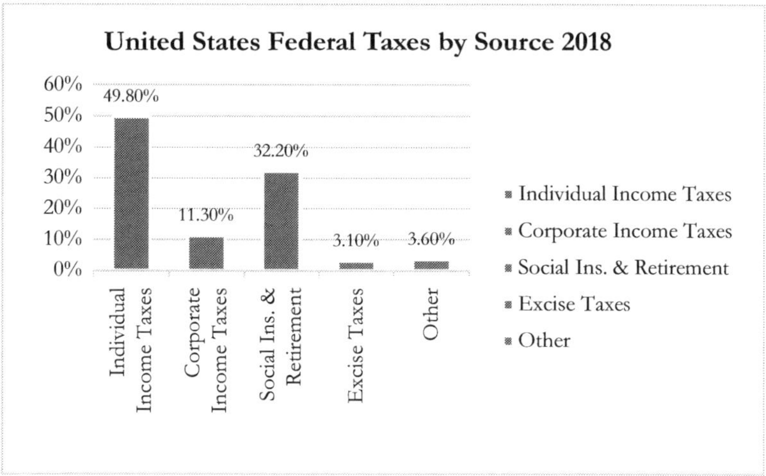

Figure 10.6 Distribution of United States federal tax revenues by source.
Source: Author created based on data from Tax Foundation (https://bit.ly/3gavRui).

Summary of Revenues

At the national level, we note that while the US government relies mostly on personal income tax as a source of revenue, the Chinese government relies mainly on VATs and sales taxes. No doubt, this difference is tied to the administrative ease with which China's government can collect taxes at the company level compared to the difficulty of collecting taxes from individual citizens—many of whom work in the informal economy or in the agricultural sector, where subsistence farming is still important.[12] China relies more heavily on tax collection at the corporate level through a VAT—a tax whose incidence may, in the end, fall heavily on consumers, since it is— in effect—a sales tax. The VAT system is not used in the United States.[13] This difference may help to explain, in part, China's low level of consumption (and higher personal savings) compared to the United States.

While the United States relies largely on individual income taxes at the federal level, state and local governments rely on intergovernmental transfers and sales and property taxes. Given the hierarchy of funding based on local income (starting from the central government in China, and moving down to the villages), we can also see why, beginning with provincial-level officials, political leaders are so eager to attract industries with high value-added production to their areas. Increasing production provides additional sources of steady revenue via the shared VAT.

Property taxes in China have not yet become as widespread a source of local income as in the United States, but the various fees related to the use of property in China are an important revenue source for local governments.[14] Furthermore, personal income as a share of national income is substantially higher in the United States than in China. Simply put, tax revenues are relatively higher where the tax base is higher. As we discussed in Chapter 5, businesses produce a disproportionate amount of income in China. US property taxes are used to fund local public services, particularly education. Chinese localities, where the land is not owned by private citizens or corporate entities but leased from the government, rely heavily on revenue sharing (via shared taxes and grants) and a sales tax on service and fees related to the use of land.[15] Private property ownership of land improvements (such as a building or home) is a fairly recent phenomenon.

The fact that localities in China lack an assured source of revenue (i.e., via property taxeso) has led many localities to rely on various user fees and the sale of land rights to the private sector. This practice, in turn, has triggered a number of conflicts related to excessive burdens on the local population, as well as issues of corruption and fairness related to land use rights. In recent years, even after tapping into the sale of land rights, local governments have still encountered funding shortfalls. The creation of local government financing vehicles (LGFVs), also known as Special Purpose Vehicles (SPVs), has become another source of finance for local governments. These LGFVs were created to bypass legal restrictions approved in 1994 that prohibited localities from running budget deficits.

LGFVs raised funds from banks, other financial institutions such as the China Development Bank (see Chapter 6), and the public. This practice, of course, presents its own challenges—as seen in the GFC in the United States, in which SPVs were part of a shadow banking sector tied to mortgages. Recognizing the funding problems that localities and provinces face, China's central government placed heavy restrictions on the use of SPVs and moved to the more transparent and market-oriented system of provincial bond issuance in 2014. In a 2015 reform, local governments were given de facto permission to run budget deficits—they were formally permitted to borrow via bond issuance under a formal central government approval process. As to bank and LGFV debt, provinces were instructed to begin converting these liabilities into bonds. In other words, the illiquid and risky loans of various lender types were to be converted into more liquid, market-priced bonds. To date, local government bonds remain closely held by institutions, rather than by the general public. We discuss China's bond market in a broader context in Chapter 11. Finally, local governments were encouraged to participate in public-private partnerships. With no regulatory structure guiding these partnerships, however, new risks have emerged related to corruption and lending to politically-connected private enterprises—hints of this occurred in China's fiscal response to the GFC, discussed below.

In recent decades in China, four important factors have placed tremendous financial stress on localities:

1. Inability to raise taxes locally
2. Central government mandates that local governments cover many expenditure categories
3. A reward system from the central government for local officials who achieve their growth targets (which requires local investment expenditures)
4. The assumption that central government tax and revenue sharing efficiently and fairly trickles down to the lowest levels of government: the townships and villages

China's system of a heavy reliance on hierarchical funding (from the central government to provinces to localities) leads to a great deal of intra-governmental negotiation. It also results in an ongoing effort to show evidence that one's own province or district is more deserving of funding than another. In past decades in China, raw economic growth has been the coin of the realm in this context. In the United States, much of the negotiation for funding takes place within and between Congress and the Executive Branch, and it has come to be known as "pork barrel" budgeting.[16]

Government Expenditures in the United States vs. China

Table 10.12 provides a breakdown of expenditures for China by the largest central government categories. China classifies its government expenditures across 21 different ministries.[17] In the United States, government expenditures are aligned with 15 Cabinet positions, albeit more loosely. In the aggregate, expenditures by China's provincial/local governments are at least five times larger than expenditures by the central government; while, in the United States, federal expenditures are about one-third larger than state and local expenditures. The largest share of China's expenditures at the central level are for national defense (34 percent of the budget), followed by interest payments on national debt (13 percent), science and technology (9 percent) and public security (5 percent). Table 10.13 shows that provincial/local expenditures are for education (17 percent), social insurance and other human services (14 percent), urban and community affairs (12 percent), and natural resources (11 percent).

Total 2017 (RMB Millions)	2,985,715	100%
National Defense	1,022,635	34%
Interest on Debt	377,769	13%
Science and Technology	282,696	9%
Public Security	184,894	6%
Grain, Oil, Materials Reserve	159,748	5%
Education	154,839	5%
Public Security	139,838	5%
General Public Service	127,146	4%
Transportation	115,642	4%
Social Security and Employment	100,111	3%
Financial Regulation	85,321	3%
Agriculture, Forests, and Water	70,874	2%
Diplomacy	51,967	2%
Housing Security	42,067	1%
Other	59,012	2%

Table 10.12 Distribution of China central government expenditures, 2017.
Source: Author created based on data from CEIC.

Total 2017 (RMB Millions)	17,322,834	100%
Education	2,860,479	17%
Social Security and Employment	2,361,057	14%
Urban & Rural Community Affairs	2,056,155	12%
Natural Resources	1,838,025	11%
General Public Services	1,523,890	9%
Health and Family Planning	1,434,303	8%
Public Security	1,061,233	6%
Transportation	951,756	5%
Housing Security	613,182	4%
Environmental Protection	526,677	3%
Resources, Power, and Information	466,021	3%
Science and Technology	444,002	3%
Culture, Physical Education and Media	312,101	2%
Interest on Debt	249,538	1%
Other	624,415	3%

Table 10.13 Distribution of China local expenditures, 2017.
Source: Author created based on data from CEIC.

For the United States, Medicare, Medicaid, Social Security, and national defense represent about two-thirds of the federal budget. Interest on the national debt represents about 7 percent of the budget. Most local education expenditure (elementary, secondary, and higher) is spent at the local level, and it represents about one-third of local budgets. Public welfare follows at 21 percent; but, as mentioned earlier, America's substantial human services component is largely channeled locally, though financed from the national budget.

Both countries must grant substantial funds from the central government to localities, but China transfers relatively more as a share of both central and local government revenues. The purposes of these grants appear to be different; in China, most transfers are conducted for the actual provision of services at the local level by local governments (about 80 percent of all grants), while in the United States the transfers represent cash payments in the form of either income support, unemployment benefits, or provision of funds to health-care providers (Medicaid or Medicare) for services rendered (about 80 percent of all grants).[18] Figure 10.7 shows that, compared to both the advanced economies and other emerging markets, China's government spends a relatively low share of GDP on health, education, and welfare (discussed in the next section) at all levels. In the United States, transfer payments from all levels of government to individuals—including Social Security payments—amounted to US dollars (USD) 3.1 trillion, or about 15 percent of GDP. This difference in spending profiles helped shape each country's response to the recent COVID-19 crisis (also discussed below).

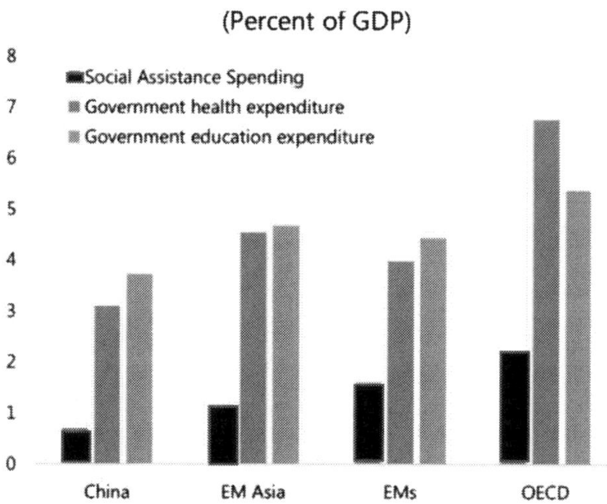

Figure 10.7 Among all economies around the world, China spends relatively less as a share of GDP on health, education, and welfare.
Source: Wingender (2018) Intergovernmental Fiscal Reform in China (https://bit.ly/3gbU5n6). International Monetary Fund.
Note: EM is "emerging markets."

As we have seen, most grants from the national government to local governments and citizens in the United States are mandated; that is, by law they must be transferred for specific purposes. In China, there is more flexibility in how much and for what purposes the funds are to be used—a question of negotiation among the various layers of government. The tradeoffs involve using intermediaries to manage these resources and invest on behalf of citizens (the agency problem) versus giving citizens direct benefits mandated by the national government.[19] The Chinese system allows for greater flexibility and adaptability, while the US system is more predictable in terms of direct benefits to citizens and avoiding agency costs. The Chinese system also offers an incentive system to implement goals mandated under the Five-Year Plan.

China's Social Safety Net

Public Pensions

China's vast social welfare and insurance programs were introduced in the 1990s, almost 100 years after Chancellor Otto von Bismarck introduced the first major social insurance program in Germany. China introduced its own set of measures in response to the major socio-economic changes that began in 1978. Workers and retirees could no longer rely on the "iron rice bowl" security provided by communes and SOEs. Retirees and vulnerable workers, such as the unemployed, now operated in a benefit vacuum. These problems accelerated with the massive layoffs resulting from closures and turnarounds of SOEs in the 1990s. Meanwhile, another leg of the social support system was being undermined; more and more of the younger generation—who had in the past supported their parents in old age—were moving away from rural areas seeking jobs in towns and cities. Demographic changes resulting from China's one-child policy have made the welfare of retirees an even more pressing issue. In Chapter 5, we discussed China's aging population, which will put an increasing burden on the public pension system in the coming years.

China's first approach to the problem came in the form of a Coasian solution (see Chapter 11); the 1994 Labor Law and later contract laws specified what the relationship between workers and employers should be, and it assumed that each of those parties could rationally negotiate their interests and reach equitable agreements. This approach failed: workers were at a disadvantage in the vast majority of cases. In turn, the Chinese Ministry of Labor and Social Security (established in 1949) and State Council embarked on a regulatory approach, rolling out a series of social insurance programs. Table 10.14 lays out a typical basic social insurance program (Shanghai's) for China, showing the contribution share between employers and employees and their date of implementation.

Program	**Employer Wage Deduction (%)**	**Employee Wage Deduction (%)**	**Year Commenced**
Pension	8	16	1997
Medical	2	9.5	1998
Unemployment	0.5	0.5	1981, reformed 1999
Maternity	0	1	2002
Injury, Work-Related	0	0.16–1.52	2003
Total Percent	10.5	28–30	
Ceiling for Monthly Salary*	RMB 24,633		
Housing Provident Fund**	7	7	1999
Housing Ceiling for Monthly Salary*	RMB 2,290–3,924		

Table 10.14 Social insurance programs, China, 2019 (Shanghai).
Source: Author created based on Price Waterhouse Coopers (https://pwc.to/2WFiwlK) and China Labour Bulletin, (https://bit.ly/2z8rqzm).
*Beyond this ceiling, no withdrawals from salary are required.
**Operated by Ministry of Urban and Rural Development.

The largest social insurance program is for pensions, which are activated at retirement (60 years for males, 50 years for females at enterprises, and 55 years for female civil servants). By 2010, virtually the entire elderly population was covered by some form of pension insurance. But the pension amount varies widely by type of public pension plan and province, and the payout is on average low. There are separate public pension plans for 1) salaried workers in urban areas including SOE employees, 2) public sector employees, and 3) rural area workers and non-salaried workers in urban areas. The IMF estimates (Lam et al. 2017) that about 60 percent of the elderly receive an average annual pension of RMB 1,000, which is less than 3 percent of per capita GDP. Public sector retirees receive the most generous annual benefit package at about 61 percent of per capita GDP, but that group only makes up about 4 percent of the population. Figure 10.8 shows that participation in the salaried urban area plan has steadily increased since 1997, and by 2018 it had reached 69 percent of the urban workforce.

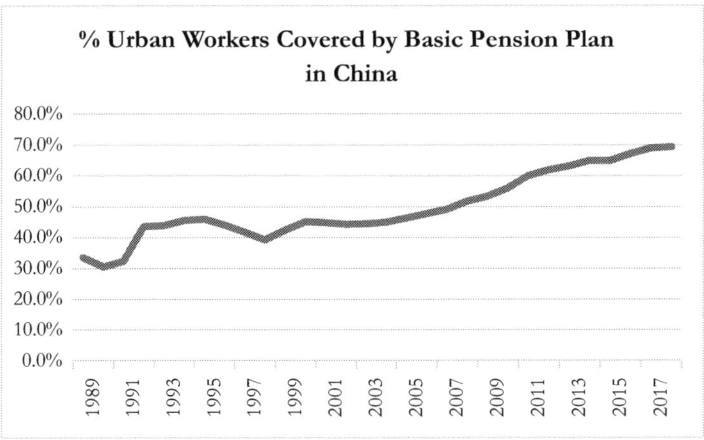

Figure 10.8 The formal measure of pension coverage for urban workers has more than doubled since 1989 in percentage terms. That number belies the fact that many urban workers, such as migrant workers, are not covered by the relatively generous urban pension scheme.
Source: Author created based on data from NBS.

A minimum of 15 working years participation is required to receive benefits, with annual benefits approximately pro-rated based on year of retirement. For both the pension and medical insurance programs, there is both a pooled component funded at the local and provincial levels (similar to social security in the United States) and a dedicated individual component (analogous to a 401K pension plan in the United States). In response to inadequate support for rural residents under the original rural/non-salaried plan, a New Rural Pension Scheme (NRPS) was introduced in 2009. The central and local governments provide a subsidy to this plan. To participate in the NRPS, at least one child must enroll his/her parents and pay premia out of his/her salary. Chen et al. (2020) suggest that rural participation in the NRPS falls far short of what would be expected given the costs and benefits of the program. They explore possible explanations for this shortfall in rural areas including lack of understanding of the program and mistrust of its administration.

A number of challenges face the social insurance program in China. The size of underfunding of the system in the coming years is estimated at around 125 percent of GDP. Two main causes of underfunding relate to the aging population and the large number of legacy retirees who contributed very little or nothing to the system (which commenced in 1997). In response to underfunding, contribution rates are very high by international standards, and they are regressive (take a larger share of income out of low wage earners). In Table 10.14, we see that combined contributions from employer and employee average about 24 percent of personal income. The average for emerging markets is 15 percent, and for advanced economies it is 20 percent (Lam et al. 2017). In the

United States, the combined contribution is 12.4 percent. Paradoxically, social security contributions in China as a share of GDP (2.9 percent) are low relative to OECD economies (e.g., 4.9 percent in the United States); while the contribution burden on salaried individuals in China is high, the low contribution of non-salaried workers (40 percent of the workforce) and the low share of personal income (discussed extensively in Chapters 4 and 5) lead to the low share of GDP anomaly. We can infer from the above discussion that policy-makers will eventually be forced to raise the retirement age in China to make the system viable. Other measures, including continued direct subsidies to the system from the general government budget, will also continue to be necessary.

Medical Coverage

Figure 10.9 shows medical coverage participation in China. Remarkably, by 2018, virtually the entire population had some form of medical coverage. The initial basic coverage implemented in 1998 had limited reach in terms of coverage of migrant urban and rural residents, self-employed workers, and unemployed workers. As a result, the authorities introduced supplementary medical coverage that offers very minimal benefits in 2007. In Figure 10.9, the steep rise in participation after 2007 reflects the inclusion of those with the new bare-bones coverage. By 2018, about 75 percent of individual coverage was of the supplementary type. The remaining share was part of the more formal basic medical coverage. Though both the basic and supplemental programs call for direct payment to providers by the government program, the reality is that most patients pay out-of-pocket and must then seek reimbursement.

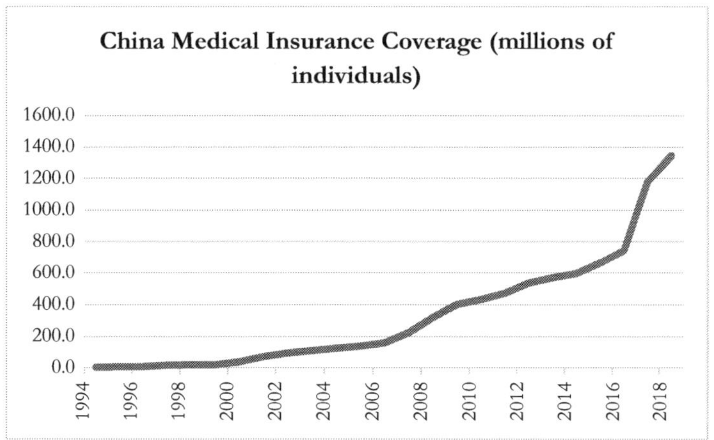

Figure 10.9 Almost all Chinese citizens now have some type of publicly provided medical insurance. The rural supplementary medical insurance plan, however, only provides bare bones reimbursements.
Source: Author created based on data from CEIC.

Unemployment Insurance

Figure 10.10 shows that, by 2018, only about one-fourth of the workforce had unemployment insurance. While the various forms of social insurance coverage discussed above require employer and employee participation in principle, we see that actual coverage falls short in terms of either breadth (number of participants) or depth (benefits provided). Problems enforcing these regulations in the many gray areas of China's labor markets—migrant workers without *hukous*, self-employed workers, household workers, independent contractors, construction workers, part-time workers, and vocational students—contribute to vast leakages out of the social insurance system (Brown 2016). The fact that unemployment benefit participants represented just 25 percent of the workforce in 2018 provides one measure of the shortfall in breadth of coverage. Coverage in the United States is far higher—in part due to far fewer self-employed workers (who, incidentally, also are not covered by unemployment insurance in most states).

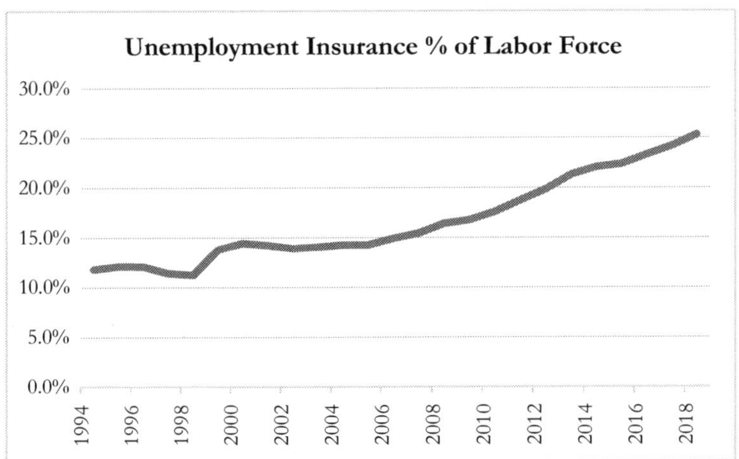

Figure 10.10 The low rate of unemployment insurance for the labor force suggests a large part of the workforce operates in the less formal part of the economy, such as self-employment or migrant work.
Source: Author created based on data from CEIC.

Social Safety Net Summary

We can infer from the above discussion that China's social safety net has expanded in breadth over the past two decades, but lacks depth in terms of benefits received. For example, medical benefits actually received from supplementary medical coverage can fall far short of what is actually needed to cover medical bills. In some cases, unemployment insurance benefits come in the form of training rather than actual cash income. One expects that, as we see more consolidation (mergers and acquisitions resulting in larger enterprises) within China's business sector over time, more employees will become part of a formal salaried sector, and the scope of coverage for the various social insurance programs will increase. Whether the depth of benefits will also increase will be a function of improved bargaining power of labor (for example, union strengthening) and a political consensus on enhancing benefits—an outcome that is less certain.

Case Study 10.4: China's *Dibao* (低保)—Is it a *Hongbao* (红包)Program?*

The most important poverty reduction program in China is known as *dibao*, or Minimum Livelihood Guarantee Program. The program provides non-conditional cash payments to households whose income and assets are deemed sufficiently low to qualify.[20] The threshold for receiving benefits from the program is determined locally, but since 2007 a central government mandate has required all local governments—both rural and urban—to provide a *dibao* mechanism. Shanghai was the first major city to introduce a *dibao* in 1993, and this was followed by a number of urban *dibaos* across the country. Over time, a number of rural communities began to experiment with *dibao* mechanisms as well. Currently, China's *dibao* program is one of the largest cash mechanisms for poverty reduction in the world. By 2018, there were over 10 million urban residents and over 35 million rural residents receiving benefits (1.3 percent and 6.2 percent of total urban and rural populations, respectively—China's official estimate for the rural poverty rate in 2018 was 1.7 percent). At its peak in 2011, 3.3 percent of urban residents and 8 percent of rural residents benefitted from *dibao* participation. Rural and urban *dibao* programs are administratively different.

Though the *dibao* legislative framework suggests that the *dibao* is to provide a guaranteed minimum income, the reality is that it is a program intended to target relatively poor households. The goal of the *dibao* system is to move those whose income falls below some local poverty threshold above that threshold toward the average income of the locality. Localities have different thresholds for what constitutes a minimum income required to be out of poverty. For example, in 2018, the overall the average poverty line for China was around an income of RMB 490 per month. Across localities, there was a wide range of poverty line thresholds, highly correlated with average per capita incomes. For example, the Shanghai threshold was around RMB 970 per month, compared to the average of the poorer Xinjiang province of RMB 353. But eligibility is not determined solely on the basis of family income relative to the poverty line. Village councils decide on a case by case basis who is eligible to receive *dibao* benefits based on other factors such as family assets and non-economic considerations. That local guidelines for receipt of benefits can be subjective and at times arbitrary can create problems, which we discuss below. Furthermore, villages generally have a shortage of funds necessary to meet the needs of all those who may qualify. As a result, local officials must ration *dibao* benefits. For example, recipients might be offered benefits in alternate years.

Over the past decade, average *dibao* payments in rural areas nearly doubled, with average per capita monthly transfers to rural individuals at about RMB 184 in 2018. Urban average transfers for the same year were more than double that of rural average transfers, standing at about RMB 387. A number of excellent studies have looked at the effectiveness of the *dibao* program. For example, Kakwani et al. (2019) consider how effective the program is in terms of targeting the poorest members of rural communities. Exclusion error (E) is the percent of the poor not selected to receive *dibao.* Leakage error (L) is the percent of *dibao* participants who are in fact not eligible to participate (their standard of living is already high enough). The relationship between the two is:

$$L = 1 - H / B \times (1 - E)$$

Where (H) is the actual number of poor individuals in a local community and (B) is the size of *dibao* program (in terms of slots available for participation). For example, if the number of those in poverty equals the number of slots ($H / B = 1$), then the percent of poor excluded (E) will equal the percent of recipients who objectively should be excluded (L). They find that, in the past, *dibao* selection has been virtually random (not truly means tested), with about 87 percent of the poor excluded and about 82 percent of those that receive benefits not truly qualified. Furthermore, they estimate a measure of the social rate of return, or the ratio of social welfare benefits to the cost of *dibao* administration. They find the social rate of return either very low or negative. Notwithstanding these findings, they also find that there is some impact of *dibao* in reducing poverty within rural society.

Other authors such as Golan et al. (2017) reach similar conclusions, but they find a very limited poverty reduction impact from the rural *dibao* program—whether measured by the number of poor residents or by the size of the gap between the poverty line threshold and *dibao* enhanced incomes. They recommend universal data-driven guidelines to determine program eligibility with more centralized control of local eligibility decisions—something that seems increasingly feasible in China's artificial-intelligence-data-analytic economy. They also suggest that expanding the breadth of the program (more participants) rather than depth (higher *dibao* payments) would be a better expansion priority. Meanwhile, Gao et al. (2015) examine the urban *dibao* program and try to measure whether that program enhances measures of well-being. They argue that the design of the program fails to achieve improvement in standard measures of well-being, in part, due to the stigma attached to being selected and participating in the program.

Overall, most authors agree that while the goals of the program are worthy, program design results in outcomes falling far short of those goals. The very good news, however, is that solutions to these problems seem to be very easy to implement; and, with time, China is edging toward making the *dibao* programs (urban and rural) better.

*Recall that a *hongbao* is a red envelope containing cash and given as a gift during the Spring Festival.

Summary of Public Finance

An important tenet of public finance is that, to the extent possible, the devolution of public services to localities is a desirable goal (Tiebout 1956; Oates 1972). This idea stems from the notion that localities are better able to understand and meet the needs of citizens at the ground level. It is also suggested that devolving power to localities can create a healthy competition between provinces (states) and allow for greater experimentation and innovation. By contrast, too much decision making at the central government level may lead to monopoly-like behavior and stagnation. Both China and the United States provide considerable leeway for provinces and states to experiment, learn and copy from one another.

However, it is also recognized that empowering local governments to fund local public services will result in unequal distribution of funding because some localities are richer than others. It is here that revenue sharing and redistribution (mandated from the central government) can play a role. China has devolved the responsibility for the provision of public services to localities more than any major economy in the world (https://bit.ly/2ZfNySU); the tradeoff here may be greater inequality across localities and provinces.

Furthermore, though mandated by the central government, the collection of taxes at the local level relies on the cooperation of local officials and the SAT. Much public expenditure—especially expenses related to health, education, welfare, and (importantly) agricultural support—is the responsibility of local governments even though it is mandated by the central government. Central government responsibilities include the traditional roles of national defense, foreign affairs, diplomacy, key infrastructure and construction projects, and overhead expenditures. In China, transfer payments from the central government are principally made to local governments, while in the United States they are principally made directly to individuals. This partly explains why there is virtually no income redistribution impact via transfers in China; whereas, in the United States, the impact is substantial. Consistent with earlier themes in this textbook, transfers in China serve the purpose of creating new investment, jobs, and ultimately supply; in the United States, transfers mainly provide income support that ultimately creates demand in the form of consumption.

Macro Finance Insight 10.3: Global, Multinational, or Transnational Structure

Large corporations with worldwide operations must decide how to structure the management of their often-complex global operations. Similarly, countries must develop different methods of economic governance for national versus provincial or local control.

Companies with a global (centralized) structure tend to conduct most decision making at headquarters, across all functions (e.g., finance or marketing), allowing subsidiaries to carry out mandates from the center. Companies with a multinational (decentralized) structure tend to allow subsidiaries a great deal of autonomy in decision making, with profits and losses (for example) deemed a local responsibility and a measure of local performance. For transnational companies (which fall somewhere in between), certain decisions are made at headquarters (e.g., strategic financial decisions) while other local decisions are made by subsidiaries (e.g., marketing). There is no single correct structure for all companies. For example, a company such as Shell would be categorized as "global," while a large international accounting firm may be considered "multinational," and Nestle Inc., "transnational." Relevant factors that determine an optimal structure include:

- Need for localization or local customization
- Need for coordination of activities
- Need for technology transfer between subsidiaries
- Level of international competition
- Homogeneous versus non-homogeneous product
- Brand recognition
- Foreign operations based on market access or local cost structure
- Economies of scale
- Establishing a brand
- Standardization of production
- Cross-subsidization by subsidiaries (mutual insurance)
- Diversification across subsidiaries (which is a form of self-insurance)

In a comprehensive discussion of China's institutions and internal governance structure, Xu (2011) states that China's governance structure is unique particularly in the relationship between the central, provincial, and local governments. Neither a centralized Soviet system nor an American-style federal system, Xu suggests that China falls somewhere in between and goes well beyond mere fiscal revenue sharing. Instead, China's system is regionally decentralized, yet authoritarian, and it relies on a great deal of local provision of government services and collection of local revenues while encouraging local experimentation, innovation, and competition among provinces. Key personnel decisions (appointments of provincial and local leaders), however, are made at the central or national level in Beijing. Senior officials are regularly rotated around the country for new positions, and promotions rely on prior performance at the local level. Furthermore, strategic decisions are made via the Five-Year Plan at the central level.

Xu suggests that this hybrid structure between national strategy and local autonomy has played a critical role in China's phenomenal economic growth. Local initiatives, such as the household responsibility system (introduced in the 1970s to promote market-based practices in the agricultural sector in provinces such as Anhui and Guangdong) or the town and village enterprise structure (launched in the 1980s to introduce collective privatization of small- and medium-size enterprises in place such as Wenzhou or Xiamen), percolated up to the national level. But while the unambiguous goal of numerical economic growth has been achieved, the system has tradeoffs in terms of inequality in income distribution and the provision of social services. On balance, it appears that China has both inherited and adopted a global structure for fiscal budgets and Five-Year Plans, incorporating elements of a multinational structure for policy implementation—an overall transnational structure. This structure has a number of consequential outcomes—both good and bad.

Case Study 10.5: China's *Fapiao* (发票)

Foreign travelers in China are often confused by the small piece of paper they receive when they purchase goods or services. The paper typically contains an official stamp; Chinese characters, a serial number, and a small gray scratch-off box (see Figure 10.11). First introduced in mainland China in the 1980s, and even earlier in Taiwan, a *fapiao* (发票) is an official invoice, receipt, tax document, and lottery ticket all rolled into one. Presented to a company or the tax authorities, it provides evidence of an expense. As recorded by the tax authorities, it provides a basis for the VAT, sales tax, and business tax (a tax on services, e.g., a meal at a restaurant—which explains why it is often given with hesitation). The lottery element (included on some types of *fapiao*) is a clever tax authority effort at incentivizing the customer to ask for a *fapiao*; who wouldn't want to win a lottery, and incidentally trigger a tax liability for the seller?

In the past, a huge market in counterfeit *fapiao* has developed. These counterfeits are used to defraud employers and tax authorities—notwithstanding the risk of the death penalty for defrauding the government. Sellers charge a commission (2 percent or more, depending on quality of face value) for the counterfeit item. In recent years, thousands of individuals, enterprises, gangs, and even government officials have been arrested for promoting or participating in the counterfeit *fapiao* market. In 2012, a businessman in Zhejiang province was arrested for helping 315 companies evade millions of dollars in taxes with fake *fapiaos*.

Low civil service salaries and the continued predominance of cash transactions are some of the reasons why fake *fapiaos* exist. Of course, one cannot dismiss outright greed and the entrepreneurial spirit as further causes.

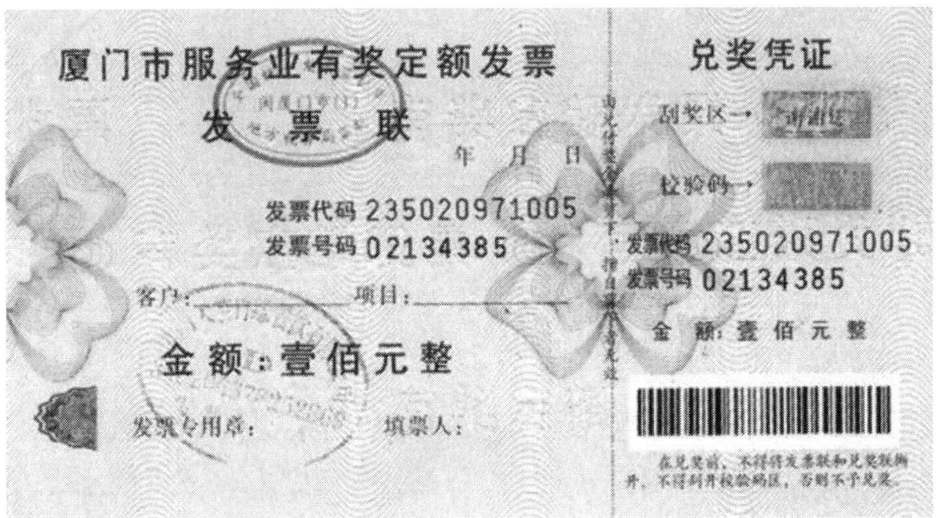

Figure 10.11 *Fapiao* is a receipt used for reporting sales revenue to the tax authorities in China.
Source: Author created.

China's unique fiscal accounting for expenditures does not give a complete picture of central and local government spending on current (consumption) versus investment-related activities. Especially murky is the role of SOEs, which conduct investment activity on behalf of the government. We do know that China's government, at all levels, devotes substantially more of its tax and borrowing funds to investment (hard assets), while the United States devotes a significantly larger proportion to individuals, social services, and national defense. Both countries, out of necessity, seem to be incrementally moving toward some average of these two extremes.

Finally, we note that in the United States, total government spending as a share of GDP is about 33 percent, while in China the figure is actually lower, at 25 percent. This figure, however, ignores the output of SOEs that produce a range of goods and services for the private sector.

Fiscal Policy in Action

Three fundamental factors distinguish China and the United States in terms of the causes of business cycles and the resulting counter-cyclical policies on the demand side.

First, China remains below its steady-state in a Solow context (as we saw in Chapter 4) compared to the United States, which is arguably at its long-run steady state. Second, China's sources of demand have historically been weighted more toward exports and investment. This distribution contrasts with that of the United States, where consumption is a principal source of demand. Third, as we have discussed, China's government has greater direct control over economic activity (especially investment) than does the US government. The second and third factors combined mean that, on the demand side, China is more vulnerable to external sector shocks, while the United States is relatively more vulnerable to investment shocks.[21] Recall from Chapter 6 that investment in the United States is three times more volatile than in China (coefficient of variation); government mandated (stable) investment is a remaining vestige of China's planned economy. Let's discuss the first two factors now (the role of government is discussed throughout this chapter, and in Chapters 7 and 8).

Macro Finance Insight 10.4: Growth Cycles vs. Business Cycles

Economies such as China's, which are still building up their capital stock via high savings rates, tend to experience growth rates in output that far exceed those of developed economies in the OECD (such as the United States). The possibility of those growth rates dipping below zero (becoming negative) are remote for countries such as China, but quite possible for those with rates hovering around 3 percent, such as the United States. However, we normally define a recession in terms of prolonged and widely dispersed negative growth (a negative first derivative) for such key economic indicators as GDP, industrial production, retail sales, and a corresponding increase in unemployment. In this sense, it is unlikely that China will experience an outright recession (or business cycle fluctuation, as it is commonly defined). Instead, China has experienced and will likely continue to experience growth recessions (periods in which economic growth dips below trend growth), causing a persistent and widespread negative second derivative in economic performance. Table 10.15 provides a record of US recessions as measured by the National Bureau of Economic Research (a non-governmental research institute located in Cambridge, MA). Figure 10.12 provides a record of growth cycles based on a set of algorithms employed by the OECD. A value of 1 represents a growth recession, and a value of 0 represents a period of growth recovery. (For China, the most recent growth recession was from February, 2018 through December, 2018.) Although roughly similar in their intent, the former is a measure of fluctuations in absolute output (the traditional measure of business cycles), while the latter is based on fluctuations in growth rates. Some stylized facts about business cycles and growth cycles do emerge from both tables. First, recoveries are longer than contractions.* Second, growth cycles occur more frequently than more traditional business cycles.

Specific to China, we see two prominent growth contractions in Figure 10.12: one occurring before and during the Asian Financial Crisis (1994–1999), the other in 2014–2016—a period of transition in China related to long-term factors, such as an excessive reliance on investments and exports. In between those two were several other growth contractions, including one corresponding to the dot-com bubble of 2000–2002, which was compounded by China's own banking crisis. All told, since 1979, China has experienced ten growth cycle recessions. In the same period, the United States has had five traditional business cycles.

*A common feature of time-series series data is that growth rates fluctuate substantially more than levels of data.

Business Cycle Reference Dates		**Duration in Months**			
Peak	**Trough**	**Contraction**	**Expansion**	**Cycle**	
(Quarterly Dates are in Parentheses)		*Peak to Trough*	*Previous Trough to this Peak*	*Trough from Previous Trough*	*Peak from Previous Peak*
	December 1854 (IV)	--	--	--	--
June 1857(II)	December 1858 (IV)	18	30	48	--
October 1860(III)	June 1861 (III)	8	22	30	40
April 1865(I)	December 1867 (I)	32	46	78	54
June 1869(II)	December 1870 (IV)	18	18	36	50
October 1873(III)	March 1879 (I)	65	34	99	52
March 1882(I)	May 1885 (II)	38	36	74	101
March 1887(II)	April 1888 (I)	13	22	35	60
July 1890(III)	May 1891 (II)	10	27	37	40
January 1893(I)	June 1894 (II)	17	20	37	30
December 1895(IV)	June 1897 (II)	18	18	36	35
June 1899(III)	December 1900 (IV)	18	24	42	42
September 1902(IV)	August 1904 (III)	23	21	44	39
May 1907(II)	June 1908 (II)	13	33	46	56
January 1910(I)	January 1912 (IV)	24	19	43	32
January 1913(I)	December 1914 (IV)	23	12	35	36
August 1918(III)	March 1919 (I)	7	44	51	67
January 1920(I)	July 1921 (III)	18	10	28	17
May 1923(II)	July 1924 (III)	14	22	36	40
October 1926(III)	November 1927 (IV)	13	27	40	41
August 1929(III)	March 1933 (I)	43	21	64	34
May 1937(II)	June 1938 (II)	13	50	63	93
February 1945(I)	October 1945 (IV)	8	80	88	93
November 1948(IV)	October 1949 (IV)	11	37	48	45

Business Cycle Reference Dates		**Duration in Months**			
Peak	**Trough**	**Contraction**	**Expansion**	**Cycle**	
(Quarterly Dates are in Parentheses)		*Peak to Trough*	*Previous Trough to this Peak*	*Trough from Previous Trough*	*Peak from Previous Peak*
July 1953(II)	May 1954 (II)	10	45	55	56
August 1957(III)	April 1958 (II)	8	39	47	49
April 1960(II)	February 1961 (I)	10	24	34	32
December 1969(IV)	November 1970 (IV)	11	106	117	116
November 1973(IV)	March 1975 (I)	16	36	52	47
January 1980(I)	July 1980 (III)	6	58	64	74
July 1981(III)	November 1982 (IV)	16	12	28	18
July 1990(III)	March 1991(I)	8	92	100	108
March 2001(I)	November 2001 (IV)	8	120	128	128
December 2007 (IV)	June 2009 (II)	18	73	91	81
Average, All Cycles:					
1854–2009 (33 cycles)		17.5	38.7	56.2	56.4*
1854–1919 (16 cycles)		21.6	26.6	48.2	48.9**
1919–1945 (6 cycles)		18.2	35.0	53.2	53.0
1945–2009 (11 cycles)		11.1	58.4	69.5	68.5

Table 10.15 A mature economy, such as the United States', has a long record of business cycle recessions and recoveries.
Source: National Bureau of Economic Research.
*32 cycles.
**15 cycles.

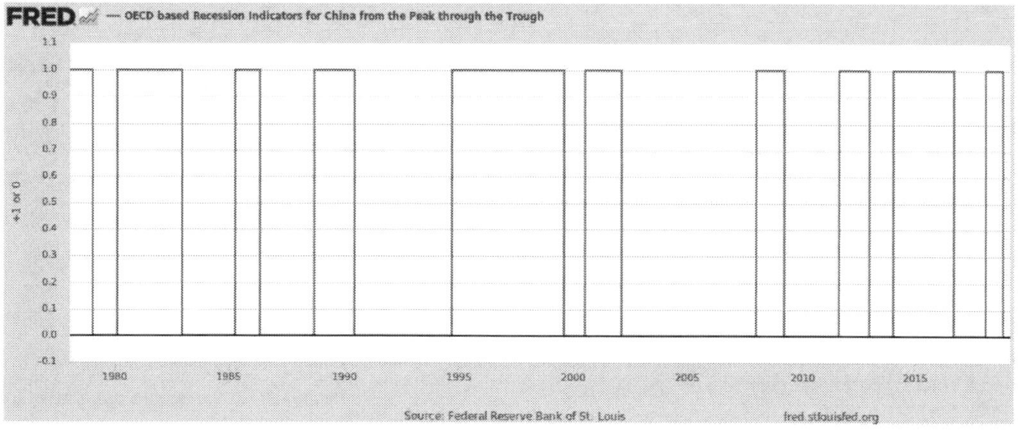

Figure 10.12 China experiences growth recessions (index value of 1) and rarely experiences an outright business cycle recession.
Source: Federal Reserve Economic Database.

Policy Responses

The Trump Trade War and COVID-19

As discussed in Chapter 3, the Trump trade war with China has the potential to have a significant impact on China's economic growth. The IMF estimates (https://bit.ly/3dN96dg) a decline below baseline GDP growth of about 1.6 percentage points in 2019, with a smaller harmful effect on the United States. In response, China has committed to an additional USD 163 billion in infrastructure spending (https://bit.ly/3bEzWDz), about 2.7 percent above and beyond an already-rapid growth rate, to boost demand. Much of this expenditure is financed through accommodative monetary policy and a surge in lending. One of the many projects includes a new USD 19.9 billion high speed rail line (https://bit.ly/2VwZKfo) linking Chongqing and Kunming in southwest China. We discussed issues surrounding rail construction and quality of growth in Case Study 4.7. Meanwhile, year over year monetary growth once again surged to 18 percent—close to the rates seen during the GFC.

In the throes of the COVID-19 pandemic, both countries executed predictable fiscal responses to the crisis. It is anticipated that China's response will be an estimated USD 390 billion (significantly smaller than the GFC response) in expenditure on infrastructure investments tied to China's 2025 goals. Meanwhile, in the United States, various aid packages—including the CARES Act (https://bit.ly/2WIhzJw)—were approved by the United States Congress and are estimated to provide at least USD 3 trillion in support for small businesses and families. The legislation was a mix of direct income transfers to individuals (about 26 percent of the total), loan support and grants for businesses (about one-third of the total), and funding to local governments and public health programs.[22] True to form, during the COVID-19 crisis, each country is following the same playbook as in prior crises. China's response is supply-enhancing investment; the US response is an effort at propping up demand and increasing income support for individuals in need of food and shelter. It is apparent that each country could benefit by using the other's playbook and relying less on their own.

Great Financial Crisis

The Great Financial Crisis challenged policy-makers to respond aggressively in both China and the United States. Figure 10.13 shows growth in the money supply (monetary policy) and real government expenditures (fiscal policy) compared to real GDP growth in China between 2000 and 2018. Of particular note is the surge in money and expenditures in response to the GFC (2008–2009). Government expenditures surged again in response to the growth recession of 2014–2016. Over the long run we can see that both the monetary and fiscal stance has been expansionary in the past two decades.

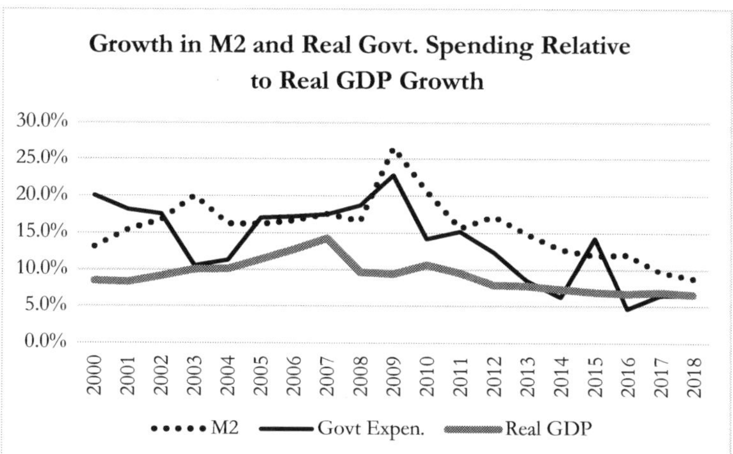

Figure 10.13 Monetary growth and real government spending have exceeded real GDP growth, suggesting overall expansionary monetary and fiscal policies. We see both policies surge during 2008–2009 in the midst of the Global Financial Crisis.
Source: Author created based on data from the Federal Reserve Economic Database and CEIC.

In the GFC, China's central government announced a series of fiscal measures that cumulatively added RMB 4 trillion (USD 585 billion) in spending from 2009 to 2010. This addition amounted to an average of 12 percent of GDP for 2008–2009, and it is estimated to have increased real GDP by 3.1 percent and 2.7 percent for those years (Cova et al. 2010). Of this amount, 90 percent was used for investment at all levels of government and 10 percent was used in various transfer payments. As also seen in Chapter 9, there was substantial and accommodating growth in the money supply (26 percent nominal growth in 2009 alone). These policies triggered similar responses to those seen during the Asian Financial Crisis (see discussed below).

In an insightful paper that sheds light not just on fiscal policy during the GFC but also on the growth of shadow banking in China, Bai et al. (2016) show that while the central government may have given the green light for stimulus spending, most of the action actually occurred at the local level.[23] Given our earlier discussion of the outsize expenditure burden that localities carry, this should be unsurprising. The authors estimate that at least three-fourths of stimulus spending occurred locally and was financed using LGFVs, which was primarily funded by banks. They base their results on the large negative gap between the reported increase in general government budget deficits and the actual increase in investment spending by localities during the GFC. What is more, the authors state that most of this spending took the form of off-balance sheet loans to "select" private enterprises (which were granted regulatory relief) within the localities. About 60 percent of the stimulus spending went to municipal construction and transportation infrastructure. In summary, local governments used LGFV financing to pay for local investment projects undertaken by private companies and to fund local budget deficits. These private companies were a precursor of the public-private partnerships described above in the section on government revenues. The authors point out that, by 2010, spending via these LGFVs accounted for 10 percent of GDP, and much of that was for private commercial projects. Meanwhile, the stimulus caused a surge in the investment rate (by 5 percent of GDP) and a three- to four-fold increase in LGFV debt between 2008 and 2015.

Bai et al. tie together three critical policy changes that we have discussed in this chapter and in Chapter 7 to explain the key involvement of localities and LGFVs in the GFC stimulus plan: the 1994 fiscal reform, which placed a heavy expenditure burden on localities without a corresponding increase in tax revenues; the 1994 law prohibiting local budget deficits; and the Silent Banking Crisis of 2000–2003, which led to rules that broke the tight relationship between local government officials and local branch bank managers. The kicker was a set of new rules in 2009 which formally allowed local governments to create LGFVs. Once again, whether this chain of events turns out to be good or bad for China hinges on the question of quality, not quantity, of growth. We note the lengthy discussion in Chapter 4 regarding declining returns on investment since 2008. Bai et al. point out a dispersion of returns across industries, suggesting that the stimulus program resulted in economic inefficiency.

In response to the financial crisis unfolding in the United States, the Obama administration introduced the American Economic Recovery and Investment Act in February, 2009. A set of tax relief and spending measures were announced that amounted to USD 787 billion—or about 5.6 percent of that year's GDP.[24] By early 2012, approximately USD 750 billion had been disbursed. Of this latter amount, about 40 percent was tax benefits, and the remaining 60 percent was evenly divided between government spending and transfer payments (entitlements). As discussed in Chapter 8, the Federal Reserve increased the monetary base by almost a factor of five through the acquisition of troubled assets and by substantially broadening the range of assets acquired beyond Treasury instruments. Monetary growth surged in the United States during the GFC. In both countries, there was nearly a doubling of the M2 growth rate as the crisis unfolded in 2009–2010.

Wen et al. (2019) show that China, despite a drop of 45 percent in exports (about a 17 percent drop in trend GDP) during the GFC, was able to rebound back to its trend GDP, while the United States and other Western economies did not. China accomplished this via accelerated growth rates above trend ("Z-shaped growth"), while the Western economies only experienced trend growth ("V-shaped growth") during the recovery stage. The authors suggest that this outcome was the result of the hand-in-glove relationship between monetary and fiscal policy in China—state-owned banks surged credit (as discussed in Chapters 7 and 8), which immediately financed state-directed investment by SOEs. It should be noted, however, that most United States recoveries have also experienced accelerated growth rates (above trend) when in recovery mode—the 2008–2009 crisis was an exception, no doubt because this was a financial crisis as opposed to a typical demand or supply-shock recession. In contrast, China experienced a classic demand-shock style recession (an exogenous drop in export demand) and a classic Z-shaped recovery in growth rates. Finally, we once again remind the reader of the question of quality of growth; a short-run stimulus package in China heavily tilted toward investment demand raises questions of positive and sustainable returns over the long run.

Asian Financial Crisis

The Asian Financial Crisis that began in Thailand in 1996 moved rapidly through the Philippines, Indonesia, Taiwan, and South Korea, and it inevitably impacted China. Chinese policy-makers were proactive in their response, raising budget expenditures 12 percent over programmed expenditures. The central government issued construction bonds to raise funds that were transferred to local governments for capital improvement projects (investments). Because tax revenues remained close to budgeted amounts, the expansionary impact was substantial (increasing GDP by at least 1.4 percent). From late 1998 through 1999, the PBC also had a very accommodative monetary policy (with monetary growth rates of over 35 percent in 1997) and a surge in the money supply, as discussed in Chapter 8. Taken together, these figures are clear indications of expansionary fiscal and monetary policies imposed in response to the Asian Financial Crisis. These effects, recalling both the investment-savings/liquidity-money (IS/LM) framework and the aggregate supply/aggregate demand framework of Chapter 9, show a substantial Keynesian-style stimulus.

Similarities and Differences in the Policy Response to Economic Shocks

We see that China's response to economic slowdowns has been a mix of orthodox policies—expansionary fiscal policy combined with accommodative monetary policy—and an array of heterodox policies, such as directed credit to specific industries and projects. A depreciation of the RMB (nearly 8 percent during the trade war) has been added to the mix. What is most remarkable about the responses of China and the United States to the 2008–2009 financial crisis is how similar they were, not just qualitatively but quantitatively. In both cases, fiscal stimulus as a share of GDP reached roughly 6 percent; and, in both cases, M2 growth rates nearly doubled. However, while the end product looked very similar, beneath the surface were fundamental differences based on the underlying economies.

In China, most of fiscal stimulus during the GFC came in the form of investment, with only 10 percent representing transfer payments. In the United States, close to 70 percent of the stimulus came in the form of tax relief or unemployment benefits and other transfer payments. Only a small share of the US stimulus package came in the form of investment. In other words, while China's fiscal stimulus consisted mostly of government-sponsored investments, most of the US package likely resulted in greater consumption. At one level, these differences simply reflect the disparity in sources of demand between the two economies. Looking deeper, we see that it would be very difficult to stimulate demand in China through tax policies. In China, personal taxes are an insignificant part of personal income, and personal income, as discussed in Chapter 5, represents a smaller share of national income (by international standards). Thus, stimulating the economy through lower taxes would have a muted effect. Establishing systems for transfer payments related to retirement, health, or unemployment benefits are structural reforms requiring time to implement.

As a nation of savers, the fiscal multiplier from tax cuts in China is likely small. In the United States, however, consumption represents a large component of aggregate demand. Changes in tax rates that impact consumption can have a substantial impact on demand. Given the simple multiplier (M) with a propensity to consume of (c) and a tax rate of (t) we have:

$$M = 1 / (1 - (c\,(1 - t)))$$

Then, the change in the multiplier with respect to tax rate changes, is:

$$\Delta M / \Delta t = -c / (1 - (c\,(1 - t)))^2$$

Thus, the smaller the propensity to consume factor (*c*), the smaller the impact of lowering tax rates; as we have discussed, China has a smaller (*c*). Because corporations already devote a sizeable share of their income to investment, tax credit policies would also be relatively ineffective in China.

At a political level, there is a pronounced bias toward consumer-driven fiscal policy as opposed to "big government" in the United States. China's already-large government involvement in the economy makes such concerns more or less moot. While the short-run economics of such stimulus approaches make sense for each country, they do present problems in terms of long-run policy goals. In the United States, key long-run policy goals include reducing the deficit and government debt, increasing savings, and increasing investment. In China, the most recent Five-Year Plan calls for increasing consumption, reducing the share of GDP devoted to investment, and enhancing the social safety net. Clearly, the short-run responses we have just described run counter to these long-run goals. In other words, the GFC, Trump trade war. and now COVID-19 crises were setbacks from the perspective of longer-term policy goals for both countries. The Trump trade war added another wrinkle to China's efforts at achieving solid and stable growth. On one hand, it moved China closer to its stated long-run goal of rebalancing from export-led growth to the more stable base of local consumer-led demand. But, in the short run, just as in the GFC, it was a step backward in that domestic investment once again surged—making the economy even more unbalanced.

Both fiscal and monetary policies appear to be more direct and to have a greater impact in China than in the United States. On the fiscal side, government spending does not suffer from the leakages from tax cuts and transfer payments, which are partly saved (the propensity to save, *s)*—especially in a weak economy—and do not create demand. On the monetary side, directing credit for targeted purposes or industries and then channeling money through state-owned banks is more likely to lead to spending than would the complex transmission system. In the latter case, represented by the IS/LM framework, monetary policy must clear several hurdles before impacting demand. China's use of monetary policy is closer in spirit to the quantity theory of money, in which money is channeled directly into demand (specifically government and investment demand).

While China's policy-makers have been quite adept at using a mix of orthodox and heterodox policy tools to respond to the external short-run demand shocks described above, it is important to recognize that many of China's fundamental economic challenges are internal, long-term, and related to long-run supply. We have discussed these long-term structural problems extensively in the first half of this textbook: the shrinking and aging of the population, diminishing returns, the increasing economic drag of depreciation, and the need for quality growth rather than quantity of growth. No amount of short-term stimulus can offset these challenges in a sustainable way. Levels of domestic debt have already reached troubling levels, and they now constrain the government's margin of maneuver. Rather, long-term solutions—including the full gamut of technological progress tools—will be needed. Greater progress is also required in rebalancing the economy away from investment and exports toward greater consumption and investment in human capital.

Macro Finance Insight 10.5: Ownership, Control and the State

It may seem odd to students of finance that ownership of shares in a company does not necessarily impart proportionate control in major decisions, such as how the company's assets are deployed and sold. But a long line of literature ranging from Jensen and Meckling (1979) to Short (1994) to Dyck and Zingales 2004) shows that this is indeed the case. This is broadly defined as the "principal-agent problem," where the principal is the owner of an entity and the agent putatively acts in the owner's behalf. The literature deals with the question of under what circumstances the interests of the principals (owners) would be fully aligned with those of the agents (controllers). A specific variation on this problem is when minority shareowners have majority control (voting rights) in a company. This can happen when there is substantial cross-shareholding among companies (companies own shares in each other), or when there is a pyramid structure. Pyramid structures are situations where a small company holds ownership in a larger company, and that company owns shares in another larger company, and so on. Cross-shareholding is a common practice in Japanese corporate governance to achieve greater control of a company than warranted by shares held. Pyramid structures also yield the same result and are common in East Asia, particularly Thailand. Noll et al. (2016) find that both pyramid and cross-shareholding structures are important across East Asia, but they point out the need for more data and research on this topic as it relates to China.

When there is a large difference between those who control a company's decisions versus those who actually have ownership, perverse incentives are created. Controllers act in ways that benefit their interests at the expense of owners. This is referred to as self-dealing. Controllers may take on excessive debt while paying high dividends to themselves—all at the expense of owners (looting); they may sell assets to related parties at below market prices (tunneling). Controllers may not care about the overall value of the company, but rather their own personal enrichment. The true shareholders of the company are left holding the bag.

Various authors attempt to measure the gap:

Self-Dealing Potential = f(Control of the Company – Ownership of the Company)

This equation shows self-dealing potential as a function of the difference between how much control or power a set of shareholders has versus actual financial ownership of the company. Researchers approach the problem of measuring control and ownership from different angles. Dyck and Zingales (2004) find, in their empirical work for companies around the globe, that the value created for controllers (at the expense of owners) is substantial.

Applying these concepts to SOEs in China is an interesting challenge. Claessens and Fan (2003) argue that the central and local governments are controlling owners of SOEs, and they go on to say that "the state is not the ultimate owner but rather the agent of the ultimate owners—the citizen" (10). These are two different views of the governance structure of an SOE. As a controlling owner, the above gap would be 0—there would not be an issue of self-dealing (control = ownership). But, in the case where the government acts as the agent of citizens (control = 100 percent and ownership = 0), there are very large concerns for self-dealing on the part of the government. Of course, various legal mechanisms can be proposed to mitigate the potential for self-dealing, as well as economic solutions. For example, allowing governments to increase their share of cashflow directly from the enterprise (actually increase their ownership share) would by definition reduce the potential for self-dealing.

The discussion becomes even more interesting at the macro finance level. Politicians (governments) control the nation's assets, but in theory they have a minimal ownership stake. What political mechanisms are available to prevent self-dealing? Ziobrowski (2004) shows that United States senators have significantly higher portfolio returns than does the average citizen. While they attribute this higher return to the use of inside information, it would also be useful to investigate whether these abnormally high returns are the result of more proactive decisions. For example, do senators actually make policy decisions to benefit their own portfolios at the expense of the citizen-owner?

As we have seen throughout this text, the role of government in the Chinese economy is substantial—it has a great deal of control. If the government believes it has a stake in economic performance (has both control and ownership), it will more likely promote quality growth. If it only has control without any stake (claims) in performance, problems of self-dealing could very well arise. In financial theory, one proposal to keep agents in check is for firms to take on more debt. Lenders may keep a careful watch to prevent decisions harmful to the overall company, and they may impose legal constraints (bond covenants) in order to ensure performance. Meanwhile, the threat of bankruptcy may serve as a further damper to those who control the company. In the macro finance context, debt may serve the same purpose with international lenders and the IMF monitoring economic performance to help mitigate the risk of national bankruptcy and the threat of IMF intervention.

Challenging Questions for China (and the Student): Chapter 10

1. Go to the Federal Reserve Economic Database (FRED) and update the chart, "General Government Gross Debt for China."
2. Decentralization of government spending and taxation has always been a basic principle guiding public finances. Describe what issues arise with decentralization in China's system of public finances.
3. Consider fiscal policy responses to the Great Financial Crisis of 2008–2009:
   a. Explain the different fiscal policy responses in the United States and China.
   b. Explain whether the short-run policies in (a) are consistent with the longer-run goals of each country.
   c. Compare and contrast monetary policy responses in the United States and China.
4. Based on estimates of China's Taylor rule response function (as described in Chapter 9), compare and contrast China's and the United States' likely policy responses to future inflation and output shocks.
5. It is argued in this chapter that both fiscal and monetary policy are more likely to have an immediate impact in China than in the United States. Explain.
6. With respect to the relationship between provinces (states) and the central government, compare and contrast China and the United States in terms of their global, multinational, or transnational structures.
7. Revenue sharing in the United States mainly involves federal revenue sharing with individual citizens at the local level. In China, revenue sharing mainly involves intragovernmental transfers.
   a. Explain why there is a difference.
   b. Explain the different implications for consumption and investment.
8. Based on what you have learned in this chapter, explain why there are such great tensions over land rights at the local level in China.
9. What are the major challenges for the Chinese economy in the coming years? Compare and contrast with those of the United States.
10. Should government officials in a country be encouraged to hold a broad portfolio of the nation's assets (e.g., a stock market index)? Why or why not?
11. Using the self-dealing gap of control-ownership in Macro Finance Insight 10.4, explain the difference between SOEs acting as agents of citizens versus actual government ownership of SOEs. Why does this difference matter? Recommend policy solutions in the case where there is potential for self-dealing.

12. Discuss the pros and cons of using net borrowing by the government as a measure of the fiscal deficit, as opposed to simply calculating (revenues – expenditures). What is the difference between the two measures?
13. In Case Study 10.5, suppose the exclusion ratio (*E*) (the percent of the poor excluded from receiving a *dibao*) equals 1. What will the leakage ratio be? Explain in words.
14. A massive loss of jobs occurred in both countries during the COVID-19 crisis. Explain how each country provided direct income support for individuals and why their approaches differed.
15. Provide a formula (an identity) linking 1) social pension contribution as a share of GDP, 2) social pension contribution as a share of personal income, and 3) personal income as a share of GDP. For each element of the formula, provide a numerical estimate for China based on data in this Chapter and Chapters 4 and 5.

References

Bai, C. E., C. T. Hsieh, and Z. M. Song. 2016. "The Long Shadow of a Fiscal Expansion." Brookings Papers on Economic Activity no. w22801, National Bureau of Economic Research.

Barboza, David. 2013. "Coin of Realm in China Graft: Phony Receipts." *New York Times,* 4 August.

Bartlett, Christopher, and Sumantra Ghoshal. 1997. "Evolution of the Transnational." In *Current Issues in International Business*, edited by Iyanatul Islam and William Shepherd, Cheltenham: Edward Elgar, pp. 113–36.

Brown, R. 2016. Chinese Workers Without Benefits. *Richmond Journal of Global Law and Business*, 15 (1), pp. 21–53.

Chen, X., L. Hu, and J. L. Sindelar. 2020. "Leaving Money on the Table? Suboptimal Enrollment in the New Social Pension Program in China." *The Journal of the Economics of Ageing*, 15.

China Labour Bulletin. 2019. "China's Social Security System." https://clb.org.hk/content/china's-social-security-system.

Claessens, S., and J. P. Fan. 2003. "Corporate Governance in Asia: A Survey." *SSRN*, 28 April, http://dx.doi.org/10.2139/ssrn.386481.

Cova, Pietro, Massimiliano Pisani, and Alessandro Rebucci. 2010. "Macroeconomic Effects of China's Fiscal Stimulus." IDB Working Paper no. 72, Washington, DC: Inter-American Development Bank.

Dunaway, Stephen and Annalisa Feddelino. 2006. "Fiscal Policy in China." In *China and India: Learning From Each Other. Reforms and Policies for Sustained Growth*, edited by Jahangir Aziz, Steven Dunaway, and Eswar Prasad. Washington, DC: International Monetary Fund, pp. 231–40.

Dyck, A., and L. Zingales. 2004. "Private Benefits of Control: An International Comparison." *The Journal of Finance*, 59(2), 537–600.

Fock, Achim and Christine Wong. 2008. "Financing Rural Development for a Harmonious Society in China: Recent Reforms in Public Finance and Their Prospects." Policy Research Working Paper no. WPS 4693, Washington, DC: World Bank.

Gao, Q., S. Yang, and S. Li. 2015. "Welfare, Targeting, and Anti-Poverty Effectiveness: The Case of Urban China." *The Quarterly Review of Economics and Finance*, 56, pp. 30–42.

Golan, J., T. Sicular, and N. Umapathi. 2017. "Unconditional Cash Transfers in China: Who Benefits from the Rural Minimum Living Standard Guarantee (Dibao) Program?" *World Development*, 93, pp. 316–36.

Hodge, Andrew W., Robert J. Corea, Benjamin J. Hobbs, and Bonnie A. Retus. 2013. "Returns for Domestic Nonfinancial Business." *Survey of Current Business*, 93(6), pp. 14–18.

Jensen, M. C., and W. H. Meckling. 1979. "Theory of the Firm: Managerial Behavior, Agency Costs, and Ownership Structure." In *Economics Social Institutions*, edited by Karl Brunner, Boston: Martinus Nijhoff Publishing, pp. 163–231.

Kakwani, N., S. Li, X. Wang, and M. Zhu. 2019. "Evaluating the Effectiveness of the Rural Minimum Living Standard Guarantee (*Dibao*) Program in China." *China Economic Review*, 53, pp. 1–14.

Kujis, Louis and Gao Xu. 2008. *China's Fiscal Policy—Moving to Center Stage*. Beijing: World Bank Office.

Lam, W. R., M. M. Rodlauer, and M. A. Schipke. 2017. *Modernizing China: Investing in Soft Infrastructure*. International Monetary Fund.

Liu, Y., J. Martinez-Vazquez, and B. Qiao. 2014. "Falling short: Intergovernmental Transfers in China." International Center for Public Policy Working Paper Series no. 9.

Noll, J., Y. Diefenbach, K. Park, and M. J. Hyun. 2016. "Corporate Governance: East Asian Style-A Literature Study on Typical Determinants of Corporate Governance in China, Japan, South Korea and Taiwan." *China, Japan, South Korea and Taiwan*, 17 February.

Oates, Wallace E. 1972. *Fiscal Federalism*. New York: Harcourt Brace Jovanovich.

Short, H. 1994. "Ownership, Control, Financial Structure and the Performance of Firms." *Journal of Economic Surveys*, 8(3), 203–49.

Tax Policy Center. 2012. "Tax Policy Briefing Book: A Citizens' Guide for the 2012 Election and Beyond." www.taxpolicycenter.org/briefing-book/.

Tiebout, C. 1956. "A Pure Theory of Local Expenditures." *Journal of Political Economy*, 64(5), pp. 416–24.

Wang, X. and R. Herd. 2013. "The System of Revenue Sharing and Fiscal Transfers in China." OECD Economics Department Working Papers no. 1030.

Wen, Y., and J. Wu. 2019. "Withstanding the Great Recession Like China." *The Manchester School*, 87(2), pp. 138–82.

Wingender, M. P. 2018. *Intergovernmental Fiscal Reform in China*. International Monetary Fund.

Xu, Chenggang. 2011. "The Fundamental Institutions of China's Reforms and Development." *Journal of Economic Literature*, 49(4), pp. 1076–151.

Ziobrowski, A. J., P. Cheng, J. W. Boyd, and B. J. Ziobrowski. 2004. "Abnormal Returns from the Common Stock Investments of the US Senate." *Journal of Financial and Quantitative Analysis*, 39(4), pp. 661–76.

Endnotes

1. Under the Appropriations Clause of the United States Constitution, it is the Congress that ultimately determines what specific purposes publicly raised money (tax revenues and borrowing) can be used for. The Constitution states "No Money shall be drawn from the Treasury, but in Consequence of Appropriations made by Law . . ."
2. An interesting feature of both the Five-Year Plan and One-Year Plan updates is that the elements are not publicly announced until March of the year that the Plan starts. Presumably, this allows for real time adjustments to the economic environment as needed.
3. The goal of living longer by one year is not something that even the powerful Chinese government can guarantee will be met. Some of the goals established are mandated, while others are strongly encouraged.
4. However, one could argue that, with the election of each US president to a four-year term, a set of long-term policies are implicitly established as a Four- (possibly Eight-) Year Plan.
5. Among the 40 countries covered by the OECD, China's system of taxes and fiscal transfers has the smallest impact on overall income distribution. India, South Korea, and several Latin American economies are slightly above China in terms of impact.
6. As in the case of New York City's bankruptcy in 1975, both levels of government may play a role.
7. We are taking a net savings approach here. Net savings is the difference between sources of funds (domestic savings) and uses of funds (domestic investment).
8. This is true as long as these taxes do not interfere with commerce (trade) between individual states (i.e., do not inhibit intra-state imports and exports); see the Commerce Clause of the United States Constitution.
9. Wages and salaries are taxed at a range of 3-45 percent, unincorporated businesses (small- and medium-sized enterprises) at a range of 5–35 percent, dividends from short-term holdings and capital gains and interest income at 20 percent. Dividends from long-term holdings and rental/leasing income is taxed at 10 percent. In addition there is a 14 percent tax on authors' income!
10. Since 1978, under the one-child policy, Chinese households have been more or less uniform, perhaps obviating the need for dependent deductions.
11. Corporations do pay half of the Social Security tax identified under social insurance. Under the new tax law that went into effect in 2017–2018, corporate taxes as a share of overall taxes will no doubt be even lower in 2018.

12. Though the number of SOEs is declining, the output of these state-controlled firms still makes up a large share of China's national income.
13. The US retail sales tax is on final, not intermediate, sales; and it is a local, not federal, tax.
14. As part of a pilot program, Chongqing and Shanghai have both started to impose property taxes at a rate of 0.5–1.2 percent.
15. Land lease terms typically run 40 years for offices, 50 years for industrial use, and 70 years for residential use. These terms can vary considerably within China depending on the region.
16. "Pork barrel" is a derogatory term, dating back to the American Civil War, describing excessive government largesse on behalf of citizens.
17. These ministries operate under the State Council, as do four other key entities: the National Development and Reform Commission, the National Health and Family Planning Commission, the PBC, and the National Audit Office.
18. Medicare is a federal social insurance health program for the old and disabled; Medicaid provides health coverage for the poor through direct payments to healthcare providers.
19. The "agency problem" refers to the conflicting incentives of managers and owners in using the resources of a company—or, in this context, local governments versus the central government (which is assumed to represent citizens). For example, local governments may seek to use funds for their own interests (a better office or more impressive automobile) at the expense of end-user citizens, who the central government represents.
20. Unconditional means that there is no formal work requirement or other type of activity to receive *dibao* benefits.
21. Notwithstanding the fragile condition of China's housing market.
22. It is estimated that, in the United States, a family of four with an annual income below USD 75,000 could receive an income transfer of up to USD 3,400.
23. I thank Phillippe Wingender of the IMF for directing me to the Bai et al. (2016) article and redirecting my thinking on this issue.
24. In fact, the figure was adjusted upward to USD 840 billion, reflecting accounting adjustments.

11
CHINA'S EVOLVING FINANCIAL SYSTEM

钱到公事办，火到猪焙烂

Finance is to the Firm as Fire to the Feast

In China's National Bureau of Statistics (NBS) *China Statistical Yearbook*, there are 24 chapters—Chapter 19, on financial intermediation, is the second-shortest chapter. Meanwhile, the two longest chapters relate to how finance in China is used in the real economy—investment in fixed assets and natural resources.[1] This metric may provide some indication of how far China's financial sector has yet to go in terms of directing China's vast savings into its most productive use—a central role that financial intermediation plays. China, over the past four decades, has made great strides in its financial system. We see in Figure 11.1 that uses of aggregate finance in China relative to gross capital formation has steadily increased over time, suggesting ever greater financial depth. But the efficient allocation of capital, the provision of sufficient means for individual portfolio diversification, and financial market transparency are all still areas that need much improvement.

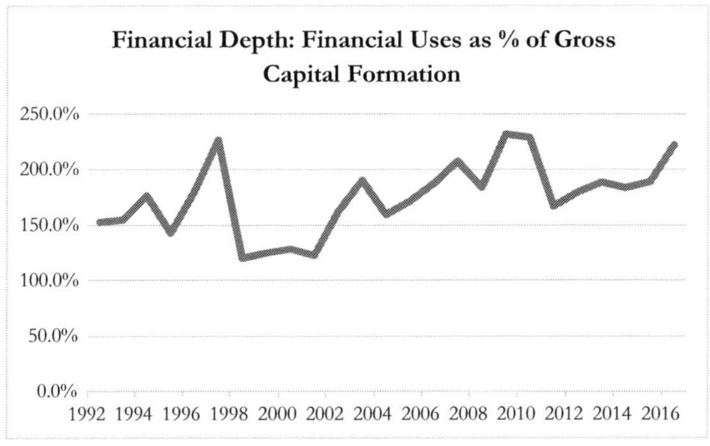

Figure 11.1 China has enough institutional depth to finance all of its investment needs; and, in recent years, that abundance has increased.
Source: Author created based on data from CEIC.

While the role of the government has been critical in institution building—it has also impacted financial reform and financial innovation via various forms of financial repression. Specifically, Chinese policy-makers have built institutions ranging from large banks to globally-significant stock and bond markets at breathtaking speed. What was once a country riddled with segmented markets in currencies, real estate, bonds, and equities has gradually moved toward greater integration with the international community. But Chinese citizens still hold a disproportionate share of their financial wealth in money (by definition, M2), and they still lack access to a wider range of assets (including international assets) that would allow for risk reduction via portfolio diversification and higher returns via a broader range of investment opportunities. The excess supply of money in the hands of the public, in the context of Walras's Law, has clear excess demand counterparts in the real estate and equity markets and the shadow banking sector.

In the following sections, we discuss China's overall sources and uses of finance (flow of funds), its banks, its bond, equity, and money markets, and some recent developments in shadow banking. In the latter, we see a great expansion of financial breadth in China. It is important to keep in mind, though, that—in the past—a large fraction of China's uses of funds was unaccounted for. Lin and Schramm (2008) estimate (for the period 1995–2006) that up to one-third of China's savings was channeled into investment without a paper trail. Unidentified (Miscellaneous) versus total use of funds in China's flow of funds presentation is displayed in Figure 11.2, suggests a recent peak in the unidentified amount in 2015 of about 29 percent. As we discuss below, growth in the shadow banking sector after 2015 may have supplanted some of this "missing finance," in a financial reporting sense.

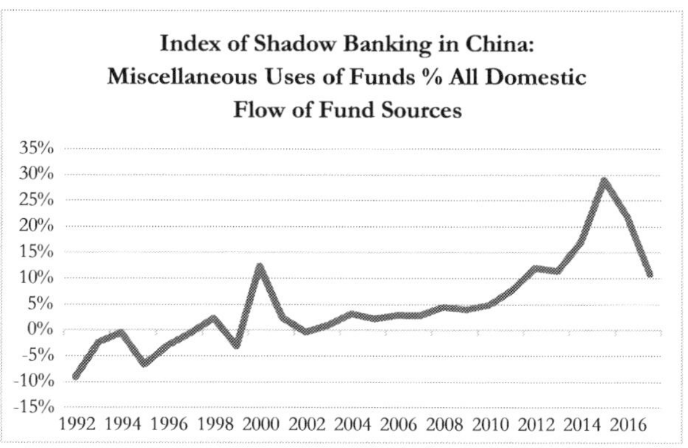

Figure 11.2 One method of estimating shadow banking is to examine miscellaneous uses of funds (uncategorized) as a share of all sources of finance for China's domestic economy. By this measure, China's shadow banking sector has grown enormously over time, but it peaked in 2015.
Source: Author created based on data from the NBS

Flow of Funds and the Financial System in the Context of the Legal Framework

One slice of the vast literature relating to how and whether financial systems impact economic growth relates to what financial systems evolve because of the legal framework in a country. Specifically, the seminal work of La Porta, Lopez-De-Silanes, Shleifer, and Vishny (henceforth "LLSV") (LLSV 1997, 1998) and the series of papers that follow posit that countries who follow a common law tradition provide more and better investor protection than do countries who operate in the civil law tradition. In turn, financial systems in each type of legal tradition can and will evolve in dramatically different ways. Common law countries will rely relatively more on external finance (for example, equity markets), while civil law countries will rely more on internal finance (for example, retained earnings). And, even within the category of external finance, there will be relative differences—civil law countries will have a greater reliance on banks and pension funds, while common law countries will have a greater reliance on equity rather than debt markets.[2] We could say that common law countries rely more on arm's-length finance, while civil law countries rely more on arms-around finance—in the latter case, we have better monitoring and control of the firm's activities from a principal/agent perspective.

A further implication of this literature is that the relatively heavier reliance on courts to independently interpret the law and decide what is fair allows common law financial systems to be more dynamic and innovative. The tradeoff, however, is that common law financial systems tend to be less predictable and are riskier than civil law systems. And these differences across the risk/return spectrum may very well reflect different cultural preferences.[3]

Where would China fall within this framework? It is first important to note that China's long and unique history has created a system which is, in fact, a mélange of heterodox and orthodox legal systems. The influences range from Confucianism to Socialism, the American Bill of Rights to Mao Zedong Marxist/Leninist thought (Beck et al. 2003). But what is clear is that, of the two frameworks discussed in the previous paragraph, China has taken a path that falls decidedly within the space of civil law—and particularly German civil law. That approach was formulated within two waves of reform: one immediately following the end of the Qing Dynasty in 1911, in which a six-part civil code and a constitution were adopted. This first wave was heavily influenced by German/Japanese civil law, with influences from the United States.

The second wave came after the death of Chairman Mao culminating in the General Principles of Civil Law, enacted 1 January, 1987 (Luney 1989). The emphasis of this collection of codes was the economic relationship between entities, including the definition of a legal person (either individual or enterprise, also in the tradition of German civil law). That civil law would be the preferred path should be no surprise given the Chinese government's decisive role in the legal process and its lack of interest in an independent judiciary interpreting laws and setting precedents in real time.

Other Views

LLSV has been a catalyst for a vast body of follow-up research in support or opposition to its central theses.[4] We have relied mostly on their approach in discussing China to organize our thoughts because their ideas seem particularly relevant to China. Other authors, using different perspectives, provide additional insights. Allen et al. (2005 and 2017) highlight the key role that non-listed and non-state-owned private enterprises have played in China's economic growth.[5] This growth occurred in the absence of any supportive legal system at all, a well-defined governance structure, or the conventional sources of finance—stock markets and banks (Levine 2005). These factors are all usually cited as necessary conditions for economic growth at every step along the way. Rather, Allen et al. suggest that private businesses in China have relied on the more traditional long-standing roles that reputation, relationships, and trust have played. They highlight the preponderance of family-owned businesses in China. These elements were buttressed by private arrangements using collateral on property, and they were sanctioned by third parties in some cases. They suggest that low barriers to entry and competition in the private sector were sufficient conditions, in this context, to achieve the large rates of growth that China has experienced. In effect, the authors (without using the term) are making a Coasian (Coase 1960) argument—private arrangements filled the institutional vacuum.

Awrey (2015), in contrast, suggests that the existence of very powerful institutions in China—particularly the central government and powerful regulators such as the Chinese Banking Regulatory Commission (CBRC)—have spawned parallel or shadow financial markets, including a large wealth management industry. Again (without using the term), this argument suggests that it is financial repression that has shaped key elements of China's financial system.

These alternative views open many avenues for empirical research into what institutional factors have truly been at work in shaping China's financial system. What all three approaches lack, however, is a greater consideration to the quality of growth rather than the mere quantity of growth. We simply cannot rely on growth rates as measures of the success or failure of financial systems and the institutions that support them; the critical question is whether these systems will support sustainable or quality growth over the long run.

LLSV and the Sources and Uses of Funds and Capital Structure

While Modigliani and Miller (Miller 1988) suggest that capital structure can be irrelevant (in terms of the value of the firm), what is suggested above is that institutional factors can push capital structure in one direction or another. Here, we examine the Chinese business sector's flow of funds and basic balance sheet (excluding intra-financial sector activity) and compare and contrast it to another major economy in the world—the United States, which follows a common law tradition.

Table 11.1 is based on China's flow of funds presentation for the national non-financial business sector. Internal funds (business gross savings) averaged 57 percent of all financing flows to the business sector for the period 2000–2017; but, by 2017, the share declined to 46 percent with the remainder from external sources. In Table 11.2, based on the United States flow of funds from the Federal Reserve Board, we see a much larger reliance on internal funds in the non-financial business sector, averaging 80 percent.[6] This would appear to contradict the LLSV proposition that internal finance should be a more important source of finance for civil law countries. LLSV implicitly assumes relatively similar macro balances on savings; but China and the United States have substantially different national savings patterns, with China saving close to half of gross domestic product (GDP) while the United States' share is only about 18 percent.[7] Historically, around half of China's national savings accrue from business savings (corporate profits). In the United States, the share contributed by business is even larger at around 75 percent of national gross savings. In other words, there is a relatively greater supply of internal funds in the United States, and thus firms are more likely to tap into that source of funds. Alternatively, households in the United States have insufficient savings to source the funding needs of businesses, while in China personal savings are abundant and channeled through the banking sector to companies.

Year	Savings (Profits)	Net Capital Transfers (% of Gross Capital Formation)	Outside Finance
2000	70.0%	12%	18%
2001	67.3%	12%	21%
2002	65.6%	11%	23%

Year	Savings (Profits)	Net Capital Transfers (% of Gross Capital Formation)	Outside Finance
2003	59.1%	10%	31%
2004	67.7%	3%	29%
2005	70.9%	3%	26%
2006	62.5%	3%	35%
2007	63.1%	2%	34%
2008	62.7%	3%	35%
2009	51.4%	2%	46%
2010	47.6%	3%	50%
2011	46.3%	2%	51%
2012	42.8%	2%	55%
2013	49.2%	2%	49%
2014	53.9%	2%	44%
2015	51.0%	2%	47%
2016	46.0%	3%	51%
2017	46.4%	3%	50%

Table 11.1 Non-financial enterprises: China flow of funds and how enterprise investment is financed (macro level).
Source: Author created based on data from CEIC and FRED.

	Flow of Funds as Percent of Combined External and Internal Finance for US						
	2009	**2010**	**2011**	**2012**	**2013**	**2014**	**Average**
INFLOWS 1/							
Gross Savings or EBD	125%	81%	74%	68%	64%	69%	80%
External Financing Net Increase in Debt Liabilities + Owner Paid-In	-25%	19%	26%	32%	36%	31%	20%
Debt Securities	13%	10%	8%	12%	9%	9%	10%
Debt Institutions	-47%	-14%	3%	5%	7%	12%	-5%
Foreign Direct Investment	8%	7%	7%	6%	5%	3%	6%
Equities	-4%	-10%	-17%	-12%	-10%	-12%	-11%

	Flow of Funds as Percent of Combined External and Internal Finance for US						
	2009	**2010**	**2011**	**2012**	**2013**	**2014**	**Average**
Other	7%	26%	31%	30%	24%	22%	23%
Proprietor Investment	-8%	7%	9%	3%	5%	1%	3%
DISCREPANCY 2/	5%	-6%	-15%	-12%	-4%	-4%	-6%

Table 11.2 Flow of funds data for the United States show that most financing in the United States still comes from internal sources.
Source: Author created based on Table Z.1 of the Federal Reserve Board.
Notes: 1/ The Breakdown of data corresponds to the following accounting identity: (Gross Savings – 1/2 Discrepancy + Net Increase in Financial Liabilities = Capital Expenditures + Net Increase in Financial Assets + 1/2 Discrepancy). 2/ We have divided the total discrepancy evenly between inflows (savings, etc.) and outflows (capital expenditures, etc.).

Examining how external sources of finance are distributed, we see the data corresponding more closely to LLSV in Table 11.3. Specifically, most of debt finance in China comes from institutions—primarily banks. In 2017, 88 percent of all sources of external finance came from institutional loans. Meanwhile, debt securities (bonds) represent a much more modest share of 2 percent. In the United States, institutions actually represent a use (outflow) rather than a source (inflow) of finance, as firms reduce their overall debt burden. United States business debt issuance averaged about 50 percent of all external finance in recent years. Equity securities represent a relatively miniscule share of finance in China, at about 8 percent of external finance in 2017. But, in the United States, equity buybacks have actually made this traditional source of finance an outflow. This practice no doubt reflects the low interest rate environment and greater efforts to acquire tax shields through debt in the United States.

Year	Loans	Bankers' Acceptance	Bonds	Stocks	FDI	Net Other
	Percent of Outside Sources					
1992	78%	0%	8%	4%	0%	10%
1993	77%	0%	1%	2%	0%	19%
1994	71%	0%	0%	0%	0%	28%
1995	75%	0%	0%	0%	0%	25%
1996	76%	0%	0%	2%	0%	22%
1997	75%	0%	0%	10%	24%	-9%
1998	75%	0%	0%	6%	27%	-8%
1999	70%	0%	1%	7%	25%	-2%

Year	Loans	Bankers' Acceptance	Bonds	Stocks	FDI	Net Other
	Percent of Outside Sources					
2000	61%	0%	1%	14%	21%	4%
2001	68%	0%	1%	9%	27%	-5%
2002	70%	0%	2%	5%	20%	4%
2003	76%	0%	1%	5%	12%	6%
2004	63%	0%	1%	6%	16%	13%
2005	65%	0%	7%	4%	22%	2%
2006	70%	0%	6%	7%	17%	0%
2007	57%	0%	5%	12%	20%	7%
2008	75%	2%	8%	5%	15%	-5%
2009	77%	4%	10%	4%	4%	0%
2010	56%	20%	10%	4%	11%	0%
2011	60%	9%	12%	5%	13%	0%
2012	66%	8%	16%	2%	11%	-3%
2013	70%	5%	12%	3%	11%	-1%
2014	71%	-1%	18%	5%	13%	-6%
2015	59%	-8%	21%	6%	11%	12%
2016	78%	-14%	26%	10%	8%	-8%
2017	88%	4%	2%	8%	9%	-11%

Table 11.3 Non-financial enterprises: China flow of funds. External financial instrument sources (micro level) show that most external funding is still institutional loans. Source: Author created based on data from CEIC and NBS.

Foreign direct investment (FDI) as a source of all finance for both economies' business sectors is similar, at about 5 to 6 percent. That FDI is of similar importance in both countries sheds further light on the LLSV approach and its limitations. Specifically, for China, FDI serves as an important vehicle for technological progress and economic growth. Furthermore, FDI has both arms-around characteristics relative to market-traded securities—joint ventures by their very nature are partnerships—but it also has arm's-length characteristics—the very definition of "foreign" suggests an investor's willingness to surrender control to a possibly very different legal/institutional framework. Future research could shed light on which effect dominates. The question is an important one for countries such as China, that follow in the civil law tradition; their ability to attract FDI and its concomitant technology may hinge on how these two effects are balanced against each other.

China's balance sheet in recent years is consistent with its flow of funds (Table 11.4). For all designated enterprises in 2018,[8] liabilities represented over 56 percent of the capital structure, and equity represented about 44 percent.[9] Some scholars in the past have suggested a "reverse pecking order" for China given the relative importance of external finance (mainly bank loans) versus retained earnings. An LLSV approach, however, makes this less of a paradox. As we saw in the flow of funds tables, internal funds (corporate savings) are of about equal importance to bank (institutional) finance. Both are forms of arms-around finance, especially in the China context. As indicated, a simple sectoral breakdown has private enterprise with less leverage relative to state-owned enterprises (SOEs). By way of contrast, we also provide the overall balance sheet for the United States' non-financial business sector in Table 11.5. Capital structure in the US is the mirror image of China's, with equity at about 64 percent and liabilities amounting to 38 percent. Of the equity portion, FDI makes up 7 percent. Marketable debt is about twice as important as institutional debt.

	All Designated	**State-Holding**	**Private Enterprises**	**Foreign Funded**	**Other**
	Industrial Enterprises	Subset	Subset	Subset	
Total Assets	100.0%	100.0%	100.0%	100.0%	100.0%
Total Liabilities	56.5%	58.7%	56.4%	54.1%	54.9%
Owner's Equity	43.5%	41.3%	43.6%	45.9%	45.1%

Table 11.4 China balance sheet for industrial enterprises with revenue over RMB 20 million in 2018. Chinese firms remain highly leveraged, but private and foreign businesses are less so.
Source: Author created based on data from CEIC and NBS data.

	2009	**2010**	**2011**	**2012**	**2013**	**2014**	**Average**
Total Assets	100%	100%	100%	100%	100%	100%	100%
Total Non-Financial Assets	51%	52%	52%	53%	53%	54%	52.4%
Total Non-FDI Financial Assets	37%	37%	35%	34%	34%	34%	35.2%
Total FDI Assets	12%	12%	12%	13%	13%	13%	12.4%
Liabilities and Equity	100%	100%	100%	100%	100%	100%	100.0%

	2009	2010	2011	2012	2013	2014	Average
Total Debt Securities	14%	14%	14%	14%	14%	14%	13.7%
Total Debt Institutions	9%	7%	7%	7%	7%	7%	7.3%
Total Other Non-FDI Liabilities	18%	18%	17%	17%	16%	15%	16.9%
Foreign Direct Investment	7%	7%	7%	8%	7%	7%	7.4%
Equity (Market Value)	53%	54%	55%	54%	56%	57%	54.6%

Table 11.5 United States non-financial corporates balance sheet. By comparison with Chinese entities, US firms are less leveraged.
Source: Author created based on data from CEIC and NBS data.

What is clear, overall, is that marketable securities (not only as a source but as a use of funds) are relatively more important for US businesses than they are for Chinese businesses, and this is fully consistent with LLSV. That US firms rely relatively more heavily on internal funds on a flow of funds basis would appear at first glance as a contradiction to LLSV. But it does not. Rather, this outcome is conditional on some critical macroeconomic and non-legal institutional differences. The small share of household savings in the US relative to China and the traditionally close relationship between the government, banks, and borrowers in China can also have a significant impact on capital structure. Finally, we note the existence of a large and unexplained gap between net financial needs of the business sector when measured from real economic flows versus financial flow of funds (at least 15 percent of capital expenditures).[10] This gap may be a type of arms-around financing reflecting financing by the shadow banking sector to small- and medium-sized firms that escapes official measurement. And this type of finance is also consistent with LLSV.

What should be apparent in the above discussion is that, if we take LLSV at face value, then an American style arm's-length stock market is not very suitable for China. It is somewhat surprising, then, that Chinese authorities have invested a great deal of time, energy, and funds in trying to develop such markets since the early 1990s. LLSV tells us that, given China's unique civil law structure, such a market is unlikely to flourish. We discuss stock market developments below. A corollary to all this is that equity as a source of finance for Chinese companies will likely look very different from that of other countries. One might speculate that a variation on private equity, wealth management funds (defined below), or large institutional investors is more likely to take root—as opposed to trading-intensive equity markets.

The Banking Sector

China's banking system, more than in any of the other major countries in the world, serves as the financial backbone of the economy. Banking institutions account for over half of China's formal financial intermediation.[11] But, beyond their important role in channeling China's vast savings into capital and the intertemporal smoothing of consumption, Chinese banks serve as a linchpin in the government's efforts at short-term macroeconomic stabilization and long-term economic development. In other words, they are a critical link in the implementation of China's Five-Year Plans, as we discussed in Chapters 7 and 8.

Background on the Rapid Evolution of the Banking System

Between 1949 and 1978, the role of commercial banks was dramatically diminished, and the central bank—the People's Bank of China (PBC)—became the sole bank operating in China. Pre-existing banks were either shut down or brought fully under the control of the PBC. Along with the dissolution of private ownership in this period, so too came the dissolution of private wealth, since there was no need for the traditional banking roles of deposit taking and commercial lending. The PBC, itself, was stripped of most of its central banking functions during the Cultural Revolution. With China's movement toward market-based mechanisms beginning in 1978, commercial banking once again became necessary. New banking activities, and some activities handled by the PBC and the Ministry of Finance, were spun off to the newly established or re-established "Big Four" state-owned banks: The Bank of China (separated from the PBC in 1978), the China Construction Bank (separated from PBC in 1978), the Agricultural Bank of China (founded 1978) and the Industrial and Commercial Bank of China (founded 1984).[12] The names imply their intended purpose, and these Big Four were initially engaged in making policy loans in support of development targets under Five-Year Plans. Ongoing financial reform, which started around 1985, led to more commercially-based activity by 1995, and the difference in lines of business between these major banks blurred.[13]

The Bank of Communications was restructured and recommenced operations in 1987, completing the set of the five large state-owned commercial banks. Three formal policy banks were later created in 1994 to take up some of the policy-related activities of the state-owned banks.[14] Another major step was the recapitalization of the state-owned banks in 1998 via a *renminbi* (RMB) 270 billion bond issuance. Though the government still holds a controlling interest in the largest banks, all of these institutions have listed on domestic or international exchanges, or both. While these banks dominated (and continue to dominate) the banking space in China, ongoing financial liberalization has allowed for the creation of other deposit-taking institutions, including joint-stock commercial banks (publicly traded with minority government stakes), city and rural commercial banks, rural and urban cooperatives, and foreign banks (incorporated in China). China's Postal Savings Banks was established in 2007 as a means for greater financial inclusion, and with 37,000 branches it has one of the widest banking networks in the country. It was listed on the Shanghai Stock Exchange (SSE) in December, 2019. By the end of 2014, there were over 2500 traditionally defined banking institutions, of which close to 1600 were relatively small rural credit cooperatives. Table 11.6 provides key dates and major steps for China's banking sector.

Years	**China Banking Sector Some Major Developments**
1978–1984	Devolution of Big Four + 1 state owned banks from the PBC and Ministry of Finance
1985–Present	Creation of numerous other banking institutions with a variety of ownership structures.
1985–95	Commercialization of the activities of the large state-owned banks and the creation of policy banks to take over policy lending
1995	Commercial Banking Law passed
1998–2003	China's Silent Banking Crisis
2001	World Trade Organization accession allowing for a five-year grace period for the banking sector
2002	Big Four state-owned banks begin to act as traditional commercial banks
2003	China Banking Regulatory Commission established
2005–Present	Foreign competition and IPOs of the Big Four banks. Foreign banks take stakes in Big Four. Foreign banks incorporated in China allowed to engage in local currency deposits and lending (2006)
July, 2013	Removal of base lending rate floors for commercial bank lending
May, 2015	Bank deposit insurance established covering virtually all bank deposits
October, 2015	Removal of deposit rate ceilings for commercial bank deposits (de jure, but not de facto)

Table 11.6 Key developments in China's banking sector.
Source: Author created based on various sources listed in references.

Size and Scope

Deposits of all financial institutions amounted to RMB 190 trillion in 2019.[15, 16] Figure 11.3 shows the tremendous growth in bank loans and deposits since 1997. In that period, deposits grew at an annualized rate of 16 percent, while loans grew at 15 percent. Figure 11.4 gives the ratio of loans and deposits to GDP. Even though deposits as a share of GDP began to surge in 1994, we can see in Figure 11.5 that, as a share of cumulative savings, they actually began to decline. Taken together, the two figures suggest greater financial inclusion up to 1994 followed by an expansion of non-institutional ways of saving—greater financial breadth via informal channels. By 2013, less than half of China's cumulative savings was in bank deposits.

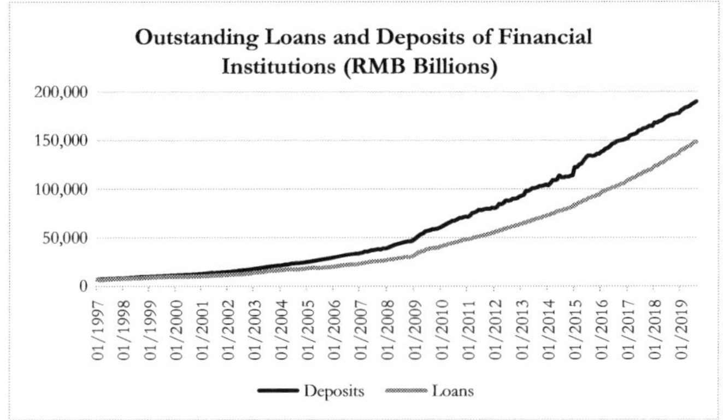

Figure 11.3 Both deposits and loans at Chinese financial institutions have grown at double-digit rates, with deposits growing faster.
Source: Author created based on data from CEIC.

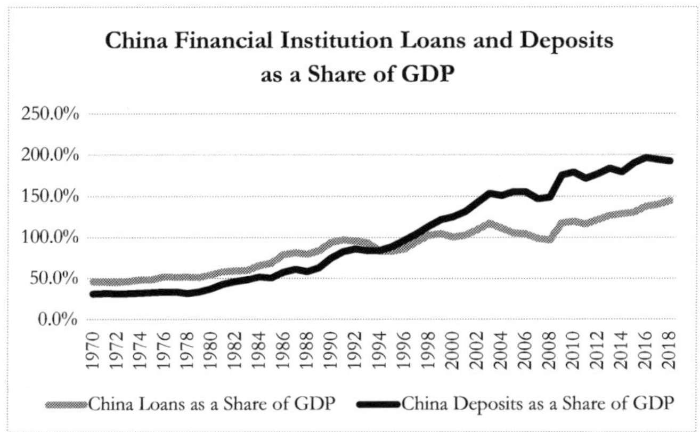

Figure 11.4 As a share of GDP, loans and deposits at financial institutions are among the highest in the world in China.
Source: Author created based on data from CEIC (and All China Marketing Data, University of Michigan, for data before 1997).

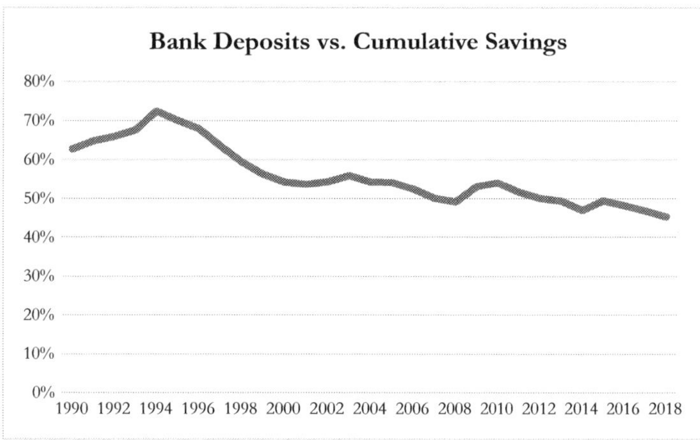

Figure 11.5 As non-bank financial institutions have grown (including shadow banking activities), banks have seen their share of cumulative domestic savings decline.
Source: Author created based on data from CEIC, FRED, World Development Indicators, and CBRC.

We also see, in Figure 11.4, that deposits as a share of GDP moved past the lending ratio in 1994. In part, this shift reflects an acceleration of China's economic growth and income but relatively stable consumption in those decades. Both individual and corporate savings contributed to increased deposits and a relatively slower growth of lending. This takeoff also corresponded to a similar path for China's current account and balance of payments surpluses and foreign exchange reserve accumulation—the latter represented as an asset on the banking system's broadly defined balance sheet. Foreign exchange reserves more than doubled in importance between 1990 and 2013 (from 10 percent of all assets in the financial system's balance sheet to 21 percent). In later years, as we see in Table 11.7, net foreign assets declined in importance to only 11 percent of the balance sheet due to the increased expansion of banks' lending activities, including bond issuance (as discussed in Chapters 7 and 8).

China Financial Sector Monetary Survey (in RMB Millions)					
	2014		**2018**		**Annualized Growth**
Assets					
Net Foreign Assets	28,777,073	21%	25,506,987	11%	-3%
Domestic Credit	107,696,218	79%	196,545,137	89%	16%

China Financial Sector Monetary Survey (in RMB Millions)					
	2014		**2018**		**Annualized Growth**
Liabilities					
Broad Money	122,837,483	90%	179,292,800	81%	10%
Other Bank Liabilities	13,635,808	10%	42,759,324	19%	33%
Total Assets or Liabilities	136,473,291		222,052,124		13%

Table 11.7 Domestic credit has an increased share of monetary sector assets, but net foreign assets remain high relative to other countries' asset holdings. Monetary sector's increased holding of bonds has increased the share of "other bank liabilities" since 2014. Source: Author created based on data from the International Monetary Fund Database.

Though not as fast as deposits, bank lending did surge in the 1990s—a phenomenon that no doubt led to the emergence of China's less-well-known Silent Banking Crisis in the 1998–2000 period. Lending in the 10 years before 1999 grew at an annual rate of 22 percent. Much of this lending was intended to support the large number of SOEs, particularly those found in China's old rust belt of the northeast. Between 2004 and 2009, bank assets grew at 20 percent per year; and, between 2009 and 2014, they grew at 16.7 percent per year. In the pivotal year of 2009, however, loans grew by an astounding 30 percent as a policy response to the global financial crisis. Unlike what is found in developed economies, the banking system continues to provide a disproportionate amount of loans for business investment rather than consumption. Even those loans to consumers remain disproportionate to housing investment. As discussed throughout this textbook, the tendency for banks to lend primarily for investment rather than to consumers continues, and it reflects broader macroeconomic imbalances and raises questions of sustainability.

The Big Four banks accounted for 40 percent of all bank assets—an important but diminished role from 2000, when their share was closer to 60 percent of all assets (Figure 11.6). As Schramm (2015) points out, while the Big Four banks are the most important source of finance in China, compared to European economies, their four-firm concentration ratio is smaller.[17]

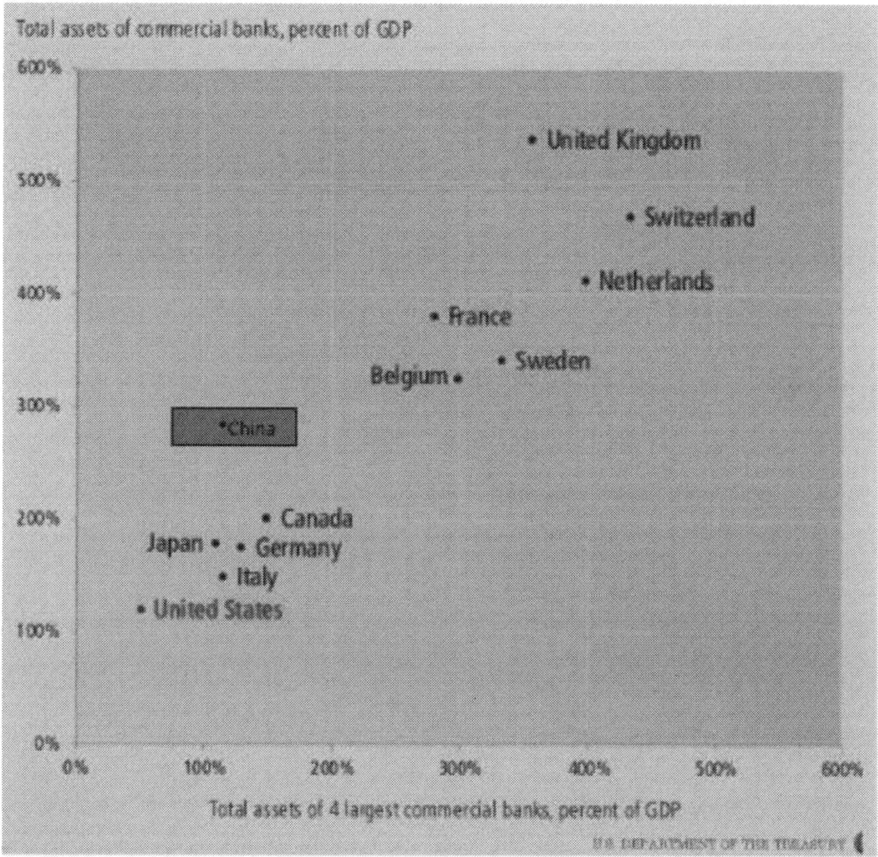

Figure 11.6 China's banking industry is not as concentrated (largest four banks) as in some European countries.
Source: Author created based on data from the US Treasury Department.

Case Study 11.1: Bank Efficiency and the Regulatory Framework

As we have seen, financial institutions have played a central role in financial intermediation in China, providing close to three-quarters of all external finance to the corporate sector. Because of the high savings rate (40 to 50 percent of GDP)—a key driver—the role of banks in the Chinese economy is even more pronounced. One key angle, related to how efficiently banks act as financial intermediaries, is how efficiently banks operate. Several studies have looked at this question from either a Data Envelope Analysis or a Stochastic Frontier Analysis (SFA) estimation approach. Both methodologies attempt to estimate how far an industry operates below the most efficient frontier. Matthews and Zhang (2009) provide a summary list of such studies, both global and specific to China. Depending on the timeframe (and this is critical, as discussed below), the results can vary.

Berger, Hasan, and Zhou (2009) analyze the 1994–2003 period using an SFA approach to compare cost and profit efficiency for the Big Four, other state-owned banks, private banks, and banks with majority and minority foreign ownership. For this period, they find that less state ownership increases profit efficiency, with the Big Four being least profit efficient and banks with a majority foreign ownership the most profit efficient. They emphasize that even foreign minority ownership has a significant impact on profit efficiency. Edging into the question of asset quality, the authors find that banks with foreign participation are also more efficient (have a smaller share of non-performing loans [NPLs]). This latter question, of course, ties in with the broader question of the quality of China's economic growth.

Meanwhile, Hsiao, Shen, and Bian (2015)—in examining banks in China for the 2007–2012 period using an SFA approach—find that, while Chinese banks are less cost efficient than their foreign counterparts, they are more profit efficient. This result is puzzling in two ways: First, how can revenue efficiency sufficiently outweigh cost inefficiency to allow for greater profit efficiency? Second, why are these results different from those of Berger et al.? In fact, the answer to both questions is the same.

The paradox posed in the previous paragraph relates to bank lending and deposit rate ceilings and their liberalization over time. Prior to 2004, both lending and borrowing rates were constrained within their own narrow band of floors and ceilings. This policy, in combination with forced policy loans up to 1995, led to China's own great banking crisis in the 1998–2003 period (discussed below). As part of the ongoing efforts at financial liberalization and what proved to be a successful effort at restoring bank profitability, the regulators removed the ceilings on loan rates and the floor on deposit rates in 2004. This change ensured a stable and large interest spread for Chinese banks.

The time period studied by Berger et al. might be referred to as a fully-regulated period that damaged bank profitability, while the period after 2003 of the Hsiao et al. study could be referred to as semi-regulated and enhancing profitability. The fact that Chinese banks principally do business in RMB (where borrowing and lending rates have been regulated) and foreign banks do relatively more business in foreign currency (where rates are unregulated) results in different outcomes for the two periods.[18] In July, 2013, floors on lending rates were removed, and the last major step to interest liberalization was the removal of the ceiling on bank deposit interest rates in 2015.[19] Basic theory suggests that this should once again realign the relationship between foreign and domestic bank profit efficiency.[20]

Banks and China's Silent Banking Crisis

In Table 11.6, we refer to the period 1998–2003 as China's Silent Banking Crisis. The quasi-halt to policy loans beginning in 1995 came too late to prevent a crisis. Numerous bad loans had resulted from earlier decades of government-mandated financing of SOEs. By 1998, the NPL ratio of China's Big Four banks had exceeded 30 percent. Taking the difference between the Big Four assets (at book value) and deposits at the end of 1998, we can infer a maximal value of bank capital (equity) of around US dollars (USD) 180 billion. The size of NPLs was larger than this amount by a factor of about 2—in other words, China's four largest banks had become fully bankrupt by 1998.

While remarkable, what is even more surprising is that the Chinese authorities could turn this situation around and avoid a full-blown economic crisis. Several key elements were involved in this process: recapitalization of the banks through cash injections, a swap of treasury bills for the bad assets, interest rate ceilings and floors (discussed above), a lack of transparency in terms of the public's awareness of the problem (there were no bank runs), and—for those citizens aware of the problem—there was an assumption that the authorities would find a workable solution. Capital injections and swapping of assets involved at least half a trillion dollars. Four asset management companies were established in 1999 to either manage or sell off the bad assets.[21] By 2008, the NPL ratio for all commercial banks in China had declined to 2.4 percent.

Figure 11.4 shows that bank loans as a share of GDP have risen well past their levels during the 1998–2003 banking crisis, but deposits as a share of GDP have risen even faster. While capital adequacy ratios continue to remain well above Basle standards, the steep growth in loans from 2009 to the present raises a red flag regarding the actual quality of loans.[22] With the NPL ratio for all commercial banks standing at 1.9 percent in 2019 (one percentage point higher than in the United States) and on the rise, China's banks face a new set of risks. The removal of interest rate ceilings in 2013–2015 was a positive step in the continued process of financial liberalization, but this comes with its own set of risks in the short run (Diaz-Alejandro 1985). Meanwhile, as discussed below, money market funds have come to compete with banks for deposits. State-owned banks, which in the past have benefitted from and grown comfortable with interest rate ceilings, must now compete for funds in more competitive markets. The United States experienced a similar phenomenon in the Savings and Loan Crisis of the early 1980s.

Bond and Interbank Markets

Valued at USD 11.5 trillion in the second quarter of 2019, China now has the world's third-largest bond market, following Japan and the United States. But outstanding debt instruments (bonds) relative to GDP is still only about 28 percent of the United States ratio.[23] Figure 11.7 and Figure 11.8 show the enormous growth in the market since 1997—China's bond market value now surpasses that of all emerging markets combined. China's bond market is now (as of 2019) over 1.7 times larger in value than its equity market. The government bond market grew by 24 percent per annum between 2015 and 2019, driven by an astounding increase in local government outstanding bonds of 315 percent. Localities have been encouraged to restructure their debt away from institutions (special purpose financing institutions and banks) to negotiable instruments. Notwithstanding the increase, interest rates actually fell as a result of the central bank's stimulatory monetary policy: The PBC began to push down policy rates and lower bank reserve requirements beginning in 2014.

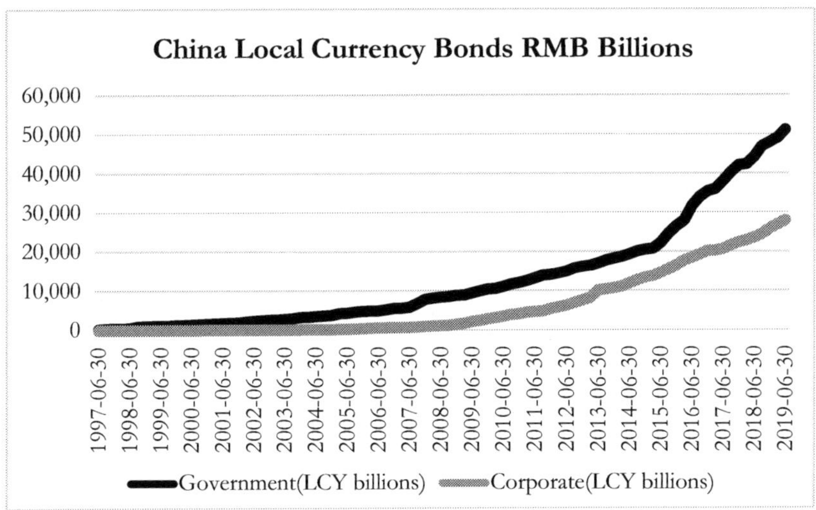

Figure 11.7 China's bond market is now the world's third-largest, but it is still dominated by government bonds.
Source: Author created based on data from the Asian Development Bank.

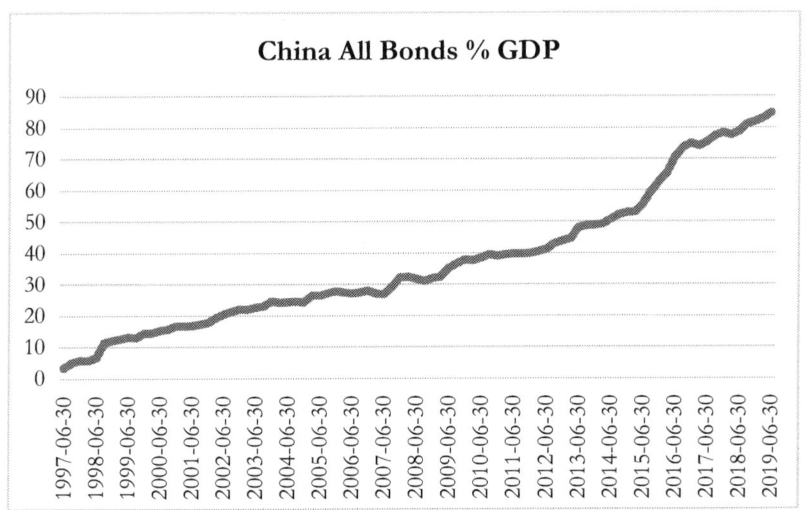

Figure 11.8 Bonds are a far more important asset than publicly traded equity in China.
Source: Author created based on data from the Asian Development Bank.

China began issuing bonds in the early 1980s. Prior to 2005, virtually all issuers were from the central bank, treasury, SOEs, development banks, and commercial banks (also state-owned). By 2005, corporate issuance had commenced with mostly short- and medium-term maturities.

Macro Finance Insight 11.1: Excessive Leverage and Financial Ratios

Earlier chapters have detailed that—as a result of long-term quantity of growth goals and the recent short-term shocks of the Great Financial Crisis (GFC), the Trump trade war, and now COVID-19—the Chinese authorities have fully opened the throttle on investment in plant, property, equipment, and public infrastructure over the past several decades. The financial counterpart to that real economic activity has been a rapid increase in bank lending, corporate bond issuance, and debt levels. Maliszewski et al. (2016) detail the rapid growth of credit in China and the accompanying risks to the economy. Between the GFC and 2015, private credit surged at a rate of 20 percent per year—well above GDP growth. Meanwhile, the ratio of credit to GDP rose by 50 percentage points to 200 percent. The authors point out that such above-trend increases (credit gaps) are comparable to what happened in countries such as Spain, Thailand, and Japan, which all experienced ensuing severe financial crises. They cite research showing that, in 38 out of 43 countries with overall growth in credit above 30 percent in a five-year period, severe financial problems arose—NPLs, bankruptcies and recessions.

In the same International Monetary Fund (IMF) report, Maliszewski et al. examine three financial ratios that give some measure of the debt burden:

1. Liabilities to earnings before interest and taxes (EBIT): China is too high at around 20.
2. EBIT to interest obligations (coverage ratio): China is too low at around 4.
3. Debt to equity (leverage): China is too high at around 4.

All of these ratios are far from where we would expect a company to safely operate and still be able to raise capital (in part, this explains the role that the government is playing in funding many SOEs). What is more, much of the credit surge has been to SOEs and supplied via the unregulated shadow banking system. And as we have chronicled in Chapter 4, this lending explosion has occurred in an environment of declining company returns, which peaked around the GFC. Roberts and Zurawski (2016) suggest that more profitable firms in China simply do not turn to external finance (a pecking order argument). This is another way of saying that the government, via the banking system, has become, by default, the lender of last resort to underperforming SOEs.

How this seemingly dire situation will get resolved is of great national and international importance. While China has taken steps to shut down or rein in "zombie" enterprises, a more structural approach to curbing and redirecting lending will be needed. Going forward, economic stimulation ought to occur via lending to households/consumers and small- and medium-sized enterprises with a consumer focus. Meanwhile, China continues to rely on its one key driver—a high national savings rate—to mitigate the troublesome situation. But this core strength can only mask the severe debt problems in the short run while lulling policy-makers into continuing value destruction over time. In the long run, rebalancing to consumption and quality economic growth need to be key parts of the solution.

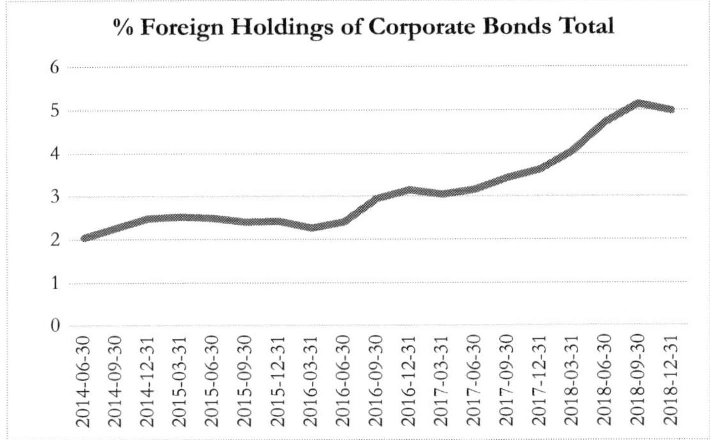

Figure 11.9 Foreigners hold an increasing but small share of Chinese bonds.
Source: Author created based on data from Asian Development Bank.

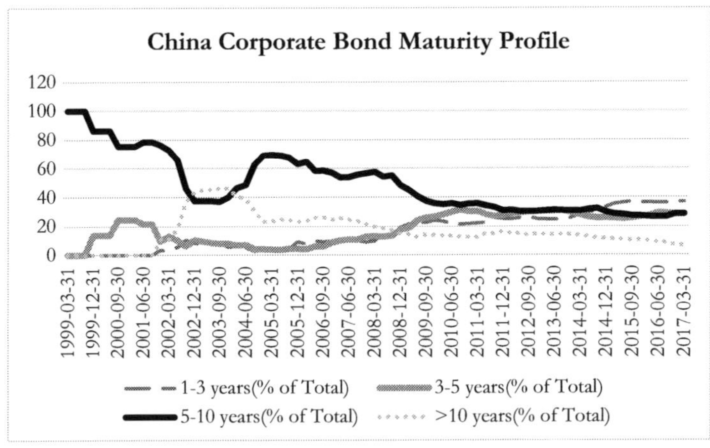

Figure 11.10 Short- and medium-term bonds still dominate the maturity profile in China.
Source: Author created based on data from the Asian Development Bank.

Onshore, around 65 percent of debt instruments represents government securities, while the remainder represents a growing number of corporate borrowers issuing a variety of instruments; most of the corporates are SOEs.[24] Bonds are now the third main source of funding for enterprises, following internal funds utilization and bank loans. Commercial banks hold around 55 percent of all bonds, followed by other non-bank financial institutions including trusts and mutual funds.[25] For all bonds, foreign ownership is less than 3 percent. Figure 11.9 shows that, by 2018, about 5 percent of corporate bonds were held by foreigners, but that amount has been steadily rising since 2014. In Figure 11.10, we see that maturities have shortened over the past decades; in 2017, about 65 percent of outstanding debt had a maturity of less than 10 years, with the largest share in the 1–3-year range. Treasury bonds are issued by the Ministry of Finance with 2-, 5-, and 7-year maturities, and they serve as benchmarks for pricing other maturities and securities. The PBC also issues central bank bonds and bills.[26] Financial bonds are issued by development banks, including the all-important China Development Bank—China's second-largest issuer after the Ministry of Finance.[27] Another facet of China's bond market is the range of international types of bonds: "Dim Sum" are RMB-denominated instruments traded in Hong Kong. "Panda bonds" are issued by foreigner borrowers in China in RMB. "Mulan bonds" are issued in special drawing rights, typically by international organizations raising funds in China, such as the World Bank. "Belt and Road bonds" are issued by development banks and companies engaged in China's Belt and Road project. Table 11.8 provides a recent yield curve for maturities for China Treasury bonds, which are treated as risk-free. Because of the segmented nature of the market and its lack of liquidity in the secondary market, a truly representative yield curve has yet to develop.

Maturity	Yield (%) Daily Average
1 Year	2.14
3 Year	2.63
5 Year	2.76
10 Year	3.00
30 Year	3.14

Table 11.8 China Treasury bond interbank yield curve (September, 2019).
Source: Author created based on data from CEIC.

Macro Finance Insight 11.2: Creative Bond Financing (But in the Republic of China)

Though we have said that China began to issue bonds beginning in the early 1980s; in fact, after the collapse of the Qing Dynasty, the newly established Republic of China issued a series of bonds to finance the new government and its modernization efforts, including railroad construction. Figure 11.11 displays one such 1913-issued "reorganization" bond with final payment due in July, 1960 (coupons not displayed). The amount borrowed is for payment in UK sterling 25 million, or the equivalent amount (at contemporaneous gold standard exchange rates) for German marks, French francs, Russian rubles or Japanese yen. Principal and interest (5 percent) were payable by the Chinese authorities to the lender in whichever of the above currencies the lender selected, regardless of the currency in which the loan was made.

What is interesting here is the historical context of the gold standard and the sophisticated nature of the bond when compared to the current plain vanilla character of Chinese bonds. The 1913 bond holds a multicurrency implicit option value for the bearer (the lender), and it in turn presents currency option exposure for the borrower (the Republic of China). If, for example, the German mark were to devalue against an ounce of gold, it would also devalue against all the above-mentioned currencies; if each currency's value is fixed against gold, it is also fixed against the other currencies. The bond bearer would then naturally exercise his implicit option to demand payment in any of the more valuable currencies whose price did not weaken against the value of gold. In the problem set at the end of the chapter, we consider the implications for bond pricing in the context of the gold standard where currencies were technically fixed against the value of gold.

In the four decades of turmoil that followed the issuance of these bonds, they were all fully in default by 1938. After the founding of the People's Republic of China, the issue of repayment was mostly forgotten until the start of the Trump trade wars. The current value amount of debt in default, by some estimates, adds up to around USD 1 trillion (https://bloom.bg/3cdEzVs) once interest and penalties are included. Perhaps not coincidentally, this is an amount comparable to what the United States owes China (an estimated USD 1.1 trillion in 2019). But history suggests that while the memory of spurned creditors is long, lenders usually come up short when it comes to actual compensation.

Figure 11.11 A Republic of China bond issued in 1913 with embedded currency options.
Source: Author created.

Bonds are traded on two separate platforms and regulated by two different sets of regulators. Close to 95 percent of trades occur in the interbank market, which is regulated by the National Development and Reform Commission and the PBC. Trading also occurs on stock exchanges (regulated by the Chinese Securities Regulatory Commission (CSRC)). The latter market is somewhat illiquid, with low volumes of trading for some instruments. Because of the separate platforms with different regulations, these platforms are not fully integrated, creating inefficiencies and arbitrage opportunities.

Unlike markets in the United States, Jiang et al. (2017) argue that listed firms who seek external finance prefer issuing equity rather than bonds (a reverse pecking order). They cite several reasons for this anomaly: 1) the low level of dividends that firms need to pay, 2) the low cost of equity (historically high price earnings ratios), and 3) the relatively illiquid market in long-term debt (or, conversely, the bias in the market toward shorter debt maturities). They go on to argue that traditional models of capital structure (e.g., Jensen and Meckling 1979) are less relevant in China due to regulatory restrictions and weak enforcement of bankruptcy laws (implying that borrowing is relatively expensive).

But it may not just be issuer preferences that need to be considered in discussing the limited role for bonds in China. And we have already seen that equity finance is relatively insignificant in China. The bond market, overall, appears to conform to some of the LLSV ideas presented earlier in this chapter. That maturities in this market tend to be short would be typical when default risks and lender protections are low (as would be true in civil law countries). What is more, long-term maturities in China are, by and large, offered via bank loans rather than the bond markets—consistent with the notion of arms-around rather than arm's-length finance. Finally, the fact that the main holders of these bonds are commercial banks and other state-owned institutions (e.g., Central Huijin Finance) precludes an active and liquid secondary bond market; these institutions tend to hold onto these assets for long periods as a stable component of their asset base. LLSV predicts that active secondary markets are unlikely to thrive in civil law countries.

Macro Finance Insight 11.3: Grade Inflation

At present, there are five major credit rating agencies within China, three of which have relationships with foreign firms (as indicated).[28] They are:

1. China Chengxin International Credit Rating Co., Ltd. (Moody's Investors Services)
2. China Lianhe Credit Rating Co. Ltd. (Fitch Ratings)
3. Dagong Global Credit Rating Ltd.
4. Shanghai Far East Credit Rating Co. Ltd.
5. Shanghai Brilliance Credit Rating and Investor Service Co., Ltd. (Standard & Poor's)

Typical ratings range from AAA to C with nine gradations. Close to 93 percent of companies in China receive a rating of AA or better, compared with only 1.4 percent in the United States. Many Chinese companies receiving these high ratings are rated lower by offshore credit rating agencies (Law 2015). In fact, Bloomberg's own analytical model suggests that about 57 percent of China's AAA rated companies should be given junk status BB or BA and lower; (Bloomberg 2016b).

Up until recently, only qualified foreign institutional investors (QFIIs) were permitted to invest in Chinese bonds; but, in 2015, the authorities announced that foreign investors would be allowed to tap into the relatively high-yielding Chinese market. The discrepancy in cross-border ratings soon became a matter of interest. The lack of informational content in Chinese ratings presents not just a problem of the efficient allocation of capital, but also creates the potential for the use of inside information. The true creditworthiness of the underlying companies is known to only part of the market—specifically, the credit rating agencies—and, in the absence of clear guidelines related to insider trading, such activities create profitable opportunities.

Interbank Markets

The interbank market determined rates are the China interbank offer rate (CHIBOR, established 1998), based on actual transactions for Chinese banks, and the Shanghai interbank offer rate (SHIBOR, established 2007), based on a poll of 18 Shanghai banks' estimated cost of funds on eight different maturities ranging from overnight to one year. Meanwhile, in the United States, the interbank rate is called the federal funds rate. When banks lack available reserves (usually due to open market operations of the central bank or, in the case of China, reserve requirement changes), they tend to cut back on lending to one another in order to increase their own reserves. This impacts interbank interest rates.

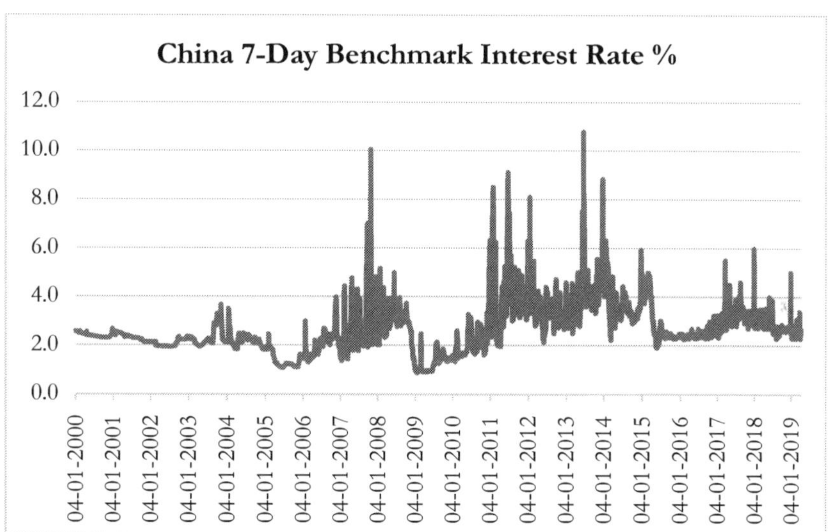

Figure 11.12 CHIBOR and SHIBOR are measures of Chinese interbank market-determined rates. The 7-day tenor serves as a benchmark for pricing other instruments.
Source: Author created based on data from the Federal Reserve Economic Database.

Figure 11.12 provides the benchmark 7-day maturity interbank rate for China. We note the rate trough in January, 2009, representing the monetary stimulus reaction to the GFC. In China, the various facilities—including the medium-term standing lending facility and the traditional discount window—provide an upper bound (corridor ceiling) on interbank lending interest rates (CHIBOR and SHIBOR) for different maturities. The standing lending facility has come to supplement traditional discount window lending. The discount rate also serves as a signaling device for changes in the monetary policy stance. Figure 11.13 shows China's discount window interest rate since 1990. The interest rate paid on excess reserves held by banks and the rate offered for PBC-initiated reverse repurchase agreements provides a floor for interbank lending rates. Figure 11.14 provides rates on 7-day reverse repurchase agreements over the past decade. The PBC offers at least five different maturities up to half a year. We note the flat (non-random) nature of rates found in Figure 11.13 and Figure 11.14 compared to the volatile rates found in Figure 11.12. The difference helps us to visualize the policy (non-market) determined rates in the former and the market-determined rates in the latter.

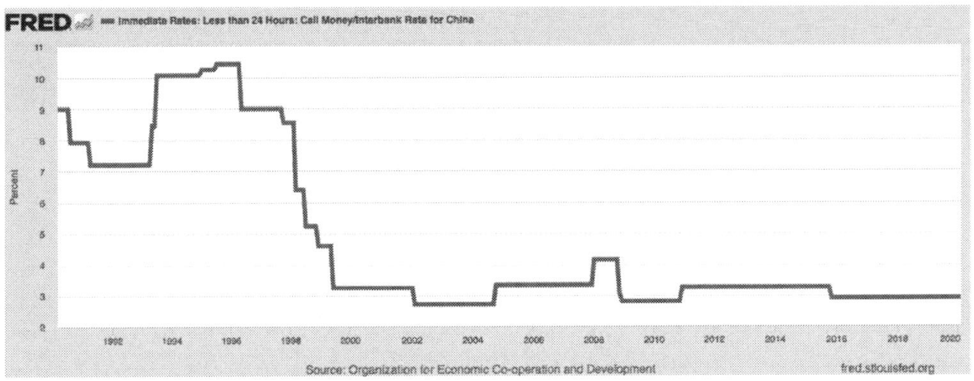

Figure 11.13 The discount rate is the PBC short-term lending rate, which provides one type of ceiling for interbank interest rates.
Source: Author created based on data from the Federal Reserve Economic Database.

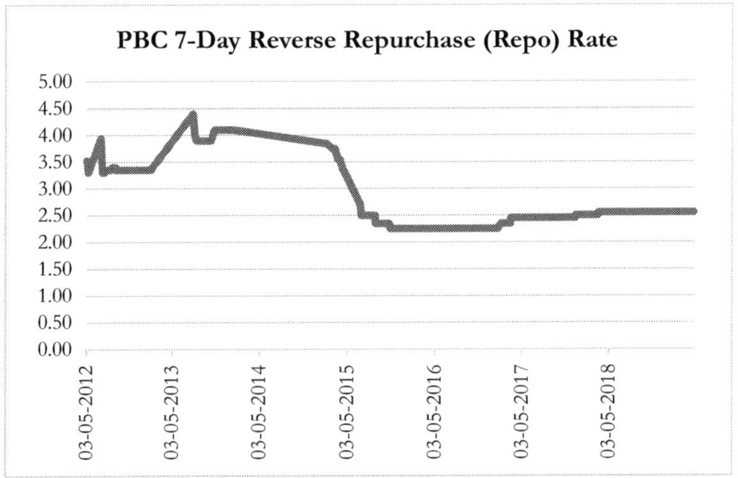

Figure 11.14 A reverse repo is a form of collateralized borrowing by the PBC, and it thus provides one type of ceiling for interbank market rates.
Source: Author created based on data from the Federal Reserve Economic Database.

Beyond the Big Four commercial banks and smaller banks, money market funds—such as Alibaba's Yu'E Bao (https://bit.ly/3ewF1iZ)—are also participants in the interbank market. They have both short-term borrowing and lending needs, which can be met by the highly-liquid interbank market. One way that money market funds invest their assets is in the repurchase agreement ("repo") market. Repos allow for collateralized borrowing on a usually short-term basis. China has two venues for trading repos: the interbank market (commenced trading in 1997) and the stock exchanges (mainly the SSE, which commenced trading in 1991). While the interbank market still represents about three-fourths of the market in repos (consistent with its leadership in bond trading), the stock exchanges have seen nearly 70 percent per annum growth in recent years.[29] Since the exchanges have standardized products, while interbank market repos are customized, exchange-traded instruments provide a clearer picture of short-term money market rates. Specifically, the 7-day exchange-traded repo is used as a benchmark rate in other markets. Over 80 percent of repos are overnight or 1-day, with the 7-day repo a distant second in terms of maturity.

While close to 90 percent of the bonds used as repo collateral are government or policy bonds, the repo market is larger than the underlying bond market itself in terms of both daily volumes and amounts outstanding—suggesting a substantial recycling of the underlying securities used as collateral.[30] In the stock exchange repo market, approximately three-quarters of the collateral represents government or policy bank bonds, with about 18 percent of enterprise bonds used as collateral (Shevlin and Chang 2015). In both markets, risky local government debt serves as part of the collateral. The danger here is a cascade effect should some shock hit the markets causing a rush for liquidity on the part of lenders. The combination of recycled repo collateral, money market participation with risky non-liquid assets, unreliable credit ratings, and value destruction in the real economy presents dangers reminiscent of the GFC in the United States. No doubt the various regulators, ranging from the PBC, CSRC, CBRC, and the China Securities and Depository Clearing Corporation (CSDC, regulating the stock market) are all working vigorously toward ensuring the continued smooth operation of these markets.

Case Study 11.2: Internet Finance in China and Inclusive Finance

Internet finance in China, unlike in the United States, grew in tandem with the financial sector itself. As we have discussed in earlier chapters, mobile payment applications, such as Alibaba's Alipay and Tencent's WeChat Pay, were an outgrowth of e-commerce and social media platforms.

The majority of transactions in China today are conducted using a mobile device employing either the Alipay or WeChat Pay platforms employing a QR code. Alipay's internet payment mechanism was launched in 2004, and WeChat Pay was launched in 2014. Though CreditEase (https://bit.ly/2WRz5eh), a peer-to-peer internet lending platform, was launched in 2005, internet finance in China only began to make steep inroads into traditional financial activities around 2013–2014. Leveraging the vast volume of transactions on their platforms, companies introduced money market funds offering higher yields than the traditional state-controlled banking sector. For example, Alibaba—through its financial arm Ant Financial—introduced their Yu'e Bao money market fund in 2013. By 2015 these companies were already providing loans to online participants in tandem with ever-more sophisticated data analytics and credit scoring. The combination of financial repression (discussed in this and earlier chapters), an inchoate regulatory framework, the implicit encouragement of the government, and information technology helped to fuel the remarkable developments in China's internet finance sector.

Huang et al. (2016) present evidence that China's internet financial revolution has resulted in a more inclusive financial system. About 62 percent (https://bit.ly/3gxt2DD) of the population in China now has access to the internet, and the vast majority rely on a mobile device for a connection. The authors apply a variety of measures, employing Peking University's Institute for Internet Finance Index (https://bit.ly/2BhIaoJ) to gauge the progress and impact of this nascent part of the financial sector. Table 11.9 shows that China still has potential to expand financial inclusion relative to the United States based on some relevant metrics.

But, with the opportunity for greater access to the financial system—particularly in rural areas—comes the risk of fraudulent activities (https://reut.rs/3bV1ILW). For example, by 2016, there were close to 4,000 peer-to-peer lending platforms—most of which were under-capitalized, did not have the fund manager's capital at risk, and—in some cases—guaranteed (fraudulently) returns on investment and capital preservation. Beginning around 2017, the authorities began to close down many of these smaller platforms and tightly regulate the remaining few. Huang et al. go on to suggest that these internet activities broaden access rather than cut into the business of the traditional state-owned banking sector. Needless to say, banking regulators and the PBC are carefully considering the impact of this type of spontaneous financial liberalization. It is well known that rapid financial liberalization and/or rapid financial innovations can be accompanied by severe and painful disruptions to the financial system (Diaz-Alejandro 1985).

Percent of Population of 15 Years of Age (2017)		
	United States	**China**
Conducted an Online Purchase	70.4	45.3
Made Digital Payments	89	60.9
Owned a Debit Card	80.2	66.8
Referenced Account Balance on Mobile Phone or Online	71.4	39

Table 11.9 Though China has made grade strides in online banking and internet commerce, there is still much room to grow when compared to the United States.
Source: World Bank Development Indicators for Financial Inclusion.

China's Equity Markets

China has three stock exchanges, the Shanghai Stock Exchange (mentioned above, SSE), the Shenzhen Stock Exchange (SZE) and the Hong Kong Stock Exchange. We limit our discussion to the mainland exchanges, the SSE and SZE. The SSE commenced operations in 1990, and the SZE followed in 1991. As can be seen in Figure 11.15, Figure 11.16, and Figure 11.17, growth has been tremendous. Eight companies were listed in Shanghai in 1990— by 2016 that number approached 1,100. Shenzhen saw an increase from six companies listed in 1991 to over 1,700 in 2016. Figure 11.16 shows that, by 2019, total market capitalization for both indices stood close to USD 7 trillion. SZE has smaller-sized companies; via its ChiNext board, SZE serves as an exit venue for private equity and venture capital funds. Figure 11.17 shows that, similar to its bond market, China's stock market as a share of GDP falls far below that of the United States (by over 100 percentage points). Again, at least at this point in time, the shortfall provides support for LLSV propositions regarding arm's-length financing in China via equity markets.

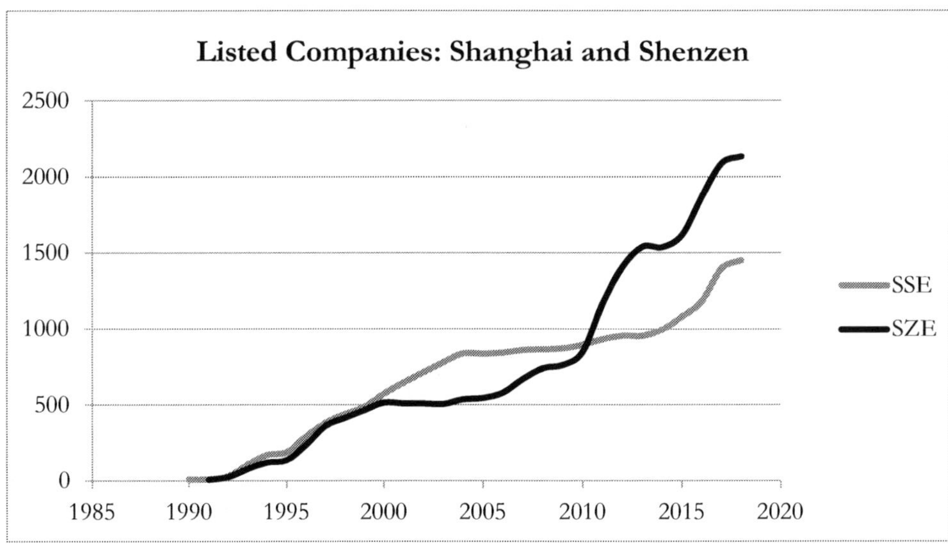

Figure 11.15 Chinese companies began listing on the two major stock exchanges of Shanghai and Shenzhen in 1990 and 1991.
Source: Author created based on data from the Hong Kong Stock Exchange.

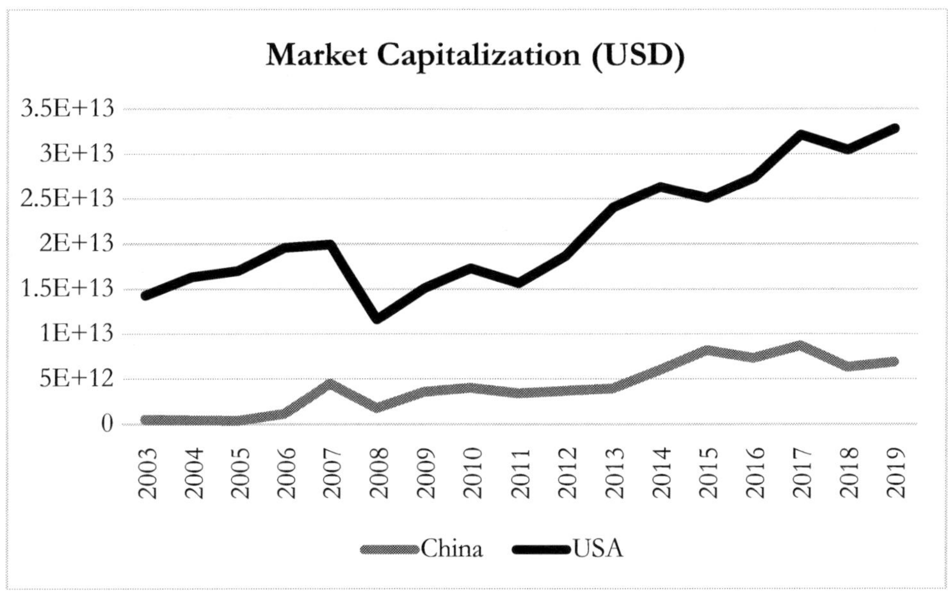

Figure 11.16 China's stock market capitalization (negotiable shares) had grown to about USD 6.9 trillion by 2019, but growth has stagnated since the GFC.
Source: Author created based on data from World Bank World Development Indicators.

Figure 11.17 China's stock market capitalization as a share of GDP remains far below that of the United States.
Source: Author created based on data from World Bank World Development Indicators.

China's stock markets can be viewed from several different angles, all of which represent specific types of market segmentation. One type of market segmentation is the negotiable/non-negotiable nexus, the other is the A/B share nexus. Negotiable shares are shares that are actually traded on public markets following an initial public offering (IPO). Non-negotiable shares are those closely held and not yet made available to the investing public. Typically, the non-negotiable counterpart to the tradeable (negotiable) shares have been held by the central government's State Council, and they include "Legal Person" shares of the central or local governments held by state-controlled institutions (such as Huijin Investment Ltd., a government-owned holding company).

"A shares" are RMB-denominated and available to Chinese citizens and large QFIIs; "B shares" are available to global investors and purchased with USD (Shanghai) or Hong Kong dollars (Shenzhen).[31] In addition, Chinese companies incorporated in the mainland but listed in Hong Kong are referred to as "H shares"; these shares can be bought and sold by anyone using Hong Kong dollars. Companies whose main operations are in China but trade in Hong Kong are referred to as "Red Chips." Similarly, Chinese companies incorporated in London or New York that issue shares are referred to as "L" or "N shares." Though adding complexity, the broader goal here has been to ensure some measure of consistency with the policy trilemma (Obstfeld 2015); China seeks to control its money supply, domestic interest rates, inflation, and economic growth while simultaneously maintaining control of its exchange rate. In turn, it must give up a degree of international capital mobility—thus, the unwillingness to allow unfettered capital movements into and out of the country—and, in this case, equity markets. Meanwhile, international investors have had an appetite for exposure to China's equity markets and strong potential for growth; China, itself, hopes to benefit from an international investor base. The A/B share dichotomy has served this purpose to some extent though international interest in listed B shares has been lackluster (Darrat et al. 2010).

Figure 11.18 show the increase in the percentage of negotiable shares for Shenzhen and Shanghai—the second major form of segmentation in equity markets. A target of 74 percent negotiable/tradable shares by 2009 was set by the CSRC, and that appears to have been met. The CSRC moved to convert many of the non-tradable shares into tradeable shares in the period 2005–2006 (Beltratti et al. 2016). At the time, approximately two-thirds of the outstanding shares were non-tradable. The existing holders of tradeable shares required compensation ranging from 30 to 50 percent of tradeable value for the increase in negotiable (tradeable) shares offered. That such compensation would be required when there was no change in the underlying assets or basic capital structure suggests a lack of depth/liquidity in the market. Figure 11.18 shows the delayed impact of the reform, since there was a "lockup" period of one year and a spate of other restrictions to limit the liquidity impact. Figure 11.18 shows that, by 2017, 78 percent of all shares had been converted to some form of tradeable instrument.

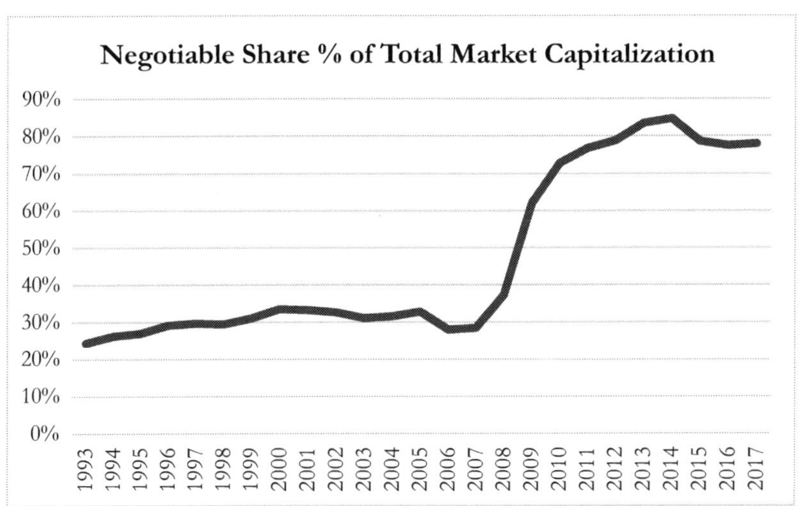

Figure 11.18 Negotiable shares are shares that are actually traded on China's exchanges (not closely held)—since reforms commenced in 2005, the proportion of negotiable shares has increased.
Source: Author created based on data from the Hong Kong Stock Exchange.

In most cases, compensation took the form of non-traded shares being offered to tradeable shareholders. Interestingly, the authors find that, in the three days before an announcement by the authorities of companies selected to change share status, there was a sharp increase in prices. The authors explain this phenomenon in terms of "informational leakage." We discuss questions of market efficiency below. An offsetting factor, not considered by the authors, is that the conversion also had important corporate governance implications—specifically, the rights of minority shareholders (pre-existing tradeable shareholders) were significantly enhanced by the conversion—as they in effect became part of a majority class. Thus, the very act of conversion should have made their shares commensurately more valuable.

The CSRC again relaxed rules related to non-negotiable share listing in the first half of 2009. This relaxation had the effect of substantially increasing market capitalization (in 2009, at least RMB 8 trillion in value was converted from non-negotiable to negotiable).[32,33] By 2016, 87 percent of shares were tradeable in Shanghai and 70 percent of shares were tradeable in Shenzhen. But, even after the great strides made in converting non-tradable into tradeable shares, the percentage of tradeable shares being held by institutions controlled by the government that are still illiquid is likely large. Recent government interventions in the market discussed below (the National Team effort) provide some context for this situation.

Market Efficiency and Government Involvement

Beyond meeting the needs of different types of investors, the great diversity of share classes also offers economists an opportunity to study such issues such as market efficiency, asset pricing models, and market integration (Eun and Huang 2007; Fernald and Rogers 2002). For example, we see in Figure 11.19 the performance of the Hang Seng AH share index, which is the ratio of A share prices (onshore) to H Share prices (Hong Kong offshore) in the same currency. *Ceteris paribus*, since we have the same underlying security with identical claims on cash flows, the prices should be the same, or at 100. Differing prices provide some indication of market segmentation between Hong Kong and the mainland. More specifically, perhaps, we also get a measure of how tightly international capital mobility is being enforced between the two areas. We see that, since the fourth quarter in 2014, the index has been consistently well above 100 (approaching 150 in 2015, and still hovering around 130 in 2019), suggesting much higher valuations for the same company in the mainland. Greater controls on capital outflows from China due to earlier foreign exchange outflows and restrictions on short sales no doubt contribute to this huge pricing disparity (and pseudo-arbitrage opportunity).

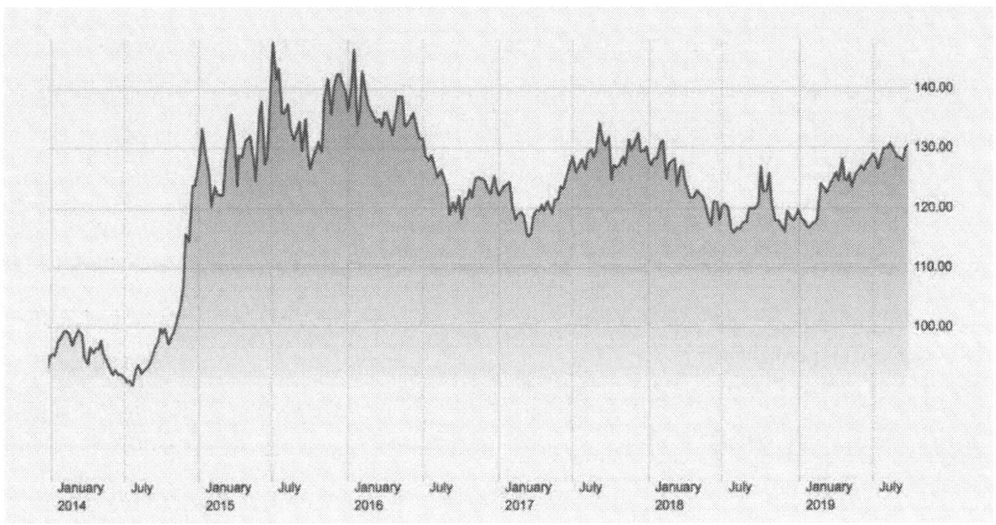

Figure 11.19 The Heng Seng AH Premium Index provides a good measure of government-imposed controls on capital mobility between China and the rest of the world (higher levels suggests greater control).
Source: *Financial Times*.

Given China's stock markets' relatively short existence, the question of market efficiency is a natural one to consider. Charles and Darné (2009) examine daily returns and test for weak form market efficiency. Specifically, they employ a variety of variance ratio tests to see whether China's stock markets follow a random walk. They find, like several other earlier studies, that A shares do but B shares do not—that is, future movements of the latter are predictable based on past movements of the time series. For example, Chen and Hong (2003) find that the market had become more efficient over time, but that A share pricing was more efficient (based on volatility clustering) than B share. Chong et al. (2012) find that technical rules generally do not create excess returns under a variety of estimation models when one considers commissions. Furthermore, after the reforms involving non-tradable shares discussed above, excess returns are substantially diminished. Groenewold et al. (2003) found evidence of efficiency employing unit root and autocorrelation tests. Meanwhile, Thiele (2014) found market inefficiency by looking at subsamples of data over a longer time horizon than some of the above studies and detected autocorrelations and long memory of returns.

Most studies have examined Chinese market efficiency from the perspective of weak form market efficiency. Malkiel (2007), in a comprehensive look at market efficiency, concludes that Chinese stock markets are generally inefficient using the more restrictive definitions of market efficiency. In terms of weak form inefficiency, he cites some of the studies mentioned above, but he also identifies several other studies that show "calendar effects"—that is, predictable holiday and seasonal patterns. In terms of broad market efficiency (prices reflecting fundamental factors), Malkiel identifies price discrepancies for the same shares traded in Shanghai and foreign exchanges, except in Hong Kong. As discussed earlier, China's financial markets remain segmented from international financial markets. Finally, Malkiel examines the performance of actively managed funds in China compared to index funds. Generally, the latter should outperform the former in efficient markets because such assets would be fairly priced in an efficient market. He finds that in China the reverse holds—actively managed funds appear to outperform passive index funds. He suggests that those actively managed funds with inside information do even better—a red flag when it comes to the use of inside information and the presence of strong form market efficiency.

Zhao et al. (2014) examined the impact of short sale restrictions on overvaluation of securities and market efficiency. In December, 2011, the CSRC began a pilot program allowing for short sales of qualifying securities. By August, 2015, 495 stocks had become eligible for short sale. The authors find that allowing short sales both reduced overvaluation and enhanced weak form market efficiency.

Macro Finance Insight 11.4: Are There Any Cheerleaders for the National Team?

After climbing by over 150 percent from late 2014 to early 2015, the stock market in China fell into a steep decline from its June, 2015 peak, with the SSE eventually losing about 60 percent of its value. In mid-June, in an effort at supporting the market, the government instructed a select "National Team" of state-owned funds, institutions brokerages, and other investors to buy shares. On 8 July, new rules on short sales and rules against selling shares (if any single owner held 5 percent or more of a company's shares) were announced. Rules restricting new offerings were also put in place. Central bank funds totaling an estimated USD 236 billon (https://bloom.bg/2VeZ6TB) were used to buy shares. While initially proposed to last only six months, the continued drop in the market (see Figure 11.20) and steep declines in early January (possibly in anticipation of the lifting of regulations on sales) resulted in Chinese authorities extending the rules indefinitely.

At one level, government intervention does not necessarily violate technical definitions of market efficiency—one could simply argue that this was a series of random unanticipated shocks to the market—no different than a surprise announcement on interest rate policy by the Federal Reserve in the United States. We note that the US Federal Reserve has been explicit in stating that the stock market is not a policy target. Future research will no doubt delve deeper to see if the policy was anticipated (as suggested above in the discussion on managed funds performance) and, in turn, if stock price movements anticipated the series of government generated events (suggesting market inefficiency, by definition). Daily volatility, in fact, increased after government intervention in June of 2015.[34] But here we need to step beyond the financial definition of market efficiency to the economic concept of allocative efficiency. If government intervention resulted in the cost of capital being too low for listed companies, financial theory suggests overinvestment relative to the optimal level; in other words, the misallocation of capital in China.

Given the large participation of retail investors and the possibility of significant losses in wealth for small investors—especially those who entered the market near its peak—government policy was aimed at creating a floor, or providing investors with an implicit put option on the market.[35] As long as the market did not plummet further, the authorities would no doubt be content with the outcome regardless of daily volatility. We note that the program may have provided an unintended form of support for the market. Since an implicit floor (put) was created and greater volatility resulted, the value of the put to current shareholders was enhanced—thus reducing the incentive to sell shares. In the period of intervention in the last half of 2015, there were continued losses in equity markets totaling USD 5 trillion. In the first half of 2016, China's National Team sold off its holdings. The overall impact of the entire period of government action in the market raises questions about governments and their efforts at supporting stock prices; perhaps a cautionary tale for the Trump administration and its undue focus (https://cnn.it/2Yxm8aw) on stock market valuations in recent years.

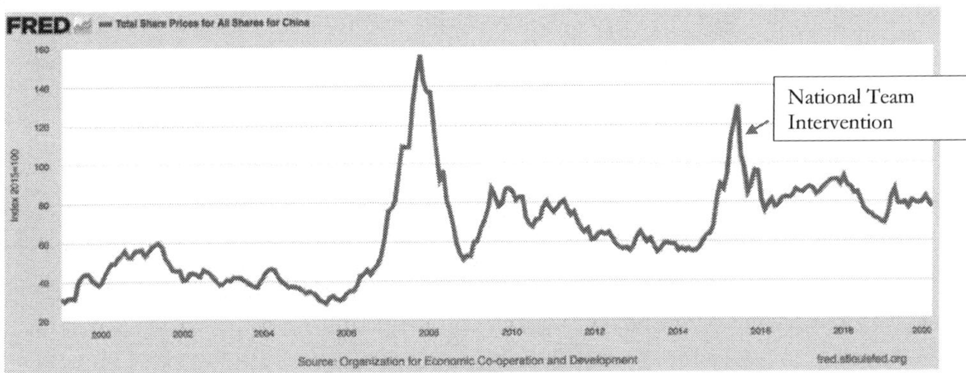

Figure 11.20 China's "National Team" began the process of supporting the stock market in China beginning around the second quarter of 2015.
Source: Author created based on data from the Federal Reserve Economic Database.

When we consider market efficiency in the broader economic context (beyond the financial definition), we are asking whether markets are channeling society's limited savings into their most productive use. This balance requires that stock prices on average or over the long run accurately reflect the value of the underlying assets and their accompanying cash flows given a market-determined rate of social discount (the pricing kernel). But government intervention in the market is one more form of financial repression, creating a false signal about pricing for a prolonged period. Volatility increases because of both the uncertainty created and the lack of liquidity (in the case of various selling restrictions). In this situation, which can persist for prolonged periods of time, it is likely that savings will not be channeled into their most productive use. In this context, Luo et al. (2015) compare fundamental factors that should impact valuations (such as net income and firm size) to actual market valuations and find consistent discrepancies in China, especially when compared to the United States markets. They do, however suggest that those discrepancies have diminished somewhat since the 2005 reforms discussed above. Chinese savers have limited ways to invest their wealth (markets are quite incomplete).[36] Viewed from an international integrated financial market angle, it is apparent that Chinese equity markets overvalue assets and, in turn, likely oversupply the economy with investment—the latter stood at an extraordinary 47 percent of GDP in 2013.

Recent Developments in Registration, Corporate Governance, and Dividends

Since the establishment of public markets in 1990–1991, firms wishing to raise funds via an IPO needed approval from the CSRC. In December, 2019, the authorities—in a comprehensive reform of market regulations (https://bit.ly/2ZOQ4A7)—announced that beginning in March, 2020, firms would be allowed to list under a registration (or market-determined) system similar to the process found in the United States. Rather than seeking regulatory approval to list, exchanges would establish their own guidelines for listing and market forces would then determine what price and quantity was acceptable for a successful IPO of a company's shares. The policy change was intended to prevent political favoritism and deter the government from attempting to pick winners who could list. The newly implemented registration system is intended to allow a market-driven process for firms hoping to raise equity finance, with greater economic efficiency as the end result.

Corporate governance in China remains an area in need of a great deal of reform (Allen et al. 2017). Though following the European two board model—a supervisory board (three or more members) and a board of directors (five to nine members)—non-controlling shareholders, labor, and other stakeholders are generally underrepresented, if they are represented at all. Due to regulatory constraints and the strong position of majority shareholders, takeovers and mergers rarely occur, limiting the ability of minority shareholders to correct bad company decisions. The lack of strong institutional investors is another check on corporate misbehavior that is missing. Finally, as discussed throughout this text, the role of the government as both a shareholder and a controller places minority investors at a severe disadvantage.

Jiang et al. (2017) cite two regulatory changes that have impacted China's still relatively low dividend payout ratios (discussed in Chapter 5). The first encouraged greater dividend payments: Beginning in March, 2001, in order for existing firms to raise more equity capital (seasoned equity offering), the regulatory authorities required firms to have paid dividends to shareholders in the three previous years. The second change inadvertently reduced dividend payouts: The 2005 requirement to convert non-tradeable shares into tradeable shares allowed share owners to rely less on dividends and more on capital gains as a source of income via sale of the formerly non-tradeable shares.

Shadow Banking[37]

"Be careful what you wish for" may be an appropriate axiom for Western economists who conduct China-related research. In the past, the lack of ways to hold wealth for China's beleaguered savers has often been bemoaned as a critical bottleneck to China's economic growth and future prosperity. In the mid-1990s, about 70 percent of China's financial wealth was held in traditional banking institutions as deposits;[38] Figure 11.5 shows that, in 1994, that figure began a secular decline, falling below 50 percent in 2008. The absence of alternative investment vehicles hindered the vital role that finance plays in an economy—channeling a nation's scarce savings into its most productive use. Moreover, the absence of additional ways to diversify wealth caused disproportionate amounts of both personal and corporate savings to be channeled into property and equity markets or offshore, creating unsustainably high prices or pent up demand for other asset classes. In turn, fewer ways to diversify wealth holdings and reduce risk has no doubt led to even higher savings as a compensating buffer against uncertainty.

Since 2009, when it was around 15 percent of GDP, non-bank finance's share of importance has increased to about 60 percent of GDP, or around RMB 40 trillion (USD 6 trillion). In absolute terms, financing in China from this sector has grown by a factor of five since the global financial crisis.[39] We generally refer to the non-bank financial sector for a country as its "shadow banking sector."[40] We see in, Figure 11.21, that notwithstanding bank's declining importance in financial intermediation in China (Figure 11.5), total social financing has risen relative to the nation's savings. While informal finance has been part of China's economy over the centuries, its most recent reincarnation traces its roots all the way back to 1994. Recall from Chapter 10 that, at that time, a major fiscal reform placed a heavy expenditure burden on provinces and localities without adequate funding support from the central government. In turn, these local governments found creative ways to finance their expenditures, ranging from the creation of special purpose lending institutions to land sales. This was, in fact, the start of China's modern shadow banking sector.

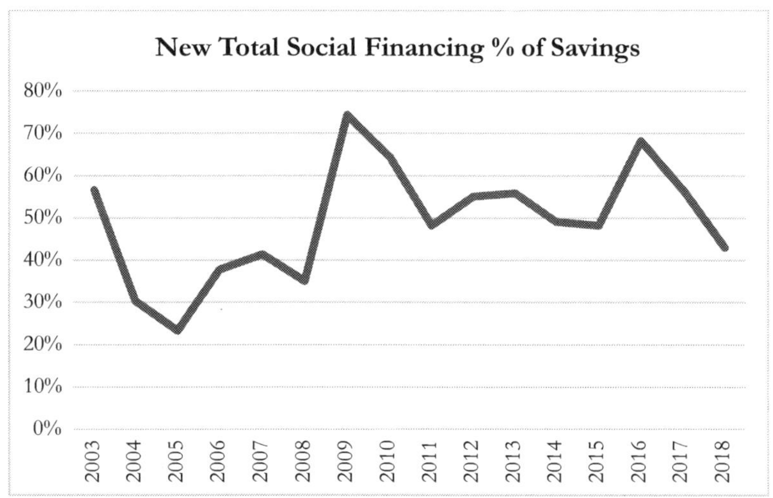

Figure 11.21 Financial intermediation has been on the rise in China relative to savings. How long China's vast savings can act as a buffer against its huge credit expansion is an open question.
Source: Author created based on data from CEIC and FRED.

We could think of the shadow banking sector as being either lightly regulated or not regulated at all. Both dynamic and innovative, shadow banking institutions often excel at information gathering (the coin of the realm in finance) and providing specialized areas of expertise that investors desire. But shadow banking investment activities can be unduly risky, with the potential for causing systematic risk—financial crises. The latter characteristic derives from the absence of a direct lender of last resort—the PBC—a backstop that traditional banks do have. Furthermore, shadow institutions operate without explicit government guarantees of principal invested, such as deposit insurance. We have already seen in Chapter 8 (Chen 2018) that the shadow banking sector has the potential to play havoc with PBC monetary policy: when the PBC tightens monetary policy, shadow banking loans actually rise due to regulatory arbitrage.

While China's sector is still relatively small by international standards (the United States shadow banking share of GDP is estimated to be 2 to 3 times larger), its rapid growth and now globally-significant size does raise some red flags. In this section, we will highlight special characteristics of shadow banking in China, the opportunities and risks that they present, and how we think the entire sector will evolve in the coming years.

Key Institutions and Activities in the Evolving Chinese Shadow Banking Landscape

Money Market Funds

Though money market funds have been present in China since at least 2003–2004, they achieved tremendous growth with the introduction of internet banking. In response to China's Silent Banking Crisis of 1998–2003, regulators implemented a series of measures to recapitalize China's traditional banking system.[41] One such measure was the imposition of interest rate ceilings on deposits and floors on loans—virtually guaranteeing a spread of profitability to the effectively bankrupt banking system. While successful in returning banks to profitability, such forms of financial repression come at a cost—financial disintermediation. Money market funds provided an avenue for higher returns and liquidity. Bundled with internet banking, convenience was thrown into the mix—24-hour access to an account with only a few cellphones clicks needed. Viewed from another angle, money markets funds in China allowed for the pooling of the funds of many small depositors into one large deposit at banks.[42] As a result, money market funds could negotiate a deposit rate well above the regulated bank rate. Thus, most money market funds invest in banks which, in turn, invest in bond reverse repurchase agreements in the interbank market. Recall that a reverse repurchase agreement is a form of collateralized borrowing by banks and other large institutions (where the collateral is typically a government security).

Macro Finance Insight 11.5: Yu'e Bao has Bad News (余额宝有恶报)

Yu'e Bao, China's largest money market fund, was founded in 2013; and, by December of that year, it already held about USD 30 billion in assets. More spectacularly, by March, 2018, its value peaked at USD 268 billion to become the world's largest money market fund. But by the end of 2019, its net asset value had fallen by over 40 percent. Yu'e Bao (which means "spare cash") had its roots in the cash balances held by Alibaba customers; Alibaba is the world's largest e-commerce retail company. Via a chain of ownership linking Alibaba to Ant Financial, Alipay, and finally Tian Hong Financial Holdings, Yu'e Bao attracted customer deposits away from banks by paying higher interest rates than bank-regulated deposit rates.

Figure 11.22 shows that, initially, returns were about 2 percentage points higher than those found for one-year deposits at banks. What is more, making mobile payments for purchases using a Yu'e Bao account was seamless and convenient. Money market funds such as Yu'e Bao were able to aggregate small savers into large bank deposits, and they could therefore negotiate a more favorable (higher) return from banks. Banks typically find small depositor accounts expensive to service, so the aggregation of many accounts into large deposits proved economical for banks as well. The mix of financial technology and mobile applications with financial repression of banks (including deposit rate ceilings and reserve requirements) fueled huge growth in money market funds like Yu'e Bao in a short period of time. By 2019, over one-third of the population (https://on.wsj.com/2TQn874) had an account with Yu'e Bao.

But a number of forces have come to play in reducing Yu'e Bao's attractiveness and net asset value (McLoughlin and Meredith 2017). Beginning in 2017, regulators began to tighten controls on how money market funds are invested both in terms of asset quality and maturity matching; virtually all money market funds' de facto goal is to preserve investor capital (maintain a fixed value per investment unit) while providing short-term liquidity on deposits. Interest rate ceilings on deposits were deregulated in 2015, and banks began to offer their own money market funds with similar mobile convenience. Finally, Ant Financial placed a differentiated mix of other money market funds on its platform, in effect competing with itself. Figure 11.22 shows that, by 2019, the return differential had narrowed to under 1 percentage point—giving investors a pause in enthusiasm for the opaque financial disclosure of Yu'e Bao when compared to government guaranteed deposits at highly regulated banks.

In the United States, Fidelity and JP Morgan offer the two largest money market funds and a full array of other mutual funds. Money market funds in the United States invest in a well-defined set of short-term financial instruments ranging from banker's acceptances, certificates of deposit, commercial paper, repurchase agreements, and US Treasury bills. The range of assets in China for short-term investments is much narrower (primarily bank- and government-issued), less liquid, and less integrated with markets outside of the interbank market. In addition, money market funds in China are significantly leveraged, relying on bond finance for some of their funding. Once again, LLSV provides some evidence of greater institutional-based finance in China, rather than arm's-length liquid market finance. What matters is whether money market funds in China and the United States provide short-term financing tools to create value while allocating risk among the various participants in an efficient way. Recently, Ant Financial has moved from iconoclastic to conventional finance and entered the formal banking industry itself with MYBank (https://reut.rs/3ewyaGc). By 2019, MYBank had an estimated value of RMB 24 billion.

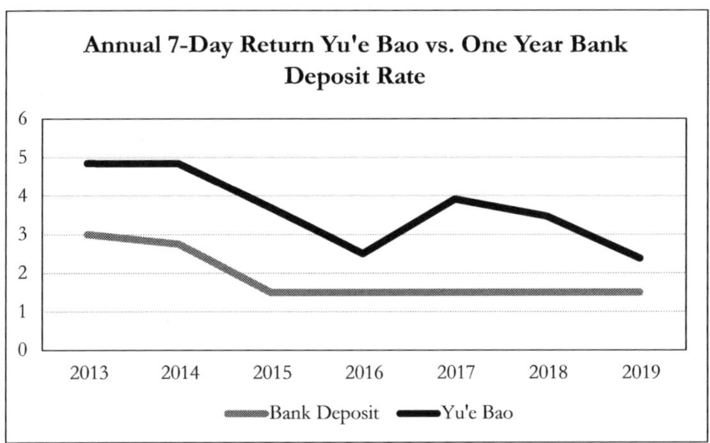

Figure 11.22 The gap between money market fund returns, such as Yu'e Bao's, and bank deposits has narrowed, causing savers to return to banks.
Source: Author created based on data from CEIC and FRED.

Trusts

A trust is another institution that accepts investments (minimum RMB 1 million) from wealthy individuals or institutions. They invest in property developers, local government projects, stocks, bonds, and other products offered up in the shadow banking industry. They are typically linked to banks via a banks' wealth management products (WMPs, discussed below), and—in some cases—they have banks as the major shareholder. They pay interest to their investors at an unregulated interest rate. In some ways, these trusts are like the private equity firms found in the West, but the investment profile is more opaque. Unlike traditional private equity firms, investors in trusts have implicit guarantees of capital preservation—a characteristic of debt rather than equity. They pool investments into structured WMPs to be offered to investors, but with loose guidelines on what the nature of those investments will be. Trusts are descendants of the earlier provincial/local government sponsored trust and investment corporations discussed briefly below. Some of these earlier institutions went bankrupt.[43]

Wealth Management Products

WMPs are short-term financial products, offered by both banks and trusts, that yield higher fixed-rate returns than bank deposits while investing in a pool of assets ranging from money market funds to local government debt.[44] In this sense, WMPs represent a form of securitization of underlying loans and investments, but without the marketability (liquidity) that accompanies the securitization typically found in the West. Of an estimated 9,000 WMPs currently offered by banks across China (at the start of

2009 there were only 176), about 60 percent do not guarantee the invested principal (Li 2014a). For some WMPs, banks offer an implicit guarantee to "top off" the interest rate should the return dip below what investors had been explicitly or implicitly promised. But many investors assume a firm guarantee is in place, and WMPs represent a significant portion (over 50 percent) of the total value of deposits for some of China's largest banks.

Entrusted Loans

Making up the largest share (about 15 percent of GDP) of the core shadow banking sector are entrusted loans, or company-to-company loans. Banks act as intermediaries or brokers for these types of loans in which amounts, interest rates, maturities, and counterparties are all customized. Uses of funds range from working capital to property development. The participation of the bank adds a level of comfort for both borrower and lender. Meanwhile, the transaction is typically off-balance-sheet, and it allows for the bank to collect fees plus a share of the interest paid. As mentioned earlier, Lin and Schramm (2008) estimate that about one-third of China's savings in the period 1995–2005 could not be accounted for on a flow of funds basis. They speculate that a significant portion of this gap represents intra-company lending. It now appears that this type of lending has moved from the undocumented deep shadows to the better documented entrusted loan segment of shadow banking.[45] Another area of financial repression is at play here: SOEs have traditionally had access to finance from the Big Four state-owned banks at below-market interest rates. SOEs can and do then lend these funds out to other firms via entrusted loans, including small- and medium-sized enterprises.

Estimates of the Size of Shadow Banking

Table 11.10 provides some rough estimates of the size of each of these shadow banking sectors in 2016 based on a variety of sources (Li 2014a). The IMF (https://bit.ly/3drsTzT) estimates that the core shadow banking sector (narrowly defined to include entrusted loans, trusts, and bankers' acceptances) was only about 27 percent of Chinese GDP (USD 3.7 trillion) in 2018. This was a decline from 2014, when the estimated size was 33 percent of GDP. A broader estimate (https://reut.rs/2Mgief3)—which includes WMPs, money market funds, hedge funds, and various non-bank asset management products—was 82 percent of GDP in 2017 (USD 10 trillion): also a decline in share from what is presented in Table 11.10 for 2016. Meanwhile, total social financing (https://bit.ly/3drsTzT) (or "aggregate finance," a broad measure of financial source flows excluding intra-financial institution activities) had grown steadily from 190 percent to an estimated 238 percent of GDP in the period 2014–2020. We can infer that bank lending, bond finance, and equity finance have risen in importance in recent years at the expense of the shadow banking sector. The relative decline in shadow banking reflects both a consolidation of operators within this sector and an increase in government regulation. In particular, new CBRC regulations (https://bloom.bg/2yIH58g) require banks to move many off-balance sheet activities (in particular, WMPs and trust activities) back onto their balance sheets beginning in 2018. The impact of these regulations in the context of M2 measurement was also discussed in Chapter 7.

Product	**Amount (in Trillions) and Estimated Share of GDP 2016**
Wealth Management Products	RMB 26 (35 %)
Trusts	RMB 18 (24 %)
Entrusted Loans	RMB 13 (18 %)
Money Market Funds	RMB 5 (7 %)
Security Firms Financing from Banks	RMB 2 (3 %)
Total	RMB 64 (87%)

Table 11.10 China's shadow banking sector peaked in importance around 2015, and since then it has seen greater competition from the traditional financial sector and greater regulation. But, by 2020, some see a loosening of restrictions.
Source: CEIC, *Financial Times*, *Bloomberg News* (various issues), and author's estimates.

Risks of the Shadow Banking Sector in China

China's shadow banking sector has characteristics that could, in fact, describe any shadow banking sector around the world:

- It is not a beneficiary of government-sponsored deposit insurance.
- It does not have any direct liquidity backstop—that is, a central bank line of credit such as a discount window—to access when liquidity in financial markets dries up.
- It is either not regulated or lightly-regulated compared to traditional banks.

In other words, shadow banks are not banks, and they are therefore much riskier for depositors than banks. But the average Chinese investor in the shadow banking system is not fully aware of the difference in risk between traditional and shadow banking. In fact, there have been a number of cases where some shadow banking firms have made false claims of government connections or implied government guarantees. There is, however, at least one worrisome similarity that shadow banks have with traditional banks: a maturity mismatch—long-term investments and short-term liabilities—both have exposure to liquidity risk. Finally, the relationship between shadow banks and traditional banks is symbiotic—they rely on each other for deposits and investments.

These factors combine to create some clear systemic risks for the Chinese and global economies. A loss in principal or liquidity squeeze (inability to liquidate investments in an orderly fashion) could propagate across the financial system (including banks) and, of course, the wider economy. Over the past several years, Chinese regulators have been taking a tougher stance toward this sector of the financial industry, shutting down or aggressively regulating firms that have the potential to create financial harm to individuals or the economy.

Summary and Outlook

Shadow banking in China branches off into two fundamental directions. One is institution-based, where we have money market funds, trusts, venture capital, private equity firms, and investment banks channeling funds directly into companies (investment banking)—a role similar but, as we indicated, different in a variety of ways from traditional banks. The other branch is related to asset management, involving securitization and the creation of marketable securities based on pools of underlying assets. WMPs and the use of repurchase agreements and working capital management all contain elements of securitization. In the same way that the equity market is influenced by legal systems (as we discussed above), China's shadow banking sector reflects the nation's legal system in being more likely to thrive at the institutional investment banking (arms-around) level than at the arm's-length (marketable) securities finance level. Common law economies, such as the United States and the United Kingdom, can deal more easily with the dynamism of marketable security arm's-length finance. Courts are better able to cope with financial innovation in real time, while in civil law countries (such as continental Europe), relying on legal codes is more suitable for arms-around institution-based financial intermediation. China, legally and politically, clearly follows in the civil law tradition of rules and regulations. The role of courts acting as independent judges of what is fair and efficient in financial markets is an unlikely modus operandi for China in the coming years.

Challenging Questions for China (and the Student): Chapter 11

1. Go to the Federal Reserve Economic Database (FRED) and find "Total Credit to Private Non-Financial Sector" (percent of GDP). Also find "Credit to Private Non-Financial Sector by Banks." Transform the latter as a percent of GDP, and then compare to the "Total Credit to Private Non-Financial Sector" (percent of GDP) series. Are banks becoming more or less important in lending to the private sector in China?
2. Discuss which factors will come to play a dominant role in shaping China's financial system in the future: the legal framework, a regulatory and institutional vacuum, or financial repression?
3. Discuss how three out of four key drivers for the Chinese economy came into play for China's Silent Banking Crisis of 1998–2003. Be sure to identify resulting implications for the Chinese economy.
4. In his classic article on financial risk, Hyman Minsky (1992) identifies three stages of debt, each of which are successively riskier: the Hedge Stage, the Speculative Stage, and the Ponzi Stage. Go to either the original article or the 2014 BBC (https://bbc.in/2M8h8Ca) summary for a description of each. With reference to Macro Finance Insight 11.1, discuss which stage you believe China is currently in.
5. Recall the bond with embedded currency options in Macro Finance Insight 11.2.
    a. Suppose the Japanese yen (and only the yen) appreciated in value relative to an ounce of gold. Describe the required principal and interest payments in this situation (in Chinese yuan equivalent).
    b. Given the historical context, why was the interest rate set at 5 percent regardless of the currency of repayment?
    c. Since a currency option's value is higher the greater the volatility of the exchange rate, how would you value the embedded currency options in this bond? (Hint: Keep in mind the historical context.)
6. How is a surprise change in interest policy by the Fed any different from the National Team acquiring stocks to support equity markets in China?
7. Assuming the LLSV set of propositions, what will the shadow banking sector come to look like in China in the coming years?
8. Discuss: It is better to have a shadow banking sector that is documented and recorded than it is to have one that is undocumented, as was the case in China pre-2005.

References

Allen, Franklin, Jun Qian, and Meijun Qian. 2005. "Law, Finance, and Economic Growth in China." *Journal of Financial Economics*, 77(1), 57–116.

Allen, Franklin, Jun Qian, and X. Gu. 2017. "An Overview of China's Financial System." *Annual Review of Financial Economics*, 9, pp. 191–231.

Awrey, Dan. 2015. "Law and Finance in the Chinese Shadow Banking System." *Cornell International Law Journal*, 48(1), pp. 1–49.

Beck, Thorsten, Asli Demirgüç-Kunt, and Ross Levine. 2003. "Law and Finance: Why Does Legal Origin Matter?" *Journal of Comparative Economics*, 31(4), pp. 653–75.

Beltratti, A., B. Bortolotti, and M. Caccavaio. 2016. "Stock Market Efficiency in China: Evidence from the Split-share Reform." *The Quarterly Review of Economics and Finance*, 60, pp. 125–37.

Berger, A. N, Iftekhar Hasan, and Mingming Zhou. 2009. "Bank Ownership and Efficiency in China. What will Happen in the World's Largest Nation?" *Journal of Banking & Finance*, (33)1, pp. 113–30.

Bloomberg News. 2016a. "China Said to Weigh Tighter Rules on Wealth-Management Products." *Bloomberg News*, 26 July, https://www.bloomberg.com/news/articles/2016-07-27/china-mulls-tightening-wealth-product-rules-21st-century-says.

Bloomberg News. 2016b. "Look Closer: 57% of China AAA Bond Issuers Have Junk-Like Risks." *Bloomberg News*, 23 May, http://www.bloomberg.com/news/articles/2016-05-23/look-closer-57-of-china-aaa-bond-issuers-have-junk-like-risks.

Carpenter, J. N., F. Lu, and R. F. Whitelaw. 2015. "The Real Value of China's Stock Market." NBER Working Paper no. 20957.

Charles, A., and O. Darné. 2009. "The Random Walk Hypothesis for Chinese Stock Markets: Evidence from Variance Ratio Tests." *Economic Systems*, 33(2), pp. 117–26.

Chen, Kaiji, Jue Ren, and Tao Zha. 2016. "What We Learn from China's Rising Shadow Banking: Exploring the Nexus of Monetary Tightening and Banks' Role in Entrusted Lending." NBER Working Paper no. 21890.

Chen, Kaiji, Jue Ren, and Tau Zha. 2018. "The Nexus of Monetary Policy and Shadow Banking in China." *American Economic Review*, 108(12), pp. 3891–936.

Chen, Max and Yongmiao Hong. 2003. "Has Chinese Stock Market Become More Efficient? Evidence from a New Approach." *Lecture Notes in Computer Science*, 2658, pp. 90–98.

Chong, T. T. L., T. H. Lam, and I. K. M. Yan. 2012. "Is the Chinese Stock Market Really Inefficient?" *China Economic Review*, 23(1), pp. 122–37.

Coase, Ronald H. 1960. *The Problem of Social Cost.* London: Palgrave Macmillan.

Darrat, A. F., O. Gilley, Y. Wu, and M. Zhong. 2010. "On the Chinese B-share Price Discount Puzzle: Some New Evidence." *Journal of Business Research*, 63(8), pp. 895–902.

Diaz-Alejandro, C. 1985. "Good-Bye Financial Repression, Hello Financial Crash." *Journal of Development Economics*, 19, pp. 1–24.

Elliott, Douglas, Arthur Kroeber, and Yu Qiao. 2015. "Shadow Banking in China: A Primer." Economic Studies at The Brookings Institution, 13, pp. 1–29.

Eun, C. S., and W. Huang. 2007. "Asset Pricing in China's Domestic Stock Markets: Is There a Logic?" *Pacific-Basin Finance Journal*, 15(5), pp. 452–80.

Fernald, J., and J. H. Rogers. 2002. "Puzzles in the Chinese Stock Market." *Review of Economics and Statistics*, 84(3), pp. 416–32.

Groenewold, N., S. H. K. Tang, and Y. Wu. 2003. "The Efficiency of the Chinese Stock Market and the Role of the Banks." *Journal of Asian Economics*, 14(4), pp. 593–609.

Hsiao, Cheng, Yan Shen, and Wenlong Bian. 2015. "Evaluating the Effectiveness of China's Financial Reform—The Efficiency of China's Domestic Banks." USC-INET Research Paper no. 15-15, http://dx.doi.org/10.2139/ssrn.2611235.

Huang, Y., Y. Shen, J. Wang, and F. Guo. 2016. "Can the Internet Revolutionise Finance in China?" In *China's New Sources of Economic Growth: Volume 1—Reform, Resources and Climate Change*, edited by Ligang Song, Ross Garnaut, Cai Fang & Lauren Johnston, Canberry: Australian National University Press, pp. 115–138.

Jensen, M. C., and W. H. Meckling. 1979. "Theory of the Firm: Managerial Behavior, Agency Costs, and Ownership Structure." In *Economics Social Institutions*, edited by Karl Brunner, New York: Springer, pp. 163–231.

Jiang, F., Z. Jiang, and K. A. Kim. 2017. "Capital Markets, Financial Institutions, and Corporate Finance in China." *Journal of Corporate Finance.* https://doi.org/10.1016/j.jcorpfin.2017.12.001.

Kim, J. H., and A Shamsuddin. 2008. "Are Asian Stock Markets Efficient? Evidence from New Multiple Variance Ratio Tests." *Journal of Empirical Finance*, 15(3), pp. 518–32.

La Porta, Rafael, Florencio Lopez-de-Silane, and Andrei Shleifer, and Robert W. Vishny. 1997. "Legal Determinants of External Finance." *Journal of Finance*, 52(3), pp. 1131–50.

La Porta, Rafael, Florencio López de Silanes, and Andrei Shleifer. 1998. "Law and Finance." *Journal of Political Economy*, 106(6), pp. 1113–55.

La Porta, Rafael, Florencio Lopez-de-Silanes, and Andrei Shleifer. 2008. "The Economic Consequences of Legal Origins." *Journal of Economic Literature*, 46(2), pp. 285–332.

Law, Fiona. 2015. "Can All Chinese Debt Be Rated Top Quality?" *Wall Street Journal*, 26 July, http://www.wsj.com/articles/can-all-chinese-debt-be-rated-a-1437942674.

Levine, Ross. 2005. "Finance and Growth: Theory and Evidence." *Handbook of Economic Growth*, 1, pp. 865–934.

Li, Cindy. 2014a. "Shadow Banking in China: Expanding Scale, Evolving Structure." *Journal of Financial Economic Policy*, 6(3), pp. 198–211.

Li, Cindy. 2014b. "China's Interest Rate Liberalization Reform." *Asia Focus*, Federal Reserve Bank of San Francisco.

Lin, Guijun, and Ronald M. Schramm. 2008. "A Decade of Flow of Funds in China (1995–2005)." In *China and Asia: Economic and Financial Interactions*, edited by Kar-Yiu Wong and Yin-Wong Cheung, New York: Routledge, pp. 26–43.

Luney, Percy R. 1989. "Traditions and Foreign Influences: Systems of Law in China and Japan." *Law and Contemporary Problems*, 52(2), pp. 129–50.

Luo, Y., J. Ren, and Y. Wang. 2015. "Misvaluation Comovement, Market Efficiency and the Cross-Section of Stock Returns: Evidence from China." *Economic Systems*, 39(3), pp. 390–412.

Luttrell, David, Harvey Rosenblum, and Jackson Thies. 2012. "Understanding the Risks Inherent in Shadow Banking: A Primer and Practical Lessons Learned." *Dallas Fed Staff Papers*.

Maliszewski, W., M. S. Arslanalp, J. Caparusso, J. Garrido, M. S. Guo, J. S. Kang, W. R. Lam, Daniel Law, W. Liao, Nadia Rendak, Philippe Wingender, Jiangyan Yu, and Longmei Zhang. 2016. *Resolving China's Corporate Debt Problem*. International Monetary Fund.

Malkiel, B. G. 2007. "The Efficiency of the Chinese Stock Markets: Some Unfinished Business on the Road to Economic Transformation." Center for Economic Policy Studies Working Paper no. 1031.

Matthews, Kent, and Nina Zhang. 2009. "Bank Productivity in China 1997–2007: An Exercise in Measurement." Cardiff Economics Working Paper no. E2009/14.

McLoughlin, K., and J. Meredith. 2017. "The Rise of Chinese Money Market Funds." *Reserve Bank of Australia Bulletin*, pp. 75–84.

Miller, Merton H. 1988. "The Modigliani-Miller Propositions after Thirty Years." *The Journal of Economic Perspectives*, 2(4), pp. 99–120.

Minsky, H. P. 1992. "The Financial Instability Hypothesis." *The Jerome Levy Economics Institute Working Paper* no. 74.

Obstfeld, Maurice. 2015. "Trilemmas and Trade-Offs: Living with Financial Globalisation." BIS Working Paper no. 480, https://ssrn.com/abstract=2552572.

Roberts, I., and A. Zurawski. 2016. "Changing Patterns of Corporate Leverage in China: Evidence from Listed Companies." In *China's New Sources of Economic Growth: Volume 1—Reform, Resources and Climate Change*, edited by Ligang Song, Ross Garnaut, Cai Fang, and Lauren Johnston, Canberra: Australia National University Press, pp. 271–312.

Schramm, Ronald M. 2015. *The Chinese Macroeconomy and Financial System: A US Perspective.* New York: Routledge.

Schramm, Ronald M. 2017. "Shadow Banking in China Casts a Long Shadow." *Asian-Pacific Affairs Council Journal.*

Shevlin, Aidan, and Andy Chang. 2015. "China's Repo Markets the Structure and Safeguards of China's Largest, Most Liquid Money Market Instruments." *JP Morgan*, 26 June. https://am.jpmorgan.com/blob-gim/1383258499796/83456/WP-GL-China-repo-market.pdf.

Thiele, T. A. 2014. "Multiscaling and Stock Market Efficiency in China." *Review of Pacific Basin Financial Markets and Policies*, 17(4), pp. 1–22.

Turner, Grant, Nicholas Tan and Dena Sadeghian. 2012. "The Chinese Banking System." *Bank of Australia Quarterly Bulletin*, September, pp. 53–64.

Wei, Shen. 2015. "Wealth Management Products in the Context of China's Shadow Banking: Systemic Risks, Consumer Protection and Regulatory Instruments." *Asia Pacific Law Review*, 23(1), pp. 91–121.

Wu, W., and M. Frazier, eds. 2018. *The SAGE Handbook of Contemporary China*. New York: SAGE Publications, Ltd.

Zhao, Z., S. Li, and H. Xiong. 2014. "Short Sale Constraints, Disperse Pessimistic Beliefs and Market Efficiency—Evidence from the Chinese Stock Market." *Economic Modelling*, 42, pp. 333–42.

Endnotes

1. The section on government finance is of about the same length. Both chapters relating to finance share an equal number of pages with a special chapter devoted to Macao.
2. In fact, the ordering of types of finance across types of legal systems very much mirrors the "pecking order" ranking. The differentiator for the latter ordering, however, is typically asymmetry of information.
3. Japan (civil law) and the United States (common law) would be prototypical of these differences in preference.
4. As of 17 March, 2016, their 1997 *Journal of Finance* article had been cited by close to 8,500 other authors.
5. Broadly defined to include the wide variety of business structures in China, from collectives to partnerships to single-proprietor and foreign-funded enterprises.
6. In 2009, during the financial crisis, firms in the United States relied heavily on internal finance, but we do not see the same effect in China. This difference is suggestive of the LLSV arms-around source of finance found in China.
7. An alternative assumption would be that there is international financial integration that would mitigate the effects of different national savings rates.
8. These are enterprises with revenues greater than RMB 20 million. Before 2011, the threshold to be included in the NBS survey was RMB 5 million.
9. Consistent with the flow of funds, we might assume that about 6 percent of equity reflects FDI.
10. For example, in the 2018 NBS Statistical Yearbook, we compare external financing needs based on real transaction flows (Table 3-14) with identified financing flow needs (Table 3-15) and arrive at a difference of about RMB 9.5 trillion. This is about 32 percent of gross capital formation. We halved this difference for various years to arrive at a conservative estimate of the potential size of the shadow banking discrepancy.
11. Author's estimate based on China's flow of funds accounts (NBS 2013: Tables 3-27 and 3-28). This estimate assumes that two-thirds of China's domestic savings are intermediated through formal channels as a source. Bank-based uses are 2013 demand and time deposits. The actual estimate is about 61 percent. Applying the same procedure, but using a macro accounting measure for national savings, we arrive at a figure of 51 percent.
12. For example, the Bank of China was established in 1912 with the founding of the Republic of China, and at times it served both commercial and central banking

functions. It was reestablished as an independent entity in 1983. Similarly, prior to 1949, there was a Farmers Bank, and this became the template for the Agricultural Bank of China. The China Construction Bank was founded in 1954 as a part of the PBC.

13. In 1995, China's Commercial Banking Law was adopted—it set out guidelines for deposit and asset management.
14. They were the China Development Bank, the Agricultural Development Bank (ADB), and the Chinese Export-Import Bank (CHEXIM). The ADB and CHEXIM have moved in recent years toward greater commercial lending, but they remain in the context of policy mandates such as Five-Year Plans.
15. Banking institutions include policy banks, the China Development Bank, large commercial banks, joint stock commercial banks, urban and rural commercial banks, cooperatives and credit cooperatives, some non-bank financial institutions (such as corporate finance agencies, trusts, consumer and auto leasing agencies, and money market brokerages), foreign banks, new rural financial institutions, and the Postal Savings Bank.
16. If we exclude policy banks and the China Development Bank, the figure is RMB 156.7 trillion, or about a 10 percent decrease.
17. The flatter the slope of a line through the origin and the specific country, the higher the four firm concentration ratio. But we need to acknowledge here the increasing integration (at least at the lending level) of Eurozone banking; so, perhaps the statement in the text is of more historical interest.
18. Other important explanations include the great economies of scale and scope that locally-owned banks enjoy and their greater experience in working with the banking authorities.
19. Both process and circumstance made full liberalization of interest rates inevitable. Since 2009, the appearance of large firms—such as Alibaba, Tencent, and small peer-to-peer lenders—has hastened the process of financial disintermediation, about which the monetary authorities have grown increasingly concerned. For example, in August, 2015, the CBRC issued a new set of regulations aimed at internet-based banking activities.
20. The introduction of depositor insurance (up to RMB 500,000) in May, 2015 led the way for liberalization of the deposit ceiling. But banks still seem hesitant to raise rates beyond PBC guidelines, suggesting an ongoing role for window guidance from the banking authorities.

21. Huarong, Great Wall, Orient, and Cinda Asset Management Companies were each assigned the task of taking on the bad assets of each of the Big Four banks.
22. The core tier 1 capital adequacy ratio stood at 10.6 percent in 2013–2014.
23. The value here represents only onshore debt instruments. Offshore RMB were valued at around USD 60 billion in 2013, representing both Chinese and foreign issuers.
24. Most offshore market debt is issued by state-owned corporates as well.
25. We note that many trusts are, themselves, owned by commercial banks.
26. The PBC stopped issuing bills in 2013.
27. At the end of 2014, the China Development Bank had about RMB 6.4 trillion in issued debt instruments, or between 20 and 25 percent of all debt securities in China.
28. In total, there are nine credit rating agencies in China, but the remaining four are relatively small.
29. Bonds that are traded on either the exchanges or the interbank market can serve as collateral for repos.
30. Shevlin and Chang state that daily trading volume of repos is eight times that of the underlying bond trading in the combined interbank/stock exchange market.
31. B shares have a face value in RMB, and Chinese residents with foreign currency bank accounts are permitted to buy B Shares.
32. *China Daily*, 10 July, 2009. "Negotiable market value of A-Shares back to 10 Trillion Yuan."
33. Including a second Bank of China IPO offering of 171 billion shares.
34. Volatility has been significantly greater in the government intervention period to date compared to the same-length period prior to 15 June, 2015.
35. Large investors trade around 60 percent of their shares in over-the-counter block transactions, bypassing the stock exchanges.
36. One important asset class that is limited is ownership of foreign assets through restrictions on capital mobility. The inability to sufficiently diversify can, in part, explain the high price earnings ratios traditionally found in equity markets and real estate (the other major asset class) in China.
37. This section summarizes a forthcoming article by Schramm in the Spring, 2017 issue of the *Asian-Pacific Affairs Council* journal published at Columbia University's School of International and Public Affairs.
38. We loosely define financial wealth in China as national savings cumulated each year since 1982.

39. And, in the decade following 2003, the sector has grown by an even larger estimated factor of 30 (Elliott et al. 2015).
40. Some definitions of shadow banking exclude insurance companies, pension funds, and government-sponsored investment vehicles. For China, however, we need to keep in mind that the latter category includes many government-sponsored venture capital funds; and venture capital funds are most often included in the definition of the shadow banking industry. We exclude bond and equity financing from our definition of shadow banking.
41. In this period, China's four largest banks (all state-owned) were sufficiently laden with bad loans (policy-related) to push bank equity fully into the negative range. The crisis was silent because there were no bank runs and most of China's citizens were unaware of the dire condition of their banks.
42. The average deposit of Chinese depositors at banks is relatively small, about one-tenth of the size of an American deposit—imposing large fixed costs per asset in China.
43. The Guangdong International Trust and Investment Corporation raised funds internationally on behalf of the local government, but by 1999 it was unable to repay creditors and was shut down by the central government.
44. Some offer floating rate returns or more complex return formulas.
45. Excluding bank, stock, and bond financing, shadow banking made up about 23 percent of all total social financing in China in 2014. Total social financing is a broad measure of all financial intermediation in China, and it is about half of national savings; it does not include the savings of companies (profits) that are retained and invested by the company.

APPENDIX: USEFUL WEBSITES FOR CHINA AND OTHER EMERGING ECONOMIES

Asian Development Bank Bond Finance
https://asianbondsonline.adb.org
Bank of China
https://www.boc.cn/en/
Bank Deposit Interest Rates
http://www.deposits.org/
CEIC
https://www.ceicdata.com/en
Economic Report of the President
https://www.whitehouse.gov/wp-content/uploads/2019/03/ERP-2019.pdf
Federal Reserve Economic Database
https://fred.stlouisfed.org
Hong Kong Stock Exchange
https://www.hkex.com.hk/Mutual-Market/Stock-Connect/Statistics/Hong-Kong-and-Mainland-Market-Highlights?sc_lang=en#select3=0&select2=8&select1=29
International Monetary Fund Article IV
https://www.imf.org/en/Publications/CR/Issues/2018/07/25/Peoples-Republic-of-China-2018-Article-IV-Consultation-Press-Release-Staff-Report-Staff-46121
International Monetary Fund Database
https://data.imf.org/?sk=388DFA60-1D26-4ADE-B505-A05A558D9A42&sId=1479329328660
International Monetary Fund Measures of Financial Access
http://data.imf.org/?sk=E5DCAB7E-A5CA-4892-A6EA-598B5463A34C
International Monetary Fund World Debt Tables
http://databank.worldbank.org/data/source/international-debt-statistics

International Monetary Fund World Economic Outlook
https://www.imf.org/external/pubs/ft/weo/2018/01/weodata/index.aspx
National Bureau of Statistics of China
http://www.stats.gov.cn/tjsj/ndsj/2017/indexeh.htm
United Nations Data
http://data.un.org
United States Bureau of Economic Analysis
https://www.bea.gov
United States Census Bureau International Database
https://www.census.gov/data-tools/demo/idb/region.php?N=%20Results%20
&T=12&A=separate&RT=0&Y=2050&R=-1&C=US
World Bank Financial Inclusion Indicators
https://databank.worldbank.org/reports.aspx?source=1228
World Bank Global Governance Indicators
https://databank.worldbank.org/source/worldwide-governance-indicators
World Bank World Development Indicators
https://databank.worldbank.org/reports.aspx?source=2&series=CM.MKT.LCAP.
GD.ZS &country=
World Federation of Stock Exchanges
https://www.world-exchanges.org/our-work/statistics

Index of Subjects and Authors

Z

About the Author

Professor Ron Schramm has spent over 30 years teaching master's students, PhD candidates, and undergraduates around the world. Most of his career was spent teaching MBA students at Columbia Business School of New York, where he taught the widest range of courses of any faculty member. He has also taught at numerous Chinese universities, including the University of International Business and Economics (UIBE) in Beijing (as a Fulbright scholar), Hong Kong University of Science and Technology, Chinese European International Business School (CEIBS), Xian Jiao Tong Liverpool University's International Business School of Suzhou (IBSS) (created and directed their PhD program), and Shanghai Jiao Tong University (taught the first course ever in corporate valuation). In addition, he spent three years as an economist at the International Monetary Fund working on debt workout for heavily indebted emerging economies.

Made in the USA
Las Vegas, NV
06 April 2022